Religion in America

Expansion of the United States with Dates When New States Became Part of the Union

WA 1889
OR 1859
ID 1890
MT 1889
ND 1889
MN 1858
WI 1848
MI 1837

NV 1864
UT 1896
WY 1890
SD 1889
IA 1845
IL 1818
IN 1816
OH 1803
WV 1863*

CA 1850
AZ 1912
CO 1876
NE 1868
MO 1821
KY 1792
VA

NM 1912
KS 1861
AR 1836
TN 1796
NC

TX 1845
OK 1907
MS 1817
AL 1819
SC
GA

LA 1812
FL 1845

THIRTEEN ORIGINAL

NY
PA

VT NH 1791
ME 1820*
MA
RI
CT
NJ
DE
MD

AK 1959

HI 1959

*Maine was originally part of Massachusetts, and West Virginia part of Virginia.

States added by 1830 to constitute the U.S. during the Jacksonian era.

States added by mid-century when California became an outpost of the Pacific. Ten years later, when Lincoln was elected president, Minnesota and Oregon had been added to the Union.

JOHN CORRIGAN

WINTHROP S. HUDSON

RELIGION IN AMERICA

An Historical Account of the Development of American Religious Life

SEVENTH EDITION

PEARSON

Prentice Hall

Upper Saddle River, New Jersey 07458

Library of Congress Cataloging-in-Publication Data

Corrigan, John
  Religion in America: an historical account of the development
of American religious life / John Corrigan, Winthrop S. Hudson—
7th ed.
      p. cm.
  Includes bibliographical references and index.
    ISBN 0-13-092389-3
  1. United States—Religion.   I. Hudson, Winthrop Still
II. Title.
BL2525.C695 2004
200'.973—dc21

2003002297

To
Charles M. Nielsen
friend and colleague

Editorial Director: Charlyce Jones-Owen
Acquisitions Editor: Ross Miller
Production Liaison: Fran Russello
Editorial/Production Supervision: Bruce Hobart
  (Pine Tree Composition, Inc.)
Manufacturing Manager: Nick Sklitsis
Assistant Editor: Wendy Yurash
Editorial Asistant: Carla Worner
Prepress and Manufacturing Buyer:
  Camille Tesoriero
Marketing Director: Beth Gillett Mejia

Marketing Manager: Claire Bitting
Marketing Assistant: Kimberly Daum
Copy Editor: Carolyn Ingalls
Interior Image Specialist: Beth
  Boyd-Brenzel
Cover Designer: Bruce Kenselaar
Cover Art: St. Sara's Serbian Orthodox
  Church outside Jackson, California,
  Andrew McKinney, Dorling Kindersley
  Media Library.

This book was set in 10/12 Baskerville by Pine Tree Composition, Inc and was printed and
bound by Courier Companies, Inc. The cover was printed by Coral Graphics.

Earlier editions copyright © 1965, 1973, and 1981 by Charles Scribner's Sons;
copyright © 1987 by Macmillan Publishing Company.

© 2004, 1999, 1992 by Pearson Education, Inc.
Upper Saddle River, New Jersey 07458

Printed in the United States of America
10 9 8 7 6 5 4

ISBN: 0-13-092389-3

Pearson Education Ltd., London
Pearson Education Australia PTY. Limited, Sydney
Pearson Education Singapore, Pte. Ltd
Pearson Education North Asia Ltd, Hong Kong
Pearson Education Canada, Ltd., Toronto
Pearson Educación de Mexico, S.A. de C.V.
Pearson Education—Japan, Tokyo
Pearson Education Malaysia, Pte. Ltd
Pearson Education, Upper Saddle River, New Jersey

Contents

Preface

This is a story about religion in America. But it is not the only story about religion in America. At certain points in the telling, it corresponds with other stories about people, places, and religious things. Sometimes, on the other hand, this story takes turns that distance it from these other stories. Like all other stories of a nation's past, it is an intertwining of many threads of narrative. Here and there those threads are woven into a relatively sturdy, even fabric. In other places, the warp and woof are uneven, ragged, or fragile. History is complex, to some extent indeterminate, and is subject to constant revision. This history of the development of American religious life is, accordingly, a work in progress.

A story changes with each telling, and this story is no different. In preparing *Religion in America* for a seventh edition, I have added several new sections, and have enlarged and detailed others. In this edition I note the important Reformation and Catholic Reformation backgrounds to Christian missionizing in North America, and especially the way in which the struggles between Protestants and Catholics in Europe translated in certain ways to the vigorous Jesuit and Franciscan and Sulpician ventures on this side of the Atlantic. The legacy of the Spanish presence in colonial North America—in the form of a distinctive Hispanic Catholicism—is also the subject of a more detailed discussion. This treatment is particularly appropriate in view of the recent dramatic growth of that part of the population whose background is Hispanic.

The careful work undertaken by historians in recent years to enlarge our understanding of African American religious history has made possible a broader and deeper picture of that aspect of the story. Drawing on this ongoing research, I have added material on the emergence of the African American denominations, on the role of religion in African American social movements (from mutual aid societies to the Convention Movement), on the formation of black women's religious societies, and on the growing popularity of Islam and Islamic movements among African Americans.

Historical scholarship continues to confirm the primary roles of women in sustaining religious institutions in America. In a new section on the "female majority," I describe some of the roles played by women, as well as the resistance that they encountered, as they sought to expand the scope of their religious activities in antebellum America. In discussing this period, I also address in greater detail the ways in which Catholics and Jews organized their religious life and the ways in which that life changed as those communities grew and diversified. There likewise is a fuller discussion of the most important of nineteenth-century national revivals, the Businessmen's Revival (or, Union Revival) of 1858, which served at one level to accentuate ethnic, gender, class, and age differences in religious groups at the same time that it fostered unity on another level.

Pentecostalism has proven to be one of the most vital and fast-growing branches of Christianity, both in America and in many other parts of the world. The story in this edition takes more time with the beginnings of Pentecostalism in America, noting the ways in which Pentecostalism, over the course of the twentieth century, has moved from the periphery of American religious life into the mainstream of popular culture. By the same token, Islam has developed from its status as a religion practiced solely by first- and second-generation immigrants to a faith embraced by a broad base of Americans, and especially as a religion that appeals to African Americans. I address this development in greater detail, noting the differences in styles of Islam in America and the ways in which it has been connected or disconnected with Islam as it is practiced elsewhere. I likewise note how the events of September 11, 2001, have affected the relationship between Muslims and non-Muslims in America.

The essential pattern of this history, for all of these additions, remains the same. Three overlapping contexts frame the story. First, religion is pictured in its relations with other aspects of American life. Religious traditions and communities exercise a profound influence on the formation of culture in America. Religion, in turn, is constantly being shaped by forces outside the church, synagogue, mosque, and meetinghouse. Religion in America addresses religious life as a whole as it arises in the context of this reciprocal relationship.

Second, the transatlantic dimension forms a key part of the story. Although religions in America exhibit distinctive features, most religionists engage in practice that bears the mark of a predominantly European background. After the initial migration of Europeans to America, the European influence was sustained in various ways and most conspicuously through waves of immigration. It is true as well that in the course of being translated to an American context, religion that originated in Europe was modified. In some cases the change was minimal, and in other cases the process of adaptation resulted in dramatic recastings of religious belief and practice. In the twentieth century, the migration of persons from Asia and from Latin America—added to communities of various sizes already established within the national borders of the United States—enlarged this other dimension of influence. But even in these cases, the religious background of immigrants was often substantially shaped by European religions. The majority of Asian immigrants, for example, are Christian. The most significant case of religious influence of a non-European stripe is the other transatlantic pathway, the African diaspora, which brought persons to the Americas as slaves. After the European influence, the African influence has been most significant. As greater numbers of Buddhists, Muslims, Hindus, Sikhs, and others settle in the United States and establish centers of religious practice, they have further complicated the religious pluralism of the nation. We ought to expect that as these communities grow and participate more fully in the give and take of public life, they will help to shape the religious landscape in new ways. Just what those shapes will be, however, we do not yet know.

Third, the story of religion in America emerges out of the interaction of many religious groups. At times that interaction was manifest in cooperative projects of missionizing, education, and reform. On other occasions, conflicts in the form of nativism, heresy accusations, and regional differences, alongside an assortment of race, class, and gender issues, broke the surface of denominational life. In early America, patterns of interaction were relatively simple because the religious spectrum was narrow. With the full-scale development of the institution of slavery, and as religious and ethnic diversity increased during the nineteenth century, relations between religious groups invariably became more complex. In the early twenty-first century, complexity born of a broad pluralism appeared as an exclamation point to the story. The durability of that pluralism was tested by the terrorist attacks of September 11, 2001. For some, such as Florida pastor and Southern Baptist Convention leader Rev. Jerry Vines, the attacks illustrated the principle that Islam was a demonic religion and that the nation's problems were caused precisely by religious pluralism.[1] For others, the vigorous and ongoing public discussion of religion in the wake of the attacks led to a more hospitable and understanding view of non-Christian and minority religions in America. One poll indicated that a

[1]"Vines Condemns Islam," *The Florida Times Union* (June 12, 2002), 1.

much greater percentage of Americans viewed Islam positively after the attacks than before them.[2]

Finally, it is important to recognize that much religion in America began as popular religion, as "religion of the people" (*populus*). Religious groups such as Christian Science, Jehovah's Witnesses, Mormonism, and many others began as popular religious movements. And individuals who have located their religious life largely within the confines of well-established denominations have, nevertheless, sometimes also embraced popular religious ideas and participated in religious rituals of a popular sort. American interest in religious entrepreneurialism and the "customizing" of religious life—through innovation, borrowing, and adaptation—is a leading theme of the nation's religious history.

My work on this book has required that I constantly attempt to see the material as would a person just beginning the study of religion in America. I am grateful to those colleagues who, from their positions in the classroom trenches, communicated to me their suggestions on enriching and clarifying the story.

I am especially indebted to the following reviewers for their help: Sandy Duane Martin, The University of Georgia; Paul P. Parker, Elmhurst College; and Elaine McDuff, Iowa State University. I also thank Howell Williams and Heather Nicholson for their help in preparing the manuscript for publication, and Art Remillard for his excellent work on the Index. I have had many outstanding copy editors over the years, but Carolyn Ingalls's work was simply extraordinary.

John Corrigan

Tallahassee, Florida

---

[2]"Post September 11 Attitudes: Religion more prominent; Muslim-Americans more accepted," a survey conducted by The Pew Research Center for the People and the Press, December 6, 2002, available at: http://people-press.org/reports/display.php3?ReportID;144. The survey of 1,500 adults was based upon data gathered in mid-November, 2002.

Introduction: Land, People, and Nation

There is such a place as the United States. It has a history. It is situated in North America, between two oceans, bordered by other nations, in a neighborhood of the world that includes another large land mass, South America, to which it is connected by a region known as Central America. The trajectories of United States history—the pathways by which past events shape the present—are both long and short, some well known for generations, others recently identified, others still to be discovered. As we study the nation's religious past, we should bear in mind that historical investigation is an ongoing project, and that we are always in the process of interpreting the manner in which events have shaped the course of history. Just as the nation itself has changed over time, so have our conceptions of it.

As communications technology, population migration, commerce, and politics shrink the globe and precipitate cultural encounters on an unprecedented scale, spatial and temporal conceptions of the United States undergo corresponding revision. Sometimes such revisions are highly visible and publicly manifested. The North American Free Trade Agreement (NAFTA), in proclaiming the mingled economic destinies of the United States, Mexico, and Canada, reconceived North America as a shared space, and framed the present in terms of a past defined by an extended and enriched timeline of historical events. Sometimes, reconceptualizations of the United States as a place and time are more subtle and complicated, as in Senator Robert Dole's 1996 Republican presidential campaign call for "a bridge to the past," or in initiatives to extend voting rights to citizens of other nations who reside in the United States.

The story of religion in America is the story of many religions, some claiming large memberships, some numbering only a few followers. It is about the relationships between persons and groups who have embraced widely varying beliefs. And it includes recognition of the ways in which the nation has created some measure of common cause and understanding among its citizens in the face of religious differences. It is about religious change, and our perceptions of that change, as well as centuries-old continuities.

The Geography of the Nation

The exploration of the North American continent was undertaken by native peoples long before the arrival of Europeans. They knew the land, drew maps, and claimed space. The Spanish, French, Dutch, Portuguese, and English who came to the New World in the sixteenth and seventeenth centuries brought with them their own understandings of space, and deployed a wide range of rituals to consecrate their colonies, to mark their possession of the lands that they explored. The English built gardens and fences, the Spanish created strings of missions, and the Portuguese planted crosses. The French planted the cross, too, and embellished the moment with a complex of theatrical displays.[1] These groups encountered each other in the New World, claiming, defending, losing, and reclaiming space for over 250 years before there was a United States.

The United States began as a slender fringe of 13 states along the Atlantic coast that declared their independence from Britain in 1776. Even this is deceptive, for the colonists inhabited mostly a fringe of a fringe. Settlement in Georgia was limited to the coastal lowlands and up one bank of the Savannah River not far beyond present-day Augusta; Massachusetts' district of Maine was mostly wilderness; western Virginia above the Shenandoah was unsettled; and central, western, and northern New York had not been opened to settlement.

By 1840, 13 more states—mostly carved out of the territory east of the Mississippi River ceded by Britain in 1783—had been added to the new nation. Thereafter the United States became a patchwork quilt with many of the patches yet missing. In 1845, Texas and Florida became part of the Union, but Oklahoma did not until 1907. When California became a state in 1850, a foothold on the Pacific was gained, but it was a foothold far removed from the rest of the nation. The southern tier of states was not completed until 1912, when Arizona and New Mexico were received as members of the Union. Two decades earlier, in 1889 and 1890, the empty

---

[1] Patricia Seed, *Ceremonies of Possession in Europe's Conquest of the New World, 1492–1640* (Cambridge University Press, N.Y., 1995).

spaces of the northern frontier had been filled when the Dakotas, Montana, Idaho, and Washington became member states of the nation. Utah remained a missing patch of the quilt until 1896. Not until 1959 did Alaska and Hawaii become constituent parts of the United States.

The Ethnography of the Nation

If the United States at the outset was small in geographical extent, it was also limited in the diversity of its population. It is true that at the beginning there were the Native Americans, the "Indians," who were treated (mostly mistreated) in a variety of ways and progressively displaced. Of the white population at the end of the colonial period, 85 percent came from the British Isles. By the beginning of the twenty-first century, however, the United States was a land of minorities, with a population drawn from every continent and almost every country of the world. Thirty-four million of its citizens have distant antecedents in Africa. Much more recent are the 35 million people referred to by the Census Bureau as being of Spanish origin. These peoples are more commonly known as Hispanics or Latinos.

Few of the 35 million Hispanics are from Spain. About two-thirds are of Mexican origin, and most Mexicans identify Mexico as an Indian (i.e., American Indian) nation. Many Hispanics (3.5 million) are from Puerto Rico, and about 1 million are from Cuba. The rest are from other countries of Latin America, the numbers swelling in proportion to the hazards of life in their homelands—a reason many from all parts of the world became Americans, blacks being the notable exception.

The Spanish presence in the United States came relatively late. When Florida became one of the United States in 1845, only a few archeological survivals remained of early Spanish settlements on this then-desolate peninsula. Texas under Spanish and then Mexican rule was also virtually an unoccupied land from the European point of view (the Indians, as usual, were ignored), with only three small permanent settlements. First Spain and then Mexico sought to entice settlers to Texas from the United States and Germany with grants of land. In 1845, when the Republic of Texas, after nine years of independence, was annexed and admitted as a state, the Mexican population that remained was far outnumbered by the newer arrivals. The 1850 census reported a Texas population of 212,595, with Protestants (mainly Baptists and Methodists) predominant among the religiously affiliated. The report added laconically that the annexation "only brought back into the Union those who had migrated thither a short time before." California thus was the first state to introduce an established Spanish presence into the life of the nation.

In this land of minorities, in addition to the Scots, Welsh, English, and Irish from the British Isles, major segments of the population were drawn from every area of Europe. One need only call the roll: Germany, Italy, Scandinavia, eastern Europe, and the Balkans—with Greece, Portugal, and the Netherlands each making its own important contribution. Descendants of the early French Huguenots constitute a remote French connection, and the twentieth-century influx of French Canadians supplied a more tangible presence.

Nearly 11 million Americans are from east and south Asia and the islands of the Pacific, and the number keeps increasing: Asian Indians, Chinese, Filipinos, Japanese, Koreans, and Vietnamese, to name the largest groupings. A medley of peoples also have come from what technically should be regarded as part of Asia and Africa but is more commonly labeled the Near East or Middle East. And then, to return to the beginning, half-forgotten by many, are the 2.5 million survivors of the Native Americans of the forests and plains who were displaced and isolated and yet continued to exist, as did the blacks for so many years, on the periphery of the "white man's world."

Religious Pluralism

There was religious diversity (and much irreligion) from the start. By the twentieth century, the diversity was so expanded that it was renamed "pluralism," a term more appropriate to describe the situation when a nation had become a sampler of all the religions of the globe. These include all the major faiths in their multifarious expressions as well as the lesser-known religions and the innovative constructs of belief and devotion of independent and often indigenous origin.

Apart from the obvious concentrations of specific religious groups in early New England, Pennsylvania, and Virginia, differences within and between separate denominations were not so noticeable in the early years of the republic, a fact attested to by Alexis de Tocqueville as late as the Jacksonian era. Traveling itinerants in the colonial period, such as Francis Makemie, Samuel Davies, Henry M. Muhlenberg, Shubal Stearns, Francis Asbury, and a host of others—including above all "the grand itinerant," George Whitefield—blurred the boundaries between the colonies and often between the churches. New England, to be sure, retained a distinctive character as it moved from a Puritan to a Yankee society, but it shared much of its religious ethos with other sections of the evolving nation through migration, missionary activity, and educational influence. It was not until the 1830s that a north side and a south side of religion began to develop and to divide the republic. In spite of this cleavage, Protestants north and south in the late 1850s were still able to join in sponsoring "union prayer meetings."

Real religious pluralism began to emerge in a small way with the innovating groups produced by the indigenous religious ferment of the 1830s and 1840s, and with the beginning of what was to be a mounting tide of immigration from abroad following the European revolutions of 1830 and 1848 as well as the potato famine in Ireland. Decade by decade the immigration increased, until it reached its peak in the years preceding the outbreak of war in 1914. The full spectrum of religious belief, however, did not become apparent until a major influx of peoples from Asia, begun after World War II, contributed both directly and indirectly to a mushrooming pluralism. Asian faiths became more prominent and helped foster in part additional home-grown religious groups or communes during the late 1960s and early 1970s.

Regionalism

Following the Civil War, regional differences in religious faith and practice were accentuated. The Old South remained a bastion of an evangelical Protestantism untouched by the changing patterns and relationships introduced by growing urbanization and large-scale immigration in other parts of the country. Immigration also created enclaves of Roman Catholics and Lutherans, which in the course of time expanded to become what Martin Marty called "empires," centers of predominant regional strength. The concentration of Lutherans in Wisconsin, Minnesota, and the Dakotas is an obvious example of such regional strength. There are also urban areas of Jewish concentration, which in similar fashion have given a distinctive tone or ethos to these localities. By the middle of the twentieth century, the most tightly knit regional religious bastion was the intramountain Mormon empire, which had spilled over the border of Utah into neighboring states. Two additional areas of regional religion have been commonly overlooked, namely Appalachia and the Pacific coast.

Unlike the mountains of New England and New York, which were largely denuded of population—and unlike northern Appalachia in Pennsylvania as well as in much of West Virginia and Kentucky, which was robbed of its innocence by coal mines, coke ovens, and steel mills—southern Appalachia had mountaineers who remained where they were, isolated from the rest of the world in their narrow valleys behind rugged ridges for a century and more. Even the architecture of their cabins remained unchanged, betraying the pilgrimages of their ancestors from Scotland and Ireland. In the same way, their folk religion preserved a faith and practice that reflected eighteenth-century religious life, with some embellishments of their own that had developed over the years. This is the reason, one assumes, that in the twentieth century the whole region, when discovered by holiness and pentecostal preachers, yielded a ready harvest once the seed was sown. In this region, thereafter, its own homegrown brands of pentecostalism then flourished.

The Pacific coast, most notably California, provides a quite different example of geographically and culturally conditioned regional religion. Culturally it is, to use a colloquial expression, "laid-back" and future-oriented. Southern California as early as the 1920s and 1930s gained the reputation in religion of being the twentieth-century equivalent of the "burned-over district" of central and western New York in the 1830s and 1840s. A profusion of novelties flourished, and interest in the new and exotic spread up the West Coast in the decades that followed.

Why this should be so is difficult to determine. Only a series of "perhaps," with a focus on California, can suggest a partial answer. Perhaps the distance across the plains was too great and the difficulty in breaching the mountains too arduous to give ready access for the old-line churches to become as deeply rooted as elsewhere. Perhaps the get-rich-quick spirit of those who participated in the Gold Rush and the quick wealth amassed by the railroad and banking elite of Sacramento and San Francisco contributed to a cosmopolitan mood and an entrepreneurial lack of interest in rootage. The early settlers were not stay-at-homes. They were people on the move and, unlike the settlers who came later to the plains east of the mountains, were uninterested in replicating the farms and villages whence they had come. Perhaps the fact that southern California became old-folks territory in the 1920s—people who were far removed and cut off from the former securities of family and church back in Iowa and elsewhere—had something to do with receptivity to religious novelty. Perhaps the influx of refugees from the "dust bowl" in the 1930s helped augment a pervasive restless and rootless spirit. Perhaps early trading contact with the Orient and Eastern religions made a difference. Perhaps the movement of troops through the ports and of their wives into the munitions plants during World War II gave an added complexity to West Coast society. The presence of Hispanics (Chicanos) and Asians after the war, as major segments of the population, added another element to an already cosmopolitan region.

Finally, the Southwest has always had a unique personality. The deep Indian roots and centuries of Spanish influence have been reinforced over time by immigration from Mexico. Many Roman Catholic churches in the region embody a ritual life and devotion that is distinctive. And certain popular religions of the second half of the twentieth century—some being of the "New Age" variety and others with more traditional backgrounds—have taken root throughout the Southwest. The stunning landscape between Texas and southern California has been home to a large number of such movements, from the Branch Davidians in Waco, Texas, to the Heaven's Gate cult in California, with the centers of lively religious ferment such as Sedona, Arizona, and Sante Fe, New Mexico, in between.

Religious Difference and National Vision

Differences between religious groups and between regions are key parts of the story of religion in America. But they are not the only differences. Racial, ethnic, gender, and class differences have been fundamental to the course of American history as well. Consequently, there have been ample tensions and frequent conflicts. The story of religion in America, like the broader history of the nation, nevertheless, includes the themes of commonality, like-mindedness, and unity. Sometimes those themes appear alongside conflict, such as in the cross-denominational alignments of churches for and against slavery in the nineteenth century. Sometimes in the organization of support for certain causes, there has been very broad cooperation, as in the crusade for temperance. At other times, a relatively small body of religious persons and groups have led many others to take a common action, as in the campaign for civil rights in the mid–twentieth century.

Since the time of the constitutional conventions in the late eighteenth century, there has been lively, ongoing discussion about what America is, and what kind of a nation it should become. Religious groups have been key participants in that discussion, helping to forge consensus, challenging power, and articulating a broad assortment of visions of the nation's future. The connective tissue that historically has linked those visions has been the assumption that America is, in fact, a nation, ethnically diverse, regional in its emphases, plural in its religions, complex and at times contradictory, but a nation nevertheless. At the beginning of the twenty-first century, "global" awareness challenges "national" purpose in models for thinking about the possibilities for collective human life. Adaptability and inventiveness, hallmarks of religion in America, which have been refined over many generations, provide a foundation for addressing that alteration, and other changes of the new millennium.

But we are ahead of the story. Let us begin with a time in which there was not yet a United States.

PART ONE

Religion in a Colonial Context
1492–1789

CHAPTER ONE

Backgrounds and Beginnings

Native Peoples

Ferdinand Columbus, the son of Christopher Columbus, described his father's landing on the island of San Salvador in 1492 in the following way:

> At daybreak they saw an island about fifteen leagues in length, very level, full of green trees and abounding in springs, with a large lake in the middle, and inhabited by a multitude of people who hastened to the shore, astounded and marveling at the sight of the ships, which they took for animals. These people could hardly wait to see what sort of things the ships were. The Christians were no less eager to know what manner of people they had to do with. Their wishes were soon satisfied, for as soon as they had cast anchor the Admiral went ashore with an armed boat, displaying the royal standard. . . . Many Indians assembled to watch this celebration and rejoicing, and the Admiral, perceiving they were a gentle, peaceful, and very simple people, gave them little red caps and glass beads, which they hung around their necks, together with other trifles that they cherished as if they were precious stones of great price.[1]

For Ferdinand—and his father—the encounter between Europeans and the North American natives was in essence a meeting of Christians with

---

[1] *The Life of the Admiral Christopher Columbus by his Son Ferdinand*, translated and annotated by Benjamin Keen (New Brunswick, N.J., 1959), 59, 60. See also *The Diario of Christopher Columbus's First Voyage to America 1492–1493*, trans. Oliver Dunn and James E. Kelley, Jr. (Norman, Okla., 1989), 63–69.

non-Christians. European explorers and settlers in the New World fixed their identities within the frameworks of specific cultures: Spanish, Portuguese, French, English, Dutch. Yet in gauging their relationship with the inhabitants of the Americas, Europeans conceived themselves above all as representatives of Christian culture. Accordingly, Columbus and those who followed him undertook the exploration of the New World under a conceptual umbrella that equated Christianity with civilization and that viewed indigenous cultures as "primitive" aggregations of "customs and ceremonies." Such a view was reinforced over the centuries in a shorthand that identified persons as either Christians or Indians. Censuses, captains' logs, mission registers, royal charters, plantation reports, military communications, and virtually every other official document of colonial rule repeatedly drove home the perception of the essential difference in the casual usage of those two words, "Christian" and "Indian."[2]

The Taino story of what they saw that day has been lost. These people who met Columbus in the West Indies farmed and fished; played ball on rectangular courts; danced; organized authority in complex systems of chiefdoms; extolled the deeds of their ancestors; looked to shamans to heal their sick; and worshipped Yucahu, the lord of Cassava and the sea, and Atabey, his mother, who was associated with fresh water and human fertility.[3] The Tainos were but one language group among hundreds in North America, and one small fraction of the continent's 15 million inhabitants.[4] Over a period of thousands of years, their ancestors had explored the great American land masses, built civilizations, and developed distinctive religious worldviews.

A Distinctive Worldview

The Tainos were a tribal community, a society organized with respect to family relationships. North America at the time of Columbus was a quilt of tribes with a diversity of languages and religions and ways of life. Most North American tribes hunted. Some relied upon agriculture as well; others fished; some gathered food in other ways. The seasonal ebbs and flows of the many climatic zones of the North American continent shaped native cultures in the same way that geographical factors such as altitude, proximity to waterways and the sea, and types of vegetation conditioned the rhythms of everyday life. Through their experiences of nature, geography,

---

[2] For a discussion of the manner in which Columbus and the European explorers who followed him sought "the universal victory of Christianity," see Tzvetan Todorov, *The Conquest of America: The Question of the Other*, trans. Richard Howard (New York, 1984; New York, 1992).

[3] Irving Rouse, *The Tainos: Rise & Decline of the People Who Greeted Columbus* (New Haven, 1992), 5–25.

[4] See "On Pre-Columbian Settlement and Population," in David E. Stannard, *American Holocaust: Columbus and the Conquest of the New World* (New York, 1992), Appendix A, 261–68.

and climate, as well as through their experiences within the tribe and with other tribes, and, when they came, with the Europeans, Native Americans fashioned religious worldviews. Those worldviews, which were grounded in questions and answers about human origins and destiny, frequently overlapped from one tribe to another. But these worldviews, nevertheless, always encoded distinct meanings for the local community.

In order to speak of a North American "primal religious tradition," we must recognize that our understanding of it is necessarily qualified in several ways. First, Native American religion is in fact remarkably diverse. We should not expect, for example, that representations of the sacred among North American tribes translate intact from one context to another. A medicine bag containing snake rattles, cactus needles, white stones, scorpion carapaces, eagle feathers, and juniper berries is not likely to be recognized as a repository of sacred power in a place where there are no rattlesnakes, cacti, quartz, scorpions, and so forth. Second, primal worldviews are not always susceptible to analysis in Western terms. So, for example, the complex of meanings associated with the power of manitou (Big God; Spirit; Cosmic force) among the Algonquin simply do not fit traditional Judaeo-Christian-Islamic categories of theological investigation. We cannot expect to appreciate the intricacy of Native American religions unless we are willing to suspend some of our habits of thought about the phenomenon of religion. Third, we know only a part of the story. Our knowledge of Native American religions comes to us primarily through oral and ritual traditions and material culture. It is gleaned from stories passed by word of mouth from generation to generation and through the examination of the artifacts of ritual and everyday life: weaponry, dress, pottery, architecture, art, and so forth. Westerners, who traditionally have relied upon literary accounts to recover traces of the historical past, are only beginning to understand how to "read" a culture's history in the slope of a roof or in a story told around a fire.

As the key unit of social organization, the tribe manifests various kinds of familial relationships. The experience of those relationships informs reflection about relationships between persons and nature, which likewise are conceived as familial bonds. The rationales for this ordering of relationships are imbedded in myths about the creation of the world, about heroes and tricksters, about monsters and ghosts, and about the end of time. Native American myths overflow with representations of kinship among nature and people; of marriages between creatures of different species; of parenting by the sun, moon, and stars; and of the remembrance of ancestors by Earth itself.

A Penobscot Indian story about the origins of humanity, corn, and tobacco begins in this way: "Kloskurbeh, the All-Maker, lived on Earth, there were no people yet. But one day when the sun was high, a youth appeared and called him 'Uncle, brother of my mother.'" An Osage story of creation establishes at the outset a similar conception of kinship: "Way beyond the

Earth, a part of the Osage lived in the sky. They wanted to know where they came from, so they went to the sun. He told them that they were his children. Then they wandered still farther and came to the moon. She told them that she gave birth to them and that the sun was their father." Conversations, arguments, and marriages between animals and people are grounded in this vision of family relatedness. A Sioux story comments on the bonds between people and rattlesnakes: "We Sioux think of rattlesnakes as our cousins. They always give warning before they strike, as if they wanted to say: 'Uncle, don't step on me; then we'll get along.'" Sometimes in these encounters, the parties change their shapes, becoming like the other creature. A myth of the Potawatomi tells of a couple who had lost their only child. One day, the woman caught a fish, sang to it, and petted it, whence it turned into a baby. In other instances, people might become like other creatures even without actually changing shape, as in the case of a Pomo myth about the girl who married a rattlesnake, bore him four human boys, and eventually became more rattlesnake than human herself—although she remained human in appearance.[5] In Native American cultures, nature—including humanity—is conceived as an interconnected web of family relations. And it is this vision that underlies the association of each clan of a tribe with a certain animal, fish, or other living thing.

Judaeo-Christian-Islamic cosmogonies are about the creation of the universe from nothing. Native American myths sometimes are structured in a similar way, with a cosmic creator playing the key role. That creator might be identified as seemingly impersonal as the Cherokee Someone Powerful, or, as, in this Cheyenne cosmogony, as Great Medicine: "In the beginning the Great Medicine created the Earth, and the waters upon the Earth, and the sun, moon and stars. Then he made a beautiful country to spring up in the far north. . . . In this beautiful country the Great Medicine put animals, birds, insects, and fish of all kinds. Then he created human beings to live with the other creatures."[6] Among the Yakima, the Great Chief Above performs the work of creation. And in Yuma myth, there is Kokomaht the Creator, who would seem to be named but who is described as "bodiless, nameless, breathless, and motionless," and is two beings—twins—at once.

There are many kinds of Native American creation myths. Sometimes the creator is identified as female. In a Hopi tale of creation, two goddesses, a Haruing Wuhti of the east and another in the west, caused the waters to recede, fashioned people out of clay, and taught them language. In other cases, the first man is said to have followed from woman, as in a myth of the Plains tribes in which a woman bore the first man after she was unknowingly impregnated by the sun while picking berries with her

---

[5] Richard Erdoes and Alfonso Ortiz, eds., *American Indian Myths and Legends* (New York, 1984), 12, 119, 404, 397–98; John Bierhorst, *The Mythology of North America* (New York, 1985), 228.

[6] Erdoes and Ortiz, eds., 111.

mother one day. And the Apache story of Gomoidema Pokoma-Kiaka tells of a maiden who survives a killing flood and conceives a daughter from sun and water, who, in turn, conceives the Son of God.[7]

Frequently, creation stories weave together the exploits of an extended cast of characters, each of whom has a role to play in creation. Many feature an earth-Diver, an animal who dives deep into the waters and returns with a lump of sod. Earth-Diver tales, which are among the oldest Native American myths, are distributed throughout the continent. These myths, which differ substantially from Western accounts of an all-powerful God who creates the world from nothing, sometimes take a tone that Westerners would find surprising. A tale among tribes in the Northeast recounts how a gluttonous and licentious trickster figure, Mesho, told Mink to dive beneath the waters and return with earth. Mink returns on the verge of death but with a mouthful of mud. Mesho revives him by administering artificial respiration to his anus, during which the mud pops from Mink's mouth and is distributed to form the Earth.[8]

Other creation myths tell of the emergence of people and animals from places beneath the surface of the Earth. A Jicarilla Apache myth is representative: "In the beginning the Earth was covered with water, and all living things were below in the underworld. The people could talk, the animals could talk, the trees could talk, and the rocks could talk." The animals and people played a game that ended in their building mounds that enabled them to crawl through a hole out onto the surface of the Earth. Here, as in virtually all Native American mythology, the Earth is a living creature, sharing with humans experiences of pleasure and pain, joy and sadness. As an Okanagon myth explains, "The Earth was once a human being, and she is alive yet; but she has been transformed. . . . the soil is her flesh; the trees and vegetation are her hair; the rocks, her bones; and the wind is her breath. . . . She shivers and contracts when cold, and expands and perspires when hot."[9]

Creation stories tell more than how the world was created. They give meaning to everyday tribal life, orienting a people to the land and to spiritual values at the same time. In narrative and in symbols, these stories stake out the spiritual and moral landscape with reference to the physical landscape. A mountain canyon, a river, a grove of trees, and a certain formation of rocks are important in everyday life as living reminders of the power of the sacred that is manifest in the myths of creation. The hole in the Earth's crust through which the Jicarilla Apache originally climbed

---

[7] Erdoes and Ortiz, eds., 115–17, 150; Natalie Curtis, *The Indians' Book: An Offering by the American Indians of Indian Lore, Musical and Narrative, to Form a Record of the Songs and Legends of Their Race* (New York, 1987), 330–31.

[8] Bierhorst, 208.

[9] Erdoes and Ortiz, eds., 83; John Bierhorst, ed., *The Red Swan: Myths and Tales of the American Indians* (New York, 1976), 55.

into the light of day is at the same time an actual geologic feature of the land, the physical center of the culture, the standpoint by which the people orient themselves to their lives of work, play, sleep, celebration, and mourning. Landscape and myth overlap as a perennial reality, mutually reinforcing perceptions of what is valuable and good, and confirming the identity of the people and the order of the world.

The beings who populate cosmogonies and other myths perform heroic deeds, exercise enormous power, change shape, speak wisdom, and create beauty. Like humans, they also get angry, seek revenge, and are lazy, underhanded, and duplicitious. Mythological beings range from those that are readily recognizable—bear, eagle, beetle, muskrat, salmon—to those that bear little physical likeness to animals or people. In between are personified forces of nature, including plant life, geological features, bodies of water, and other elements of the natural world. Often there is fluidity in conceptions about the manner in which the sacred appears: for the Sioux, Wakan at times is a spiritual power that enlivens all of nature, whereas at other times it is identified as Wakan Tanka, a personification. In either case, the immediate and direct relationship to nature and the spiritual dimension of that experience are paramount to Native American cultures.

The religious life of Native Americans is rich with symbol, with the experience of the sacred, and with visions of kinship with people, animals, the land, and all of nature. In its ordering of the world, mythology also provides a template for morality, for guidelines about how people ought to act. A Cheyenne hero-myth begins in this way: "A long time ago the people had no laws, no rules of behavior—they hardly knew enough to survive. And they did shameful things out of ignorance, because they didn't understand how to live."[10] To know "how to live," to know the way of life of the tribe and to embrace it, is to live a moral life. But "moral" here is considerably broader in its implications than in the meanings of the word in Western monotheistic religions.

Belief and Performance

Hunting, fishing, and food gathering and preparation were parts of the way of life of the Native Americans who greeted Columbus. So also were games, sleeping, and the manufacture of art. All of these activities are to some extent holy exercises, governed by certain understandings of their place in an ordered world, and also demanding certain perspectives and procedures. Morality accordingly is not a separate or discrete area of tribal life. It is not a code that is abstracted from work and play and then read back into daily activities. It is, rather, an informing fact of daily existence. To live the tribal way of life is to live morally.

[10] Erdoes and Ortiz, eds., 199.

Ritual transmits and confirms tribal knowledge. It expresses a religious worldview through dramatic performances, ranging from hunting rites to ritual quests for visions. Ritual is no less a language than the spoken word in terms of its effectiveness in communicating the religious meanings of events and in locating everyday life within the context of myth. In fact, tribal ritual in general is the performance of myth, the acting out of myth before an audience familiar with it. In ritual performances, persons listen to and repeat myth, shape it in new ways, adapt it, and confirm their belief in it. In ritual, a community identifies itself and rededicates itself to the tribal way of life.

Hunting, planting, warfare, and other activities important to the survival of the tribe are richly clothed in ritual forms. So also are the four principal passages experienced by persons in the course of the life cycle: birth, puberty, reproduction (marriage), and death. Tribal understanding of the meanings of each of these important events is embedded in myth. And in each case, ritual communicates those meanings to persons undergoing the passage, as well as to the community as a whole.

Pregnancy, although not usually attended with public celebrations, is nevertheless a time of life requiring rituals involving the mother and the father, and sometimes other members of the family as well. Power, mystery, and danger all are associated with a pregnant woman; even her glance could hearken disorder and disease. Accordingly, she frequently is secluded, sometimes in a structure outside the house. Both parents, recognizing that their words and actions affect the fortunes of the child, regulate their behavior in such a way as to ensure that the child's path in life is set toward good and not evil. Among the Shoshoni, the father rises early, bathes in cold water, and moves around, thus making it easier for the child to do the same after birth.[11]

A few days to a few months following birth, a child is presented to the community, in celebrations marked by prayers and dedications. At this time or thereabouts, the child is given a name that is usually inherited from a dead ancestor. For the Inuit, or Eskimos, the soul of a dead ancestor accompanies its name, reincarnating in the body of the child. Inuit parents accordingly treat their children with great sensitivity in order to avoid offending the ancestor, who might decide to evacuate the body, leaving it lifeless. Among the Tlingit, reincarnated ancestors must be cleansed of the disease that killed them. Therefore, a Tlingit baby is made to vomit, thereby evacuating the disease, before the baby is allowed to nurse. A name represents connections across generations, defines relations between the individual and the tribe, and provides direction for personal growth by suggesting character traits thought appropriate for a person. The name given at birth may change over time, as part of the flux of the

---

[11] Ake Hultkrantz, *Shamanic Healing and Ritual Drama: Health and Medicine in Native North American Religious Traditions* (New York, 1992), 75.

circumstances of a life and the ongoing reinvention of personal realities. As persons take on new social roles or succeed in various undertakings, they are given additional names to reflect their achievements and status. In all cases, naming is rich with religious meaning: Names are foundations from which to view the order and harmony of creation, standpoints from which persons both observe and participate in the tribal way of life.

At puberty, males and females actively participate in rituals that formally initiate them into tribal life. These complex rituals bring revelations of religious truth, sacred knowledge about the people and the landscape, and an awareness of one's responsibilities as an adult member of the tribe. For girls, the rites that mark the passage from childhood to adulthood follow the onset of menstruation, whereas for boys, the time of initiation generally is calculated with respect to their proven ability to provide food, succeed in battle, encounter the sacred in dreams or visions, or other such accomplishments.

One of the most richly detailed Apache ceremonies is the puberty rite for girls. As is the case in many other tribes, a girl is removed from the everyday life of the community when she begins to menstruate. She must observe various dietary taboos, is kept awake by singing, and is instructed in the responsibilities of womanhood by a senior female relative. Over a course of four or five days, and sometimes longer, the tribe feasts and celebrates while the girl is pledged to the most solemn and serious behavior. Central to the ritual process is the invocation of Changing Woman, who is recognized in myth for her role in the creation of the world. The girl prays to Changing Woman for the powers that will sustain her social roles and spiritual status within the tribe. She reinforces her identification with Changing Woman by representing in dance the impregnation of Changing Woman by the sun, as that event is expressed in Apache myth.

The Oglala warrior Crazy Horse was known to proclaim before a battle, "A good day to fight and a good day to die!" Indians view death as a passage into afterlife, although there are exceptions. Coming at the end of a long life, death is in certain respects the beginning of a new life. In some cases, the afterlife is envisioned as a continuation, on some level, of contact with the world that one has left, as in Pueblo belief that a person might become a rain-bearing cloud or a kachina spirit (rain spirit). Other tribal cultures envision the afterlife as a shadowy existence in a world deep in the Earth, on a mountain, or otherwise at some distant site from the land of the living.

Last rites vary in detail from tribe to tribe, but in every case they are conceived as necessary to the passing of a person from the world. These rites of passage for the Shoshoni include self-inflicted wounds and the cutting of hair among mourners. The body is dressed in fine clothes, with certain ornamental touches depending on the sex of the deceased. The dead person's clothes and belongings are given away, except for those that will be placed at the grave, such as headdresses and the family tent. In the case of a dead male, the man's best horse is killed at the burial site so that it can be of use to the deceased in the land of the dead. A woman likewise is buried with her kitchen utensils. Mourning may continue for up to six months, at which time the grieving family is reintegrated with the tribe: The mourners are painted with red, brought to a dance, and told to be happy again.[12]

Some other tribes, such as the Navajo, have little interest in the afterworld, do not believe in heaven or hell, and, accordingly, perform no ceremonies to ease the passage of the deceased into another world. A body is buried without fanfare somewhere off the beaten path. The shovels can never be used again, nor can the hogan, or house, if death occurred within it. The deceased's name is stricken from the speech of the tribe, and the gravediggers must be ritually purified before they can be readmitted to everyday tribal life. Navajos believe that the ghosts of persons may return to settle outstanding accounts with the living; and, in general, the notion of the return of a person to the world in any form is fearful and abhorrent for them. Accordingly, the Navajo were indisposed to Christianity, which centers on the resurrection and second coming of a dead man, Jesus. They likewise were uninterested in the Ghost Dance movement that began in the 1870s because it included the expectation of a reunion of the dead with the living.[13]

Hunting was essential to the livelihood of most tribes, and as such was conceived as an activity requiring various ritual purifications, prayers for both the hunters and the game, and ceremonies to celebrate the hunt's success. Hunting was a sacred activity. As a toddler, an Ojibwa male was presented with a bow and arrow. He was given a feast after his first kill, and thereafter each time that he successfully hunted a new species of animal. His puberty rites included spiritual exercises that increased the likelihood of his success in the hunt. The seclusion of girls during the rites of puberty was undertaken for the same purpose. Indeed, the ritual life of the Ojibwa was almost entirely focused on ceremonies and observances related to the hunting of large game.[14]

War, like hunting, was clothed in spiritual meanings. The Pawnee (meaning "wolf"), one of a group of Plains Indians, mimicked the behavior of wolves while on the warpath. A Pawnee man during war sometimes broke company with his fellow warriors and, like a wolf, operated alone. The Coyote Warrior Song expressed his loneliness in that endeavor and sought supernatural protection: "O great expanse of the blue sky, / see me roaming here / Again on the warpath, lonely; / I trust in you, protect me!"

[12] Ake Hultkrantz, *Native Religions of North America: The Power of Visions and Fertility* (San Francisco, 1987), 65–66.

[13] Christopher Vecsey, *Imagine Ourselves Richly: Mythic Narratives of North American Indians* (New York, 1988), 123.

[14] Vecsey, 87.

The warrior seeking protection might also directly invoke the power of Tirawa, the One Above, in a dance song: "The father, him I saw / Wearing a bonnet of war, / Wearing emblem of power— / Father him I saw, / Yea, 'twas the father I saw."[15] Protection was also available in the form of medicine bundles, sacred stones, and shields that were decorated with emblems of the supernatural so as to deflect bullets and arrows.

Combat was itself part of a ritual process of maturation, of building a reputation, and of manifesting spiritual power. Prayers, ceremonies, and ritual purifications were an integral part of war, as both preparation for battle and as part of a process of recognizing a successful warrior's rise in status within the tribe. Some warriors possessed stronger medicine than others in this regard. Chief Roman Nose, a Sioux, "had a powerful war medicine, a magic stone he carried tied to his hair on the back of his head. Before a fight he sprinkled his war shirt with sacred gopher dust and painted his horse with hailstone patterns. All these things, especially the magic stone, made him bulletproof." Chief Roman Nose did not come by such power without certain ritual precautions and preparation. He could not touch anything metal while eating. He ate from stone or clay pots, using a carved horn or stick of wood, and his meat had to be cooked in a buffalo's pouch or other nonmetal container. The day that Roman Nose, in his haste, overlooked this precaution, he died of a bullet in the chest.[16]

Many Native American tribes believe that at death the soul leaves the body through the head. "Soul loss" could be permanent, as in death, or it could be a temporary condition leading to physical illness. In the latter case, a medicine man or medicine woman might be able to recover the soul and bring it back to the body. Entering into a trance, a shaman—a religious professional skilled in travel outside the body or in other spiritual feats—could track the missing soul in its wanderings outside the body, even to the land of the dead if the shaman was of exceptional skill and could return with the soul to the everyday world. In this way the disease of the body would be cured. Another kind of illness comes about through witchcraft, through the manipulation of malevolent power by one's enemies so as to cause one harm. In such cases, a shaman must locate the various lethal "objects" that a witch has embedded in a person's body and then must remove them by ritual means. Tainos in the West Indies relied on the skill of a bohuti (a shaman) to suck the object from the person's body. Still another kind of illness is a combination of aspects of the first two: the theft of a body part, especially the heart, by a witch. In order to effect a cure, the medicine person must battle the witch and recover what had been stolen. In all cases, healing is understood as a complex process involving spiritual power, psychological status, social bonds, and relationships to the land and nature. And the purpose of healing is to restore a person to

---

[15] Curtis, 111–12.

[16] Erdoes and Ortiz, eds., 256.

wholeness by reestablishing interdependencies within and among these key areas of a person's life.

Indian art frequently is connected with healing, either as preventive medicine or as therapy for a specific ill. Indeed, Native American art overflows with religious meanings of many sorts. Among the best-known examples is the totem pole, carved from wood into the shapes of animals sacred to the tribe or a smaller family group. Totem poles are erected for a variety of reasons. A pole placed at the edge of the village welcomes visitors or warns enemies. A frontal pole sometimes stands guard outside a house or lodge, whereas a memorial pole displaying certain crests and figures might be erected to honor the memory of a chief. Mortuary poles, carved with the crests of the deceased, serve as depositories for the bodies or the cremated remains of persons. Some poles feature humanlike "watchmen" figures together with animals. Others incorporate mythical creatures such as the Kolus, a supernatural bird with a large curved beak found in tribes along the Northwest coast, or the Thunderbird, which can represent a range of meanings from war to fertility, depending on its geographical context.

The specific connection of art with healing is dramatically illustrated in the Navajo sandpainting rite. Conceived as a means of removing dangerous supernatural influences from a person, this approach to healing involves remaking persons in such a way as to bring them back into harmony with the cosmos. After a medicine person has painted from memory a number of mythical figures inside a circle on the sand floor, the personages associated with the figures are beckoned by ritual means into the circle of the painting. The sick person, who sits in the center of the circle, then ritually reestablishes proper relationships with those personages through contact with the sand painted in their images. At the end of the ceremony, the sandpainting is destroyed, its artistic, aesthetic value inseparable from its religious purpose.

A Myth of Purity and Decay

Native American cultures are grounded in a worldview, in an understanding of existence that differs in many ways from the European way of seeing the world. Characteristic of that worldview is an intuition of wholeness and harmony that invests even seemingly mundane activities of life with religious meanings. This worldview is manifest in myths and performances that represent the timeless interconnectedness of sacred forces, the land, and people.

The cultural language of Native Americans—the myths, rituals, symbols, medicine, art, and all the other overlapping concerns of religion and everyday life—was not the language of Columbus. When European explorers thought about sound, motion, space, cause and effect, logic, and time, they did so in ways that did not translate easily, if at all, into a Native American idiom. Five hundred years later, it is clear that the categories of the

Western worldview do not align well with the vision of primal religious traditions.

Columbus's gift of little red hats and glass beads, so valued by the Tainos, were trifles to the Spanish. Some missionaries eventually came to understand that cultural difference was more far-reaching than estimations of the value of hats and beads. Other missionaries did not grasp the depth of the rift. Beginning with the reports of Father Ramon Pane, whom Columbus commissioned to study the religion of the Tainos, European attempts to understand Native American religions have been akin to trying to fit the square peg of Indian religion into the round hole of Christianity. History has shown that the endeavor sometimes will succeed but that the process will alter the shape of both religious worldviews.

Europeans had hoped to find paradise in the Americas. Their initial exploration of the continent was fueled by sincere hopes for the discovery of the innocent, blessed, and pure: the Fountain of Youth, the Garden of Eden itself. This myth of a pristine land has influenced the historical appraisal of European encounters with Native Americans. In one telling of the story, Native American religions—like the Edenic land itself—are cast as having been pure and ingenuous in the precontact period. The same story suggests that Indian religions have lost the elements that made them precious in the first place, that as a result of European contact they have suffered mutation and corruption over time, and so they bear little resemblance to their pure, precontact forms. Clearly there has been a certain amount of syncretism and accommodation between Native American religions and the religions brought to the Americas by Europeans. But the religions of the American Indians and the religions that came with the Europeans remain distinct. And strands of tradition that secure the worldviews of the present time to the North American religious world before 1492 remain strong.

Catholic Missionaries

The Protestant Reformation and the Council of Trent

Spain and France undertook the missionary enterprise in the New World during a period of vast religious reform in Europe. The Reformation of the sixteenth century, in all of its various manifestations, marked a decisive turn in the religious history of Europe and shaped the European migration to the New World of the Americas. The Reformation is most commonly associated with Martin Luther, a Roman Catholic priest and a member of the Augustinian order of monks in Germany, and John Calvin, the French translator and theologian who worked largely in Geneva. These two dissidents were responsible for much of the biblical commentary, constructive theology, and practical instruction about religious life and morality that became the core of the Protestant challenge to Roman Catholicism. But a great many other writers and organizers also contributed to the Reformation, making it a broad and complex historical event that unfolded in different ways in different places. And the century of Reformation also included significant change within the Roman Catholic church, as forces and ideas that had been percolating within Catholicism for several centuries spilled over into a program of renewal and reconstruction—the Catholic Reformation—and coalesced as new patterns of devotion, institutional organization, and religious ideology.

The Reformation did not come about overnight. It did not suddenly materialize out of the religious atmosphere of Wittenberg when Martin Luther, on October 31, 1517, nailed to the door of the cathedral there a list of his objections to Catholic ideas and religious practice. The emergence of humanism; the invention of the printing press and improvement of the manufacture of paper; sharpened regional political differences; the development of new schools of philosophical thought; restructurings of social class; and debates about the nature of civil and ecclesial authority all set the stage for the sweeping changes of the sixteenth century. The flashpoint was popular perception of several related problems: corrupted morals among the clergy, papal greed, and vast financial treachery on the part of the church. But even before Luther ritualistically named those failings in his act of defiance in 1517, a host of popular religious movements had dotted the map of Europe. These popular religious movements within Christianity were fueled equally by disenchantment with the Roman church and embrace of the residue of agrarian folk traditions and pagan religious cultures. They ranged from the quasi-official women's order of Beguines to heretical movements that were investigated by the Inquisition in the centuries leading up to the Reformation and for a period of time thereafter. There was apparently little shortfall of religious piety. New churches were founded, the faithful pilgrimaged to holy sites, and the devotions to saints remained strong. But one aspect of that piety, its manifestation in movements organized and embraced by laity, increased steadily, both a sign of the religious vitality of Christians and a mark of their dissatisfaction with Catholic religious leadership. In-house reforms were ineffective. And Protestantism, as historian Lucien Febvre observed, emerged as "a remedy for the disturbed consciences of a good number of Christians . . . to propose to men, who seemed to have been waiting for it for years and who adopted it with a sort of haste and greed that is very revealing, a solution that really took account of their needs and spiritual condition. It offered the masses what they had anxiously been searching for: a simple, clear, and fully effective religion."[17]

---

[17] Lucien Febvre, "The Origins of the French Reformation: A Badly-Put Question?" in *A New Kind of History and Other Essays*, ed. Peter Burke (New York, 1973), 60; Steven Ozment, *The Age of Reform 1250–1550: An Intellectual and Religious History of late Medieval and Reformation Europe* (New Haven, 1980).

That clear and simple truth of Protestantism of course took many forms, but in one of its theological embodiments, it was Martin Luther's insistence that a person was "justified by faith." By this, Luther meant that a person could anticipate union with God through believing, rather than the performance of officially sanctioned acts of religious devotion. Inasmuch as this claim challenged the complex and richly detailed ritual framework for Catholicism, it was considered heretical, and Luther was excommunicated. But his emphasis on interiority, on inner piety in religious life, struck a strong chord with many, and his recommendation for the dramatic revision of Catholic liturgy—reducing the seven Catholic sacraments to three (baptism, the Lord's Supper, and penance), and rejecting the central Catholic ritual of the mass—took hold among those who followed him, the Lutherans. John Calvin, by the same token, made straightforward proposals, thought no one who engaged his weighty tome, the *Institutes of the Christian Religion*, would have thought his theological system simple in any sense of the word. Calvin's theology was, in a sense, the other side of the coin from Luther's emphasis on interiority. Though Calvin, like Luther, embraced a Christianity steeped in soulful piety (he declared that God "wins us by the sweetness of his goodness"), he is best known for his insistence on the strict ethic of a Christian life (which was an emphasis in Luther's writings as well). That ethic was enforced by authorities who, together with those they supervised, took the law of the church as the law of the land. Calvinism accordingly developed a characteristic attention to detail in the everyday lives of the faithful, and Calvinists came to understand themselves engaged in a covenantal relationship with God, a kind of bargain, in which the community's moral disciplining of each and every member was a condition of the pact with God.

Lutheran and Calvinist theologies shared more than an antipathy to Roman Catholicism. They shared ideas, reinforced each other, and offered up an assortment of theological building blocks to other leaders who customized their own Protestant viewpoints in acts of borrowing as much as through theological invention. They also prodded and challenged each other to be more precise, more encompassing, and relevant to Christians who inhaled the Reformation as one would breathe fresh air. As they claimed an increasingly broad and committed following, the reformers—Luther, Calvin, the various Anabaptists, English and Scottish innovators, and others—likewise kept the Roman Catholic church to some extent off balance and provoked the convening of Catholic leaders from all over Europe in Trent, in northern Italy, in the middle of the sixteenth century. At the council, Catholics reaffirmed their doctrines in the face of Protestant criticisms, reformed many of the clerical abuses that had discouraged the allegiance of the rank and file, and recognized the importance of education to moral life. This last emphasis was developed to a great extent by the order of Jesuits, founded by Ignatius Loyola in Paris in 1534, and was at the heart of a centuries-long investment in missionizing the indigenous populations of the New World. Together with the efforts of other Catholic clergy, Jesuits shaped a world of colonial encounter in the Americas that was recognizable as much for its instances of compassion as for its cruelties, its religious compromises, and its intractable religious differences. French and Spanish Catholics were the first to launch missionary campaigns in the Americas, and those campaigns, full of religious devotion, aspirations for personal achievement, and the desire for personal salvation, even in the form of martyrdom, bore with them a memory of the religious conflict in Europe. Reemergent under the umbrella of Trent, Catholic leadership looked across the Atlantic to the new proving ground for religious doctrine, to the prospect of claiming the inhabitants of the New World for Rome. Infused with the spirit of Trent, they crossed the Atlantic flush with confidence that they would make over the Americas as a Christian land.[18]

The Spanish Religious Interest

Old Spain and New Spain

Spanish first impressions of the Americas, as well as the visions and ambitions that they excited, varied greatly. We have read from one account of what Christopher Columbus saw when he came ashore at San Salvador in 1492. Thousands of other Spanish explorers saw other beaches, other forests, other birds and mammals, other villages and cities. Accounts of those impressions sometimes corresponded. Frequently, however, they did not. Even when groups of Spaniards viewed the same terrain, they saw it differently—but equally "truly"—and often professed as much. An example is the preamble in a letter sent to Don Tristan de Luna, the regional governor, by a group exploring the Florida interior in 1560: "Inasmuch as accounts given by each one in particular, although very true, cannot fail to disagree in something because ordinarily the judgments and opinions which many persons have of one and the same thing are diverse . . . we have agreed to relieve your Lordship of the confusion . . . [by reporting] with one opinion. . . ."[19]

---

[18] An animated, interactive map of Spanish and French missions in colonial North America, north of the current border with Mexico, that includes a wide range of data (missions populations, names of missionaries, dates of foundings and closing, commodity production, epidemics, etc.) in John Corrigan and Tracy Leavelle, *Spanish and French Missions in Colonial America* (Berkeley, CA: Electronic Cultural Atlas Initiative and California Digital Library, http://www.ecai.org/).

[19] Fray Domingo de la Anunciacion and others to Luna, Coosa, August 1, 1560, in *Earliest Hispanic/Native American Interactions in the American Southeast*, ed. Jerald T. Milanich (New York, 1991), 223.

Different views of the New World sparked different plans for exploiting it. The Crown, together with aspiring importers and merchants, saw gold, slave labor, and commodities for trade. The military saw opportunities for establishing reputation, a stage for distinction and personal honor, *pundonor*. The church saw an unprecedented harvest of converts. But even within these groups, there was much difference of opinion about the role of Spain in the New World. Especially where religion was concerned, Spaniards struggled in coming to terms with the meaning of their mission. Various explorers sought out in the Americas the keys to the restoration of life and harmony: the Fountain of Youth, the Golden Cities, and the Garden of Eden itself. The church likewise saw in the New World a chance to restore itself, to reinvent itself, to close ranks in one monumental venture that would demonstrate unity and purpose—and in the process, to purify Christianity of the ambiguities, contradictions, and conflicts apparent everywhere in its Spanish incarnation. This part of the mission, like the search for the Fountain of Youth, failed.

Spanish Christianity in the fifteenth century embodied several distinct personalities, and those personalities, even though sometimes contradictory, survived into later centuries. Religious orthodoxy was enforced through draconian measures, yet attraction to rituals and beliefs outside orthodox Christianity remained lively and widespread. Church and state were closely linked, yet sometimes broke out into open warfare with each other. Spanish Christianity was shaped by a keen ethnocentric sense of superiority, yet in comparison with that of other Christian nations, it was the most outspoken in its defense of the human rights of non-Europeans. Spain itself, on the eve of the voyages of Columbus, existed as an ambiguous union of the kingdoms of Aragon and Castile-Leon, ruled, respectively, by Ferdinand and Isabella. These monarchs, though married, presided over their respective realms with a significant degree of independence from each other.

Spain advanced significantly in power and prestige in 1492—not because of the discovery of America by Cristóbal Colón, but as a result of the Christian kingdoms' victory over the Moorish state of Granada to the south. Undertaken in the spirit of the medieval crusades against Islam, the war had dragged on for decades and in the process had sharpened the militant, authoritarian, and formal elements of Roman Catholicism in Spain. It also made more familiar the crusader's simple designation as a "Christian"—a prelude to "Christian" as a generic term for those who later encountered the native inhabitants of the Americas. Religious unity, which was deemed essential to political unity, at last seemed possible. And so, having driven out the Moors, the Catholic rulers delivered an ultimatum to those Spanish Jews who had not converted to Christianity: convert or be expelled.

Jews and Muslims in Iberia, in fact, had been converting to Christianity for hundreds of years. Converted Jews were known as *conversos*, and

Muslims as *moriscos*. But as Spain began to coalesce as a political and religious entity in the years before the conquest of Granada, leaders of both church and state had begun to question the authenticity of Jewish and Muslim conversions. The instrument that they settled upon to investigate suspicious conversions was the Inquisition, which had been in existence in parts of Christendom for 250 years and was imported to Castile in 1481. From there it was extended in 1570 to New Spain (Mexico) and other parts of the Americas to police the faith of the colonists. Though not directly aimed at Indians, it set the tone for dealings with them. The well-known excesses of the Inquisition—the slightest deviation of a person from Christian orthodoxy could lead to torture and execution—made it a poisonous gift to Spanish society. Yet in the Inquisition is revealed the full devotion of early modern Spain to the ideals of pure doctrine, formal ritual, and the moral authority of the church.

Alongside this embrace of orthodoxy, Spanish Christians—from the aristocracy to the peasantry—constructed their everyday religious lives out of beliefs and rituals that did not always square with official traditions. Spanish devotions included worship at local shrines, pilgrimage to those farther away, and the cultivation of visions of the saints in heaven. The faithful anxiously sought relics—ranging from the bones and clothes of saints to splinters of the cross on which Jesus was crucified—and prized them for their ability to cure illnesses, relieve doubt, and free persons from the controlling powers of demons. The pursuit of mystical experiences frequently outpaced interest in learning catechism, and some practices that were of scant interest to Catholic authorities in Rome (or even discouraged by them) were essential to Spanish devotions. Of particular importance were rituals associated with death. Blending Christian doctrine with folk beliefs and local funeral customs, such rituals ranged from "masses for the dead" performed in ornate cathedrals to rural ceremonies involving ancient notions of the land, fertility, and the cycle of seasons.[20]

Sixteenth-century Spanish mystics St. Teresa of Avila and her friend St. John of the Cross represented some of these patterns of religious life in their own lives. Both invested themselves in the institutional life of the church, but they also manifested the monastic ideal of withdrawal from the world and the quest for communion with God through solitude and meditation. Both adhered strictly to formal church doctrine but interwove it with their own beliefs about the nature of spiritual advancement. And Teresa's corpse eventually became a relic. Her followers reported that her body did not undergo corruption after death and that an intoxicating jasmine and violet perfume emanated from it, even after it was exhumed in 1583, nine months after burial. Shortly thereafter began the process of carving her body into relics, and in time her body was distributed piece-

---

[20] On rituals of death, see Carlos M. N. Eire, *From Madrid to Purgatory: The Art and Craft of Dying in Sixteenth Century Spain* (New York, 1995).

meal to Christians around the globe. Pieces of her bones accordingly entered into the religion of private devotions, relics, and folk/agrarian rituals and ceremonies—a Spanish style of "popular religion"—that existed alongside the more formal, bureaucratic, and authoritarian Catholic orthodoxy. This blending of impulses—the mixed but not necessarily contradictory messages of popular and formal religion—set an example for Spanish missionaries in the New World. So, for example, we discover Bishop Juan de Zumárraga reporting in 1531 that he had engineered the destruction of 500 temples and 26,000 idols in New Spain—at the same time that Christian and Aztec myths were being represented alongside each other in the decoration of Catholic churches there.

Just as there was a good bit of play between formal elements of religion and those derived from extraecclesiastical sources, so also was there a significant amount of give and take between church and state in Spain. The state and the church were closely linked throughout the period of the Spanish empire in the Americas, but during that same time, the conflicting interests of the two parties frequently made for an abrasive relationship.

State control of the church increased as Spain's star rose in Europe, so that by the latter sixteenth century, during the reign of Philip II, the crown exercised authority over not only clerical appointments, but also over church finances, the interpretation of doctrine, and the implementation of papal and conciliar directives. Spanish religious leaders and state officials joined forces under the assumption that a well-funded church, a regulated clergy, and the coordination of moral teachings with civil policies were essential to the stability of both church and state. Rome assisted in the process by granting the crown the rights to all religious offerings collected in the New World, as well as a central role in the appointment of church officials there.

Against the background of this relationship between the church and the crown, a continuous series of conflicts severely tested the resolve of each party to uphold the arrangement. Debates between clerics and royal authorities about Spanish policies in the Americas frequently revealed fissures in the church-state alliance.[21] Church leaders on occasion were forced to choose between their loyalty to Rome and their duties to a Spanish monarchy that sometimes snubbed its nose at Rome. When riots broke out in Madrid in 1766, the government blamed the Jesuits (from whose dress came the name the "Hat and Cloak Riots"). The state subsequently undertook to expel the Jesuits from Spain and its overseas empire, and also to confiscate Jesuit property, which was enormous. Those proceedings reaped a whirlwind of ill will among some New World populations that had worked constructively with the Jesuits. In response, the government strove

---

[21] See Rev. Maynard Geiger, O.F.M., "The Franciscan Conquest of Florida (1573–1618)" in *The Missions of Spanish Florida*, ed. David Hurst Thomas (New York, 1991), 252–57.

even more determinedly to reduce the power of the church. The clergy, in turn, protested individually and collectively in various ways. Clergy in the New World sometimes advocated radical responses, as in the case of Miguel Hidalgo, a native priest who led the first Mexican war of independence.

For the Spanish, the project of converting the inhabitants of the Americas to Christianity began with the second voyage of Columbus. On board the ship was a Benedictine priest charged with the evangelization of the Indians. Representatives of other religious orders followed, especially Dominicans, Franciscans, and Jesuits. Spanish domination exacted an immense toll in lives—especially as it brought European diseases to populations that carried no immunities to them—but by degrees the missionary enterprise unfolded. Spreading outward from the Caribbean, it developed along the paths of conquest in the Americas.

From the beginning, the Spanish debated how the natives were to be evangelized and introduced into the fold of Spanish culture. The hard-line approach, which was taken by the government and by contingents within the clergy, proposed that Native Americans were to be forcibly brought into the church. Juan Gines de Sepulveda declared that the scriptural passage "force them to come in" (Luke 14:24) be acknowledged as a guide to relations between Christians and Indians; and the Jesuit Alonso Sanchez argued that the New World would be Christianized only through Spanish domination.[22] This approach rested on assumptions about the Indians themselves and above all on the view that Indians were incapable of choosing what was best for them. Missionaries concluded that the New World "noble savages" had to be resettled into communities centered upon the church, and there they would be immersed in Christianity until they agreed to embrace it. The spectacle of a Spanish garrison outfitted in armor frequently expedited the process of conversion. But such conversions even then were frequently challenged. The Council of Lima (1552) decided to withhold the eucharist from Indians because it viewed their conversions as superficial.[23] Moreover, the problem sometimes arose from the methods of the missionaries themselves: Pedro de Gante's announcement that he baptized 14,000 Indians in a single day suggests a style of evangelizing that counted heads first and asked questions later.

Some of the clergy advocated the return to a view of missionary work common in Europe before the fields of missionary glory were opened in the Americas. This view conceived of evangelizing as an enterprise that allowed potential converts to choose freely to become Christian. Alongside of this they proposed sweeping revisions in the treatment of Indians: the

---

[22] Charles H. Lippy, Robert Choquette, and Stafford Poole, *Christianity Comes to the Americas 1492–1776* (New York, 1992), 124.

[23] See John McManners, "The Expansion of Christianity (1500–1800)" in *The Oxford Illustrated History of Christianity*, ed. McManners, (New York, 1990), 300–12.

abolition of slavery, respect for native cultures, and civil justice. These threads of protest were intertwined as a movement to defend Indians from the cruelties of Spanish conquest. The movement to defend them, which grew to significant proportions in the sixteenth century, included a wide assortment of clergy and lay advocates. Preeminent among those who argued the case for the Indians was Bartolomé de las Casas, a priest and plantation overlord (*encomendero*) in Hispaniola and Cuba. In 1514, las Casas suddenly renounced his office as *encomendero*, took up the cause of the Indians, and over the course of the next twenty years experimented with new models for relations between Indians and missionaries. He also immersed himself in the study of theology and authored groundbreaking works on the nature of the missionary enterprise. Returning to Spain, he gained influence at court and helped to bring about the New Laws of 1542, which put an end to further enslavement of the Indians and mandated far-reaching reforms in the *encomienda* system.

"The Friars Were Watching"

As conquistadores and explorers widened the sphere of Spanish influence in the New World, gold and other commodities, shipped eastward on the swift Atlantic current, found their way into the treasuries and storehouses of the government. The arrangement between church and state dictated that from this treasure the crown would fund missions to the Indians. The church organized a system by which to search out candidate populations for conversion and to administer the ecclesiastical apparatus once it was put into place. The enthusiasm and determination of the religious orders in this regard brought them renown, but at the same time, it kindled conflicts with the military and the supervisors of commerce over exploration priorities and the distribution of resources. But the clergy continued to see the New World in their own way, or, as an observer to an expedition in Florida wrote in 1560, "And the friars were watching, hoping that a greater population might be discovered to convert and maintain in the Christian creed."[24]

Florida disappointed the hopes of the Franciscan friars who traveled with the military along its coast and across the interior. Some of Spain's most accomplished explorers, including Juan Ponce de León and Hernando de Soto, came looking for treasures, but the land yielded neither a Fountain of Youth nor golden cities. An incentive for the settlement of Florida was found, however, in the 1560s, when the discovery of French Huguenot settlements nearby to the north alarmed the sensibilities of both the friars and their military escorts. Spain subsequently established a base for operations against the Protestant French, naming it San Agustín, in keeping with the occasion of the first Roman Catholic mass offered

---

[24] "Narrative of Fray Augustin Davila Padilla (1560)" in Milanich, ed., 232.

there, the feast of St. Augustine, in 1563. Its Jesuit founders were replaced by Franciscans in 1566, who operated missions in San Agustín and other coastal towns for the next century. Their labors occasionally were rewarded by dramatic mass conversions but were plagued by equally dramatic mass defections.

Spanish missionary activity in Florida developed very slowly. In 1680, the Province of St. Helen (the Franciscan administrative designation for the region of Florida) was the smallest of the seventeen provinces in the Americas, numbering only eleven houses and a total of ninety friars. The mission compounds were of humble wattle-and-daub construction, not the commanding structures that would be built on the other side of the continent. The Indians, by the eighteenth century, were beginning to discover the benefits of alliance with the English and so drifted away from the influence of the Spanish clergy. The Franciscans themselves were plagued by internal conflicts, the most important being the erosion of cooperation between clergy who were born and trained in the Americas and those imported from Spain. Governor Manuel de Montiano in 1738 described the situation as a "deep abyss of enmity and disunion" between the two groups.[25] When Florida passed into the hands of the English in 1763, little more than an empty husk of Catholicism remained.

New Spain, or Mexico, proved more profitable to both church and state than Florida. The spectacle of the magnificent Aztec civilization fired the imaginations of the government bureaucrats and clergy, who dreamed of empires of gold and God, respectively. The religious orders found their work less difficult in New Spain because Spanish domination in the region was decisive, and the environment accordingly offered a greater measure of stability and familiarity than did Florida. But the interests of neither clergy nor crown could be confined to familiar territory. Tales of fabulous wealth to the north began circulating in Mexico City—some from the mouth of Alvar Núñez Cabeza de Vaca, a shipwrecked bureaucrat who had walked across half the continent on his way back to Mexico City. In 1540, a soldier by the name of Francisco Vásquez de Coronado, together with Fray Marcos de Niza, a young priest, led an expedition northward from New Spain on a journey that would take them all the way to Kansas. Although they found no streets paved with silver and gold, they discovered in the Pueblo villages and the camps of Plains Indians a target population for evangelization.

The Franciscan missionary ventures in New Mexico began in 1581, eight years after the Spanish Ordinances of Discovery outlined a strategy replacing "conquest" with "peaceful and charitable" encounters with Indians. By 1598, whatever regulation the Ordinances might have brought to exploration of the lands north of Mexico City was subverted when Juan de Oñate was granted a contract to colonize New Mexico. Oñate, the son of a

[25] Geiger, 247; Thomas, 301.

fabulously wealthy Spanish silver-mine owner in Mexico, visited a host of cruelties upon the Pueblo Indians in the course of establishing Spanish authority in the region. The Franciscans who accompanied Oñate in turn portrayed themselves to the Indians as powerful wonder-workers, who could bring rain, heal the sick, and attract game. And they did not hesitate to remind the Indians of the Spanish conquest by regularly staging dramatic reenactments of it (in which the Indians played the roles) and by requiring that Indians greet a priest by kissing his feet. Such rituals clothed the friars with an authority over public life. That authority was essential to the efforts of Franciscans to bend the life of the people into a strict framework of Christian moral behavior—especially in the area of marriage and sexual relations—for it was the Franciscan strategy to reach the soul by first changing the behavior of the outer person.

However, as was the case in Spain, the exercise of ecclesiastical power and the drive for conformity (at least in terms of everyday behavior) was accompanied by flexibility in certain areas. Franciscans adopted a strategy of introducing Indians to Christian rituals by performing those that bore the appearance of similarity to Indian rituals. Also, the missionaries sought out ways in which to absorb native conceptualizations of religious power into their presentations of Christianity. Accordingly, Christian chapels were constructed on the sites of Indian shrines. The kachina cult—the Pueblo devotion to a variety of powerful spirits—was blended with the Christian veneration of the saints. Native rituals celebrating the passage of persons from childhood to adulthood, and others connected with the fertility of the land and the abundance of game likewise were allowed to mix with Christian practices. The Pueblo prayer-stick coalesced with the Christian cross. The calendar for the celebration of Christian feasts and holy days was adjusted to fit the cycle of Pueblo ceremonialism, so that Christmas and the rituals of the winter solstice were merged in the Pueblo mind. The drama of the crucifixion of Christ paralleled the ritual ordeals required of tribal leaders and male warriors. In short, the missionary endeavor in New Mexico, and, consequently, the religion of the converted, were characterized by a complex blending of strictness and adaptation. New Mexico was not Spain, however. In Castile, a certain amount of ambiguity in religion did not pose a threat to church or state because the culture had deep roots in Christianity. In New Mexico, the circumstances of Pueblo conversion were markedly different: Recent domination, not a long history of shared cultural presuppositions, proved inadequate as a glue to hold together the tensions present in the Christianity of the Indians.[26]

The superficiality of the Pueblo Christianization became apparent in 1680 when the Indians revolted and chased the Spanish from New Mexico. Reflecting on the event, the Franciscans maintained that the Antichrists—

---

[26] See Ramón A. Gutiérrez, *When Jesus Came the Corn Mothers Went Away: Marriage, Sexuality, and Power in New Mexico, 1500–1846* (Stanford, 1991), 46–94.

the colonial governors—were responsible for the revolt because they poisoned the relationship between the missionaries and Indians by their brutality in establishing dominion over them. This accusation against the civil authority, which had made possible the missionary enterprise from the start, was in keeping with the conflicted relationship between church and state in Spain at the time. The accusation also significantly altered the plans of missionaries for how they would go about their work.

Christianity returned to New Mexico, but very slowly, since the environment had been poisoned by Spanish rule. Missionary initiatives in adjacent areas (Texas and Arizona) met with limited success. By the late seventeenth century, about the time that the Franciscans were driven from New Mexico, the Jesuits had carved out a thriving mission enterprise of their own among the Yaqui Indians, in the rich mining country of northwestern New Spain. Jesuit influence extended northward into the Pimería Alta in the person of Eusebio Kino, who founded a mission among the Pima Indians near present-day Tucson, Arizona. Kino proved more effective as an itinerant evangelist and sometime rancher than as a mission administrator, however, and in any event, the changes he brought to the religious life of the Indians were largely diminished by the Yaqui revolt of 1740. In Texas, on the other hand, a battle between Mexicans and American settlers in 1836 brought lasting fame to a mission—the Alamo—that otherwise was undistinguished.

Prior to their expulsion from the Spanish dominions in 1767, the Jesuits had established a string of missions in Baja California. The Franciscans took control of these in 1768. The following year, news of Russian posts in the Pacific Northwest made its way to the chambers of José de Galvéz, a representative of the crown in New Spain. Galvéz subsequently ordered the settlement of California to buffer Russian encroachment on Spanish interests. Guided by Fray Junipéro Serra and his successor Fermín Lasuén, the Alta California venture eventually numbered eighteen missions, founded between 1769 and 1823. The mission buildings that have survived evoke moods both of this-worldly practicality and other-worldly spirituality, and are frequently cited as evidence of the success of Spanish missionaries in the land that became the United States. In fact, there were fewer missions in California than in either Florida or Texas, and the efforts of numerous extraordinary missionaries in California resulted in no extraordinary record of Christianization of the Indians.

What, then, is the legacy of the Spanish mission to the Indians in America? The Spanish missionaries faced a number of exceedingly difficult challenges in the New World. Indian cultures were strange to them, and the translation of religious language into the native idioms proceeded slowly and imperfectly, especially when notions such as the Christian Trinity were involved. The mission enterprise was usually shorthanded, only occasionally well funded, and always locked in a complicated relationship with military and commercial interests. Large-scale missionary ventures had not been a part of Spanish Catholicism for hundreds of years, and so the friars and priests were forced to improvise almost every step of the way. Finally, Spanish missions in Florida, California, and the Southwest suffered as operations located on the periphery of real Spanish interests far to the south.

Against this background it is more appropriate to speak of the significance of the Spanish missionary enterprise than of its success. It is significant because it set the tone for a style of Christianity grounded in the interpenetration of Catholic orthodoxy and local traditions. The reinterpretation of the Virgin Mary as a nurturing goddess, the coincidence of specific saints with local deities, the confluence of ritual traditions, the connections between Indian and Spanish religious objects, and a host of other instances of religious syncretism characterized the Catholicism of the Indians. The remnants of this syncretism are still alive within twentieth-century Hispanic Catholicism in America—in celebrations of the Day of the Dead, in the deemphasis of institutional Catholicism, in the attention given to the passion of Christ, and in numerous other ways.

French Missions and Institutions

Religious Disagreements and the Problem of Organization

French exploration of North America began with the voyages of Jacques Cartier, whose reconnoiterings in the Gulf of St. Lawrence and the St. Lawrence River in 1534 and 1535 set the stage for permanent French settlement in the New World. The islands and land mass charted by Cartier were not the sites of initial French ventures, however. Failed attempts in Brazil and, as we have seen, by French Huguenots in Florida preceded the founding of Acadia at the mouth of the St. Lawrence in 1604. Now included in the Canadian maritime province of Nova Scotia, Acadia—with its trading center of Port Royal—was settled by both Catholics and Protestants, and it was geared from the outset to the exploitation of commercial possibilities rather than religious missions. Clergy, who were present at the founding, died or returned to France. The Huguenot merchant underwriters of the colony balked at sending Catholic priests to Acadia, and when Jesuits finally did arrive in 1611, their doctrinal and personal quarrels with Protestants undermined the missionary work of both parties. The repercussions of those public disputes over doctrine were not lost on Samuel de Champlain, founder of Quebec (1608), explorer of the St. Lawrence River, and namegiver of Port Royal. Champlain reported to Cardinal Richelieu years afterward that "the Indians sometimes took one side, sometimes the other, and the French taking sides, according to their different beliefs, said everything that was bad of both religions."[27] When the English captain Samuel Argall of Virginia reduced Port Royal in 1613, thereby ending for a while the French experiment in Acadia, French missionary policy in North America was still without a blueprint.[28]

The floundering start of French missionaries in the New World was not simply the consequence of personality conflicts, language barriers, and English terrorism. Church authorities who envisioned the spread of Christianity in the New World were slow in developing a strategy for evangelization because of complex and deep-rooted problems in France. Not the least of those problems was the diversity of Christian belief. The dawn of the seventeenth century witnessed not only the obvious differences between Catholics and Protestants in France but also a considerable latitude in belief among Catholics themselves. Old agrarian traditions in the form of "folk beliefs" lived alongside official Catholic doctrines in the everyday lives of many French, and the combination was vexing to church leaders. The clergy lamented the ignorance of the peasantry, the shabby education of priests, and the ineffective efforts of church leaders to engage and channel the religious interest of the populace. Typical was the complaint of a priest of Nanterre that his congregation was ignorant of "those most common things that one must absolutely understand in order to receive the sacraments and be saved."[29] Though clergy sometimes exaggerated in their estimations of the religious state of affairs, such sorry judgments about religious education at home help to explain why French missions abroad in North America fared poorly. In neither case was there a proven strategy of religious education.

In contrast to the Catholic state of affairs (and it was not limited to France) was the Protestant world of concisely articulated doctrines, compact ritual, and church organization that favored strict local control of religious life. In France, Protestantism took the form primarily of the Hugenots, or French Calvinists, who after a period of conflict with Catholic authorities lived more or less peaceably alongside the majority Catholic population in the early seventeenth century. In time, however, as Catholicism was renewed in France, this arrangement deteriorated. The production of a lively culture of Catholic devotion, guided by the earlier reforms of the Council of Trent (1545–1563), together with government maneuvers to consolidate power, nurtured the political will of French Catholicism. One consequence was renewed persecution of Huguenots, most of whom fled to neighboring kingdoms, though some sought refuge in North America. After Cardinal Richelieu consolidated his power over

---

[27] Cited in Elizabeth Jones, *Gentlemen and Jesuits: Quests for Glory and Adventure in the Early Days of New France* (Toronto, 1986), 25.

[28] See ibid.; W. J. Eccles, *The Canadian Frontier 1534–1760* (New York, 1969); and the excellent survey by Robert Choquette in H. Lippy, Choquette, and Poole, 131–242.

[29] Jean Delumeau, *Le Catholicisme entre Luther et Voltaire* (Paris, 1971), 256–57.

government in the 1630s, Huguenots and other Protestants were forced to leave French territories even in North America.

The religious changes in France in the first half of the seventeenth century included reforms in several areas. French clerics and lay persons organized an assortment of men's and women's religious orders, the church enlarged seminary education and more diligently enforced church discipline, and the nation experienced a resurgence of pride in the distinctive features of the "Gallican" (French) church. Among the religious orders for women that were founded or greatly expanded during this time were the Ursulines, the sisters of the Congregation of Notre Dame, and a congregation of sisters organized by Jean Eudes in 1641. Counterpart male orders were the Recollects, Capuchins, and Sulpicians. All found work in New France alongside the Jesuits, although their associations were marked by disagreements about the relation of church to state, claims to financial resources, and the nature of the missionary enterprise.

Catholicism in the St. Lawrence Valley

In spite of their disagreements, French missionaries made significant progress in organizing Catholicism in the St. Lawrence Valley. Immediately after the reoccupation of Quebec, which had been in English hands from 1629 to 1632, missionary activity in New France unfolded primarily as a Jesuit enterprise. Jesuit missions to the Huron and to the Five Nations of the Iroquois met alternately with success and disaster, but even the failures succeeded in producing tales of heroism, suffering, and martyrdom. Those tales enshrined as legendary servants of God the "Black Robes," such as Jean de Brébeuf, Isaac Jogues, and Charles Garnier, and nurtured missionary zeal for generations of Canadian clergy and laypersons. At the same time, the Society of Jesus (the Jesuits) launched a series of initiatives aimed at developing an institutional base for Catholicism in New France. Fundamental to these efforts was the support of the Compagnie du Saint-Sacrement, a powerful society that was founded by wealthy Catholics in France in the mid-1630s and that was so secret in its operations that it remained invisible to historians for three hundreds years. With influential friends in France and with hostilities with the English to the south temporarily suspended, Jesuits in Quebec were able to found a college, the Còllege des Jésuites (1635), a seminary for French and Indian males (1636), and, in joint ventures with Augustinian and Ursuline nuns, a hospital and a convent school (1639). At the same time, they developed means by which to nurture the faith of French Catholics, through religious instruction and the administration of worship, and in other ways to fashion a religious infrastructure to serve their stated purpose of building "A New Jerusalem, blessed by God and made up of citizens destined for heaven."[30] English Protestants, recently arrived in Massachusetts Bay, were at that very moment using virtually identical language to describe their own vision of Protestant destiny in North America.

Quebec thrived as a fur-trading center and soon became the hub of French activity in North America. From there the French moved again up-river to settle Montreal in 1642. Under almost constant siege by the Iroquois, Montreal managed so little progress in commerce that in a matter of just a few years, the balance of power in administrating the town shifted from representatives of the Company of New France to Jesuits who were determined to preserve Montreal as a base from which to evangelize the Indians. The religious infrastructure, accordingly, began to grow. Marguerite Bourgeois, who was canonized a saint in 1984, founded a school for girls. Jeanne Mance established a Catholic hospital. Various other enterprises slowly advanced, so that by the late 1650s, Montreal boasted four hundreds residents (half the population of Quebec), a growing contingent of priests and nuns, a government that favored local control, and at least one miraculous healing.

Jesuit missions among the Hurons to the west rose and fell, depending on the mood of the powerful Iroquois, who waged intermittent campaigns against Hurons and French alike. And the fur trade that was carried on in the territory between Montreal and Lake Superior was unsteady and would remain so until the glut of beaver fur at the end of the century finally caused the bottom to fall out of the European market. Nevertheless, the French settlement of North America, in its religious as well as governmental aspects, had begun to evidence the rough contours of a colonial order, as if the blueprint lacking at Acadia had at last been discovered and implemented. Catholicism in New France, carried forward by the financial and political support of pious Catholics back in France, was essentially shaped neither through sparkling achievements in the mission field nor through partnership in a thriving trade venture; rather, it defined itself in the relentless elaboration of institutional religious life in churches, schools, hospitals, ecclesiastical hierarchy, a college, a seminary, boardinghouses, and the formalized sharing of power with civil magistrates. In short, it began to approximate the religion of its Catholic benefactors in France.[31]

Institutional Support

The development of institutional support lurched ahead in 1659 with the arrival of François de Laval as the first bishop of New France. Laval urged the crown to intercede in North America, in order to unite Quebec, the maritime colonies (some of which were under the control of the English),

---

[30] Quoted in W. J. Eccles, *Essays on New France* (Toronto, 1987), 27.

[31] See Choquette, in Lippy, Choquette, and Poole; Eccles, 56ff; Elaine Allan Mitchell, *Fort Timiskaming and the Fur Trade* (Toronto, 1977).

and the semiautonomous settlement of Montreal under the umbrella of royal authority. In 1663, with France at peace with its European neighbors and with Louis XIV's power consolidated at home, Louis took control of New France from its merchant board of governors and made it a royal province. The subsequent reconfiguration of power in New France proved advantageous for the church in at least one sense, namely, that the authority of the bishop to shape policy was formally recognized alongside that of the governor and intendant (or "chief manager"). Royal control also provided a kind of ballast for the ship of state that enabled it to endure the growing disagreements among Jesuits, Sulpicians (who began arriving in 1657), Ursulines, Recollects, and the missionary priests trained at the Paris Seminary for Foreign Missions (founded in 1663). On the negative side, the church discovered that its enhanced status was sometimes not sufficient to carry forward its programs against the interests of a strengthened civil government. Typical was the case of Laval's proposed banning of the brandy trade with the Indians, a measure that was overruled by the civil magistrates.

The development of French interests in North America, including the activities of French missionaries, was significantly broadened after 1663. Expeditions to survey the Great Lakes and their tributary waterways set off from Montreal and Quebec with increasing frequency. Jesuits played a key role in many such ventures. Jacques Marquette arrived in Wisconsin in 1669, and a few years later, paired with Louis Jolliet, came upon the Mississippi River, exploring it as far as its junction with the Arkansas River. In 1682, René-Robert Cavelier de la Salle charted the remainder of the river to its labyrinthine delta at the Gulf of Mexico, naming the territory after the King of France. This Louisiana Territory eventually made its way into the United States, after a period of occupation by the Spanish, when it was purchased during the presidency of Thomas Jefferson in 1803.

Between 1663 and 1803, the work of priests and nuns in French territories progressed in fits and starts. In the valley of the St. Lawrence, missionaries continued to approach Indians who had shown only slight interest in Christianity. Occasionally, their efforts would be rewarded, as in the case of a Mohawk woman, Kateri Tekakwitha, who was baptized in 1676 by Jesuits. At the age of twenty, she relocated to the Christian Indian village of St. Francis Xavier near Montreal, where she remained until her death a few years later. Her example of piety impressed French and Indians alike, and her remains were brought to the Indian reservation of Kahnawake, where they have been revered as relics. In the west, a string of forts and missions in the Great Lakes region had appeared by 1690. Jesuit priests such as Claude Allouez, Claude Dablon, Henri Nouvel, and Charles Albanel worked among the Illinois Indians; and Jesuits visited the Cahokia, Tensa, Natchez, and other tribes along the length of the Mississippi from its source to New Orleans, which was founded in 1718. By the early eighteenth century, however, the turf war between Jesuits and the seminary-trained priests had reached a critical juncture. Neither group wished to share mission territory with the other, and the Jesuits balked at teaching the native languages to their missionary competitors. As the number of priests trained in the seminaries in Paris and Quebec grew, the influence of religious orders was diminished, so that by 1704, all Jesuits were gone from Louisiana, and those who remained in the mission field were limited in their activities by policies hatched in Quebec.

Back in Quebec and in the towns in the St. Lawrence valley, Christianity was by no means well established. The supply of locally trained clergy was insufficient to meet all of the religious needs of Canadian Catholics. By 1700, just 60 secular priests (i.e., those not associated with a specific religious order) served a population of 15,000. There was one church for every 223 persons, a difficult situation for a population scattered over a very large area. The formal machinery of ecclesiastical bureaucracy had been put into place, but the state of affairs at the parish level was less than what church leaders had hoped. Jacques de Meulles, the intendant in New France, reported in 1683 that the French inhabitants rarely attended church and that their knowledge of Christianity barely surpassed that of Indians encountered by missionaries.[32] Partly to blame were the paltry funds appropriated for the support of parish priests, and many clergy opted for the mission fields to the west and south. Of more importance, the experiences of many settlers simply did not correspond with the clergy's visions of a religious future. The notion of a "New Jerusalem" meant little to traders who gathered periodically at Montreal's fur fairs or to soldiers (a substantial part of the population) who polished their bayonets and counted the days before they could return to France. Other events further complicated the situation. When war with Britain ended with the capitulation of New France in 1760, the British enacted anti-Catholic measures, chasing entire religious orders back to Europe and hobbling the remaining ecclesiastical bureaucracy—a process expedited by the suppression of the Jesuits in France and its territories in 1764. In 1774, on the brink of conflict with its American colonies, England sought to shore up its position with Canadians by restoring civil rights to Catholics. And so, church leaders once again flexed their political muscle, the ranks of the clergy grew, and the infrastructure of religious life was revived.

The steady growth of Catholicism in Canada after 1780 did not go unnoticed in the United States. From the early days of the English settlement of Massachusetts, Protestants in New England looked suspiciously upon their Catholic neighbors. England's war with the French and Indians in North America during the 1740s to the 1750s was fueled by inflammatory British rhetoric about the designs of French Catholics to overrun and dismantle the Protestant regime in New England. In the nineteenth century, church

---

[32] Eccles, *Canada Under Louis XIV*, 224; *Essays on New France*, 29.

leaders in the United States again characterized Canadian Catholicism as a danger to the destiny of Protestantism in North America. And in the late nineteenth century, the growth of Protestant churches in Canada itself brought Protestant Anglo-Saxon prejudice to English-speaking Ontario. That prejudice, or nativism, was particularly evident during periods of internal migration of French Catholics from Quebec to Ontario. Canadian Catholics, in turn, closed ranks and embraced a distinctly conservative and ultramontane (i.e., characterized by a close adherence to Roman leadership) Catholicism. Some Catholics, including clergy, left Canada for the United States. In fact, by the late twentieth century, the number of Franco-Americans of Canadian origin exceeded the number of French Canadians in Canada.[33] Some of these immigrants settled in places where the French legacy remained strong, such as Louisiana, northern New England, and parts of the Midwest. Others mingled with immigrant Catholics recently arrived in the United States from various European countries, including France.

The projects of French Catholics in North America differed from those of the Spanish. Like their Spanish colleagues, French missionaries saw in North America a potential harvest of souls for Christianity. Both the Spanish and French spilled blood—their own as well as that of the indigenous peoples—in the process of claiming those souls. French missionaries, more so than Spanish, were encouraged in their work by stories about martyrdom, including the possibility of their own. And the Black Robes who were active in New France typically undertook their evangelization of the Indians as an ongoing series of forays into Indian villages and lands, rather than through the establishing of mission complexes to which Indians were invited for catechizing and acculturation (although these strategies were also used). Nevertheless, the French in Quebec, like the Spanish in Mexico, produced enduring and highly elaborated machinery for the administration of Catholicism in the New World. For the French, that machinery developed in the service of French colonists, so that even as missionary efforts brought discouragement, the institution-building continued in the centers of French trade. The fact of the durability of those Catholic institutions, together with recurrent ultramontanism in Canada, shaped the development of Catholicism both north and south of the Canadian border. That Catholicism, in presenting theological and ideological challenges to Protestants in the United States, has at the same time influenced the formation of Protestant understandings of nationhood.

---

[33] For a summary of the French-Canadian diaspora, see J. E. Robert Choquette, "French Catholicism in the New World," in *The Encyclopedia of the American Religious Experience*, ed. Charles H. Lippy and Peter W. Williams, vol. 1 of 3 vols., (New York, 1988), 233–37.

CHAPTER TWO

England and America

Our roots as a nation go back to the remarkable burst of colonizing activity that transformed the Atlantic Ocean into the *Mare Nostrum* of western Europe. There is little that we, as Americans, can claim as exclusively our own. Our language is not our own, nor are our tables of weights and measures. Our most familiar proverbs and nursery rhymes have been inherited from others. Our concept of trial by jury came to us from abroad. Indeed, our whole legal system, with its guarantees of liberty and provisions for constitutional government, is the product of a longer history than ours. Even after our declaration of political independence, we remained part of this larger society—reading the works of European poets, studying the writings of European philosophers, listening to the music of European composers, utilizing the discoveries of European scientists, reaping the benefits of European capital invested in our railroads and mines, recruiting European "hands" for our mills and factories. In almost every respect we have been part of Europe. This tendency is as true in religion as it is in literature, law, philosophy, art, or science.

The religious heritage that links us to Europe is immediately apparent to any visitor to the British Isles. When Americans walk down the street of an English city, they will be reminded of home as they pass Anglican (Protestant Episcopal), Presbyterian, Baptist, Methodist, and Roman Catholic churches. They may be handed a Plymouth Brethren tract, encounter a Salvation Army lassie, or find a Quaker meetinghouse or Jewish synagogue half hidden in a side street. Traveling north of the Tweed River, they will discover that many of the Presbyterian divisions at home had their origin in Scotland.

But it is not from the British Isles only that our churches have come, for there are German, Swedish, Danish, Norwegian, and Finnish Lutheran churches; German, Dutch, and Hungarian Reformed churches; Mennonite, Moravian, and Dunker communities. And more recent immigration from central and eastern Europe has swelled the Roman Catholic and Jewish populations in the United States and has introduced the numerous national churches of Eastern Orthodoxy into the American scene. At the end of the twentieth century, immigration continued to reshape the population. Asian religious communities and various Islamic groups, aided by the reform of immigration laws, have become highly visible components of the religious landscape.

With only a few exceptions, the varied religious groups of America have their rootage abroad. But this fact must not obscure the parallel fact that we are Americans. There have been modifications and adaptations of the European influence from the beginning. And although the European heritage gave American religious life its initial shape and substance, and influences from around the globe over time have altered the religious profile of the nation, the purpose here is to focus attention upon the distinctive ethos and character of the religious development of America.

England as the "Bridge" from the Old World to the New

As early as 1622, John Donne was asserting with remarkable prescience that England, which hitherto as an island had been "but as the suburbs" of Europe, was destined to occupy a much more central position in the future as the "bridge" between the Old World and the New.[1] His words were prophetic as far as the Atlantic coast of North America was concerned, and the most obvious conditioning factor in American religious life has been its English beginnings. The thirteen colonies were English colonies, the vast proportion of the population was of English stock, and the American Revolution was fought—so the colonists asserted—to defend and preserve their rights as Englishmen.

Protestant Predominance

The fact that the American colonies were English colonies meant, first of all, that the colonists in background if not always in active affiliation would be predominantly Protestant. Even the non-English minorities—Scots, Scotch Irish, Germans, Dutch, French, and Swedes—were almost wholly

[1] Louis B. Wright, *Religion and Empire* (Chapel Hill, N.C., 1943), 111.

Protestant in background. Only in Maryland were there a significant number of Roman Catholics, and even in Maryland they were a minority. Judaism was limited to a handful of tiny congregations. Thus, to the extent that the mind of colonial America was shaped by a religious faith, it was shaped perforce by Protestantism.

This overwhelmingly Protestant religious orientation was equally true of the new nation as its borders pushed westward. The French trading posts on the Great Lakes were not rooted deeply enough to become centers of a continuing cultural or religious tradition, and a permanent non-Protestant area of settlement was confined to a relatively small enclave at the southern tip of the vast area embraced in the Louisiana Purchase of 1803. It was not until the nineteenth century was well advanced, when their numbers began to be augmented by large-scale immigration, that Roman Catholics became a numerically significant segment of American life; and it was not until the end of the nineteenth century that major Jewish and Eastern Orthodox communities came into existence.

As a consequence of Protestant predominance, even non-Protestant groups tended to take on a somewhat Protestant coloration in the American environment. The earnest "moralism" of American Roman Catholicism has often been attributed to the influence of a Protestant culture; and on occasion, American Roman Catholics have had to defend themselves against charges of undue "Americanism," a term that usually implied the adoption of Protestant presuppositions. A more complete adjustment was represented by Reform Judaism, which initially adopted even the forms of Protestant Sunday worship. Nor has Eastern Orthodoxy remained unaffected. A spokesman for the Greek church, after staunchly defending at an ecumenical gathering the unchanging integrity of the Orthodox witness, commented privately that the Orthodox in America scarcely dare admit even to themselves the extent to which their life has been modified by an encounter with Protestantism.

After World War I, to be sure, the older Protestant predominance had been so greatly reduced by the shifting tide of immigration that influences that once moved only in one direction tended to become reciprocal. Not the least of the influences—for example, reshaping the Protestant understanding of the pastoral office and Protestant liturgical practice—has been the influence exerted by Roman Catholicism.

The Puritan Heritage

Although the United States by virtue of its English antecedents and character was predominantly Protestant throughout its early history, it was an English Protestantism with a difference. At home the great majority of the people were Anglicans, members of the Church of England; and the "Dissenting" interest composed of Presbyterians, Congregationalists, Baptists, and Quakers was relatively small. In the colonies this situation was reversed. By the end of the colonial period, the Congregationalists and the Presbyterians were the two largest American denominations. The Baptists and the Anglicans were roughly equal in size, and the Quakers—widely dispersed throughout all the colonies—ranked fifth in number of adherents. It was this difference in the religious makeup of the population that Edmund Burke had in mind when he noted in his speech *On Conciliation with the American Colonies* (1775) that "the people [of the colonies] are Protestants, and of that kind which is the most adverse to all implicit subjection of mind and opinion."

What was the character of this early American Protestantism? Although diverse in outward ecclesiastical form, its diversity found expression mostly within the limits of the common faith of English Puritanism.[2] The tendency in popular mythology to stress the priority of Plymouth at the expense of Jamestown is not historically accurate, but in a deeper sense it is a true recognition that the religion of the English colonies had its fundamental rootage in a Puritanism that Americans have found most easy to identify in terms of New England.

André Siegfried, a French observer of twentieth-century America, confirmed the estimate that is implicit in the prominence given to the story of the landing of the Pilgrims when he asserted, "If we wish to understand the real sources of American inspiration we must go back to the English Puritanism of the seventeenth century." James Bryce also emphasized this feature of American life in 1888 as he sought to describe the American commonwealth to his fellow countrymen at home. "There is a hearty Puritanism in the view of human nature which pervades the instrument of 1787," he wrote. "It is the work of men who believed in original sin, and were resolved to leave open for transgressors no door which they could possibly shut. Compare this spirit with the enthusiastic optimism of the Frenchmen of 1789. It is not merely a difference of race and temperaments; it is a difference of fundamental ideas."[3]

The same verdict had been expressed by Philip Schaff in 1844 when, shortly after his arrival from Germany, he sought to analyze the main features of American religious life. "Puritan Protestantism forms properly the main trunk of our North American church," he declared in his inaugural address as professor of church history in the Mercersburg Theological Seminary. "Viewed as a whole," the American church "owes her general characteristic features, her distinctive image, neither to the German or Continental Reformed, nor to the English Episcopal communion," but to the Puritans of New England. "To this New England influence must be added indeed the

---

[2] See David Hall, "Understanding the Puritans" in *Religion in American History*, eds. J. M. Mulder and J. F. Wilson (Englewood Cliffs, N.J., 1978), 1–16.

[3] André Siegfried, *America Comes of Age* (New York, 1927), 33. James Bryce, *The American Commonwealth* (New York, 1910), I, 306.

no-less important weight of Presbyterianism, as derived subsequently from Scotland and Ireland. But this may be regarded as in all essential respects the same life. The reigning theology of the country . . . is the theology of the Westminster Confession." A few years later, he asserted that "the six north-eastern states included under the name of New England . . . are . . . in regard to culture and Christianity, the garden of America" and from this seedbed has come "the leading religious influence in the Union," exerting "a powerful influence upon the religious, social, and political life of the whole nation."[4]

Schaff's only error was to identify this Puritanism so exclusively with New England. Puritanism was far from monolithic. In England it was a many-faceted movement that embraced Presbyterians, Congregationalists, Baptists, large numbers of Episcopalians, and even the Quakers. It is a mistake, therefore, to limit Puritan influence in America to New England Congregationalism, for in other forms of English dissent, it was strongly represented in all the colonies. As Schaff noted, the Presbyterians—including those from Scotland and Ireland—stood shoulder-to-shoulder with the Congregationalists at every important point. This pattern was equally true of the Baptists who also had adopted a modified form of the 1647 Westminster Confession[5] as their statement of faith. Nor was colonial Anglicanism for the most part "the high-flying Anglicanism" of the Restoration divines; it was "the Calvinistic Low Church Anglicanism of the period before Laud."[6] Whether in Virginia or in New England, the same books of religious edification were read, the same doctrines were taught from the pulpits, and the same laws were passed to enforce religious duties. When the Quakers, who represented the left wing of the Puritan movement, are brought into the picture, it is evident that the Puritan influence in early America was dominant. So pervasive was its influence that, as Schaff reports, even many of the Lutheran churches were remade in the Puritan image.[7]

---

[4] Philip Schaff, *The Principle of Protestantism as Related to the Present State of the Church* (Chambersburg, Pa., 1845), 114; quoted by J. H. Nichols, *Romanticism in American Theology* (Chicago, 1961), 2. Philip Schaff, *America: A Sketch of Its Political, Social, and Religious Character*, ed. Perry Miller (Cambridge, Mass., 1961), 54, 89, 107; see also 116–17.

[5] The Westminster Confession, with modifications made by Congregationalists, is reproduced in Williston Walker, *The Creeds and Platforms of Congregationalism* (New York, 1893). The Baptist recession is in W. L. Lumpkin, *Baptist Confessions of Faith* (Philadelphia, 1959). John Witherspoon, president of Princeton, noted the basic unity of the denominations in this tradition when he described the religious situation in New Jersey at the close of the Revolution. "The Baptists," he said, "are Presbyterians in all other respects, only differing in the point of infant baptism; their political weight goes the same way as the Presbyterians." *Essays on Important Subjects* (Edinburgh, 1805), IV, 203.

[6] The comment is William Haller's in *The Constitution Reconsidered*, ed. Conyers Read (New York, 1938), 136. This "Calvinism" owed more perhaps to Zurich than Geneva, the term being used as shorthand for the whole Reformed tradition.

[7] Schaff, *America*, 93, 150–54.

Shaker women of the Canterbury, New Hampshire, community. Puritanism was one expression of religious impulses that shaped the Anglo-American world over two hundred years. Some of the same impulses that gave birth to Puritanism were involved in the genesis of other religious groups, such as the Shakers. *(Courtesy, The Winterthur Library: The Edward Deming Andrews Memorial Shaker Collection.)*

One further word of caution needs to be spoken. What was labeled as Puritan by Schaff, Bryce, and Siegfried was not a static theological point of view.[8] As the Calvinism of the early Puritans was not precisely the same as the Calvinism of Geneva, so the Puritanism of nineteenth-century America was not that of seventeenth-century England, and it might more properly be described as Evangelicalism. There was constant modification and

[8] Some recent scholarship has stressed the imprecision of the label "Puritan." See David D. Hall, *Worlds of Wonder, Days of Judgement* (New York, 1989), and Charles Lloyd Cohen, *God's Caress* (New York, 1986).

change and development. But there were also large elements of continuity; and even when theological foundations were altered or eroded, habitual ways of thinking and feeling persisted and continued to give form and structure to the common life.

Religious Diversity

The fact that the American colonies were English colonies also explains in large measure the multiplicity of religious bodies that was so prominent a feature of the English colonial scene in contrast to the religious uniformity that prevailed in the French and Spanish domains, for a deliberate policy of religious toleration was adopted by the English colonial authorities.

At the outset, to be sure, it was assumed that there would be and should be uniformity of religion in the new settlements; but in keeping with the whole system—or lack of system—of English colonial administration, the instructions at this point were not always observed. The Separatists who landed at Plymouth in 1620, for example, had set sail with the permission of the Virginia Company to establish a settlement within its territory, even though the second Virginia charter stated that no one, such as the Separatists, who refused to take the Oath of Supremacy should be allowed to embark for Virginia. In colonies other than Virginia, English administrative laxity was transformed into an explicit policy of toleration, and in no colony other than Virginia did the English authorities even attempt to impose a pattern of religious uniformity. When such attempts were made, as in Massachusetts Bay, it was by the colonists themselves, and it was in spite of, rather than because of, English policy.

One important factor determining the tolerant attitude of the English government was the economic advantage to be gained by a policy of toleration. The colonies were regarded as commercial ventures designed to contribute to the wealth and prosperity of the mother country. The great need if they were to be profitable was to attract settlers who would provide the labor to exploit the untapped resources of field and forest. Jails were emptied to provide colonists, the impoverished were sent out, adventurers were enlisted. But it soon became obvious that those who suffered from disabilities at home because of their religious profession would be prime recruits if they could be induced to leave the homeland by the prospect of greater freedom abroad.

The Dutch had early discovered the economic folly of adopting rigorous measures to suppress religious dissent, and Peter Stuyvesant was rebuked for attempting to institute such a policy in New Amsterdam. The Dutch authorities informed him that his "vigorous proceedings" should be discontinued lest he "check and destroy" the population. The secret of the prosperity of old Amsterdam, he was reminded, was the moderation displayed by the magistrates in dealing with religious minorities, with the result that "people have flocked" from every land "to this asylum." He was informed that a similar policy should be pursued in New Amsterdam. "It is our opinion that some connivance would be useful; that the consciences of men, at least, ought ever to remain free and unshackled."[9]

English policy was of a piece with the Dutch. This similarity is self-evident in the grants that were made to Lord Baltimore and William Penn, but the clearest statement of the motivation that lay behind the policy is to be found in a communication from the Lords of Trade in London to the Council of Virginia: "A free exercise of religion . . . is essential to enriching and improving a trading nation; it should be ever held sacred in His Majesty's colonies. We must, therefore, recommend it to your care that nothing be done which can in the least affect that great point."[10] Non-English settlers were welcomed, and some were even recruited with the promise of freedom to establish their own religious institutions. Most of these non-English groups arrived relatively late in the colonial period[11] and constituted, proportionately, a small segment of the total population, but they did serve to give added variety to the religious spectrum.

Economic advantage alone, however, does not explain the relative equanimity with which dissent was viewed by both the Dutch and the English. A major contributing factor was the fact that the "maxims of moderation" were already being practiced at home. The English were more halting in their progress in this direction, but throughout the colonial period, England was moving steadily toward an ever-broadening toleration of religious dissent. At times the toleration at home was within narrow limits. At other times, as during the two decades following the meeting of the Long Parliament in 1640, it was very broad. For brief periods under Charles I and Charles II, there were efforts to impose a rigid conformity, but these efforts were never wholly successful and were not long pursued. With the adoption of the Act of Toleration in 1689, the acceptance of religious diversity within the limits of trinitarian Protestantism became the settled domestic policy of the English government. Thus its religious policy in the colonies was in many ways merely a reflection of a policy that was being developed at home, and in the end, England did little more than export her own religious diversity.

A New Beginning in a New Land

Although the English inheritance was the most important single influence determining the form and substance of religious life in the colonies, both the necessities and the opportunities of life in the New World introduced

---

[9] The text of the letter is printed in W. W. Street, *Religion in Colonial America* (New York, 1942), 151–52.

[10] *Historical Collections Relating to the American Colonial Church*, ed. William S. Perry (Hartford, Conn., 1871–1878), I, 379–81.

[11] The great influx of the Germans and Scotch Irish, the major non-English elements in the population, occurred during the last third of the colonial period.

changes of emphasis and modifications of practice. Faced with the task of beginning anew, the leaders of the churches found themselves far more dependent upon the laity than had hitherto been true, and they were forced to concede to the laity far greater powers than the laity had previously enjoyed. Furthermore, the long sea journey had removed many of the inhibitions and restraints to which most of the churches had been subject, leaving them free to experiment in reshaping their life to conform more closely to long-cherished convictions than had been possible at home. Finally, given the view of history that prevailed, the mere fact that a new beginning could be made cultivated an eager expectancy that this was "the Lord's doing" and was but a foretaste of the near-approaching time when all things would be made new.

The Importance of the Laity

The Protestant Reformation with its emphasis upon the priesthood of believers and its appeal to the plain testimony of Scripture tended to elevate the laity in the life of the church. The tendency was arrested, however, by the establishment of national churches, sanctioned and maintained by the state. The clergy, being appointed by and responsible to the state, took charge and left to the people a passive role. Thus, within the limits of state control, the church tended to become a clerically dominated institution. In England, to be sure, the post-Reformation struggle for dominance between contending parties within the church necessitated appeals for lay support and gave added influence to the laity,[12] but this influence was always limited by ordered structures of church life. In the colonies, on the other hand, the restraint of an established church order was reduced to a minimum.

One of the facts of life in the New World was that a new beginning had to be made, and for most of the churches, this new beginning had to be made by individual clergymen recruiting their own congregations out of a population that was largely unchurched. The ready-made congregations of early New England and the parishes created by legislative fiat in Virginia were not typical. Elsewhere there were neither closely knit bodies of believers already in existence nor parishes established by law. Nor was there any ecclesiastical body close at hand to supervise and regulate the life of the churches. Furthermore, because of the diversity that prevailed, the clergy often had to compete for the allegiance of the people. Far removed from the status-giving context of an ordered church life and dependent upon what support they could enlist among the laity for both the formation and the maintenance of the congregations they served, the only real authority that the clergy possessed was the authority they could command by their

[12] See James F. Maclear, "The Making of the Lay Tradition," *Journal of Religion,* 33 (1953), 113–36.

powers of persuasion and the force of their example. Given these circumstances, it is not surprising that the laity began to exercise a decisive voice in church affairs, with "everything," as Pennsylvanian Henry M. Muhlenberg explained, dependent "on the vote of the majority."[13]

Even in New England, where churches had been constituted at the outset with ministers as a "speaking aristocracy" and congregations reduced to a "silent democracy," this state of affairs did not long persist. Men who had gained independent status as property holders by clearing their own land with flintlocks close at hand were not the type to be unduly submissive, and their self-assertiveness soon stripped the New England clergy of much of their independence. The same process was at work in Virginia, where lay vestries gained effective control by neglecting to present the clergy to the governor for permanent induction into office, thus retaining, as the Archbishop of Canterbury complained, the right to hire and fire them like "domestic servants."[14]

A further consequence of lay predominance in church affairs was the strong support that was given to what was later described as "local autonomy." With single congregations beginning of necessity as independent self-governing units, resistance developed when attempts were made to subordinate them to larger units of ecclesiastical control. This trend was especially true in places where church structures tended to be relatively weak, as in the middle colonies. The laity were fearful of losing the prerogatives they possessed in the local church. Thus in Virginia and other southern colonies, where the Anglican laity had gained decisive powers in local "vestries," there was vigorous opposition to the attempt to establish an episcopate in America. A similar apprehension among the Congregational laity in Massachusetts thwarted the proposal to complete the Congregational structure there with a yearly consultative synod, and the Presbyterians in 1758 were forced to come to terms with this sentiment by conceding extensive powers to local presbyteries at the expense of synodical authority.

Thus, whatever the denomination and whatever the polity that was ostensibly professed, all colonial churches tended to be characterized by a strong emphasis upon local autonomy and lay control. This emphasis persisted and was only partially curtailed in the nineteenth and twentieth centuries through strenuous efforts of Presbyterian, Methodist, and Roman Catholic clergy alike to have all church property transferred to and vested in presbytery, conference, or bishop. The objective was to limit local lay power by gaining control of the church property.

---

[13] *The Journals of Henry Melchior Muhlenberg* (Philadelphia, 1942), I, 67. For a perceptive discussion of this point, see Sidney E. Mead in *The Ministry in Historical Perspectives*, eds. H. Richard Niebuhr and D. D. Williams (New York, 1956), 212–18.

[14] Elizabeth Davidson, *The Establishment of the English Church in Continental American Colonies* (Durham, N.C., 1936), 19.

The Breakdown of the Parish System

A further consequence of the conditions that prevailed in the New World was the shattering of the parish system of ecclesiastical organization and the transformation of all the churches into what are usually described as "gathered" churches.

For almost a thousand years in western Europe, it had generally been assumed that every member of society was automatically a member of the church. Richard Hooker (1554?–1600), speaking of the situation in England, had voiced this common assumption in these words: "There is not any member of the Church of England but the same man is also a member of the commonwealth; nor any member of the commonwealth which is not also [a member] of the Church of England."[15] For purposes of worship, instruction, and discipline, people were divided geographically into parishes. This was the basic unit of church life, established and maintained by the state. It was in marked contrast to a self-supporting congregation whose membership was defined by voluntary affiliation.

Only in Virginia and in New England did a parish system, designed to embrace a total community, function with any success, and in Virginia the success was limited. The pattern of settlement in Virginia was the major problem. With population thinly distributed on large plantations bordering navigable rivers, a single parish could be 30 miles in length. In such a situation, it was difficult for the parish incumbent even to keep in touch with his parishioners, to say nothing of maintaining regular services of worship and a systematic program of instruction for them. In New England the pattern of settlement on small landholdings gathered about a village center was more conducive to an effective parish system, and it was maintained largely unimpaired until the inroads of dissent destroyed the religious homogeneity of the population.

Elsewhere in the colonies, the religious diversity that was present from the beginning compromised any attempt to establish a system that presupposed that the whole community would belong to a single church. A thin façade of parish structure was maintained by legislative action in Maryland, the Carolinas, Georgia, and the environs of New York City, but none of these parish churches could claim more than a minority of the population. South of Virginia most parishes existed only on paper, never having been supplied with clergymen. The only thing that made possible even the pretense of maintaining a parish system was governmental authority, and the moment it was withdrawn, the whole flimsy structure toppled. By this time the Anglicans had become a minority even in Virginia, and the adoption of Thomas Jefferson's "Bill for Establishing Religious Freedom" (1786) was equally effective in exposing as fiction the notion that the

---

[15] *Hooker's Ecclesiastical Polity: Book VIII*, ed. R. A. Houk (New York, 1931), 156.

Anglican parishes there were anything more than "gathered" churches composed of voluntary adherents.

The New England story was somewhat more complex, for in New England the attempt was made to preserve "gathered" churches within a parish structure. This posed no great problem during the early years when the total population was largely a "sifted" people. But when the children of believers were unable to exhibit the minimum qualifications for church membership, the problem became acute. In an effort to preserve the parish concept, a form of "birthright" membership was adopted, and by this means, the collapse of the parish system in New England was deferred until the increase of dissent made its defense a hopeless cause. A full century before disestablishment stripped away the lingering traces of the parish structure in New England, Jonathan Edwards (1703–1758) recognized that its days were numbered and called upon his fellow Congregationalists to return to their initial emphasis upon the church as a covenanted community of convinced believers. Although certain privileges were retained until the first decades of the nineteenth century, the defenders of the attenuated "establishment" that survived during these final years found it necessary to adopt all the techniques of the "gathered" churches in order to carry on a rearguard defense of its few remaining prerogatives.

The "techniques of the 'gathered' churches" is a key phrase, for it calls attention to the necessity that was laid upon the churches to win support and gain recruits by voluntary means. No longer could they depend upon people automatically being members of the church and subject to its discipline. The churches had to utilize all their powers of persuasion if they were to maintain and perpetuate themselves. The techniques they devised to this end were many and varied: the fostering of revivals, the organization of mission societies, the establishment of Sunday schools, the development of programs of visitation, the publication of tracts, and later the utilization of advertisements in periodicals. But above all, preaching was the means by which churches survived as voluntary organizations. Effective preaching was the very cornerstone of Protestantism, and it played an important role as well in the development of Roman Catholicism and Judaism in America. This vigorous evangelistic and instructional activity, imposed upon the churches by their status as "gathered" groups of convinced believers, was to become one of the most distinctive features of American church life.

The Possibility of Thoroughgoing Reform

The prominence of religious radicals and left-wing groups in America has frequently been noted, and it is not surprising that they should have come to the New World in disproportionate numbers. Members of the established churches in Europe could only view the situation in America with some dismay, for the necessity to make a new beginning forced them to improvise and served to shatter many of their previously cherished patterns of ecclesiastical life. In New Amsterdam, for example, Jonas Michaelius was acutely conscious of the coercions imposed by the conditions of life in a new land, and he felt compelled to explain the irregularities that attended the formation of his church. "One cannot," he wrote to the authorities at home, "observe strictly all the usual formalities in making a beginning under such circumstances."[16] The nonestablished churches of Europe, however, were in a reverse situation. They welcomed the opportunity to make a new beginning free from the restraints to which they were subjected at home. This was the great attraction that enticed the Mennonites and the Moravians to risk the hazards of beginning life anew in the American wilderness. It was this prospect also that exerted so strong an appeal to that hardy band of Pilgrims who settled at Plymouth in 1620 and that encouraged the founders of Massachusetts Bay Colony in 1629 to undertake their "great migration."

The necessity to make a new beginning was seen by these minority groups as more than mere negative release. It was an opportunity to undertake a positive work of construction. William Penn never could have launched his "holy experiment" in England where the existing patterns and institutions of a settled community would have dictated compromises from the start. He needed a place to begin anew where there would be "room," as he put it, for "such an experiment." It was this opportunity that was given him in America.

The significance of the opportunity to make a new beginning can be seen most clearly through the eyes of those who sailed with the Winthrop fleet to Massachusetts Bay. Michaelius had to "make do" in New Amsterdam, but the early New Englanders had had to "make do" at home. In England they had been compelled to adjust to the irregularities imposed upon them by the requirements of the established church, and the shift to the New World was viewed by them as a release from this bondage. "It is one thing," explained John Cotton, "for . . . members of the church loyally to submit unto any form of [church] government when it is above their calling to reform it"; it is quite another matter for them to "choose a form of government and governors discrepant from the rule." The Great Migration had been organized with the specific purpose of providing them with this freedom to "choose." John Winthrop standing on the deck of the *Arbella* made explicit the duty that was laid upon them. It was to "bring into familiar and constant practice" that which they previously had been able to "maintain as truth in profession only." The purpose was clear. "We

---

[16] His letter is printed in *A Documentary History of Religion in America*, ed. E. S. Gaustad (Grand Rapids, Mich., 1982–1983), I, 82–83.

go," said Francis Higginson, "to practice the positive part of church reformation."[17]

America was for them, as it was to become for others, a land of opportunity, a land where a "wide door" of "liberty" had been set open before them. No longer were they to be compelled to resort to devious expedients, as they had been at home, in order to avoid "corruptions." This necessity had been lifted. But more important was the freedom they possessed to undertake a radical reconstruction of church life to conform to what they regarded as the plain prescriptions of God's "most holy Word."

The Sense of Expectancy

A new beginning is always a heady experience that breeds an eager expectancy among those who participate in it. Hopes are kindled and, as imagination takes over, the future becomes pregnant with possibility. This tendency was doubly true of the new beginning that was made in America, for European peoples had always lived with the hope—sometimes faint but never absent—that the Lord's promise in Isaiah and Revelation to "make all things new" would some day be fulfilled. And the very term "New World," which was used to describe the setting in which they were making their new beginning, was calculated to remind them of the Lord's promise.

Since every Englishman had been taught from childhood to view the course of history as predetermined by God's overruling providence, no one could regard the colonizing activity in America as an ordinary venture. As early as 1613, William Strachey was insisting that God had kept America hidden for a purpose and that those who had established the small settlement in Virginia were but pursuing a course of action that God had foreseen and willed and was now carrying to its foreordained completion.[18] In New England, Edward Johnson (1598–1672) declared that the northern colonies were "the place where the Lord will create a new heaven and a new earth in, new churches and a new commonwealth together."[19] John Winthrop reminded New Englanders that they were to be "a city set upon a hill" to demonstrate before "the eyes of the world" what the result would be

---

[17] See Perry Miller, *Orthodoxy in Massachusetts* (Cambridge, Mass., 1933), 137, 146. Winthrop's address, "A Model of Christian Charity," is printed in *The Puritans,* eds. Perry Miller and T. H. Johnson (New York, 1963), I, 195–99.

[18] Perry Miller, *Errand into the Wilderness* (Cambridge, Mass., 1956), 111, 117.

[19] *Johnson's Wonder-working Providence, 1628–1651,* ed. J. F. Jameson (New York, 1910), 23, 25. A portion of Johnson's narrative is in *The Puritans,* eds. Perry Miller and T. H. Johnson (New York, 1963), I, 143–62.

when a whole people was brought into covenant with God.[20] William Penn was equally convinced that God intended his "holy experiment" to be "an example . . . to the nations," and Samuel Purchas's history of Virginia, written in 1625, began its account of that colony's varied experiences with Adam and Eve in order to "show how God had so managed the past that English colonization in the present was the fulfillment of his plan."[21]

This understanding of the decisive role that America was to have was appropriated and popularized in the eighteenth century by leaders of the Great Awakening. (For the Awakening, see Chapter 3.) Jonathan Edwards, reflecting upon the outbreak of the revival, was convinced that "this work of God's Spirit, so extraordinary and wonderful, is the dawning or at least a prelude of that glorious work of God so often foretold in Scripture, which in the progress and issue of it shall renew the world of mankind." He saw the Awakening, after so many successive disappointments, as the vindication of the expectation that the final act of God's work of redemption would begin in America. And if "in any part of America," he continued, "I think if we consider the circumstances of the settlement of New England, it must needs appear the most likely of all American colonies to be the place whence this work shall principally take its rise."[22] Whatever other leaders of the revival may have thought of Edwards's speculation as to the point at which the new age would first manifest itself, they shared his belief that God's Spirit was making itself felt in an unusual way and that God had a special destiny in store for America.

This mood of eager expectancy was to continue to be characteristic of American religious life. Having escaped in so many ways the limitations of a bounded existence, men and women were easily persuaded of the reality of unlimited possibilities. The hope of all things being made new, in the course of time, was often subtly secularized and frequently restated in political terms (America as the agent for the establishment of democratic liberties around the globe; the mandate to settle territories to the west). But the conviction remained that somehow this was God's country with a mission to perform. For the churches this sense of mission was the source of much of their restless energy as they sought to keep abreast of the western tide of migration and to make sure that the United States would fulfill its calling as a godly nation.

---

[20] Perry Miller discusses this "errand" in *Errand into the Wilderness*, 11 ff. It should not be overlooked, however, that many Puritans discovered themselves unable to negotiate the demands of life in the New World and returned to England. Others, weary from their struggles with English authorities, merely sought in America refuge from their problems. See Andrew Delbanco, *The Puritan Ordeal* (Cambridge, Mass., 1989) and Theodore Dwight Bozeman, *To Live Ancient Lives: The Primitivist Dimension in Puritanism* (Chapel Hill, N.C., 1988).

[21] Miller, *Errand into the Wilderness*, 115. See also Wright, 115–33.

[22] *The Works of Jonathan Edwards*, Vol. IV, *The Great Awakening*, ed. C. C. Goen (New Haven, 1972), 353, 358.

The Outsiders

One should keep in mind, as a continuing feature of the American context, two segments of the population that were unable to share the eager expectation of the dominant majority. The Native Americans quickly became strangers in the land with no heady vision of the future to sustain them. To evangelize the Indians and make them joint-heirs of the promise had been one of the motives of colonization, and there was intermittent missionary activity. For the most part, however, Indians were treated as an alien presence to be pushed back beyond the forward-moving edge of "civilization." In similar fashion, captives brought from Africa as slaves were outsiders who had little reason to view the future as pregnant with the possibility of all things being made new.

Mostly only at times of sporadic revolt did the outsiders achieve momentary visibility as persons. It is true that some Indian missions were successful, with converts being accepted and assimilated to new modes of life, but this was not the typical outcome of the encounter between the colonists and the first Americans. A few blacks also gained visibility in churches of their own in the years surrounding the American Revolution. The dating is shadowy, but two black Baptist preachers, David George and George Liele, gathered a congregation in 1775 at Silver Bluff, South Carolina. Three years later there was a black congregation downriver in Savannah. With the British evacuation at the end of the American Revolution, David George was carried to Nova Scotia where he gathered a church in 1784, and Liele escaped to Jamaica to carry on Baptist activity there. The first permanent African Baptist church in Savannah was established in 1788 by Andrew Bryan.[23] Meanwhile, in 1776, a black church was founded at Williamsburg, and in 1780, another black Baptist church was formed in Petersburg, Virginia. By the 1790s, there were also black Methodist churches in Philadelphia and New York City. Despite these beginnings, a century and a half elapsed before either Native Americans or blacks achieved sufficient visibility and power to become participants in the shaping of a future for all Americans.

Religious Characteristics
of the Different Colonies

The thirteen colonies came into being as a result of two great waves of English colonizing activity separated by the twenty distracting years (1640–1660) of the English civil wars and the regime of Oliver Cromwell. Virginia, Maryland, and the several New England colonies were products

---

[23] See Albert J. Raboteau, *Slave Religion* (New York, 1978).

of the early years. Following the restoration of the Stuarts to the English throne in 1660, the gap between Maryland and New England on the Atlantic coast was closed by the capture of New Netherlands from the Dutch in 1664 and by the founding of New Jersey in 1674, and of Pennsylvania and Delaware in 1681 and 1682. The southern frontier was extended by the settlement of Charleston in 1670 in accordance with a proprietary patent to the territory which was later divided into the royal colonies of South and North Carolina. Georgia, the last of the thirteen colonies, was founded in 1733.

The Southern Colonies

Virginia, the earliest of the colonies, was unique in several other respects. In Virginia alone of all the colonies did the Anglicans command a clear majority of the religious population; in Virginia alone was Anglicanism the established religion from the beginning; and in Virginia alone was provision made to enforce conformity to the Church of England. The instructions of James I in the first charter of Virginia were explicit. "The true word and service of God" was to be "preached, planted, and used" in the new colony "according to the doctrine, rights [rites?], and religion now professed and established within our realm of England."[24] Chaplains were appointed by the Company, and repeated legislation required everyone to attend the services of the church. It is true that these laws were seldom rigorously enforced, but the intention was that there should be no toleration of dissent.

The first major break in the pattern of religious uniformity in Virginia came after 1660 when Quaker missionaries were successful in establishing scattered communities of adherents, but it was not until the later decades of the colonial period that the Anglican predominance was sharply reduced and then surpassed as new population flowed into the area that lay beyond the tidewater region. The surge of non-Anglican strength was partially the result of Anglican neglect to provide a ministry for the new arrivals, but it was more largely due to other factors. Many of the new settlers who spread out in the territory adjacent to the Shenandoah were Scots from northern Ireland, some were Germans, others were from New England. The potential Presbyterian strength represented by the Scotch Irish was marshaled with great effectiveness by Samuel Davies, who had been sent to Virginia by the Synod of New York in 1748 and who continued to spearhead the Presbyterian advance until 1759 when he became president of the College of New Jersey (now Princeton). The moderate growth of the Baptists was transformed into a phenomenal expansion by the exciting

[24] Peter G. Mode, *Source Book and Bibliographical Guide for American Church History* (Menasha, Wis., 1920), 10.

preaching of a transplanted New Englander, Shubal Stearns, who began his activity in Virginia in 1754. The success of these dissenting groups was facilitated by the tension that existed between the older and the newer areas of settlement. Anglicanism suffered because of its identification with the early planters of the tidewater region, whose descendants had become a ruling aristocracy that controlled the Assembly, denied full representation to the upcountry districts, and refused to heed their grievances. Moreover, attempts to suppress dissent by this time could be countered by an appeal to rights guaranteed by the English Act of Toleration of 1689.

From the standpoint of religion, North Carolina, South Carolina, and Georgia had little in common with Virginia beyond a nominal establishment of Anglicanism as the official faith of the three colonies. Religious toleration was granted at the outset, and the population had little homogeneity. The settlement of North Carolina was haphazard, and it resembled Pennsylvania in its religious diversity. The early inhabitants were runaway servants from Virginia. For many years Quakers were the largest religious group. Later the Scotch Irish sweeping up the Shenandoah Valley gave Presbyterians major strength in the southern colonies, and Baptists were active and growing rapidly at the close of the colonial period. Strong German communities—mostly Lutherans and Moravians—were found in both North Carolina and Georgia. Only in South Carolina was there any significant Anglican strength south of Virginia. In 1704, "by dint of political trickery" an act was passed by the South Carolina Assembly providing for an Anglican establishment. Its provisions, however, were never fully carried out because of lack of clergymen, and at best it was a highly precarious establishment depending upon shifting majorities in an Assembly controlled at intervals by the dissenting groups. A similar establishment was secured in North Carolina in 1715 and in Georgia in 1758, but in neither colony did the establishment become operative in more than a handful of parishes.

Maryland, founded in 1634 by the second Lord Baltimore, had many affinities with the middle colonies, both geographic and otherwise. Its proprietor was Roman Catholic; and like the Quaker William Penn, he was as interested in providing a place where his coreligionists could settle as he was in making his colony a profitable financial investment. For both these reasons, like Penn, he pursued a forthright policy of religious toleration. For the first decade or two, Roman Catholics were the only persons in Maryland who received any benefit from this toleration, for there were no other dissenting groups. The non-Catholic Christians there were Anglicans, and one can scarcely speak of tolerating in English territory a church whose "supreme governor" was the English monarch. Indeed, the charter presupposed that churches would be "dedicated and consecrated according to the ecclesiastical laws of our kingdom of England."

The Roman Catholics who participated in the colonization of Maryland were a minority of even the first contingent that sailed for the new colony;

and in order not to jeopardize the charter, they were instructed by the proprietor that "no scandal nor offense" was "to be given any of the Protestants." On shipboard they were "to cause all acts of the Roman Catholic religion to be done as privately as may be" and were "to be silent upon all occasion of discourse concerning matters of religion."[25]

The wise precautions by which the proprietor sought to secure the toleration of his coreligionists were not entirely successful, for Roman Catholics were disenfranchised for a brief period in the 1650s after their leaders had proclaimed allegiance to Charles II in opposition to the authority of English Parliament. And after the expulsion of James II from the English throne because of his efforts to subvert the Protestant faith, Roman Catholics in Maryland were again subjected to various disabilities. Nevertheless, they remained one of the most important and influential segments of Maryland society.

By 1677 both Roman Catholics and Anglicans had been reduced to the status of minority groups if credence is given Lord Baltimore's report to the Privy Council concerning the shifts that had occurred in the religious affiliations of the Maryland populace. The greatest part of the inhabitants of that province (three of four at least) "do consist of Presbyterians, Independents, Anabaptists, and Quakers; those of the Church of England, as well as those of the Romish, being the fewest."[26] In spite of this numerical inferiority, the overthrow of James II in 1688 marked the beginning of a vigorous campaign to secure an Anglican establishment in Maryland, an objective achieved in 1702 when the Board of Trade and Plantations in London was finally satisfied that the rights of other minorities would be safeguarded. By this time Presbyterians, Baptists, and Quakers were becoming more numerous, and German Protestants were soon to spill over the border from Pennsylvania.

The New England Colonies

Plymouth, the first New England colony, was almost immediately overshadowed by, and in 1691 absorbed into, Massachusetts Bay Colony, and its religious history differed little from its larger neighbor. Both colonies were established by Congregationalists—Plymouth by Separatist Congregationalists; Massachusetts Bay by Nonseparatist Congregationalists—but in the New World, this difference was not of great moment.

A degree of intrigue and perhaps deception lay behind the establishment of Massachusetts Bay. In 1629, when the repressive ecclesiastical measures of William Laud, bishop of London (later archbishop of Canterbury) and chief advisor to the king, were making life in England difficult for

---

[25] "The Calvert Papers," no. 1, *Maryland Historical Society Proceedings* (Baltimore, 1889), 132.

[26] L. J. Trinterud, *The Forming of an American Tradition* (Philadelphia, 1949), 26.

them, a group of Nonseparatist Congregationalists obtained from Charles I a royal charter for the Massachusetts Bay Company. For some reason the usual clause that required the headquarters of such a company to be in England and thus subject to the immediate control of the crown was omitted from the charter. This omission could scarcely have been an oversight, for when the great Winthrop fleet sailed in the summer of 1630, it carried with it all the officers and stockholders of the company together with the charter itself. With charter and company in America, the colony was in effect an independent republic. The stockholders were called "freemen," and they became the electorate; the directors, or "deputies," became legislators; and the governor of the company became the chief executive of the colony. When it became inconvenient for the whole body of freemen to attend the annual meeting, or "general court," of the company, a representative system was devised whereby their "assistants" became a second house of the legislative assembly. When the English authorities finally discovered what had occurred, efforts were made to have the charter returned and the status of the colony regularized. Tactics of delay, however, were adopted; the turmoil of the two decades from 1640 to 1660 intervened, and it was not until 1684 that the charter was finally revoked and a royal governor appointed.

With freedom to pursue an independent course, the early settlers of Massachusetts Bay were in no mood to permit dissent from the "due form" of ecclesiastical government they had established. Having forsaken their homes to found a new Zion in the American wilderness, they saw no reason why their endeavor should be compromised by dissidence. Others, they contended, had full liberty to stay away; and they noted that there was ample room elsewhere in America for them to establish settlements of their own. As early as 1635 the first of a long succession of heresy trials imposing banishment as the most common penalty was held.[27]

The attempt to suppress dissent in Massachusetts Bay was never wholly successful for several reasons. The mere fact of space, even in Massachusetts, made policing difficult. And the policy of banishment created centers just across its borders from which the contagion of dissent filtered back to the older settlements. Furthermore, their fellow Congregationalists in England were embarrassed by their proceedings and exerted constant pressure upon them to adopt a more liberal policy. But the major reason was the fact that within the heart of New England Puritanism there was a steady and persistent acknowledgment that "the Lord hath more light yet to break forth out of his Holy Word" and that therefore they must ever be ready "to receive whatever truth shall be made known . . . from the written Word of God." These were the words of John Robinson

---

[27] Among those banished were Roger Williams, Samuel Gorton, William Coddington, John Wheelwright, and Anne Hutchinson.

(1576–1625), pastor of those who came to Plymouth in 1620 when they were exiles at Leyden, but these words represent the basic assumption upon which the whole Congregationalist enterprise was founded. In the light of this fundamental principle, it is not surprising that Congregationalism was forever spawning its own dissidents—men and even women who defended themselves by appealing to the truth that had been made known to them from "the written Word of God." Moreover, given the fact that the average New Englander heard over seven thousand sermons preached in the course of a lifetime, there was more than ample opportunity for men and women to hear and reflect upon Scripture.[28]

Although these factors reduced the effectiveness of the attempt by Massachusetts Bay to enforce conformity, the leaders persisted in their endeavor until 1684 when the loss of the charter made it impossible to proceed independently of English authority. Three years later the end of Congregational monopoly in the colony was dramatically signalized in Boston when the governor forced the Congregationalists to permit the Old South meetinghouse to be utilized for Anglican worship. By the end of the century, Massachusetts had been drawn by the terms of a new charter into a closer orbit around old England, and this process included having to come to terms with religious diversity, as a consequence of the English Act of Toleration (1689).

New Hampshire, in its pattern of church life, was little more than an extension of Massachusetts Bay. This tendency was also largely true of Connecticut, founded by Thomas Hooker in 1635 and later incorporating the smaller colony of New Haven. Connecticut in one respect was more conservative than Massachusetts. The *Saybrook Platform* of 1708 provided a more centralized control over the churches.

Rhode Island was a different story. The territory around Narragansett Bay had become the refuge for many of those expelled for reasons of religious dissent from Massachusetts Bay. Roger Williams, who was to be briefly a Baptist and then a Seeker, made his way there in 1636.[29] Anne Hutchinson, the "antinomian" prophetess whose trial shook the whole ruling hierarchy of the Bay colony, arrived with a number of her adherents in 1637. John Coggeshall and William Aspinwell came in 1638, and a little

---

[28] Cotton Mather, *Magnalia Christi Americana* (Hartford, 1855), I, 64. For a discussion of the frequency with which New Englanders heard sermons preached, see Harry S. Stout, *The New England Soul: Preaching and Religious Culture in Colonial New England* (New York, 1986), 4.

[29] For Williams, see Perry Miller, *Roger Williams: His Contribution to the American Tradition* (Indianapolis, 1953), and W. C. Gilpin, *The Millenarian Piety of Roger Williams* (Chicago, 1979). For a brief account, see "Introduction" to his *Experiments of Spiritual Life and Health*, ed. W. S. Hudson (Philadelphia, 1951). For a discussion of Roger Williams set in the context of religious liberty in America, see William Lee Miller, *The First Liberty: Religion and the American Republic* (New York, 1986).

later were joined by John Clarke and William Coddington. Williams, fearful lest the leading of God's Spirit and one's faithfulness to Christ be impaired by the sinful corruption of men, was a firm advocate of complete religious freedom. On this basis he succeeded in bringing together the disparate religious elements represented in the communities at Providence, Portsmouth, Newport, and Warwick to form the colony of Rhode Island and Providence Plantations, traveling to England in 1643 to secure the necessary patent from the English Parliament. Although Baptists initially were the largest group in Rhode Island, they were soon rivaled and then surpassed by the Quakers, who utilized the freedom the colony afforded as a base from which to attempt the evangelization of other parts of New England.

The Middle Colonies

When the English took over control of New Netherlands in 1664, the new colony was the most religiously heterogeneous area in America. The Dutch Reformed church quite understandably was the largest single religious group, and throughout the seventeenth century it was to continue to have more adherents than all other groups combined. But, as Governor Dongan (a Roman Catholic) reported in 1687, there were also French Calvinists, German Lutherans, Congregationalists from New England, several varieties of Quakers, Mennonites, Baptists, some Roman Catholics, and a few Jews. "In short," he explained, "of all sorts of opinion there are some, and of the most part none at all."

The terms of capitulation to England provided that the Dutch should have freedom of conscience, worship, and church discipline. This was interpreted to mean that the Dutch Reformed church retained a measure of its established character, and the early English governors considered that the Dutch Reformed ministers were entitled to support from public funds. The Duke of York, to whom the colony had been granted by royal patent, also issued instructions that no one who professed the Christian faith was to be in any way disturbed for differing judgment in religious matters. Thus the policy of religious toleration that hitherto had prevailed was continued, with only the status of the Jews left in doubt.

After the Glorious Revolution of 1688, which brought William and Mary to the English throne, the governor of New York was instructed to secure an Anglican establishment in the colony. After repeated rebuffs, the Assembly was finally induced in 1693 to adopt a measure that stipulated only that a "sufficient Protestant minister" should be supported by an annual tax in each of six parishes to be set up in New York City and three adjoining counties. The governor interpreted the act (contrary to the intention of the Assembly) as a legal establishment of the Church of England. It was a small victory, for there were too few Anglicans in the colony to give it much substance. As the chaplain of the English garrison reported, there were only 90 Anglican families in the entire colony, in contrast to the 1,754 Dutch Reformed families and the 1,355 families of various types of English dissent.

The colony of New Jersey had a checkered development. Initially it was part of the grant to the Duke of York in 1664, but almost immediately he gave it to two friends. A few hundred Dutch and New England émigrés were already there, and to attract more settlers, laws were promulgated that provided for freedom of conscience and assembly. In 1674, West New Jersey was sold to two Quakers, who let William Penn become one of the proprietors. It was not until 1702, when New Jersey became a royal colony, that the two sections were reunited. Delaware was purchased by Penn from the Duke of York in 1682 and was administered jointly with Pennsylvania until given a separate assembly in 1704.

William Penn founded Pennsylvania in 1681. Son of an admiral, Penn was converted to Quakerism in 1667 at the age of twenty-three. Penn was eager to secure a colony where, free from the pressure of bad example and worldly corruption, he could carry out a "holy experiment" in establishing a society fashioned in accordance with Quaker ideals. His share of West (New) Jersey did not satisfy his ambitions; a tactful reminder to the Duke of York of a debt to his father that had not been repaid led to his becoming the proprietor of the vast slice of territory that was given the name Pennsylvania.

The settlement of the new colony began without delay. A few Swedes, Finns, and Dutch were already there, and large-scale Quaker immigration set in at once. Other English-speaking inhabitants were enticed by the easy terms for the purchase of land described in Penn's promotional brochure, *Some Account of the Province of Pennsylvania* (1681). The prospect of religious freedom attracted several German minority religious groups (see pp. 77–81); the lure of economic advantage drew other Germans from the economically depressed Palatinate. Large numbers of Scotch Irish Presbyterians also arrived driven from home by the economic consequences of the Woolens Act of 1699 and by religious disabilities imposed in 1704. Quakers, however, continued to set the tone of the colony and, because of unbalanced representation in the Assembly, Quakers long maintained political dominance.

The English-speaking Denominations

The Church of England was drastically reformed at the time of the Protestant Reformation. Ties with Rome were severed, monasteries suppressed, prayers for the dead abolished, altars replaced by tables, the liturgy reshaped and rewritten, worship conducted in English, and the monarch acknowledged as "supreme governor" of the church. Although the English church was indebted to the major Reformed theologians—Bucer, Bullinger, and Calvin—for its theology, the impact of the variant form of Calvinism known as Arminianism[30] began to be felt soon after the first colonies were settled. During the reigns of Elizabeth I (1558–1603) and James I (1603–1625), a strong Puritan movement developed within the church which sought to remove a few remaining popish "ornaments," to promote godly preaching throughout the land, and to secure greater self-government for the church. Church government, and the relation of church to state, remained difficult issues, provoking violence and blood-shed until the Act of Toleration in 1689. Henceforth the Church of England was to be in fact and in law the church of only part of the English people. A further anomaly for an "established" or "state church" was the fact that the monarch when in Scotland ceased to be an Anglican and became a Presbyterian.

The Anglicans

In colonial America, Virginia was the great center of Anglican strength. And Anglicanism served well to promote stability and social solidarity in the tidewater, beginning with the arrival of the first minister in Jamestown, who brought spiritual milk to those who had survived the "starving time" of the settlement's first years. The first ministers were chaplains sent out by the Virginia Company, but between 1619 and 1622, a rudimentary parish system was set up with assessments levied and land set aside for parochial support. Lay vestries with responsibility for ordering parish life probably were introduced at this time. They were given statutory authority in 1643 when the Assembly ordered that vestrymen should be chosen by the voters of each parish. Later the vestries became self-perpetuating bodies, the preserves of the socially and economically privileged.

There was a perennial shortage of ministers throughout the colonial years, which was partly due to the fact that the establishment of a college to train a native ministry, though earnestly sought, was long delayed. Although Harvard College was founded as early as 1636, it was not until 1693 that Virginia was able to secure a similar institution for training its clergy. Even after the College of William and Mary opened its doors, the problem was not wholly solved. Since a bishop alone could ordain, young Anglicans

---

[30] Jacob Arminius (1560–1609) was a Dutch Calvinist who opposed the hyper-Calvinism of the late sixteenth century. Later the term *Arminian* was used in England to designate a "Romish" tendency to stress the human role in redemption. A century later John Wesley used the term with a still different connotation. See the portion of his "What Is an Arminian?" printed in H. E. Fosdick, *Great Voices of the Reformation* (New York, 1952), 514–17.

who wished to enter the ministry were compelled to undertake the long and hazardous journey to England to secure ordination.

Among expedients used to entice ministers to Virginia was the payment of a bounty of 20 pounds to anyone who would transport a "sufficient minister" to the colony. Later the bounty was paid directly to the minister. Clergymen secured by such means were of uneven quality. Several were of unusual ability, although many were not. But even the competent and faithful had a difficult time. Parishes were large, population was scattered, and a legal technicality frequently deprived them of security and authority. A 1629 act directed the governor to "induct" a minister "into any parish that shall make presentation of him." Vestries discovered that by neglecting to present their ministers for induction, the parish remained technically vacant and the minister could be made subservient by hiring him on a yearly basis. If the faithful and competent had a difficult time by being subjected to the whims of the vestry, clergy of less zeal and devotion found the absence of Episcopal supervision a distinct advantage. Charges of indolence, drunkenness, and immorality were not uncommon. Although abuses were not as widespread as some suggested, there were few means by which they could be corrected. In this regard there was a significant difference from New England, and it stemmed partly from the fact that Virginia was settled primarily as a trading colony, not as a refuge for religious visionaries.

The Anglican clergy in the colonies were nominally under the supervision of the bishop of London, but, apart from certain formalities, his jurisdiction was not given practical implementation until after the Revolution of 1688 when Bishop Compton began to delegate his disciplinary authority to resident "Commissaries," the most notable of whom were James Blair in Virginia and Thomas Bray in Maryland. Although they did much to improve the condition of both church and clergy, they lacked the full episcopal powers that were indispensable to a fully developed church life. Bray was one of the first to make an earnest plea for an American episcopate, but despite continuing agitation, this was to remain an unrealized hope throughout the whole colonial period. Much of the opposition to the appointment of a bishop came from the laity, who felt that he would jeopardize their prerogatives. William White, who became one of the first bishops of the newly formed Protestant Episcopal Church after the American Revolution, declared in 1782 that "there cannot be produced an instance of laymen in America, unless in the very infancy of the settlements, soliciting the introduction of a bishop." Even the clergy in the southern parishes were opposed to the establishment of an American episcopate, Samuel Auchmuty reported, since without a bishop they were "their own pastors."[31]

[31] William White, *The Case of the Episcopal Churches in the United States Considered*, ed. R. G. Salomon (Philadelphia, 1954), 29. Carl Bridenbaugh, *Mitre and Sceptre* (New York, 1962), 249.

The missionaries sent out by the Society for the Propagation of the Gospel (S.P.G.) after 1701 presented a brighter picture than did the general run of the parish clergy. The primary objective of the Society was to provide for "the administration of God's Word and the sacraments" in those areas where there were no settled Anglican clergy. From the time of its inception until 1783 when it officially ceased operations in the newly independent colonies, 84 of its missionaries labored in New England, 58 in New York, 54 in South Carolina, 47 in Pennsylvania, 44 in New Jersey, 33 in North Carolina, 13 in Georgia, 5 in Maryland, and only 2 in Virginia. In all, 309 missionaries were recruited to serve in these colonies, and well over $1 million (£227,454) was raised in England for their support.[32] These funds provided an excellent return on investment in 1722, when Timothy Cutler, president of Yale College, together with several of his friends, left the Congregational church for Anglicanism after assurances from the Society that they would support him.

The Congregationalists

The "congregationalism" of the early New Englanders was the product of the peculiar history of the English Reformation, which in several respects was an "arrested" reformation. Some of the early advocates of a more thoroughgoing reform, especially liturgical reform, broke from the parish churches and established independent churches of their own. These were the Separatists.[33] They restricted church membership to convinced believers and insisted that, since all members were equally priests, all should share in the determination of church affairs. Others who were dissatisfied with the slow pace of official reform found a considerable measure of freedom to carry out their desired reforms within the established parishes. As long as they engaged in no concerted organizational activity, both Elizabeth I and James I were content for the most part to leave them to their own devices. When pressure was applied, they found patrons to aid them, and they became adept at defending their rights in the common-law courts. They did not reject the Church of England as a false church, although they acknowledged that in many ways it was deformed and tainted with corruptions.

This point of view was made explicit in the words Francis Higginson is reported to have said on shipboard as the shores of England faded from view:

---

[32] C. S. Pascoe, *An Historical Account of the Society for the Propagation of the Gospel* (London, 1901), 86–87.

[33] Robert Browne (1550?–1633?), author of *Reformation without Tarrying for Any[one]* (1582), was the early leader.

> We will not say as the Separatists are wont to say at their leaving England, "Farewell Babylon, Farewell Rome" but we will say, "Farewell dear England, Farewell the Church of God in England and all the Christian friends there." We do not go to New England as Separatists from the Church of England, though we cannot be separate from the corruptions in it.[34]

Prior to Higginson's departure in 1629, these Nonseparatist Congregationalists had elaborated the theory that in the hidden essence of its constitution, the Church of England was basically congregational in structure. They differed from the Presbyterians at two points. Since they had had unworthy and unwanted ministers thrust upon them in their parish churches, they were unwilling to concede the power of ordination even to a presbytery, reserving it to the local congregation alone. Furthermore, since they had been pressured on occasion by the threat of excommunication wielded by a bishop, they were insistent that this power also must be reserved to the local congregation so that an individual might be tried by those who knew him best and not by any higher judicatory.

The Separatists provided the nucleus of the settlement at Plymouth; those who came to Massachusetts Bay were Congregationalists of the Nonseparatist variety. The difference between the two groups was not great, and soon they formed a single denomination. There were a few isolated individuals like Roger Williams, of course, who insisted that they should repudiate the Church of England in profession as well as in practice, but this counsel was rejected as politically inexpedient.

Unlike other religious groups, the Congregationalists in America were well supplied with ministers from the beginning, with no fewer than 130 graduates of Cambridge and Oxford having come out to serve the churches prior to 1647. "Such a concentration of educated men within a new settlement in proportion to the population," it has been stated, "has never occurred before or since," and one of the first concerns of the early settlers was to make provision for the future supply of educated ministers. *New England's First Fruits* (1643) emphasized this point in its account of the founding of Harvard in 1636.

> After God had carried us safe to New England and we had builded our houses, provided necessaries for our livelihood, reared convenient places for God's worship, and settled the civil government; one of the next things we longed for and looked after was to advance learning and perpetuate it to posterity, dreading to leave an illiterate ministry to the churches when our present ministers shall lie in the dust.[35]

---

[34] Mather, I, 362. For an elaboration of the Separatist-Nonseparatist distinction, see Perry Miller, *Orthodoxy in Massachusetts*, 53–101.

[35] A portion of *New England's First Fruits* is printed in *The Puritans*, ed. Miller and Johnson, II, 70–77.

So successful were they in this endeavor that of the 1,586 ministers who served the Congregational churches of New England during the colonial period, only 79 were not college graduates.

"The convenient places for God's worship" that were erected were called meetinghouses so that people would not be confused and make the mistake of thinking that the church was a building. These houses in which the church met were plain structures, often beautiful in their simplicity, with the people gathered about the table which stood at the center and with a high pulpit on one side for the reading and preaching of God's Word. The worship was equally plain, with the singing of psalms, a long prayer, the reading of Scripture, and a sermon being the principal features. The government of these churches was given its classic definition in the *Cambridge Platform* of 1648,[36] a document drafted and adopted in response to a "Remonstrance" that challenged the Congregational way of proceeding and threatened an appeal to the English Parliament if the restrictions upon church membership and voting were not liberalized. The synod that framed the *Platform* also adopted as a statement of the Congregationalist doctrinal position the Confession of Faith that had just been issued in England by the Westminster Assembly of Divines.

The *Cambridge Platform* had sidestepped one issue with regard to church membership that had begun to trouble the churches, and it proved to be an issue that could not long be ignored. According to Congregational theory, both the believing adult and his or her infant child belonged to the church, the latter being "federally holy" and entitled to receive baptism. On reaching the age of discretion, however, the child was required to give an account of his or her own repentance and faith in order to qualify for full communicant standing, including the right to partake of the Lord's Supper and to vote at church meetings. It was understood that true faith, even among the weakest Christians, would be confirmed by some specific experience of God's redeeming grace, and that in the absence of such an experience, a person was not to be admitted to full membership. This practice posed no problem until grandchildren began to be born whose parents were but "half-way" embraced within the covenant community and the question was raised as to whether their children were "federally" related to the church and qualified to receive baptism.

The controversy that ensued was heated—whatever the decision, one of two equally cherished "goods" would be sacrificed. If baptism were denied to children of unregenerate parents, the integrity of the churches as gathered communities of convinced believers would be preserved, but an increasing proportion of the population would be removed from the

---

[36] A portion is reprinted in H. S. Smith, R. T. Handy, and L. A. Loetscher, *American Christianity* (New York, 1960–63), I, 128–40. The full text is in Walker, *Creeds and Platforms of Congregationalism.*

discipline of the church, and the endeavor to fashion a holy common-wealth in the American wilderness would be endangered. If baptism were granted, the churches would be in danger of becoming "mixed multi-tudes" of the regenerate and unregenerate. Seventeen ministers from Massachusetts and Connecticut met in Boston in 1657 and announced that they were persuaded that the children of halfway covenanters should be baptized. Their decision was hotly debated for five years, but in the end it prevailed.

The decision of the synod opened the door to further laxity. Within lit-tle more than a decade, the restriction that kept unregenerate church members from partaking of the Lord's Supper began to break down. Solomon Stoddard, pastor at Northampton, became the chief advocate of lowering the bar at this point. He insisted that the germ of grace is latent in all the children of the covenant and that it should be nourished by par-taking of the Lord's Supper as soon as possible. To him it seemed contra-dictory that those who were in need of grace should be denied this means of grace because of their weakness in grace. His arguments were persua-sive to many, and his practice was widely adopted.

A further breach was effected in Boston toward the close of the century. The instigators were two Harvard tutors, William Brattle and William Lev-erett. They insisted that all distinctions among church members should be discarded and that even those who could not testify to an experience of grace should be allowed to participate in the government of the church, including the right to vote in the selection of the minister. The Brattle Street Church was formed in Boston in 1699 on that principle, and it with-stood the attacks of conservatives over the next decade.

Though defeated in Massachusetts, the conservative party was more suc-cessful in Connecticut, where Yale College had been founded in 1701 with the aid of the Mathers (Increase and his son, Cotton) as a counter to the lax influences emanating from Harvard. The *Saybrook Platform* of 1708 em-bodied all the essential features of the *Massachusetts Proposals.* It provided that the churches of each county were to be formed into a Consociation that was to have disciplinary oversight over them and from whose decision there was to be no appeal. These churches were further bound together by a General Association made up of delegates from each of the local Associa-tions. The approval of the colonial authorities was secured by including the proviso that no church should be compelled to join the "united churches" or hindered, if allowed by the general laws of Connecticut, from exercising discipline in its own way.

As a result of the stabilizing influence exerted by Yale and the achieve-ment of a measure of disciplinary oversight of the churches, Connecticut became the citadel of Congregational orthodoxy. Over the course of time, many of the Connecticut Congregationalists came to feel a greater sense of kinship with the Presbyterians than they did with their fellow Congrega-tionalists of Massachusetts, who had been unable to complete their system with any connectional body and thus pursued a more independent development.

The Presbyterians

The classic form of Presbyterianism, with its presbyteries, synods, and general assembly, took shape in Scotland, where the Reformation had been carried forward under the leadership of John Knox, after his return from John Calvin's Geneva. It did not differ greatly from the structures devised by the other Reformed churches on the Continent. Incipient presbyterian tendencies had long been present in English Puritanism, and they came to the fore when the Long Parliament met in 1640. One reason for the strength of the Presbyterian party that emerged at that time was the influence of the Scottish Commissioners. The meeting of Parliament had been precipitated by a Scottish invasion, which in turn had been occasioned by an attempt to impose "Laud's liturgy" upon the Scottish churches. The Scots supported Parliament in its controversy with the king, but they insisted, as a condition of their support, that the Church of England be brought into conformity with the Church of Scotland so that occasion for future strife might be avoided.

Presbyterian sentiment was constantly cropping out in early New England and gained strength from the course of events at home. Hingham and Newbury were two notable centers, and several Presbyterian churches were established by migrating New Englanders—first on Long Island and then in New Jersey, Pennsylvania, Maryland, and South Carolina. Several of these churches were brought together to form the Presbytery of Philadelphia in 1706. Ten years later three additional presbyteries were organized and the Synod of Philadelphia was established. Although there were scattered groups of Scotch Irish in the colonies as early as the 1680s, the great influx of population from northern Ireland that contributed so greatly to Presbyterian strength did not begin until 1720. Those who settled in the back country of New England tended to be absorbed into the Congregational churches, but the major flow of Scotch Irish was into the middle colonies and down the Shenandoah Valley into the Piedmont region of the South, and these areas became the great centers of Presbyterian strength and influence.

Francis Makemie, a Scotch Irishman with strong ties to both England and New England, was the key figure in the early growth of American Presbyterianism. He was in effect a missionary-at-large, itinerating widely to gather churches and to supervise their work. He had been sent to the colonies in 1683 by the Presbytery of Laggan in Ireland, but after 1691, he served as an agent of the newly formed United Brethren (Congregationalists and Presbyterians) in London.

In 1707, Makemie became one of the heroes of the struggle for religious freedom. He had been arrested by the governor of New York for unlicensed preaching, and he responded that "to give bond not to preach" was one thing he did not dare do. He appealed to the Boston ministers for help; they enlisted the aid of the United Brethren in London, and the case became a cause célèbre.[37] Makemie was acquitted after a brilliant defense, but the governor forced him to pay the costs of his own prosecution—the rather considerable sum of £83/7s/6d. This injustice so incensed the colonial legislature that an act was passed prohibiting the assessment of such costs in the future. Charges were also brought against the governor, which led to his being recalled to London in disgrace.

Makemie died in 1708, and the subsequent history of the Presbyterians in colonial America was to be inextricably entangled in the story of the Great Awakening. This was true even of the Adopting Act of 1729[38] by which the Synod of Philadelphia established the Westminster Confession of Faith as the doctrinal standard of American Presbyterianism, since freedom was given the presbyteries to distinguish between the essential and nonessential doctrines contained therein.

The Baptists

The English Baptists were another offshoot of the Puritan movement. Baptists were Congregationalists who had become convinced that if churches were to be composed of believers only, then baptism should be restricted to those who were able to give some account of their own faith. Prior to 1640, the Baptists in England were few in number. It was during the decade that followed that they became a significant and influential group, with their most notable strength being gained among the officers and men of Cromwell's army. Some of the Baptists—the General Baptists—were Arminian in theology, deriving their name from their adherence to the doctrine of a general atonement. What was destined to be the major Baptist body, however, was firmly rooted in the Calvinistic tradition that found its classic expression in the Westminster Confession of Faith.[39]

Baptist beginnings in America closely paralleled those of the Presbyterians. It was not the intention of the founders of New England to foster dissent, but dissent there was from the start, and the considerations that had led some of the English Congregationalists to become Baptists were equally persuasive to some New Englanders. Henry Dunster, for example, rejected infant baptism in 1654 and was forced to resign as president of Harvard. The key figure initially, however, was Roger Williams, who was instrumental in forming a Baptist church at Providence in 1639, three years after establish-

---

[37] An account of Makemie's apprehension and examination is printed in *The Presbyterian Enterprise: Sources of American Presbyterian History*, ed. M. W. Armstrong, L. A. Loetscher, and C. A. Anderson (Philadelphia, 1956), 13–18.

[38] Printed in Armstrong, Loetscher, and Anderson, eds., 30–32. See also Jonathan Dickinson's *Remarks* in Smith, Handy, and Loetscher, I, 262–68.

[39] The several strands of Baptist life are discussed in *Baptist Concepts of the Church*, ed. W. S. Hudson (Philadelphia, 1959), 11–29.

ing a settlement there. Williams soon abdicated his Baptist leadership, for he became convinced that all existing churches, including the newly established Providence church, lacked a proper foundation, a defect that could be remedied only by a new apostolic dispensation in which new apostles, authoritatively commissioned and divinely authenticated, would appear to reestablish the true church. A more important person in early Baptist history was John Clarke, who had gathered a church at Newport, Rhode Island, in 1641. It was Clarke's *Ill News from New England* (1652) that gave notoriety to the case of Obadiah Holmes, who was publicly whipped by the Massachusetts authorities for conducting unauthorized worship in Lynn.

Although Rhode Island remained a center of Baptist activity and a Baptist church was organized in Boston as early as 1665, the major Baptist growth prior to the Great Awakening stemmed from the formation of the Philadelphia Baptist Association in 1707. This Association was founded almost simultaneously with the Presbytery of Philadelphia and was similar in character to the presbytery although it lacked the latter's "authoritative" judicial power. Initially the Association was composed of churches in New Jersey, Pennsylvania, and Delaware; later it also included churches in Connecticut, New York, Maryland, and Virginia; ultimately subsidiary Associations were formed in Massachusetts and Virginia, and a relationship was established with the Charleston Association in the Carolinas. The Association carried on vigorous missionary activity from Nova Scotia to Georgia, and it established the College of Rhode Island (later named Brown University) as a training center for its ministers. The Philadelphia Confession of Faith of these American Baptists was a slightly amended version of the Westminster Confession of Faith, following the changes introduced by the Savoy Declaration (1658) of the English Congregationalists with an additional modification at the point of baptism.[40]

Although the growth of the Baptists was substantial during the first half of the eighteenth century, the large-scale accessions that made them one of the major religious groups in America occurred just prior to and during the American Revolution.

The Quakers

The Society of Friends, as the Quakers are more properly termed, emerged in England around 1650 out of the turmoil and confusion of the religious controversies that had accompanied the English civil wars.[41]

---

[40] "The Platform of Government," which the English Congregationalists had appended to the Savoy Declaration, was incorporated in the body of the Confession by the Baptists.

[41] For the Puritan antecedents, see G. F. Nuttal, *The Holy Spirit in Puritan Faith and Experience* (Oxford, 1946). Two standard accounts of the Quakers are Howard Brinton, *Friends for 300 Years: The History and Beliefs of the Society of Friends* (New York, 1952), and F. B. Tolles, *Quakers and the Atlantic Culture* (New York, 1960).

During these years many people had pursued what was in effect a spiritual pilgrimage from one group to another. In the end there were many who became completely disenchanted by the welter of competing claims and, like Roger Williams, became Seekers waiting for a new apostolic dispensation when the true Church would be restored. Others, whom Oliver Cromwell was to describe as "happy finders," believed that the new dispensation, in the form of a new age of the Spirit, had already arrived. It was from among these "happy finders" that George Fox gathered the people known as Quakers. They were a plain people—plain in dress, plain in speech, and plain in behavior. They gathered in silence for worship until one of their number was led by the Spirit to speak. Many of them became itinerant "publishers of truth," moving from place to place to declare that Christ had already returned to reign, that he was rising up as the "Christ within" in innumerable sons and daughters, and that the terrible day of the Lord was at hand when the whole creation would be purged of dross and corruption.

Few groups exhibited the intense missionary zeal that characterized the early Quakers. In many ways they were a most attractive people of simple honesty and integrity, but in terms of their missionary activity, they were frequently the most troublesome of people. It became customary for them to invade churches and to interrupt the sermon with denunciations of false worship and the folly of seeking God through empty forms and human inventions. A few felt called by the Spirit to even more bizarre behavior, such as going naked through the streets of a town as a "sign." By 1700, however, the early excesses had disappeared and Quakerism entered a period of "quietism." Henceforth they were to be the most restrained of people in their behavior and were to become increasingly esteemed for their humanitarian sympathies and concerns. John Woolman is the most famous representative of this latter tendency. The journal in which he tells of his itinerant ministry in bearing testimony against slavery is a moving testament of devotion.[42]

The first Quaker missionaries to reach the New World were two women, Mary Fisher and Ann Austin, who arrived in Boston in 1656 and were followed a few weeks later by eight additional publishers of truth. The following year Quaker missionaries made their appearance in New Amsterdam and Virginia. Everywhere, except in Rhode Island, they were harried with fines, imprisonment, and deportation. The most savage persecution occurred in Massachusetts, where a law was enacted subjecting Quaker missionaries who returned to the colony, after once having been banished, to the death penalty. Four suffered martyrdom before Charles II intervened in 1661 and put an end to the executions.

Rhode Island and Long Island, where the followers of Anne Hutchinson had been embryonic Quakers for twenty years, quickly became centers of

---

[42] *The Journal of John Woolman* (Chicago, 1950).

Quaker strength. By the time George Fox arrived for a missionary tour in 1672, persecution had practically ceased, and Quaker "meetings" were to be found in every colony from New Hampshire to South Carolina. Two years later, when West (New) Jersey came under the control of Quaker proprietors, the flow of Quaker settlers to the New World set in, and the number of Quaker immigrants swelled to a great tide after Pennsylvania was established as a Quaker domain in 1681. As a result of the earlier missionary activity and the later migration, Quakers ranked fifth numerically among the various religious bodies at the close of the colonial period.

As the number of Quakers increased, zeal tended to diminish. The passage of time and growing prosperity took their toll. In 1764, an aged Quaker minister summarized the decline that had taken place over the past sixty years. He well remembered, he declared, that in the early days

> Friends were a plain lowly minded people and that there was much tenderness and contrition in their meetings; and that at the end of twenty years from that time, the Society increasing in wealth and in some degree conforming to the fashions of the world, true humility decreased and their meetings in general were not so lively and edifying; that at the end of forty years many of the Society were grown rich, that wearing of fine costly garments and with fashionable furniture, silver watches became customary with many and with their sons and daughters, and as these things prevailed in the Society and appeared in our meetings of ministers and elders so the powerful overshadowings of the Holy Spirit were less manifested amongst us . . . and that the weakness amongst us in not living up to our principles and supporting the testimony of truth in faithfulness was matter of much sorrow.[43]

With the passing of the first generation, there were many who were Quakers by birth rather than conviction. This tendency was both accelerated and sanctioned by the action of the London Yearly Meeting in 1737 which permitted "the wife and children to be deemed members of the Monthly Meeting of which the husband or father is a member, not only during his life but after his decease." Thus the Quakers with their "birthright membership" were pursuing the same path as New England Congregationalists with their progressive lowering of the bars to church membership after the adoption of the Half-way Covenant.

The Roman Catholics

Of all the churches that took definitive shape at the time of the Reformation, the Roman Catholic Church was by far the largest. As certain elements in the pre-Reformation church had been made normative for Lutherans by the Augsburg Confession and the Formula of Concord, so

[43] F. B. Tolles, *Meeting House and Counting House* (Chapel Hill, N.C., 1948), 123–24.

other elements were made normative for Roman Catholics by the decrees
of the Council of Trent (1545–1563). In spite of their predominance in
many parts of Europe, the Roman Catholics were a small minority in England. Although their faith was proscribed by law, few Roman Catholics
found the hard conditions of life in America an attractive prospect. In
England they were mostly landed gentry, and they had friends at Court to
offer them protection. Consequently, enjoying at least modest comfort and
relative security, these English Roman Catholics did not bulk large in the
colonizing activity of their compatriots. Since there was to be no significant Roman Catholic immigration from the Continent until after the
American Revolution, the Roman Catholic population in the colonies was
largely limited to Maryland, where the proprietor had granted large
manors to his Catholic friends. There were a few Roman Catholics in New
York and a larger number in Pennsylvania, but elsewhere only isolated individuals were to be found.[44]

When the *Ark* sailed from England late in 1633 with the first contingent
of settlers for Maryland, it stopped briefly at the Isle of Wight to pick up
two Jesuit priests, Fathers Andrew White and John Altham, who were to
distinguish themselves in the new colony by their earnest pastoral care and
by their missionary activity among the Indians. Later they became involved
in controversy with the proprietor because of their zeal in attempting to
proselyte among non-Catholics and because of their purchase of land directly from the Indians. In different ways both of these proceedings appeared to threaten Lord Baltimore's authority, and when he carried the
issue to Rome, they were ordered to yield to his demands. The resolution
of the controversy was hastened by the arrival of two secular priests in 1642
to replace the dissident Jesuits. In 1669, the proprietor complained that
only two priests remained in the colony, and as a result two Franciscans
were sent out in 1673; they were joined four years later by three additional
Franciscans and three more Jesuits. Within a few years Catholic families
were moving northward into Pennsylvania, and in 1706, the Jesuits opened
a mission near the border of Pennsylvania and for a brief period conducted a school there. This school was apparently the only Catholic educational venture until the founding of Georgetown Academy in 1791.

Denominations of Continental Origin

With the exception of African slaves and Native Americans who had little
opportunity to develop independent religious institutions, there were only
three nationality groups of measurable size at the end of the colonial period that were of non-British stock. These were the Germans with roughly

---

[44] John Tracy Ellis, *Catholics in Colonial America* (Baltimore, 1965).

9 percent of the white population; the Dutch, 3 percent; and the French, 1.7 percent.[45] Of these, the Dutch and the French were the earliest arrivals, with most of the latter initially being French-speaking Walloons. Practically all these people, whether Dutch, French, or German, were of Protestant background.

The Dutch and the French Reformed

Reformed Protestantism had no single outstanding early leader. It originated in the reforming activity of such men as Huldreich Zwingli, Henry Bullinger, Martin Bucer, and William Farel. Later John Calvin emerged as the most influential of the Reformed theologians, and his *Institutes of the Christian Religion* became the most representative statement of the Reformed understanding of the Christian faith. Almost everywhere the Reformed churches had to struggle for existence, and in the face of unrelenting persecution, they stressed the sovereignty of God and man's duty to glorify him by full and unyielding obedience.

In 1609, the Dutch achieved independence from Spain. Free of persecution by the Spanish, the Reformed churches flourished in the Netherlands. So also did Dutch seafaring trade.

With energies released by the winning of independence, the Dutch Republic became the great trading power of Europe with the largest and most efficient merchant marine in the world. Dutch traders were everywhere, reaching Java as early as 1595. In the next few decades, they ejected the Portuguese from most of their trading posts in the Far East, conquered Brazil, and occupied several islands in the West Indies. Their attention had been called to the possibilities of the fur trade in North America by the pioneering voyages of Henry Hudson, and in the same year that they gained control of Brazil, they established a trading post at the present site of Albany on the Hudson River. Two years later, in 1626, another trading post—New Amsterdam—was established on the tip of Manhattan Island.

New Amsterdam was a typical sailors' town. Many of the inhabitants were rough and boisterous, and the lot of the early ministers was far from easy. Not until Peter Stuyvesant became the director of the colony in 1647 did the ministry receive any real support from the governing authority. Stuyvesant, the son and son-in-law of Dutch Reformed ministers, was a zealous churchman and a strict disciplinarian. He restricted the sale of liquor, ordered strict observance of the Sabbath, and required all persons to attend the services of the church. Stuyvesant's zeal included an attempt to impose a rigid religious uniformity upon the colony, but his treatment of Lutherans, Quakers, and Jews earned him a stern rebuke, and he was ordered to leave any dissenter "unmolested as long as he is modest, moderate, [and] his political conduct irreproachable."

[45] John Tracy W. L. Sperry, *Religion in America* (New York, 1946), 266–70.

By the time the colony was surrendered to the English in 1664, there were 11 Dutch Reformed churches in the colony that included settlements in what was to be New Jersey. Although the shift to English control involved problems of readjustment, the Dutch churches continued to grow with the natural increase in the Dutch population; and it is estimated that there were 120 Dutch Reformed congregations at the time of the Declaration of Independence.

Beginning in the 1660s, members of French Reformed churches, or Huguenots, began making their way to America. The largest number settled in New York and South Carolina. Several Dutch Reformed ministers made it a practice to preach in French, and the French Reformed in New York generally became members of the Dutch churches. In 1683, however, the French Reformed in New York secured a pastor of their own, and congregations also were formed at New Rochelle and New Paltz. By the end of the century, there were five or six French Reformed churches in the vicinity of New York City. Another church had been formed in Boston, at least one in Virginia, and several in South Carolina. The tendency everywhere was for the Huguenots to disperse and to become denationalized, partly perhaps because of an eagerness to forget the language and customs of the land that had subjected them to such relentless persecution. In the South they tended to become Anglicans. In New York they were absorbed by the Dutch Reformed; the "French church" at New Paltz, for example, kept its records in Dutch after the first fifty years of its existence.

Mennonites, Dunkers, and Moravians

Pennsylvania was the great center of German immigration to the colonies, for William Penn's efforts to recruit settlers found an eager response among the inhabitants of the Palatinate (an area between the upper Rhine and France), which had repeatedly been ravaged and devastated by the armies of Louis XIV.

Of all the Reformation groups, none had been subjected to more bitter persecution than the Anabaptists. They were earnest people, deeply devout, who rejected infant baptism and sought to practice full obedience to the commands of Christ, refusing among other things to take oaths, hold public office, or bear arms. They had managed to survive in small scattered communities throughout the Rhineland from Rotterdam to the valleys of Switzerland. The earliest Mennonites, a group that took its name from Menno Simmons (1492–1559), arrived in Pennsylvania from Krefeld, Germany, in 1683. Most of this initial contingent had been won to Quaker views prior to their departure, and separate Mennonite worship was not established until 1690. The Swiss Mennonites who began arriving around 1710 settled in what is now Lancaster County, and this became the principal Mennonite center. Each Mennonite congregation conducted its own affairs, frequently choosing its officers—a bishop, elders, and deacons—by lot. Consequently they were seldom troubled by lack of ministerial leadership, and they never needed to await the arrival of a minister in order to organize their church life.

The Dunkers (Church of the Brethren) in many ways were not unlike the Mennonites. They also were a "plain" people who sought to live in strict obedience to New Testament precepts. Their founder was Alexander Mack, a man of some means who had come under Pietistic influences after reacting against the spiritual lethargy of the German Reformed church in which he had been reared. At Schwarzenau in Hesse-Kassel, Germany, in 1708 he formed into a church the little group he had gathered for Bible study, and other congregations were soon formed in neighboring provinces. Unlike the Mennonites, many of whose practices they adopted, the Dunkers baptized by a threefold immersion rather than by pouring. It was this practice that gave them their popular name. Their worship centered in the Lord's Supper, which was preceded by a "love feast" and the washing of feet, and was concluded with the "holy kiss of charity" and the "right hand of fellowship." The Dunker migration to America was initiated in 1719 by the congregation at Krefeld, and four years later their first church in America was formed at Germantown, Pennsylvania.

A Saxon nobleman, Nicholas Ludwig, Count von Zinzendorf (1700–1760) was the key figure in the story of the Moravians. He was a Lutheran who also had come under the influence of Pietism, a movement that, in reaction to the seeming lifelessness of Lutheran and Reformed orthodoxy, stressed the importance of religious experience and the devotional life.[46] Its most characteristic feature was the gathering of earnest Christians in small groups to study the Bible, sing hymns, and engage in prayer. The Pietists were neither hostile to the churches nor heterodox, but they found theological discussion distasteful and regarded it as a source of division and strife among Christians. Christianity was a life, they insisted, not a creed. Thus Pietists tended to sit loosely to their confessional traditions, to emphasize the common experience of Christ that bound all Christians together, and to possess a strong missionary fervor. It was this spirit that Zinzendorf imbibed, and it led him to welcome to his estates any refugees among whom he espied any signs of true piety.

The Moravians, or the Unitas Fratrum, had their origin in the evangelical movement that sprang from the preaching of John Hus of Prague in the fifteenth century.[47] They had been buffeted by persecution for more than two centuries when Zinzendorf offered them asylum in 1722. Zinzen-

---

[46] Pietism stemmed from the activities of Philip J. Spener (1635–1705) and August H. Francke (1663–1727). The former gathered small groups for Bible study in his home at Frankfort. The latter developed a similar ministry among students at the University of Leipzig. The founding of the University of Halle in 1691 by the Elector of Brandenburg provided them with a center for the dissemination of their views.

[47] See Edward Langton, *History of the Moravian Church* (London, 1956), and J. R. Weinlick, *Count Zinzendorf* (New York, 1956).

dorf, together with other Lutheran Pietists whom he had gathered about him, soon became deeply involved in the activities of the Moravian community. He gradually emerged as their leader and was consecrated Bishop in 1737. Under his leadership the Moravians launched a far-flung missionary campaign that had several objectives—the conversion of the heathen, the renewal of spiritual life among nominal Christians, and the reuniting of all Christian groups in a single spiritual communion. An early project had been the establishment of a Moravian settlement in Georgia in 1735 where some missionary work was carried on among the Indians and blacks. Their refusal to bear arms, however, aroused the opposition of the colonial authorities, and in 1740, the Moravians moved to Pennsylvania where they established the towns of Nazareth and Bethlehem. Later Salem, North Carolina, became a major Moravian center.

In the meantime Zinzendorf, having been charged with harboring religious fanatics and promoting views contrary to accepted Lutheran standards, had been banished in 1738 from his estates. He utilized his banishment as an opportunity to embark on a missionary tour that brought him to Pennsylvania in 1741. His immediate objective was to draw together the various German Protestant denominations in Pennsylvania to form what he called "the Church of God in the Spirit." Although he failed in that endeavor, he was able to organize missionary activity among the Indians before he returned to Europe in 1743.

The German Lutherans and the German Reformed

Germans immigrated from the Palatine in increasing numbers during the corrupt reign of Louis XIV in the latter part of the seventeenth century. However, organized church life among the German Lutherans and German Reformed was not effected immediately for several reasons. For one thing, they migrated as individuals and not as religious communities. They generally had no financial resources of their own, and they had no group to help provide the expense of travel. Many of them came as "redemptioners," given free passage by shipowners who recouped themselves financially by selling their passengers for a term of service as indentured servants. Others were assisted by the English government, which recognized the need for settlers but had placed restrictions upon the emigration of English subjects lest the homeland should be impoverished. Most of these Germans had no strong religious interest, and neither the Reformed nor the Lutherans had a tradition of lay initiative in church affairs. Consequently, their adherents tended to be dependent upon outside help for leadership in the formation of churches.

Although a Swedish Lutheran church had been formed in 1639 and the Dutch Lutheran church in New Amsterdam had secured a minister as early as 1658, the first German Lutheran church was not organized until 1703. And it was not until 1742, when Henry Melchior Muhlenberg arrived, that Lutheran churches were linked in common cause. Within six weeks Muhlenberg mastered the situation and was installed as pastor of the Philadelphia Lutherans. He soon took additional churches under his care, and ultimately seven churches looked to him for pastoral leadership. Whenever possible he responded to calls for help from more distant places and frequently was asked to arbitrate church quarrels. The regular reports that he sent to Halle, Germany, stimulated further interest in his work and brought reinforcements in both men and money. Muhlenberg's most important achievement was the forming of the Ministerium of Pennsylvania in 1748. This was the first permanent Lutheran synod in America, and its influence became decisive in the developing life of the churches.

Whereas most of the Lutheran population in the colonies stemmed from the influx of Germans into Pennsylvania, being largely a dispersion from this center, the Salzburg Lutherans in Georgia were the product of an independent odyssey. They had been driven from their homes in Austria in 1731 by the Roman Catholic archbishop of Salzburg. Fourteen thousand of them in the dead of winter made the long trek to Prussia, where they had been promised refuge. When accounts of their sufferings aroused interest in England, provision was made to send some of them to Georgia, where they arrived in four contingents between 1734 and 1741. The first group was accompanied by two ministers who had been trained at Halle, and they had a vigorous church life from the beginning.

The plight of the German Reformed in America was much the same as that of the Lutherans. They also came without pastors and with meager resources. The first churches to be formed among them were an exception to the general rule of waiting until a minister appeared on the scene. John Philip Boehm had settled in Pennsylvania in 1720 as a farmer. He was the son of a Reformed minister at Frankfort-on-the-Main, and he had taught school for a period of twelve years. After his arrival his neighbors persuaded him to conduct religious services for them. Five years later the three informal congregations he had gathered pressed him to assume the pastoral office. With some reluctance he agreed to do so, although he was not ordained. When a German Reformed minister, George Michael Weiss, arrived two years later, he was scandalized by Boehm's action, challenged his right to assume ministerial prerogatives, and attempted to take over his congregations. The people rallied to Boehm's support, appealed to the Dutch Reformed ministers in New York for advice, and were referred by them to the Classis of Amsterdam for a decision. In due time an answer was received that approved Boehm's emergency assumption of pastoral duties but advised him to seek ordination. He was ordained by the Dutch Reformed ministers of New York on November 23, 1729. Weiss was present at the ordination, and afterward the two worked together in complete harmony.

People of German Reformed background were rapidly increasing in numbers, being augmented by an influx of settlers from Switzerland, and they were becoming widely dispersed in the back country of the colonies. Most were without either ministers or churches. In 1746, Michael Schlatter, a Swiss who had been educated and ordained in the Netherlands, was sent to Pennsylvania as the representative of the Dutch synods with instructions to visit existing congregations, to form new ones where needed, and to bring them together as soon as possible in a presbytery (or "coetus") subject to the synods of Holland. He immediately made a tour of the churches and discovered that in Pennsylvania there were four ordained men to care for an estimated German Reformed population of 15,000. Within a year he had organized the "coetus," and in 1751 he returned to Europe to plead the cause of the German Reformed churches. When he returned, he brought with him six young ministers, 700 Bibles, and the promise of an annual subsidy of 2,000 gulden from the states of Holland and West Friesland.

The Jews

With the exception of such transient groups as the Sandemanians, Rogerenes, and the Ephrata community, the Jews were the smallest of the religious minorities in colonial America.[48] Twenty-three Jews, fleeing from Brazil when the Portuguese regained control from the Dutch, arrived in New Amsterdam in 1654. Most of them failed to remain, but those who did were not permitted to maintain public worship until after the end of Dutch control. Their number gradually increased, and by 1695, they were worshiping in a rented room. Thirty-five years later, in 1730, a synagogue was built and dedicated. There were isolated Jews in New England as early as 1649, and a community was gathered in Newport, Rhode Island, about 1658. This early congregation had disappeared by 1690 and was not revived until about 1750. The beautiful synagogue, which still survives in Newport, was erected in 1763. Apart from these two centers, the only other congregations in America prior to the American Revolution were at Savannah (1733), Philadelphia (1747), and Charleston (1749). Moreover, none of these congregations included a rabbi until the nineteenth century.

Popular Religious Beliefs

Not all of the religion that was transplanted to America was defined by denominational boundaries. Some religion took a "popular" form that supplemented and sometimes contradicted the religious life associated with

---

[48] See Jacob R. Marcus, *Early American Jewry*, 2 vols. (Philadelphia, 1951–1953).

the churches. This popular religion was in no ways organized, but instead was threaded through colonial American culture as an exceedingly broad set of beliefs and behaviors.

Colonists brought popular religion from Europe as part of their cultural baggage. In England and on the Continent during the centuries leading up to the settlement of North America, men and women viewed the world as a setting for manifestations of diverse supernatural forces. Life was marked by mysterious and unearthly events—some proved favorable to physical and spiritual health, and others crippled or destroyed life. Astrology, magic, prophecy, fortune telling, various forms of divination and supernatural healing, and witchcraft thrived in the religious atmosphere of Europe on the eve of the American colonization. Colonists also reported and closely followed stories of mermaids, rattlesnakes that hypnotized persons with their eyes, and sinister disappearing black dogs.[49]

In America the clergy condemned much popular religion, and especially witchcraft, as superstitious evil. This treatment did not prevent the laity from believing in it, however. Americans and Europeans in the seventeenth century blamed witches for a host of scourges ranging from diseased livestock to hallucinations. In a few instances, entire communities were aroused to vigilance against witchcraft. Such was the case at Salem, Massachusetts, in the 1690s, when numerous suspected witches were imprisoned and some were executed.[50] Belief in witchcraft was as widespread in other North American colonies as it was in New England. Belief in occult healing also took root in American soil. Reverend Cotton Mather of Boston lamented in 1720 the widespread use of charms and magic words in attempts to cure disease. Among spoken charms, he singled out the word *Abracadabra* as a particularly "famous" example, while condemning as well attempts to cure toothaches by wearing around the neck a folded paper with strange sayings scrawled upon it. Particularly upsetting to Mather was his realization that even the faithful used charms to overcome illness: "But this impiety, how commonly it is practiced: Even among those who have been baptised for God. . . ."[51]

Not all popular religion earned the scorn of the clergy, however. Some aspects of popular religious belief did not directly challenge church doctrine and were not considered detrimental to the soul. Such was the case with wonder stories, or tales of remarkable and supernatural happenings. Protestants had long believed that it was through God's "providence" that

---

[49] Herbert Leventhal, *In the Shadow of the Enlightenment: Occultism and Renaissance Science in Eighteenth-Century America* (New York, 1976); Jon Butler, *Awash in a Sea of Faith: Christianizing the American People* (Cambridge, Mass., 1990), 7–36; and David D. Hall, *Worlds of Wonder, Days of Judgment: Popular Religious Belief in Early New England* (New York, 1989), 71–116.

[50] See John Putnam Demos, *Entertaining Satan: Witchcraft and the Culture of Early New England* (New York, 1982).

[51] Cotton Mather, *The Angel of Bethesda*, ed. Gordon W. Jones (Barre, Mass., 1972), 293–301.

the natural world in all of its operations was upheld. This included not only such regular events as the rising and setting of the sun, but the seemingly odd or freakish events that occurred in nature that amazed and bewildered mere mortals.[52]

The lore of wonders was generated in part from the New World experiences of the colonists, but a substantial part of the lore was transmitted from England through newspapers, almanacs, and books. The clergy rarely opposed the lore because the telling and retelling of wonder stories served to keep people's attention focused on the supernatural in general and oftentimes God in particular. When men and women repeated to each other stories of frightening earthquakes or destructive fires or extraordinary deliverances from lightning bolts or fateful carriage accidents, the clergy rested. In wonder stories, the God who ruled the universe saved from harm those who were steadfast in their faith, and punished those who strayed.

Popular religion, as represented by wonder lore, witchcraft beliefs, the use of magical charms, and numerous other ideas and behaviors, was one component of the religious life of Americans. It not only was more important at some times in the nation's history than at other times but also was more visible in certain social and geographic contexts than in others. It never replaced denominational religion, nor did it even challenge it in any significant way. In its various and ever-changing forms over the years, however, it consistently expressed the vitality and diversity of religious belief in ways that are not always apparent in more organized forms of religion in America. It also historically represented something of the fluidity and adaptability of religious faith in America, particularly when it was connected with patriotism in a kind of "civil religion."

This account of denominational beginnings in America can be misleading. Although there was a profusion of religious groups, most of the people belonged to no church at all. It was not until the Great Awakening, when America experienced its "national conversion,"[53] that this situation began to change.

[52] Hall, 75–80, 91–94.

[53] The term is supplied and explicated by H. Richard Niebuhr, *The Kingdom of God in America* (New York, 1959), 126.

CHAPTER THREE

The Great Awakening

The Great Awakening, which was to exert a decisive and far-reaching influence upon the development of American religious life, was but one manifestation of a general spiritual quickening during the eighteenth century. There were scattered "awakenings" of new religious life in England, Scotland, and Wales, as well as in America. These several awakenings reinforced each other and initiated the great tide of evangelical religion that swept through the English-speaking world, reaching a crest of influence in the latter half of the nineteenth century before it began to ebb away. Churches of all denominations were caught up in the surge of religious fervor and were profoundly affected by its impact. A new type of preaching dominated the pulpits, the structure of public worship was altered, and the "revival" became the most widely accepted means of introducing people to the Christian life.

Although the immediate effect of the Awakening was to arouse opposition, split congregations, set minister against minister, and divide most of the denominations, the opposition in the end was almost everywhere overwhelmed, and the ultimate consequence was to mold the various denominations to a common pattern, to subordinate differences, and to make possible wide-ranging cooperative endeavors.[1] Above all, this surging tide

---

[1] A common pattern of religious life in New England and elsewhere already existed in the form of popular religion, and this served to some degree to mitigate the effects of controversy over doctrine that took place during the Awakening and in the years immediately following. See David D. Hall, *Worlds of Wonder, Days of Judgment: Popular Religion in Early New England* (New York, 1989), and Jon Butler, *Awash in a Sea of Faith: Christianizing the American People* (Cambridge, Mass., 1990).

of evangelical religion supplied the dynamic that emboldened the Protestant churches of America to undertake the enormous task of Christianizing a continent, nerved those of the British Isles to assume a similar responsibility for an expanding population at home and overseas, and led both the British and the American churches to join forces in a vast mission to the entire non-Christian world.

Why the spark provided by any one of the local quickenings should suddenly have ignited a general conflagration is something of a mystery. The early drive and enthusiasm of the Puritan movement sprang from a transforming experience of God's grace and a consequent dedication to warfare against sin, together with a strong tendency to introspection and self-critical reflection. This brand of Protestantism, which was transplanted to America in the seventeenth century, guided the lives of the faithful there, such as New Englander Elizabeth White, who wrote as follows in the 1660s: "When I have seen a spider, which of all things is most loathsome to me, I have been ready to wish myself such a one, esteeming of it to be in a far happier condition than I was."[2] But this religion had moved to the periphery of religious life, for some of the consciousness of entering the Christian life through a "new birth" had been replaced by an insistence upon mere assent to orthodox beliefs as the foundation of the Christian life. Others stressed the reasonable character of the "grand essentials" of all religion and emphasized moral behavior as the distinguishing mark of the Christian. The theological problem faced by the successors of the Puritans was to draw the emotional component of religion inward from the periphery, and to blend it with doctrine and morality. In addressing this problem they were mostly unsuccessful, with "head" predominating over "heart." This is not to say that ministers and laypersons were satisfied with their efforts. When Jonathan Edwards spoke of "the time of extraordinary dullness in religion" that preceded the outbreak of the revival in Northampton, Massachusetts, he was but echoing the lament that had been voiced by many of the New England clergy for the better part of a century. And from time to time there had been local awakenings—even in Northampton under the preaching of Solomon Stoddard—when consciences would be touched, faith awakened, and people brought into the churches in unusual numbers. But no general revival had occurred.

Nor is the suggestion that the revivals were the product of the unsettled conditions of frontier life an adequate explanation of a phenomenon that was equally widespread in both Britain and America. Furthermore, the communities in America where the revivals first appeared were centers of an

---

[2] For the definition of Puritanism as a "revival," see Alan Simpson, *Puritanism in Old and New England* (Chicago, 1962), 103–10. For an interpretation of revivalism as a "revitalization" of the Puritan "culture core," see William G. McLoughlin, *Revivals, Awakening and Reform: An Essay on Religion and Social Change in America, 1607–1977* (Chicago, 1978). Elizabeth White, *Experiences of God's Gracious Dealing* (Boston, 1741). White wrote the lines in the 1660s.

established agrarian economy rather than frontier settlements. Even after re-vivalism became an accepted feature of American religious life, revivals sel-dom occurred in an area until the frontier period was over; and they manifested themselves with equal power in many of the oldest communities.[3]

It is true that the revivals were initially welcomed and later eagerly pro-moted as an answer to the problem posed by the fact that a large part of the population, in both England and America, stood outside the churches altogether. In England the parish system, which through custom and tradi-tion provided the possibility of long-term nurture and instruction in the Christian faith, had broken down.[4] And in America, with the possible ex-ception of New England, the parish system had never been successfully es-tablished. Even in New England the loss of the charter in Massachusetts had made it clear that little confidence could be placed in external guar-antees that were designed to ensure that at least the outward formalities of religion would continue to be observed. Thus the churches were con-fronted by a clear-cut summons to missionary endeavor. Given the circum-stances that prevailed, the time was ripe for a type of preaching that would prick the conscience, convict people of sin, and lead them through the agony of repentance into a personally apprehended experience of the new life that was to be found in Christ. The mystery nonetheless remains, for such preaching had never completely disappeared. The novelty of the Awakening was the widespread response it suddenly elicited, a response so unexpected that it surprised even those who sought it.

Transatlantic Influences

The Transmission of Ritual Forms

A practice of great future significance was introduced at the beginning of the eighteenth century, when Scotch Irish Presbyterians began to migrate to America in large numbers. Some settled in New England, but the major-ity came to the middle colonies, and especially to northern New Jersey and to the area around Philadelphia. The new arrivals did not agree in all articles of religious doctrine. They did share, however, a belief in the importance of religious ritual, as it had emerged among Irish Presbyteri-

---

[3] The appearance of revivals in postfrontier areas is documented in the illuminating study of Whitney R. Cross, *The Burned-over District: The Social and Intellectual History of Enthusiastic Reli-gion in Western New York, 1800–1850* (Ithaca, N.Y., 1950), 75–76. See also Paul Johnson, *A Shopkeeper's Millennium: Society and Revivals in Rochester, New York, 1815–1837* (New York, 1978); Richard W. Pointer *Protestant Pluralism and the New York Experience: A Study of Eigh-teenth-Century Religious Diversity* (Bloomington, Ind., 1988).

[4] For the significance of unaltered parish boundaries in relationship to England's shifting population, see Winthrop S. Hudson, *The Great Tradition of the American Churches* (New York, 1963), 99–100.

ans over the course of the previous half-century. And as they formed communities and established churches along the Atlantic seaboard, they continued to organize their religious life around that ritual.

A key component of this Presbyterian ritual was the Lord's Supper, or "communion." In Scotland, it was an occasion that unfolded over the course of several days and attracted several thousand, and sometimes over ten thousand people. The ritual as it was performed differed in detail from one context to another, and the communion "season" could last anywhere from two days to ten days.

A typical performance of the ritual generally began with observance of a day of fasting together with one's own congregation. The following day, persons from different congregations would travel to the outdoor site of the communion they were to have together to hear a group of ministers preach a series of sermons, lasting as long as twenty-four hours. This mostly extemporaneous preaching would be followed by a day of preparation for the Lord's Supper itself, a process that included personal prayer and soul-searching, examination by ministers or church elders, and a renewal of commitment to piety and morality. On Sunday, following further preaching, prayer, and psalm singing, the participants were seated at tables arranged in front of the pulpit and were served the bread and the wine. On the last day, ministers preached thanksgiving sermons and reminded persons of the solemnity of their rededication to spiritual striving.[5]

Typically, in the course of the communion ritual, some persons experienced religious conversions, and others rediscovered their faith. The ritual stage for these experiences—lengthy outdoor services attended by great crowds, extemporaneous preaching by numerous ministers, a mood of intense prayerful self-examination and reflection—also promoted an intense community piety.[6] In America, as the communion season was re-created, it helped to structure a context for the outburst of emotional religion known as the Great Awakening.

Theological Change and Public Piety in New England

By the beginning of the eighteenth century, new currents in English scientific and religious thought had crossed the Atlantic Ocean to the colonies. The scientific view of the world as a rational, ordered, interconnected whole was manifest in writings by Robert Boyle, William Derham, and John Ray, and in the works of English "latitudinarian" writers (so called because they promoted latitude, or tolerance, in religion) such as John Tillotson.

[5] See Leigh Eric Schmidt, *Holy Fairs: Scottish Communions and American Revivals in the Early Modern Period* (Princeton, 1989), 21–59, 70–73; Marilyn J. Westerkamp, *Triumph of the Laity: Scots-Irish Piety and the Great Awakening 1625–1760* (New York, 1988), 28–35, 136–44.

[6] Westerkamp, 31.

Americans gradually became acquainted with these writings, and some of the clergy were profoundly influenced by them.

In New England, a group of ministers who had encountered the new thinking as students at Harvard College began to articulate a fresh theological viewpoint that emphasized the "whole person." These ministers, led by Benjamin Colman of the newly organized Brattle Street Church, proposed that reason and the emotions operated together in fostering spiritual development. Stressing the unity of creation, these ministers rejected the assumption—which had emerged within many of the churches in New England in the preceding decades—that emotion was essentially a private aspect of religion. Rather, they argued that public worship, and community life in general, ought to be animated by a heartfelt piety. For them, emotional piety and a rational morality grounded in Scripture were complementary components present in both private and public life.[7]

As part of their program to restore to religion a balance of head and heart, these Boston-area ministers promoted a style of worship aimed at arousing the emotions, or "affections." Believing in a world wherein all things were interconnected in the whole, they proposed that the emotions of the soul could be enlivened through the stimulation of the senses. Accordingly, they argued for the institution of preaching techniques and forms of worship that suited that purpose. As Colman wrote, "Our spirits being imbodied are naturally come at by impressions from our senses, and more particularly by the eye and the ear."[8]

Colman and his colleagues promoted psalm singing, public recitation of prayer, expressive reading of scripture, and other methods they believed would serve to inflame the religious affections of their audiences. In addition, they advocated preaching that used colorful images and a direct, animated style of address. Of most importance, they stressed that the public gathering in the meetinghouse was the ideal setting for arousing the affections. As Colman's colleague Thomas Foxcroft wrote, "The union of many devout souls in a joint presence, mutually raises and enlivens their affections. As a collection of many dispersed *rays* into a narrow compass, gives them greater light and heat . . . even so the concurrence of a multitude in the solemnities of God's house tends to kindle and diffuse a common ardour in the worshipping assembly."[9]

The emphasis that Foxcroft and Colman and their Boston-area colleagues placed on emotional public worship helped prepare the New England soil for the itinerant ministers who scored such successes there. But even those members of the Boston clergy who endeavored to raise the emotional

---

[7] John Corrigan, *The Prism of Piety: Catholick Congregational Clergy at the Beginning of the Enlightenment* (New York, 1991).

[8] Benjamin Colman, *The Government and Improvement of Mirth* (Boston, 1707), 152.

[9] Thomas Foxcroft, *The Character of Anna* (Boston, 1723), 35.

temperature of their congregations could not have anticipated the suddenness or the magnitude of the revival of religion that was soon to take place.

The First Stirrings of Revival

The Great Awakening in America had its antecedents in local revivals that developed among the Dutch Reformed churches of northern New Jersey under the leadership of Theodore J. Frelinghuysen; among the Presbyterian churches of the same general area under the leadership of the Tennents, father and sons; and in Northampton and other communities of the Connecticut valley under the leadership of Jonathan Edwards. Although these local revivals were not consolidated into one great movement until George Whitefield arrived on the scene, they provided a foretaste of what was to come and did much to shape the subsequent outburst of religious fervor.

Theodore J. Frelinghuysen

The "beginner of the great work"[10] in America was a German born near the Dutch border, educated under Dutch auspices, ordained to the ministry of the Dutch Reformed church, and sent to America in 1719 to become a pastor in the Raritan valley of New Jersey. Although sometimes described as a German Pietist, his real affinities were with Dutch Calvinists who had been deeply influenced by the experimental piety of the English Puritans.[11]

When Frelinghuysen assumed his new responsibilities, he discovered, to his dismay, that most of his parishioners were content with a perfunctory orthodoxy that had become for them more a symbol of their Dutch nationality than an expression of any deep-seated Christian conviction. He immediately embarked on a program of reform, seeking to rouse them from their lethargy by a strict enforcement of the provisions of the Reformed discipline with regard to admission to the Lord's Supper, by personal conferences in their homes, and above all by pointed evangelistic preaching that sought to induce the members of his congregations to take seriously the understanding of the Christian faith they ostensibly professed.[12] Many were scandalized by his bluntness, and his congregations were disrupted and thrown into turmoil. The cause of the disaffected was championed by the Dutch ministers of New York, one of whom visited them in their homes to encourage their opposition. Frelinghuysen,

---

[10] The phrase is Whitefield's; quoted by L. J. Trinterud, *The Forming of an American Tradition*, 34.

[11] For the absence of Pietist influence, see *ibid.*, 54–57.

[12] His program of reform is illustrated in a sermon, a portion of which is printed in H. Shelton Smith, Robert Handy, and Lefferts Loetscher, *American Christianity*, vol. I, (New York, 1960–1963), 316–21.

however, refused to be daunted, and conversions became so frequent in the heated atmosphere that opposition within his own congregations was silenced. By 1726, the revival was at its height and had spread to other Dutch communities; and within the next few years, Frelinghuysen gained the support of the majority of the Dutch ministers.

The Tennents

William Tennent and his sons were key figures in the outbreak of the revival among the Presbyterians. A graduate of the University of Edinburgh and an unusually able teacher and scholar, the father followed Irish precedent in giving his sons their theological training in his own home while he was a pastor at Bedford, New York, from 1720 to 1727. Gilbert Tennent, his eldest son, received a Master's degree from Yale in 1725, perhaps in partial compensation for his father's disappointment in not being named to succeed Timothy Cutler as president of that institution. Two years later the father moved to Neshaminy, Pennsylvania, where he established an embryo college of his own. Deeply indebted to the Puritan devotional classics for his own understanding of the Christian faith, the elder Tennent succeeded in transmitting his earnest concern for a vital inward faith both to his sons and to the graduates of his "log college" at Neshaminy.

The chronology of the awakening among the Presbyterians is somewhat obscure, for Gilbert Tennent reports that his brother John had the first actual revival. This event must have been sometime in 1727, or 1728. Later, when John Tennent was pastor at Freehold, New Jersey, another revival occurred that was carried forward after John's death by his brother William, Jr. The most important of the brothers, however, was Gilbert. He was the outstanding preacher and the natural leader of the men his father had trained.

In 1726, Gilbert Tennent was called to the Presbyterian church at New Brunswick, New Jersey, where the revival among the Dutch Reformed was at its height. He and Frelinghuysen immediately recognized each other as kindred spirits. Tennent's ministry, by his own account, was not conspicuously successful at first, but Frelinghuysen encouraged him, and Frelinghuysen's success served both as a rebuke and as an inspiration. After a period of sickness, during which he was "exceedingly grieved" that he had "done so little for God" and had vowed to "promote his kingdom" with all his might if God would be pleased to spare him for this purpose, Tennent began to secure the response his father had taught him to seek.

The nub of the problem, as Tennent defined it, was what he called the "presumptuous security" of those who professed to be Christians. They had been baptized, catechized, and inducted into full membership in the church. They affirmed orthodox doctrines and were fully persuaded that one is saved by faith and not by works. But faith was interpreted as merely assent to orthodox ideas and was quite unrelated to most of the Christian graces. There was little of the inwardness and transforming power of the

Christian faith to be found among them. To counter this complacency, Tennent adopted the Puritan technique of preaching for "conviction"—an acknowledgment of one's own sinful estate. He insisted that no one ever became a Christian without first being subjected to the terrifying realization that one is not a Christian. One must first know oneself as a sinful creature, estranged from God and rightfully subject to condemnation, before one can apprehend and receive God's forgiveness and acceptance.

Tennent's preaching had the desired effect. By 1729, scattered Presbyterian congregations from New Brunswick to Staten Island began to throb with new life under his leadership. Other products of his father's tuition, notably Samuel Blair, were equally active. The participation of Presbyterian ministers of New England background, such as Jonathan Dickinson at Elizabeth and Aaron Burr at Newark, was also enlisted. By the end of the 1730s, there had been eight or ten local revivals of some degree of intensity. In the meantime Gilbert Tennent was gaining a wider hearing through the 1735 publications of three of his sermons. Earlier in the same year two sermons by John Tennent with an account of the revival at Freehold had also been published.

Jonathan Edwards

The third manifestation of religious excitement occurred in the Connecticut valley with Jonathan Edwards playing the central role. Edwards, one of the most brilliant and original minds that America has produced, scarcely conforms to the popular image of the revivalist. His interests seem to have been largely academic, and he spent long hours each day in his study. His sermons were tightly knit and closely reasoned expositions of theological doctrine, which he read rather than speaking extemporaneously. But his preaching struck a nerve among his listeners, and from that sprang a revival of extraordinary power.

Edwards had been educated at Yale, graduating in 1720 at the age of 17. For some years he served there as a tutor, leaving in 1727 to assist his grandfather, Solomon Stoddard, who was pastor of the church at Northampton, Massachusetts, and succeeding him two years later when he died. Edwards was greatly distressed by the "licentiousness" that so generally prevailed among the youth of the town.

> Many of them [were] very much addicted to night walking, and frequenting the tavern, and lewd practices. . . . It was their manner very frequently to get together in conventions of both sexes for mirth and jollity, which they called frolics, and they would often spend the greater part of the night in them.

Furthermore, many of them were "indecent in their carriage at meeting." Edwards began to meet with the young people in their homes. They in turn responded to his pastoral concern; reformation in behavior set in, and by 1733, Edwards was able to report that they had grown "observably more decent in their attendance on public worship."[13]

In the meantime he had become alarmed by the complacency engendered by the spread of "Arminian" principles. The notion of human ability, he believed, undercut a dependence upon divine grace, which was at the heart of the Christian faith. To counter this threat, he preached a series of five sermons in 1734 on justification by faith alone. Those sermons, Edwards reported, were attended by "a very remarkable blessing of heaven to the souls of the people in this town." A young woman of questionable morals was converted, other young people were stirred by her example, the tempo of religious interest increased, and conversions multiplied.

> This work of God . . . made a glorious alteration in the town, so that in the spring and summer following (anno 1735) the town seemed to be full of the presence of God. It never was so full of love, nor so full of joy, and yet so full of distress, as it was then. There were remarkable tokens of God's presence in almost every house. It was a time of joy in families on the account of salvation being brought unto them; parents rejoicing over their children as new born, and husbands over their wives, and wives over their husbands.

There had been other revivals in the valley, most notably those that occurred under the ministry of Edwards's grandfather, Solomon Stoddard. None of them, however, proved to be contagious. With the quickening of 1734, it was otherwise. News was carried to other communities, visitors came to Northampton, Edwards was invited to preach in neighboring churches, and by 1736, the revival had spread throughout the Connecticut valley. But by 1737, the revival in Northampton had come to a halt, ceasing almost as abruptly as it had begun. Even this, Edwards interpreted as further evidence of God's mercy, for by withdrawing his Spirit to other places he was but demonstrating "how entirely and immediately the great work lately wrought was his" and "how little we can do and how little effect great things have without him."[14]

Edwards's fame as a revivalist was the product in part of his *Faithful Narrative of the Surprising Work of God in the Conversion of Many Hundred Souls in Northampton,* published in London in 1737 and reprinted in Boston in 1738. John Wesley read it as he walked from London to Oxford, and George Whitefield read it during his first brief visit to Georgia in 1738; it had a decisive effect upon both men. More important than the stimulation that the book provided was the way in which it shaped subsequent revival

---

[13] *A Faithful Narrative of the Surprising Work of God in the Conversion of Many Hundred Souls in Northampton and Neighboring Towns* (London, 1737), reprinted in *The Works of Jonathan Edwards,* vol. IV, *The Great Awakening,* ed. C. C. Goen (New Haven, 1972), 146–47.

[14] Quoted by Edwin S. Gaustad, *The Great Awakening in New England* (New York, 1957), 22.

efforts by the precise and detailed account it gave of how the revival at Northampton actually developed. The duplication of this pattern, of course, became a major objective of those who followed him. Even the conversion process itself tended to become stereotyped. Less influential but of greater inherent significance was the series of writings—*The Distinguishing Marks of a Work of the Spirit of God* (1741), *Some Thoughts Concerning the Present Revival of Religion* (1742), and *A Treatise Concerning Religious Affections* (1746)—in which he analyzed with psychological insight and scientific precision the twin phenomena of conversion and revival.

The Great Awakening

It was not until 1740 that the local manifestations of intense religious interest and concern were transformed into a Great Awakening that was to spread throughout every colony from Nova Scotia to Georgia and to touch every area—urban and rural, tidewater and back country—and every class—rich and poor, educated and uneducated—before its power was finally dissipated. There had been interconnections, to be sure, between the revival movements led by Frelinghuysen, the Tennents, and Edwards. Frelinghuysen and Gilbert Tennent actively supported one another. Edwards was at Yale when William Tennent was sufficiently well known there to think of himself as a possible choice for the presidency and when Gilbert Tennent received a degree. In his *Faithful Narrative*, Edwards mentions an earlier revival "under the ministry of a very pious young gentleman, a Dutch minister, whose name as I remember was Frelinghuysen." But these were mostly tenuous connections, and the revivals remained local in character until they were consolidated into a single movement by the itinerant activity of George Whitefield.

"The Grand Itinerant"

A recent graduate of Oxford University where he had been an intimate friend of the Wesleys and a member of the "Holy Club," George Whitefield had spent a few months in Georgia in 1738. Upon his return to England, he had adopted, much to the dismay of John Wesley, the expedient of preaching in the open air. Both men had come to look upon "all the world" as their "parish" to the extent that they were convinced that, wherever they chanced to be, it was their "bounden duty to declare unto all that are willing to hear the glad tidings of salvation"; hence, Whitefield's expedient had the distinct advantage of making it unnecessary to secure an invitation from a local parish church in order to have an opportunity to preach. Moreover, Whitefield's preaching in the open air met with such success that by the time he returned to America late in 1739, he had persuaded Wesley to "become more vile" and to preach in his stead to the great throngs he had assembled in the vicinity of Bristol, England.

The Old Court House in Philadelphia. From this courthouse George Whitefield preached to great throngs. Benjamin Franklin paced off the distance at which Whitefield's voice could be heard and estimated that, on the basis of two square feet per person, he could easily be heard by 25,000 people. *(Courtesy of the Library Company of Philadelphia.)*

Whitefield arrived in Philadelphia on November 2, 1739. He was a "slim slender youth," twenty four years of age, with a strong but mellow voice, perfect enunciation, a keen sense of the dramatic, and an ability by subtle inflection to clothe almost any word with emotion. Later it was said that by merely pronouncing the word *Mesopotamia*, he could bring tears to the eyes of his listeners. Although his intention had been to proceed immediately to Georgia to look after the affairs of his projected orphanage, Whitefield was prevailed upon to preach first in the Anglican church and then in other churches, and finally he spoke to great crowds each evening from the steps of the courthouse. The response was astonishing. Even Benjamin Franklin was impressed, both with the young man himself and with the good moral effect of his preaching. Franklin later reflected that "it seem'd as if all the world were growing religious." William Tennent visited him and persuaded him to make a rapid evangelistic tour of the area between Philadelphia and New York, which already had been stirred by revivals. Conscious of the new opportunity that had opened before him, Whitefield determined to preach his way to Georgia, traveling by land instead of going by ship. After a brief period in Savannah, he was back in the Philadelphia area from the middle of April to the middle of May to collect funds for the building of his orphanage, announcing his intention to visit New England in the autumn on a similar mission.

Whitefield arrived at Newport, Rhode Island, in September 1740, having sailed from Charleston three weeks before. His arrival had been well publicized, and the Boston newspapers carried advertisements of numerous books and tracts by and about Whitefield. During the next 73 days he traveled 800 miles and preached 130 sermons. He was met everywhere by great throngs. The ministers of Boston gave him an enthusiastic welcome (Charles Chauncy may have had some reservations); Harvard and Yale threw open their doors; the visit to Jonathan Edwards at Northampton was a triumphant pilgrimage; and by the time Whitefield had made his way through New York and New Jersey to Philadelphia, he was convinced that America was to be his "chief scene of action."[15] He preached whenever and wherever he could find anyone to listen, and in this, as well as in his extemporaneous preaching, he had many imitators. He died in Newburyport, Massachusetts, during his fifth tour, in 1770.

The Mounting Opposition

By 1740, the revival had taken some turns that provoked concern in many churches. That concern was transformed into outright opposition after Gilbert Tennent's sermon on *The Danger of an Unconverted Ministry*, delivered at Nottingham, Pennsylvania, in March 1740. Published before the year was out, it was viewed by many as a step across the boundary of church order. Even though he had been goaded into a denunciation of "pharisee-teachers" by the persistent efforts of unsympathetic preachers to sabotage his father's "log college," Gilbert Tennent's response only served further to inflame them. "Is a blind man," he asked,

> fit to be a guide in a very dangerous way? Is a dead man fit to bring others to life? . . . Is an ignorant rustic that has never been at sea in his life fit to be a pilot? . . . Isn't an unconverted minister like a man who would learn others to swim before he has learned it himself, and so is drowned in the act and dies like a fool?

The sermon ended with an open invitation for people to forsake the ministry of "natural" men and to seek out instead a congregation where they would receive profitable instruction.[16]

In the middle colonies, as well as in New England, where Tennent toured with Whitefield for three months beginning in December 1740, ministers rose in opposition to Tennent. Moreover, about this time, printed copies of Whitefield's journal of his New England tour were found

---

[15] Joseph Tracy, *The Great Awakening* (Boston, 1842), 112. For Whitefield's life, see Stuart C. Henry, *George Whitefield: Wayfaring Witness* (New York, 1957).

[16] A major portion of the sermon is reprinted in Smith, Handy, and Loetscher, I, 321–28.

to contain disparaging comments about the caliber of many New England ministers. Whitefield, to be sure, had paid tribute to the general level of religious life in New England, which he regarded as exceeding that of any other part of the world, but he said many who preached did not "experimentally know Christ," and consequently their preaching was judged uninspired and uninspiring:

> The ministers' preaching almost universally by note is a certain mark they have in a great measure lost the old spirit of preaching. . . . It is a sad symptom of decay of vital religion when reading sermons becomes fashionable where extempore preaching did once almost universally prevail.

Whitefield echoed Tennent's denunciation of unconverted ministers. The reason that congregations have been dead, he wrote, is that "dead men preach to them," and "how can dead men beget living children?" God may, if he chooses, "convert people by the Devil," and he may also "by unconverted ministers," but "he seldom or never makes use of either of them for this purpose." Nor could one look to the New England colleges, Harvard and Yale, to supply ministers of different caliber, said Whitefield, for "their light is become darkness, darkness that may be felt and is complained of by the most godly ministers."[17]

Opposition was further aroused by the fanatical spirit and emotional extravagance of James Davenport, who projected himself on the scene at this junction. The revival preaching, to be sure, was highly emotional, and on occasion people were known to cry out, to weep and sob, and even to faint and swoon. But the leaders of the revival were careful to restrain such public displays and to cast doubt upon them as evidence of conversion. Thomas Prince reported that he did not "remember any crying out or falling down or fainting, either under Mr. Whitefield's or Mr. Tennent's ministry all the while they were here [in Boston]."[18] It was otherwise with James Davenport, who did so much to bring the revival into disrepute by encouraging all manner of excess.

The grandson of the founder of New Haven and a graduate of Yale, Davenport had been called to a pastorate on Long Island in 1738. Stirred by the revival excitement, he crossed to Connecticut in the summer of 1741 to follow the itinerant path blazed by Whitefield and Tennent. His sermons were marked by invective, incoherent ejaculations, and indiscriminate denunciations of ministers. He sang as he made his way through the streets to the place of worship. He claimed to be able to distinguish infallibly the elect from the damned, publicly greeting the former as "brethren" and the latter as "neighbors." He perhaps was unbalanced mentally, and the leaders of the revival immediately sought to dissociate themselves from

---

[17] Gaustad, 30; C. C. Goen, *Revivalism and Separatism in New England, 1740–1800* (New Haven, 1962), 49.

[18] Goen, 18.

him. But the damage was done, and the revival cause was brought into further disrepute when Davenport invaded Massachusetts the following summer. He had been arrested in Connecticut and transported under guard out of the colony. In Massachusetts he was jailed, again adjudged insane, and sent back to Long Island. In the end his sanity seems to have been restored, and through the friendly counsel of Eleazar Wheelock and Solomon Williams, he came to see the error of his ways. In 1744, he published his *Confessions and Retractions,* expressing the hope that this would remove the prejudices that his extravagant behavior had evoked. It was a vain hope, for those who had been affronted by Whitefield's ill-considered observations were only too happy to utilize Davenport's excesses as a weapon to discredit the revivalists as a whole.

Charles Chauncy (1705–1787) led the attack and blasted the revival from the pulpit of the First Church of Boston in a sermon entitled *Enthusiasm Described and Cautioned Against.* This was followed in 1743 by a more extended denunciation, *Seasonable Thoughts on the State of Religion in New England.* The Harvard faculty was also incensed. When Whitefield had first visited Boston, he had been entertained and commended by the president of the college, and the overseers had set aside a day of thanksgiving for the beneficent effect of his labors. When he returned in 1744, the doors of the college were closed to him, and the faculty issued a statement, later endorsed by the Yale faculty, blistering his message, his methods, and his character.

The situation was confused and the ministers badly divided. One group, under the leadership of Chauncy, feared that the enthusiasm of the revival might undermine the authority of the churches, and so for a time they emphasized the rational and moral aspects of religion as an antidote. Another group of ministers, loosely clustered around Edwards, favored the revival and participated wholeheartedly in it, but they also remained aware of its potential effects on the order of the Congregational churches. Only a handful were ready to insist upon emotional manifestations as evidence of conversion and to defend itinerancy and lay preaching. The others were uncommitted. These responses to the revival predicted the course of religion in New England well into the next century. At one end of the spectrum eventually appeared a style of religion that accented the capabilities of human reason and the central importance of morality. The other end of the spectrum was anchored by advocates of highly emotional, effervescent religion that was focused on conversion but that was significantly less concerned with systems of doctrine. And in the middle were various shades of the legacy of both Chauncy and Edwards, persons who sought to combine the emotional element in religion with an emphasis on discipline, clerical authority, and formal worship.

Although the movement was fairly general throughout New England, the real stronghold of the "Separate" or "Strict" Congregationalists was in eastern Connecticut. It has been suggested that this was a lower-class revolt, but a careful examination of the Separate churches has revealed that they were composed of a representative cross section of the population and included prominent and even wealthy members of their respective communities.[19] The constant factor was the earnestness of their religious concern. In all, no fewer than 98 Separate churches were formed, and there were at least 32 temporary separations. But this observation scarcely indicates their full strength, for the strong and ultimately overwhelming tendency was for the Separates to become Baptists. The doctrine of believers' baptism, of course, was a fitting expression of the Separates' conception of the church as a community of "experienced" Christians. At least 19 of the Separate Congregational churches became Baptist, but a better indication of the Separates' strength is the additional 130 Baptist churches that were formed by disaffected Congregationalists. Although not participating directly in the earliest New England revivals, the Baptists reaped the largest harvest, siphoning off the strength of the remaining Separate churches to such an extent that they tended to dwindle and die.

The Southern Phase of the Awakening

In the South the Awakening developed more slowly. Although Whitefield preached to large numbers in the South, the way had not been prepared for him by earlier revivals, and there was little leadership to conserve the results he obtained. The old, established areas of Virginia were Anglican territory, and the Anglican clergy were unsympathetic and even hostile.[20] Other areas were more recently settled, and without existing centers of church life, there had been scant opportunity for revivals to develop. Thus, throughout the South, Whitefield blazed the way for the spread of the Awakening instead of consolidating existing interest into a single movement as he had done elsewhere. Later, when the revival took root in Virginia, class differences between Anglicans in the eastern parts of the colony and Baptists and Methodists in the west complicated matters, as they became associated with antirevivalist and prorevivalist sentiments, respectively.

The earliest spiritual quickening in Virginia occurred east of the mountains in Hanover County. As a result of Whitefield's influence as he made his way overland to Georgia in December 1739, a few lay people began to meet in private homes to read some of Whitefield's sermons and other devotional literature. A spontaneous revival broke out. As religious concern spread, the homes of the leaders became too small to hold the gatherings, and "reading houses" were erected. This was the situation when William Robinson, a graduate of William Tennent's "log college," was sent by the New Brunswick Presbytery on a missionary tour of Virginia during the

---

[19] This is the conclusion reached by Goen as a result of his thorough and careful research; *Revivalism and Separatism*, 188–91.

[20] Rhys Isaac, *The Transformation of Virginia: Community, Religion, and Authority, 1740–1790* (Chapel Hill, N.C., 1982).

winter of 1742–1743. Those who had erected the "reading houses" invited him to preach and became Presbyterians. Robinson was followed by a succession of revivalist itinerants sent out by the Synod of New York, the most important of whom was to be Samuel Davies, who succeeded Robinson at Hanover in 1747. Under his leadership the revival spread rapidly; numerous churches were organized and brought together in 1755 to form a new presbytery. After Davies's departure in 1759 to become president of Princeton, the Presbyterian activity became less pronounced.

In the meantime the revival broke out in another quarter. In 1754, two brothers-in-law, Shubal Stearns and Daniel Marshall, came to Virginia from Connecticut. They had been converted by Whitefield, became Separate Congregational itinerants, and were then ordained as Baptist preachers. Within a year of their arrival in Virginia, they were told of people across the border in North Carolina, where there was no preaching, who would travel 40 miles to hear a sermon. From among these people a church was gathered at Sandy Creek, and from this center no fewer than 125 ministers were raised up in little more than a decade, fanning out in all directions to preach the gospel. Marshall went on to Georgia where, assisted by the "exhortations" of his wife, he labored with almost equal success. From Virginia to Georgia, Separate Baptist churches multiplied at an astonishing rate. At first tension existed between the hyperenthusiastic Separate and the old "regular" Baptist churches formed or reorganized by evangelists from the Philadelphia Baptist Association. By 1787, however, this breach was being healed, first in Virginia and then later in North Carolina, Kentucky, and elsewhere. Devereaux Jarratt, Anglican rector at Bath, preached a revival in Dinwiddie County in the 1760s. By the early 1770s, with the help of lay preachers sent from England by Wesley, Jarratt began to itinerate and attracted large assemblies to his open-air sermons. Jesse Lee, one of his young converts, reported:

> I have been at meetings where the whole congregation would be bathed in tears, and sometimes their cries would be so loud that the preacher's voice could not be heard. Some would be seized with trembling and in a few moments drop on the floor as if they were dead, while others were embracing each other with streaming eyes and all were lost in wonder, love, and praise.[21]

With the assistance of several lay preachers, Jarratt was busily forming converts into "methodist" societies. By 1777, as a result of their activity, there were 4,379 members of the societies in Virginia and adjoining counties of North Carolina, yet the total for all the colonies was only 6,968. After the Revolution when the societies broke with Anglicanism and formed the Methodist Episcopal Church in 1784, Jarratt expressed resent-

---

[21] W. W. Sweet, *Methodism in American History* (New York, 1954), 76.

ment at the separation. He felt that he had been deceived by the assurances of loyalty that he had received from the lay preachers. Within a few years his bitterness was gone, but he remained within the Anglican fold where his influence contributed greatly to the strength of the evangelical movement within the newly formed Protestant Episcopal Church.

The Impact of the Awakening

The Awakening was much more than the activity of a few conspicuous leaders. It was "Great" because it was general. People everywhere were caught up in the movement, and its influence was spread by innumerable local pastors, passing itinerants, and lay exhorters. Few could escape the excitement or avoid the necessity to declare oneself as friend or foe.

And because the Awakening was general, it played an important role in forming a national consciousness among people of different colonies whose primary ties were with Europe rather than with one another. As a spontaneous movement that swept across all colonial boundaries, generated a common interest and a common loyalty, bound people together in a common cause, and reinforced the conviction that God had a special destiny in store for America, the Awakening contributed greatly to the development of a sense of cohesiveness among the American people.

Institutional Consequences

No exact estimate can be made of members added to the churches by the Awakening, but the number in all denominations was large. Interest in Indian missions was revived. A wide variety of charitable projects, including schools for Indians and the children of indentured servants, were initiated. The role of the laity in the churches was enhanced. The setting of minister against minister undermined ministerial authority at a time when a stress upon a self-authenticating religious experience was freeing the individual from dependence upon clerical opinion. On the other hand, quite paradoxically, the ministerial office was also given added luster by the fame of the revivalists, and the number of young men drawn into the ranks of the ministry rapidly mounted.[22]

A consequence of marked future significance was the remarkable success of Baptist and Methodist itinerants in the conversion of blacks to Christianity. This was the result of their energetic efforts to evangelize the slaves, a task hitherto neglected and not seriously attempted by other Protestant denominations (not even by the Quakers) until plantation missions were organized after 1830. Blacks responded to the exciting preach-

---

[22] Patricia U. Bonomi emphasizes the health of religious institutions in the eighteenth century in *Under the Cope of Heaven: Religion, Society and Politics in Colonial America* (New York, 1986).

ing of the itinerants and were welcomed into Baptist and Methodist churches on the basis of a surprising degree of equality. They were given formal responsibilities, and the talents of the gifted were utilized as exhorters and preachers in evangelistic endeavors. There often were more black than white members of local churches. Some all-black congregations were formed, and a few blacks served as pastors of mixed congregations.[23]

Apart from the multiplication of churches and the incorporation of blacks within the Christian community, the major institutional survivals of the Awakening came from the impulse that was given to higher education by the necessity to provide educational opportunities for the swelling number of ministerial recruits. Presbyterians were especially active in this endeavor, and many of their ministers established classical academies, similar in character to William Tennent's "log college" and patterned after the small private Presbyterian academies of Ireland and the Dissenting academies of England, which at this time enjoyed an educational reputation that was greater than that of the ancient universities. Several colleges—Washington and Lee, Washington and Jefferson, and Dickinson—trace their ancestry back to these early academies. In 1746, the Synod of New York secured a charter for the College of New Jersey (Princeton), which was designed as the capstone of the Presbyterian educational structure, and in 1776, the Hanover Presbytery in Virginia established Hampden–Sydney College. Baptists also organized several academies and in 1764 founded the College of Rhode Island (Brown University) as their major center for training of ministers. In 1766, prorevivalists among the Dutch Reformed obtained a charter for Queen's College (Rutgers University). Dartmouth, an outgrowth of an Indian charity school, was incorporated in 1769.

Although the clergy of the English settlements along the seaboard did not have the opportunity to duplicate the work of the priests who accompanied the French traders and trappers on their far-ranging travels through the interior of the continent, the evangelization of those tribes with whom the English came into contact did not suffer neglect.[24] The effect of the Awakening was to pour new enthusiasm into this task. Eleazar Wheelock, Samuel Kirkland, David Brainerd, and for a time Jonathan

---

[23] For an account of this phase of the Awakening, see W. S. Hudson, "The American Context as an Area for Research in Black Church Studies," *Church History*, 3 (1983), 159–70. Baptists and Methodists encountered much opposition and hostility because of their tampering with other people's property, an activity that among other facets of their behavior has caused them to be labeled as a major countercultural force in the South. See R. R. Beeman and Rhys Isaac, "Cultural Conflict and Social Change in the Revolutionary South," *Journal of Southern History*, 46 (1980), 533–34; Isaac, 161–77.

[24] Anglicans lost heart for Indian missions for many years after the 1622 massacre of 300 colonists, but others did not. For Indian missions, see R. P. Beaver, *Pioneers in Mission* (Grand Rapids, 1966); F. P. Purcha, *Americanizing the American Indians* (Cambridge, Mass., 1973); and Henry W. Bowden, *American Indians and Christian Missions: Studies in Cultural Conflict* (Chicago, 1981).

Edwards were among those who devoted themselves to Indian missions. Brainerd's diary, edited by Edwards, is a moving testament of devotion that tells the story of his experiences among the Indians, and it inspired many others to give themselves to mission work.

The Theological Temper Generated by the Awakening

Evangelicalism, to use the term by which the new surge of spiritual life is usually described, has often been interpreted as a revolt against Calvinism. Although this may have been its ultimate consequence, it was far from that in the beginning. The understanding of the Christian faith as set forth in the great Reformed Confessions was taken for granted. John Wesley was an important exception but, in many respects, even Wesley stood within the Genevan tradition. Evangelicalism, however, was much more a mood and an emphasis than a theological system. Its stress was upon the importance of personal religious experience. If it was a revolt against anything, it was a revolt against the notion that the Christian life involved little more than observing the outward formalities of the religion.

Only in New England was significant theological discussion provoked by the Awakening, and only in New England did clearly defined theological alignments appear. From a theological standpoint the "Consistent Calvinists," or Edwardseans, made the most impressive contribution to the debate. This "New England Theology" was fashioned by Jonathan Edwards and his two most influential disciples, Joseph Bellamy and Samuel Hopkins, in an effort to buttress the revival by a bold and intellectually rigorous restatement of those doctrines that they were convinced had been verified by the revival.[25] The truth that redemption was effected by God's sovereign grace alone was to be defended at whatever cost to human pride, and all attempts to substitute moral attainments for the righteousness that comes only as a gift were to be resolutely opposed. Arrayed against them, especially in the vicinity of Boston, were those charged with being "Arminians"—ministers who regarded Edwardsean doctrines as unduly harsh and as an affront to common sense in that they tended to undermine all morality. The doctrine of original sin, pictured in terms of innocent infants burning in hell, was denounced as inhuman, unreasonable, and indefensible; and the doctrine of predestination was condemned as destructive of all moral effort. Between the embattled extremes was a varied group of middle-of-the-roaders known as "Old Calvinists." Whether more traditionally oriented or more liberally inclined, members of this group were distressed by theological wrangling, viewing it as the consequence of an overly fussy concern for "theological niceties" and advocating instead a "large measure of charity." Ezra Stiles was

---

[25] See Joseph Haroutunian, *Piety Versus Moralism, the Passing of the New England Theology* (New York, 1932); and Conrad Wright, *The Liberal Christians* (Boston, 1970).

typical of their point of view when he announced that the reigning theological debate was only a verbal dispute.

> Interrogating so-called Arminians, he found they believed in the redemptive grace of Christ; inquiring of so-called Calvinists, he learned that they did not deny the importance of good works. On the whole, "I cannot perceive any very essential real difference in their opinions respecting the fundamental principles of religion."[26]

In this lack of concern for careful theological distinctions and in the emphasis upon "the fundamental principles of religion," the moderates were more closely akin to the general spirit of Evangelicalism than were the Edwardseans. Evangelicalism as a whole tended to prize a "warm heart" and to be impatient with theological controversy. What distinguished the Edwardseans from other Evangelicals was their firm conviction that a warm heart was not enough. In keeping with the earlier Puritan heritage, they insisted that both heart and head—faith and reason, grace and law—must be brought together in the service of God. Thus the Edwardseans were to provide the major portion of whatever intellectual content Evangelicalism was to have. Without the influence of this theological structure that Evangelicalism took largely for granted, Evangelicalism would have had small staying power. Reduced to little more than sentiment, its thrust would quickly have evaporated. It is of particular importance for American history that Evangelicalism was formed as a compound of an emotional experience of "rebirth" and a commitment of obedience to God's law. This framework for evangelical religion, which took shape in the eighteenth century, also incorporated a view of preaching as a means to promote religion in both of these areas. Various styles of preaching came about in the later history of the denominations, but evangelical preaching of the sort that emerged from the religious ferment of the eighteenth century proved the most durable and appealing over time.

The Denominational Concept

What has been called the "denominational" concept of the church had been elaborated a century earlier by the Dissenting Brethren of the Westminster Assembly of Divines.[27] This concept was to be of decisive future importance

---

[26] Gaustad, 130. Stiles was a representative figure through whom many of the tendencies of the age are to be seen. A graduate of Yale, he was pastor at Newport, Rhode Island, and Portsmouth, New Hampshire, before returning to Yale in 1778 as president of the college. See Edmund S. Morgan, *The Gentle Puritan: A Life of Ezra Stiles, 1727–1795* (New Haven, 1962).

[27] The Assembly was summoned in 1643 by the Long Parliament to advise the Parliament in its task of effecting a religious settlement for the nation. Presbyterian sentiment was predominant among the assembled clergy. The Congregational minority became known as the Dissenting Brethren. The case for "denominationalism," as developed by these dissenters, is discussed in Russell E. Richey, ed., *Denominationalism* (Nashville, 1977), 19–42. Jacob Neusner provides an unusually incisive discussion of the same concept in *Understanding American Judaism* (New York, 1971), II, 259–77.

in the shaping of American religious life. Denominationalism, as these men used the term, was the opposite of sectarianism. A "sect" regards itself alone as the true Church. By definition a "sect" is exclusive. "Denomination," on the other hand, was adopted as a neutral and inclusive term. It implied that the group referred to is but one member, called or denominated by a particular name, of a larger group—the church—to which other denominations belong. Gilbert Tennent stated the concept with clarity and incisiveness when he declared the following: "All societies who profess Christianity and retain the foundational principles thereof, notwithstanding their different denominations and diversity of sentiments in smaller things, are in reality but one Church of Christ, but several branches (more or less pure in minuter points) of one visible kingdom of the Messiah."[28]

On the basis of this understanding of the church that acknowledged the unity that existed within the diversity of outward ecclesiastical forms, the Protestant churches were able to develop a functional catholicity that was to find expression in the creation of a whole system of voluntary societies for the promotion of a host of worthy causes. There were societies devoted to missions, Bible and tract distribution, education, charitable enterprises, and a wide-ranging spectrum of moral and social reforms. These societies were to be the instruments into which much of the evangelical fervor released by the Awakening was subsequently to be channeled when the Protestant churches jointly addressed themselves to the task of spreading churches and schools across a continent while devoting themselves, at the same time, to reforming the nation. From a modern perspective, two of the more important causes forwarded by these societies were the abolition of slavery and the emancipation of women. In many ways the full promise for slaves and for women was to remain unfulfilled, but, if much remained to be accomplished, significant progress was made. From the perspective of the early nineteenth century, however, in contrast to that of a later time, the missionary task in its various ramifications was regarded as fundamental to the achievement of all other objectives.

All this, however, was in the future. The immediate problem at hand was the relationship of the colonies to England.

---

[28] Leonard J. Trinterud, *The Forming of an American Tradition* (Philadelphia, 1949), 132.

CHAPTER FOUR

The Birth of the Republic

When Edmund Burke in 1775 sought to help his fellow members of Parliament understand the "love of freedom" and "fierce spirit of liberty" that had occasioned the uproar in the colonies over sugar and stamps and tea and taxes, he reminded them that "the people of the colonies are descendants of Englishmen." And then he added:

> England, Sir, is a nation which still I hope respects, and formerly adored, her freedom. The colonists emigrated from you when this part of your character was most predominant; and they took this bias and direction the moment they parted from your hands. They are therefore not only devoted to liberty, but to liberty according to English ideals, and on English principles.

Representative institutions in harmony with English practice had indeed developed very early in all the colonies. Some of the colonial charters were explicit in guaranteeing that the settlers would have "the rights of Englishmen," and the colonists had become accustomed through long practice to the idea that they could not be taxed by their own consent as expressed in the colonial assemblies.

Religion and Politics

Although the "love of freedom" had deep and ancient roots in English society, it had been nurtured and transformed into a "fierce spirit of liberty" during the first half of the seventeenth century when the religious issue had come to the fore and had become inextricably intermingled with the liberties of Englishmen. During the course of the constitutional struggle in England, it became evident to the participants that certain theological convictions had definite political implications, and these implications were rather fully explored and explicated by both royalists and parliamentarians before the nation finally regained its equilibrium. It was the emotion and spirit generated in the struggle between king and Parliament that Burke had in mind when he noted that the colonists were not only Englishmen but "Protestants, and of that kind which is the most adverse to all implicit subjection of mind and opinion."

The Puritan Political Heritage

Those Protestants whom Burke described as "the most adverse to all implicit subjection of mind and opinion" had their rootage in Reformed or Calvinist Christianity. It has been said of the early Calvinists that they feared God so much that they could not fear any man, be he king or emperor. And they had much to fear from men, for almost everywhere the Reformed churches were "churches under the cross"—suffering persecution and struggling to survive. But they remained undaunted, sustained in part by a firm confidence in God's overruling providence and impelled by a strong conviction that the chief end of man is to glorify God and insisting that God is glorified by full and complete obedience. When John Knox informed Queen Mary that "right religion takes neither origin nor authority from worldly princes but from the eternal God alone" and then told her that subjects therefore must not "frame their religion according to the appetite of their princes," he was speaking in an accent that was familiar to all sons of Geneva.[1]

The Reformed churches were prodded into political theorizing. Although they remembered the apostle Paul's admonition that Christians must be subject to "the powers that be," they were not of a temper patiently to endure bloody repression if a plausible excuse for active resistance could be found. Goaded by the burnings in England under Mary Tudor, the persecution in Scotland under Mary Stuart, the wars of religion in France, and the massacre of the Dutch by the Spanish troops of the Duke of Alva, the Reformed leaders explored every possible concept that could be utilized to justify resistance and rebellion. Rights derived from natural law and from the origin of government in a compact between the

---

[1] See John T. McNeill, "The Democratic Element in Calvin's Thought," *Church History* (1949), 153–71; and W. S. Hudson, "Theological Convictions and Democratic Government," *Theology Today* (1953), 230–39.

ruler and the ruled were explicated, and the role of lesser magistrates as guardians of the liberties of people was carefully defined. Even tyrannicide, in exceptional circumstances, was defended.[2]

Doctrines of resistance and rebellion were purely negative features of Reformed political thought. From a positive point of view, a distinct preference was exhibited for the checks and balances of a "mixed state." Noting with characteristic irony that "it very rarely happens that kings regulate themselves so that their will is never at variance with justice and rectitude," Calvin himself had suggested the importance of broadening the franchise so that the self-interest of the one may be checked by the self-interest of the many. "It is safer and more tolerable for the government to be in the hands of the many that they may afford each other mutual assistance and admonition, and that if any one arrogate to himself more than is right, the many may act as censors and masters to restrain his ambition." "No kind of government is more happy than this, . . . and I consider those most happy people who are permitted to enjoy such a condition" in which they have the right and the duty to "exert their strenuous and constant efforts" to preserve their liberties.[3]

This was the seedbed of the Puritan political thought that reshaped the English constitution through the ordeal of civil war and became so deeply rooted in the consciousness of Englishmen that the ejection of James II from the throne in 1688 was effected by a "bloodless" revolution. Defenders of the royal prerogative had few doubts as to the source of the rebellious and seditious notion of the time. Richard Bancroft, chaplain to Elizabeth I's archbishop of Canterbury and soon to be archbishop himself, pointed an accusing finger at Geneva in his book *Dangerous Positions and Proceedings* (1593). James I echoed the accusation at the Hampton Court Conference in 1604. And in 1663, Robert South repeated it, saying this: "In our account of the sons of Geneva, we will begin with the father of the faithful (faithful, I mean, to their old antimonarchical doctrines and assertions), this is, the great mufti of Geneva—John Calvin."

The fact that this "fierce spirit of liberty" was part of the intellectual baggage carried to the New World by the Puritans has been obscured by two much-quoted statements of John Winthrop and John Cotton. "A democracy," said Winthrop, "is among most civil nations accounted the meanest

---

[2] See, for example, *A Defense of Liberty Against Tyrants: A Translation of the* Vindiciae contra Tyrannos, ed. H. J. Laski (London, 1924), and John Ponet, *A Shorte Treatise of Politike Power,* facsimile reproduction in W. S. Hudson, *John Ponet: Advocate of Limited Monarchy* (Chicago, 1942).

[3] John Calvin, *Institutes of the Christian Religion,* IV, xx, 8; and *Commentary on Micah,* 5:5. For a later explication of the necessity for checks and balances, see the preface to John Cotton's *The Keys of the Kingdom of Heaven* (1644), reprinted in A. S. P. Woodhouse, *Puritanism and Liberty* (London, 1938), 293–98.

and worst of all forms of government." "Democracy?" Cotton asked rhetorically. "I do not conceive that ever God did ordain it as a fit government either for church or commonwealth."[4] Winthrop and Cotton, of course, used the word in its classical meaning, which had no connotation of indirect representation. The democracy they repudiated was not the "mixed" government that the nineteenth century became accustomed to calling democracy. Cotton's inclusion of "church" in his rejection of democracy should make it clear that a definition of terms is required, for Cotton was a major architect of the "congregational" form of church government.[5] Even Thomas Jefferson did not believe that democracy "would be practicable beyond the extent of a New England township."[6] What Winthrop and Cotton were advocating, and what the Founding Fathers sought to establish, was a "mixed government" with a separation of powers that would provide "guards for their future security."

No one was more aware than John Cotton that all men and especially men in power are prone to corruption. "Let all the world," he declared, "learn to give mortal man no greater power than they are content they shall use, for use it they will. . . . It is necessary that all power that is on earth be limited. . . . It is counted a matter of danger to the state to limit prerogatives, but it is a further danger not to have them limited." Winthrop told the men of Hingham that in signing the covenant, they had agreed to submit to the rulers that were thus set over them for their own good, but this admonition had an important qualification—unless they could prove that their rulers were violating the good they had been appointed to serve.[7] This was the common conviction. Thus, although minority rights were not cherished with equal ardor by all Protestant churches in America, most of them through tradition, conviction, and experience had developed an ingrained antipathy to arbitrary rule and had been taught that upon just occasion, people had the right and even the duty to rebel.

---

[4] R. C. Winthrop, *Life and Letters of John Winthrop* (Boston, 1869), II, 430; and John Cotton's "Letter to Lord Say and Seal," in *The Puritans,* ed. Perry Miller and Thomas H. Johnson, I, (New York, 1963), 209.

[5] It has often been noted that experience gained in self-governing New England Congregational churches contributed to the political views of the colonists. Less seldom recognized was the "fierce spirit of liberty" generated by the Anglican "vestry system" in the southern colonies and also the familiarity with representative government in Presbyterian and other churches.

[6] *The Constitution Reconsidered,* ed. Conyers Read (New York, 1938), 106.

[7] John Cotton, *An Exposition of the Thirteenth Chapter of Revelation* (London, 1656), 72, as reprinted in *The Puritans,* ed. Miller and Johnson, I, 213. For Winthrop, see Perry Miller, "From the Covenant to the Revival," in *The Shaping of American Religion,* ed. J. W. Smith and A. L. Jamison (Princeton, 1961), 334–35. It is made clear by Edmund Morgan, *The Puritan Dilemma: The Story of John Winthrop* (Boston, 1958), that Winthrop's (and also Cotton's) emphasis was usually upon the duty of obedience.

Fears Generated by Anglican Aggressiveness

In the colonies the Puritan political heritage had not been allowed to fade into the past as mere ancient history, nor had the memory of distant events that surrounded that heritage with deep emotion been permitted to grow dim. Provoked by an Anglican aggressiveness that aroused old fears of ecclesiastical tyranny, both pulpit and press rehearsed past history to counter what was considered a present threat. And because the royal power and the episcopal pretensions were so closely linked, the controversy generated a widespread spirit of disaffection that in the course of time was transformed into a deeply rooted rebellious temper. Since the most prominent of the immediate grievances that led to the American Declaration of Independence were economic and political, the importance of the ecclesiastical issue as a major factor in precipitating the American Revolution frequently has been neglected.[8]

The Glorious Revolution of 1688 that brought William and Mary to the English and Scottish thrones had a marked effect upon Anglican fortunes in the New World. Under James II, the Church of England had been given scant support in the colonies, numbered few adherents, and had been officially established only in Virginia. This situation was altered by the Revolution. Dissenting "dissidence" at home was temporarily quieted by the Act of Toleration, and the Anglican bishops were freed from their almost complete preoccupation with the domestic problems created by a Roman Catholic king. Thus the way was cleared for a more aggressive Anglican policy in the colonies. With the support of a sympathetic Court, it now became possible to marshal sufficient pressure to secure Anglican establishments in Maryland, South Carolina, and the city of New York, with North Carolina and Georgia later being brought into line.

The Society for the Propagation of the Gospel (S.P.G.) was designed to spearhead and implement the new Anglican thrust. It had been organized in 1701, with royal and archiepiscopal blessing to send "orthodox clergymen" to the colonies to instruct such as lacked "the administration of God's Word and Sacraments" in the "principles of true religion." If the clause in the charter that defined the purpose of the Society had been interpreted to mean providing a ministry for the numerous communities in the middle and southern colonies that lacked any ministry whatsoever, the Society would have aroused little opposition. The Society, however, was determined that Anglicanism should shed its regional character, and this undertaking meant expansion into the older, settled areas north of Mary-

---

[8] Carl Bridenbaugh, *Mitre and Sceptre: Transatlantic Faiths, Ideas, and Politics, 1689–1775* (New York, 1962), explored in detail this aspect of the Revolutionary background. For another aspect, see Norman C. Hatch, *The Sacred Cause of Liberty: Republican Thought and the Millennium in the American Revolution* (New Haven, 1977). For a discussion of fears about the possible loss of ecclesiastical independence, see Bernard Bailyn, *Ideological Origins of the American Revolution* (Cambridge, Mass., 1967).

land. Consequently, the charter was interpreted as a directive to proselyte members of other communions. In 1750, for example, one-third of the S.P.G. missionaries were stationed in New England where there already was at least one "orthodox minister" in every town and where the converts to Anglicanism were drawn almost exclusively from the ranks of professing Christians. Elsewhere in the colonies, S.P.G. activity was similarly restricted to a great degree to older communities that already had a settled ministry, and the zeal of its missionaries was primarily engaged in making Anglicans out of Quakers, Presbyterians, Baptists, Lutherans, and Reformed.

Under such circumstances it is scarcely surprising that friction developed—a friction that was augmented, as Jonathan Edwards and the "Associated Ministers of Hampshire" explained, by the "uncharitable and unchristian spirit" of the missionaries in "intimating that our ministry is no ministry, not having had episcopal ordination," and thereby inferring with self-evident satisfaction that all other "churches are no churches of Christ, and that our people are to be looked upon as strangers to the commonwealth of Israel—a tenet or principle which came from Rome and which in years past has been disclaimed in England and is still by all the other reformed churches in Europe." The "grand business" of the missionaries, a correspondent of the *Boston Evening Post* declared, "seemed to be not to convert men from paganism to Christianity but to proselyte Protestant Dissenters to the Church of England, as if they imagine there can be no salvation out of that church."[9]

Other irritations and grievances, some of them profoundly disturbing, stemmed from what William Smith, Jr., of New York called the Anglican "lust for dominion." Anglican clergy in the middle and northern colonies sought to impress the local populace by holding their conventions in the presence of the governor and by having them preceded by a public procession of the clergy in gowns and cassocks. This ostentation was a minor annoyance, but it was not calculated to reduce friction. More serious were deliberate harassments, such as the arrest of Francis Makemie for preaching in New York City; the ejection of a Presbyterian minister at Jamaica, New York, with an S.P.G. missionary installed in his place; repeated interventions of the S.P.G. to prevent non-Anglican churches in New York from being incorporated so that title to their property might be secure; the order of the Board of Trade that no schoolmasters from England were to be permitted to teach in New Hampshire without a license from the Bishop of London; the attempt of the missionaries to thwart the founding of the College of New Jersey by the Presbyterians, their efforts to subvert the interdenominational character of King's College and the College of Philadelphia, their scheming to gain control of Harvard and Yale, their role in frustrating the establishment of a Presbyterian college in North Carolina; and the successful intimidation of printers so that for a time

---

[9] Bridenbaugh, 79–80, 90.

there was no freedom of the press for non-Anglicans in New York. Even the granting of a charter to enable Congregationalists to carry on mission work among the Indians was denied. Ill feeling was intensified when news was received that the plight of the Dissenters in England had worsened after Queen Anne came to the throne, with the disabilities imposed by the Occasional Conformity Act and the Schism Act being added to those of the Test and Corporation Acts.[10] Nor were reports of the burning of Dissenting meetinghouses by English mobs reassuring.

It was, however, the persistent efforts of S.P.G. missionaries to persuade the British government to establish an Anglican episcopate in America that did more than anything else to awaken old fears and to spread a spirit of dissaffection. The proposal to send bishops to regularize the status of colonial Anglicanism seems innocuous enough if one fails to take into account the close link that existed between Anglican ecclesiastical authority and British political authority. To many of the colonists, bishops were a symbol of incipient tyranny; and Anglican activity in America had done little to disabuse them of the notion that powers, once granted to bishops, would be extended and abused. Jonathan Mayhew put the point succinctly when he stated, "People have no security against being unmercifully priest-ridden but by keeping all imperious bishops and other clergymen who love to lord it over God's heritage from getting their feet into the stirrup at all."[11] Even so, the traditional fear of bishops might not have evoked such a long-sustained campaign of opposition had the proposal not been promoted as part and parcel of a plan to secure a tax-supported Anglican establishment in all the colonies and had it not, in order to facilitate this goal, involved a scheme for regrouping the colonies in more efficient administrative units that would necessitate the withdrawal of the existing colonial charters. The struggle against bishops thus came to be regarded by many as a struggle to defend both the civil and the religious liberties of the colonists.

A further alienation occurred when the S.P.G. missionaries sought to advance their cause by suggesting that an American episcopate would bind the colonists more closely to England. No argument could have been better calculated to antagonize the other churches, for its plain implication was that their members were disloyal people. Nor did the missionaries hesitate to spell out this implication. In seeking to counter the antibishop attack, they accused "dissenting" leaders of being "avowed republicans," "enemies to monarchy," and a "restless and turbulent faction," whereas if

---

[10] The Test and Corporation Acts excluded non-Anglicans from governmental positions. The Occasional Conformity Act tightened this restriction, and the Schism Act required all teachers to be licensed by a bishop and to teach nothing but the Anglican catechism. Had the latter act been enforced, it would have suppressed all schools run by Dissenters and would have taken from Dissenters the education of their children.

[11] A. L. Cross, *Anglican Episcopate* (New York, 1902), 145.

the Church of England were properly established, the populace would quickly be reduced to "passive obedience," since the Anglican clergy "inculcate the great principles of loyalty and submission to government." An article in the *Boston News-Letter* in 1750 reached back to the Hampton Court Conference of 1604 to find the proper slogan to state the case for episcopacy as the indispensable support of monarchy: "The good old saying, 'No Bishop, no King,' however, grating it may be to some people, ought to be the standing maxim of the English government."[12]

Although the tactical skill and political connections of the Dissenting Deputies[13] in London thwarted successive schemes to secure an American episcopate, the fears aroused created a smouldering fire of discontent and provided repeated occasion for preachers to utilize their sermons for purposes of political instruction. The campaign for bishops had been launched by the first S.P.G. missionaries and had been pushed with intermittent vigor in succeeding decades, but in the 1760s, the agitation was stepped up, and a mounting militancy reached its peak in 1770. This coincided with the new economic and political policies of the government, which were to result in a general conflagration. Within this context, according to the *St. James's Chronicle*, "stamping and episcopizing" were commonly regarded as "only different branches of the same plan of power"; and Ezra Stiles indicated that much of the opposition to the Stamp Act was based on a recognition that if "a Parliamentary revenue had been established independent of the [colonial] Assemblies," the door would have been opened to the appropriation of funds "for half a dozen bishops on this continent." John Adams put it more bluntly: "If Parliament could tax us, they could establish the Church of England with all its creeds, articles, tests, ceremonies, and tithes; and prohibit all churches as conventicles and schism shops."[14]

In the seventeenth century, the Church of England had reaped a whirlwind of disaster when Archbishop Laud identified it so completely with the ill-considered economic and political policies of Charles I that the church became an equal victim with the crown in the Revolution that followed. In the eighteenth century, the role was reversed. The colonial structure came tumbling down at least partly because the Church of England identified the crown so intimately with its own "lust for dominion" that it became an albatross about the neck of the government. The precise weight to be given ecclesiastical grievances as a contributing cause of the American Revolution is

---

[12] Bridenbaugh, 102, 181, 262.

[13] A committee of lay representatives of "the Three Denominations" (Congregationalists, Presbyterians, and Baptists) which was formed in 1732 to direct the political agitation of English Dissenters in their struggle to secure the repeal of restrictive legislation. See B. L. Manning, *The Protestant Dissenting Deputies* (New York, 1952).

[14] Bridenbaugh, 239, 259; Anson Phelps Stokes, *Church and State in the United States* (New York, 1950), I, 234.

impossible to determine, but John Adams, the most reflective and perceptive participant in the events that led to war, always insisted that "the apprehensions of episcopacy contributed . . . as much as any other cause to
arouse the attention not only of the inquiring mind but the common people and urge them to close thinking on the constitutional authority of parliament over the colonies." Such apprehensions took on a particularly
urgent tone as Americans increasingly perceived the English church and
crown both as hopelessly corrupt and as an imminent threat to subvert by
their influence the religious superstructure of America.[15]

Deism

Although a pervasive Puritanism as recast by Evangelicalism was the dominant religious emphasis in colonial America, a minimal faith known as
Deism had become fashionable in some upper-class circles during the
decades immediately preceding the American Revolution. Sophia Hume,
a Quaker writer in South Carolina, had vigorously warned her countrymen
of "infidelity and deism" as early as 1748.[16] Several of the most conspicuous
leaders of the struggle for independence (George Washington, Thomas
Jefferson, Benjamin Franklin, and Thomas Paine were notable examples)
were Deists.

Deism had a double rootage. It may be traced back to seventeenth-
century men of "latitude" in England who sought to overcome division
among Christians by suggesting that only those affirmations on which all
Christians agree are essential articles of faith. Rejecting dependence upon
biblical revelation and appealing only to unaided natural reason, Deists reduced the "essentials" of religion to a simple fivefold affirmation that God
exists, that he is to be worshiped, that the practice of virtue is the true worship of God, that people must repent of wrongdoing, and that there are future rewards and punishments. To these five points American Deists added
a belief in God as a governing and overruling Providence who guides and
determines the destinies of nations.

If Deism was partly the product of latitudinarian sentiment, it was also
related to the rationalism associated with the "Age of Reason" or the "Enlightenment." The period from the Peace of Westphalia (1648) to the
French Revolution (1789) was a time of rapid scientific advance, best epit-
omized in the work of Sir Isaac Newton. To many contemporaries, Newton
seemed to have solved all the chief problems of astronomy, optics, physics,
and mathematics. Alexander Pope voiced this estimate when he wrote,

> Nature and Nature's Law lay hid in night.
> God said 'Let Newton be!' and all was light.

---

[15] *The Works of John Adams,* ed. C. F. Adams (Boston, 1850–1856), X, 185.

[16] Sophia Hume, *An Exhortation to the Inhabitants of South Carolina* (Philadelphia, 1748), 137.

As a result of his studies, Newton was thought to have discovered "a universal law of nature" that banished mystery from the world.[17] The universe was simply a vast mechanism—intelligible, harmonious, and thoroughly rational—the product of God the Great Mathematician. It was within this context that two chief publicists of Deism, John Toland in *Christianity Not Mysterious* (1696) and Matthew Tindal in *Christianity as Old as Creation* (1730), affirmed that the "essentials" of religion are those truths that can be known by human reason alone without the aid of any special revelation.

The alliance of Christians with Deists in carrying forward the Revolution was not as strange as it may seem to be, for Deists did little more than appropriate Puritan political ideas. English Puritans as early as the 1640s had made a distinction between the realm of nature and the realm of grace, between natural revelation and special revelation. By the end of the seventeenth century, this distinction had become integral to the thinking of representative figures ranging from Increase Mather through Jonathan Edwards and his heirs to Jonathan Dickinson, Samuel Davies, and John Witherspoon.[18] As long as Deists made no direct attack upon "revealed" religion (see Chapter 6), Christians had no difficulty uniting with Deists for common political ends on the basis of the shared assumptions of "natural" religion.

William Penn, Algernon Sidney, and John Locke served as transmitters of Puritan political ideas to the Revolutionary generation. Locke was perhaps the most important. His influence was exerted by his *Treatises on Government* (1690) and his *Letter Concerning Toleration* (1689), both of which were written in connection with the Revolution of 1688. In the former he asserted that all peaceful governments were established by the consent of the governed in order to protect their natural rights to life, liberty, and property, and that whenever this trust is betrayed, the people have the right to resist. The statement of the "antient" (ancient) rights of Englishmen in the Magna Carta (1215) formed the historical point of reference for this line of thinking.

Locke's political views were largely a distillation of concepts that had long been current coin in Calvinist political theory—a fact that John Adams acknowledged[19]—and had become fundamental postulates of a large portion of the English people in earlier conflicts between king and Parliament. Although Thomas Jefferson wrote the Declaration of Independence, the key paragraph that justified the resort to arms could quite easily

---

[17] Newton had no such idea, for he spent much of his time doing "biblical arithmetic" in an attempt to date the millennium.

[18] See Conrad Wright, *The Liberal Christians* (Boston, 1970), 17–20.

[19] *Works*, VI, 4. For an explication of this point, see W. S. Hudson, "John Locke: Heir of Puritan Political Theorists," in G. L. Hunt, *Calvinism and the Political Order* (Philadelphia, 1965). For Penn, see W. S. Hudson, "William Penn's *English Liberties:* Tract for Several Times," *William and Mary Quarterly* (1969), 578–85.

have been written by a Puritan divine. When it came to writing a constitution for the new nation, the happier view of human nature implicit in John Adams's assertion that unaided reason is "a revelation from its maker which can never be disputed or doubted" gave way to a more pessimistic estimate.[20] Even those who thought people were good enough to win heaven by their own efforts were skeptical about statesmen making the grade and insisted that the exercise of power must be checked by adequate safeguards. The stories illustrating the adage "power corrupts" that came to Americans in the form of the popular English publication *Cato's Letters* drove this point home in dramatic fashion.

The Winning of Independence

During the years prior to the Revolution, "rational religion" exerted little influence in America except among "intellectuals" of the coastal ports and some plantation owners of the South. Few of those who regarded themselves as emancipated from traditional Christian doctrine had any desire to promote their views among the populace at large. Believing that orthodox religion served to inculcate principles of private and public morality among the common people, the rationalists tended to maintain at least a nominal connection with the existing churches and to contribute to their support. Thus to the extent that religious concerns played a decisive part in enlisting mass support for the colonial cause, this support of necessity was marshaled by the orthodox churches.

The Attitude of the Various Denominations

Not all the churches, of course, supported the war with Great Britain, nor did any single denomination present an unbroken front. There were both Tories and Patriots in every religious group, as well as many who were apathetic. Nevertheless, the general attitude that was to characterize each of them would not have been difficult to predict.

The Church of England had a long tradition of intimate identification with the English government, and in the colonies this governmental relationship constituted its major source of strength. It is not surprising, therefore, that the Anglican clergy, with a few notable exceptions, were zealous Tories who condemned the conflict as an unjustified rebellion against constituted authority. The Anglican laity in the South, on the other hand, gave strong support to the struggle for independence. The pacifist groups—Quakers, Mennonites, Moravians, and Dunkers—held themselves aloof as

---

[20] For an analysis of the basic Puritan-Calvinist assumptions reflected in the U.S. Constitution, see H. Richard Niebuhr, *The Kingdom of God in America*, (New York, 1959), 48–87. See also Henry F. May, *The Enlightenment in America* (New York, 1976), 48–65, 88–99, 155–64.

a matter of principle. The Dutch and German Reformed and the Lutheran churches had no real stake in the perpetuation of British rule. Whereas many sought to avoid taking sides in the conflict, the majority ranged themselves on the side of the colonists. This arrangement was also true of Roman Catholics and Jews, with Charles Carroll among the former contributing notable service to the colonial cause. These latter groups, however, were relatively small. The more significant support came from the Congregational, Presbyterian, and Baptist churches.

The Congregationalists had early nurtured a tradition of independence in the colonies that they had founded, and later British rule came to be associated in their minds both with Anglican proselyting activity and with pressure to give increased recognition to the status of the Church of England as the official church of the governing authority. But above all, Congregationalists had been fed a steady diet of "election sermons" that emphasized concepts of fundamental law, constitutional rights, limited government, and the duty to resist abuses of power—all of which were notions calculated to create a climate of opinion opposed to any infringement of the people's liberties.[21]

The Presbyterians and the Baptists embraced these ideas the more zealously because of the disabilities to which they had been subjected in several of the colonies. Even in New England where Congregationalists often made life difficult for Baptists, the Baptists responded by accusing the Congregationalists of being disloyal to their own tradition and by asserting that the Baptists were the true heirs of the founders of New England.[22] In Virginia both Presbyterians and Baptists were thrown into a perpetual state of disaffection by irritations arising from Anglican tactics of oppression. The attitude of the Scotch Irish among the Presbyterians was further colored by bitter memories of the ill treatment their fathers had received at the hands of the English in northern Ireland.

The Role of the Clergy

In 1781 when arch-Tory Peter Oliver reviewed the course of the Revolution in his *Origin and Progress of the American Rebellion,* he suggested that if one wished to understand the inflamed public opinion that swept the colonies into war, one must look to "Mr. Otis's black regiment, the dis-

---

[21] Election sermons belonged in the class of "occasional sermons" that were preached not only on election days but on other public occasions as well, such as ordinations, funerals, and so forth. "Regular" sermons, which usually differed in tone from occasional sermons by virtue of their emphasis on piety, made up the vast majority of the sermons audited by colonists, especially in New England. See Harry S. Stout, *The New England Soul: Preaching and Religious Culture in Colonial New England* (New York, 1986), 27–31, 54–56.

[22] This was the whole thrust of the argument of Isaac Backus in his *History of New England, with Particular Reference to . . . the Baptists* (Boston, 1777–1796).

senting clergy."[23] They certainly were key figures, for their influence penetrated remote communities that were seldom reached by newspapers and books. And if it is true, as a British official reported of the people of rural Connecticut, that "they are all politicians and Scripture learnt," this was the result of the work of the preachers. Practical politics may have been learned at the town meeting, but the undergirding political theory was picked up from the Sunday sermon and the weekly lecture as well as from the annual election sermon. So well rehearsed were these common folk in political thought that they knew all the arguments, delighted in the subtleties of debate, and were familiar with the facts of past crises that pointed up the present moral. Ezra Stiles could refer to "half a dozen bishops on this continent and a long string of &c. &c. &c.," in perfect confidence that the reader would recognize the allusion to be to the "Et cetera Oath" that had troubled the consciences of Englishmen more than a century before. Thus a few cliché-studded sentences were often sufficient to evoke a broad context of meaning. Perhaps the general run of the populace was best informed in New England, but elsewhere less widespread literacy and less ample access to the press made people even more dependent upon the preachers for information concerning issues of the day.[24]

The role of the clergy was not restricted to fostering and perpetuating notions of fundamental and "inalienable" rights. What Peter Oliver had in mind when he spoke of the importance of "Mr. Otis's black regiment" was the indispensable aid they provided in enlisting active support by "preaching up" the Revolution in innumerable "fast day" and recruiting sermons. This they did in a curiously roundabout fashion. Although American rights were defended, there was little stress upon American righteousness and few direct and forthright attempts to enlist divine aid against the British. Their understanding of God's relationship to his people in terms of a covenant that involved more responsibilities than privileges left scant room for such unabashed presumption, and they knew that a simple invocation of the powers of heaven was no way to secure the assistance of a Supreme Governor whose favor was far from capricious.[25]

The preachers and those taught by them knew that under the providential government of God, the occasion for troubles and disasters must be sought within rather than without. Thus they viewed the present affliction visited upon the colonies as less the result of the iniquity of the British than the consequence of the infidelity of the Americans. The remedy, therefore was to confess their sins and to mend their ways. Only then

---

[23] James Otis, a Boston lawyer, was one of the most conspicuous and effective leaders in arousing anti-British sentiment.

[24] Bridenbaugh, 189, 259.

[25] For an analysis of this type of approach, see Perry Miller, "From the Covenant to Revival," in *The Shaping of American Religion*, ed. J. W. Smith and A. L. Jamison, 322–68.

could they expect that God would impart the necessary wisdom, energy, and will to push the war to a successful completion.

The successive "recommendations" of the Continental Congress that days of "public humiliation, fasting, and prayer" be observed played upon this theme as a repetitive refrain, expressing the hope that "we may with united hearts and voices unfeignedly confess and deplore our many sins, and offer up our joint supplications to the all-wise, omnipotent, and merciful Disposer of all events; humbly beseeching him to forgive our iniquities, to remove our present calamities, to avert those desolating judgments with which we are threatened" (1775); summoning the colonists to "implore the mercy and forgiveness of God, and beseech him that vice, prophaneness, and exortion and every evil may be done away and that we may be a reformed and happy people" (1777); lamenting the fact that "too few have been sufficiently awakened to a sense of their guilt, or warmed with gratitude, or taught to amend their lives and turn from their sins, so he might turn from his wrath" (1779); and asking God's gracious intervention "to make us sincerely penitent for our transgressions; to prepare us for deliverance, and to remove the evil with which he hath been pleased to visit us; to banish vice and irreligion among us, and to establish virtue and piety by his divine grace" (1780).

Religious Freedom

Of the original thirteen colonies, four—Rhode Island, New Jersey, Pennsylvania, and Delaware—had long been fully committed to a policy of religious liberty, and the Anglican establishments in five of the remaining colonies—in New York, Maryland, North Carolina, South Carolina, and Georgia—quickly toppled after the outbreak of hostilities when the supporting prop of English authority was withdrawn. The speedy action of New York in repealing all laws or acts that "may be construed to establish or maintain any particular denomination of Christians" was typical. Indeed, the North Carolina Assembly anticipated the repudiation of British authority when it refused in 1773 to renew the Vestry Act, an action that had the practical effect of bringing the establishment there to an end. Only in Virginia, and in Massachusetts, Connecticut, and New Hampshire, was there any delay; and even in these four areas the struggle for religious liberty was carried on during the war years as part of the revolutionary struggle itself. In Virginia as early as June 12, 1776, an effort was made to forestall the popular tide and to preserve some remnant of the establishment by adopting a "Declaration of Rights" that asserted that "all men are equally entitled to the free exercise of religion."[26]

---

[26] The motion for its adoption was made by a conservative, Edmund Pendleton, who viewed the declaration as a means of relieving the pressure for the more radical action of disestablishment. Stokes, I, 380.

Anonymous, Baptism of George Washington (1908). Religion, the American Revolution, and the myth of the American "Promised Land" are here interwoven. *(William Jewell College, Gano Chapel)*

Obviously the urgent necessity that the war imposed to find a basis of unity among people who were religiously diverse was a compelling consideration in this rapid shift of many of the former colonies to a policy of full religious freedom. But the story is much more complex than simple necessity would suggest. For one thing, the shift was facilitated by a growing spirit of harmony and goodwill among many of the denominations. The Great Awakening had done much to promote this irenic ecclesiastical temper, bridging religious barriers in much the same way as it had tended to dissolve colonial boundaries by the sweeping tide of new religious life and activity. At the same time, the major non-Anglican religious groups also were being drawn together to resist Anglican encroachments, and both a catholic spirit and a developing national consciousness were fostered by the interdenominational and intercolonial committees of correspondence that were set up to coordinate this resistance. But an even more important factor in the movement toward full and complete religious freedom was a developing awareness among the colonists of the meaning of the American experience.

Although all non-Anglican churchmen cherished the security and safety they had found in the vast expanse of the New World, the classic interpretation of their common experience that gave meaning to the American adventure was fashioned by the New Englanders.[27] As clear a statement as any of this meaning was supplied by Cotton Mather in an election sermon before the General Court of Massachusetts early in the 1690s. "What went ye into the wilderness to see?" the forefathers were asked rhetorically.

> And the answer to it is not only too excellent but also too notorious to be dissembled. Let all mankind know that we came into the wilderness because we would worship God without that Episcopacy, that Common Prayer, and those unwarranted ceremonies with which the "land of our forefathers' sepulchres" had been defiled. We came hither because we would have our posterity settled under pure and full dispensation of the gospel, defended by rulers that should be ourselves.

It is true that these early settlers were seeking freedom for themselves and not for others, but they were constantly being needled by their fellow Congregationalists in England to adopt a more liberal policy than that of reminding those who differed from them that they had equal freedom to establish settlements of their own in the American wilderness. By the early decades of the eighteenth century, this more liberal policy had been forced upon them by the concessions they had been compelled to grant Anglicans, Baptists, and Quakers. Thus the tables were turned when the Anglicans launched their drive for ecclesiastical power in New England. Formerly the Congregationalists had squirmed under charges of intolerance, but now they could pin the label of bigotry upon the Anglicans and could remind them that the New England Congregationalists conceded more freedom to Anglicans than the Anglicans in England were willing to concede to Congregationalists.

---

[27] This was in spite of the fact that the economic model of development that eventually triumphed in America originated in the Chesapeake and the South. See Jack P. Greene, *Pursuits of Happiness: The Social Development of Early Modern British Colonies and the Formation of American Culture* (Chapel Hill, N.C., 1988).

Under the Anglican pressure, New Englanders increasingly turned to re-casting the story of their past to bring it into accord with the necessities of the present. The Founding Fathers were pictured as apostles of liberty, and the need to maintain intact the liberties that had been bequeathed to them was constantly reiterated.

By 1760 Ezra Stiles was declaring that

> The right of conscience and private judgment is unalienable; and it is truly the interest of all mankind to unite themselves into one body for the liberty, free exercise, and unmolested enjoyment of this right. . . . And being pos-sessed of the precious jewel of religious liberty, a jewel of inestimable worth, let us prize it highly and esteem it too dear to be parted with on any terms lest we be again entangled with that yoke of bondage which our fathers could not, would not, and God grant that we may never, submit to bear. . . . Let the grand errand into America never be forgotten.[28]

And five years later, in an essay on canon law, John Adams rehearsed once again the history of New England and issued a preemptory summons: "Let the pulpit resound with the doctrines and sentiments of religious liberty," for there is "a direct and formal design on foot to enslave America."

In New York, William Livingston shrewdly included the Dutch forefa-thers with the English when he reminded the governor in 1755 that

> the greatest number of our inhabitants are descended from those who with a brave and invincible spirit repelled the Spanish tyranny in the *Netherlands*, or from those who for their ever-memorable opposition to arbitrary measures of King Charles I were constrained to seek a refuge from the relentless sword of persecution in the then inhospitable wilds of AMERICA. From such ances-tors we inherit the highest relish for civil and religious LIBERTY.

The following year the Anglican William Smith of Philadelphia sent word to London that "the impartial Presbyterian historian," William Smith, Jr., of New York, had explained the prevailing discontent of the people as the product of their desire "for an equal universal toleration of Protestants" and their aversion to "any kind of an ecclesiastical establishment." Twelve years later Livingston asserted that all good and loyal Protestants affirm "the natural right of every man to choose his own religion." Everywhere the religious issue was inextricably entangled with the revolutionary strug-gle. From South Carolina the Anglican Commissary, Charles Martyn, re-ported to the Bishop of London that the principles of most of the colonists "are independent in matters of religion as well as republican in those of government" and that "it would be as unsafe for an American bishop . . . to come hither as it is at present for a distributor of stamps." The watchword

---

[28] Bridenbaugh, 3.

that united them all was "liberty, both civil and religious." Little wonder
that, with the cry of religious liberty having been constantly upon their
lips, the Assemblies in those areas where Anglicanism had been established took immediate steps at the outbreak of war to give substance to
one of the major slogans under which the colonists were being called
upon to do battle.[29]

The crucial struggle for religious liberty advanced most rapidly in Virginia. Although the penalties imposed on religious dissent in Virginia were
progressively eliminated during the war years as a result of Baptist and Presbyterian pressure, the Anglicans who dominated the "unreapportioned" Assembly had continued to fight a rearguard action in defense of the
establishment. Their last endeavor was the attempt in 1784, after the coercion imposed by the necessity to maintain united support for the war effort
had been removed, to regain some measure of tax support for the Anglican
church by levying a "general assessment," to be distributed impartially
among all Christian churches. It was this "general assessment," again as a
result of Baptist and Presbyterian pressure, that was defeated as inconsistent with the principles of liberty. Since the proposed benefits would be restricted to Christian churches, the point was made that the state would be
required to determine what constitutes Christianity and thus would be compelled to set up its own standard of orthodoxy. Furthermore, "the same authority which can establish Christianity in exclusion of all other religions
may establish with the same ease any particular sect of Christians in exclusion of all other sects" and "the same authority which can force a citizen to
contribute threepence only of his property for the support of any one establishment may force him to conform to any other establishment." In January 1786, the issue was settled with the adoption of the "Bill for
Establishing Religious Freedom," which rejected the whole idea of any multiple establishment as well as any religious test for public office.[30]

When the delegates assembled to draft the U.S. Constitution, the controversy in Virginia had been brought to an end, and for most Americans
the issue of religious liberty was no longer a subject for debate. If the Constitution in its primary form failed to deal with the issue beyond providing
that "no religious test shall ever be required as a qualification to any office
or public trust under the United States," it was not because there was any
question at this point but because the instrument of 1787 gave the federal
government no powers to deal with religious matters and it was assumed
that no other guarantee was needed. As soon as it became apparent that
an affirmative statement was necessary to win ratification by reluctant
states, the necessary affirmation was promptly made by amendment—an

---

[29] *Ibid.*, 167, 176, 249, 304.

[30] The arguments were presented in the "Memorial and Remonstrance" of 1784 drafted by
James Madison. Both documents are in Edwin S. Gaustad, *A Documentary History of Religion*,
I, (Grand Rapids, MI, 1982–1983), 259–67.

amendment carefully devised to establish religious freedom, defined in terms worked out in Virginia, as binding national policy. The restrictions of the federal Bill of Rights did not apply to acts of the individual states; but only Massachusetts, Connecticut, and New Hampshire, with their emasculated Congregational establishments, remained out of step with the rest of the country. Long before the courts by invoking the Fourteenth Amendment (1868) imposed federal policy upon the states, Connecticut (1818), New Hampshire (1819), and Massachusetts (1833) had fallen into line with guarantees in their own constitutions that gave all religious groups a purely voluntary status.

Separation of Church and State

A curious misunderstanding was to develop concerning the First Amendment: "Congress shall make no law respecting an establishment of religion nor prohibiting the free exercise thereof." A *New York Times* editorial of April 23, 1960, began with these words: "We start with the premise, shared by every American who believes in the constitutional principles on which our country is founded, that religion has no proper place in American politics." This was a curious statement because when the First Amendment was adopted, no one thought that "separation of church and state," to use the terminology of the Supreme Court, implied any separation of religion and politics. The colonial clergy, according to their differing convictions, both "preached up" and "preached down" the American Revolution. They debated, for example, the issue of God-given rights. Since then, political issues have never been absent from American pulpits. In similar fashion, political leaders cast their thought within religious categories and used religious rhetoric to express political convictions.

The separation of church and state is a separation of institutions—a separation of "church" and "state." Ecclesiastical institutions have no connection with the state. They shall not be "established"; that is, they shall receive no state support, patronage, or privilege. Nor shall religious institutions be subject to any state control. Any interference with the "free exercise of religion" is strictly forbidden. No individual shall be penalized for belief or unbelief. Churches shall be wholly voluntary, dependent upon purely persuasive powers to marshal support to maintain themselves and to make their influence felt.

This arrangement seems very clear, plain, and simple, but the terms should be plural rather than singular. Americans have neither a monolithic church nor a monolithic state. What we do have are churches and a multiplicity of governmental units that come into contact at many different points and in many different ways. The principle of separation is clear, but the line of separation follows a meandering course that must be repeatedly defined, adjudicated, and applied under a variety of circumstances in specific cases. What must be kept in mind is that the principle of institutional separation and its strict application has been of great utility both to the nation and to the churches. It has contributed to public peace and tranquillity by avoiding the religious antagonisms that have lacerated public life in Europe. At the same time, under conditions imposed by the American constitution, many religious institutions have flourished and exerted influence in the shaping of American society.

African Traditions and Christianization

The winning of independence did not apply to all persons. Africans toiled as slaves on plantations in the South and were put to work in a variety of contexts in the North. Slave-owners undertook to wipe out African religious belief along the way, leading to what one historian has termed the "African spiritual holocaust."[31] This attempt was largely successful, although certain remnants of African traditions remained alive within a broader context of Christianity.

The Atlantic slave trade brought approximately 12 million persons, primarily from the west coast of Africa, to the New World. The majority of these, five out of every six, were sold to planters and households in the Caribbean and South America. In the English colonies of North America, the slave population nevertheless increased rapidly in the first half of the eighteenth century, and especially so in the South. Even in the mid-Atlantic, in a colony such as Maryland, the slave population accounted for over half the population in some counties by 1750.[32] Because slaves were drawn from diverse tribal societies and dispersed across the broad geography of the New World, the slave population of a single county could represent dozens or even hundreds of cultural backgrounds. And although there was always common ground, the slave-owners' deliberate intermixing of Africans with different backgrounds guaranteed that discrete traditions would not endure. Certain aspects of African theology and ritual eventually were secured within the multidimensional context of religious life in slave communities, but no tribal religions survived the forced migration intact. Some burial ceremonies, healing rituals, practices related to courtship and marriage, means of communicating with spirits, styles of personal decoration, and other such rudiments remained. But they functioned independently of the African systems in which they originated. And, increasingly with the passing of time, they were altered as they came into contact with Christianity.

Slaveholders initially showed no interest in Christianizing slaves. They sought to maintain a meaningful distance between themselves and African slaves, and that distance was represented most effectively in the area of reli-

---

[31] Jon Butler, *Awash in a Sea of Faith*, (Cambridge, MA, 1990), 129–63.
[32] *Ibid.*, 131.

gious difference. At the beginning of the eighteenth century, however, the
Church of England enlarged the scope of its missionary endeavors, target-
ing various New World populations, including slaves. The process of establishing contact with slave communities was not easy for missionaries.
Slave-owners feared that Christian baptism might embolden slaves, encouraging them to press cases for better treatment or outright manumission, or
that baptism might unnecessarily complicate the commercial purpose of
the institution of slavery. Francis Le Jau, who traveled South Carolina as a
missionary for the Society for the Propagation of the Gospel (S.P.G.), complained that masters "wou'd not have me urge of Contributing to the Salvation, Instruction and human usage of slaves and ffre [sic] Indians" and
noted that when he recommended "to the Masters that care be taken of
their [slaves'] Souls, some submit to my Exhortation (few indeed) and all
Generally seem to be more Concerned for loss of their money."[33] Language
barriers, the difficulty of travel to rural or island locations, and the sheer
length of a slave's day of labor likewise frustrated the efforts of missionaries.

In 1727, the bishop of London directly addressed the concerns of slave-
owners in declaring that the Christianization of slaves in no way affected
their status as property. That understanding was reinforced in the mission
field, where slaves would be schooled in their continuing obligations to the
master. Le Jau required slaves undergoing baptism to pledge "in the presence of God and before this Congregation that you do not ask for holy baptism out of any design to free yourself from the Duty and Obedience that
you owe to your Master while you live."[34] Elias Neau, the founder of a
school for slaves at Trinity Church in New York City, urged enactment of a
statute that explicitly disconnected baptism from any change in civil status,
for fear that slave-owners would prohibit slaves from receiving religious instruction.[35] The work of missionaries accordingly was eased somewhat with
the church's clarification of the issue of human chattel, but Christianization nevertheless proceeded slowly and unevenly. Missionary efforts lacked
coordination, and that shortcoming could lead to confusions and outright
contradictions, such as when the Quakers entered the mission field and encouraged potential converts to challenge the legitimacy of slavery.

The mission enterprise was advanced significantly by the Great Awakening as it developed in New England and the Southern colonies in the 1740s
and 1750s. The Awakening foregrounded the emotional experience of conversion as the essential building block of the Christian life, and this understanding, as it was diffused through the colonies, proved more attractive to

---

[33] Cited in William E. Montgomery, *Under Their Own Vine and Fig Tree: The African-American Church in the South 1865–1900* (Baton Rouge, La., 1993), 5.

[34] *Ibid.*, p. 6.

[35] Albert J. Raboteau, *Slave Religion: The Invisible Institution in the Antebellum South* (New York, 1978), 98–99, 123–124, 227–228; A. Leon Higginbotham, *In the Matter of Color, Race and the American Legal Process: The Colonial Period* (New York, 1978), 125–129.

potential converts than a course of catechismal instruction. Moreover, the populist character of the Awakening made it inviting to persons of different social backgrounds. Presbyterian, Methodist, and Baptist preaching was well received by blacks, and even in Puritan New England, Jonathan Edwards noted the conversion of several blacks early on in the revival there.

The revivalist enterprise in the South between the Revolution and the Civil War brought tens of thousands of black southerners into Baptist and Methodist churches by 1800. The "born-again" revivalist message stressed spiritual status reversal, and this understanding was easily construed as applicable to social life. Accordingly, conversion led not only to a rebirth of the spirit but also to reconstructed self-understanding as a person deserving of divine blessings in a measure equal to society's elites. Literacy, property, family name, manners, and other such conventional distinctions of social position proved no barrier to conversion. Revivalism did not reduce class stratification or cause southerners to suspend their faith in money and bloodline as markers of social rank. It did, however, force a redefinition of social order by challenging traditional notions of virtue. One result was that "*respectable* came to mean 'pious' or 'moral,' rather than 'capable of eliciting respect by reason of social rank'; and *vulgar* came to mean 'impious' or 'immoral,' rather than indicating commonness or 'low social rank.'"[36]

The enthusiasm and expressiveness manifest in the revival setting likewise contributed to the attractiveness of evangelicalism for slaves. Revivalism helped to bridge African religious backgrounds to Christianity by providing rough analogies to trance, spirit possession, singing, dancing, drumming, and mediumship. The ecstatic performance of revival included profession of encounters with the Holy Spirit, energetic preaching, Christian prophecy, and the singing of hymns, as well as an assortment of physical exercises—clapping, jumping, jerking, shouting, and barking. As such, it was present to slaves in a manner that recalled core elements of their African backgrounds.

Black preaching was one nexus of Christianity and African religions. The African tradition of the "good talkers," who traveled the coast of West Africa acquiring reputations for their teaching and storytelling performances, blended with the practice of itineracy that became a defining feature of evangelical Protestantism during the Great Awakening. Black preachers, in developing techniques of rhythm, repetition, singing, demonstrative and physical display, and exploitation of biblical images, likewise fused tribal backgrounds with Protestant styles of worship. The crucible for this cultural mingling was the preacher himself or herself, who brought deep emotional involvement to the enterprise, and was acknowledged as effective to the extent that the auditors' responses were affective. George White, who was licensed by the Methodist church as a "coloured preacher" in 1807, reported that during one meeting where he was exhort-

[36] Donald G. Mathews, *Religion in the Old South* (Chicago, 1977), 35.

ing, "a numerous body of people . . . fell prostrate under the divine power. . . . at which my own heart glowed with inexpressible joy, and renewed resolution to proceed in obedience to my Master's command; exhorting to repentance all I met with."[37]

The emotionalism of revivalistic Christianity among slaves was especially well represented in spirituals. Transmitted orally among slave communities, spirituals were constructed of images derived from a variety of sources, including the experience of nature, labor in the fields, relations with slave-owners, and the Bible. Spirituals frequently arose spontaneously as part of the process of worship among slaves and were connected to a larger performance that included dancing, shouting, foot-stamping and hand-clapping. The pattern of response to preaching—in which congregations would repeat or reinforce the words of the preacher in intervals of listening and speaking—helped to generate spirituals, as did prayer itself, which often followed a similar pattern of singsong declamation. A generation after emancipation, a participant described this process:

> Minutes passed, long minutes of strange intensity. The mutterings, the ejaculations grew louder, more dramatic, till suddenly I felt the creative thrill dart through the people like an electric vibration, the same half-audible hum arose—emotion was gathering . . . then, up from the depths of some "sinner's" remorse and imploring came a pitiful plea . . . sobbed in musical cadence. From somewhere in the bowed gathering another voice improvised a response . . . then other voices joined the answer, shaping it into a musical phrase; and so, before our ears, as one might say, from this molten metal of music a new song was smithed out, composed then and there by no one in particular and by everyone in general.[38]

Some spirituals were directly drawn from preaching, whereas others were composed collectively. As they were transmitted orally from community to community, they were abridged, enlarged, or altered in order to fit new contexts. The themes of spirituals varied, but the majority were grounded in Old Testament stories about divine intercession on behalf of the oppressed, about Moses and the prophets, and about justice. Accordingly, God as a figure who meted out justice, protected the faithful, and rewarded the righteous frequently appeared in spirituals. In some cases, the slaves' yearning for heavenly reward dovetailed with their hopefulness for civil freedom, and was coded in double meanings in the words of the spiritual, as in "Steal Away to Jesus." Civil freedom for African Americans, however, was many years away.

---

[37] George White, "A Brief Account of the Life, Experience, Travels, and Gospel labours of George White, an African," in *Black Itinerants of the Gospel: The Narratives of John Jea and George White*, ed. Graham Russell Hodges (Madison, Wisc., 1993), 61.

[38] Quoted in C. Eric Lincoln and Lawrence H. Mamiya, *The Black Church in the African American Experience* (Durham and London, 1990), 349. See also 346–81.

Part Two

The New Nation
1789–1865

CHAPTER FIVE

The Republic and the Churches

The winning of independence presented to the American people a prospect that was at first exhilarating and then sobering. The initial exuberant optimism was voiced by Ezra Stiles in the Connecticut election sermon of 1783, entitled *The United States Elevated to Glory and Honor.*

> This will be a great, a very great nation, nearly equal to half Europe. . . . Before the millennium the English settlements in America may become more numerous millions than that greatest domain on earth, the Chinese Empire. Should this prove to be a future fact, how applicable would be . . . [our] text [Deut. 26:19] when the Lord shall have made his American Israel high above all nations which he has made—in numbers, and in praise, and in name, and in honor.
>
> I am sensible some will consider these as visionary utopian ideas; and so they would have judged had they been told . . . at the battle of Lexington that in less than eight years the independence and sovereignty of the United States should be acknowledged by four European sovereignties, one of which should be Britain herself. How wonderful the revolutions, the events, of Providence! We live in an age of wonders; we have lived an age in a few years; we have seen more wonders accomplished in eight years than are usually unfolded in a century.

Nor was Stiles dismayed that the churches were to be dependent solely upon their powers of persuasion, for he was confident that in a free market truth would prevail. "Here Deism will have its full chance; nor need libertines [any] more to complain of being overcome by any weapons but the gentle, the powerful ones of argument and truth. Revelation will be found to stand the test to the ten thousandth examination."[1]

But when the exhilaration of the moment was past, there were second thoughts. The war left the former colonies exhausted, impoverished, and disorganized. Soon the government of the Confederation was mired in confusion, and the very grounds of promise—expanse of territory, multiplying population, and diversity of interest—came to be seen as dangers that threatened the nation. Hopefulness gave way to anxiety. Several decades were to elapse before it seemed clear that the multiple experiment in independence, republicanism, federal union, and religious liberty would be crowned with success. In the interim, Americans were sustained by the conviction that had nerved them in the struggle for independence—the belief that God had a special vocation in store for America.

The Mission of America

It is somewhat misleading to speak of the religious pluralism of the United States. From the beginning there was a pluralism of religious bodies, denominations, churches. But most of these had a common understanding of the Christian faith, an understanding that under the impact of the Awakening came to be known as "evangelical" religion. In addition to the common faith of the churches, there was also a "general" religion that was not pluralistic; a "civic" religion that was the religion of most people; a "religion of the republic" with its own beliefs, myths, and symbols, its own ceremonies and rituals, its own days of remembrance and thanksgiving. The religion of the churches and the religion of the republic existed side by side. Since they were regarded as mutually supportive, the distinction between them often was blurred. Still, the operating assumption was that the nation had its own independent religious vocation.[2]

The Religion of the Republic

The theoretical basis for distinguishing between the vocation of the nation and the vocation of churches had been developed in the 1640s by English Puritans, who were dismayed that religious differences should result in civil war. They posited a distinction between the realm of nature and the

---

[1] The sermon is reprinted in John W. Thornton, *The Pulpit of the American Revolution* (Boston, 1860). See pp. 440–41, 471.

[2] See R. N. Bellah, "Civil Religion in America," *Daedalus*, 96 (1967), 1–19. See also Elwyn A. Smith, *The Religion of the Republic* (Philadelphia, 1971); Conrad Cherry, *God's New Israel* (Englewood Cliffs, N.J., 1971); and S. E. Mead, "The Nation with the Soul of a Church," *Church History*, 36 (1967), 262–83.

realm of grace. The realm of nature was God's "great kingdom, the world." The realm of grace was "his special or peculiar kingdom, the kingdom of grace." In the first, God rules "every natural man" by "the light of nature to a civil outward good and end." In the second, God rules the Christian by his special revelation in Christ to an inward and a spiritual end. Whereas the religion of the churches is available only to the "saints" through the gift of faith, natural religion is available to all men through "natural reason," that is, through the lessons of history, including the history of the Hebrew people, that make plain the manner of God's providential dealings with civil communities. "General religion," William Penn called it; beliefs and principles, including the Ten Commandments (the epitome of natural law) common to Christian and Jew alike. By the end of the seventeenth century, this distinction had received its most influential expression in John Locke's famous *Letter Concerning Toleration* (1689).[3]

Throughout the colonial period many Americans had viewed themselves as sharing in some decisive way the role in history that they believed God had reserved for England. The Revolution brought about a shift in thinking at this point, making it clear to the citizens of the new republic that a headstrong and heedless England had forfeited her place in God's plan for the nations. Even prior to the war some Americans were audacious enough to believe that the colonists alone were God's new Israel. After the war this became the general conviction. Through his providential control of events, God had fashioned the United States as a new instrument to effect his purposes for mankind. Thomas Jefferson, Benjamin Franklin, John Adams, and other members of the Constitutional Convention were as vigorous as any clergyman in asserting that the United States had come into being as a grand design of Providence for "the illumination of the ignorant and the emancipation of the slavish part of mankind over all the earth."[4]

The faith of the new republic was neither sectarian nor parochial. Its roots were Hebraic. Its explication was cast in Hebraic metaphors—chosen people, covenanted nation, Egyptian bondage, promised land. Its eager millennial expectation was expressed in the vivid imagery of the Hebrew prophets. Its potentially unbridled exuberance was kept in partial check by an Hebraic awareness that divine displeasure could quickly bring divine judgment upon the nation.[5] Nor was the faith of the republic parochial. Members of the Revolutionary and post-Revolutionary generation frequently referred to themselves as "citizens of the world." The blessings they had won were blessings that of right belonged to all people. And the

---

[3] For this distinction, see A. S. P. Woodhouse, *Puritanism and Liberty* (London, 1938), Introduction, 38–43. For Locke, see George L. Hunt, *Calvinism and the Public Order* (Philadelphia, 1965), 115–16, 118–24.

[4] *Works of John Adams*, ed. C. F. Adams (Boston, 1850–1856), I, 66.

[5] See W. S. Hudson, "Fast Days and Civil Religion," *Theology in Sixteenth and Seventeenth Century England: Papers Read at a Clark Library Seminar, February 6, 1971* (Los Angeles, 1971).

cautionary reminder that "the eyes of the world are upon you" remained a standard item in the rhetoric of the nation.

There were two versions of the mission of America. The initial version stressed the role of the United States as "a light to the nations," forwarding the emancipation of mankind by the contagion of its example and the power of its attraction. The second and later version emphasized the American role as "the liberator of the oppressed."

The firm belief in the contagious influence of American example was never more eloquently expressed than by Lyman Beecher in an address at Plymouth in 1827.

> To accomplish . . . changes in the civil and religious condition of the world, revolutions and convulsions are doubtless indispensable. . . . To the perfection of this work a great example is required of which the world may take knowledge, and which shall inspire hope and rouse and concentrate the energies of man. But where could such a nation be found? It must be created for it had no existence upon the earth. Look now at the history of our fathers and behold what God hath wrought . . . , a powerful nation in full enjoyment of civil and religious liberty, where all the energies of men . . . find scope and excitement on purpose to show the world by experiment of what man is capable. . . .
>
> When the light of such a hemisphere shall go up to the heavens it will throw its beams beyond the waves; . . . it will awaken desire and hope and effort and produce revolutions and overturnings until the world is free.
>
> From our revolutionary struggle proceeded the revolution in France and all of which followed in Naples, Portugal, Spain, and Greece. And though the bolt of every chain has been again driven, they can no more hold the heaving mass than the chains of Xerxes could hold the Hellespont vexed with storms. Floods have been poured on the rising flame, but they can no more extinguish it than they can extinguish the fires of Etna. Still it burns, and still the mountain heaves and murmurs. And soon it will explode with voices and thunderings and great earthquakes. Then will the trumpet of Jubilee sound, and earth's debased millions will leap from the dust, and shake off their chains, and cry, "Hosanna to the Son of David."[6]

In the interim preceding that glorious day, the United States would continue as an "asylum for the oppressed," drawing to herself the tired, the poor, the huddled masses yearning to be free. Likewise, by the simple power of attraction, the new nation would bring the blessings of liberty to all North America as settlers in more distant parts of the continent petitioned to be received into the Union.

The second version of the mission of America was no less idealistic. Unlike the "example to the nations" theme, the second version stressed a

[6] For Beecher's address, see W. S. Hudson, *Nationalism and Religion in America* (New York, 1970), 99–105.

more active role. This was the servant image of a nation called to help liberate the captive and the oppressed. It was foreshadowed in Thomas Jefferson's purchase of Louisiana, and it found expression in Andrew Jackson's determination to "extend the area of freedom," in subsequent military adventures, and in the sacrificial foreign mission activity of the churches. The latter enterprise, among other objectives, sought to banish ignorance, superstition, poverty, and disease in far corners of the earth as a prelude to Beecher's day of Jubilee when the oppressed everywhere would shake off their chains and the whole world would be free.

Unfortunately, a servant image is easily transmuted into a master image, with the master image being justified (through benefits conferred) as no more than an extension of the servant role. Still, a tension remained between those who wished simply to liberate and those often equally idealistic, who viewed themselves as tutors to mankind. Senator Albert J. Beveridge, who insisted that God had made Americans stewards of civilization and their brothers' keepers, was a conspicuous exemplar of the muscular Americanism that sought to impose American ways, institutions, and enterprise on peoples who were less than willing to receive them. This robust self-righteous vision of America's mission always encountered resistance. The resistance was not always successful, but it had sufficient rootage in tradition to maintain a degree of ambivalence in the public mind as to America's role in world affairs, whether it was to be that of an example, a servant, or a benevolent master.

The major counter to an uninhibited imperialist thrust was an acknowledgment, deeply grounded in American consciousness, that America's election was conditional. "Covenant mercies" presuppose "covenant duties" was the way John Higginson phrased it in his preface to Cotton Mather's *Magnalia*. The sense of divine vocation was paralleled by a sense of divine judgment, by an awareness that the judgment of God is harshest on those who are most favored. Again and again Americans were cautioned that desolation and destruction is the fate of a wayward people, that the United States has no unqualified promise from God that it will endure, and that God is prepared to raise up another people unto himself if those entrusted with his mission should fail him.

Church Religion

A distinction of "civil religion" from "church religion" is helpful in understanding both within the context of the American sense of mission. "Civil religion," the "religion of the republic," was *public* religion, a religion available to all through natural reason. "Church religion," although technically not a privatized religion, nevertheless was more intensely personal and focused above all on individuals and their salvation rather than the nation and its mission. The one provided a bond that united the nation and gave it a reassuring sense of a God-given vocation; the other rescued individuals from sin, reconciled them to God, and established them in the paths of virtue.

Although civic religion and church religion could be viewed as somewhat autonomous, they were not unrelated. Both fell within the scope of God's ultimate purpose for mankind, and their respective millennial visions often became intermingled. Moreover, both were generally regarded as mutually supportive. Church religion, free and unconstrained, depended upon the devotion to liberty that stood at the heart of the national faith. On the other hand, it was clear to most proponents of "reasonable" religion (including Benjamin Franklin, for example) that, for the rank and file of the populace, a more personal "experienced" religion was indispensable in a society based largely on voluntary obedience.

Both church religion and civil religion operated under the umbrella of the American understanding of national mission. That sense of mission was grounded in the belief that the benefits of life in America as "the Promised Land" were sustained by virtue of the ongoing covenant. The covenant, however, was a delicate instrument, and the relationship that it structured between God and the nation was liable to deterioration in the event that Americans failed to live up to their obligations. Most Americans assumed that by vigilance and diligent effort they could fulfill the conditions of the covenant. Accordingly, they were relatively optimistic about the nation's future. Others, however, worried that the nation was straying from the intentions of the founders, and consequently took a decidedly pessimistic view of the possibilities for continued security and prosperity under the covenant. Optimism about national destiny has been present in much revivalism, while premillennialism has represented the pessimistic view of the mission.

The Reordering of Denominational Life

Although no denomination escaped the disruption and dislocation of the war years, all survived the conflict with varying fortunes. Anglicans, Quakers, Mennonites, and Moravians suffered most. Congregationalists and Presbyterians were less affected. Baptists and the as-yet-unorganized Methodists actually prospered, multiplying in number. The Revolution was a time of troubles for the peace churches. Often their members were subjected to fines, abuse, and public opprobrium. Conflicting loyalties led to defections that reduced their membership. Moravians, Mennonites, and Dunkers withdrew into greater isolation as small enclaves within the larger society. This tendency was less true of Quakers, who lacked the defensive rampart of another language. Quakers on occasion were to move into the world to exercise an influence far greater than their numbers warranted, but the war helped introduce the internal divisions that ushered in what

Howard Brinton called their period of "conflict and decline." Never again were Quakers to be one of the major religious denominations in America.

Anglicans

The Church of England was the greatest casualty of the American Revolution, stripped almost overnight of its privileges, prestige, and support. As the church of the royal officials, it was disliked and distrusted, and its unpopularity was augmented by the ardent Toryism of many of its clergy, most of whom "to the utmost of their power opposed the spirit of disaffection and rebellion." Its ranks were also depleted by the Methodist defection in the South and by the emigration to Canada of "United Empire Loyalists" in the North. In the end only a remnant survived the war, and this remnant continued to diminish.

The surviving Anglicans faced a triple coercion. First, to be indigenous to America, an explicit break with the church that acknowledged the King of England as its "supreme governor" was required. Second, since supervision by the Bishop of London's Commissaries had ended, a new governing structure had to be devised. Most urgent was the problem posed by a shortage of clergymen, most of whom had fled. At this point Anglicans were plagued by dependence upon England. Not only was it impossible to secure ordination in America, English ordination required an oath of allegiance to the British crown.

An American bishop was the basic requirement. Samuel Seabury, urged by ten Connecticut clergymen, secured episcopal consecration from the nonjuring bishops of Scotland, but this independent action was resented. The major roles in organizing an American church were played by William White and William Smith. White was rector of Christ Church in Philadelphia and chaplain to the Continental Congress. Smith's long association was with the College of Philadelphia, but at the time he was in Maryland as rector at Chestertown. White was the one who rallied support, and Smith did the committee work. As a result of their efforts, a General Convention met in 1785 to frame a constitution for the Protestant Episcopal Church, to revise the liturgy, and to arrange for consecration of bishops. White and Samuel Provoost of New York were sent abroad to be consecrated, reconciliation with Seabury was effected, and a fully equipped church met for the first time in the General Convention of 1789.[7]

Still the new church looked forward to no very hopeful future. Bishop Provoost relinquished his episcopal duties in 1801, convinced that the church would "die out with the old families." Others also believed that no more than a languishing life of brief duration could be expected.[8] It was not until a new generation of men—most notably Bishops Griswold,

---

[7] F. W. Mills, *Bishops by Ballot: An Eighteenth-Century Ecclesiastical Revolution* (London, 1978).

[8] See L. W. Bacon, *A History of American Christianity* (New York, 1907), 213, 232.

Moore, Chase, and Hobart—infused new vigor into its leadership that the Protestant Episcopal Church began to make a significant recovery.

Congregationalists, Presbyterians, and Baptists

At the time of the formation of the new nation, the "three old denominations" of English Dissent, linked to one another by common adherence to the doctrines of the Westminster Confession, were the largest American denominations. In contrast to the Anglicans, they had survived the war with increased prestige, each having been strongly identified with the colonial cause. At the beginning of the conflict, Congregationalists had the largest number of churches and members, with Presbyterians ranking second. Baptists lagged considerably behind in a virtual standoff with the Anglicans. But whereas Anglican strength disintegrated during the war, Baptist strength multiplied with astonishing rapidity. So marked was Baptist growth that by 1800, Baptists, as the popular wing of the Puritan-Reformed phalanx, had become the largest American denomination. Congregationalists, on the other hand, experienced internal dissensions that weakened them and that resulted in diverting their energy to fighting rearguard defense of the special privileges they possessed in New England.

Presbyterians were equally well equipped for independence. They too had numbers, wealth, learning, and able leaders. They also enjoyed the prestige of being strongly identified with the winning side of the war some had labeled a Presbyterian rebellion. "When the war is over," an agent of Lord Dartmouth had declared, it will become apparent that "Presbyterianism is really at the bottom of the whole conspiracy."[9] Furthermore, Presbyterians had the advantage of numerical strength on what was to be the growing edge of the country—a fact that led Theodore Roosevelt to call the Scotch-Irish Presbyterians America's first frontiersmen. Moreover, with the breach between the Old and New Side factions healed in 1758, Presbyterians were able to move quickly to fashion an effective structure to meet the needs of an expanding nation—local presbyteries being drawn into four regional synods and these in turn linked to a national General Assembly that met for the first time in 1789. Finally, as population moved westward, Presbyterians were to inherit considerable Congregational strength.

Of real significance was the fact that by the end of the colonial period, most Presbyterians and Congregationalists had come to think of themselves as a single denomination. Ministers moved freely between the pulpits of the two groups, and the first three presidents of the Presbyterian college at Princeton were New England Congregationalists. In the years

---

[9] Leonard J. Trinterud, *Forming of an American Tradition*, (Philadelphia, 1949), 250. "Presbyterianism," of course, was used in the broad sense, which included Congregationalists.

immediately preceding the Revolution, these intimate fraternal relationships produced a variety of joint committees, and this bond was formalized by an exchange of official delegates between their respective church judicatories. The common identification was further reinforced by the tendency of Congregationalists, especially in Connecticut and Rhode Island, to refer to themselves as Presbyterians. The arrangement was formalized between Congregationalists and Presbyterians by the 1801 Plan of Union, which virtually joined the two denominations for three decades.[10]

In New England two factors forced Congregationalists to be content with the church structure they had been able to forge prior to the war. For one thing, their status as state churches in Massachusetts, Connecticut, and New Hampshire inhibited them from fashioning any official structure that would have provided a link across state lines. Moreover, a strong emphasis upon local autonomy had developed that fostered vigorous resistance to the surrender of local prerogatives. The jealous defense of local rights was most pronounced among those who were not church members but who, as inhabitants of the towns, controlled many of the outward affairs of the state-established churches.

The major weakness of Congregationalism was division within its own ranks. The Great Awakening created a split between revivalists and antirevivalists. This led to schisms with large numbers of the revival faction being siphoned off into "Separate Congregational" and Baptist churches. As early as 1760, Ezra Stiles reported that there were already 22,000 Baptists in New England compared with 60,000 to 70,000 Congregational church members. During the next fifty years, the gap steadily narrowed. There also had been an upper-class defection to Anglicanism, and by 1800, Methodists were making significant inroads.

The growing diversity in New England was accompanied by unrelenting attack upon the remnants of the Congregational establishments, and Congregationalists became preoccupied with defending what remained of the "Standing Order." At best this was a delaying action, for acts of disestablishment were passed in Connecticut in 1818, in New Hampshire in 1819, and in Massachusetts in 1833. It was only then that Congregationalists found "in their new insecurity and nakedness a kind of self-respect and self-reliance that made for good health."[11] A degree of doctrinal unity was restored by the conversion of the moderate conservatives to a revivalist point of view and by the defection of the Unitarians. By this time, however, the opportunity that had been theirs had been lost. Although New England exported vast segments of its population to the West, much Congregational blood in the newer regions was flowing through Presbyterian veins

---

[10] The Plan of Union is printed in H. Shelton Smith, Robert Handy, Lefferts Loetscher, *American Christianity*, I, (New York, 1960–1963), 545–47.

[11] E. S. Gaustad, *Historical Atlas of Religion in America* (New York, 1962), 42.

as a result of the agreement between the two denominations, which did not fall apart until after 1837.

By 1800, Baptists had become the largest of the "three old denominations" of English Dissent, with twice as many adherents as any other religious group. In spite of striking gains they were to make in the West, Baptists were far from a frontier phenomenon. The greatest gains were made in the East. Throughout the nineteenth century most centers of Baptist strength were along the seaboard—in Maine, New Hampshire, Massachusetts, New York, Pennsylvania, the Carolinas, and Georgia.

Noah Worcester, a Congregational minister, was puzzled by the surge of Baptist growth, and in 1794 he sought to account for it in his *Impartial Inquiries Concerning the Progress of the Baptist Denomination*. As reasons for their success, he mentioned the "coldness" of ministers and members of other denominations, the sympathy and respect gained from persecution, the advantage they had been able to take of revivals, the confident use they made of "irrelevant" Scripture, and finally "the want of qualifications in some Baptist teachers." Baptists did profit from revivals, for a stress upon the necessity for a "conversion" experience gave added weight to the doctrine of believers' baptism, and the appeal to Scripture was persuasive to those who had been taught to accept Scripture as their final authority. But Worcester's explanation of the influence exerted by "some Baptist teachers" who lacked "qualifications" (i.e., education) probably missed the point. "Many people," he said, "are so ignorant as to be [more] charmed with sound than sense."

> To them the want of knowledge in a teacher . . . may easily be made up and overbalanced by great zeal, and affecting tone of voice, and a perpetual motion of the tongue. If a speaker can keep his tongue running . . . and can quote memoriter a large number of texts from . . . the Bible, it matters not to many of his hearers whether he speaks sense or nonsense.

Except in the back country of the South, not many of the Baptist preachers were unusually emotional in their preaching, nor did they prize an unlearned ministry. As Baptists multiplied in the closing decades of the eighteenth century, they were busy with projects for establishing academies and a college, and after the turn of the century, they became increasingly active in promoting ministerial education. But, overwhelmed by the rapidity of their growth, Baptists had little opportunity to enforce educational standards. Mature men who exhibited gifts of leadership were called into service, and this readiness to utilize what leadership was available was one of the secrets of their growth. As was to be true of the Methodists, the Baptists helped fill the vacuum left by the shortage of ministers among those denominations that adhered more rigidly to formal educational requirements.

Methodists and "Christians"

Prior to 1784, Methodists were not a church but only a "religious society" nominally related to the Church of England.[12] Local Methodist societies had been formed in America during the decade prior to independence, mostly in the Chesapeake Bay region and southward through Virginia to North Carolina. One would suppose that the Revolution would have had the same disastrous effect upon Methodists as it had upon other Anglicans, for John Wesley was equally vocal in his opposition to American independence. Furthermore, all but one of the lay preachers Wesley had sent out to the colonies returned to England after the outbreak of hostilities. Francis Asbury was the significant exception. Though he was personally authoritarian in his overseeing the development of early American Methodism, Asbury rejected any notion of the office of minister as a representation of gentlemanly refinement and elevated class or social status. Rather, lay preachers under Asbury's direction engaged the lower classes on their own terms, preaching in the vernacular, accepting popular idioms into worship, and offering persons not only a sense of belonging and involvement in the movement but also the opportunity to join its leadership. Asbury's mission accordingly was in step with the mood of emergent democracy, and Methodism, like other populist movements that were to appear in the first part of the nineteenth century, made large numbers of converts utilizing what Nathan Hatch has called "the democratic art of persuasion."[13]

American Methodists seized upon the winning of independence as an opportunity to form themselves into a separate church. With so many of the Anglican clergy gone, John Wesley was prevailed upon in 1784 to ordain ministers for his American brethren so that they would not be denied the consolation of the sacraments. Although he was violating the laws of the Church of England, Wesley was convinced that ordination by presbyters was valid when dictated by necessity, and he found justification for it in the practice of the ancient church at Alexandria where presbyters had even ordained bishops. Thomas Vasey and Richard Whatcoat were the two men ordained, and they sailed for America accompanied by the Rev. Thomas Coke, whom Wesley appointed to be "joint superintendent" with Asbury "over our brethren in North America." After their arrival, the "Christmas Conference" of 1784 was convened at Baltimore, Asbury was ordained, and the new Methodist Episcopal Church was constituted.

"The Revolutionary War now being closed and a general peace established," wrote Jesse Lee, the first official historian of Methodism, "we could

---

[12] John Wesley's tracts. *A Plain Account of the People Called Methodists* and *The Character of a Methodist,* are reprinted in Harry Emerson Fosdick, ed., *Great Voices of the Reformation* (New York, 1952), 499–513.

[13] Nathan O. Hatch, *The Democratization of American Christianity* (New Haven, 1989), 13; and Asbury quoted on page 85 of Hatch.

James Varick (c. 1750–1827), cofounder and first bishop of the African Methodist Episcopal Church Zion. Unable to secure full ordination for African Americans in the Methodist Episcopal church, Varick and his colleagues organized a new church. *(Star of Zion.)*

go into all parts of the country without fear; and we soon began to enlarge our borders and to preach in many places where we had not been before."[14] The borders were enlarged and numbers also. In 1784 at the time of the Christmas Conference, Methodists had numbered almost 15,000. Six years later, in 1790, there were 57,631 members. By 1820, they had overtaken the Baptists and had become the largest American denomination. A major reason for the astonishingly rapid spread and growth of Methodism was the adoption of the "circuit system" that Wesley had devised for his English societies. Thus the new church was equipped with a highly mobile ministry of traveling preachers who covered a vast territory instead of being tied to a single locality. The more intimate nurture of the flocks they gathered was provided by local lay preachers and class leaders. No system was more admirably designed for moving quickly into new territory, whether that territory was in older settled regions of the seaboard or over the mountains into the new communities of the frontier. In both areas Methodists met with equal success. Had they not put down deep roots in the East, they would not have been able to move so boldly into the West with the initial tide of migration.

[14] Jesse Lee, *Short History of the Methodists* (Baltimore, 1810), 84.

Some persons sought to achieve religious unity by avoiding "party names." This sentiment surfaced in 1784 among a group of Virginia Methodists led by James O'Kelly. Impressed by the revivalist emphasis upon the name "Christian" as the bond that unites, they resolved to be known by no other name. In 1801, a similar movement was initiated in New England when Abner Jones, a Vermont Baptist, became convinced that "sectarian names and human creeds should be abandoned and that true piety alone . . . should be made the test of Christian fellowship and communion." Three years later in Kentucky the happy relationship with Methodists in the great camp meeting revivals persuaded several Presbyterian ministers, including Barton W. Stone, that Christians could and should live together in love, and they resolved to be known by no other name. A fourth point of origin was in western Pennsylvania where Thomas Campbell settled after his arrival from Ireland in 1807. As a student at Glasgow, he had been deeply influenced by Scottish Evangelicalism, and he was dismayed that in America he was not permitted to invite all Christians to participate in the communion service. In 1809, he organized the "Christian Association of Washington County, Pa.," and issued a *Declaration and Address* to summon Christians of every denomination to abandon unscriptural doctrines and usages and to restore the original unity and purity of New Testament Christianity. A month later he was joined by his son Alexander, who became the best-known leader of the western "Christians," or "Disciples of Christ."

There was little communication between the eastern and western "Christians." In the East the "Christians" were gradually brought together in the General Convention of the Christian Church, a body that united with Congregationalists in 1931. In the West the Campbellites and the Stoneites coalesced to form the larger "Christian" group. (The Campbellites tended to prefer the name "Disciples of Christ.") Although the Christian movement failed in its objective to unite all Christians, it did succeed in becoming one of the larger Protestant denominations.

"Christian" churches were partly the product of a Wesleyan concern to bridge divisions among denominations, but there was more explicit evidence of the spreading influence of Wesleyan theology. From a small beginning in New Hampshire, Free-Will Baptists penetrated much of the New England hinterland and upstate New York. Nor was the German-speaking population of the mid-Atlantic states immune to Wesleyan influence. Jacob Albright became a Methodist in 1790, began to preach among the Germans of the mid-Atlantic area in 1796, and, after forming his converts into what came to be called the Evangelical Association, was elected its bishop in 1807. Philip William Otterbein, a German Reformed minister in Baltimore, also appropriated Methodist theology and techniques, forming the United Brethren in Christ Church in 1800.[15]

---

[15] In 1946, the Evangelical Association and the United Brethren combined to form the Evangelical United Brethren Church.

Roman Catholics

Unlike Judaism, whose adherents were not greatly augmented numerically until after the Civil War, Roman Catholicism experienced steady growth after the Revolution. Prior to independence, Roman Catholics were a small minority, many of them landed gentry, concentrated almost exclusively in Maryland and Pennsylvania. The Quebec Act of 1774 had placed the territory between the Ohio and Mississippi rivers within the province of Quebec; this act aroused ill feeling among some ardent patriots who regarded it as evidence that the British government was ready to surrender this vast inland empire to Roman Catholicism, and it was used as a religious issue to whip up anti-British feeling. By the end of the war, however, apprehensions thus generated had been largely forgotten. Charles Carroll had rallied his coreligionists in Maryland to the colonial cause, and Irish Catholics in Pennsylvania had demonstrated their unwillingness to dishonor the memory of their fathers by any hesitancy to fight the English. This display of loyalty plus French military support allayed former suspicions, and the birth of the republic ushered in an era of general good feeling.

The Roman Catholic Church in the colonies had been under the jurisdiction of the Vicar Apostolic in London; but independence made this arrangement inappropriate. In 1784, John Carroll, a cousin of Charles Carroll, was appointed "superior of the missions" with full responsibility to direct the affairs of the church in the United States, and six years later he was elevated to episcopal rank. In 1808, the diocese of Baltimore was given metropolitan status with Carroll as archbishop.

In the new republic the Catholic Church experienced many growing pains. The number of adherents mounted rapidly, partly as the result of the acquisition of older settlements along the Mississippi but more largely a consequence of new immigration from Ireland and southern Germany. Tension between older members and more recent arrivals was often acute, and this complicated the task of maintaining an orderly development of church life. The installation of refugee priests from France as pastors of Irish congregations also aroused resentment.

"Lay trustees" posed one of the more serious problems. All churches in America had been vexed by the self-assertiveness of the laity, and the Roman Catholic Church was no exception. In the immediate postwar years, Americans in general were especially conscious of their "rights" and "liberties" and were determined not to be pushed around. The effect of this pervasive spirit upon Roman Catholics was explained by Archbishop Ambrose Maréchal of Baltimore in 1818:

> The American people pursue with a most ardent love the civil liberty which they enjoy. For the principle of civil liberty is paramount with them, so that absolutely all the magistrates from the highest to the lowest are elected by popular vote. . . . Likewise all the Protestant sects . . . are governed by these same principles, and as a result they elect and dismiss their pastors at will.

Catholics in turn, living in their midst, are . . . exposed to the danger of admitting the same principles of ecclesiastical government.[16]

Not only were they exposed to the danger; many in fact succumbed to it. As early as 1786, the trustees of St. Peter's Church in New York City asserted their right to choose and dismiss their pastor, and three years later the congregation of Holy Trinity Church in Philadelphia followed the example of St. Peter's in choosing their own pastor. Similar acts of disobedience occurred elsewhere. A congregation at Norfolk went so far as to assert that the bishop, according to the "civil rights and religious liberties" guaranteed by the laws of Virginia, had no authority to interfere in the affairs of any congregation or in "any of their religious matters whatever." Even where overt defiance was absent, chronic friction was frequent. It was not until the custody of property was transferred to the bishops that the situation was finally regularized.

The flood of Roman Catholic immigrants constituted the greatest problem of the church during these years. No fewer than 1 million immigrants of Roman Catholic background arrived in the United States between 1790 and 1850. Had it not been for extensive assistance from abroad in the form of both funds and personnel, the task of ministering to these new Americans would have been completely impossible. As early as 1791, the French Sulpicians founded St. Mary's Seminary in Baltimore to provide training for a native priesthood, but throughout the nineteenth century major reliance had to be placed upon men sent from Europe. The religious orders rendered notable service, especially in the field of education. Colleges, academies, and parochial schools were established. By 1840, there were at least 200 parochial schools, staffed in part by American sisterhoods that had been growing in number since 1800. The controversy over tax support for parochial schools that was to agitate the life of the nation for more than a century was initiated in 1840 when Bishop John Hughes of New York petitioned for Roman Catholics to be given a proportionate share of New York City public education funds for their parochial schools.

By 1852, when the First Plenary Council of American bishops was held, the Roman Catholic Church had become the largest ecclesiastical body in the nation, and a number of noteworthy converts testified to its growing indigenous character. Among these converts were Elizabeth Bayley Seton, who founded the Sisters of Charity; Orestes A. Brownson, whose pilgrimage led him from Presbyterianism into the Universalist and then the Unitarian ministry before he became a Roman Catholic in 1844; and Isaac Hecker, a colleague of Brownson at Brook Farm (see Chapter 8), who became the founder of the Paulist Fathers. Compared with total membership, however,

---

[16] J. T. Ellis, ed., *Documents of American Catholic History*, (Milwaukee, 1955), 219. For a discerning account of the tensions, see James Hennesey, "Square Peg in a Round Hole," *Records of the American Catholic Historical Society of Philadelphia* (1973), 167–95.

converts did not bulk large. Throughout the rest of the century, Roman Catholicism continued to gain its great strength from immigration.

Estimating the Influence of the Churches

Although Roman Catholicism made notable numerical gains during the first half of the nineteenth century, Protestantism in its varied ecclesiastical forms remained overwhelmingly predominant. Religious pluralism as a significant feature of American life was a post–Civil War development that reached its culmination in the twentieth century. By then, non-Protestant groups had burgeoned as a result of new patterns of immigration, and Protestantism itself had become fragmented into separate camps by geographical, racial, and theological lines of demarcation that had little to do with the earlier denominational divisions. Unlike the earlier denominationalism, the new lines of Protestant division progressively eroded the earlier Protestant consensus.

Any estimation of the influence of the churches in the nineteenth century must come to terms with two important facts. First, only a third of the nation's population practiced church religion in a consistent manner. This adherence, calculated over the period of a century, shows a rate of 17 percent in 1776, 34 percent in 1850, 37 percent in 1879, and, in the midst of a great wave of immigration, 45 percent in 1890.[17] It therefore is questionable whether institutional life was the dominant framework for religious observance. Second, large numbers of African slaves and numerous tribes of Indians practiced a religious life that bore little or no resemblance to the Sunday worship of white Protestants and Catholics. Some slaves converted to Christianity as did some Indians, but even among converts, worship and ritual and belief often differed significantly from official church doctrine and performance.

Religious denominations were important in nineteenth-century America. They influenced the course of the nation in terms of developments at home as well as in international affairs. They clarified and reinforced belief in the myth of a national mission to serve as both a platform for the growth and export of democratic government and as a moral example to the world. For persons who conceived their lives under the umbrella of that myth, the churches remained influential. But for those whose circumstances put them on the periphery of the national myth, because of their class or race or their geographic isolation or foreign tongue, the churches were less influential, and, in certain cases, outrightly antagonistic. To reach these groups, the churches generated an assortment of strategies and programs in the course of the nineteenth century. As we shall see, the movement westward proved a stimulus to innovation.

---

[17] See table in Roger Finke and Rodney Stark, *The Churching of America, 1776–1990: Winners and Losers in Our Religious Economy* (Rutgers University Press, New Brunswick, N.J., 1992), 16.

CHAPTER SIX

Protestant Expansion and Consolidation

It took most Protestant churches until about 1800 to regroup and reorder their forces. The initial gloom, shared by Congregationalists and Episcopalians, was voiced by the Presbyterian General Assembly in 1798 when it bewailed the "general dereliction of religious principle and practice among our fellow citizens." Hidden behind the lamentation of prevailing impiety was a demoralizing recognition that these denominations were rapidly being outpaced in number of adherents by Baptists and Methodists. Still, there was sufficient conventional irreligion to disturb those who believed that the health of society depended upon moral principles and virtuous habits inculcated by true religion. More alarming was the aggressive Deism of Thomas Paine, Ethan Allen, and Elihu Palmer, for they launched a frontal attack upon the whole concept of revealed religion.[1]

Deist sentiment was not new in America, but hitherto it had been confined to an aristocratic elite who frowned upon widespread dissemination of their views because they believed that the "superstitions" of revealed religion did little harm and actually had the beneficial effect of promoting morality among the common people, thereby helping preserve good order in society. In the first flush of enthusiasm evoked by the French Revolution, however, Deism was transformed into a popular movement. Pamphleteers began to attack the churches as enemies of progress. Although Robert Baird later spoke of the French Revolution as that "volcano" that for a time "threatened to sweep the United States into its fiery stream," the

---

[1] See G. A. Koch, *Republican Religion* (New York, 1933).

danger was more apparent than real.[2] It is true that "deistical societies" were formed and college students took delight in shocking their elders by calling each other Voltaire and Rousseau, but in retrospect it is clear that this "radicalism" had no deep rootage. Unlike in Europe, there was no deep-seated anticlerical sentiment to nourish such activity. At the time, however, the danger posed by French "infidelity" seemed real and threatening. The depraved "state of nature" that engulfed France following 1793 dismayed Americans generally and was utilized to discredit the Deist movement. It also provided churchman with an effective hortatory device to rouse the churches and summon them to action.

By 1800, the churches had become aware of another problem that was of continuing concern—the problem presented by the flow of population into the fertile valleys beyond the mountains. Even prior to Independence, small pockets of settlement were to be found south of the Ohio River. After 1790, this westward migration became a stampede. Population spread quickly to the Mississippi River. Kentucky was admitted as a state in 1792, Tennessee in 1796, Ohio in 1803, Louisiana in 1812, Indiana in 1816, Alabama in 1817, Illinois in 1818, Mississippi in 1819. By 1821, the Mississippi River was sufficiently breached for Missouri to become a state. Then, without waiting for the intervening territory to be occupied, the rush to the Pacific began.

As early as 1760, Ezra Stiles had called attention to the importance of the West, and a sense of alarm was created when it became apparent that soon the balance of political power would be in the hands of those who were migrating in such numbers to the newer settlements. The great fear was that the people of the West, being far removed from the civilizing and Christianizing influence of the settled communities of the East, would revert to "barbarism" and subvert the moral order of society. Throughout the first half of the nineteenth century, an insistence upon the urgent necessity to find means of countering the lapse of the West into barbarism was a repetitive refrain on the lips of earnest churchmen.[3] John England, Roman Catholic bishop of Charleston, South Carolina, recognized the crucial importance of what was to become the heartland of the nation when he declared, "Give us the West, and we shall take care of the East."[4]

Establishing churches and providing a ministry in the newer settlements was to be a task of overwhelming magnitude, but it would be a mistake to draw too sharp a distinction between the East and the West, between conditions of life in the older settlements and on the frontier. The frontier

[2] Robert Baird, *Religion in America* (New York, 1844), 102.

[3] The most eloquent statement of the threat was Horace Bushnell's *Barbarism, the First Danger* (New York, 1847). See also Lyman Beecher's *A Plea for the West* (Cincinnati, 1835).

[4] Philip Schaff, *America*, (Cambridge, Massachuccetts, 1961), 187.

rapidly receded, and the new settlements quickly assumed the characteristics of the areas from which the settlers had come. Life in the Kentucky and Tennessee hills did not differ greatly from life in the back country regions of Virginia and the Carolinas. Plantations of the southern seaboard were duplicated in Alabama and Mississippi. Replicas of the mansions of Charleston dotted the banks of the Ohio. Farther north, along the trail of westward-migrating Yankees through western New York, Ohio, Michigan, Illinois, and Iowa, farmhouses and villages were almost indistinguishable from those of New England.

Nor did the manner of life differ greatly after the first years. It was a rural society both East and West, and in both there was relative isolation for those who desired it. A European traveler in the East was apt to be as impressed with stretches of woodland as with expanses of open fields. In 1790, there were only six communities with as many as 8,000 inhabitants—New York, Philadelphia, Boston, Charleston, Baltimore, and Salem—and these as seaports were far from typical. And the West almost immediately began to produce port cities of its own. By 1820, Cincinnati and New Orleans were cities of consequence. By 1830, Pittsburgh, Rochester, Buffalo, Louisville, and St. Louis were thriving centers with a population that ranked them among the top cities of the country. A decade later, Cleveland, Detroit, Chicago, and Milwaukee had become boomtowns of importance.

There were differences, to be sure. The population in the West was younger and more uninhibited. Migration was a selective process. As a rule only the more adventurous and sturdy spirited were willing to undertake the long trek to unsettled areas. But basically the population mirrored its own background. Where there were many who tended to be crude, turbulent, and illiterate, as was true along the tributaries of the lower Ohio River, they did not differ greatly in these respects from the inhabitants of the regions whence they had come. In religion, the strands linking the West to the East were equally evident. Methodists tended to be exuberant wherever they were. Kentucky revivalists were mostly products of Virginia and North Carolina. The revivalists who preceded and followed Charles G. Finney in western New York made repeated tours of New England. Lyman Beecher on one occasion, it is true, said that if Finney ever came to New England, he would meet him at the border and fight him all the way to Boston. But later it was Beecher himself who invited Finney to come to Boston. Edwin S. Gaustad has called attention to the fact that during the first half of the nineteenth century, the churches were engaged not only in a "conquest of the West" but also in a "reconquest of the East," and both of these conquests were closely interrelated and can be understood only as part of a single surge of new religious life and activity.[5]

[5] Edwin S. Gaustad, *Historical Atlas of Religion in America* (New York, 1962), 37, 42.

The Second Awakening

As was to be expected in the light of past experience, an initial reaction of Protestant churches to the need for action was a renewed emphasis upon the tried and proved expedient of revivalistic preaching. This preaching, in turn, helped provoke the great wave of revivals, known as "the Second Great Awakening," which swept back and forth across the country for almost two generations.

The onset of the Second Awakening is difficult to chart,[6] for it appeared in many localities almost simultaneously. The earlier colonial Awakening had continued to some degree among both Baptists and Methodists. And during the 1790s, scattered revivals had appeared among Congregationalists in more remote sections of New England. In Virginia the most significant event was a revival among students at Hampden–Sydney and Washington colleges in 1787, which sent thirty to forty men into the Presbyterian ministry. Joined by James McGready, a graduate of the "log college" at Washington, Pennsylvania, these young men fanned out into the Carolinas, Kentucky, and Tennessee, and they were responsible for the quickening religious interest that culminated in 1800 in a widely attended revival in Logan County, Kentucky. Excitement generated in Logan County spread rapidly throughout Kentucky and Tennessee; back into the Carolinas, Virginia, and western Pennsylvania; then northward into new settlements beyond the Ohio River. In central and western New York there were revivals of sufficient scope in 1800 for local annalists to refer to that year as the year of "the great revival." And in 1802, there was a revival at Yale where, as the result of a notable series of chapel sermons by Timothy Dwight, a third of the students professed conversion. President Dwight stumbled into the revival inadvertently. Distressed by "freethinking" views among the students, he boldly launched an attack to demonstrate that the only alternative to godliness was first anarchy and then despotism. The intensity of the response was surprising. It convinced Dwight that revivals could be exploited as an effective antidote to "infidelity," and this he proceeded to do.

The revival at Yale was significant for several reasons. Dwight commanded wide respect among conservatives, and under his leadership the heirs of the moderate antirevivalist party in New England were brought into the revivalist camp. It was also significant in terms of the students it sent out to become leaders of the revival campaign, most notably Lyman Beecher and Nathaniel W. Taylor. Beecher was to be the great organizer and promoter of the New England Awakening, and Taylor was the theologian who worked out the appeal and provided the intellectual defense.[7]

---

[6] See B. A. Weisberger, *They Gathered at the River* (Boston, 1958); and J. B. Boles, *The Great Revival, 1787–1805: Origins of the Evangelical Mind* (Lexington, Kentucky, 1972).

[7] See S. E. Mead, *Nathaniel W. Taylor* (Chicago, 1942).

Finally, through the contagion of Yale's example, the revival spread to other colleges and became an established institution on most American campuses with the number of "hopeful converts" being regularly reported. In this way additional leadership was recruited.

The new revivalism was markedly different from the revivalism of the first Awakening under Jonathan Edwards when the outpouring of God's spirit was regarded as a by-product of the faithful preaching of God's Word. Christians "waited" for these earlier revivals, Calvin Colton remarked, "as men are wont to wait for showers of rain, without even imagining that any duty was incumbent upon them as instruments."[8] In the Second Awakening, a change began to be introduced. More and more preachers sought to provoke a revival by utilizing "means" that were calculated to cause hearers to make a decision and to make it right. Thus the revival became a technique—a technique that had been taking shape earlier, but never had it been quite so instrumental in character. Heretofore the revival had always in a sense been an end in itself. Now it became an adjunct to other ends, and a discourse could be written on "The Necessity of Revivals of Religion to the Perpetuity of Our Civil and Religious Institutions."[9]

The early revivals in the West were not dissimilar in character to those in the East, but there was a more effervescent emotionalism. The western revivalists were dealing with a moving, floating, migrating population, and they were operating in areas where opportunities for Christian nurture were few and often nonexistent. Consequently they had to push for much quicker decisions than their eastern contemporaries. Subject to this coercion, revivalists in the West tended to turn on all the heat they could and make a concentrated appeal to the emotions. This was especially true in Kentucky and Tennessee where much of the early population was unusually rough, turbulent, and unlettered. In the upland regions of the South, whence they had come, opportunities for schooling had been scant, and uninhibited displays of religious emotion frequent. Many of them were like Augustus Longstreet's "honest Georgian" who "preferred his whiskey straight and his politics and religion red hot."

Camp Meetings

A distinctive feature of frontier religious life was the camp meeting,[10] a technique developed by the fiery Presbyterian minister James McGready. McGready stormed into Kentucky in 1796 to become pastor of three small congregations in Logan County on the Tennessee border—a section Peter Cartwright labeled "Rogue's Harbor." Of the area, Cartwright said: "There

[8] Calvin Colton, *History and Character of American Revivals of Religion* (London, 1832), 2–6.

[9] It was published as an article in *The Spirit of the Pilgrims* of 1831.

[10] C. A. Johnson, *The Frontier Camp Meeting* (Dallas, 1955); and D. D. Bruce, *And They All Sang Hallelujah: Plain-folk Camp-meeting Religion* (Knoxville, 1974).

was not a newspaper printed south of the Green River, no mill short of forty miles, and no schools worth the name. We killed our meat out of the woods, wild; and beat our meal. . . . As for coffee, I am not sure that I ever smelled it for ten years."[11] Among these backwoodsmen, McGready's impassioned preaching elicited a growing response. Many, he reported, were stuck with "an awful sense of their lost estate." But it was not until 1800 that their pent-up emotions burst loose.

A four-day sacramental meeting was held at Red River in June. Two Presbyterian ministers, William Hodges and John Rankin, were there to assist McGready, and the two McGee brothers—William, a Presbyterian minister, and John, a Methodist minister—were also present. During the first three days McGready, Hodges, and Rankin spoke, and several times the audience was reduced to tears. On the final day, John McGee—the Methodist brother—could restrain himself no longer. He rose and began to exhort the people "to let the Lord Omnipotent reign in their hearts." When a woman "shouted" for mercy, he moved to her side.

> Several spoke to me: "You know these people. Presbyterians are much for order. They will not bear this confusion. Go back and be quiet." I turned to go back and was near falling, [but] the power of God was strong upon me. I turned again, and losing sight of fear of man, I went through the house shouting and exhorting with all possible ecstasy and energy.

Soon the floor was "covered by the slain" and "their screams for mercy pierced the heavens." According to McGready, the most notorious "profane swearers and Sabbath-breakers" were "pricked to the heart" and many were "crying out 'what shall we do to be saved?'"[12]

News of the excitement at Red River spread rapidly, and it was duplicated at Gasper River in July where makeshift tents were erected to accommodate people coming from distances as great as 50 and 100 miles. Underbrush was cleared away so services could be held out-of-doors. Success at Gasper River led to the staging of other camp meetings, which drew larger and larger crowds. The most famous of them all was at Cane Ridge in Bourbon County the following summer, when the number attending was variously estimated from 10,000 to 25,000. Even 10,000 was a striking total at a time when Lexington, the largest settlement in the state, had only 1,795 inhabitants.

Whatever the actual numbers may have been at the camp meetings, there was abundant confusion. Preachers of every denomination attended and were encouraged to exhort the throng simultaneously from preaching stands erected at suitable distances. People would drift from

---

[11] Cartwright was a Methodist circuit rider, and his *Autobiography* is a vivid and fascinating account of frontier life.

[12] Johnson, 34–35.

one stand to another. They would gather in smaller groups to hear recent converts relate their experiences, then burst into hymns of praise. With "the traditionally slow cycle of guilt, despair, hope, and assurance" being compressed into a few days or even hours, the emotional stress was agonizingly intensified, and it cut deep into normal restraint. Not only were there outbursts of weeping and shouts of joy; but also in the frenzied excitement of the moment, individuals were suddenly swept into physical "exercises"—falling, running, jumping, jerking, barking—which were attributed to the smiting power of the Holy Spirit. Accounts of these physical manifestations were undoubtedly exaggerated by both friendly and hostile witnesses but were sufficiently numerous to arouse misgivings in the minds of many.

The camp meetings caused the faithful to rejoice. There is no way to prove that they elevated the moral tone of communities along the tributaries of the Ohio, but in 1801, George Baxter, president of Washington College in Virginia, had no doubts on this score.

> I found Kentucky . . . the most moral place I had ever been. A profane expression was hardly ever heard. A religious awe seemed to pervade the country. Upon the whole, I think the revival in Kentucky the most extraordinary that has ever visited the church of Christ; and all things considered, it was peculiarly adapted to the circumstances of that country. . . . Something of an extraordinary nature seemed necessary to arrest the attention of a giddy people who were ready to conclude that Christianity was a fable and futurity a dream. This revival has done it. It has confounded infidelity, awed vice into silence, and brought numbers beyond calculation under serious impressions.[13]

More tangible evidence of the beneficent effect of camp meetings was the swelling membership of the churches. In Kentucky alone between 1800 and 1803, Baptists gained more than 10,000 members, and Methodists had an equal number of accessions. Presbyterian growth may have been as large, but it was obscured and then reduced by a triple secession.

Many Presbyterians were disturbed by the camp meeting extravagances they had helped foster. In 1805, the General Assembly expressed stern disapproval when it announced that "God is a God of order and not of confusion, and whatever tends to destroy the comely order of his worship is not from him." The disenchantment of the General Assembly had been hastened by the tendency of Presbyterian camp meeting revivalists to accept "the doctrine of grace as held by the Methodists" and by their laxity in enforcing educational standards for ordination. Both issues led or were leading to schism. The first, centering on doctrine, was the "New Light" schism

---

[13] Quoted from the *Methodist Magazine* (London, 1803), 93, by L. W. Bacon, *A History of American Christianity* (New York, 1907), 237.

of 1803 that, under the leadership of Barton W. Stone, was quickly transmuted into the Kentucky wing of the "Christian movement." The second
had its beginnings in 1805 when the Cumberland presbytery was dissolved
by the Synod of Kentucky for ordaining "illiterate" exhorters. The problem of the presbytery had been to find ministers for mushrooming
churches. When repeated appeals to the General Assembly proved unavail-
ing, revivalist members of the presbytery formed what was to become the
Cumberland Presbyterian Church. A third secession took place in 1805
when Shaker emissaries from New York won a considerable number of
Presbyterians in Kentucky and southern Ohio, including three ministers,
to the peculiar tenets of Ann Lee (see Chapter 8).

If Presbyterians had trouble handling the energies generated by camp
meetings, Methodists did not. They were accustomed to noise and excitement and to "on-the-job" training for their preachers. Furthermore, the
theology of camp meeting exhorters with its implicit rejection of predestination and its explicit emphasis upon salvation as potentially available to
all, which proved so divisive among Presbyterians, posed no problem for
Methodists. This was the gospel they had preached from the beginning. At
Gasper River it was Methodist preacher John McGee who set the theological tone for camp meetings by demonstrating that the hardest sinners
would respond if it was made clear by a blunt approach that in winning
one's way to heaven, the help of the Holy Spirit would not be denied the
truly penitent.

Within a few years camp meetings had become almost a Methodist preserve. By 1811, Methodists were holding their own camp meetings—at
least four hundred of them scattered throughout the country. As camp
meetings were domesticated by Methodists and adapted to conditions of
life in other sections of the nation, much of the frenzied excitement of
the first years disappeared. Grounds were policed, admittance was restricted, crowds were carefully controlled, and the meetings became
much more sober, dignified, and orderly. By the 1830s, even among
Methodists, camp meetings had become occasions when the faithful gathered to combine an annual outing with an opportunity to listen to inspi-
rational addresses. Ultimately the camp grounds—at Chautauqua, New
York; Ocean Grove, New Jersey; Junaluska, North Carolina; Oak Bluffs,
Massachusetts; Bayview, Michigan; and elsewhere—became conference
centers or summer resorts.

The camp meeting as such did not play a great part in the development
of American religious life because it was the product of the scattered population and isolated life of frontier society. When this isolation was replaced
by settled communities with a social life of their own, the death knell of
the camp meeting as an effective evangelistic technique had been
sounded. A new technique—the protracted meeting—was developed to
marshal the group pressure that camp meetings had demonstrated to be
so successful in inducing conversions.

New Measures

A distinctive thrust of the Second Awakening took shape in central and western New York under the aegis of Charles G. Finney.[14] Until Finney appeared, the northern phase of the Awakening, for the most part, had been kept firmly in the hands of settled ministers, and only ordinary "means of grace" had been used. Even when the "gifts" of a traveling evangelist such as Ashahel Nettleton were utilized, the evangelist stayed with the local pastor, preached the Sunday sermons, delivered an extra lecture or two, participated in the prayer meeting, and visited the homes. Disorder and confusion were discouraged. If an audience began to show signs of undue emotion, the people were apt to be dismissed and the distraught counseled in private. Finney was too impatient to put up with such restraint. Before his conversion in 1821, Finney did not think Christians were really sincere. How could they believe that people "were on the verge of hell and yet be so indifferent in regard to this terrific fact"? If he were ever converted, he said, he would be a Christian in earnest and "pull men out of the fire."

At twenty-nine, Finney, a lawyer in Adams, New York, was by his own confession a sinful, worldly man. He attended the Presbyterian church, led the choir, and debated theological points with the pastor. But the dazzling insight that led to his conversion was the product of his own reflection. While walking to his office one morning, it dawned upon him that salvation was much simpler than he had supposed. All that was needed to receive it was "my own consent to give up my sins and accept Christ." As he remembered it, he stopped in the middle of the street and said to himself, "I will accept it today or I will die in the attempt." He recalled the Scripture: "Then shall ye go and pray unto me, and I will hearken unto you" (Jer. 29:12). To Finney this was a contract, and that night his prayers were answered with a "mighty baptism" that overwhelmed him. "The Holy Spirit descended upon me in a manner that seemed to go through my body and soul. . . . I wept aloud with joy and love; and I do not know but I should say, I literally bellowed out the unutterable gushings of my heart." The next morning when a deacon of the church reminded him of a case in court that was set for ten o'clock, Finney's response was immediate and decisive: "Deacon B_____, I have a retainer from the Lord Jesus Christ to plead his cause, and I cannot plead yours."[15]

Finney pursued his theological studies under George W. Gale, the Presbyterian pastor at Adams, and began to make preaching expeditions to

---

[14] Whitney R. Cross, *The Burned-over District: The Social and Intellectual History of Enthusiastic Religion in Western New York* (Ithaca, New York, 1965), a case study of the westward transit of New England culture, details Finney's activities.

[15] Finney's account of his conversion is printed in H. Shelton Smith, Robert Handy, and Lefferts Loetscher, *American Christianity*, II, (New York, 1960–1963), 19–24.

nearby communities. In 1824, a Female Missionary Society sent him on a missionary tour of Jefferson County. He began at Evans Mills and Antwerp, where he converted "the great mass of the population." He had equal success in other communities. Six feet two inches in height, with great piercing eyes that had an uncanny hypnotic effect, he was a commanding figure in the pulpit. He had few mannerisms. He spoke the simple language of everyday life. He said that he merely talked about things that the preachers preached about, but he did it with a bluntness few could evade. In 1825, he moved into the Mohawk River valley. The village of Western caught fire. Then Rome exploded, and Utica, Boonville, and Vernon were swept by the conflagration. By this time Finney was attracting national attention. He was wanted everywhere at once. In 1827, he went to Wilmington, Delaware, spent the winter in Philadelphia, and in 1828 made a foray into New York City.

Finney is said to have arrived in New York City with "his backwoods invasion of civilization" at about the time Andrew Jackson entered the White House. The comment is misleading, for neither Finney nor Jackson was a back country rustic. Finney was trained as a lawyer, had mastered the points of theology with sufficient thoroughness to write a highly regarded book on systematic theology, and ended his career as a professor and then president of Oberlin. His great talent was to make complicated doctrines as clear and sensible as the multiplication table. He noted that his success was greatest with business and professional classes. Rochester, scene of his greatest triumph, was typical in this respect. "The exceptional feature," Whitney Cross observed, "was the phenomenal dignity of this awakening. No agonizing souls fell in the aisles, no raptured ones shouted hallelujahs. . . . The great evangelist, in an unclerical suit of gray, acted like a lawyer arguing . . . before a court and jury, talking precisely, logically, with wit, verve, and informality. Lawyers, real-estate magnates, millers, manufacturers, and commercial tycoons led the parade of the regenerated."[16]

The controversial feature of Finney's revivals were his "new measures." As a lawyer, he refused to be inhibited from winning his case by being restricted to conventional means. His were the tactics of a trial lawyer. He said "you" instead of "they" when speaking of the wicked, and on occasion did not hesitate to mention a notorious sinner by name. The "convicted" were brought forward to the "anxious bench"—a front pew roughly analogous to the witness stand—where attention was centered upon them and where they dramatized the struggle for heaven in the soul of everyone. Women, to the scandal of many, were encouraged to testify and pray in public. The greatest "innovation" was Finney's adaptation of the revival to an urban environment. The entire community was mobilized by bands of workers visiting the homes. Prayer meetings were held at "unseasonable

[16] Cross, 155. For a detailed analysis, see P. E. Johnson, *A Shopkeeper's Millennium* (New York, 1978).

hours"—unseasonable, that is, for farmers. And the conventional routine of stated services—Sunday sermons and a weekday lecture—was displaced by special services held each night and prolonged for hours in inquiry sessions. This was the "protracted meeting"—a community-wide revival campaign of several weeks duration—which was designed to marshal the group pressure in settled areas that the camp meeting had been so effective in fostering on the frontier. In a real sense, the protracted meeting was the camp meeting brought to town.

The protracted meeting also was representative of revivalism as a "results-oriented" activity. Evangelical preaching was aimed at awakening the heart of the listener as well as presenting a coherent view of the nature of the relationship of the individual to God. It also made no secret of the fact that preaching itself was the most effective means by which to bring about the intended results (e.g., a new birth and moral enlightenment). It was this view that guided Finney when he wrote this of religious revival in 1834: "It is not a miracle, or dependent on a miracle, in any sense. It is a purely philosophical result of the right use of the constituted means—as much so as any other effect produced by the application of means."[17]

Although the urban phase of the Second Awakening can be seen most clearly in the person and activity of Finney, it must not be supposed that it was the work of a single man.[18] There were others who were already proceeding along the path he was able to take, and Finney gathered about him many zestful young graduates of the revival-infected colleges, and he established training institutes for other young converts. In more remote areas his methods were widely copied—among Lutherans and Dutch Reformed as well as among Presbyterians, Congregationalists, Baptists, and Methodists. Even Quakers under the leadership of a visiting Englishman, Joseph John Gurney, conformed to the general pattern.[19] In 1832, Albert Barnes of Philadelphia reported that there was scarcely "a city or town or peaceful hamlet" in the country that had not been "hallowed" by a revival. A decade later Robert Baird noted that revivals had become "a constituent part of the religious system" to such an extent that "he who should oppose himself to revivals, as such, would be regarded by most of our evangelical Christians as, *ipso facto,* an enemy to spiritual religion itself."[20]

---

[17] Charles G. Finney, *Lectures on Revivals of Religion* (New York, 1835), 12. A description of the "new measures" is also included in the book. For a broader discussion of the sort of "scientific" view of religion that Finney represented in an early form, see Theodore Dwight Bozeman, *Protestants in an Age of Science: The Baconian Ideal and Antebellum Religious Thought* (Chapel Hill, N.C., 1977).

[18] Daniel Nash, Jedediah Burchard, James Boyle, Luther Myrick, Jabez Swan, and Jacob Knapp were a few of the better-known men who actively promoted the revival.

[19] See D. E. Swift, *Joseph John Gurney* (Middletown, Conn., 1962).

[20] Quoted by S. E. Mead in *The Ministry in Historical Perspectives,* ed. H. R. Niebuhr and D. D. Williams, 226, 227.

Role of Women

A striking feature of the revivals was the predominance of women among the converts. Women may or may not have been more religious than men, but for women a conversion experience could provide some release from the constraints of male domination. It could be something of a declaration of independence, for it was a renunciation of the past and involved a resolute determination to pursue a new independent pattern of life. "The new birth," Donald G. Mathews has said, "was just what it was represented to me, a new entry into a new kind of life," often to the consternation of those upon whom a woman had been psychologically dependent.[21]

The ritual following conversion and preceding church membership also contributed to a woman's sense of self-confidence. She was expected to stand before the congregation and publicly profess her faith by relating her conversion experience. In many circles, women, like children, were expected to be seen and not heard. For a woman to become the center of attention by engaging in an act of public speaking to an attentive audience conferred upon her a claim to respect and honor. "She had stood up in meeting on her own," says Mathews, and expressed "some of her most private thoughts which were accepted by the community as significant and praiseworthy." She also had learned to cite biblical texts and the preacher's opinions to counter pronouncements of other males, thus finding room for additional maneuver.

More important than these primary aspects of evangelical religion in creating psychological and social space for women was the way in which evangelists such as Finney used females in the organizational work of the revivals. In similar fashion, female auxiliaries to the voluntary societies provided opportunities for women to participate in affairs outside the home, assume responsibility, and perfect leadership skills. Initially the auxiliaries were local groups, primarily responsible for accumulating funds for charitable and missionary projects, but in the end they served as channels to participation in affairs on the national scene. Moreover, on occasion women in a more direct fashion would burst the bonds of male authority to function in a mixed society. This event occurred when a woman's account of her conversion was so profoundly moving that she would be asked to repeat her testimony and thus become in effect a traveling evangelist. This phenomenon was most common among Wesleyan groups (i.e., groups with a Wesleyan theology such as Methodists and Free-Will Baptists), although it had long been commonplace among Quakers. Mrs. Chloe Willey's conversion by a Baptist itinerant in New Hampshire—a story replete with faintings, visions, and extraordinary discernments of good and evil in the world—had set something of a standard for the genre when it was published in 1807. Such stories effectively established women's

---

[21] See Donald G. Mathews, *Religion in the Old South* (Chicago, 1977), 103–9.

reputations and led to some women to become "prophetesses" with groups of their own.[22]

Finally, imbued with the sense of mission generated by evangelicalism, the enthusiasm of women readily spilled over into their own specific concerns, the most prominent of which were female education and woman's suffrage.

Missionary and Educational Activity

Although revivals swelled membership rolls and generated enthusiasm and energy, Protestant expansion was primarily the product of missionary activity. This was the principal means employed as the frontier marched westward to the Pacific. This was true even in the camp meeting territory bounded by the watershed of the Ohio. Even among Methodists who utilized camp meetings most widely, the meetings did no more than supplement the regular work of churches carried on from day to day by circuit riders and class leaders.

With the stampede to the West that began in 1790, distances became too great and new settlements too numerous to be left to the haphazard and intermittent efforts of pastors on leave as short-term missionaries. For a task so large, the full resources of the churches had to be marshaled. Recognition of this need coincided with the onset of the Second Awakening, which quickened missionary interest and concern. The consequence was that the energies released by the revivals were channeled into a new missionary thrust.

Early Missionary Societies

It has often been noted that whenever the English are confronted by an urgent need, the instinctive reaction is to form a committee or "voluntary society" of like-minded friends to do what needs to be done. In England this had been the technique of securing quick and concerted action throughout the seventeenth century, and in the eighteenth century, societies had been formed for a variety of ends, including the reformation of manners, the promotion of Christian knowledge, and the propagation of the gospel. With the rise of new evangelical zeal at the end of the century, this folk pattern of response found expression in the formation of foreign mission, Bible, and tract societies. Nor had the colonists been oblivious to the advantages of the voluntary society technique. They used it to promote Indian missions, to forestall an American episcopate, to mobilize resistance to the Stamp Act, and—through committees of public safety—to initiate the Revolutionary struggle.

---

[22] Mrs. Chloe Willey, *A Short Account of the Life of . . . Mrs. Chloe Willey* (Amherst, N.H., 1807).

With this heritage, it was inevitable that voluntary societies would be formed to enable the churches to match the increasing pace of settlement with a more systematic and widely supported missionary endeavor.[23] The beginning of the new era in mission activity is usually dated from the founding of the New York Missionary Society in 1796 by Presbyterians, Baptists, and Dutch Reformed. The primary object of this society, however, was to promote Indian missions. The Missionary Society of Connecticut, organized by Congregationalists in 1798, was the first society to undertake the establishment of churches in frontier areas. Baptists followed suit with the Massachusetts Baptist Domestic Missionary Society in 1802. Presbyterians were more ambivalent. For more than a generation they were unable to make up their minds whether to channel their efforts through voluntary societies or the General Assembly. Actually they did both. They formed the Western Missionary Society in 1800, they participated in several New York societies, and at the same time the General Assembly in 1802 appointed a Standing Committee on Missions. Episcopalians were preoccupied with internal problems. Not until 1821 was their Domestic and Foreign Missionary Society organized. Methodists were also tardy in forming their first missionary society (1819), but they had little need of this type of organization, since every conference was in effect a missionary society and every itinerant a missionary. As soon as a traveling elder was recruited, a circuit would be laid out that would take him to the newest settlements no matter how remote. A Presbyterian missionary in Kentucky paid tribute to the effectiveness of the Methodist system when he reported that wherever he went, a circuit rider had preceded him.

> I at length became ambitious to find a family whose cabin had not been entered by a Methodist preacher. . . . I traveled from settlement to settlement . . . , but into every hovel I entered I learned that the Methodist missionary had been there before me.[24]

Nothing daunted the circuit riders. This fact was made clear by the common remark, when people wished to describe the severity of a blizzard or cloudburst, that "nobody was out but crows and Methodist preachers."

The touring missionaries, whether Presbyterian, Congregational, or Baptist, functioned in much the same way as the circuit riders.[25] They preached wherever they could gain a hearing and had an ample supply of books and pamphlets to distribute. Instead of forming "classes," they formed any small cluster of hopeful Christians into a "conference." The goal of the missionaries was to transform one of the conferences as soon as

---

[23] C. I. Foster, *An Errand of Mercy: The Evangelical United Front* (Chapel Hill, N.C., 1958).

[24] A. H. Redford, *History of Methodism in Kentucky* (Nashville, 1868–1876), 530.

[25] See M. W. Armstrong, ed., *The Presbyterian Enterprise*, (Philadelphia, 1956), 106–8, for an extract from the journal of a Presbyterian "circuit-rider."

Abby Kelley. This antislavery lecturer did not hesitate to criticize Protestant church leaders for their unwillingness to support women in the ministry. *(Courtesy, American Antiquarian Society.)*

possible into a church and to win sufficient support to become settled pastors. This process allowed the sending society to utilize its funds to send out additional missionaries. For his part, the former traveling missionary provided supervision to neighboring conferences, seeking to nurture them into full-fledged churches.

The transition from conference to church was not always easy to effect, for this implied assuming responsibility for paying the preacher, and money was scarce. But if money was scarce, land was not. Life was simple and one could readily become self-supporting. Ministers often supplemented their meager stipend by tilling a few acres. Sometimes they supported themselves until a church was strong enough to maintain them. The latter practice was most common among Baptists, particularly on the southern frontier. Typical in this respect was Joab Powell of Tennessee, who experienced a call to preach as a Baptist minister. Not waiting for a missionary society to send him, he went to Missouri where he spent twenty years farming and preaching, before moving on to Oregon where he gained fame as an itinerant revivalist. As early as 1757, the Synod of Philadelphia noted that Presbyterians in the newer settlements "were highly pleased with the prevailing principle that gospel ministers should work for their living and preach for charity" with the result that many have "struggled and earned their bread in a great measure with the sweat of their brows."[26] Three-quarters of a century later in Illinois, a Baptist missionary encountered the same spirit. He had preached 69 sermons and baptized 22 persons, and the people had said to him, "We love to hear you preach. Come as often as you can." But when he reminded them that "the laborer is worthy of his hire," they began to grumble about "missionary-beggars" and "money-hunters."[27]

There were grumblings about the quality of missionary preaching as well, often from other missionaries. John Mason Peck, pioneer Baptist missionary in southern Illinois and Missouri, reflected this bias when he declared that one-third of the preachers in this region were "doing positive injury to religion" and another third were able to render no more than "minor service."[28] Given these conflicting views, it is understandable that antimission sentiment should have arisen. Still it was localized and, apart from enclaves among Baptists, did not long endure.

Voluntary Societies and a National Strategy

The initial decades of the nineteenth century witnessed, first, the proliferation of voluntary societies and, then, their coordination in the interest of a unified strategy for the nation as a whole.[29]

The earliest societies were local and regional missionary societies devoted to establishing churches. Other societies serviced the mission enterprise—Bible and tract societies furnished necessary literature, Sunday school societies provided religious instruction for children, and education societies established colleges and seminaries to supply trained missionary personnel and pastors. A third group of societies promoted humanitarian

[26] *Ibid.*, 69.

[27] C. B. Goodykoontz, *Home Missions on the American Frontier,* (New York, 1971), 205.

[28] *Ibid.*, 33.

[29] For the unified strategy, see Foster, 160. It is placed in context by R. T. Handy, *A Christian America* (New York, 1971); Nathan Hatch, *The Democratization of American Christianity* (New Haven, 1989).

causes and projects for moral and social reform. Societies became so numerous and varied that Orestes Brownson complained that "matters have come to such a pass that a peaceable man can hardly venture to eat or drink, to go to bed or get up, to correct his children or kiss his wife" without the guidance and sanction of some society.[30]

The picture of confusion that one might gain from the multiplicity of societies would be misleading. There was purpose in the apparent disorder. To understand this, one must appreciate what was regarded as the peculiar genius of the voluntary society. The voluntary society, first of all, was an instrument for quick and concerted action by concerned individuals with no need to wait until some official body could be persuaded to act. A few friends could take the initiative and then, through the society they created, proceed to enlist the broadest possible support for the attainment of a single objective. The possibility of its energies being diverted and diluted by other concerns would be avoided. "Concentrated action is powerful action" was the way the manifesto of the American Bible Society put it. Finally, the voluntary societies that united "the best hearts, the most willing hands, and the most vigorous and untiring enterprise" in common tasks were regarded as the heaven-sent means by which the divided denominations could pool their efforts to meet particular needs.[31]

Four factors converged to give the voluntary societies their distinctive character. First, Protestants had become increasingly conscious of the ties binding them together. S. S. Schmucker of the Lutheran seminary at Gettysburg declared that whereas each evangelical "denomination must naturally prefer its own peculiarities," it is a "dangerous error" to regard "these peculiarities as equal in importance with the great fundamentals of our holy religion held in common by all." In similar vein Samuel Miller at Princeton said "it would never occur to us to place the peculiarities of our creed among the fundamentals of our common Christianity." Albert Barnes was even more explicit, asserting that "the church of Christ is not under the Episcopal form, or the Baptist, the Methodist, the Presbyterian or the Congregational form exclusively; all are, to all intents and purposes, to be recognized as parts of the one holy catholic church."[32]

Second, the revival campaigns stressed a doctrine of "disinterested benevolence" that had been elaborated by Samuel Hopkins and Nathaniel W. Taylor.[33] Sin was defined as including "selfishness," and the effect of

---

[30] Stow Persons, *American Minds* (New York, 1958), 160.

[31] H. Shelton Smith, Robert Handy, and Lefferts Loetscher, *American Christianity*, I, (New York, 1960–1963), 555; and Lyman Beecher writing of national needs in *The National Preacher*, 3 (1829), 154.

[32] Schmucker, Miller, and Barnes are quoted by S. E. Mead in *The Ministry in Historical Perspectives*, ed. H. Richard Niebuhr and D. D. Williams, (New York, 1956), 222–24.

[33] See selection from Hopkins illustrating his view in Smith, Handy, and Loetscher, I, 539–45. For Taylor, see *ibid.*, II, 28–36.

conversion was to shift "the controlling preference of the mind" from a "preference for self-interest" to a "preference for disinterested benevolence." If one's conversion was genuine, it was insisted, this shift in the preference of the mind would express itself in action. The conversion experience, therefore, was not the end of the Christian life but only its beginning. Working was as necessary as believing, and working meant participating fully in every good cause.

Third, in clarifying their understanding of conversion as a transformed life, the revivalists sought to place Christian perfection in line with older Puritan ways of thinking. Nathaniel W. Taylor and Lyman Beecher led the way in making the adjustment, but Asa Mahan and Charles G. Finney gave widespread currency to perfectionist ideas among non-Wesleyan Protestants and elaborated them in ways that were congenial to Methodist piety.[34] The result was a blending of a rational outline of doctrine and duties with emotional religion.

Fourth, the concern of churches was not simply to evangelize individuals but also to remake society. They were heirs of the millennial tradition voiced by Mark Hopkins, president of Williams College, when he declared that the time was coming when "wars, and intemperance, and licentiousness, and fraud, and slavery, and all oppression" shall be brought to an end "through the transforming influence of Christianity."[35] Although this was to be "the Lord's doing," Christians could help speed the coming of the perfect society by promoting revivals, establishing churches, and participating in the host of societies designed to counter the evils Hopkins had listed as well as others he had neglected to mention.

The societies had local beginnings but were pulled together into national organizations to coordinate their work throughout the country. This trend was particularly true after 1818 when the fight to save the establishment in Connecticut was lost, thus permitting Lyman Beecher—the real architect of the voluntary system in America—to devote full attention to transforming the societies into "a gigantic religious power," thoroughly "systematized" and "compact" in organization.[36]

There was little difficulty in combining most local reform and service societies into national organizations on an interdenominational basis. The American Bible Society and the American Education Society were the earliest, formed in 1816; the American Colonization Society was next in 1817; then the American Sunday School Union was formed in 1824, the American Tract Society in 1825, the American Temperance Society in 1826, the American Peace Society in 1828, and the American Antislavery Society in 1833. Unlike the reform societies, the Sunday school and tract societies

---

[34] See Timothy L. Smith, "The Doctrine of the Sanctifying Spirit," *Wesleyan Theological Journal,* 13 (1978), 93–94.

[35] Ralph Gabriel, *The Course of American Democratic Thought* (New York, 1940), 36.

[36] Gilberg H. Barnes, *The Anti-Slavery Impulse, 1830–1844* (New York, 1933), 17.

had to take extra precautions to preserve their interdenominational character. The publishing committee of the American Tract Society, for example, was composed of an equal number of Baptists, Congregationalists, Dutch Reformed, Episcopalians, and Presbyterians who were charged with protecting their denominational "peculiarities," it being believed that there was sufficient common ground to load each tract with an ample measure of "divine truth." The missionary and education societies were of a different character. Their task was to establish churches and train ministers. This necessitated organization on a denominational basis. The Presbyterian United Domestic Missionary Society was reorganized in 1826 as the American Home Missionary Society, and it became the arm of the Presbyterian-Congregational coalition. Similar national societies were formed for the other denominations.

The whole cluster of national societies has sometimes been referred to as the "benevolent empire." Their activities were closely coordinated through a series of "interlocking directorates." Most of the leadership at the national level was concentrated in a relatively small group; and the annual meetings, held in New York in May, were so scheduled that one could participate in most of them. They did not act alone, an auxiliary society assured its members in 1826. They moved together "harmoniously" and thus formed "so many parts of the grand whole" in seeking to fulfill "that last command of our ascended Lord, 'Go and spread the influence of the gospel over every creature.'"[37] They were particularly effective in doing so in the cities and in the West.

Contributions to Education

It was in the area of secondary and higher education that the churches made their greatest contribution. Presbyterians and Congregationalists were the most active in founding academies and colleges. Baptists followed their example, as did Methodists after a delayed beginning. Other denominations made contributions in proportion to their numbers. For the greater part of the nineteenth century, most secondary and collegiate education was carried on under denominational auspices. Of the 516 colleges and universities founded before the Civil War, only a few had no religious affiliation.

Founding of theological seminaries was another Protestant activity. Prior to 1800, specifically theological education, as distinguished from the classical education given aspiring ministers in the colleges, was commonly acquired under the direction of older clergymen. Such supervised training combined advanced study with practical experience, but there was a growing conviction that more adequate preparation could be given in a graduate professional school. New Brunswick Theological Seminary, which

[37] Foster, 143, 154.

traces its beginnings to 1784 when instruction was initiated in New York City, antedated the general movement, which is usually considered to have begun with the founding of Andover Theological Seminary in 1808. In the next few years the movement spread rapidly in most denominations.

Part of the energy generated by revivals was directed toward efforts to provide educational opportunities for females and blacks. Emma Willard's Troy Female Seminary (1821) and Mary Lyon's similar endeavor at Mt. Holyoke (1837) are the most frequently cited examples of the former concern, but many female seminaries flourished in the South and elsewhere.[38] Lincoln University in Pennsylvania, founded in 1854, and Wilberforce in Ohio, founded in 1856, are specific examples of the latter concern—provision of educational opportunities for those of African antecedents who had gained their freedom. Earlier, New York Central College, established in 1843 in McGrawville, New York, by abolitionist Baptists, regarded the education of blacks, who constituted a significant portion of its student body, as central to its mission. But it was Oberlin College (1832) that put the whole thrust of evangelical religion together.

Oberlin was dedicated to "universal reform," being rescued financially in 1835 by the Tappan brothers, New York City merchants who stipulated that Finney serve as professor of theology and that the student rebels expelled from Lane Theological Seminary because of antislavery activity be accepted as students. Both women and blacks were admitted to the course of instruction. Its name[39] and the words *learning and labor* on its seal indicated that, like many evangelical colleges of the time, Oberlin was founded as a manual labor school to put into practice the latest educational theory, which stressed the blending of head, hand, and heart in the instructional process. Although the central purpose of Oberlin, in keeping with its revivalist concerns, was to send out well-equipped ministers and missionaries, there was scarcely a reform proposal that did not find ready reception and nurture in the congenial "perfectionist" atmosphere of the college.

The Mood of the South

Although academies and colleges multiplied in the South as they did in other parts of the country, there was less self-generated activity by the voluntary societies. Perhaps the climate, before the advent of air conditioning, slowed the pace of life. More likely the absence of the highly organized and systematic procedures of the bustling cities of the North

---

[38] Leonard I. Sweet, "The Female Seminary Movement and Woman's Mission in Antebellum America," *Church History*, 54 (1985), 41–55.

[39] *A life of the Swiss Protestant Johann Frederick Oberlin* (1740–1826), which gave impetus to the manual labor movement, was published by the American Sunday School Union in 1830. A year later Lewis Tappan and others founded the Society for Promoting Manual Labor in Literary Institutions.

was responsible. It could not have been because the mood in areas of the South where evangelical religion was strong was any less exuberant and optimistic than in the North. Baptists, Methodists, and Presbyterians may have had fewer resources in the South than elsewhere, but they had done their work well.

Andrew Johnson, the future president but at the time a youthful adherent of Andrew Jackson, reflected the eager optimistic spirit of the time. Johnson was addressing his constituents in the First Congressional District of Tennessee. He told them that democracy and Christianity

> are going along, not in divergents, not in parallels, but in converging lines—the one purifying and elevating man religiously, the other politically. . . . At what period of time they will have finished the work of progress and elevation is not now for me to determine, but when finished these two lines will have approximated each other—man being perfected both in a religious and a political point of view.

As he continued, Johnson became lyrical in his vision of the future, noting that as the lines converge, then can

> proclamation be made that the millennial morning has dawned and that the time has come when the lion and the lamb shall lie down together, when the "voice of the turtle" shall be "heard in our land," when ". . . the glad tidings shall be proclaimed . . . of man's political and religious redemption," and that there is "on earth, peace, good will toward men."[40]

Overseas Missions

Thus far, attention has been centered on the new nation, but the religious enthusiasm of the Second Awakening could not be contained within national boundaries. Not only the nation but also the world was to be redeemed. News of the Orient had been seeping back into New England during the early years of the Awakening. This was the era of the clipper ships and the Pacific trade, and every ship that returned to Salem or Boston brought tales of distant lands and strange people. Also, exciting reports of William Carey's pioneering missionary venture in India were being published in the religious press, and funds were being collected in Philadelphia and elsewhere for his support. In 1810, the "banding" of a number of students at Andover Theological Seminary—not far from Salem—to offer themselves for foreign-mission service led to the founding

---

[40] Dixon Wector, *The Saga of American Society* (New York, 1937), 100. L. P. Graf and R. W. Haskins, eds., *The Papers of Andrew Johnson* (Knoxville, 1970), II, 176–77. For discussion of the home as a center of piety and as a safe context for the expression of emotion, see Jan Lewis, *The Pursuit of Happiness: Family and Values in Jefferson's Virginia* (New York, 1983), and D. G. Mathews, *Religion in the Old South* (Chicago, 1977).

of the American Board of Commissioners for Foreign Missions.[41] Two years later, five of the students—Samuel Newell, Adoniram Judson, Luther Rice, Samuel Nott, Jr., and Gordon Hall—set sail for India. Judson became persuaded of the validity of Baptist contentions while on shipboard, and when he arrived in India, he discovered that Rice had come to share his views while sailing on board another ship. When Judson went on to Burma, Rice returned to America to enlist Baptist support for Judson's mission. By 1850, the foreign mission work of all denominations called for an annual expenditure of about $650,000.

Protestant expansion in America during the decades that followed the formation of the new nation was part of a much larger movement of Protestant resurgence whose achievements led Kenneth Scott Latourette to describe the nineteenth century as "the great century" in the history of Christianity.[42] In Britain and on the continent of Europe, as well as in America, a sweeping tide of evangelical religion brought new life to Protestant churches at a time when the Roman Catholic Church was waging a defensive struggle against the forces of nationalism and "liberalism" in Roman Catholic lands. It was not until the end of the century that the Roman Catholic Church, either in America or elsewhere, was to be able to abandon its defensive posture. In the meantime, the Protestant churches in America were not without pressing problems of their own.

[41] See W. E. Strong, *The Story of the American Board* (Boston, 1910). An overseas mission had been anticipated by David George when he sailed for Sierra Leone in 1792 after having established a black church in Nova Scotia. Jamaica, Haiti, and Liberia also became scenes of missionary activity by blacks from America.

[42] Latourette's primary focus was upon the achievements of the far-flung missionary enterprise. Only by a repetitive refrain of superlatives could he describe what had taken place. "Never before in a period of equal length had Christianity or any other religion penetrated for the first time as large an area as it had in the nineteenth century." "Never before had any religion been planted over so large a portion of the earth's surface." "Never before had Christianity, or any other religion, been introduced to so many different peoples and cultures." "Never before had so many hundreds of thousands contributed voluntarily of their means to assist the spread of Christianity or any other religion." "Never before . . . had Christians come so near the goal of reaching all men with their message." "Never had it exerted so wide an influence upon the human race." "Measured by geographic extent and the effect upon mankind as a whole, the nineteenth century was the greatest thus far in the history of Christianity." Kenneth Scott Latourette, *A History of the Expansion of Christianity* (New York, 1937–1945), IV, 1, 4; V, 469; VI, 442, 443, 450; VII, 450.

CHAPTER SEVEN

The Broadening of Denominational Life

The evangelical religion of the first part of the nineteenth century bred a spirit of cooperation that was expressed both in the revivals of the period and in the activities of the voluntary societies. The societies were explicitly designed to secure the broadest possible base of participants. And indispensable to the success of a revival in any community was the participation of a major portion of the churches, for without this broad participation, the necessary psychological climate and group pressure could not be created. "The spirit of sectarianism," therefore, was the great "hindrance" and "quencher" of revivals; and Finney constantly warned his helpers not "to dwell upon sectarian distinctions or to be sticklish about sectarian points."[1] With Christians working side by side in the revivals and in the societies, further impetus was given to the development of cordial relations among the major denominations.

There were discordant notes, however, in the midst of the harmony. The Great Awakening of the colonial period, with its "New Lights" and "Old Lights," and "New Sides" and "Old Sides," had demonstrated that revivals could divide as well as unify. And the Second Awakening was equally productive of controversy and division. The reactions were quite diverse. The doctrinal harshness of revivalist preaching, on the one hand, contributed to the Unitarian and Universalist defections; the doctrinal looseness of revivalism helped produce a reaction that led to a revived confessionalism. And while many, in considering revivalism, debated the role of emotion,

[1] Calvin Colton, *History and Character of American Revivals*, 116–17. Finney, *Lectures on Revivals of Religion*, 2nd ed. (New York, 1835), 369.

the place of reason, the authority of the clergy, and the importance of ritual, other forces of diversity were at work. African Americans began organizing themselves as separate religious communities in a fashion closer to the denominational patterns of white churches. The efforts of women to broaden their roles in religious life, though they met with limited success, established a base from which women could more effectively criticize groups that excluded them from full participation. Roman Catholic and Jewish communities became more visible, especially in large urban environments, all while Methodism established itself as the fastest-growing denomination in America.

Unitarians and Universalists

Although Unitarianism (i.e., antitrinitarianism) in Boston was the product of many influences, its roots went back to the "liberal" tendencies that developed during the time of the first Great Awakening; and during the succeeding years, there had been a steady but barely perceptible drift toward greater emphasis upon the human role in redemption.[2] By the time Ashbel Green, a young Presbyterian minister from Philadelphia who was later to be president of Princeton University, made a tour of New England in 1791, he found many of the Boston ministers to be unsound in the faith. Among them, he reported, were Arminians, Universalists, Arians, and one professed Socinian. Ten years later Archibald Alexander, then president of Hampden-Sydney College in Virginia, found the situation in Boston even more dismaying. Heretical notions of all types abounded, and the only agreement he could discover was a rejection of the doctrine of the Trinity.[3]

The reports of Green and Alexander are somewhat misleading, because heretical doctrines were not being openly proclaimed. The only overt break occasioned by the theological ferment had occurred not among the Congregationalists but at King's Chapel, the former church of the royal governor. In 1782, the Episcopalian proprietors of the Chapel, being unable to obtain a minister, had invited James Freeman, a recent graduate of Harvard, to serve as reader. In deference to his scruples, the liturgy was revised to eliminate trinitarian references, and the Athanasian and Nicene Creeds were omitted. Then, in 1787, the congregation proceeded to ordain Freeman as its pastor. The Congregational clergy were much more cautious. Without the problem posed by a set liturgy, most of them were content to let "sleeping dogmas lie." Orthodox doctrines were not openly opposed and rejected; rather, they were quietly ignored. A clear-cut party

---

[2] See Conrad Wright, *The Beginnings of Unitarianism in America* (Boston, 1955); and E. M. Wilbur, *A History of Unitarianism . . . in America* (Cambridge, Mass., 1952). Fresh perspectives are provided by Wright in *The Liberal Christians* (Boston, 1970).

[3] Wilbur, 399.

alignment appeared only when Henry Ware, a known liberal, was elected to the professorship of divinity at Harvard in 1805, thereby leading to the founding of Andover Seminary in 1808.

A definite separation did not take place until after 1815. The event that brought the uneasy truce to an end was the publication in Boston of a chapter from the *Memoirs of Theophilus Lindsey*, which reproduced letters that had been written to the English Unitarian leader by several of the New England "liberals." One letter noted that, although most of the Boston clergy were Unitarian in sentiment, "the controversy is seldom or never introduced into the pulpit." But now names had been named and sentiments had been exposed, and there was little hope of preventing an open breach. A pamphlet war ensued, with Jedidiah Morse writing a tract entitled *Are You of the Christian or the Boston Religion?* and John Lowell replying in kind with one entitled *Are You a Christian or a Calvinist?*

The classic exposition of Unitarian doctrine was William Ellery Channing's Baltimore sermon on "Unitarian Christianity," which he delivered in 1819 at the ordination of Jared Sparks.[4] The foundation was the inspired Word of God made manifest in the Scriptures; but, being "written for mankind" and "in the language of men," the meaning of Scripture must be sought "in the same manner as that of other books." The special divine office of Christ as Savior was not questioned. Though Jesus was not God, he was sent by the Father to effect the "moral and spiritual deliverance" of humankind, that is, to rescue people "from sin and its consequences, and to bring them to a state of everlasting purity and happiness." The basic issue that set Unitarians apart was their optimistic view of human nature. There is an "essential sameness" between God and man, declared Channing, and "all virtue has its foundation in the moral nature of man." The great significance of Jesus is that he leads and entices men to divine perfection. Having been made for "union" with the Creator, the "infinite perfection" of the Creator is "the only sufficient object and true resting place for the insatiable desires and unlimited capacities of the human mind." Later the Unitarian position was to be summarized in James Freeman Clarke's "Affirmation of Faith": "The fatherhood of God, the brotherhood of man, the leadership of Jesus, salvation by character, and the progress of mankind onward and upward forever."

Publication of the extract from Lindsey's *Memoirs* precipitated a struggle for the possession of church property. Often the Trinitarians constituted a majority of church members, but the courts ruled in 1820 that church property was vested in the "parish," which embraced both church members and nonmembers. In many instances, with all eligible voters of the parish or town participating in the decision, even a minority Unitarian faction among church members was able to gain title to the property. Oliver

---

[4] The sermon has been reprinted many times. A portion of it is in H. Shelton Smith, Robert Handy, and Lefferts Loetscher, *American Christianity*, I, (New York, 1960–1963), 493–502.

Wendell Holmes's poem "One-Hoss Shay" was supposed to be a symbol of the sudden crumbling of "Calvinism," but it collapsed only in eastern Massachusetts; and even there only momentarily, for within a brief time, orthodox Congregational churches were reestablished in almost every parish. When the American Unitarian Association was formed in 1825, it numbered 125 churches, 100 of them in Massachusetts and most within 40 miles of Boston, a fact that led the irreverent to quip that the Unitarians believed in the fatherhood of God, the brotherhood of man, and the neighborhood of Boston.

Unitarianism, on the whole, was the faith of well-to-do, urban New Englanders who rejected the notion of human depravity. Universalism was its counterpart among less urbane, rural folk who were repelled by the idea of eternal damnation and thus led to affirm the doctrine of universal countervailing salvation. Their mood in part was reflected in this reaction of a seventeen-year-old New Hampshire girl to uninhibited revivalist preaching: "We went this evening to hear Lorenzo Dow, a famous Methodist preacher, his appearance was enough to frighten one and his preaching disgusted all—the meeting house was crowded full. Think we should have been as wise if we had staid home."[5]

Although Universalism had been brought to America by John Murray in 1770, it did not gain much headway until after Elhanan Winchester, a Baptist minister, was converted in 1781. The next year, Charles Chauncy's Universalist-flavored *Salvation for All Men* appeared in print. Later, under the leadership of Hosea Ballou, whose *Treatise on Atonement* was published in 1805, Universalists adopted an antitrinitarian position and, except for social status, became indistinguishable from Unitarians. As a lower-class denomination, the Universalists competed with Methodists and Wesleyan-oriented Free-Will Baptists for the allegiance of the common people. Although the Universalists were concentrated initially in rural New England, they moved into the newer settlements of the West with such success that by 1850, they had more than twice as many churches as the Unitarians.

The Resurgence of Old School "Confessionalism"

By the late 1820s, Calvinists among the New England Congregationalists were deeply concerned about liberal influence. That concern was succinctly expressed in the slogan "Shall we sustain our Calvinism or see it run down to the standard of Methodists and laxer men?"[6] At Andover, Jedidiah

---

[5] Alice Felt Tyler, *Freedom's Ferment* (Minneapolis, 1944), 29.

[6] S. E. Mead, *Nathaniel W. Taylor*, 221.

Morse persuaded the followers of the seminary to "guard against the insidious encroachments of innovation" by shackling the institution to the Westminster Shorter Catechism and the so-called Andover Creed based upon Samuel Hopkins's restatement of the views of Jonathan Edwards. The center of the controversy was in Connecticut, where a Pastoral Union was formed in 1833 and steps were taken to found a new seminary to combat the influence of Yale. The following year, the (Hartford) Seminary was established at East Windsor, and Bennet Tyler was summoned from Portland, Maine, to assume the presidency. The integrity of both the Pastoral Union and the seminary was carefully guarded by Articles of Agreement that defined Calvinism in terms that would exclude any New Haven sentiments. The rift, which was to continue for many years, amounted to an open schism among the loosely organized Congregational churches.

A similar alarm among Presbyterian conservatives precipitated the formation of what came to be known as the Old School party in opposition to the New School, or New Divinity, men. The Presbyterian conservatives worked in close alliance with the strict Calvinists of New England, and as early as 1827, the Presbyterian *Christian Advocate*, published in Philadelphia and edited by Ashbel Green, was accusing the professors at Yale of promulgating doctrines that subverted the principles of orthodoxy. The ensuing controversy was marked by a whole series of heresy trials, beginning in 1831 when charges were brought against Albert Barnes in Philadelphia and ending in 1835 with the arraignment of Lyman Beecher before the Presbytery of Cincinnati. In each instance, after appeal to higher judicatories, the charges were dismissed, but the trials contributed greatly to the inflamed climate of opinion which led in 1837 to the exclusion of four New School synods in New York and Ohio from the Presbyterian church.[7]

Although the theological issue was the most obvious factor in the division of 1837, the division was partly the product of a geographically based power struggle within the Presbyterian denomination, and lurking in the background was the disruptive issue of slavery. From the beginning, Pennsylvania had been the center of power and prestige within the Presbyterian fold, but by 1828, its position of dominance had been badly eroded. In that year Green noted that, whereas there were 196 licentiates and ministers in Pennsylvania, New York had 426. The damaging aspect of this imbalance was the fact that the New York ministers were within the New England rather than the Pennsylvania orbit of influence. Beecher, who had gone west to become president of the newly established Lane Theological Seminary, was certain that his trial for heresy was triggered by men of the Philadelphia-Pittsburgh axis who were alarmed at the prospect of a New England man rising to leadership in Cincinnati.

---

[7] The Old School–New School controversy is illuminated by documents reproduced in Maurice W. Armstrong ed., *The Presbyterian Enterprise*, 146–71. See also G. M. Marsden, *The Evangelical Mind and the New School Presbyterian Experience* (New Haven, 1970).

Political battles grew out of dissatisfaction with the Plan of Union, but as much as it might complain, the Old School party was not able to gain leverage until 1837. The balance of power was represented by Princeton Theological Seminary, and the faculty there hesitated to commit its influence to any program that would divide the church. Princeton regarded itself as the theological center of Presbyterian life, and it had looked with misgiving upon the establishment of Auburn Seminary in 1818 and Lane in 1829. But it was the founding of Union Theological Seminary in New York by New School men in 1836 that threw Princeton, though not without some reservations, behind the political program of the Old School party. The new seminary in New York City could be regarded only as a direct challenge to Princeton's central role in the life of the church.

During the months preceding the General Assembly of 1837, the Old School faction organized carefully to obtain a maximum representation; and when the Assembly met, it proceeded with dispatch to carry out the Old School program. The "union" with the Congregationalists was abrogated, the relationship with the American Home Missionary Society and the American Education Society was severed, and three synods in New York and one in Ohio were expelled from the church. The following year, after attempting unsuccessfully to gain readmittance, the New School Presbyterians organized as a separate body that, with the adherence of scattered presbyteries and churches in other parts of the country, was roughly equal in size to the Old School body.

Although he took no great part in the division of 1837, Charles Hodge became the great theologian of Old School Presbyterianism. He had been appointed to a professorship at Princeton Seminary in 1822 and remained there for fifty years, sharing in the training of over 3,000 ministers and contributing more than any other single person to the shaping of American Presbyterianism. He was deeply influenced by Swiss orthodoxy, and a strong confessionalism became the hallmark of his theology. Hodge was convinced that "no such thing exists on the face of the earth as Christianity in the abstract. . . . Every man you see is either an Episcopalian or a Methodist, a Presbyterian or an Independent, an Arminian or a Calvinist. No one is a Christian in general."[8] His theological system was based solidly on the Westminster Standards and other Reformed confessions, which he sought faithfully to expound and defend. It was with this purpose in mind that he boasted that "a new idea never originated" at Princeton Seminary while he was there. His great monument, as well as the source of much of his later influence, was his three-volume *Systematic Theology*, explicitly designed as a defensive rampart against all doctrinal aber-

[8] *Biblical Repertory and Theological Review*, 8 (1836), 430.

rations.[9] Although Hodge attempted to keep Presbyterianism in a theological straitjacket, it has been pointed out that his learning, doctrinal rigor, respect for confessional tradition, and insistence upon intelligible discussion did much in succeeding years to prevent antiintellectual tendencies, sentimentality, and emotional partisanship from overwhelming theological concern.

During the 1830s, the Baptists also were torn by an Old School–New School division that was in part a reaction to the growing influence in their ranks of the New England Theology.[10] The Baptist Old School party, however, failed to capture the denominational machinery that, above the associational level, existed solely in the form of voluntary societies. A defection thereupon occurred both in the East and in the West, but the defensive posture that these "Primitive Baptists" adopted became so permeated by an antimission spirit that the defecting churches and associations were left to eke out no more than a dwindling existence.

A revived confessionalism among the Reformed and the Lutherans came from another quarter. Both groups had been heavily infiltrated, first by Wesleyan doctrines, then by the more moderate evangelicalism of early Princeton, and finally by Taylorism and its associated Finneyite "new measures." In 1822, five ministers withdrew on doctrinal grounds from the Dutch Reformed Church, but their adherents were able to maintain only a meager church life until 1857, when the Christian Reformed Church was established on a strong confessional base by Dutch immigrants in Michigan. Not only did the new church prosper, but also its influence had the effect of drawing the older Dutch church back to a more conservative position.

A theological shift among the German Lutherans followed much the same pattern. S. S. Schmucker, graduate of Princeton and president of the Lutheran seminary at Gettysburg, was the great symbol of the Lutheran adjustment to the American theological climate.[11] It was Schmucker who

---

[9] It is necessary to speak of "later" influence, for Hodge's *Systematic Theology* (New York, 1872–1875) was not published until the last years of his life. Prior to this time, his influence was mediated primarily through the classroom and in his articles in the *Biblical Repertory and Theological Review* (later known as the *Princeton Review*).

[10] The theological issue was clearly delineated by Thomas Smiley (1759–1832), who was to become an Old School leader, in a letter to John Davis, April 27, 1811, and in his manuscript "History of the Chemung Association," 88–102, both of which are in the Samuel Colgate Baptist Historical Collection. Smiley, a pastor on the New York–Pennsylvania border, was shocked and dismayed by "the high Hopkinsian or all but fully Arminian sentiments" of the "Eastern missionaries" sent out by the Baptist board in Boston. For the missionaries' account of their tours through the Chemung River area, see the *Massachusetts Baptist Missionary Magazine*, 2 (1808–1810), 302–7; and the *American Baptist Magazine*, 1 (1817–1818), 269–71.

[11] See J. A. Brown, *The New Theology* (Philadelphia, 1857); Vergilius Ferm, *The Crisis in American Lutheran Theology* (St. Louis, 1987); and E. Clifford Nelson, ed., *The Lutherans in North America* (Philadelphia, 1975).

issued in 1838 a *Fraternal Appeal* summoning all branches of evangelical Protestantism in America to unite in a single Apostolic Protestant Church. His leadership met opposition, especially from a recently arrived group from the Saxony region of Germany, who, at a meeting in Chicago, formed the Evangelical Lutheran Synod of Missouri in 1847. Other equally conservative synods were formed by immigrants from other parts of Germany—the Buffalo Synod in 1845, the Wisconsin Synod in 1850, and the Iowa Synod in 1854. Although these synods engaged in doctrinal controversy among themselves, the conspicuous leader who influenced them all and who played a large part in the reshaping of American Lutheranism as a whole was Carl F. W. Walther. As his biographer reports, Walther was "easily the most commanding figure in the Lutheran church in America during the nineteenth century." Another scholar has noted that Walther "stood almost alone in the nineteenth century American theological scene as one fully aware of the crucial importance of the problems of Law and Gospel to the Christian faith." In this respect he anticipated "the emphasis of Karl Barth and the 'Luther renaissance' of the next century, but by the same fact he doomed himself to attack and misunderstanding in his own time."[12]

The great wave of German immigration did not leave Lutheranism in the eastern part of the United States unscathed. Not only was pressure exerted by the newer synods in the West, but immigration also altered the theological complexion of the older synods in the East. By the 1850s, even at Gettysburg, Schmucker was displaced in influence by Charles Philip Krauth, who was urging the churches to maintain their fidelity to the traditional Lutheran standards.

The Emergence of African American Denominations

The development of African American Christian religious life from informal communities to institutions moved decisively ahead one Sunday morning in November 1787. While worshiping at St. George's Methodist Church in Philadelphia, Absalom Jones, Richard Allen, and other black members of the congregation were forced by white church trustees from the front rows of the gallery and directed to seating farther back. After a brief consultation, the African American membership as a whole exited the church. Allen subsequently began leading meetings in the blacksmith shop that he purchased. That congregation, which was formed largely out of the Free African Society, was dedicated in 1794 by Bishop Francis Asbury as the Bethel African Church. Five years later Asbury ordained Allen

---

[12] D. H. Stephens, *Carl F. W. Walther* (Philadelphia, 1917), 10; Sydney E. Ahlstrom, "Theology in America," in *The Shaping of American Religion*, eds. J. W. Smith and A. Leland Jamison, 275.

a deacon. By 1803, the Bethel Church had over four hundred members, and two years later the congregation was meeting in a brick building on the corner of Sixth and Lombard Streets.[13] So began the African Methodist Episcopal Church (AME).

The organization of the AME, like the founding of other black denominations, emerged directly out of discrimination practiced by the white membership of the churches. Blacks in many established churches on the eastern seaboard experienced the indignities of second-class citizenship within their own congregations, including the denial of burial in church grounds, segregated seating, reception of communion after whites, and other forms of explicit discrimination. Prior to 1787, Allen, then in his midtwenties, already had voiced his concern over the need for a separate church to be formed from the city's population of 1,600 African Americans, and he had succeeded in persuading several others to consider the possibility. During the late 1780s, prompted by "a love to the people of their complexion whom they beheld with sorrow because of their irreligious and uncivilized state," he explored this option with several other black Methodists, and together they formed the Free African Society as a mutual aid association and parareligious organization. Assisted by Benjamin Rush, the prominent Philadelphia physician and signatory to the Declaration of Independence, the group in 1791 drafted a statement outlining their principles of faith and their plan for church government. The incident in the gallery at St. George's proved to be the flashpoint for action, and the views of white members of the congregation so thoroughly alienated some black worshipers that they decided to leave not only the congregation but also the denomination. In 1794, they formed, just twelve days prior to the dedication of the Bethel church, St. Thomas's Episcopal Church, with Absalom Jones, who was ordained the first black Episcopal priest in the United States, as pastor.[14]

Allen, however, wished to remain within Methodism, and so by degrees he worked toward the realization of a black Methodist denomination. His contact with Daniel Coker, the leader of the Colored Methodist Society formed by blacks who had declared their independence from white churches in Baltimore, encouraged him in this regard. News of Allen's progress in Philadelphia, including a victory in the Pennsylvania Supreme Court that finally ratified the incorporation of the Bethel Church apart

[13] "Some Letters of Richard Allen and Absalom Jones to Dorothy Ripley," *Journal of Negro History* 1 (1916), 441; Will B. Gravely, "African Methodisms and the Rise of Black Denominationalism," in Russell E. Richey and Kenneth E. Rowe, eds., *Rethinking Methodist History: A Bicentennial Historical Consultation* (Nashville, 1985), 111–24; E. Curtis Alexander, *Richard Allen: The First Exemplar of African Methodist Education* (New York, 1985).

[14] Albert J. Raboteau, *A Fire in the Bones: Reflections on African American Church History* (Boston, 1995), 79–102; Gary B. Nash, "New Light on Richard Allen: The Early Years of Freedom," *William and Mary Quarterly*, 3rd. Ser., Vol. 46, No. 2 (Apr., 1989), 332–40.

from St. George's, likewise was warmly received in Baltimore. Allen eventually determined that the problems encountered by black Christians might be addressed in a gathering of delegations from black congregations. On April 7, 1816, representatives from sixteen African American groups, representing congregations that had separated from white churches in New Jersey, Delaware, and Maryland, gathered in Philadelphia. After deliberating about who should lead the church, five ordained ministers, including Absalom Jones, consecrated Allen as bishop of the African Methodist Episcopal Church on April 11.

Several black churches within the Protestant denominations were also organized during this period of time. The first African American Baptist congregation was gathered on the plantation of William Byrd II in Lunenberg, Virginia, in the late 1750s. Though it lasted only a year, it was reorganized in 1772, with the ordination of four black preachers, including three brothers, Moses, Benjamin, and Thomas Gardiner. We have already seen how the black Baptist preacher George Liele organized churches in the 1770s in South Carolina and in Savannah, Georgia. The church in Savannah was reorganized by an ex-slave, Andrew Bryan, in 1788, as the First African Baptist Church; and by the 1830s, it counted over 2,000 members, some slaves and some free blacks. By 1818, The Sunbury Baptist Association, which grew out of the Savannah River Association, included five black churches and six mixed churches. During the Civil War, those black congregations formed the Zion Baptist Association with churches from Florida and South Carolina. The Joy Street Church, the first black Baptist congregation in the northern states, was founded in New York in 1805, and it was followed by the Abyssinian Church in 1807. Black Baptist churches were founded in Philadelphia (1808), Trenton (1812), Wood River, Illinois (1818), and Albany (1821); and associations such as the Providence Baptist Association and the Colored Baptists Association (Illinois) began appearing in the 1830s. In 1807, John Gloucester founded the First African Presbyterian Church in Philadelphia.

Other Christians found white control of denominational life so overbearing that they created, as Richard Allen did, new African American denominations. Peter Spencer, protesting discrimination at the Asbury Methodist Church in Wilmington, formed the Ezion Methodist Church in 1805. Differences intensified with Asbury, and in the midst of legal wrangling, Spencer and his congregation left Asbury completely and formed the Union Church of Africans in 1812. In New York, Peter Williams, George Collins, James Varick, and Christopher Rush organized what would become the African Methodist Episcopal Zion Church. Frustrated by white refusal of voting and preaching status to black members of the congregation, blacks left the John Street Methodist Episcopal Zion Church, gathered separately with the approval of Francis Asbury, and eventually built their own church in 1800. By 1813, the church had divided, the newer congregation calling itself the Asbury Church. William

Stillwell, a white member of the John Street Church, ministered to both groups. In 1821, what would eventually be called the AMEZC (a name officially adopted in 1848) was formally constituted in a gathering of representatives from six black Methodist churches from Philadelphia, Newark, New York, and New Haven. With a white minister presiding over the meeting, the nineteen preachers in attendance ordained James Varick as the first bishop of the church.

The organization of black denominations and the gathering of black congregations was as much a political act as it was a religious movement. In Philadelphia, New York, and other places in the North where blacks had acted boldly to remove themselves from the authority of religious groups that discriminated, the African American clergy challenged slavery openly, criticizing it in statements of church discipline as well as from the pulpit and in publications such as the *Christian Recorder*, the oldest African American newspaper. The black churches likewise condemned immorality of other sorts, with some black clergy supporting temperance and others involving themselves in various reform campaigns. Allen founded the Society of Free People of Color for Promoting the Instruction and School Education of Children of African Descent in 1804, and AMEZ leaders in New York organized a society to aid fugitive slaves. All such activity was in keeping with the early-nineteenth-century impulse—visible across the spectrum of the Protestant denominations—for the reform of society through involvement in the work of voluntary organizations. A vast number of causes, ranging from orphanages to hospitals, young women's improvement clubs to societies for the promotion of virtue, marked the landscape of Protestant public life during this period. The themes of moral reform that emerged within the African American denominations and churches focused on those issues of most concern to blacks.

The initiative and social visions of African American religious groups was not received as simply one more contribution toward the moral improvement of the nation, however. Black leaders were regularly criticized for their public stances, and white legislatures increasingly acted to limit the power of blacks. Typical of such backlash against the perceived rise of black influence were the Black Laws passed in Ohio in 1804 and 1807 that required blacks to provide proof that they were freemen and to post a $500 bond as surety that they would behave in a law-abiding manner. When the city of Cincinnati decided on short notice vigorously to enforce the laws in the next decade, a three-day riot broke out in "Bucktown" that ended in deaths and injuries to both whites and blacks.[15] Racial riots sporadically broke out elsewhere, including in Philadelphia in 1829. The development of fugitive slave laws and the institutionalization of slave patrols in the South darkened the scenario even further, so that in 1830, Hezekiah

---

[15] Eddie S. Glaude, Jr., *Exodus!: Religion, Race, and Nation in Early Nineteenth-Century America* (Chicago, 2000), 112–13.

Grice of Baltimore broached in a letter to black leaders the idea of a national convention. The convention subsequently met in Philadelphia that year, at the Bethel Church, with Richard Allen presiding over the forty attendees.[16]

The 1830 convention was the first organized political gathering of free blacks. Those who attended discussed discrimination, poverty, and the tensions with whites that came with black organizing. The convention ratified the church as the most important institution in black life. Black congregations grew, churches coalesced in their identities as black churches separate from white churches, and linkages between black churches were forged through the ongoing convention movement. Not unexpectedly, black churches also were increasingly a focal point for white criticism of African Americans. And in some cases, the suspicions and fears of whites spilled over into violence. Such was the case at St. Philip's African Episcopal Church in New York, which was destroyed by a mob in July 1834. The 1830 meeting, which inaugurated the nineteenth-century convention movement among African Americans, was a religious and civic enterprise, a "secular adjunct of the black church, an extension into a broader public space of the black religious impulse of self-reliance and social uplift."[17] The convention movement, which organized black activism for a generation of African Americans and which for a while was called the American Moral Reform Society (1835–1842), debated the pros and cons of racial designations in the pages of *The Colored American*, a newspaper founded by African Americans in 1837, and supported an assortment of causes. Preeminent among those causes was abolitionism, and the black leader best known for his abolitionist exhortations within the convention movement was the Presbyterian preacher Henry Highland Garnett. Delegates of the convention movement, gathering in Buffalo, New York, in 1843 for the National Negro Convention, heard Garnett proclaim "let your motto be resistance, resistance, RESISTANCE!" That motto was imported into a host of enterprises within the black churches in the nineteenth century, in both North and South, informing morality at personal and collective levels, as resistance to the temptations of Satan as much as resistance to racism. Hanging like a canopy over much of African American religious life, "resistance" set the tone for black self-determination and the struggle for civil rights in the twentieth century, as it was richly represented by the black clergy in images drawn from Old Testament texts.

Though domestic issues of slavery, discrimination, and economic status drew the majority of the attention of African American voluntary societies, interest in missionary work grew steadily. Lott Carey, an ex-slave, played a role in organizing the Richmond African Baptist Missionary Society in

---

[16] Sally Hadden, *Law Enforcement in a New Nation: Slave Patrols and Public Authority in the Old South, 1700–1865* (Cambridge, Mass., 2001).

[17] Glaude, 113.

1815, and in 1821, he sailed to Liberia. The American Colonization Society (ACS), which was founded late in 1816 for the purpose of raising money to compensate slave-owners and to resettle ex-slaves in Africa, conceived of the community of repatriated slaves as a Christianizing force in Africa. In 1820, the ACS sent Daniel Coker of Baltimore and another ninety blacks to Sierra Leone. While at sea, Coker organized a shipboard branch of the AME Church. The grand missionizing plans of the ACS were never realized, however; and under the criticism of Richard Allen and the abolitionist William Lloyd Garrison, and divided by competing visions, it ceased operating in the 1850s. Up to that time, it nevertheless was responsible for the migration of over ten thousand African Americans to what became known as Liberia. Among the churches there was the First Baptist Church of Monrovia, which was gathered in Virginia in 1821, a few days before the voyage to Africa. John Boggs of the AME arrived in Liberia in 1824, the first step in what eventually became a larger church effort in the 1840s and afterward, when the General Conference of the AME church established the Parent Home and Foreign Missionary Society. All of these efforts spent in organizing missions were slow in realizing their potential. It was not until Reconstruction that African Americans turned more determinedly to missionary activity in Africa. As one historian has observed, "After 1870, black Americans could not resist the call for African missionaries."[18]

Despite all the pioneering achievements of men within the black churches, it was often the case that women performed the crucial work of organizing the "mutual benefit societies," the voluntary associations that oversaw the welfare of black communities on the local and everyday level. The aid societies were closely intertwined with the churches, as we have seen in the case of the Free African Society, which formed the St. Thomas Episcopal Church in Philadelphia. The mission of the Free African Society to the community was not lost with the founding of the church, however. It was reconstituted as the Female Benevolent Society of St. Thomas, and, together with the American Female Bond Benevolent Society of Bethel (1817), the Daughters of Aaron (1819), the Daughters of Africa (1812), and other black associations, it shaped networks of mutual aid that profoundly influenced black social experience. The membership of African American mutual aid societies in Philadelphia—of which there were over a hundred by 1838—was two-thirds women, and as these societies continued to emerge out of the black churches, they served as a focal point of women's involvement in the community and as a framework for female leadership. In the first few decades of the nineteenth century, women built networks of societies throughout the North. The female Wesleyan Association of Baltimore, the Abyssinian Benevolent daughters of Esther in New

---

[18] Sylvia M. Jacobs, "The Historical Role of Afro-Americans in American Missionary Efforts in Africa," in *Black Americans and the Missionary Movement in Africa*, ed. Sylvia M. Jacobs (Westport, Conn., 1982), 17.

York, and the Colored Female Charitable Society of Boston engaged in various sorts of care-related activities in those cities. Some, such as the African Dorcas Association, founded in New York in 1827 to provide clothing to black schoolchildren, had a specific focus. Religious and moral concerns were always at the center of such societies' business, however. The Colored Female Religious and Moral Society of Salem, Massachusetts, was committed to prayer and religious reading as well as to sickness and death benefits; and the New Orleans Colored Benevolent Society of Louisiana in its 1846 charter declared itself for "the suppression of vice and inculcation of virtue among the colored class" as well as its intention to furnish insurance to the community. The centrality of these societies to African Americans cannot be overestimated. After the Civil War, they proliferated in black communities in the North and South, so that by the end of the nineteenth century, they were so ubiquitous as to lead W. E. B. Du Bois to observe that "the woman who is not a member of one of these [benevolent societies] is pitied and considered rather out of date."[19] One of the most successful of those African American female benevolent societies was the Order of St. Luke, which was founded in 1867 by Mary Prout, an ex-slave, and ably administrated by Maggie Lena Walker. With over 100,000 members in twenty-eight states by 1920, it included a bank; a weekly newspaper; a department store; a girls' scholarship program; and a long record of battling for suffrage, racial equality, and other causes of deep concern to African Americans and women.[20]

Some African American women entered into community service in more formally religious fashion, as Roman Catholic nuns. The first of these orders was the Oblate Sisters of Providence, a congregation that grew out of the need for the religious instruction of black children in the Baltimore area. In 1793, there were over fifteen thousand black Roman Catholics in Maryland. When in July of that year, another five hundred fleeing the revolution in Haiti and San Domingo joined them, the local Sulpician priest, Jacques Joubert, decided to mount a campaign to teach the refugees and others to read. Joubert, who was serving at St. Mary's Seminary in Baltimore, taught Sunday school to blacks and eventually proposed to Elizabeth Lange, Frances Balis, and Miss Bogue that they form a religious group devoted to the education of girls. In 1829, after advancing by degrees to formally authorized Roman Catholic Sisterhood, the three took vows, with Lange assuming the role of Mother Superior of the Order. St. Frances Academy, their school, initially enrolled twenty-four girls. Students from Washington, D. C., and Philadelphia boarded at the school, and together with students from Baltimore, the school counted annually

---

[19] Quoted in Walter Weare, "Mutual Benefit Societies," in *Black Women in America: Religion in America*, ed. Darlene Clark Hine (New York, 1997), 136–41.

[20] Ibid., 140.

between fifty and a hundred pupils who learned arithmetic, English, penmanship, religion, and housekeeping. The school thrived, and the Order broadened its mission after 1900, eventually operating elementary and secondary schools in thirteen states, Cuba, and Costa Rica.[21]

The Sisters of the Holy Family, founded by Henriette Delille in New Orleans in 1842, was the largest of the three orders of black nuns. Delille, who was descended from free black families in Louisiana, was educated by nuns, and in part because of the example of one of them, she was determined to organize an order of religious women "to teach and to do whatever other social work was needed, such as caring for the aged and orphaned."[22] Delille's vision ran against the grain of expectations for women in New Orleans, where only white women were thought of as candidates for membership in a religious order. Her determination to see the congregation recognized sustained her through seventeen years, leading up to the official founding of the sisterhood. By the time of the Civil War, the community numbered six nuns, but rapid growth in the latter part of the nineteenth century—as the order expanded its reach to other parts of the state—led in the twentieth century to a string of educational institutions across the South from Florida to California. Other black women's religious congregations founded in the nineteenth century, such as the Franciscan Handmaids of Mary, also contributed to the welfare of African Americans. And people in Roman Catholic towns that were founded by blacks across the country, from California (Nuestra Sonora de Los Angeles, 1781), to Florida (Gracia Real de Santa Theresa de Mose, 1784), and as far north as New York and Illinois, organized their lives in similar fashion, with women taking a leading role in educating children and knitting together the matrices of mutual support that sustained those communities.

The Female Majority

The involvement of African American women in religiously based missions of welfare and teaching in black communities was one part of a broadening of women's religious and social activism that gathered momentum in the nineteenth century. Already by 1817, the General Assembly of the Presbyterian Church had observed, "It is among the distinguished glories of the commencement of the nineteenth century, that PIOUS Females are more extensively associated and more actively useful in promoting evangelical and benevolent objects, than in any former period of the world."

---

[21] Theresa A. Rector, "The Impact of Black Women in Education: An Historical Overview," in *Journal of Negro Education*, Vol. 51, No. 3 (Summer, 1982), 240–44; Gloria Marrow, "Oblate Sisters of Providence," in Hine, ed., 175–76.

[22] Quoted in Rector, 246.

The sudden visibility of women was less a matter of an unexpected surge in the involvement of women in religious work, than it was an instance of male leadership glancing out from behind its patriarchal blinders for a moment to see what was actually happening in the churches.[23] As historian Ann Braude has explained, religion in America has been characterized by the involvement of the "female majority," who have done the work of religion at the same time that they have been excluded from much religious life, as well as from the offices and roles associated with institutional leadership and community influence. In short, women have

> made religious institutions possible by providing audiences for preaching, participants for rituals, the material and financial support for religious buildings, and, perhaps most important, by inculcating faith in their children to provide the next generation of participants. There could be no lone man in the pulpit without the mass of women who fill the pews. There would be no clergy, no seminaries to train them, no theology to teach them, and no hierarchies to ordain them, unless women supported all of these institutions from which they historically have been excluded.

For Braude, "American religious history is founded on a paradox: its institutions have relied for their existence on the very group they have disenfranchised."[24]

Women created over the course of several centuries in North America various ways in which to exercise some form of initiative, some means by which to make possible their participation in religious communities. In some cases, they succeeded through sheer determination in claiming authority vested in formal roles and offices within their denominations. We have seen how African American women founded orders of nuns. White women did the same: Elizabeth Bayley Seton, for example, began the Sisters of Charity in 1809. But as they were excluded from positions of authority and leadership in both church and civil government, women shared "informal" public space with men, and increasingly turned in the early nineteenth century towards the formation of counterpublics—that is, they formed associations that represented their own public life in ways ambiguously related to institutional structures that were dominated by males in the masculinized "public realm."[25] Such associations might be prayer groups, local aid societies, mothers' clubs, children's welfare alliances, or

[23] Quoted in Lois A. Boyd and R. Douglas Brackenridge, *Presbyterian Women in America: Two Centuries of a Quest for Status* (Westport, Conn., 1996), 3.

[24] Ann Braude, "Women's History *Is* American Religious History," in *Retelling U.S. Religious History*, ed. Thomas A. Tweed (Berkeley, 1997), 89, 90.

[25] See Mary Ryan, *Women in Public: Between Banners and Ballots, 1825–1880* (Baltimore, 1990), and *Civil Wars: Democracy and Public Life in the American City during the Nineteenth Century* (Berkeley, 1997); Linda K. Kerber, Nancy F. Cott, Robert Gross, Lynn Hunt, Carroll Smith-Rosenberg, and Christine Stansell, "Beyond Roles, Beyond Spheres: Thinking About Gender in the Early Republic," *William and Mary Quarterly* 46 (July, 1989), 565–85.

other benevolent organizations. Such activity was visible in both Protestant and Roman Catholic churches, and in Jewish communities as well: Jewish congregations in Cincinnati, for example, founded the Ladies Benevolent Society in 1838, the German Ladies Benevolent Society in 1842, and the German Ladies Relief Society in 1850.[26] Such organizations offered various kinds of relief to needy persons in the community. More far-ranging, in geographic terms as well as in terms of women's progress in entering a public domain traditionally overseen by men, were women's involvements in missionary societies, which led to a large-scale women's missionary movement in the latter part of the century. The rapid increase in the number of women missionaries after midcentury—half of the missionaries commissioned were women—set the stage for the founding of the Women's Union Missionary Society (1861) by Sarah R. Doremus, the Women's Board of Missions (1869), and a host of denominational and regional women's missionary societies during and after the Civil War. But even cast as missionary work, the public role of women in antebellum America was grounded in irony. That role was made possible by their willingness to efface themselves, or, as historian Amanda Porterfield has observed, "humility and self sacrifice provided antebellum women an avenue to public life." And it followed that "while women's proficiency in humility and self sacrifice justified their place on a larger, more public stage, it also limited the degree to which they could enjoy and capitalize upon their success."[27] Some women served as missionaries overseas, but domestic missionizing, conceived as the Christianizing of America, remained the focus of females preparing to serve the cause of religion. So, when Mary Lyon founded Mount Holyoke Female Seminary in 1836, she anticipated that some graduates would travel across the globe, and many did so, to Persia, India, Ceylon, Hawaii, and Africa. Many more stayed in America to teach virtue, shape the moral sensibilities of children and men, and reform society.

Lyon's Mount Holyoke was not the only female seminary. Before the Civil War, many such institutions were begun for the education of women, ranging from Troy Female Seminary in New York, founded by Emma Willard in 1821, to the Female Institute of the Seminary West of the Sewanee, in Florida, in 1858. The best of them, such as Troy or Mount Holyoke, taught science, mathematics, and history alongside theology, conversational French, and other subjects traditionally a part of the education of women. But the founding of such seminaries was not in response to a sudden need for women ministers, nor did their founding lead to a change in the formal status of women within the Protestant churches. Trained in theology, knowledgeable of doctrine, educated in history and science, and able to speak

[26] See Karla Goldman, "The Public Religious Lives of Cincinnati's Jewish Women," in *Women and American Judaism: Historical Perspectives*, eds. Pamela S. Nadell and Jonathan D. Sarna (Hanover N. H., 2001), 107–27.

[27] Amanda Porterfield, *Mary Lyon and the Mount Holyoke Missionaries* (New York, 1997), 6.

before an audience, the graduates of the seminaries were not ordained. They sometimes served in auxiliary posts within church organizations, but for all of their training, they did not make inroads into the ministry. Men controlled the ministry, and they actively excluded women from it.

Women's efforts to obtain denominational authorization to preach initially was not linked to formal education. Rather, women claimed a "call" to preach, a vision or an inspiration leading them to the pulpit, or, more commonly, to the center of a room, a spot under a tree, or the back of a wagon. Until the 1840s, evangelical female preachers tended to be from the lower or lower-middle class, rarely boasted educational credentials, and addressed their auditors in an emotional, spontaneous style. As Catherine Brekus has written, "female preachers were no more refined in their speech or gestures than the men. . . . Aiming their sermons at ordinary workers and farmwives, they cultivated a colloquial, even crude style that shocked middle-class sensibilities."[28] They preached pointedly for religious conversions, and they utilized whatever means they thought fit to excite the affections of their audiences and to provoke them to religious experiences.

Nancy Towle began her nondenominational ministry following a dream that she believed God had given her, that she would "one day become religious, and bear testimony to the word of God's grace over the earth." During the 1820s and 1830s, as an itinerant preacher, she addressed audiences of men and women in formal settings such as churches or schoolhouses, as well as in fields and homes. Preaching like a man—that is, claiming the authority that had been reserved exclusively for men—she spoke from the pulpit and responded to those who criticized her "masculine" style by upbraiding them for their small-mindedness and conceit. Challenging deep-rooted traditions of male religious authority, Towle anticipated a future in which "female warriors," raised up by God, would carry the battle to those who sought to diminish the social and religious status of women. Abigail Roberts, a well-known preacher in New York and New Jersey in the early nineteenth century, was so effective a public speaker that four Christian Connection churches were formed out of converts in her meetings. Raised as a Quaker, she became an evangelical Christian and sometimes presided at meetings that included both Quakers and evangelicals. The Christian Connection was a primitivist movement that sought to restore the practice of Christianity to the ways in which it was depicted in the New Testament. Some female preachers in the denomination—which included Charlotte Hestes, Rachel Macomber, Deborah Pierce, Sabrina Lambson, Abigail Stone, Elizabeth Stiles, Sally Waldren, and Hannah Peavey Cogswell—as well as female preachers in other denominations, looked to Quakers and certain popular male itinerants such as Lorenzo Dow for models on how to conduct themselves as religious leaders. Quaker women spoke in meet-

[28] Catherine A. Brekus, *Female Preaching in America: Strangers and Pilgrims, 1740–1845* (Chapel Hill N. C., 1998), 199.

ings, when called by God to do so, and though silence was also valued among Quakers, female involvement in the public worship was considerably more in evidence than in most other denominations. The influence of that model was seen in the fact that evangelical women preachers tended to adopt the simple gowns and bonnets worn by Quaker women. At the same time, women cultivated the preaching style of Dow and David Marks, less concerned for the good order of the meeting than in pursuing whatever options presented themselves as means to effect conversions.[29]

Dreams, visions, and callings of various sorts grounded many women's determination to preach in the early nineteenth century. Women's authority was reinforced, in many cases, by demonstrations of their abilities as leaders. Mother Ann Lee, the Shaker leader who came to America in 1774, was known for her commanding voice, ability to see spirits, prophecies, and healings. Her followers recalled that "so great was the manifestation of the power of God in Mother . . . that many were unable to abide in her presence. Her words were like flames of fire and her voice like peals of thunder." Like many other women, she had experienced a vision that led her to theological innovation, including the notion of a masculine-feminine deity. But those who were drawn to her remembered her charisma, her public performances of preaching, as being overwhelmingly dramatic and commanding, compelling to both men and women.[30] In the early nineteenth century, women such as Harriet Livermore, Jarena Lee, and Abigail Roberts followed in the footsteps of Mother Ann Lee. They began their ministries on the basis of calls that they experienced to preach, and over time they solidified their authority through their effectiveness as preachers, earning the respect and support of many clergymen, even while the leadership of the larger denominations resisted their entry into the ranks of those formally ordained or commissioned.

Only a few women were accepted into the clergy. The first of these was Antoinette Brown, who was fully ordained in the Congregational Church in Butler, New York, in 1853. But none followed her until late in the nineteenth century, and even then with difficulty. Anna Howard Shaw, who in 1889 was the first woman ordained by the Methodist Protestant Church, had her ordination revoked, subsequently found a local conference willing to defy the ruling of the General Conference, and finally resigned her Massachusetts pulpit in 1885. Eventually she became the president of the National American Woman's Suffrage Association, where she served from 1904 to 1915. One hundred years later, in 1980, Marjorie Matthews was elected by the United Methodists as their first woman bishop. But the road from Shaw to Matthews was complicated, gradual, and marked by frequent setbacks in the cause for female clergy.

---

[29] Ibid., 5, 182–3, 197, 198–9, 202, 343–346.

[30] Jean M. Humez, ed., *Mother's First-Born Daughters: Early Shaker Writings on Women and Religion* (Bloomington, Ind., 1993), 18, 19–38.

Antebellum Roman Catholicism

Unlike Judaism, whose adherents were not greatly augmented numerically until after the Civil War, Roman Catholicism experienced steady growth after the Revolution. Prior to Independence, Roman Catholics were a small minority, many of them landed gentry, concentrated almost exclusively in Maryland and Pennsylvania. The Quebec Act of 1774 had placed the territory between the Ohio and the Mississippi Rivers within the province of Quebec; this placement aroused ill feeling among some ardent patriots who regarded it as evidence that the British government was ready to surrender this vast inland empire to Roman Catholicism, and it was used as a religious issue to whip up anti-British feeling. By the end of the Revolution, however, apprehensions thus generated had been largely forgotten. Charles Carroll had rallied his coreligionists in Maryland to the colonial cause, and Irish Catholics in Pennsylvania had demonstrated their unwillingness to dishonor the memory of their fathers by any hesitancy to fight the English. This display of loyalty, along with French military support, allayed former suspicions, and the birth of the Republic ushered in an era of more genial relations.

The Roman Catholic Church in the colonies had been under the jurisdiction of the Vicar Apostolic in London; however, Independence made this arrangement inappropriate. In 1784, John Carroll, a cousin of Charles Carroll, was appointed "superior of the missions" with full responsibility to direct the affairs of the church in the United States, and six years later he was elevated to episcopal rank. In 1808, the diocese of Baltimore was given metropolitan status with Carroll as archbishop.

In the new Republic, the Catholic Church experienced many growing pains. The number of adherents mounted rapidly, partly as the result of the acquisition of older settlements along the Mississippi but more largely a consequence of new immigration from Ireland and southern Germany. Tension between older members and more recent arrivals was often acute, and this situation complicated the task of maintaining an orderly development of church life. The installation of refugee priests from France as pastors of Irish congregations also aroused resentment.

"Lay trustees" posed one of the more serious problems. Many churches in America had been vexed by the self-assertiveness of the laity, and the Roman Catholic Church was no exception. In the immediate postwar years, Americans in general were especially conscious of their "rights" and "liberties," and they were determined not to be pushed around. The effect of this pervasive spirit upon Roman Catholics was explained by Archbishop Ambrose Marechal of Baltimore in 1818:

> The American people pursue with a most ardent love the civil liberty which
> they enjoy. For the principle of civil liberty is paramount with them, so that

absolutely all the magistrates from the highest to the lowest are elected by popular vote. . . . Likewise all the Protestant sects . . . are governed by these same principles, and as a result they elect and dismiss their pastors at will. Catholics in turn, living in their midst, are . . . exposed to the danger of admitting the same principles of ecclesiastical government.[31]

Not only were they exposed to the danger, but also many succumbed to it. As early as 1786, the trustees of St. Peter's Church in New York City asserted their right to choose and dismiss their pastor, and three years later the congregation of Holy Trinity Church in Philadelphia followed the example of St. Peter's in choosing their own pastor. Similar acts of disobedience occurred elsewhere. A congregation at Norfolk went so far as to assert that the bishop, according to the "civil rights and religious liberties" guaranteed by the laws of Virginia, had no authority to interfere in the affairs of any congregation or in "any of their religious matters whatever." Even where overt defiance was absent, chronic friction was frequent. It was not until the custody of property was transferred to the bishops that the situation was finally regularized.

The flood of Roman Catholic immigrants constituted the greatest problem of the church during these years. No fewer than one million immigrants of Roman Catholic background arrived in the United States between 1790 and 1850. Had it not been for extensive assistance from abroad in the form of both funds and personnel, the task of ministering to these new Americans would have been completely impossible. As early as 1791, the French Sulpicians founded St. Mary's Seminary in Baltimore to provide training for a native priesthood, but throughout the nineteenth century, major reliance had to be placed upon men sent from Europe. The religious orders rendered notable service, especially in the field of education. Colleges, academies, and parochial schools were established. By 1840, there were at least two hundred parochial schools, staffed in part by American sisterhoods that had been growing in number since 1800. The controversy over tax support for parochial schools that was to agitate the life of the nation for more than a century was initiated in 1840 when Bishop John Hughes of New York petitioned for Roman Catholics to be given a proportionate share of New York City public education funds for their parochial schools.

The consolidation of authority within Catholicism in the Republic was significantly advanced by the First Provincial Council, held in Baltimore in 1829. Catholics of English descent had controlled the development of institutional life from that most powerful of American dioceses, and during the council they attempted to extend further their authority by requiring

---

[31] J. T. Ellis, ed., *Documents of American Catholic History* (Milwaukee, 1955), 219. For a discerning account of the tensions, see James Hennesey, "Square Peg in a Round Hole," *Records of the American Catholic Historical Society of Philadelphia* (1973), 167–95.

priests who belonged to religious orders to submit to the authority of local bishops. Bishops were also given the deeds to all church property. Measures were passed organizing record-keeping, and efforts were made to enforce a uniform catechism. In the wake of the council, the bishops met every three years in order to determine ways in which to foster uniformity within American Catholicism. Those efforts were important, as ethnic differences made more visible by increasing immigration posed the constant threat of factionalizing the church.

Between 1776 and 1820, the Roman Catholic population grew from a community of 25,000 served by 23 priests, to approximately 160,000, including 122 priests and 208 nuns. About half of the Catholic population lived in the Baltimore diocese, but the other eight dioceses were growing rapidly. Well over a hundred Catholic churches served as focal points for the Catholic communities across the nation by 1820, and many more were added as new territories were annexed (Louisiana Purchase [1803]; Texas [1845]; Oregon Territory [1848]; and Mexican Cession [1848]). Such annexations sometimes illustrated important differences in Catholic styles. When Jean-Baptiste Lamy was appointed to the new diocese of Santa Fe in 1853, he struggled to coordinate the Spanish and Mexican traditions of the membership there with his own French-flavored Catholicism. The ongoing efforts of Catholic leadership—in their triennial meetings, in establishing seminaries and schools, in supporting the development of religious orders geared to particular forms of service, and in imposing catechetical and ritual uniformity on the national membership—gradually acquired the momentum necessary to unify in important ways a relatively understaffed church that was spread out over a vast land. But differences remained, and these would take the form, throughout the nineteenth and twentieth centuries, not only of liturgical and devotional variation but also as divergent ways of thinking about the relation of laity to clergy, and of American Catholicism to Rome. In some cases, the solutions to such problems represented the embrace of the principles of republicanism, as in the case of John England, who was installed as the bishop of Charleston in 1820. In the interest of definitively negotiating a common understanding of the nature of authority within his diocese, he offered to the clergy and laity in 1823 a constitution that provided for the election of lay trustees in the parishes and that established a practice of annual meetings between clergy, trustees, and other laity to discuss church affairs. Those meetings, as far as England was concerned, were grounded in an understanding that "the laity are empowered to cooperate but not dominate." The annual meetings continued until England's death in 1842, a sign of the trust that they built between the various parties involved.[32]

---

[32] Quoted in Jay P. Dolan, "The Search for an American Catholicism, 1780–1820," in *Religious Diversity and American History: Studies in Traditions and Cultures*, Walter H. Conser, Jr., and Sumner B. Twiss, eds. (Athens, Ga., 1997), 44.

In Baltimore and in some other places, there was resistance to incorporating a republican ethos into the emergent Catholic Church in America. Ambrose Maréchal became the archbishop of Baltimore in 1817. As we have seen, he embraced the Tridentine Catholic tradition (that is, the style of Catholicism established by the Council of Trent in the mid–sixteenth century) of a hierarchy of authority that left little role for the laity. Maréchal opposed John England's innovations in Charleston, condemning them as "democratic," and he urged a return to a monarchical model of church authority. The case was similar in Kentucky, where Stephen Badin, a Frenchmen ordained to the priesthood in America in 1793, worked with the three French bishops in the state to centralize authority and to shape a Catholic piety grounded in a strict French Catholic morality. That morality shared much with the evangelical Protestantism of the region—an aversion to dancing, frivolous entertainments, and luxury, and also a deep sense of human sinfulness. And although not all Catholics in Kentucky were comfortable with the French model, enough eventually embraced it so as to make possible a degree of religious understanding across denominations—in terms of morality if not in terms of church government—that might otherwise have been more difficult.[33]

By 1865, there were 3.5 million Catholics in the United States, and Catholicism was the largest denomination. If Bishop John England was correct, in estimating in 1836 that 3.75 million American Catholics had left the church, we might venture that a residue of Catholic culture influenced a great many more people than was reflected in parish membership rosters.[34] The influence of English Catholics, who earlier had presided over the development of American Catholicism from their base in Maryland, declined. The predominant Catholic groups were now the Irish and the Germans. The shift was represented most visibly in the appointment of the Irish-born Francis P. Kenrick as the archbishop of Baltimore in 1851. The rising number of conversions likewise changed the character of the church, and in significant ways in some locales. Tens of thousands of converts in the decades leading up to the Civil War, including many from the Unitarian and Episcopal churches and a fair number of socially prominent and educated persons, significantly broadened the cultural base of Catholicism. Among those converts were Elizabeth Bayley Seton, who, as we have seen, founded the Sisters of Charity; Orestes A. Brownson, whose pilgrimage led him from Presbyterianism into the Universalist and then the Unitarian ministry before he became a Roman Catholic in 1844; and Isaac Hecker, a colleague of Brownson at Brook Farm, who became the founder of the Paulist Fathers.[35]

---

[33] Ibid., 46.

[34] Debra Campbell, "Catholicism from Independence to World War I," in *The Encyclopedia of the American Religious Experience*, eds. Charles H. Lippy and Peter W. Williams, vol. 1 (New York, 1988), 364.

[35] Campbell, 364–5.

Jewish Communities

Judaism grew slowly in the new nation, hindered by a shortage of rabbis and complicated by the competition between Jews from Spain (Sephardim) and those who immigrated from Central and Eastern Europe (Ashkenazim). Intermarriage, a practice forced upon Jews by the shortage of prospective Jewish spouses, especially in westerly regions, likewise affected the development of Judaism in America, particularly in view of the fact that the children of intermarried Jews tended to identify as Protestants.[36]

In 1800, the Jewish population was 1,600. By 1860, it had grown to 150,000, or about one-half of a percent of an overall American population of 31 million. Immigrant Jews from Central Europe often began as peddlers—a line of work that did not require large inventory or warehousing of items because the peddler carried his wares on his back—with funds provided by Jewish congregations. In the large seabord cities as well as in places such as Albany and Rochester, Cleveland, Milwaukee, and St. Louis, Jewish entrepreneurs often developed larger retail businesses in collaboration with other members of the community. Some of those businesses grew into department stores such as Gimbel's, Filene's, Sears and Roebuck, Neiman Marcus, Bloomingdale's, Altman's, and others. Jewish settlers in Cincinnati, who supported five synagogues by the 1850s, made the city a center of garment manufacturing.[37]

The development of the Jewish community in Cincinnati illustrates the manner in which Reform Judaism came to occupy a central place in antebellum American Judaism. As Jews moved westward with other settlers, they naturally found themselves increasingly detached from the synagogue life of the urban centers of the eastern seaboard. Typical of this predicament, and illustrative of frontier solutions to it, is the case of Joseph Jonas, who came to the United States from England and then made the two-month migration to Cincinnati in 1817. He soon managed to persuade two of his brothers and two male friends to join him there, and in 1819, these formed a *minyan*, that is, a group (Hebrew: *number*) of Jewish males sufficiently large to hold Sabbath services. Little did it matter that Jewish law required a quorum of ten males for a *minyan*; on the frontier, pioneers made adjustments. Five years later, the Jewish population of Cincinnati had grown large enough to justify a congregation, Bene Israel. That congregation, and especially the German Jewish B'nai Jeshurun, which was gathered in 1840, having been formed in circum-

---

[36] Abraham J. Karp, "The Emergence of an American Judaism," in Lippy and Williams, eds., vol. 1, 274.

[37] Gerald Sorin, *Tradition Transformed: The Jewish Experience in America* (Baltimore, 1997), 22–3, 27.

stances that required innovation, were understandably receptive to reform when Isaac Meyer Wise, who has been described as "master architect" of Reform Judaism in America, arrived in the city in the 1850s.[38] At B'nai Jeshurun, Wise embarked on a sweeping plan for change within Judaism. Borrowing from the Reform movement in Europe and by adapting European ideas to the American context, Wise succeeded in forging a consensus among the various American Jewish congregations that had been experimenting with reform. (The Beth Elohim congregation in Charleston, South Carolina, had begun debating broad reform as early as 1824.) His most important contribution was the *Minhag America*, the "American Rite" Jewish prayer book that he completed in 1857 and that many congregations adopted. Under Wise's leadership, synagogues in various parts of the country took a more pragmatic approach to their religion, choosing to pray in English or German rather than Hebrew, to abandon distinctive Jewish dress, relax dietary laws, and to downplay the notions of Messiah and return to Zion. For Wise and those who followed him, America was Zion, and in this Zion, the nation's capital, Washington, D.C., became the equivalent of Jerusalem. Accordingly, Wise opposed the establishing of an independent Jewish state in Palestine. But Wise insisted on the centrality to Jewish life of the divine revelation to Moses, and he frequently and openly criticized Christian theology and the efforts of Christian evangelicals to convert Jews. His view was that "there is but one revelation, that at Sinai, and that all men must return to it in the end, Christians as well as Jews."[39]

Other Jews also articulated their frustrations with Christian efforts to convert them. Mordecai Manuel Noah, a thoroughly Americanized Jew born in Philadelphia, attempted to establish a refuge for Jews on an island in the Niagara River, in New York, in 1825. He envisioned the island, which he named "Ararat," as a place where Jews could escape Christian proselytizing. Although his experiment failed to attract followers, he remained a leading figure in the Jewish attempt to understand and to explain to others the differences and similarities between Judaism and Christianity. Unlike Wise, he argued for the restoration of the Jews to Palestine, and he challenged Christians who looked forward to the coming of a divinely ordained millennial era to cooperate in that project of restoration as way of hastening the events called for in the timetable of cosmic events. He challenged a Christian audience in such a way, proposing, "why not ask yourself the great and cardinal question whether it is

[38] Moshe Davis, "Jewish Religious Life and Institutions in America," in *The Jews: Their History, Culture, and Religion*, ed. Louis Finkelstein, vol. 1 (Philadelphia : Jewish Publication Society of America, 1949), 366.

[39] Quoted in Egal Feldman, *Dual Destinies: The Jewish Encounter with Protestant America* (Urbana, Ill., 1990), 80; Max Dimont, *The Jews in America: The Roots, History, and Destiny of American Jews* (New York, 1978), 124–5; Karp, vol. 1, 275.

not your duty to aid in restoring the chosen people as Jews to their promised land?"[40]

Reform leaders believed that Judaism should be democratized, or "Americanized." Some who were more traditionalist, such as Isaac Leeser of Congregation Micveh Israel in Philadelphia, also recognized the necessity of incorporating certain aspects of American culture into Judaism. In their endeavors to bring about change—in whatever fashion and to whatever extent they variously envisioned—they all embraced hope for a united American Jewry. Judaism, however, proved to be too diverse for them to make much progress in realizing that vision. In the first place, ethnic differences remained strong through the antebellum period. The Ashkenazim who came to America were not only from Germany. Some were from Holland—where many Jews had gone after their expulsion from the Iberian peninsula in 1492—and others from England and Poland. In New York City, which had a Jewish population of about three hundred in 1825, there were by the late 1840s synagogues specifically oriented toward differing German, Dutch, and Polish Ashkenazic traditions, in addition to the original Sephardic Shearith Israel congregation. Differences were also apparent between immigrants who arrived in the later part of the antebellum period and those Ashkenazim who had migrated earlier in the century. The former tended to be more educated and better informed about Jewish tradition. And there were differences among the Reformers, as well. Wise, for all of his determination to Americanize Judaism, was unwilling to go as far as was David Einhorn of Baltimore, an ideologically keen rabbi who had been educated in Bavaria, whose declarations for Radical Reform lost him a succession of posts in Germany. Einhorn opposed Wise's every step toward uniting American Jews under the banner of a moderately reformed worship. Wise was at the same time criticized by traditionalists for too far-reaching reform. In the midst of such debate and differences, plans to form national associations of Jews proved too difficult to implement. Such organizational activity would not bear fruit until later in the century.

Rationalists, Scientists, and Transcendentalists

The emergence of Deism in the eighteenth century, as we have seen, was fueled by Enlightenment theories about knowledge and claims for the capability of human reason. The empirically oriented worldview of much of the Enlightenment supported departures from the authority of religious revelation. Just as the laws of the universe—eternal and immutable—were

---

[40] Quoted in Feldman, 77; Jonathan D. Sarna, *Jacksonian Jew: The Two Worlds of Mordecai Noah* (New York, 1981).

perceptible through the cultivation and exercise of reason, so too were the moral laws of the universe available to human scrutiny. Laws of gravity, motion, and thermodynamics, as well as the rules of virtue, justice, and compassion, were aspects of an interlocking cosmic network of phenomena grounded in a divine plan for the universe. The Deistic reliance upon the power of reason as a guide to morality—and the hopes of Deists such as Thomas Paine and Thomas Jefferson for the achievements of reason— were represented in the literature, architecture, and art of the period after the War of Independence.

Jefferson's editing of the Bible represents the spirit of this rationalistic religion. In *The Life and Morals of Jesus* (ca. 1819), Jefferson strung together excerpts from the Gospels that illustrated, as far as he was concerned, the most valuable lessons of the Bible. He emphasized historical and moral narratives in the Gospels—stories about Jesus as moral teacher and exemplar—while omitting references to miracles, resurrection of the body, and other accounts that he considered corruptions or embellishments of historical events. For Jefferson, religion was properly about the practical business of moral life, not about transcendence, supernaturalism, or the nonrational. Jefferson accordingly was suspicious of institutional religion, of organized Christianity, because it violated the canons of natural philosophy and fostered dangerous enthusiasms, superstitions, fear, and guilt. Arguing that if the "mere Abracadabra" of the "priests of Jesus" could be translated into terms understandable through reason, the priests themselves would be far from satisfied, because "their security is in their faculty of shedding darkness, like the scuttle fish, thro' the element in which they move, and making it impenetrable to the eye of a pursuing enemy (i.e. an octopus inking the water). And there they will skulk, until some rational creed can occupy the void which the obliteration of their duperies would leave in the minds of our honest and unsuspecting brethren."[41] Jefferson's advocacy of freedom of religion was grounded in such a view of clerical leadership as potentially duplicitous as much as it was in his understanding of the necessity for civil freedoms in a democratic republic. He nevertheless did not hesitate to make impressive mention of God in some of his most important writings, and, upholding the rights of his fellow citizens to practice their religion as they pleased, he recognized the positive influence of organized religion in the moral society.

Deism lost most of its momentum as a formal religious option in the first two decades of the nineteenth century. But the ideas and moods that it embodied were carried along in a variety of ways throughout the antebellum period. The development of science in America made discussion of Enlightenment theories about the working of the universe a regular occurrence in newspapers and magazines, and, as the public became more engaged in that discourse, in pulpits and lecture halls as well. Although that

---

[41] Thomas Jefferson to Francis Adrian Van der Kamp, 30 July 1816.

science was not yet what science would become by the twenty-first century, throughout its development as various methods and theories—some successful, others failed—it served as a constant provocation to American religious writers and practitioners to come to terms with the Enlightenment. It was through engagement with science, both as laboratory discovery and as armchair interpretation, that rank-and-file American religionists eventually were forced to think about the reliability of revelation, of doctrines of the supernatural, and of what lay beyond the grave. The controversy and enthusiastic public debate that accompanied the publication of Charles Darwin's *On The Origin of Species* in 1859 revealed the power of the evolutionary theory to focus the attention of Americans on those issues. But that book is best seen as the exclamation to several decades of ongoing, and at time inflamed, discussions among Americans about reason and revelation, religion and science.

One of the most important of the various movements that incorporated select rationalist elements into religion, and one that eventually came to form a major part the religious legacy of the Enlightenment, was Transcendentalism. Beginning as the "Transcendental Club" that met in the Boston home of Unitarian pastor George Ripley, it included clergymen Ralph Waldo Emerson, Theodore Parker, James Freeman Clarke, Frederic Henry Hedge, William Ellery Channing, and Orestes Brownson. They were ably abetted by several influential lay recruits, such as Bronson Alcott, Henry David Thoreau, Margaret Fuller, and Elizabeth Palmer Peabody. Repelled by what they regarded as the cold logic of their Unitarian elders and deeply influenced by Samuel Taylor Coleridge's *Aids to Reflection*, the Transcendentalists sought to reconcile the rationalism of their fathers with the romanticism of their age by introducing a strong note of mysticism into Unitarian formulations.[42]

Since they were eclectic in their approach to truth, it is difficult to characterize the Transcendentalists. No two of them agreed at every point; and although some exhibited intense individualism, others displayed a passionate zeal for communal life. James Freeman Clarke on one occasion suggested that their group might be called "the Club of the Like-Minded" because "no two of us thought alike." They were, nonetheless, bound together by what they called "the spiritual principle"—a principle that was articulated in three major agreements: an insistence upon divine immanence, a dependence upon intuitive perception of truth, and a rejection of all external authority. Every created thing had deep religious meaning, and they found "sermons not just in stones but in bean rows at Walden Pond and mud puddles on Boston Common." They were called Transcendentalists, said Ripley, because they believed "in an order of truths which transcends the sphere of the external senses." Since "the truth of religion

---

[42] William R. Hutchinson, *The Transcendentalists Ministers* (New Haven, 1959). For basic documents, see *The Transcendentalists: An Anthology*, ed. Perry Miller (Cambridge, Mass., 1950).

does not depend on tradition, nor historical facts, but has an unerring witness in the soul," they refused to acknowledge any authority beyond themselves. The Transcendentalist, Emerson declared, "believes in miracles, in the perpetual openness of the human mind to the new influx of light and power; he believes in inspiration and ecstasy." The individual soul is linked to God, and through the gift of intuition—instinct, imagination, insight—the soul can penetrate beyond the outer shell of life and consummate union with God by participating in the life of the "oversoul."[43]

Andrews Norton and other old-line Unitarians were horrified by this "latest form of infidelity" and were restrained from ejecting the Transcendentalists from the Unitarian fellowship only by an awareness of the scandal that a heresy trial among the Unitarians would create. Consequently, the members of the club were permitted to proceed in their churches with their program of reformation. Unlike John W. Nevin, the Presbyterian expositor of the "Mercersburg theology" who had been spurred by Coleridge to move in a more sacramental and churchly direction, the Transcendentalists were led by their romantic vision to a quite contrary emphasis. They sought to turn their churches into free religious associations in which the distinction between clergy and laity would disappear and worship would be so ordered that leadership might be rotated.[44] Furthermore, their goal was a comprehension that would embrace the best elements of all former religious systems and within which radical movements would not be looked upon as heresies but as "providential" clues to some need that God wished the churches to fulfill.

The Union Revival

The revivalist spirit among Protestants, and especially as it flourished within Methodism (in a form condemned by their opponents as camp meeting delirium), remained strong in the decades leading up to the Civil War. Earlier defections to Methodist views and techniques had produced a cluster of new ecclesiastical bodies such as the United Brethren, the Evangelical Association, the Free Will Baptists, the Cumberland Presbyterians, and the greater part of the Christian movement. But more significant than these defections was the fact that the Calvinism of the other denominations was becoming so diluted as to be unrecognizable. Taking their lead from Nathaniel W. Taylor, the revivalists had placed such emphasis upon the ability of the sinner to acquire conversion as, in effect, to transform

---

[43] Hutchinson, vii, 29; Tyler, 48; O. B. Frothingham, *George Ripley* (Boston, 1882), 84–5.

[44] Transcendentalism was not so enamored of the notion of "free association" as to overlook the importance of structure in social life. See Anne Rose, *Transcendentalism as a Social Movement, 1830–1850* (New Haven, 1981).

Calvinism into an operational Arminianism. Finney illustrated the progression. He was first a Presbyterian and then a Congregationalist, but his theology became more and more that of the Methodists until he finally embraced the Wesleyan doctrine of Christian perfection. By midcentury, Robert Baird was testifying that it was necessary in all progressive churches "to preach to sinners as if they believed them to be possessed of all the powers of moral agency, capable of turning to God, and on this account, and no other, inexcusable for not doing so."[45]

Curiously enough, Baird's comment appeared in—of all places—the *Princeton Review.* Old School Presbyterians had been greatly distressed by the infiltration of Arminian views and Finneyite techniques—the "results oriented" religion—into their denominational life, but after the break of 1837, they exhibited astonishing alacrity in climbing on the bandwagon and turning again to revivalism as "the only effective weapon in the church's arsenal for turning back the tide of uncouthness, materialism, and moral disintegration."[46] Ultimately, Barnes, Beecher, and even Finney were defended in the pages of the *Princeton Review,* and James W. Alexander could refer with equal approval to the Calvinist and Arminian revivals of the past, saying, "Accidents may vary but the essence is the same."[47] Charles Hodge was the architect of the theory that permitted Old School Presbyterians to reverse their basic commitment. He did this by adopting Jonathan Edwards's distinction between natural ability and moral inability, and then glossing over the distinction to such an extent that his position was not dissimilar to that of New School revivalists.[48] With even Old School Presbyterians no longer untainted, it is apparent that "the Methodist age" of American Protestantism was reaching maturity.

The extent to which the notion of conversion as an acquired characteristic of religious life—the practical view that conversion could be experienced as a result of participation in revival—was made manifestly clear in the Revival of 1858. Beginning in New York and Boston on the heels of a catastrophic national economic crash in 1857, the revival spread quickly through the northern states before making inroads in the West and South. Organized by the laity, it featured noon-hour prayer meetings in cities, with businessmen leaving their places of work in order to pray together in churches, theaters, lecture halls, and other buildings capable of accommodating large audiences. The revival was not as emotional as earlier Methodist camp meetings had been (and still were), and so it did not feature the falling-down, shouting, and barking exercises well-known as markers of evangelical piety. Participants in the revival prayed fervently and

---

[45] Robert Baird, *Princeton Review* 22 (1850), 204.

[46] Elwyn A. Smith, *The Presbyterian Ministry in American Culture* (Philadelphia, 1962), 214.

[47] Ibid., 215.

[48] For a discussion of the Old School "capitulation," see Smith, 220–24.

sometimes wept, but rarely did the performance of emotion develop beyond those behaviors. The practicality of the revival was unmistakable in the manner of its typical unfolding. Those who gathered for the prayer meeting would make specific requests for divine blessings, imploring peace of mind, forgiveness, and strength of character, as much as a new job, the cure of a sick child, or the reform of an alcoholic spouse. The requests, which sometimes were written on paper and deposited in a basket prior to the meeting, were made before the assembled worshipers, and collective prayer was offered for them. Conversions took place during of after the meetings, but not in as dramatic a fashion as some previous revivals. The mood tended to be serious, somber, and controlled. Women participated as well as men, and in many places in rather larger numbers than men; but it was the fact of significant male participation, and especially the role of young males—the apprentices and young clerks who had migrated from the farm to the city in search of work—that gave the revival one of its names, the Businessmen's Revival.

The other name for the events of 1858 is the Union Revival. Promoters of the revival, in newspapers, sermons, and by word of mouth, stressed that the revival included persons from all the Protestant denominations. And such was largely the case, with Unitarians, Baptists, Congregationalists, Presbyterians, and other groups all claiming leadership roles in their communities as the revival preoccupied the nation. But the revival, for all of its apparent manifestation as "union" among the Protestant churches, also betrayed the growing awareness, especially in the larger cities, of social differences. Fundamental to the revival was the practice of organizing prayer meetings specifically for various identity groups: sailors, mothers, clerks, firemen, fathers, girls, students, missionaries, bankers, actors, and even ministers, among others. The designation of certain meetings for such groups represented not union—although the revival did feature impressive interdenominational cooperation—but, rather, the extent to which various groups of Americans now envisioned themselves as different from each other. The revival revealed the broadening of denominational life— the rising visibility of African American congregations, women's religious organizations, Roman Catholics, Jews, Unitarians, confessionalist groups, and many other groups that became better-rooted in the landscape in the first half of the nineteenth century. It demonstrated the degree to which social identities in post-Jacksonian America were inseparable from religious life. It also exemplified the manner in which Americans, always practical, increasingly took a businesslike approach to religion. And it predicted that the churches, in a few shorts months, would divide not as much over a theology as over the social and political issue of slavery.[49]

---

[49] John Corrigan, *Business of the Heart: Religion and Emotion in the Nineteenth Century* (Berkeley, 2002).

CHAPTER EIGHT

Visions of Religious Community

The first half of the nineteenth century in the United States was a time of eager expectancy, unbridled enthusiasm, and restless ferment. A new nation and a new world were being born, and to many people, anything and everything seemed possible. It was a period when the comet's tail was said to have swept America, and everyone went a little mad. "We are all a little wild here with numberless projects of social reform," Emerson wrote to Carlyle in the autumn of 1840. "Not a reading man but has a draft of a new community in his waistcoat pocket." The hyperbole is obvious.

Not everyone went mad. Many were sufficiently prosaic to think that nothing more than a watch belonged in a waistcoat pocket. Still, there were many who were not of the mind or spirit to keep their expectations under control. Although European visitors were impressed by the popularity and vigor of conventional religion, they were also struck by the many new ways to heaven that were being fashioned in America and by the strenuous efforts of others to give the heavenly existence earthly embodiment.

Two factors combined to produce the unusual religious ferment of these years. One factor was the social context. The other was the religious climate. In the American environment there were an absence of tradition and a sense of pregnant possibility that encouraged a spirit of experimentation. Nor was this experimentation inhibited by law. Unlimited freedom had been granted religious expression, no matter how eccentric it might be. And an abundance of cheap land and open space provided an unequaled opportunity to implement and institutionalize religious ideas. If the context was hospitable to innovation, the actual impetus that gave rise to most of the novel cults, sects, and movements was the climate of opinion generated by successive waves of revivalism.

Noah Worcester had pointed out in 1794 that the "sects" had profited from revivals, and this continued to be the case (although it was also true that revivals often functioned as catalysts for unity among the large denominations). Successive harvests were to be reaped by the Shakers, the Mormons, the Oneida community, the Millerites, the Spiritualists, and a host of smaller and more transient groups. The revivals left many individuals distraught and torn by anxiety; and, having tried without success to gain a sense of assurance in their own churches, they were in a receptive mood to listen to new prophets who offered definite guarantees of spiritual security. Although the emotional disturbance that revivalism left in its wake explains why even the most bizarre groups, once established, could garner adherents, it does not account for the origin of those groups. Here it was the spirit—ideas, attitudes, hopes—fostered by the revivals that played the creative role.

Three emphases stimulated by revivalistic preaching were of decisive importance in creating the climate of enthusiasm out of which the new cults, sects, and communities emerged. For one thing, the revivalists demanded an immediate confrontation with God. This often took the form of an ecstatic vision or a mythical illumination that could easily be interpreted as a new revelation. Second, the revivalists placed increasing stress upon the possibility of perfect sanctification, thus arousing a hunger for holiness and a life free from sin. Finally, they tended to dwell upon the ancient millennial expectation of a golden age to come, whether inaugurated by the personal return of Christ or established through the preaching of the gospel. All the groups that deviated from the norm of conventional religion during these years stemmed from at least one of these emphases, and most of the groups represented a blending of all three.[1] In the midst of the search for community, preaching remained a central feature of religious life among Protestants. Catholics continued to audit the homilies delivered by priests, and Jewish congregations increasingly came to expect some manner of exhortation. And the Hartford, Connecticut, pastor Horace Bushnell, who criticized revivalism, also found ways to incorporate aspects of it into a view of the community of faith. In so doing, he delivered a mediatory theological framework that would help set the terms for a post–Civil War Protestantism.

The Utopian Vision

A prominent feature of the first half of the nineteenth century in America was the rise and decline of a variety of communal societies. All of them were impelled by a vision of an ideal or a perfect life that they sought to

---

[1] See A. L. Jamison, "Religions on the Christian Perimeter," in *The Shaping of American Religion*, eds. J. W. Smith and A. L. Jamison (Princeton, N.J., 1961), 197–202.

actualize. These societies were never numerous, nor was the total number of adherents great. Most of them quickly appeared and as quickly disappeared. Only a few maintained themselves for any considerable period of time. Some were nonreligious in origin and orientation, and these exhibited the least staying power. Some were imported from abroad—the Rappites at "Harmony" in western Pennsylvania and later at "Harmony" in Indiana; the Separatists of "Zoar" in Ohio; the followers of William Keil at "Bethel" in Missouri and "Aurora" in Oregon; the Amana Society (The Community of True Inspiration) at "Ebenezer" near Buffalo and then in Iowa; and the community of Swedish immigrants established by Eric Janson at Bishop Hill in Illinois. With the partial exception of William Keil's Rappite seceders, all of these immigrant groups remained isolated from American life. But there also were indigenous communal societies. Of the indigenous communities where men and women sought sanctification in a perfect society, the Shaker settlements of Ann Lee and the Oneida community of John Humphrey Noyes were the most important. The Transcendentalist ventures at Fruitlands, Brook Farm, and Hopedale, on the other hand, were more typical in that they illustrated the pathos of shattered hopes that was the lot of most of the communal enterprises.

The Shakers

The followers of Ann Lee (1736–1784) provide an outstanding example of the blending of new revelation with perfectionist and millenarian ideas in the formation of a communal society.[2] Although "Mother Ann" had come to America with eight followers in 1774, the United Society of Believers in Christ's Second Appearing was not organized until 1787, three years after her death, when a former Free-Will Baptist preacher took charge and gave the Society its definitive shape.

Ann was the wife of a blacksmith in Manchester, England, and the mother of four children, all of whom died in infancy. She had become a member of a small group of Shaking Quakers who were crying out warnings of Christ's approaching second advent and predicting that famine and pestilence were about to descend upon the wicked. The distinguishing feature of their worship, which gave them their name, was the frequency with which they would be "seized with a mighty trembling, with a violent agitation of the body, running and walking on the floor, with singing, shouting, and leaping for joy."[3] In 1770, Ann became the vehicle of a

---

[2] See Edward D. Andrews, *The People Called Shakers: A Search for the Perfect Society* (New York, 1953); and Henri Desroche, *The American Shakers: From Neo-Christianity to Presocialism* (Amherst, Mass., 1971).

[3] See contemporary account in H. Shelton Smith, Robert Handy, and Lefferts Loetscher, *American Christianity*, I, 586–96. See also D. W. Patterson, *The Shaker Spiritual* (Princeton, 1980).

revelation that the root of human depravity and the source of all evils afflicting mankind was the sex act. This was the forbidden fruit, the original sin of Adam and Eve. In the words of a Shaker hymn,

> As lust conceived by the Fall
> Hath more or less infected all;
>
> So we believe 'tis only this
> That keepeth souls from perfect bliss.

The basic summons was to a celibate life, and it was about this emphasis that Ann gathered her first little company of disciples.

After leaving England and settling in Watervliet, New York, Ann gained no new adherents until 1779, when a revival at New Lebanon proved so disturbing that it brought Joseph Meacham and several members of his congregation into the fold. Other recruits were won as scattered revivals began to appear in western Massachusetts and Connecticut. During the final four years of her life, Ann was reported to have performed miracles that convinced her followers that she was Christ in his "second appearing," making manifest the female element in the Godhead and inaugurating the beginning of the millennium by gathering a faithful remnant out of the churches of Antichrist.

In 1787, three years after the death of Mother Ann, Joseph Meacham assumed leadership of the group, gathered the members into several "families" for communal living, drafted the constitution of the United Society, and elaborated and systematized Shaker doctrine. Everything was carefully regulated, and the violence of the earlier physical manifestations was subdued and reduced to a ritualistic dance (e.g., "square order shuffle"; "circle dance") in which worship was expressed by the body as well as by speech and song. In the new order that was at hand, all that had been "earthly, sensual, devilish" would become "spiritual, divine, and heavenly," and the whole endeavor of the Shakers was to live a life of perfection as preparation for the perfect state promised to them. Since there would be no further need for the propagation of the human race in the new age, the inclusion of celibacy among the twelve virtues that must be pursued and practiced did not seem unreasonable.

Under Meacham's leadership the Society experienced a surge of growth with the onset of the Second Awakening. Within five years, ten communities with more than 2,000 members had been formed in Maine, New Hampshire, Massachusetts, Connecticut, and New York. A second period of growth began in 1805 when emissaries were sent west to reap a harvest in the wake of the great Kentucky revival, including two of the prominent leaders of the revival—Richard McNemar and John Dunlavy. By 1825, there were at least twenty communities scattered throughout Ohio, Indiana, and Kentucky, as well as in New England and New York; and within a few years, the Society had about 6,000 members.

Economically the Shakers prospered from the start. Although farming was the basis of their economy, they quickly developed successful commercial and handicraft enterprises. After 1837, the various communities were troubled by a wild burst of spirit-inspired communications that created a deep fear of any further enthusiasm. After this loss of fervor and with the waning of rural revivalism, the Shakers attracted fewer and fewer new members. Although the communities remained prosperous, a steady decline in numbers had set in by 1850. A century later, only a handful of elderly men and women remained.

The Oneida Community

Whereas the Shakers were seeking perfection in celibacy, others were going to the opposite extreme with their claims to holiness and even venturing into unorthodox or curiously ordered sexual relationships. Opposed to the "spiritual wifery" that swept through certain perfectionist circles, John Humphrey Noyes was at the same time the most conspicuous perfectionist leader who placed a stamp of approval upon a departure from the accepted code of sexual relationships.[4]

Noyes was a product of the Finney revivals. A graduate of Dartmouth and the son of a successful Vermont businessman who was prominent in state politics, Noyes had begun the study of law when Finney captured him for the ministry and sent him off for a year at Andover Seminary and two years at Yale Divinity School. When Noyes asserted that conversion brought complete release from sin, he was refused ordination. This setback, however, did not keep him from preaching wherever he could find groups of like-minded perfectionists and from giving further study to what he called "the Sin system, the Marriage system, the Work system, and the Death system." After much pondering, he concluded that it was necessary to create a society in which conditions would be favorable to the practice of perfection. He was later to declare that, as "the revivalists had for their great idea the regeneration of the soul," he had as his great idea "the regeneration of society, which is the soul's environment."[5]

Noyes's communitarianism was based on three fundamental doctrines. The first was total security from sin, but this security was so defined that it did not eliminate the need of discipline and improvement. The second was the conviction that the millennium had been introduced in A.D. 70 but had been obscured by spurious postmillennial growths of the second and

---

[4] See *Lawrence Foster, Religion and Sexuality: Three American Communal Experiments* (New York, 1980); M. L. Carden, *Oneida: Utopian Community to Modern Corporation* (New York, 1977); and Louis J. Kern, *An Ordered Love: Sex Roles and Sexuality in Victorian America: The Shakers, the Mormons and the Oneida Community* (Chapel Hill, N.C., 1981).

[5] J. H. Noyes, *History of American Socialism* (Philadelphia, 1870), 24. See also Alice Felt Tyler, *Freedom's Ferment*, (New York, 1962), 186.

third centuries. The third was the insistence that, since the saints were equally yoked in dedication to their faith, the practice of primitive Christian communism—a communism that included the marriage relationship—was the only logical arrangement.

Noyes gathered a small group in Putney, Vermont, and in the early 1840s instituted a communism of property. When this communism was extended in 1846 by putting into operation his theory of "complex marriage," the local citizens were aroused; to avoid the possibility of being mobbed, the community was reestablished at Oneida, New York, two years later. A major stroke of luck was the conversion of Samuel Newhouse, the inventor of a highly effective small-animal trap. Trap manufacturing placed the community on a sound financial basis, until it was replaced as the chief industry by silverplate ("Community Plate") production. But economic considerations were incidental. The philosophy of the community was stated by Noyes in these words:

> Our warfare is an assertion of human rights; first the right of man to be governed by God and to live in the social state of heaven; second the right of woman to dispose of her sexual nature by attraction instead of by law and routine and to bear children only when she chooses; third the right of all to diminish the labors and increase the advantages of life by association.

These principles, he insisted, must find expression in "one living organization before the Kingdom of Heaven can come." Thus, personal sanctification and social regeneration went hand in hand.[6]

Although Noyes fashioned a detailed and closely supervised pattern of life for the community, including procedures for "mutual criticism" and innovations in the education of children, it was the theory and practice of "complex marriage" that gained its notoriety for the community. This theory, which regarded each woman in the group as the wife of every man and every man as the husband of every woman, was instituted on religious grounds. Noyes's followers thought of themselves as saints purified by religious experience and disciplined to the practice of absolute fellowship among themselves by a total love of God. As a consequence, they believed that there was a basic incompatibility between absolute goodwill among the regenerate and the exclusive legal and physical bonds of conventional marriage. "Sexual communion," Noyes insisted, "differs only in its superior intensity and beauty from other acts of love," and it contributes to true mutuality. But when sexual communion is restricted to acts of "special love," it becomes unsocial and dangerous to communal interests. The Oneida perfectionists resented the charge that they were practicing "free love," for sexual intercourse among them was "organized" rather than promiscuous, and they believed it was inspired by true spirituality.

---

[6] Cross, *The Burned-over District*, 335, 337. Whitney R. Cross (Ithaca, NY, 1950)

For thirty years the community remained true to its original ideals, but pressure from the outside world persuaded Noyes in 1879 to abandon the practice of "complex marriage." This event in turn led to the abandonment of communal ownership of property the following year. A joint-stock company was formed, the shares were distributed among the former communitarians, and silverplated tableware became the chief reminder of their former effort to institutionalize a sinless life and thus provide a foretaste of the kingdom of God.

Transcendentalism's "Wild Oats"

When Emerson spoke of the draft of utopia to be found in almost every reading man's waistcoat pocket, he was thinking preeminently of some of his fellow Transcendentalists, for in a curiously romantic way, they also had appropriated the perfectionist and millenarian tendencies of the time. Emerson himself remained skeptical, but others were driven by an overpowering desire to anticipate the millennium by perfecting human institutions. Three small communal societies—Fruitlands, Brook Farm, and Hopedale—were the product of what in retrospect can be seen as their moment of aberration.[7]

Louisa May Alcott's *The Transcendental Wild Oats* is a fictionalized account of the venture of her father, Bronson Alcott, in communal living at Fruitlands, near Harvard, Massachusetts, which began with high hopes in the spring of 1843 and collapsed before winter set in. Believing that "our freer, but yet far from freed, land is the asylum . . . for the hope of man," Bronson Alcott was convinced that only in America could "the second Eden . . . be planted in which the divine seed is to bruise the head of Evil and restore Man to his rightful communion with God in the Paradise of Good." This was his vision of Fruitlands. Unfortunately, what might have been at least a summer's idyl was spoiled by the domineering spirit of Charles Lane, a dour ascetic Englishman, who was determined that every natural human desire should be denied. One by one the members slipped away, the crops were left unharvested, and Lane finally departed to join the Shakers.

Brook Farm, in West Roxbury, Massachusetts, was a happier experiment. George Ripley, Unitarian minister and leading member of the "Transcendental Club," was its founder and director. In 1840, before resigning from the pulpit of his Purchase Street congregation in Boston, Ripley had told his parishioners that it was the business of Christianity to overthrow every social evil, and Brook Farm was designed to be, "if not the sunrise," at least

---

[7] See Clara E. Sears, *Bronson Alcott's Fruitlands*, (Philadelphia, 1975) with *Transcendental Wild Oats*, by Louisa Alcott (Boston, 1915); Zoltan Haraszti, *The Idyll of Brook Farm* (Boston, 1937); Adin Ballou, *History of the Hopedale Community* (Lowell, Mass., 1897); Mark Holloway, *Heavens on Earth: Utopian Communities in America* (New York, 1966).

"the morning star" of the new day in which the thinker and the manual laborer would be united in a noncompetitive society.

Most of the literary lights of the time participated at Brook Farm either as members, visitors, or supporters. The intellectual life at the Farm was exciting, and the social life, which included plays, dances, picnics, and boating parties, was lively. Since the members were better dreamers than farmers, the community was dependent upon outside support except for the income derived from its school, which was recommended by the Harvard faculty as an excellent place to send young boys who aspired to become college students. In 1844, however, the members became entranced by the ideas of the French socialist Charles Fourier (1772–1837) and decided to turn Brook Farm into a Fourierist phalanx. This undertaking necessitated conforming to a rigid theory of social organization and involved establishing industries, forming specialized labor groups, and ritualizing sexual relations. Money was borrowed, the school was neglected, and in 1846, a fire left the community insolvent. By this time many of the sponsors had lost interest, having been diverted by newer fads, and so in 1847, the community wound up its affairs. Later Nathaniel Hawthorne looked back with nostalgia to "our beautiful scheme of a noble and unselfish life" at the Farm. "How fair in that first summer appeared the prospect that it might endure for generations, and be perfected as the ages rolled by into the system of a people and a world. Were my former associates now there—were there only three or four of those true-hearted men still laboring in the sun—I sometimes fancy that I should direct my world-weary footsteps thitherward and entreat them to receive me for old friendship's sake."

The community at Hopedale was a less dilettantish effort. Established near Milford, Massachusetts, in 1841, it managed to maintain itself for fifteen years. Adin Ballou, a Universalist minister, was the founder and guiding spirit. Although he was not a member of the "Club," he was a Transcendentalist nonetheless and a friend of Channing and Parker. Since "it was one of the declared objects of Christ's labors to inaugurate the kingdom of heaven on earth," Ballou was convinced that "the imperative duty" of Christ's disciples is "to pray and to work for that sublime end." Working meant "actualizing" New Testament teachings in order to initiate a world movement toward the perfect life. Some thirty persons responded to Ballou's summons to subject themselves to "all the moral obligations" of the religion of Jesus and to take the lead in banishing from the world "all things known to be sinful against God or human nature." Ten years later the community had grown to nearly two hundred members and was a moderate financial success. But when Ballou retired from active leadership, it was decided that the common fund would be more productive if diverted to private enterprise, and in 1856, the whole project was liquidated. The failure, Ballou remarked with sadness, was not financial but "moral and spiritual"—"a deficiency among its members of those graces and powers of character which are requisite to the realization of the Christian ideal of human society."

New Visions

Utopian communities that sought to reproduce the heavenly existence in earthly institutions were but one manifestation of the religious ferment of the first half of the nineteenth century. Other variant groups came to the fore in which the perfectionist motif was more subdued. Such groups as the Mormons, the Millerites, and the Spiritualists were no less symptomatic of the energies released by the prevailing religious climate, but they found their primary orientation in some other point of emphasis—in a new and supplementary revelation, in the reduction of the millennial expectation to a definite timetable of events, in the sudden bursting of the barriers to the spirit world.

The Mormons

The Church of Jesus Christ of Latter-day Saints, which was to create for itself a great intramountain empire in the West, had its origin in the remarkable story of Joseph Smith, who in 1816, at the age of ten, had come with his parents from Vermont to the vicinity of Palmyra, New York.[8] Here he absorbed much from the religious excitement of what came to be called "the burned-over district." Smith later reported that he was greatly disturbed by the religious controversies that swirled about him. "In the midst of this war of words and tumult of opinions, I often said to myself, what is to be done? Who of all these parties be right? Or are they all wrong together?" Troubled by these anxieties, he "retired to the woods" to seek the wisdom of God. His prayer was answered by the appearance of two heavenly personages—the Father and the Son—who told him to hold himself apart from the contending denominations, for a special task was to be given him. After a period of testing in which he received a series of further revelations, Smith was guided by the angel Moroni to discover long-buried golden plates that told the story of the Nephites and Lamanites, descendants of a lost tribe of Israel, who had inhabited the American continent centuries before. Christ had appeared among them after his resurrection and had established the proper church order. The Lamanites, progenitors of the Indians, had apostatized and had defeated the faithful Nephites in a battle in which all the Nephites except Mormon and his son Moroni were slain. The records of this ancient people were buried by Moroni in the hill Cumorah, and it was there that Smith discovered them, together with the

[8] One account of Mormonism is L. J. Arrington, *The Mormon Experience* (New York, 1979). See also Jan Shipps, *Mormonism: The Story of a Religious Tradition* (Urbana, Ill., 1985).

THE

BOOK OF MORMON:

AN ACCOUNT WRITTEN BY THE HAND OF MOR-MON, UPON PLATES TAKEN FROM THE PLATES OF NEPHI.

Wherefore it is an abridgment of the Record of the People of Nephi; and also of the Lamanites; written to the Lamanites, which are a remnant of the House of Israel; and also to Jew and Gentile; written by way of commandment, and also by the spirit of Prophesy and of Revelation. Written, and sealed up, and hid up unto the LORD, that they might not be destroyed; to come forth by the gift and power of GOD unto the interpretation thereof; sealed by the hand of Moroni, and hid up unto the LORD, to come forth in due time by the way of Gentile; the interpretation thereof by the gift of GOD; an abridgment taken from the Book of Ether.

Also, which is a Record of the People of Jared, which were scattered at the time the LORD confounded the language of the people when they were building a tower to get to Heaven: which is to shew unto the remnant of the House of Israel how great things the LORD hath done for their fathers; and that they may know the covenants of the LORD, that they are not cast off forever; and also to the convincing of the Jew and Gentile that JESUS is the CHRIST, the ETERNAL GOD, manifesting Himself unto all nations. And now if there be fault, it be the mistake of men; wherefore condemn not the things of GOD, that ye may be found spotless at the judgment seat of CHRIST.

BY JOSEPH SMITH, JUNIOR,
AUTHOR AND PROPRIETOR.

PALMYRA:
PRINTED BY E. B. GRANDIN, FOR THE AUTHOR.

1830.

Title Page of the First Edition of the Book of Mormon, printed by the author. *(Courtesy of Lowell H. Fewster and the Ambrose Swasey Library, Colgate Rochester Divinity School.)*

translating spectacles that enabled him to decipher what he later described as the Reformed Egyptian hieroglyphics of the text. In 1830, Smith's translation of the Book of Mormon was published at Palmyra.

This new scripture provided a basis for resolving the sectarian jangling that Smith had found so disturbing, for it gave an authoritative judgment upon almost every issue that was in dispute. This fact was quickly recognized by Alexander Campbell, who pointed out in his *Delusions: An Analysis of the Book of Mormon* (1832) that the golden plates had anticipated and given a definitive answer to "every error and almost every truth discussed in New York for the last ten years," including "infant baptism, ordination, the trinity, regeneration, repentance, justification, the fall of man, the atonement, transubstantiation, fasting, penance, church government, religious experience, the call to the ministry, the general resurrection, eternal punishment, who may baptize, and even the question of freemasonry, republican government, and the rights of man." And the Book of Mormon even provided for the future adjudication of controversy by insisting that anyone who denies "the revelations of God" and says "that they are done away, that there are no revelations, nor prophecies, nor gifts, nor speaking with tongues and interpretation of tongues" denies "the gospel of Christ."

It is scarcely surprising that one of the first converts to embrace the new revelation was Sidney Rigdon, an ex-Disciple minister who had once contested Campbell's leadership, since the Book of Mormon stressed many of the basic themes of Campbellite preaching—free grace, free will, repentance, restoration, plainness of doctrine, opposition to "priestcraft," rejection of infant baptism, and even the distinctive Campbellite doctrine of baptism "unto the remission of sins." Nor in view of this heritage is it surprising that when young Joseph Smith on October 30, 1830, met with five friends in Fayette, New York, to restore "the Church of Christ in these last days," he should have chosen the typically Campbellite designation of "Church of Christ" for his reincarnation of the ancient order of church life. Four years later, at the instigation of Rigdon, the name was changed to the Church of the Latter-day Saints, and in 1838 it was given its present expanded form.

Another theme of the Book of Mormon, which had wide appeal to people who were stirred by the romantic nationalism of the time, was the portrayal of America as the promised land—"a land which is choice above all other lands," a land to which none shall come "save they shall be brought by the hand of the Lord." Indeed, the whole biblical setting of the drama of salvation was transferred to American soil. To the successive declarations of political, economic, diplomatic, and intellectual independence penned by Jefferson, Clay, Monroe, and Emerson was now added a declaration of religious independence. The Old World heritage was rendered both obsolete and irrelevant, for the restoration of the true church depended upon the recovery of an independent American tradition that extended back to the time of the Babylonian Exile and was validated by the postresurrection appearance of Christ in America.

Prior to forming the new church, Smith had a revelation in which John the Baptist appeared and ordained him and Oliver Cowdery[9] to the "Priesthood of Aaron, which holds the keys of the ministering of angels, and of the gospel of repentance, and of baptism by immersion for the remission of sins." Thus equipped, he was directed to form the church by a revelation that designated "Joseph Smith, Jun., who was called of God and ordained an apostle of Jesus Christ, to be the first elder of this church," and "Oliver Cowdery, who was also called of God, an apostle of Jesus Christ, to be the second elder of this church." At the first meeting of the church, Smith's full office was made clear by a further revelation that stated that he should "be called a seer, a translator, a prophet, an apostle of Jesus Christ, an elder of the church through the will of God the Father and the grace of your Lord Jesus Christ," with the added admonition that the church should "give heed unto all his words and commandments . . . for his word shall ye receive as if from mine own mouth."

By 1830, the new scripture had been published, the new church formed, and the new prophet designated with powers of immediate revelation to deal with troublesome problems as they arose. In the course of time, more distinctive doctrines were elaborated—a plurality of gods, for example, as well as of wives—which set the Mormons further and further apart from the generality of Christians. Geographically, Mormons remained apart as well, leaving New York for Kirtland, Ohio, where Sidney Rigdon's congregation provided fresh recruits, then on to Missouri, and then to Nauvoo, Illinois, gaining converts along the way. In Nauvoo, Smith attempted to establish a semi-independent domain. The tragic murder of Smith by an angry mob in 1844 while he was confined in the jail at Carthage, Illinois, precipitated one of the epic stories of American history—the heroic trek of the majority of the Mormons under the leadership of Brigham Young to a new "Zion in the Wilderness." Sheltered by the mountains surrounding the basin of the Great Salt Lake in Utah, they at last found a measure of peace and security. By 1870, the number of Mormons in the intramountain region exceeded 140,000, many of them converts who had been won abroad.

The Millerites

A severe fiscal crisis, the Panic of 1837, brought with it renewed millennial hopes for many Americans. William Miller, a farmer at Low Hampton, New York, was the key figure in the Adventist excitement of the late 1830s and

---

[9] Cowdery was Smith's clerical assistant. While in Vermont prior to moving to Palmyra, Cowdery had embraced some "extraordinary doctrines, apparently involving millennial expectations and direct revelation as well as some mysterious treasure hunting." Cross, 38–39.

early 1840s.[10] After his conversion in 1816, he had become a member of the Baptist church and began to study the Bible with particular attention to the last times. Interested in calculating the date of Christ's return, he probably found the clue that pointed to 1843 in the Boston edition of the British Christian Observer or a similar publication. By nimble arithmetic (years of 360 days—twelve 30-day months—instead of 365), he was able to prove to his satisfaction that "God in his wisdom has so interwoven the several prophecies that . . . they tell us the same things." In 1828, he felt a "call" to tell the world of his discovery that Christ would come "about 1843." "I tried to excuse myself," he later explained. "I told the Lord that I was not used to speaking . . . that I was slow of speech and slow of tongue. But I could get no relief." By 1831, he had developed sufficient courage to begin to issue local warnings by sharing his discovery with neighbors and friends. He was asked to discuss his views in a nearby church, and he suddenly found that on this one subject at least, he was eloquent. Invitations multiplied, and he began to gain a measure of local fame. Although he was never ordained, Miller's ministerial status was somewhat regularized in 1833 with a license to preach.

Although revivalism had bred a mentality that predisposed many to become ready converts to Miller's dating of the end of time, three events combined to give him a more than local reputation. The first event was the publication in 1836 of his computations in book form under the title *Evidence from Scripture and History of the Second Coming of Christ, About the Year 1843*. The second was the Panic of 1837, which created for the book an unusually receptive audience. The third was the chance discovery of Miller by Joshua V. Himes at Exeter, New Hampshire, in 1839, while Miller was on a speaking tour of New England. Minister of a Christian Connection church in Boston and an indefatigable promoter, Himes had all the gifts that a century later would be associated with Madison Avenue. Immediately sensing the potency of the message of the plain-spoken farmer, Himes attached himself to Miller as his manager and publicity agent. He equipped Miller with a great chart displaying Miller's calculations in graphic form, purchased the biggest tent in the country for Miller's meetings, edited two journals—the *Midnight Cry* in New York and *Signs of the Times* in Boston—and helped found others in Philadelphia, Cincinnati, Cleveland, Rochester, and Montreal. Other evangelists were recruited and sent on speaking tours; camp meetings were organized; children's books, catechisms, tracts, pamphlets, and even a hymn book, *The Millennial Harp*, were published. The publicity was effective: 50,000 people became believers, and as many as a million more were skeptically expectant.

Miller had been hesitant to be more specific than to say that Christ would return "about 1843," but in January 1843, he announced that this year

[10] See Ernest Sandeen's chapter, "The Millenarian Tradition in the United States, 1800–1845," in his *The Roots of Fundamentalism* (Chicago, 1970); also F. D. Nichol, *The Midnight Cry* (Washington, D.C., 1944).

(from March 21, 1843, to March 21, 1844, taking into account the change in the calendar year) must see the end of time. The tension, which mounted as the year progressed, was heightened by the appearance of a comet in the heavens. Meetings grew larger and converts more numerous, but March 21, 1844, came—and time still continued. On May 2, Miller confessed his error and acknowledged his disappointment, but one of his followers called attention to Habakkuk 2:3 and Leviticus 25:9 and announced that there obviously was to be a "tarrying time" of seven months and ten days. Thus, October 22, 1844, was to be the day of Christ's triumphant return, and people were rallied once again with the slogan "The Tenth Day of the Seventh Month." Miller was finally converted to the new date: "I see a glory in the seventh month which I never saw before. Thank the Lord, O my soul! . . . I am almost home. Glory! Glory! Glory! I see that the time is correct." The excitement revived, and the number of people living each moment as if it were their last exceeded that of the preceding summer.

With the second disappointment, most of those who had been caught up in the movement were completely disillusioned. The reaction of others was often bitter. Miller, for example, was excommunicated by the Baptist church at Low Hampton, and in 1849, he died, discredited and almost forgotten. A few became Shakers, giving that group its last important influx of new members. Some remained steadfast in their hope, believing that only a minor error in calculation had been made. They met in Albany in 1845 to form a conference that later splintered into three groups, the largest of which was the Advent Christian Church. Others, persuaded by Ellen Gould White that Christ's failure to appear was due to a neglect of proper Sabbath observance, formed the nucleus of what was to be the Seventh-day Adventist Church.

The Spiritualists

Before the Millerites had fully recovered from their disenchantment, "the Rochester rappings" of the Fox sisters in 1848 created a new sensation that led to the development of modern Spiritualism.[11] The way had been prepared by the teachings of Emmanuel Swedenborg (1688–1772), whose views had become something of a vogue among religious liberals and whose works had just been republished in a new English edition. Swedenborg claimed to have received communications from the spirit world by which knowledge of all things in the heavens and below the heavens had been given to him. Interest in his teachings was reinforced by the spread of mesmerism, which utilized the strange power of "animal magnetism" to produce a hypnotic trance

---

[11] See R. L. Moore, *In Search of White Crows: Spiritualism, Parapsychology, and American Culture* (New York, 1976); Ann Braude, *Radical Spirits: Spiritualism and Women's Rights in Nineteenth-Century America* (Boston, 1989).

that was thought to point to the basic laws of the spirit world and to give promise of unlocking the mysteries of the life beyond. All that was needed to transform these embryonic ideas into Spiritualism was a mechanism for communicating with the dead, and it was such a device that was supplied unwittingly by two young girls, Maggie and Katie Fox.

The "rappings" began at Hydesville, New York, as a childish prank that some adults took seriously and that was exploited by an older sister who lived in nearby Rochester. Soon the Fox sisters were holding public seances and notable converts were being won, including Horace Greeley, editor of the *New York Tribune.* By 1851, seven Spiritualist periodicals were being published, and six years later the number had increased to sixty-seven. The Universalists provided the most recruits, and although interest began to subside prior to the Civil War, the movement found institutional expression in a number of enduring Spiritualist "associations." Drawing upon a wide range of religious and psychological writings, and fueled as well by the emergent movement for women's rights, Spiritualism and female mediumship enjoyed several flurries of renewed enthusiasm. In 1888, the Fox sisters acknowledged their hoax and demonstrated how they had produced the "rappings" by cracking their toe joints; but this exposure had little effect upon convinced believers.

The Humanitarian Impulse

Utopian communities and novel sectarian emphases were not the only expressions of religious ferment. Most of the enthusiasm generated by the Second Awakening was devoted to more conventional enterprises in which the concerns of the evangelically awakened often paralleled those of the heirs of Channing. The revivalists were generally postmillennialists who assumed that an era of peace, justice, and goodness would precede the return of Christ. Consequently, where there were revivals, there must be reform. Every aspect of society began to be subjected to eager scrutiny in order to scour and purify the earth in preparation for God's final act of redemption. Scarcely any phase of American life was left untouched. Temperance, Sabbath observance, world peace, profanity, vice, women's rights, slavery, the condition of penal institutions, educational innovations—all became objects of concern. The whole impulse was carefully articulated in a series of related societies and was closely integrated with revivalistic efforts, as was made clear in 1835 by Theodore Dwight Weld in a letter to Lewis Tappan:

> God has called some prophets, some apostles, and some teachers. All the members of the body of Christ have not the same office. Let Delevan drive temperance, McDowell moral reform, Finney revivals, Tappan antislavery, etc. Each of these is bound to make his own peculiar department his main

business, and to promote collaterally as much as he can the other objects. I have no doubt but Finney has erred in not giving as much collateral attention to antislavery as the present emergent crisis demands. And I am equally certain that I have not done as much collaterally to promote temperance and revivals while I have been lecturing on slavery as I ought.[12]

The revivals provided the impetus, summoning men and women to battle against sin; and the reform movements were the implementation of the thrust toward the coming kingdom of righteousness. The task of those who enlisted in the struggle was put succinctly by Finney: "Every member must work or quit. No honorary members."

The Expanding Concern

Whereas initially the reforms were mainly limited to rectifying individual vices—such as infidelity, drunkenness, Sabbath breaking, dueling, gambling, and profanity—by methods of persuasion, the concern quickly expanded to include larger social issues. The masthead of the *New York Evangelist* illustrated the broadening of the reform impulse. In 1831, when it was insisting that "the emancipation of the world must engross the desires . . . and the enterprise of the world," the masthead announced that the paper was "Devoted to Revivals, Doctrinal Discussion and Religious Intelligence." In 1835, it added "Practical Godliness," and in 1837, "Human Rights." World peace was an early preoccupation, and colonization in Africa was promoted to solve the problem of slavery. Later antislavery sentiment was channeled into a demand for "immediate emancipation." Prison reform captured the interest of some, and a noted group of women spearheaded interest in female education and women's rights. The latter concerns culminated in the 1848 Seneca Falls Convention, held in the heart of Finneyite territory and convened by Elizabeth Cady Stanton, who had become acquainted with evangelical reform activity first through her cousin and then through her husband.

Although Lyman Beecher in 1827 listed "monopoly of the soil" and the factory system as twin evils to be combatted, economic problems did not bulk large in the thinking of evangelical reformers. This treatment occurred partly because they tended to think that individual conversions would remedy the ills of poverty but primarily because an abundance of unsettled land in a largely agrarian society served as an escape valve for economic discontent. Antislavery agitation had deep economic implications, of course, and some people dabbled with peripheral urban and labor problems when they established havens for out-of-work sailors and formed societies to reclaim prostitutes from their shame. The Panic of

---

[12] G. H. Barnes and D. L. Dumond, eds. *Letters of Theodore Dwight Weld* (New York, 1934), I, 243.

1837 brought further hesitant steps in the direction of a social gospel. In 1842, revivalist Edward N. Kirk stressed the need to ferret out the causes of poverty and to apply remedies. In 1851, an influential Presbyterian layman, Stephen Colwell, published *New Themes for the Protestant Clergy* in which he advocated legislative enactments to better the condition of workingmen. Two or three years later, the *Independent* began to urge programs of urban renewal that would have as their aim low rents, clean buildings, and healthy surroundings.

The Slavery Controversy

Of all the reform crusades, the one that disrupted the churches and shook the nation to its foundations was the antislavery movement.[13] Other reform movements had taken an individualistic turn that enabled the existing denominations for the most part to contain those movements. They had developed within the context of revivalism, and most of them were no more than urgent summons to individuals to free themselves from the entanglement of sin. The antislavery crusade, as conducted by the evangelicals, had begun with the same emphasis. Although the adoption of the British motto—"immediate emancipation"—seemed to imply a drastic abolitionism, it was interpreted to mean "immediate emancipation gradually accomplished" or "gradual emancipation immediately begun." The emphasis was upon persuasion and a personal renunciation of slavery as sin. The campaign of Theodore Dwight Weld and his band of rebels, which recruited at Lane Theological Seminary and later expanded to a biblical "Seventy," exhibited all the characteristics and methods of revival meetings. The immediatism they preached was an immediate repentance of the sin of any personal involvement in and support of the slave system. However gradual the emancipation was to be, there was a point at which persuasion would end and abolition would be required, and as antislavery sentiment was intensified, it became increasingly difficult to keep the movement from demanding that its moral standard be imposed and enforced by legislative action. As a convention of Christian abolitionists in Hamilton, New York, resolved in 1845, "Those who admit the sinfulness of slavery . . . and yet vote for oppression, or for those who are connected with pro-slavery parties, are guilty of the most inconsistency; and are undeserving the name Christian patriots, and unworthy to be recognized as the true friends of downtrodden Christianity."[14]

---

[13] See G. H. Barnes, *The Antislavery Impulse, 1830–1844* (New York, 1933); D. L. Dumond, *Antislavery: The Crusade for Freedom* (Ann Arbor, Mich., 1961); and Bertram Wyatt-Brown, *Lewis Tappan and the Evangelical War Against Slavery* (New York, 1971).

[14] Quoted in John R. McKivigan, *The War Against Proslavery Religion: Abolitionism and the Northern Churches* (Ithaca, New York, 1984), 147.

The disruptive effect of antislavery agitation was accentuated because it appeared at a time when an equally aggressive proslavery movement was developing. During the first third of the century, many in the South were quite as critical of slavery as was anyone in the North; but by the 1830s, this sentiment had declined, and highly vocal champions of the South's "peculiar institution" were beginning to dominate southern opinion. An influential factor in this shift was the increasing importance of cotton in the South's economy and the accompanying conviction that profitable cotton production depended upon slave labor. The bitter attacks of northern abolitionists also contributed to the consolidation of proslavery sentiment in the South, as did the anxiety aroused by the growing minority status of the slaveholding states in a rapidly expanding nation.

Thomas R. Dew, professor of political economy at the College of William and Mary, laid down the basic lines of the slavery defense in 1832 when he argued that slavery not only had been from earliest times the chief means of advancing civilization but also had been established by divine authority.[15] Southern clergymen picked up this final point and began to respond to the antislavery arguments by appealing to the sanction of Scripture and by depicting the abolitionists as anti-Christian atheists who reject the Word of God. "We defend the cause of God," Benjamin Morgan Palmer, minister of the First Presbyterian Church of New Orleans, was to declare.

The Disruption of the Churches

The disruptive effect of the slavery issue upon the churches was foreshadowed by its role in the hidden agenda of the Presbyterian Old School–New School division in 1837, and it was more clearly evident in the formation of perfectionist "union" churches and in perfectionist defections among Methodists, Baptists, and Lutherans. Although the perfectionist antislavery sentiment was to become widespread, its early focal point was in upper New York state. As early as 1835, the reorganized Central (formerly Oneida) Evangelical Association, with fifteen ministers, eight licentiates, and seven churches, was proposing that it be considered as the nucleus of a network of true churches free from all sin to which all right-minded congregations could repair as they found their old denominations entangled in unrighteousness. "Union of feeling and sentiment," ran the resolution, can never be obtained until the churches "abandon their exclusive creeds and incorporate nothing in their articles that will shut off their fellowship with any child of God." The one thing demanded by these "union" churches was an unequivocal stand against slavery, since "proslavery or apparently neutral churches are anti-Christian." By 1855, there were no

---

[15] See Thomas R. Dew, *The Pro-Slavery Argument as Maintained by the Most Distinguished Writers of the Southern States* (Charleston, S.C., 1852); and W. S. Jenkins, *Pro-Slavery Thought in the Old South* (Chapel Hill, N.C., 1935).

fewer than eighty-three of these "union" churches in New York state alone, and others were scattered through New England and the Middle West. In addition, the entire Genesee Association was read out of the Congregational fold in 1844 for its perfectionist tendencies.[16]

New York state was also the center of antislavery agitation among Methodists. In spite of the attempt of the national General Conference in 1836 to stifle discussion of the issue, hundreds of petitions demanding disciplinary rules against slavery continued to flood in from New York, especially from the Genesee conference. The bishops resorted to expulsions and discriminatory appointments in an endeavor to silence the antislavery forces, and at the 1840 General Conference, they maintained their iron-clad control in the face of petitions signed by 10,000 laymen and 500 preachers. Between 1839 and 1842, isolated groups in New England, New York, and Ohio began to withdraw from the church, and finally in 1843 at a meeting in Utica, the Wesleyan Methodist Church was formed on a typically perfectionist platform that included abolitionism as one of its tests for membership.

Baptists suffered a similar defection that extended from Maine through New York to Michigan. It took shape in the formation of a competing Baptist Free Mission Society in 1843 and in the establishment of New York Central College at McGraw, New York. Among Lutherans an antislavery faction of twenty-one perfectionist congregations in central New York in 1837 formed the Franckean Synod, which denied membership to anyone who sanctioned the principle of slavery.

These were minor schisms, and their growth was nipped by a shift in the policy of the major bodies. Responding to the increasing pressure of antislavery sentiment, the Methodist General Conference of 1844 adopted a strengthened antislavery rule that preserved the unity of the northern section of the church at the expense of the southern portion, which departed the following year to form the Methodist Episcopal Church, South. The Baptist foreign and home mission societies also were forced to take a firmer stand, which resulted in the formation of the Southern Baptist Convention in 1845. The Congregationalists, as a regional denomination, were able to move into the abolitionist camp without suffering disruption, although the Disciple or "Christian" churches were too loosely affiliated to suffer schism. The Old School and the New School Presbyterian churches, having divided in 1837, sought to muffle the controversy in order to avoid further division. The New School group succeeded in doing so for a time, but it finally split in 1857, whereas the Old School churches forestalled any break until after the Civil War began. Lutherans were torn by controversy, but the General Synod was able to steer a neutral course. The Episcopalians and the Roman Catholics tended to remain aloof from the controversy. Remaining aloof, of course, often meant that the proponents of a

[16] Cross, 261, 278–81.

slave-based social order were free to speak, whereas their opponents were urged to avoid creating dissension by remaining silent.

The division of the churches was prophetic of the political division that was to follow. By 1860, the crisis was at hand. As soon as the outcome of the presidential election was certain, the South Carolina legislature summoned a state convention that met on December 20, 1860, and unanimously declared "that the Union now subsisting between South Carolina and other states under the name of 'The United States of America' is hereby dissolved." Four months later, Fort Sumter was shelled, and the Civil War had begun.

During the agitation preceding the conflict, women had emerged for the first time to play a significant political role. Some were important in enlisting financial support; some devoted themselves to organizational tasks; and others took to the platform as eloquent advocates of abolition. The Grimké sisters from South Carolina, Sarah and Angeline, toured New England as agents of the Anti-Slavery Society. And there were others.

When Theodore Parker said that Lyman Beecher was "the father of more brains than any man in America," he was thinking not only of Beecher's sons, Henry Ward, Edward, Charles, and Thomas K., but also of his equally gifted daughters. Harriet gained fame by her writing. Catherine's great contribution was in education, desiring to secure "professional advantages of education for my sex equal to those bestowed on men." She wrote, she agitated, she established female seminaries and colleges, and she organized societies to support her educational ventures. Isabella joined forces with Elizabeth Cady Stanton and fought with equal zeal for the "great and holy work" of woman suffrage. All were opposed to slavery, but it was Harriet Beecher Stowe who probed the conscience of the nation with her emotion-laden indictment of slavery in *Uncle Tom's Cabin* (1852).[17] And after the war began, it was another young woman, Julia Ward Howe, who provided the stirring words of "The Battle Hymn of the Republic"— with its closing line "as he died to make men holy, let us die to make men free"—as the marching song of the Northern armies.

In both the North and the South, preachers marched with the troops— some to bear arms, others to serve as chaplains. Prayer meetings were a familiar feature of life in the camp. In the field, the sound of hymn singing echoed across the lines. In the Confederate armies especially, a continuing revivalistic fervor was often maintained. The concern of people at home for the troops was expressed through such agencies of churchmen as the United States Christian Commission (the Civil War equivalent of the World War II USO), whose agents distributed incidental necessities—including mittens, scarves, taffy, writing paper—and wrote letters to loved ones for the seriously wounded or illiterate. The Red Cross, under the inspiration of Clara Barton, won its spurs in assisting the personnel of the

---

[17] See Marie Caskey, *Chariot of Fire: Religion and the Beecher Family* (New Haven, 1978).

Sanitary Commission. But the most fateful features of the war were its fratricidal character and its magnitude. It was a war that bruised almost every
family in the land, changed the face of the nation, and created new problems both for the country and for the churches.

Continuity and Mediation

The Civil War disrupted the churches and led many—clergy and laity alike—
to rethink familiar understandings of the founding of the nation and to
question religious beliefs about its destiny. The war brought with it sweeping
change. But there were continuities as well. Preaching, a standard feature of
religious life for Protestants and Catholics, and increasingly for Jews, was for
most soldiers the only sign of religious life available to them during their military service. On the move and under fire, and thus rarely able to attend religious services as they had done before the war—in a house of worship, with
familiar clergy and neighbors, possessed of a Bible or other religious literature, and in a state of mind that was balanced and at ease—soldiers relied
almost solely upon irregular preaching to meet their spiritual needs. It was
not only soldiers but also civilians whose communities were directly affected
by the war who experienced religious life largely as the preaching of ministers who traveled with the troops or who otherwise appeared as itinerants.
Preaching, long a standard part of religious life, became even more important as a continuity between the practice of religion before and after war.
Likewise important was the translation of the excitement and vitality of the
revivalism into churches that had little to celebrate and much to lament as
the war took its awful toll. Horace Bushnell's theology, articulated before the
war, proved highly influential afterwards in bringing about a mediation between the spirit of revivalism and the more somber styles of worship and the-
ologizing in many of the urban churches.

The Continuing Importance of Preaching

Preaching, which was the centerpiece of the lay revival of the 1850s, was
central to the development of religion in America over the course of the
nation's history. Preaching had always been the most effective way to engender in persons a deep regard for Scripture and to impress upon them a
sense of moral obligation. After the Revolution, when a political vision
rooted in respect for the voice of the people became culturally dominant,
preaching acquired particular importance as "the democratic art of persuasion."[18] Preaching became an instrument for the proliferation of popu-

---

[18] Nathan O. Hatch, *The Democratization of Christianity* (New Haven, 1989), 211. ♦

lar religious movements, but at the same time it remained the cornerstone of religious life in those churches where authority traditionally was vested in ordained clergy.

From the earliest settlement of Massachusetts, the sermon served not only as a means for the promotion of religious doctrine but also as a vehicle for the expression of ideas about the political meaning of America. John Winthrop's exhortation to his fellow travelers on board the *Arabella* in 1629 outlined a social order grounded in faith and guided by divine providence. Winthrop's blending of religious and civil themes was a strategy common among dissenting bodies in England, and it foretold the emergence of the sermon in America as the principal means whereby the relation between religion and national identity was delineated. Not all of the thousands of sermons heard by a New Englander over a lifetime were aimed at clarifying the meanings of Winthrop's "city on a hill." Many sermons were preached simply to encourage piety or to explain points of doctrine. What mattered was the capability of the sermon to function both as an instrument of religious exhortation and teaching and as a means of expression of religio-political conceptualizations. The sermon was a versatile and fluid form of communication. That fluidity was essential to the adaptation of the sermon to a wide variety of contexts, as America grew and changed as a nation.

From seventeenth-century Puritan sermons that featured lengthy explications of doctrine, to the emotional sermons of the Great Awakening, to the unabashedly political sermons of the Revolutionary War years, the form evolved over time. In the nineteenth century, the sermon was adapted to a much wider range of functions. For John Nevin the sermon was a means to encourage ecumenism, whereas Ralph Waldo Emerson used the sermon to provoke his audiences to reflection on the beauty of God and nature. Charles Finney designed a program of "new-measures" conversionist techniques around the sermon, and William Channing sought to enlighten his audiences to the path of rational progress. In the course of working out their religious beliefs, these ministers came to understand the role of the sermon in different ways. Those diverse understandings were reflected in their various utilizations of the sermon as a dramatic device for communication.

As ministers adapted the sermon to suit their messages, certain styles of preaching became associated with certain ministers. During the Great Awakening, the personality of George Whitefield was unmistakably associated with the rousing sermons he preached throughout the colonies. The same was true with Charles Finney and his "new-measures" preaching in New York beginning in the 1820s. With the emergence in the nineteenth century of a remarkably wide range of perspectives on religion came many different styles of preaching. Many new movements sprang from the rich religious ferment of the time, as older denominations underwent change, and sometimes division, from within. As an increasingly large number of religious groups competed for members, preachers sought ever more diligently to devise styles of communication and dramatization that affected their audiences. The result, to an increasing extent, was that the personality of the preacher became the most significant component of American homiletics. By 1877, Phillips Brooks, the Episcopal bishop of Boston's Trinity Church, was informing Yale Divinity School students that preaching was the transmission of religious truth through the contagion of a strong personality.[19] In the twentieth century, and especially in the age of electronic media, this view influenced a great many religious leaders—Protestant, Catholic, and Jewish.

Preaching was an important component of the religion of Jews in America. Jews who migrated to America from Europe brought with them little in the way of a preaching tradition that corresponded to the emphases in Protestantism. The rabbi was essentially a teacher whose responsibilities revolved around the application of the Torah to the circumstances of the congregation. Jewish culture was rich with folktakes, however, that transmitted moral lessons and offered spiritual insight, and thus to some extent accomplished the sorts of things that Protestants might expect from a sermon. Under the influence of Protestantism in America, this form of Jewish sermonizing was developed to form a significant part of the religious life of a congregation. Some Jewish congregations enlarged the role of the rabbi to include regular preaching, and other congregations went so far as to create a new office in the synagogue, that of "preaching minister." Accordingly, preaching ability became an important consideration in evaluating a rabbi's talents, and the sermon eventually became a regular feature of the Jewish liturgy.

An early instance of the emergence of preaching in a Jewish congregation in America took place in a Sephardic congregation in Philadelphia. In 1829, Isaac Leeser, the newly elected cantor, began to preach regular sermons. Leeser later observed that "at that period, the duties of the minister were confined to the conducting of the public worship in the synagogue and elsewhere, and it was not accepted that he should be at the same time a preacher and exhorter."[20] Over time the congregation became accustomed to Leeser's exhortations, giving official approval to the practice in 1843. Other congregations soon afterward came to expect regular preaching, and as rabbis began to come to America after 1840, they learned to adapt to the expectations of their congregations. None was more successful in this regard than Isaac Meyer Wise, who arrived in Albany in 1846 and whose preaching, according to Leeser who visited him there, was eloquent and gratifying.

Preaching had long been an important part of Roman Catholic religious life. In the course of the Catholic liturgy, the priest traditionally had delivered a homily, which was shorter and generally less elaborate than the

---

[19] See *Lectures of Preaching* (New York, 1877); and Raymond W. Albright, *Focus on Infinity: A Life of Phillips Brooks* (New York, 1961), 187–89.

[20] Leeser is quoted in Leon A. Jick, *The Americanization of the Synagogue,* 1820–1870 (Hanover, N.H., 1976), 61.

Protestant sermon. The form of the Catholic sermon, however, was as fluid as the Protestant. Preaching from the pulpit, a priest could explain doctrine, exhort his audience to greater devotion, transmit the evolving social viewpoint of the church, promote morality, or address pressing local issues. Sometimes the priest took a verse of Scripture as a point of departure for the homily, whereas at other times he began with a message from the bishop or the Pope.

Among some Protestants, the sermon came to be understood as the primary means by which divine grace was communicated to persons. This was never the case in the Catholic Church, where the homily remained but one part of Catholic services. The American context gave rise to an increased Catholic concern with preaching, however. In fact, among some of the so-called Roman Catholic Americanists of the nineteenth century, the sermon came to occupy an elevated place in church services. In the mid-nineteenth century, Isaac Hecker of New York, a convert from Methodism and a Catholic priest, incorporated into his missionary campaign the revivalistic style of Protestant preaching, with very favorable results. Hecker later was admonished by the Vatican for seeking to "Americanize" Catholicism, but his belief in the importance of the sermon illustrates the trend toward progressively greater attention to the homily in Catholic worship. By the mid-twentieth century, Catholic seminary curriculum included a very substantial commitment to homiletics, and Catholic congregations had come to expect carefully crafted sermons as a part of their weekly services.

Preaching was particularly important in African American congregations, and the figure of the black preacher loomed large in the slave world as well as in the segregated world of free blacks. African American hopes and aspirations, as well as recollections of bondage, were focused on the figure of the preacher, who served not only as a spiritual guide and exhorter but also as the only person tolerated by whites as a voice for the African American community. "The Preacher," wrote W. E. B. Du Bois, "is the most unique personality developed by the Negro on American soil. A leader, a politician, an orator, a 'boss,' an intriguer, and idealist,—all these he is. . . ."[21]

Methodist and Baptist churches had welcomed blacks as members, and unlike many other churches they were prepared to offer them a share of the authority exercised by church leaders. Blacks with the "gift of preaching" were enlisted to serve as exhorters and, in numerous instances, as preachers and pastors. These black preachers were taught to read, and some were eventually ordained, but most commonly they continued as exhorters. Black preaching, encouraged by revivalistic Methodist and Baptist churches in the nineteenth century, featured an emotional style of preaching, oftentimes a kind of shouting, or as Du Bois wrote, a "Frenzy."[22]

---

[21] W. E. B. Du Bois, *The Souls of Black Folk* (Chicago, 1903), 190.

[22] Ibid., 191.

In addition to the evangelical themes of sin, rebirth, and salvation, black preaching was characterized by references to Old Testament stories about the enslavement of the Jews and their eventual liberation. In the hands of black preachers, these stories served not only as spiritual sustenance but also as commentary on the predicament of blacks throughout American history, and also as inspiration for continuing their struggle against racist inequality. During the nineteenth century, the sermon came to be the chief means by which African American communities expressed their disappointments, hopes, and political and social visions. It was through the sermon that Dr. Martin Luther King, Jr., inspired popular support for the civil rights movement in the 1960s.

Women who believed themselves called to the ministry but who were denied ordination in the churches also became itinerant preachers. This was by no means an easy undertaking for women, who had little in the way of models for their calling. Nancy Towle, who traveled extensively as a preacher in the 1820s and 1830s, recollected her call to preach as a confusing experience: "I sometimes felt a longing desire to go 'into all the world and preach the Gospel to every creature.' In imagination I was there; and in dreams of the night I was there. . . . But, nevertheless, I was not able to understand, how this could be, consistently required of me."[23]

Some women preached through a connection with a denomination, as was the case with Susan Humes, who acquired a reputation as a preacher at Methodist camp meetings in New England in the early 1820s.[24] Other women preachers charted new territory. Phoebe Palmer of New York, a member of the Methodist Episcopal church, undertook highly successful evangelistic tours in the United States and Canada, and she was instrumental in organizing the Holiness movement. In her lengthy defense of female preaching, *Promise of the Father* (1859), she argued that inspired preaching warranted a woman's "overstepping the precincts of her own church fold."[25] Like African Americans, women in the nineteenth century discovered that a reputation as an effective preacher could give them public standing on a level with an ordained minister. And in the religiously charged culture of nineteenth-century America, that was no mean accomplishment.

By the mid-nineteenth century, persons from all corners of society were preaching sermons of many different sorts. In practice, preaching came to represent freedom and democracy in America. In fact, one historian has concluded that by the time of the Civil War, "the sermon had become a metaphor for the culture of America."[26] It was no accident that Herman

---

[23] Nancy Towle, *Vicissitudes Illustrated, in the Experience of Nancy Towle* (Portsmouth, N.H., 1883), 22.

[24] Ibid., 37–38.

[25] Phoebe Palmer, *Promise of the Father* (Boston, 1859), 357.

[26] William B. Lawrence, "The History of Preaching in America," in *Encyclopedia of the American Religious Experience*, eds. Charles H. Lippy and Peter W. Williams, 3 (New York, 1988), 1317.

Melville presented the central theme of *Moby Dick* (1851) in a sermon preached by Father Mapple in Whaleman's Chapel. And what was Mapple's conclusion about the nature of duty to God? "To preach Truth in the face of Falsehood."[27]

The Mediating Theology of Horace Bushnell

After several false vocational starts, which included teaching, journalism, and law, a quiet conversion experience in the solitude of his own room sent Horace Bushnell to Yale Divinity School and to the pastorate of the North Congregational Church in Hartford, Connecticut, where he was to spend the rest of his active pastoral life.[28] Bushnell was both "conservative" and "liberal" in his emphases, finding much of Christian truth in the older tradition of New England and yet appropriating and incorporating into his thinking insights derived from the Unitarian critique. He could speak of "free," "self-governed" individuals and yet could emphasize the way in which individuals are bound, either for good or for evil, by the organic character of the communities—family, church, neighborhood, and nation—in which they exist. His endeavor was to be a mediator, reconciling the intimations of Christian truth to be found in diverse theological camps. Although Bushnell's views won little acceptance prior to the Civil War, they later became of major importance in preparing the way for the New Theology of the 1870s and 1880s.

Bushnell is best remembered as the author of *Christian Nurture* (1847), which, while not his most important work, was one of the most influential books ever to be published in America. It was a criticism of revivalism and a plea for what in its broadest sense could be called Christian education. With his understanding of language as a social phenomenon, Bushnell was driven to recognize the formative influence of the community of faith. No person exists in isolation. All live within a social context that shapes and determines character. There is no reason to suppose that a child of believing parents cannot "grow up in the Lord." Take any scheme of human nature that you please, Bushnell declared, and you will find nothing in it "to forbid the possibility that a child should be led, in his first moral act, to cleave unto what is good and right." Instead of assuming that "the child is to grow up in sin, to be converted after he comes to mature age," the "aim, effort, and expectation" should be that he may "grow up a Christian and never know himself as being otherwise." The great trouble with revivalism, as Bushnell saw it, is that as a result of its "jump and stir," the ordinary operations of God's grace tend to be "swallowed up and lost in the extraordinary," and people are led to

---

[27] Herman Melville, *Moby-Dick, or The Whale* (New York, 1947), 46.

[28] See Barbara M. Cross, *Horace Bushnell* (Chicago, 1958).

Three Stalwarts: Elizabeth Cady Stanton, Harriet Beecher Stowe, and Julia Ward Howe. Stanton adopted Amelia Bloomer's dress reform as well as short hair. (*Elizabeth Cady Stanton, photograph from Brown Brothers; Alanson Fisher "Portrait of Harriet Elizabeth Beecher Stowe," author and reformer (1811–1896). Oil on canvas, 1853. National Portrait Gallery, Washington, DC, U.S.A./Art Resource, NY; Julia Ward Howe, reproduced from an 1861 photograph in* Julia Ward Howe, Reminiscences, 1819–1899, *Boston, Houghton Mifflin Co., 1899.*)

believe that the only entrance into the Christian life is through a convulsive conversion experience in a revival meeting.[29]

Bushnell was not opposed to revivals. He believed that they rendered a necessary service to those who have been caught in the web of the kingdom of evil. Sin no less than virtue can be transmitted by the social context.

> Evil, once beginning to exist, inevitably becomes organic and constructs a kind of principate or kingdom opposite to God. . . . Pride organizes caste and dominates in the sphere of fashion. Corrupt opinions, false judgments, bad manners, and a general body of conventionalisms that represent the motherhood of sin, come into vogue and reign. And so, doubtless, everywhere and in all worlds, sin has in its nature to organize, mount into the ascendant above God and truth, and reign in a kingdom opposite God.[30]

With God's help and the Christian nurture provided by family and church, no one need sink into the slough of sin; but if that problem has occurred, then a drastic rebirth to change the "reigning love" is necessary. As early as 1838, Bushnell had published an article in the *Quarterly Christian Spectator* "to establish a higher and more solid confidence in revivals," an article in which he insisted that "nothing was ever achieved in the way of great and radical change without some degree of excitement; and if any one expects to carry on the cause of salvation by a steady rolling on the same dead level, and fears continually lest the axles wax hot and kindle into a flame," that person "is too timorous to hold the reins of the Lord's chariot." Although not everyone needed "a fireball shot from the moon," some did.[31]

As Bushnell reconciled revivalism to the ordered life of home and congregation, so he reconciled the major contentions of the Unitarians with an evangelical understanding of the Christian faith. He refashioned his conception of God, man, Christ, and the Atonement to take the force from the Unitarian critique, and in the process, he reached back to Jonathan Edwards for themes that helped him make his case. He reaffirmed the Trinity by acknowledging that it applied only to God as revealed and not as ultimate being, as descriptive not of his person but of the modes of self-disclosure by which he makes himself known as Father, Son, and Spirit. In similar fashion, Bushnell bridged the gap between the natural and the supernatural without allowing them to become indistinguishable. During the second half of the century, Bushnell's "progressive orthodoxy" was to sweep through many of the seminaries, and men who had been deeply influenced by him were to be among the most distinguished preachers in the land.

---

[29] Horace Bushnell, *Christian Nurture* (New York, 1923), 4, 10; "Spiritual Economy of Revivals of Religion," *Quarterly Christian Spectator* (1838), 143–45.

[30] Horace Bushnell, *Nature and the Supernatural* (New York, 1858), 135.

[31] Horace Bushnell, *An Argument for "Discourses on Christian Nurture"* (Hartford, 1847), 16.

PART THREE

Years of Midpassage
1869–1918

CHAPTER NINE

Post–Civil War America

The Civil War was a watershed between an old and a new America. The American people became much more heterogeneous in background. The advent of modern science drastically altered the intellectual climate. And the quickening pace of industrialization created new centers of power in national life.

The changing composition of the population was one of the conspicuous contrasts between the old and the new America. After 1840, a sharply increasing percentage of the population was of foreign birth. From 1850 to 1860, the number of foreign born had increased 84.4 percent. From 1860 to 1870, in spite of the dislocation of war, there was a further increase of 34.5 percent. The first great influx had come from Ireland and Germany, but before the end of the century, many nations were contributing to the growing number of new Americans. In contrast to the overwhelming predominance of British elements in the population at the beginning of the century, only a small percentge of the new arrivals were from England, Scotland, and Wales. By 1900, out of a population of 75 million, one-third were either of foreign birth or children of foreign-born parents. Of these 25 million new Americans, 8 million were German in background; 5 million were Irish; 2.5 million had come from Austria, Hungary, Poland, and Italy; another 2.5 million had come from the Scandinavian countries; 850,000 were French Canadians; and 774,000 had come from Russia. In addition to these totals, there were several million grandchildren of the immigrants who had arrived in the 1840s, 1850s, and 1860s.

A second contrast between the old and the new America was the radical shift in the intellectual climate. Geology, in the person of Charles Lyell, had been busy rewriting the Genesis account of the origin and early history of the earth. But it was the new biology, as set forth by Charles Darwin in his *On the Origin of Species* (1859), that was to become the chief symbol of the intellectual revolution. The idea of evolution was not new. It had been championed by Hegel and Comte, and the writings of Herbert Spencer were to be more important than those of Darwin in pointing up the full implications of evolutionary thinking. Spencer adopted the doctrine of evolution as a unifying philosophical principle and sought to apply it to all phenomena. *Progress, Its Law and Cause* (1857) set forth the basic thesis that was elaborated in his subsequent writings: *First Principles* (1862), *Principles of Biology* (1864–1867), *Principles of Psychology* (rev. ed., 1870–1872), *Principles of Sociology* (1876–1896), and *Principles of Ethics* (1892–1893). With this evolutionism penetrating every realm of thought, a new history began to be written that was based on the application of evolutionary theories to the understanding of the past. And this new historical understanding bolstered the developing "higher criticism" of the Bible—first in Germany and then in Britain and America—which many were to find so disturbing.

A third feature of post–Civil War America was a marked shift in the center of power. Before the war the agrarian democracy envisaged by Jefferson still reigned supreme, although the lure of the city had begun to replace the lure of the West among young men of spirit and ambition. The census statistics for the decade 1840 to 1850, which revealed that the population of the cities had increased 90 percent, whereas the population of the country as a whole had increased only 36 percent, gave a foretaste of what was to come. Ten years later, in 1860, the capital invested in industry, railroads, commerce, and urban property was greater than the value of all the farms. The Civil War had "the effect of a hothouse" on this industrial growth. Military needs and currency inflation caused the mills to roar louder and the blast furnaces to flame higher. By the time Ulysses S. Grant took the oath of office as president of the United States, there was no longer any doubt that the dominant influence in American life had shifted from the rural countryside to the burgeoning urban communities. The successive efforts of Grangers, Greenbackers, and Populists to dislodge the commercial and industrial interests from the centers of power simply confirmed the fact that they were fighting a lost cause, for they never were able to win more than regional victories.

Each of these facets of post–Civil War society was to pose critical problems for the churches, but their full significance did not become clear for a decade or two. In the meantime, there were pressing problems that demanded immediate attention.

Reconstituting the Nation

When Abraham Lincoln stood on the windswept fields of Gettysburg and spoke of those who "four score and seven years" before had "brought forth on this continent a new nation, conceived in liberty, and dedicated to the proposition that all men are created equal," he was recalling the theme that had given meaning and significance to the sense of American nationhood. But now this venture had been brought into question. Although Lincoln looked forward to the time when "this nation, under God, shall have a new birth of freedom," there was no blinking the stark, stubborn, present fact that the American people were engaged "in a great civil war, testing whether that nation, or any nation so conceived and so dedicated, can long endure."

The Bond of Religion

From the beginning of national life, religion had served as a bond of unity that helped overcome the divisive effects of competing local interests and regional concerns. The Great Awakening had done much to make the several colonies emotionally one by binding them together in a common cause, generating a common loyalty, fostering common sentiments, and thrusting forward a common leadership. But it was a theological interpretation of the American past, present, and future that had contributed most to making them one nation. What had welded together the diverse peoples of the colonies—Englishmen, Scots, and Germans; Georgians, Virginians, and New Yorkers—was the consciousness of being summoned to a God-given mission. God had "designed this continent . . . to be the asylum of liberty" and had selected America to be an example to the nations. There was scarcely anyone who had not believed with Lyman Beecher that the establishment of the United States "in the full enjoyment of civil and religious liberty" had been a "design of Heaven" to demonstrate to the world "by one great successful experiment of what man is capable" and thereby to awaken among peoples everywhere the "desire and hope and effort" that would produce "revolutions and overturnings" until the whole world was free. It was this conviction that had given Americans whatever sense of common nationality they had, and it was this conviction that gave such moving power to the few brief words spoken by Lincoln at Gettysburg.

As tension had mounted between the North and the South, there had been agonized efforts to preserve the unity of the nation by reminding people of their God-given vocation. But the slavery question proved so disruptive that not even the churches could be kept from separating, and their divisions were prophetic of the tragedy that was to follow. Few had believed that the war could come. The notion that the nation could descend to fratricidal strife was unthinkable to most Americans. "There must be no war" had been a repetitive refrain. But the war had come, and its effect was shattering. The great "experiment" had gone wrong. The protective hand of divine Providence seemingly had been removed. No longer could Americans picture themselves as an example to the nations. Nor could they ease their tortured spirits by placing the blame for the disaster upon extraneous circumstance. The responsibility could not be sought beyond the American people themselves. No outside nation was involved. No foreign influence played any part in precipitating the tragedy. The machinery of peace was at hand in the orderly procedures of national life, but it had not been utilized.

The traumatic effect of the war was doubly compounded when what had been the bond of union was twisted to serve the cause of division. It was both natural and appropriate for the churches, North and South, to provide chaplains for the combatants and to organize agencies to minister to the temporal as well as the spiritual needs of the soldiers. It was no less natural for them to seek God's blessing and to claim divine sanction for their opposing armies, but it was profoundly disconcerting and disturbing. Those on both sides of the Mason-Dixon line in theology and piety were brothers, yet they offered contradictory prayers. In both North and South, the God who had made them a nation was being reduced to the partisan of a section.[1] When the bond that had united them was being utilized by apologists in both camps to justify the resort to arms, it was clear that the war itself must somehow be brought within the scope of a larger design of God if the nation were to be reunited.

Although not many gave themselves to this latter task, Lincoln was struggling throughout the war years to find a larger meaning to the conflict than that suggested by any simple alliance of Providence with either the North or the South.[2] Displaying a deeper theological perception than many preachers, he wrote to John Hay in 1862 that "it is quite possible that God's purpose is something different from the purpose of either party;

[1] Two Presbyterian theologians, J. H. Thornwell and R. L. Dabney, were the most effective apologists in linking the position of the South with the cause of God and religion. Thornwell declared that "the Scriptures not only fail to condemn slavery, they as distinctly sanction it as any other social condition of man." To call slavery sinful, therefore, is to reject the Bible. "Our policy," wrote Dabney, must be "to push the Bible argument continually" and force the enemies of slavery to reveal their true infidel colors. Presbyterians, of course, were not alone in this enterprise. Episcopalians, Baptists, and Methodists played their part. Even John England, Roman Catholic bishop of Charleston, wrote a sturdy defense of slavery on biblical grounds. For representative statements, see H. Shelton Smith, Robert Handy, and Lefferts Loetscher, *American Christianity*, II, 177–78, 182–86, 201–10.

[2] See W. J. Wolf, *Lincoln's Religion* (Chicago, 1974); J. H. Moorhead, *American Apocalypse: Yankee Protestants and the Civil War* (New Haven, 1978); and C. C. Goen, *Broken Churches, Broken Nation* (Macon, Ga., 1985).

and yet the human instrumentalities, working just as they do, are of the best adaptation to effect his purpose. I am almost ready to say that this is probably true; that God wills this contest, and wills that it shall not end yet." Later in the same year he told a congressional delegation that he believed that God "will compel us to do right in order that he may do these things, not so much because we desire them as that they accord with his plans for dealing with this nation." And then he continued: "Sometimes it seems necessary that we should be confronted with perils which threaten us with disaster in order that we may not get puffed up and forget him who has much work for us yet to do." In his Second Inaugural Address, he reverted once again to this theme.

> On the occasion corresponding to this four years ago, all thoughts were anxiously directed to an impending civil war. . . . Neither party expected for the war the magnitude or the duration which it has already attained. . . . Each looked for an easier triumph, and a result less fundamental and astounding. Both read the same Bible, and pray to the same God; and each invokes his aid against the other. It may seem strange that any men should dare to ask a just God's assistance in wringing their bread from the sweat of other men's faces; but let us judge not, that we be not judged. The prayers of both could not be answered—that of neither has been answered fully.
>
> The Almighty has his own purposes. . . . If we shall suppose that American slavery is one of those offenses which, in the providence of God, must needs come, but which, having continued through his appointed time, he now wills to remove, and that he gives to both North and South this terrible war, as the woe due to those by whom the offense came, shall we discern therein any departure from divine attributes which the believers in a living God always ascribe to him?
>
> Fondly do we hope—fervently do we pray—that this mighty scourge of war may speedily pass away. Yes, if God wills that it continue until all the wealth piled by the bondman's two hundred and fifty years of unrequited toil shall be sunk, and until every drop of blood drawn with the lash shall be paid by another drawn with the sword, as was said three thousand years ago, so still it must be said, "The judgments of the Lord are true and righteous altogether."

Lincoln was not alone in exploring the theme of God's hand in the conflict. Of the theologians who picked it up and elaborated it, Horace Bushnell and Philip Schaff were most prominent.[3] Like Lincoln, they both saw the war as the product of the guilt of the whole nation, the humiliation of an arrogant and a boastful people, a supreme hour of trial designed to aid the nation to fulfill rather than to forfeit its destiny. Slavery had been the Achilles' heel of a nation called to exemplify what it meant for all people to be created free and equal, but slavery was not the sin of the South

---

[3] See W. A. Clebsch, *Christian Interpretations of the Civil War* (Philadelphia, 1969). Also see T. J. Pressly, *Americans Interpret Their Civil War* (New York, 1962).

alone. The evil was inherited by the whole nation. Nor was slavery the real cause of the war. The real issue was whether or not the American people were to be a true people capable of fulfilling their destiny. Hitherto—"half-loyally and half-lawlessly"—Americans had claimed a self-made and thus a false nationality. Too many had thought of the nation as their own creation and had never given themselves fully to it. The several states had "simply kenneled under the Constitution" and had not been merged and compacted into a true nation.

As the product of the collective guilt of the American people, the war was an act of divine judgment. But to Bushnell and Schaff it was more than that, for it presented the possibility of redemption and renewal. Believing that without the shedding of blood there is no atonement, they viewed the war as a sacrificial and cleansing tragedy that contained within it the possibility not only of preserving but also of regenerating the nation. The "baptism of blood" was thus to be seen as an act of divine mercy through which the nation could be reborn, purged of its sin, and recalled to its proper vocation. Upon the anvil of suffering and under the hammer of a providential God, it was hoped that what had been only a federation made up by a temporary surrender of power would be forged into a true nationhood. It seemed clear to them that nothing less than a common tragedy was sufficient to effect the reconciliation that would unify a heterogeneous population into the free and responsible society that from the beginning had been God's intention for the American people.

What Lincoln, Bushnell, and Schaff were seeking to do was to restore to the American people their former bond of union by helping them understand that even in the war itself, God's will was being worked out in the life of the nation. The verdict of the war could then be accepted with grace both by those who gained the triumph and by those who suffered defeat, for by this reappropriation and reinterpretation of the American experience, the conflict could be transmuted into something more than an occasion for future bitter memories. It was with this thought in mind that Lincoln looked forward to the future task as he brought his Second Inaugural Address to a close with words that have never been forgotten:

> With malice toward none; with charity for all; with firmness in the right, as God gives us to see the right, let us strive on to finish the work we are in; to bind up the nation's wounds; to care for him who shall have borne the battle and for his widow and orphan—to do all which may achieve and cherish a just and lasting peace among ourselves, and with all nations.

The Failure of Reconstruction

Having compressed into four years a bloody slaughter that was comparable in magnitude only to the losses inflicted over a decade and a half by the Napoleonic wars, it was to be expected that festering sores would be left that would complicate and long delay the task of binding up the nation's wounds. Still there were many factors that could be counted upon to facilitate the healing process, not the least of which was the general weariness of the people with the war. The generous spirit exhibited by Grant in victory and the dignified acceptance of defeat by Lee had the immediate effect of tending to minimize recrimination. Reconciliation was further eased by "mystic chords of memory" that stretched back beyond the strife to the common history that had been shared. Having been schooled in the providential view of history, many were prepared to accept the outcome of the war as a clear manifestation of God's will for the nation. Reduced to its simplest form, the plain implication of the providential understanding of defeat was stated by a young South Carolinian: "I think it was in the decrees of Almighty God that slavery was to be abolished in this way, and I don't murmur."[4] Other Southerners found it possible to take the more positive view articulated by Bushnell and Schaff. Stephen Elliott of Georgia and Richard H. Wilmer of Alabama were conspicuous examples of theologians who were able to find in the war grounds for gratitude of God for settling "the meaning of the Constitution," restoring to the American people "one undivided country," and making clear the true mission of the nation.[5] Within this perspective, both Lee and Lincoln had served as instruments in the hands of God to effect his purposes; and it was this understanding that made it possible for both men to be lifted from the status of partisan leaders to that of national heroes.

Unfortunately the universal esteem in which Lincoln and Lee came to be held was deceptive, for the reconciliation was destined to be incomplete, and a unified national life was never fully reestablished. However decisive the war had been, the peace proved to be inconclusive. In the absence of strong leadership, the national government could not agree on what to make of its victory. Efforts at reconstruction were delayed, confused, indecisive, and of short duration.[6] There was little evidence of that "firmness" to "strive on to finish the work we are in" of which Lincoln had spoken. Some, to be sure, sought to gain political advantage by "waving the bloody shirt," but this attempt did not conceal the increasing disposition in the North to leave the South to its own devices and to get on with the business of tapping the national till and reaping the profits of a booming economy. Seldom in history has a nation been so heedless of the fruits of victory. The issues that had stood at the center of the conflict were subordinated to partisan politics, and the task of restoring the Union by protecting the fundamental rights of all its people was neglected.

[4] Quoted by S. E. Mead, *Lively Experiment,* (New York, 1963), 143.

[5] Clebsch.

[6] See J. H. Franklin, *Reconstruction After the Civil War* (Chicago, 1961); C. Vann Woodward, *Reunion and Reaction: The Compromise of 1877 and the End of Reconstruction* (Boston, 1951); and Lawanda and J. H. Cox, *Politics, Principle, and Prejudice, 1865–1866* (New York, 1963).

As soon as it was apparent that little support was to be given the law-abiding elements in the South, unrepentant extremists became convinced that their cause was not wholly lost. Bands of hoodlums—Jayhawkers, Red Shirts, Knights of the White Camellia, and Klansmen—were recruited to intimidate law-abiding citizens by night-riding forays of pillage and torture. With amazing rapidity, unreconstructed malcontents gained control of the former secessionist states, silenced the dissent of other white Southerners, and put blacks "in their place"—a place that sometimes afforded them less protection than that of their previous status as slaves. While Lee continued to be revered, General Nathan Bedford Forrest, Grand Wizard of the Ku Klux Klan, became the romantic hero that young white Southerners of spirit were encouraged to admire and emulate.

Although the outward ties of national life had been restored by the war, the resulting unity was far removed from that true nationhood that some had dared hope would be the consequence of the baptism of blood through which the American people had passed. In 1880, to be sure, Atticus G. Haygood, Methodist president of Emory University, preached a Thanksgiving sermon on "The New South"[7] in which he re-peated the theme that had been articulated by Elliott and Wilmer. But many of his fellow Southerners did not heed his appeal to recognize that the abolition of slavery had been a blessing and that their duty now was to rejoin the Union in spirit as well as in fact. As early as 1865, an-other Methodist preacher in Mississippi had exhorted the South: "If we cannot gain our *political*, then let us establish our *mental* indepen-dence."[8] Actually, in the vacuum created by the withdrawal of national leadership, a very large degree of political independence was achieved, and this outcome fostered a growing mental independence. The suc-cessful defiance of the brief effort at Reconstruction along the lines of a national policy made it possible for many Southerners to ignore the ver-dict of the war and to cling to an understanding of the American Consti-tution that had few points of contact with either the realities of the past or the necessities of the future. This essentially romantic interpretation of the American experience left the South intellectually and emotion-ally isolated from the rest of the nation. There was no conversion to an understanding that the nation was anything more than a mere aggrega-tion of sovereign states. What unity there was had been achieved by leav-ing the major issues—as far as the South was concerned—unresolved, and from these unresolved issues a later generation was destined to reap a bitter harvest.

---

[7] Reprinted in Smith, Handy, and Loetscher, II, 372–77.

[8] K. K. Bailey, "Southern White Protestantism at the Turn of the Century," *American Historical Review*, 68 (1963), 618.

The Southern Churches

The independent regional course of development that the South was permitted to pursue following the Civil War fostered a growing sectional self-consciousness that was to manifest itself in the religious as well as in the political and intellectual life of the southern states. There were some ecclesiastical links with the rest of the nation. Denominations that had not divided over the issue of slavery prior to the Civil War experienced no great difficulty in resuming their former unified denominational life. For them there was no prewar heritage of bitterness to overcome, and they had had scant time to develop the vested interests of an independent institutional life.

The ease with which the latter denominations effected the reunion of their severed branches is illustrated by the Protestant Episcopal Church. Although a separate Episcopal church had been formed in the South following Secession, the fact that a schism had occurred was never recognized or accepted by northern Episcopalians. At the General Convention of 1862, the roll call included the southern dioceses—an action that implied that the missing bishops and deputies were only temporarily absent. The next convention was held in October 1865, six months after Lee had surrendered. Prior to the convention, the presiding bishop wrote to all the southern bishops inviting them to attend and assuring them of a cordial welcome. The response to the invitation was varied. Those who attended, however, were received with such friendly warmth that a month later the General Council of the southern Episcopal church voted that, since the circumstances that had brought it into existence had ceased, the southern dioceses were free to renew their former affiliation.

The denominations that were able to reunite, however, represented only a minority of southern church members. The three major denominations were the Methodists, Baptists, and Presbyterians. The Methodists and Baptists had gone their separate ways since 1845. Although there was much initial sentiment for reunion in both communions, the Methodist Episcopal Church, South, and the Southern Baptist Convention had become too firmly established to be quickly dismantled. Time was needed to untangle the existing institutional structures, but each year of delay made the prospect of success less promising as a result of the steadily increasing southern regional self-consciousness. By 1869, the Methodist *Richmond Christian Advocate* was declaring, "We consider reunion neither possible nor desirable."[9]

The Presbyterian division was more recent, but it was complicated by an earlier schism. Since 1837, the Presbyterians had been divided into Old School and New School bodies. In 1857, the New School Presbyterians divided over the issue of slavery, and in 1861, the southern Old School Presbyterians formed a separate church. In 1864, the New School and Old School Presbyterians in the South united. Thus at the close of hostilities

---

[9] William Warren Sweet, *Virginia Methodism* (Richmond, Va., 1955), 285.

the major body of Presbyterians was confronted by a three-way split. The first task seemed to be the healing of the breach in the North as a preparatory step to ending the schism between North and South. This undertaking occasioned delay, for negotiations initiated in 1866 were not brought to a successful conclusion until 1870. By this time an intense sectional spirit had reasserted itself in the South, and Presbyterians were to be no more successful than Methodist or Baptists in bridging the institutional barriers that had been erected.

The three large southern denominations justified their separate existence by constantly reminding themselves that Southerners were "a different people,"[10] and over the years their ecclesiastical isolation helped to give substance to their assertion. Several factors combined to produce this result. The most obvious, of course, was the mere fact of institutional separation, which left most of the southern churches out of touch with the developing religious life of the rest of the nation. Equally important in giving the religious and ecclesiastical ethos of the South its own distinctive cast was the nostalgia that caused Southerners to idealize the past and to look askance at any innovation in either thought of practice. And further heightening the insularity of the southern churches was their role as the only available vehicle for the institutional expression of sectional feeling. Politically the South was divided into several states. Economically the South was not homogeneous, and its new commercial and industrial ventures were tied to northern financial centers. Thus the southern Methodist church, the southern Presbyterian church, and the Southern Baptist Convention were the only institutional links that bound the South

---

[10] The *New Orleans Christian Advocate* was to declare in 1880 that the "civilization of the two sections, and the customs and character of the people are in many things diverse. . . . One broad distinction is that the Southerner, as a matter of honor and principle, minds his own business, while the inborn nature of the North is to meddle. The South is tolerant, courteous, and refined in its contact with people in the ordinary associations of life. The North has a prying, inquisitive disposition, and is bent on bringing every one to its way of thinking and doing."

There are also differences in religion. "There is a south side to churches and religion, not so much in regard to their creeds, articles of religion, and church polity, as in the type of piety that prevails. Methodists and Presbyterians in the South profess the same faith as Methodists and Presbyterians in the North, and yet they are not the same people. The political meddling of the Northern churches is, of course, one difference. . . . There is a secularity about them, and a style that brings them into near fellowship with worldly enterprises and organizations. They *run* things up there—churches as well as factories and railroads. The style of their preaching is in contrast with ours, and is largely of the politico-sensational order. The North has been over-run with professional evangelists, whose methods and teachings have in many instances done harm. People raised in these churches, and imbued with their spirit, if converted, are apt to be essentially defective in the higher traits of Christian character. With many excellent people and exemplary Christians among them, and with much that is good and worthy of imitation in their church work, there is a spirit and practice, and a type of religion, that we should regret to see in our southern churches." Quoted by H. D. Farish, *The Circuit Rider Dismounts* (Richmond, Va., 1938), 148–49.

together. Although the regional character of these denominations contributed to the popular esteem in which they were held throughout the South, this culturally grounded popularity tended to insulate them further from the larger Christian community.

The folk religion of the southern churches was further heightened by an adherence to the doctrine of "the spirituality of the church." This concept had first been formulated by a Presbyterian, John Holt Rice. When it became apparent in 1827 that the slavery issue was apt to disrupt church life, Rice suggested that the church should "confine itself to making good Christians" and not concern itself with matters beyond its competence, such as the civil arrangements of society. By this means a bifurcation was introduced that permitted the churches to condone slavery while condemning card playing and dancing, and that was reflected in the subsequent attitude of southern Methodist bishops who rejoiced that their church held aloof from political questions and was "satisfied to perform her own legitimate duties."[11]

Basically, however, the southern churches preserved and perpetuated the popular evangelicalism of the immediate prewar period, stressing sentimental preaching, periodic revivals, and heartfelt religion. Although outsiders could point to many defects, including a rigid biblicism that sometimes tended to become obscurantist, there were also manifestations of an impressive vitality that on occasion broke the bonds of established custom. This southern evangelicalism was not distinctive in itself. Parallel expressions were to be found in other sections of the country. What made it distinctive was its almost complete predominance throughout the South and its success in withstanding any fundamental change in either thought or practice over a long period of time.

The Churches and the Freedmen

When he assumed the presidency in 1861, Abraham Lincoln had noted the obligation imposed upon him by the Constitution to see that "the laws of the Union be faithfully executed in all the States." A month later he issued a call for 75,000 volunteers in order to fulfill this constitutional duty. Combinations "too powerful to be suppressed by the ordinary course of judicial proceedings" had arisen, and this left him with no alternative but to utilize the armed forces of the United States "to cause the laws to be duly executed." The integrity of the nation was at stake, and the fundamental issue of the conflict that followed was the preservation of the nation. The precipitating cause of the war, however, had been the issue of human bondage, and before the strife was over, the system of human slavery had been brought to an

---

[11] E. T. Thompson, *The Spirituality of the Church* (Richmond, Va., 1961), 21; Sweet, 298; S. S. Hill, *Southern Churches in Crisis* (Boston, 1968).

end by executive proclamation. As a consequence of the presidential action and the later constitutional amendment, American blacks—for the first time in any significant numbers—were given an opportunity to determine their own destiny. Legal and extralegal restrictions were to limit this freedom, and its exercise was to prove hazardous in many localities. Nonetheless, the Emancipation Proclamation marked the beginning of a new era.

The Growth of African American Churches

In the decades after the Civil War, spirituals, a key feature of black worship, became a less common feature in black congregations. This change was due in part to blacks' determination to distance themselves from slavery, and partly because their worship in the institutionalized churches that they joined was more highly structured than plantation worship and therefore less accommodating of the spontaneity that had produced spirituals. Worship remained lively, however, and singing endured as a central feature of worship within black congregations.

Black churches grew steadily in the latter half of the nineteenth century, and very rapidly in the period 1890–1930. Membership increases in the black churches far outpaced those in other churches. Prior to the Civil War, the percentage of blacks who were church members was less than half the percentage of whites who were church members. By 1916, this percentage was slightly larger, having increased from about 11 percent to approximately 43 percent of the black population. Over 90 percent of the church-going blacks were Methodist or Baptist. The popularity of the church among blacks stemmed at least in part from the fact that it was one of the few institutions that was exclusively their own. Cut off from most areas of social and political life, blacks found in the church the opportunity for self-expression, recognition, and leadership. It was hardly a coincidence that until well into the twentieth century, most of the outstanding black leaders had been ministers, for the ministry provided one of the few opportunities for leadership open to blacks. Furthermore, the church was the primary agency of self-help in the community, in a society in which the family had historically been undermined by slavery—families routinely were broken up for sale—and by the vast migration of individual family members to the North, which began in the late nineteenth century.

The emergence of black denominations in the early nineteenth century set the stage for the large-scale movement of freedmen to institutionalized religion after the Civil War. The African Methodist Episcopal Church was organized in 1816 out of a separation from other Methodists that had occurred in Philadelphia in 1784. It numbered 20,000 persons in 1864, and by 1884 had grown to a remarkable 400,000 members. The African Methodist Episcopal Zion Church, which was formed in 1821 following a separation from a New York congregation, experienced even more rapid growth, from 6,000 to 300,000 members during approximately the same period. The Colored (Christian) Methodist Episcopal Church emerged out of the Methodist Episcopal Church, South, in the 1860s, with about 50,000 members. During Reconstruction, black Baptist congregations— small, poor, and rural—arose in numbers that led quickly to a Baptist majority among ex-slaves. One feature of the Baptist churches that made them attractive was the ease with which they could be organized. African Baptist congregations had been formed in Boston in 1805, in New York in 1807, and in Philadelphia in 1809. In the West, regional Baptist associations had been established between 1835 and 1855. In the South, very few separate black churches were organized among either Baptists or Methodists before 1865, however; and most black Baptists and Methodists worshiped alongside whites in churches where whites sometimes were a small minority. Reconstruction changed that pattern. By the late 1860s, every southern state had its own black Baptist convention, and in 1886, a majority of the members of these conventions joined together as the National Baptist Convention.

The increase in black membership in the churches was an outcome of the concentrated efforts of denominational missionary societies, the involvement of the federal government through the Freedmen's Bureau, and, especially, the American Missionary Association (AMA) which was supported largely by northern Congregationalists. Lewis Tappan, treasurer of the AMA in 1861, had sent a representative, the Reverend Lewis C. Lockwood, to investigate reports of black refugees at Fortress Monroe, in Virginia, shortly after the Confederate shelling of Fort Sumter. Noting that the blacks he encountered there had "a great thirst for knowledge" and recognizing the possibilities for Christianizing them, he engaged Mrs. Mary Peake, who at the time was active in a black Baptist church in Norfolk, to teach reading, religious songs, and the Bible to black children and adults. As the initial effort of what became a missionary enterprise on a grand scale, Peake's school, and Peake herself—she rejected her physician's advice to abandon her work and died in 1862—set the tone for AMA activities among southern blacks for the rest of the century.[12]

In attempting to reach the 3.5 million freedmen after the war, the AMA had put 83 teachers into the field by late 1863. By 1867, the number had increased to 528. Among the surviving institutions that the Association begat are Fisk, Atlanta, and Tougaloo universities; Talladega College; and Hampton Institute. Methodist and Baptist organizations also contributed to establishing black educational institutions, and they were aided by modest contributions from other denominations. The fluid race relations of early Reconstruction soon gave way, however, to a hardening of sentiment

---

[12] See Joe M. Richardson, *Christian Reconstruction: The American Missionary Association and Southern Blacks, 1861–1890* (Athens, Ga., and London, 1986), 4.

against the education of blacks and to the passage of Jim Crow laws, which actively excluded blacks from white society. The AMA and other organizations continued their involvement in black education, largely through the efforts of women such as Mary Peake. These missionaries and teachers included Etta Payne, who was trained in medical schools in Boston and Philadelphia; Laura Stebbins, from the English Classical School in Springfield, Massachusetts; Eliza Summers, who had taught in public schools in Woodbury, Connecticut; and a host of female workers from Mount Holyoke Seminary, Oberlin College, and the ranks of primary and secondary schoolteachers. The AMA also continued financially to assist black congregations, typically in poor, rural areas, as in the case of a church built in Liberty County, Georgia, in 1874, which was announced in the local *Gazette* in a way that stressed the northern involvement: "The colored people below no. 3 A&G. R.R. [Atlantic and Gulf Railroad], with commendable zeal, have started to erect a large church. The building which is to be fifty feet long, and thirty-five wide, is to be located near Arcadia. . . . This enterprise, which is under the charge of the Congregationalists, has received material aid from the north."[13]

With the end of Reconstruction in 1877, black communities suffered increasing abuse and subjugation as white supremacists consolidated power in the South and the federal judicial system sanctioned segregation. Beginning in the 1890s, in the wake of a series of crop failures, large numbers of blacks began resigning tenantry and sharecropping on southern farms and moving to urban areas, especially in the North, where there was demand for factory labor. The membership rolls of black churches in Chicago, Detroit, Cincinnati, Philadelphia, Baltimore, and other cities doubled or tripled over the course of the Great Migration. Black Baptist and Methodist churches, the AME and AMEZ, and various other congregations expanded rapidly, constructing or enlarging houses of worship, organizing social programs, providing basic education, and assisting with housing. Accordingly, a primary function of these churches was to facilitate the adaptation of rural migrants to urban industrial life.

Revivalistic religion flourished in the growing black urban congregations. Pentecostal and Holiness Christianity proved particularly attractive. These "sanctified" churches, which originally included both African Americans and Caucasians, promoted a highly emotional style of religion and dictated strict standards of virtue. They also enlarged the worship service to include a variety of musical instruments and reiterated the role of shouting, dancing, clapping, and physically demonstrative praise, which

---

[13] Quoted in Thomas F. Armstrong, "The Building of a Black Church: Community in Post–Civil War Liberty County, Georgia," in *African-American Life in the Post-Emancipation South, 1861–1900,* vol. 9 of 12 vols., ed. Donald G. Nieman (Garland, N.Y., and London, 1994), 164.

were in increasingly short supply in Baptist and Methodist churches. Emphasizing a "baptism in the Holy Ghost," the majority of these congregations practiced speaking in tongues and expected healing and prophecy as "gifts of the Spirit" as well. Among the many churches that were formed along these lines, the Church of God in Christ, founded by Charles Harrison Mason, stands out. Mason, born to former slaves who had been converted during the Second Great Awakening, experienced conversion in 1880 and subsequently became a Baptist minister. In Lexington, Tennessee, in 1897, Mason preached to a growing audience, which survived the pistol and shotgun attacks during their meetings in an abandoned cotton-gin house. This audience became the core congregation of the Church of God in Christ when Mason incorporated his church later that year. Ten years later, after attending the Azusa Street Revival in Los Angeles led by the black Holiness preacher William J. Seymour, Mason introduced into his church the practice of speaking in tongues that he had witnessed among the black and white participants at Azusa Street.

During the period 1890 to 1940, an assortment of messiahs—persons claiming to be God or to possess divine powers—came to prominence in the black community. Some, such as S. D. Grace and Father Divine, developed organizations that expanded to a variety of urban settings. Others remained local and fleeting in their influence, and not all were African Americans. In 1889, Jacob Orth, a white man in coastal Georgia, convinced as many as a thousand blacks that he was the messiah and that the end of the world was imminent. The "Christ Craze" that he kindled was reinforced by a series of natural disasters, economic downturn, violent white supremacy, and a person being struck by lightning. Orth predicted that the world would end on August 16. Prior to that he was arrested and committed to the state asylum in Milledgeville. Edward James, a black man, took Orth's place, but after August 16 the Christ Craze disintegrated.[14]

While some blacks participated in movements such as the Christ Craze, others found their way into roles less messianic. In 1891, Charles Randolph Uncles became the first black Roman Catholic priest ordained in the United States. By the end of that decade, Mrs. Julia A. Foote and Mrs. Mary J. Small had become the first women ordained to the ministry in the African Methodist Episcopal Zion Church. Prince Hall Freemasonry attracted a growing number of bourgeois black men, who, like Protestant males in the white lodges, found community and identity in the fraternal rituals and programs. African Americans from churches around the country connected their religious faith to social reform and the civil rights

[14] See Thomas F. Armstrong, "The Christ Craze of 1889: A Millennial Response to the Economic and Social Change," in *Toward a New South? Studies in Post–Civil War Southern Communities,* eds. Orville Vernon Burton and Robert C. McMath, Jr. (Westport, Conn., 1982), 223–45.

cause through the National Urban League (founded in 1910) and the National Association for the Advancement of Colored People (founded in 1909). And blacks continued to invest heavily in education, founding black schools and seminaries and supporting them through their religious denominations.

Renewal of Home Missionary Concern

Apart from the South, where the white churches shared the impoverishment of their region, the post–Civil War years witnessed a marked resurgence of missionary activity. By the time the smoke had cleared from the battlefields, the earlier theological controversies had been forgotten, and the churches in the North were ready to redirect to other pressing tasks the energy that had been devoted to ministering to the soldiers. Part of this energy was preempted by needs in the South, but the needs of the West and of the multiplying cities were not forgotten.

Church Extension in the West

Three enticements that drew people to the newer West were mining, cattle, and wheat. The initial discovery of gold in California had been followed by similar discoveries—including silver and copper—in Colorado, Arizona, Idaho, and Montana. Then the discovery that cattle could live on the prairie grass that stretched from the Missouri River to the mountains and could survive the winter without shelter led to the creation of a great cattle empire. And when it became clear that it was feasible to raise winter wheat on the plains, there was a swelling influx of homesteaders. The whole development was spurred by the extension of railroads throughout the area, with the first transcontinental track being completed in 1869.

Establishing churches in the new West was an unusually difficult enterprise, for the early population was scattered and transient. In the mining camps, the inhabitants—mostly men—had been stirred by a lust for gold. They had come not to establish homes but to make a "killing." Few men could have cared less than the miners about the desirability of establishing churches. When G. A. Reeder, a Methodist missionary at Yuma, attempted to hold meetings in the schoolhouse, he found himself preaching to empty seats. It was not until he took up a "position on the chief corner of the town, having the wholesale liquor establishment for my 'backing,' all the leading saloons near by, and a score of liquor dealers and drinkers within hearing," that he was able to make any impression on the community.[15] Effective missionary endeavor was equally difficult in the cow

---

[15] W. C. Barclay, *History of Methodist Mission,* Vol. III, *Widening Horizons* (New York, 1958), 242.

country, for it also had a floating population of men who were not greatly addicted to the practice of religion. Unlike the miners, the cowhands were not even gathered into temporary communities. The homesteaders provided a more stable population, but even among them, a drought or a disastrous grasshopper infestation might provoke a further migration that would suddenly deplete the membership of a newly established church. With few exceptions, it was not until trading centers began to develop along the railroads that the churches were able to establish themselves on a permanent basis.

Methodists led the westward march of the churches, with Presbyterian, Congregationalists, and Baptists only a step behind.[16] The Methodist Church Extension Society was founded in 1864, and the Presbyterian and Baptist boards also allocated funds for the evangelization of the West. After the long period in which it had merged its interests with the Presbyterian, Congregationalism developed a resurgent denominational consciousness, and it was determined not to allow itself to be eclipsed on the new frontier. The Congregational General Council, which met in Boston in 1865, authorized the raising of a rather astonishingly large sum to be use in the West, and thereafter Congregationalists engaged in a surge of church-building activity. By 1882, there was not a western state or territory in which Congregationalism was unrepresented. Baptists pioneered in the use of "chapel cars" that were shunted onto railroad sidings and used as places of worship until church buildings could be constructed. Baptists also persuaded the Union Pacific and Central Pacific railroads to give them a site for a church in every village along their rights-of-way. C. C. Mc-Cabe of the Methodist Church Extension Society rode up and down the western lines establishing churches, and he boasted that the Methodists were building more than one Methodist church for every day in the year and proposed to make it two a day.

Other religious bodies were also represented in the West. The Disciples expanded into the new territory mostly through individual initiative until the church extension board was formed in 1884. The Episcopalians organized the whole area into missionary dioceses, but they were hampered by the problem of recruiting a sufficient number of ministers to implement their ambitious plans. Unitarians established a few churches, and the Lutherans exhibited real strength among German and Scandinavian immigrants who took up land in the West. Roman Catholics were to be found in increasing numbers in the mining centers, and their ranks were swelled by the acquisition of those territories in the Southwest that had a Spanish-speaking population (a development that would have major consequences

[16] In addition to Barclay, see R. T. Handy, *A Christian America: Protestant Hopes and Historical Realities* (Oxford, 1971); C. M. Drury, *Presbyterian Panorama* (Philadelphia, 1952); C. B. Goodykoontz, *Home Missions on the American Frontier* (Caldwell, Idaho, 1939); C. L. White, *Century of Faith* (Philadelphia, 1932).

for Catholicism in the next century). Furthermore, largely through the instrumentality of Bishop John Ireland of St. Paul, Minnesota, colonies of Roman Catholics from Ireland were established in the northern tier of states.

Urban Revivalism

While the churches were busy evangelizing the West, they continued to be concerned with the population flowing into the cities. The rural area of the nation was being enormously expanded as the frontier receded before the plows of the homesteaders, but even this expansion did not counterbalance the denuding of the older rural areas as young people left marginal farms to man the mills and the stores in the new communities that were springing up at every important railroad junction. And an even greater attraction was being exerted by the major metropolitan centers that were developing at key points throughout the country. In the 1830s, Finney, Beecher, and Barnes had experimented with conducting revivals among urban people; and the "prayer meeting" revival of 1857–1859 was an urban phenomenon. A fully systematized urban revivalism was to be a major contribution of Dwight L. Moody to American church life. Whereas Finney's great successes were won in communities where the population rarely exceeded 10,000,[17] Moody achieved fame by galvanizing into action the religious forces of cities with a million or more inhabitants. Finney's triumphs in western New York, Utica, Rome, and Rochester were duplicated by Moody in London, New York, Philadelphia, Boston, and Chicago.

If the new revivalism was shaped and systematized by Moody, it was fathered and promoted by the Y.M.C.A.[18] The move to the cities tended to relax the ties of habit, social pressure, and emotional association that had bound the new arrivals to the church in their former places of residence. The Young Men's Christian Association was a British import designed to counter this tendency among teenage boys who were striking out on their own for the first time. The Boston Y.M.C.A., organized on the British model in 1851, was quickly duplicated in other cities. Its prospectus expressed its hope of becoming "a social organization of those in whom the love of Christ has produced love to men; who shall meet the young stranger as he enters our city, take him to the church and Sabbath school, bring him to the Rooms of the Association, and in every way throw around him good influences, so that he may feel that he is not a stranger, but that noble and Christian spirits care for his soul."

---

[17] Rochester, with a population of 14,404 in 1835, was the major exception.

[18] Out of a similar concern, women in 1858 began organizing Y.W.C.A.s to surround young women in the cities with Christian influence. See C. H. Hopkins, *History of the Y.M.C.A. in North America* (New York, 1951).

Moody in England. He first gained fame in 1875 when he preached for four months at the Hippodrome in London. His great success as a revivalist in America came after his return from England. *(Courtesy of the Library of Congress.)*

Initially established as "a mission of the evangelical churches to young men," the eager members of the "Y" soon turned the tables and transformed the Y.M.C.A. into a mission to the whole community. They collected funds to aid the destitute and cared for the sick in lodging houses, but their principal activity was evangelistic—working in rescue missions, organizing Bible-study groups, distributing tracts, and going out to preach on street corners. Soon they were to become the chief agency of the churches in promoting communitywide revival campaigns. It was through participation in activities of the Chicago Y.M.C.A. that Moody was introduced to organized evangelistic work and induced to forsake his commercial pursuits to devote himself wholly to the business of conducting revivals.[19]

The "business" of conducting revivals is an appropriate term for Moody. Not only was he a businessman, but he also looked like a businessman, talked like a businessman, took things in hand like a businessman. By utilizing every technique of efficient business promotion—"planning, organization, publicity, vast sums of money, a host of workers, skillful executive direction"—Moody was able to demonstrate that citywide revivals could be produced almost at will, and in the process he became the first and foremost representative of a new breed of professional evangelists. Whitefield, Wesley, Nettleton, and Finney had made revivalism a full-time profession, but the "new breed" was distinguished by their strong emphasis not just on "results," but on the efficient business methods to be employed in obtaining them. Had Moody not been deflected from his business career, it is likely that with his ebullient energy and talent for organization, he would have carved out a financial empire for himself analogous to those of such friends and supporters as Cyrus McCormick, Marshall Field, and John Wanamaker. As it was, he made a fortune in religious work but gave it all away so that at his death his only estate was $500, which he did not know he had.

Born in Northfield, Massachusetts, Moody (1837–1899) prospered in the shoe business in Chicago, but he traded his office desk for work with the Y.M.C.A. during the Civil War, visiting army camps and supervising his mission Sunday School in Illinois. After the war, Moody became something of a civic institution in Chicago. "Every man has his own gifts," he said. "Some start things; others can organize and carry them on. My gift is to get things in motion." Operating on the basis that "it is better to get ten men to work than to do ten men's work," he soon had a host of projects under way, most of them connected with the Y.M.C.A., of which he had now become "librarian and agent." By a clever scheme of financing, he was instrumental in erecting a spacious building—including an auditorium that would seat 3,000 persons—for the work of the association. At the dedication in 1867 he gave unabashed expression to his aggressive spirit: "When we stop trying to enlarge our work for the Lord and raise money for it, we shall become stale and stupid. . . . We must ask for money, *money*, MORE MONEY at every meeting; not for the support of the Association—as it now is—but to enlarge its operations." Shortly after its completion the building burned down, and before the embers were cool, Moody solicited sufficient new subscriptions to replace it.

In the meantime, through informal talks at meetings and by shrewdly observing the successes and failures of the preachers who conducted

---

[19] See J. F. Findlay, *Dwight L. Moody: American Evangelist* (Chicago, 1969).

services at his Illinois Street Church, Moody was gaining skill as an evangelist—a skill he perfected in addresses at Y.M.C.A. and Sunday school conventions. It was a triumphal two-year tour of the British Isles from 1873 to 1875, however, that made him a public figure with a national reputation. A chance encounter with two philanthropic laymen on a visit to England in 1872 in connection with his Y.M.C.A. work had led to an invitation to come back the following year to conduct a series of evangelistic meetings. Taking Ira D. Sankey with him as his song leader, the tour began inauspiciously at York. Minor triumphs in the north of England were followed by major victories at Edinburgh and Glasgow. When London was invaded for a four-month period, the total attendance at the meetings was more than 2.5 million.

With the unbroken series of successes of the British campaign having been reported in sensational terms by the press, Moody was greeted on his return to the United States by the query as to what he would do in America. If there was a question in the minds of others, there was no question in his. He had found his vocation. As a New England country boy, he knew that "water runs down hill," and he was convinced that in the life of the nation "the highest hills are the great cities." If we can stir the cities, he contended, "we shall stir the whole nation." In the next five years he duplicated his British triumphs in America. Beginning in Brooklyn, where a skating rink was remodeled to hold the crowds, he moved on to Philadelphia for the winter, with John Wanamaker purchasing a freight warehouse to serve as an auditorium. In New York, P. T. Barnum's Hippodrome was rented; and in Chicago and Boston, where no buildings of sufficient size could be found, tabernacles were constructed. From Boston, after a period spent in the smaller New England cities, he went on to Baltimore, St. Louis, Cleveland, and San Francisco.

An editorial in the *Nation* (March 9, 1876) commented that "the Moody and Sankey services are an old-fashioned revival with modern improvements." The improvements were mostly highly efficient methods of organization. Everything was carefully planned in advance. Nothing was left to chance. There were committees for finance, prayer, publicity, home visitation, Bible study, music, tickets, and ushering. An executive committee was appointed to make sure that all the other committees functioned properly. No advertising device was neglected, and considerable sums were spent on posters and newspaper notices. When someone complained that it was undignified to advertise religious services, Moody replied that he thought it more undignified to preach to empty pews. Cities were divided into districts, and squads of workers were trained and sent out to visit each home. Notables were recruited to grace the platform. Sankey's music was a great attraction, as was that of the massed choirs. And the singing of gospel songs by the congregation was a stirring experience.

Moody indeed was accomplished at the "business" of revival, but his sermons were anything but businesslike. He employed a warmhearted, slapdash, no-nonsense, colloquial style of preaching that established complete rapport with those who attended, and he persuaded vast numbers to proceed to the inquiry rooms, where they were given "decision cards" to sign for the use of local pastors in following up the conversions that were professed. Like Finney before him and Billy Sunday who followed him, Moody was a "folksy" preacher who fashioned anecdotes into vehicles to transmit his message from the pulpit to the congregation. Indeed, so adept was Moody at relating instructive stories, that a large number of his anecdotes were collected and published. And if he did not manage to reach his audience with his stories and illustrations, he would employ other rhetorical devices, following his own advice: "If one method don't wake them up, let us try another."[20]

Moody never pretended to be anything more than a layman. Such theology as he had was rudimentary at best. His student conferences at Northfield featured an assortment of the ablest theological scholars, who were competent, as Moody was not, to address the challenges to faith that students were experiencing as a result of scientific inquiries and the new biblical studies.

Moody exerted his more lasting influence on the college campuses, where the students were greatly impressed by his openhearted spirit of devotion. A surprising feature of his student conferences at Northfield was their distinctly liberalizing effect. In spite of feeling himself singularly ill-equipped to speak to students, Moody was successful in deeply influencing many of the "first minds" of the college campuses, including Henry Drummond, George Adam Smith, John R. Mott, Robert E. Speer, Sherwood Eddy, and Charles Foster Kent.

The Sunday School Movement

The other great evangelistic enterprise of the Protestant churches following the Civil War was the Sunday School movement. Since early in the century, missionaries of the American Sunday School Union had been busy establishing Sunday schools for the children of the nation, and they had been given powerful support when Horace Bushnell, in *Christian Nurture* (1847), argued the need to supplement revivals with "more natural" and "more constant means of grace." Though the Sunday School Union continued to exist, the dynamic new agency was to be the International Sunday School Association. This was a popular lay enterprise that carried forward the whole endeavor in a burst of new enthusiasm and devotion.

As was true of so many religious movements in the latter part of the nineteenth century, Dwight L. Moody was the chief instigator, having con-

---

[20] Dwight L. Moody, *Anecdotes and Illustrations of D. L. Moody's Related by Him in His Revival Work* (Chicago, 1877); *How to Conduct Evangelistic Services and Prayer Meetings* (Springfield, Mass., 1876), 4.

ceived the idea of breathing new life into Sunday school work and having recruited B. F. Jacobs, a Chicago wholesale grocer and real-estate man, to forward the project. Described by his friends as "a steam engine of a man," Jacobs quickly became the key figure. He captured control of the informal conventions assembled at the time of the Sunday School Union meetings, and turned them into an independent organization that promoted city, county, state, and national conventions of Sunday school workers. The movement was frankly interdenominational, and its goal was to multiply through united effort the number of communities throughout the land where the influence of the Christian religion reigned supreme. This was to be done by enlisting, training, and inspiring a corps of dedicated teachers in every community to revitalize the Sunday school and to supplement its traditional instructional purpose with a definite evangelistic objective. The heart of the project was a highly efficient county-convention system that utilized mass rallies to kindle ardor and zeal while at the same time introducing the workers to new methods and providing them with a modicum of training. So great was the enthusiasm awakened at the rallies that a convention often became the occasion for a revival in the city in which it was held.

One of the major innovations, adopted at the insistence of Jacobs by the national convention in 1872, was the Uniform Lesson Plan. This was a plan proposed by John H. Vincent, who had become editor of Methodist Sunday school publications in 1868. The idea was to have each class within a Sunday school, and Sunday schools of all denominations, studying the same lesson each week. The plan had at least two distinct advantages. For one thing, "next Sunday's lesson" became a bond of union between members of different denominations and thus contributed to a growing sense of Protestant solidarity. An equally great advantage was that it facilitated lesson preparation. Teachers of all age groups of all Protestant denominations could be gathered on Saturday afternoon to study the lesson they were to teach the following day.

Vincent also was responsible for spearheading the development of teacher-training institutes. These institutes were designed primarily for prospective teachers and sought to equip them with tested methods of Bible teaching before they assumed any instructional responsibilities. The institute idea caught on quickly and swept across the country. In Chicago it found more elaborate institutional expression in the establishment of the Moody Bible Institute in 1886. At Chautauqua Lake in western New York, the summer training institute founded by Vincent in 1874 developed into the elaborate summer program of the Chautauqua Institution.

Within a very brief time, the Sunday school—benefiting from its surge of popularity—had begun to replace revivalism as the primary recruiting device of the churches. No longer was it merely a children's school. Adult classes were formed that frequently rivaled the stated services of the church in attendance. Slogans such as "Each one win one" were adopted, and the whole program of instruction marched forward inexorably each year to "Decision Day." So great was the enthusiasm that by the end of the century, annual Bible school parades had become a fixture in many communities, with the mayor and other civic notables ensconced in the reviewing stand. In 1910, when the Adult Bible Class Federation held its national convention in Washington, Congress adjourned to witness the parade. The following year at San Francisco the parade was headed by a platoon of mounted police, and there were 10,000 men in the line of march, each with a Bible, carrying banners and singing hymns and official delegation songs. Such displays should not be taken as representative of religious homogeneity, however. New Americans, and especially Roman Catholics, had by 1910 dramatically altered the religious landscape, especially in urban areas.

CHAPTER TEN

The New Americans

The influx of millions of Europeans into the United States during the fifty years from Appomattox to the assassination of Archduke Franz Ferdinand at Sarajevo was a phenomenon comparable only to the migrations that overwhelmed the Roman Empire in the fifth and sixth centuries. The invasion was spurred by the spreading ganglia of the iron horse, which had begun to bind the nation into a single economic unit on the eve of the Civil War. Even in the midst of the fighting, Congress had sped with lavish grants the advance of the railroads to the Pacific coast, thereby opening the whole continent to settlement and creating a market, national in scope, that served as a powerful stimulus to commercial and industrial growth. With free farms awaiting the enterprising, employers bidding for cheap labor, and steamship companies drumming up passengers, the surge of immigrants broke all precedents. From 1865 to 1900 no fewer than 13.5 million foreigners entered the United States. The pace at which they arrived was even greater after the turn of the century, when almost 9 million immigrants passed through the ports of entry from 1900 through 1910. What this influx meant to the life of the nation can be fully understood only when it is remembered that the population of the United States at the close of the Civil War was little more than 30 million.

The Irish and German invasions had begun prior to the war, with the incoming tide of Irish attaining major proportions during the "hungry forties" and the influx of Germans gaining momentum after the abortive Revolution of 1848. By the 1870s, when German immigration had reached flood tide and outstripped the Irish, the wave from Scandinavia had begun. Finally, from southern and eastern Europe came waves of Italians,

Poles, Croats, Czechs, Slovaks, Hungarians, Greeks, Russians, and Romanians to work the mines, man the factories, and ply the needle in the garment trades.

Many of the Germans and most of the Scandinavians pushed on to the farmlands northwest of Chicago, but the other nationality groups tended to cluster in the cities. The ethnic composition of the cities changed in startling ways. Boston ceased to be the citadel of the Cabots and the Lodges and became the stronghold of the Kellys and the O'Briens. Other cities received a strong German, Polish, or Italian coloration. New York, as the chief port of entry, became a polyglot center of many nationalities. So rapid was the change that the number of foreign-born in Chicago, for example, in 1890 nearly equaled the entire population of the city in 1880. The concentration of new Americans was even greater in some of the small industrial cities, where almost all the inhabitants had been recruited abroad to staff the mills. Charles A. Beard, in describing the impact upon American society of the incoming tide of cheap labor, commented that "not since the patricians and capitalists of Rome scoured the known world for slaves—Celts, Iberians, Angles, Gauls, Saxons, Greeks, Jews, Egyptians, and Assyrians—to serve them" had the world witnessed such a drastic alteration in the comparison of a social order as occurred in America during these years.[1]

The Response of the Older Americans

It is not surprising that so great a flood of immigrants should have created alarm among many of the older Americans. Peaceful coexistence seldom comes naturally. Tension usually develops whenever differing social groups first come into contact.

Nativist Concerns

The reasons for the sense of alarm that fostered a resurgence of nativist sentiment during the 1880s and 1890s were mixed. Apprehension built up at almost every level. There was a *cultural* concern at the introduction of differing folkways, customs, mores, and patterns of behavior. *Social* apprehensions were aroused by the poverty, illiteracy, and unsanitary habits of many of the immigrants. Whether the immigrants were herded into slums or created slums, there was widespread agreement that they constituted a social hazard. Even at best they had had a bad start. They were fleeing a

[1] Charles A. Beard, *The Rise of American Civilization* (New York, 1927), II, 247.

life of poverty; and long, unsanitary voyages across the Atlantic meant that many of them went from the ship to the hospital to be cared for at public expense. Francis J. Lally has reported that a New York almshouse commissioner sadly exclaimed, "Many of them had far better been cast into the deep sea, than linger in the pangs of hunger, sickness, and pain, to draw their last agonizing breath in the streets of New York."[2] Not only did these new Americans tax the public dole, they committed crimes far out of proportion to their number. The *political* impact of the new arrivals was expressed in the saying that the immigrants "landed on Monday and voted on Tuesday," being met at the dock by the "bosses," quickly registered, and then were shepherded to the polls. Although this saying overstated the situation, the shifting of control in the cities from the native-born to the foreign-born was bound to produce unhappy reactions even without the suspicion that the immigrant vote was being manipulated. From an *economic* point of view, the new Americans also were not an unmixed blessing. They did provide cheap labor for an expanding America, but not too many of the native-born appreciated this fact. Much more evident to them was the way in which the immigrants tended to depress wages and lower the standard of living by competing with the existing labor force.

All of these factors were heightened by the sense of an alien intrusion into American life. The various nationality groups tended to cling together in "ghettos" of their own, separating themselves from the rest of the community. Many spoke no English. They were suspected of exalting foreign ties and cherishing foreign ideals. To many of the older Americans, it seemed that the America they had known was doomed unless the immigrant invasion could somehow be checked.

In the post–Civil War period, labor leaders were the first to voice alarm at the threat posed by the incoming tide from Europe. At a later date even so uncompromising a "social liberal" as John A. Ryan (1869–1945) of Catholic University was to advocate restricting the flow of immigration. Only small victories, however, were won. The first general immigration law, adopted in 1882, excluded only convicts, lunatics, idiots, and those likely to become public charges. Nine years later, polygamists and those suffering from dangerous diseases were banned. It was not until 1917 that a literacy test was imposed, and the highly restrictive "quota" system was not adopted until 1924.[3]

---

[2] Fransis J. Lally, *The Catholic Church in a Changing America* (Boston, 1962), 29–30.

[3] The renewed immigration after World War I coincided with a period of economic recession and brought renewed agitation for restrictive legislation. A temporary measure was adopted in 1921 limiting the number of immigrants annually to 3 percent of the foreign-born of each nationality resident in the United States in 1910. Three years later the Johnson-Reed Act restricted total annual immigration to 150,000 and assigned quotas to each nationality on the basis of its present representation in the population. A complete prohibition of Japanese immigration made the exclusion of Asians almost complete.

Protestant-Catholic Tensions

Nativist sentiment frequently had religious overtones, with Roman Catholicism being depicted as part of an international conspiracy to subvert the free institutions of America. This had been the theme of Samuel F. B. Morse, inventor of the telegraph, in a series of letters entitled "A Foreign Conspiracy Against the Liberties of the United States," which he wrote to the *New York Observer* in 1834. During this early period, such prominent Protestant leaders as Lyman Beecher, Horace Bushnell, and Albert Barnes believed that there was a deliberate design by Roman Catholics to capture middle America, which was to be the great battlefield where the destiny of the world would be decided. The Order of United Americans (the "Know-Nothing" party of the 1850s) both fed upon and generated this fear, but it subsided with the onset of the conflict between North and South. The conspiracy theme was revived in 1887 with the formation of the American Protective Association (A.P.A.) at Clinton, Iowa, whose members were pledged to endeavor "to strike the shackles and chains of blind obedience to the Roman Catholic church from the hampered and bound consciences of a priest-ridden and church-oppressed people." The A.P.A. was a fringe group that flourished most in areas where Roman Catholics were least numerous, as in Iowa, Nebraska, and Kansas. Although the A.P.A. was an active political force that won local victories, it was bluntly rebuffed in its attempt to influence national politics, and it withered away within a few years. Anti-Catholic feeling, nevertheless, continued to persist among some segments of the American population.[4]

Although Joseph H. Fichter has suggested that anti-Catholicism in the United States was more largely rooted in ethnic than religious antagonisms,[5] the religious element should not be unduly minimized. It is true that much of the hostility to Roman Catholicism was generated by its "foreignness." And it is likely that native-born Catholics would have continued to be accepted, like other Americans, had Catholic immigrants not arrived in such overwhelming numbers. Moreover, nativist sentiment was not absent among Roman Catholics. Native-born Roman Catholics often were dismayed by the Irish immigrants, criticizing their lack of cleanliness, their boisterous conduct, their raucous laughter, their disgraceful fights. The Irish in turn frequently denounced the Germans with as much vigor as other nativists. In 1854, the Boston diocesan paper, the *Pilot*, welcomed a decline in immigration, urged the tightening of the naturalization laws,

---

[4] The excesses of the earlier anti-Catholic movement have been described in detail by R. A. Billington, *The Protestant Crusade, 1800–1860* (New York, 1938). For the later movement, see D. L. Kinzer, *An Episode in Anti-Catholicism: The American Protective Association* (Seattle, 1964). John Higham associates anti-Catholicism with other kinds of nativism, including anti-Semitism and racism. See John Higham *Strangers in the Land* (New York, 1960).

[5] Joseph H. Fichter, "The Americanization of Catholicism," in Thomas T. McAvoy, ed., *Roman Catholicism and the American Way of Life*, (Notre Dame, IN, 1960), 116–17.

and was of the opinion that if the Know-Nothings succeeded in obstruct-ing the Germans, posterity would overlook their crimes of bigotry. A few decades later, Archbishop John Ireland alerted the Associated Press to the "general un-American character" of the American German Catholic As-sembly. German Catholics exhibited similar hostility to still-newer immi-grant groups. And when Roman Catholics in the southern states were urged to welcome coreligionists from Ireland and Germany, they insisted that only those who would be friendly to southern interests be sent. "We must not," they declared, "warm vipers into life that may sting us when they grow warm."[6] Although all this is true, religious concerns were pres-ent in the tension between Protestants and Roman Catholics.

Protestants, of course, did not constitute a single homogeneous anti-Catholic bloc, a fact that Archbishop Ireland acknowledged and Robert D. Cross has documented.[7] Expressions of friendship and good will were not uncommon, and such organizations as the A.P.A. seldom reflected respon-sible Protestant opinion. There were nonetheless serious fears and appre-hensions, stimulated in part by the harsh anti-Protestantism of some Roman Catholics. Michael Muller, a Redemptorist Father, did little to fos-ter good feeling when he published *The Catholic Dogma: Out of the Church There Is No Salvation* (1886). His purpose in writing the book, he said, was to refute "those soft, weak, timid, liberalizing Catholics, who labor to ex-plain away all the points of Catholic faith offensive to non-Catholics, and to make it appear there is no question of life and death, of heaven and hell, involved in the difference between us and Protestants." There were other Catholics who denounced Protestants as infidels, and even the sug-gestion by a bishop in 1870 that non-Catholics could be persons of good faith and good character was sufficient to cause him to be called "a Luther or a Lucifer." Ten years later, Augustine Thébaud, a Jesuit who had been in America since 1838, insisted that Protestants who "profess to be friendly to Catholics" are not sincere. And Archbishop John Hughes of New York de-nounced as "Protestant priests" Catholic clergymen who enjoyed good re-lations with Protestants.[8]

Further antagonism was aroused by the generally negative attitude of some Catholics toward American life as a whole. The influential *Church Progress* of St. Louis was not particularly tactful when it made unfavorable comparisons between the United States and the Catholic nations of Europe, and the statement of Condé Pallen that American culture "ex-hales an atmosphere filled with germs fatal to Catholic life" was hardly

---

[6] W. E. Wright, "The Native American Catholic, the Immigrant, the Immigration," in McAvoy, *Roman Catholicism and the American Way of Life*, 213–14, 216. See also C. J. Barry, "The Ger-man Catholic Immigrant," *ibid.*, 199; and Robert D. Cross, *The Emergence of Liberal Catholicism in America* (Cambridge, Mass., 1958), 92.

[7] Cross, 30, 32–37, 44, 48, 52, 65.

[8] *Ibid.*, 51–52, 56.

calculated to win friends. This negativism was most conspicuous among German-speaking Catholics. Anton Walburg, a leading priest in Cincinnati, was emphatic in his criticism of the United States. In 1889, he depicted American culture as a "hotbed of fanaticism, intolerance, and radical ultra views on matters of politics and religion." Even the language, he insisted, was so permeated with Protestant ideas that an English-speaking Catholic could never prosper. In contrast to the United States, Walburg pointed to Germany as standing "foremost in the ranks of civilized nations," and he advised Americans to stop worrying about getting involved in European quarrels, since the United States was too weak to defeat Ecuador, let alone a European power.[9]

Although mutual animosities fostered mutual estrangement, Protestant uneasiness had its basic rootage in apprehensions concerning the changes that a continuing massive Roman Catholic immigration might introduce into American society. The existing social order, which embodied in so many ways the ideals and moralities of evangelical Protestantism, seemed to many thoughtful people to be in danger of being completely subverted. The most obvious, if perhaps the most superficial, threat was the challenge to two of the most conspicuous folk moralities of American Protestantism—Sabbath observance and temperance. The "Continental Sunday" of the immigrant groups both scandalized and spread consternation in the Protestant camp. And Protestants, long schooled in the evils of strong drink, noted with dismay that these new Americans were bringing "their grog shops like the frogs of Egypt upon us."[10]

Of more serious concern were the attacks leveled by Catholics against the public schools. Universal public education had been fostered as a counter to the project of that "old deluder Satan" to keep people from a knowledge of the Scriptures, and the "little red schoolhouse" was regarded, along with motherhood and the home, as one of the most cherished institutions of American life. Although it was understandable that Catholics might wish schools of their own, nothing could have been better calculated to raise Protestant hackles than the attempt to drum up support for parochial education by attacking public education. The public schools were described as "godless," and those who defended them were charged with being "fanatics." Bishop Bernard McQuaid called the public school system "a huge conspiracy against religion, individual liberty, and enterprise," and Michael Muller regarded it as a disease that would "break up and destroy the Christian family" and described the public schools as "hotbeds of immorality" where "courtesans have disguised themselves as school-girls in order the more surely to ply their foul vocation." Zachariah Montgomery was convinced that free love would be the ultimate consequence of free public education. "Free teaching draws after it free books,

[9] *Ibid.*, 26, 28, 72, 90.
[10] Lally, 29.

free clothes, free food, free time," he contended. "All this is going very far with the communists. . . . If we admit a right . . . to take the child out of the family, they will ask next for the wife." Other Catholics were convinced that not everyone should be taught to read, for this would serve to make them unfit for the station in life into which they had been born. Still others argued that godly innocence was more often associated with childlike ignorance than with worldly knowledge. A few, appalled by the thought of a system that mixed innocents with the "crime-steeped progeny of the low and vile," went so far as to urge that all free (i.e., public) education be abandoned.[11]

Perhaps the greatest apprehension was aroused by the fear that Roman Catholicism might serve to undermine American democracy. Although no more than a small minority of the American people may have shared the conviction of the radical nativist fringe that massive Catholic immigration was a deliberate plot to overthrow the free institutions of America, there were many who feared that the tenets and spirit of Roman Catholicism were antithetical to religious and political liberty. The memory of events in Europe after the defeat of Napoleon in 1814 and after the abortive revolutions of 1848–1849 did little to reassure them, and they were equally disturbed by the condemnations contained in the *Syllabus of Errors* of 1864 and by the decrees of the Vatican Council in 1870. Moreover, in the encyclical letter *Immortale Dei* (The Christian Constitution of States) of 1885, Leo XIII had explicitly affirmed the right of the papacy to judge when the affairs of the civil order must yield to the superior authority of the Roman Church.[12] And somewhat later the Vatican newspaper *Osservatore Romano* pointed out that "as the Pope is the sovereign of the Church . . . , he is also the sovereign of every other society and of every other kingdom."[13] Some comments by American Catholics were no more reassuring. An article in the *American Catholic Quarterly Review* in 1877 dismissed the Declaration of Independence as a flock of vague clichés, and five years later a pastoral letter of the bishops of the province of Cincinnati took a dim view of the notion that a people should rule themselves.[14]

Other Catholics, most notably Cardinal James Gibbons, Archbishop John Ireland, and Bishop John J. Keane, were as disturbed as most Protestants by the reactionary stance of the conservative wing of the Roman Catholic Church of America. They resented both the aspersions cast upon the public schools and the innuendoes that suggested that the American

---

[11] Cross, 95, 96, 98, 131–32, 135–36.

[12] For the *Syllabus of Errors,* see H. Shelton Smith, Robert Handy, and Lefferts Loetscher, *American Christianity,* II, 112–15. The constitution promulgated at the Vatican Council in 1870, and the encyclical *Immortale Dei* are reprinted in W. S. Hudson, *Understanding Roman Catholicism* (Philadelphia, 1959), 37–45, 66–90.

[13] Cited in Cross, 60.

[14] *Ibid.,* 99.

form of government was less desirable than the nondemocratic regimes of Europe. They repeatedly voiced their own approbation of American democratic principles and were forthright in condemning the antidemocratic views of some of their fellow Catholics. In contrast to the conservative Catholics, the liberals were widely acclaimed and publicly honored by Protestants. Gibbons was invited to preach in Protestant pulpits, Keane gave the Dudleian lecture at Harvard, and a Baptist minister affectionately addressed Ireland as "my archbishop." The result of the Catholic ambivalence was a degree of ambivalence in the Protestant mind, with varying opinions being held as to the future course that the Roman Church would pursue in America.

Protestant Ministries to the Immigrants

The Protestant approach to the newcomers to the American scene was motivated by a varying mixture of religious concern, humanitarian sentiment, patriotic fervor, and anti-Catholic feeling that interpreted the incoming tide as part of a carefully laid plot to capture the United States for the Pope. Many believed, however, that the "safety and welfare and Christian civilization of our country depends in no small degree upon transforming" the immigrant "into a true American," and that "nothing but Christianity, as incarnated in American Protestantism," can accomplish this end. The new arrivals, declared mission executive Charles A. Brooks, must be "born again of the American spirit."[15] In spite of attempts to enlist support for mission work among immigrants by equating Protestantism with patriotism, the literature of the time makes it clear that much of the motivation was rooted in a truly humanitarian and religious solicitude for the friendless and poverty stricken. Methodists, for example, were as assiduous in their work among Lutherans from Sweden and Calvinists from Hungary as they were among Roman Catholics from any land.

Apart from informal "welfare" or "relief" programs, the major response of Protestant churches to the presence of the new Americans was a strenuous effort to provide them with a religious ministry in their own language. Later, as a phase of their expanding humanitarian activity, the churches developed a systematized program of "Christian Americanization" or "Christian Friendliness" to assist the immigrant families in making a successful adjustment to American life. Women were enlisted to go into the homes to show mothers how to cook the food available in American stores, to teach them English, to help them prepare for naturalization examinations, and generally to befriend them.

Almost every Protestant denomination developed foreign-language ministries. Mission work was established among the Germans, Scandinavians,

---

[15] H. B. Grose, *Aliens or Americans?* (New York, 1906), 237, 255; C. A. Brooks, *Immigration: Its Extent, Its Effect on America, Its Call to the Churches* (New York, 1915), 8.

French Canadians, Italians, Poles, Hungarians, Czechs, Romanians, and Portuguese. Baptists, for example, maintained a ministry to twenty-one different nationality groups in as many different languages. The recruiting of a "native ministry" to labor among their fellow immigrants was haphazard at first, but as soon as any specific group began to arrive in significant numbers, training institutes were organized to train converts for mission work. Foreign-language "departments" were established in theological seminaries to provide more adequate ministerial training. Baptists were typical in this respect, establishing a German department at Rochester Theological Seminary in 1858; a department for Swedish, Danish, and Norwegian students at the seminary in Chicago in 1871; a French-Canadian department at the Seminary in Newton, Massachusetts in 1889; and an Italian department at Colgate Theological Seminary in 1907. "So ample were these facilities," Aaron I. Abell reported in his study of urban Protestantism, "that by 1900 a body of clergymen ready to meet all calls for independent or assistant pastorates had come into existence." As early as 1895, the problem of the Congregationalists had become one of sufficient financial support rather than of available personnel, for their home missionary society reported that the once "greatest desideratum—trained Congregational pastors—to supply these churches of foreign tongues, is now supplied in a degree almost beyond our power to use, through Oberlin and Chicago theological seminaries, whose well-equipped graduates stand ready to enlarge the field of our missionary service wherever the means are at the command of this society to employ them."[16]

Although by no means negligible, the number of non–English-speaking immigrants added to the membership of churches of British background accounted for only a small fraction of the new Americans. As was to be expected, it was the churches of their homelands that experienced the great surge of growth.

Adjustments and Tensions Within Roman Catholicism

The most spectacular development in American religious life during the latter half of the nineteenth century was the growth of the Roman Catholic Church. In spite of repeated alarm that vast losses were being suffered among those who came to America, the Roman Catholic Church was remarkably successful in retaining the allegiance of Catholic immigrants.[17] Although the number of Roman Catholics had rapidly mounted during

[16] A. I. Abell, *The Urban Impact upon American Protestantism* (Cambridge, Mass., 1943), 182, 183.

[17] The myth of vast losses was exploded by Gerald Shaughnessy, *Has the Immigrant Kept the Faith?* (New York, 1925). See also J. P. Dolan, *Catholic Revivalism* (Notre Dame, Ind., 1978).

the pre–Civil War years, giant strides in membership took place in the decades that followed. The 4 million Catholics of 1870 increased to 6 million in 1880. Ten years later the total was 9 million, and in 1900, it was 12 million. By 1920, every sixth person and every third church member were Roman Catholic.[18]

Institutional Development

The challenge presented to the Roman Catholic Church by the immigrant flood was prodigious. The immigrants were poor. They came from different countries, spoke different languages, and—within the limits of their common faith—had different traditions and customs and loyalties. Even had they not been poverty-stricken, they came in such numbers that the task of recruiting priests, erecting parishes, and building churches seemed almost insurmountable. Financial help did come from Europe. From France the Society for the Propagation of Faith had sent more than $6 million by 1914. Additional help came from similar societies in Germany, Austria, and Switzerland. But the major financial burden was carried in America. In terms of personnel, assistance from abroad was much more important and substantial. Religious orders and congregations sent over priests, lay brothers, and nuns, with Ireland, Germany, France, and Belgium contributing the greatest number. Secular priests also were dispatched. Although bishops constantly stressed the importance of encouraging vocations to the priesthood and founded seminaries to provide the necessary training, it was the recruits from abroad who made it possible for the ranks of the clergy to swell from slightly more than 2,000 in 1860 to 6,000 in 1880, to 12,000 in 1900, and to 17,000 in 1910. Nor was it an easy task to maintain effective oversight of the multiplying parishes. New dioceses were constantly being formed, and by 1914, they exceeded 100, grouped in 14 provinces.

Prior to the period from 1846 to 1850 when five new provinces were constituted, there had been but a single province—that of Baltimore—in the United States. Beginning in 1829, the bishops met approximately every three years in a provincial council to deal with their common problems. When other provinces were established, this procedure had to be altered. In place of the provincial gatherings, plenary councils of the whole American episcopate were summoned to coordinate the work of the church on a national basis. The first plenary council met in 1852, the second in 1866,

---

[18] For a scholarly account, see J. J. Hennesy, *American Catholicism: A History of the Roman Catholic Community in the United States* (New York, 1981). Key documents of American Catholicism are printed in J. T. Ellis, *Documents of American Catholic History*, rev. ed. (Milwaukee, 1962).

and the third in 1884.[19] Thereafter such national councils were either suppressed or suspended, presumably to avoid the dangers implicit in the idea of a national church. A similar concern had dictated the refusal of Rome to accede to the petition of the bishops that the archbishop of Baltimore be granted the place of primacy among the bishops in the United States. In place of these alternatives, both containing the potential hazard of undue independence, an Apostolic Delegate (papal representative) was appointed in 1893 to provide the necessary coordination and direction for the American church. With the structure of government having been thus completed and with the arrangement functioning effectively, Pius X on June 29, 1908, removed the church in the United States from the jurisdiction of the Congregatio de Propaganda Fide. The effect was to place the Roman Catholic Church in America on a basis of equality with older branches of the church in Europe and to bring to an end its missionary status.

The resources of manpower, money, and ingenuity were further taxed by the policy of developing a whole system of Catholic education. The first provincial council of Baltimore in 1829 declared it to be "absolutely necessary that schools should be established in which the young may be taught the principles of faith and morality while being instructed in letters." In 1852, the first plenary council reemphasized the need for parochial schools, and in 1884, the third plenary council decreed that schools, if possible, should be established in every parish within the next two years. Support for the program of parochial education, however, was not as uniform as these decrees suggest. German Catholics were among the most ardent proponents of parochial schools, viewing them as a means of preserving their German language and culture. Liberal prelates, such as Gibbons, Ireland, and Keane, preferred to work out an accommodation with public education as a means of integrating Catholics more fully into the mainstream of American life. A hard-fought struggle ensued, with Irish conservatives such as Archbishop Michael A. Corrigan of New York City and Bishop McQuaid of Rochester giving the Germans staunch support. Ultimately the issue was settled by papal intervention in favor of a complete system of parochial education, with deviations being tolerated if judged necessary by a bishop in the light of local conditions.

Progress in fulfilling the ideal of a school in every parish was slow. Had the Roman Catholic population not been concentrated in the major cities and in a few largely self-contained rural enclaves, the whole project would have been doomed from the start. Even with this concentration, parochial education was made possible only by the sacrificial devotion of the members of sisterhoods who were recruited to staff the schools. In spite of the

---

[19] For these councils, see Peter Guilday, *A History of the Councils of Baltimore, 1791–1884* (New York, 1932).

fact that the council of 1884 had decreed that within two years every parish must have its own school, parishes so equipped had increased only from 40 percent to 44 percent by 1892. Thereafter, with dissidence having been quelled, progress was more rapid. In 1914, the parochial schools enrolled over 1 million pupils, had over 20,000 teachers, and were maintained at a cost of over $15 million per year. But even an achievement of this magnitude was not enough, for a large proportion of Catholic children were still being educated in public schools.

Interest in secondary education lagged, with the total enrollment in 1915 being less than 75,000. Colleges and universities, on the other hand, were beginning to receive vigorous support after a long period of precarious existence.[20] Georgetown, St. Louis, Fordham, Notre Dame, and Holy Cross, among others, had become strong institutions, and in 1884, the third plenary council took action to establish the Catholic University of America as a full-fledged graduate institution to serve as the capstone of the Catholic educational structure.

"Americanism"

In addition to other problems, Roman Catholics had the difficult task of adjusting people of diverse nationality both to one another and to the American environment. Moreover, America was a mission territory under the propaganda until 1908. To weld Irishmen, Germans, Italians, Czechs, French Canadians, and many others into a single church was a taxing effort. Tension often was acute. The earlier trustee controversy was in part a rebellion of the Irish against the imported French priests who had been displaced from their homeland by the Revolution of 1789. After the Civil War the German-Irish tension came to the fore, and in the 1890s, Polish dissatisfaction produced a schismatic movement that resulted in the formation of the Polish National Catholic Church.[21] In 1914, a parallel Lithuanian National Catholic Church was organized.

The German-Irish issue, which had long smoldered and had been reflected in the school controversy, was brought to a head in 1891 when the St. Raphael Society of Switzerland, with Peter Paul Cahensly as its secretary, in a petition to Rome declared that in the United States the Roman Catholic Church had lost 10 million souls through failure to make proper

---

[20] Of 38 colleges established between 1791 and 1850, only 7 survived. Theodore Maynard, *The Story of American Catholicism* (New York, 1941), 474.

[21] In 1916, the Polish group reported a membership of 28,245. Consecration of its bishops had been obtained from the Old Catholic Church in Europe, a small Dutch group that had refused to accept the decrees of the Council of Trent. Old Catholics in Germany and Switzerland had been alienated by the dogmatic pronouncements of the first Vatican Council in 1870.

provision for them in their own language. As was true of other nationality groups, provision had been made for the establishment of German congregations under the leadership of German-speaking priests. And of the 69 bishops in 1886, 15 were of Germanic extraction. But this was not enough for the St. Raphael Society, which had been founded to aid German-speaking immigrants. In its petition to the papacy, the Society proposed that each of the nationality groups in America be organized into separate dioceses. This attempt to fragment the church in America by institutionalizing Old World divisions was rejected by the papacy, but it serves to illustrate a difference in point of view as to the proper strategy to be pursued in the United States.

Most of the German leadership was convinced that the way to hold the immigrants was to keep them isolated from American life. German culture, customs, and language were defended with the slogan "Language Saves the Faith," and it was insisted that only priests proud of being German and schools in which German was the language of instruction could save German Catholics and their children from being de-Catholicized. To those who contended that "we are apostles to bring the people to Christ . . . , not to maintain or implant a nationality or to spread a language," the *Herald des Glaubens* responded that priests who voiced such sentiments "would rather see several million Germans go to hell than forego the opportunity to convert a few hundred Yankees."[22]

The Germans, of course, were not alone in believing that the only way to prevent defections was to insulate the faithful and to resist all accommodation to the American environment. Some of the most influential Irish bishops, although not concerned with the language problem, were equally determined that no concessions should be made to American culture. There were others, however, who believed that resistance to Americanization not only created unnecessary antagonism and impeded the winning of converts but actually was a policy calculated to speed the defection of those who had been Catholics in their homelands. If being an American meant ceasing to be a Catholic, they had little doubt of the choice that many, especially their children, would make. Isaac Hecker and the Paulist Fathers, the order of missionary priests Hecker had founded in 1859, were the most conspicuous advocates of this point of view, but it also found strong support among members of the hierarchy, notably from the triumvirate of Gibbons, Ireland, and Keane.

Gibbons's *The Faith of Our Fathers* (1876) was one of the most successful Catholic apologetics ever written in English, and the response it elicited seemed a clear demonstration of the effectiveness of the Americanizing tactic. At the centenary in 1889 of Baltimore's establishment as a diocese, Gibbons reemphasized the Americanist theme, saying that John Carroll's aim had been "that the clergy and people—no matter from what country

[22] McAvoy, ed., *Roman Catholicism and the American Way of Life*, 192–94; Cross, 25–26, 91–92.

they sprung—should be thoroughly identified with the land in which their lot was cast; that they should study its laws and political constitution and be in harmony with its spirit; in a word, that they should become, as soon as possible, assimilated to the social body in all things pertaining to the common domain of civil life." And then, turning to the present, Gibbons called upon his contemporaries to emulate Carroll. Ireland was even more emphatic, believing that people unwilling to be assimilated did not deserve to be admitted to the country and that anyone who did not rejoice in the blessings of America "should in simple consistency betake his foreign soul to foreign shores, and crouch in misery and subjection beneath tyranny's sceptre."

> We should live in our age, know it, be in touch with it. . . . We should be in it and of it, if we would have its ear. . . . For the same reason, there is needed a thorough sympathy with the country. The Church of America must be, of course, as Catholic as even in Jerusalem or Rome; but as far as her garments assume color from the local atmosphere, she must be American. Let no one dare to paint her brow with a foreign taint or pin to her mantle foreign linings.[23]

But it was not simply a tactic that the liberal coterie had adopted. They were fully committed to American democracy, glorying in it, believing in it, and willing to defend it. "If I had the privilege of modifying the Constitution of the United States," declared Gibbons, "I would not expunge or alter a single paragraph, a single line, or a single word of that important instrument."

> The Constitution is admirably adapted to the growth and expansion of the Catholic religion, and the Catholic religion is admirably adapted to the genius of the Constitution. They fit together like two links of the same chain.

Furthermore, these Americanizers believed that America had a mission to the world. God intended America to be more than a "motherland," asserted Keane. "She was meant to be a teacher through whose lips and in whose life he was to solve the social problems of the Old World."[24]

The leaders of the liberal contingent also were certain that America could teach lessons in religion as well as in politics. The role of the laity was emphasized, and lay congresses were organized. Close clerical supervision and direction were minimized by a stress upon the necessity for individual initiative in the apostolate of the church. The contemplative life exalted by most of the religious orders tended to be disparaged. "An

---

[23] Theodore Maynard Roemer, *Catholic Church in the United States,* (New York, 1941), 303–4; Maynard, 511; Cross, 89.

[24] J. T. Ellis, *Perspectives in American Catholicism* (Baltimore, 1963), 124; Cross, 184.

honest ballot and social decorum," Ireland contended, "will do more for God's glory and the salvation of souls than midnight flagellations or Compestellan pilgrimages." Protestants were not to be regarded as implacable enemies but as "brothers to be brought back to the fold." Love and persuasion should replace harsh polemic. The technique of seeking to exert religious influence through the formation of a Catholic political party, a practice widely adopted in Europe, was likewise decried. Even the almost automatic identification of American Catholics with the Democratic party ("Have you heard the news? John Danaher has become a Republican!" "It can't be true. I saw him at mass just last Sunday.") was deplored on the ground that it deprived Catholics of influence because the Democrats took them for granted, whereas the Republicans felt no obligation to them.[25]

The 1880s and 1890s were heady years for the liberals, but they were also years when the issue of "Americanism" was being sharply drawn.[26] The peak of the liberal ascendancy was reached in 1893 at the seventeen-day Parliament of Religions held in conjunction with the Chicago Columbian Exposition. The American archbishops, presumably influenced by Ireland, had decided that the Parliament presented a signal opportunity to present Catholic truth to those outside the fold. At the opening session, Archbishop Patrick A. Feehan gave an address of welcome, and Cardinal Gibbons (he had received the red hat in 1886) led the assembly in the Protestant version of the Lord's Prayer. Bishop Keane presented two papers, read an address prepared by Gibbons, and presided on the day assigned for a specifically Catholic program. Although those who participated felt that a real service had been rendered the Catholic Church, others were scandalized by the appearance given by Catholic participation of waiving the Roman claim to unique and final truth. By sharing the platform with every religious sect "from Mohammedanism and Buddhism down to the lowest form of evangelicalism and infidelity," the participating bishops were accused of having taken a dangerous first step toward "indifferentism." Even prior to this event, in an article in the *American Catholic Quarterly Review*, the vicar general of Archbishop Corrigan had charged Ireland, Gibbons, and Keane of being guilty of the "liberalism" condemned by the *Syllabus of Errors*.[27]

Many issues, in addition to those strictly related to "Americanism," contributed to the coalescing of two parties in the church, each striving for

---

[25] Maynard, 514; Cross, 187.

[26] The two indispensable books dealing with the "Americanism" controversy are Cross, *Emergence of Liberal Catholicism*, and T. T. McAvoy, *The Great Crisis in American Catholic History, 1895–1900* (Chicago, 1957). The latter volume makes full use of archival material. It was reprinted under a new title, *The Americanist Heresy in Roman Catholicism* (Notre Dame, Ind., 1963).

[27] Thomas Timothy McAvoy, *The Great Crisis in American Catholic History*, (Chicago, 1957), 76–77.

ascendancy. There were differences of opinion over parochial schools and the language question, tensions between nationality groups, differing attitudes toward "temperance," and debates as to the position the church should take with regard to the Knights of Labor and the "single-tax" proposal of Henry George. The establishment of Catholic University in 1889 had been displeasing to many. Some feared it as a rival to their own institutions. Some were opposed to its location in Washington, where students would be exposed to the corrupting influences of the nation's capital. Others were dismayed that an undergraduate college for women would be adjacent to a campus where priests and members of religious orders would be pursuing graduate studies. Still others were alienated by the "progressive" auspices under which the university had been established and by the pretension of its board of trustees to serve as a standing council of the church. The latter pretension was related to a centralizing tendency that also aroused antagonism. Gibbons was being encouraged to assume the role of spokesman and unofficial primate of the church by exploiting the precedence he derived from being the archbishop of Baltimore and the only American cardinal, and the archbishops had begun to function as a committee in a way that seemed to abridge episcopal liberties. Perhaps as important as any of these issues in the process of polarization was the personal rivalry of Archbishops Ireland and Corrigan, each of whom aspired to be the next American to possess a cardinal's hat. Thus ties of friendship, common convictions and ideals, and mutual antipathies were involved in the struggle that was to take place.

When Archbishop Francesco Satolli was sent to represent the papacy at the Chicago World's Fair in 1892, he was privately instructed to adjudicate the controversies among American Catholics and to make known at an appropriate time that Leo XIII wanted him to remain in America as a resident apostolic delegate to ensure that unity would be maintained. For a variety of reasons, nearly all the bishops were opposed to the appointment of any such permanent papal representative in the United States. Ireland was the major exception to this opposition. He sensed the hopelessness of resistance and decided to seek advantage by being the first to welcome the establishment of an apostolic delegation in Washington. He was confident that Satolli could be won to be liberal cause. Ireland's confidence was buttressed by the favor he had enjoyed at Rome during a visit of the preceding year, and by Leo XIII's apparent sympathy with progressive views. Furthermore, Denis J. O'Connell, rector of the American College in Rome and a close collaborator of the liberal triumvirate, had been assured that Satolli would restore unity by driving Corrigan "to the wall."[28] Ireland therefore was far from dismayed when Satolli announced that he had received a papal commission appointing him as apostolic delegate in the United States.

[28] Cross, 180. McAvoy cites evidence that Leo did not really favor either faction in *The Great Crisis in American Catholic History*, 89–90.

James Cardinal Gibbons (1834–1921), Archbishop of Baltimore for Forty-Three Years. (Courtesy of the Library of Congress.)

For a time Ireland's hopes seemed to be confirmed. Satolli's early decisions were generally in harmony with the views of the liberals. The first indication that their fortunes were to suffer reverse came in 1895 when Leo XIII issued the encyclical letter *Longinqua Oceani* to the American church. After praising the notable accomplishments of American Catholics and noting the absence of any hostile legislation in the United States, Leo added the disturbing comment that it "would be very erroneous to draw the conclusion that in America is to be sought the type of the most desirable status of the Church." Indeed, the church in America "would bring forth more abundant fruits if, in addition to liberty, she enjoyed the favor of the laws and the patronage of the public authority." Ireland was so upset by this reprimand that he canceled a previous agreement to write an explanatory article on the anticipated encyclical for the *North American Review*. The encyclical was followed by a series of further blows. A papal warning later in 1895 against taking part in "promiscuous assemblies" was obviously directed against the liberals' enthusiasm for parliaments of religion. The most shocking rebukes were the forced resignation in 1895 of Denis O'Connell as rector of the American College in Rome and the equally involuntary resignation in 1896 of Keane as rector of Catholic University. When news of Keane's dismissal reached Bishop McQuaid, he wrote jubilantly to Corrigan:

> The failure of the University is known at last. . . . What collapses on every side! Gibbons, Ireland, and Keane!!! They were the cock of the walk for a while, and dictated to the country, and thought to run our dioceses for us.[29]

Several things had combined to change the attitude of Rome toward the liberal triumvirate. First, the appointment of Satolli had given the papal court its own independent source of information concerning American affairs, and his recommendations increasingly favored the conservatives. After initially relying on the advice of the liberal prelates, Satolli had been won to the views of their opponents through the influence of Joseph Schroeder, one of the few staunchly conservative professors at Catholic University. Second, Leo XIII himself had taken a conservative turn, having become disappointed by the failure of his liberal tactic to win support for the restoration of the temporal power of the papacy. Third, the central issues of the dispute in America had been carried to Europe, where they accentuated existing unrest and dissension. Ireland had toured France in 1892, calling upon the French to emulate the Americans; Keane had spoken in a similar vein at Brussels in 1894; Gibbons had been equally eloquent at Rome some years earlier, and many of the speeches and writings of the Americanizers had been translated and circulated in Europe. The conservatives were no less active, with William Tappert reporting in Cologne that the American liberals had surrendered to rationalism, and Joseph Schroeder telling another German audience that they were attacking the universality of the church and undermining the authority of the papacy. The net result of this dual incursion was to win some support for the liberals but also to arouse an even more powerful opposition. Fourth, a papal rebuke of McQuaid for an intemperate attack upon Ireland had given McQuaid an opportunity to make a detailed reply and to state fully the conservative concern. He warned the Pope of a

---

[29] Maynard, 518–19.

"false liberalism" in America "that, if not checked in time, will bring disaster on the Church." It may have been this communication that tipped the scales against the progressive prelates, because Rome had already witnessed the appearance of "modernism" in Europe, and was wary that America might embrace it as well.[30]

The liberal triumvirate refused to be daunted by its several defeats and immediately launched a counteroffensive, including the Fribourg Conference. This in turn provoked a detailed indictment of their views in an article in the February 1897 issue of the *American Ecclesiastical Review*. The liberals were accused of "an excessive 'flaunting' of American patriotism at the expense of Catholic loyalties; an undue reliance upon scholarship as a source of truth, coupled with a disregard for doctrinal uniformity; extreme libertarianism within the Church to the detriment of sound hierarchical principles; and a muting of Catholic truths in order to attract converts from Protestantism."[31] The article went on to declare that the church could be saved from this dangerous "American religious liberalism" only by the direct and forthright intervention of Rome. The sole liberal victory was Schroeder's forced departure from Catholic University at the beginning of 1898, but the price of this small triumph was to strengthen the demand for a formal condemnation of "Americanism." Meanwhile, the "jingoism" of the American press in the months preceding the declaration of war against Spain heightened and consolidated European opposition. It gave substance to the insistence of the Catholic conservatives that all forms of expansionism by the barbarous Americans were aimed at the destruction of the civilization of Christian Europe.

On January 22, 1899, Leo XIII issued a condemnation of what had become known as "Americanism" in the letter "*Testem Benevolentiae*," which he addressed to Cardinal Gibbons.[32] Although the purpose of the condemnation was "to put an end to certain contentions" that had "arisen lately" among American Catholics, the pretext for the letter was the controversy aroused by the publication in 1897 of an abridged French translation of Walter Elliott's *Life of Father Hecker* (1891).[33] Ireland was informed by Cardinal Rampolla, the papal secretary of state, that centering attention on the Hecker biography was designed to ease the embarrassment and humiliation of submitting to the papal directive. "The words of the letter," Ireland was told, would "allow us to say that the things condemned were never said

---

[30] McAvoy, *The Great Crisis in American Catholic History*, 124–25.

[31] Cross, 198.

[32] The encyclical is reprinted in Smith, Handy, and Loetscher, II, 336–40.

[33] Ireland had written a glowing introduction for the French translation, Keane had presented a copy to Leo XIII, O'Connell had rushed to the defense of Hecker in a speech during the summer of 1897, and Gibbons defended Hecker in a letter published in France, as "a providential agent for the spread of the Catholic faith" and rejoiced that through the biography, Europeans had an opportunity to learn more about him. McAvoy, *The Great Crisis in American Catholic History*, 173–76, 180, 182–83, 200.

or written in America" but "were set afloat in France" as a result of the translation and interpretation of the Hecker biography in a foreign language. He was further told that he should do his best "to spread this view." This was "small comfort," wrote Ireland, "but we must make the most of it." And then he added: "In my letter to the Pope, I accepted the letter, swore against all the opinions condemned in it, which I said had never been heard in America, and declared it an insult to America to have linked such extravagances with the name of Americanism."[34]

Ireland was joined by Gibbons and Keane in coupling submission with a declaration that "Americanism" was a "phantom heresy"[35] that could only have flourished abroad. The conservatives, however, knew better. The bishops of the province of Milwaukee, incensed at the suggestion that the Pope had been "deceived by false reports" and "had beaten the air and chased after a shadow," affirmed that the condemned opinions had "most assuredly and evidently been proclaimed among us orally and in writing." McQuaid publicly denounced those who said the heresy did not exist, and Corrigan rejoiced that "the monster" had been "struck down dead" by the timely intervention of the Holy See.[36] It was obvious, of course, that Leo XIII had the United States in mind as the seat of the infection. He addressed the letter of condemnation to Gibbons and not to the primate of France, and directed that it be sent to other members of the American hierarchy. Furthermore, Keane was privately but specifically instructed, when appointed archbishop of Dubuque, to heed the warnings contained in the letter to Gibbons. And Ireland was placed under leash and died without his coveted cardinal's hat.

Roman Catholics in America, of necessity, had little time for creative theological reflection. Most of the priests and bishops were forced to be "brick and mortar" men rather than theologians. Their major preoccupation was building new churches and institutions to minister to the tremendous influx of Catholics from abroad. Thus the effect of the condemnation of "Americanism" was only to accentuate the generally conservative temper of American Catholicism. Whatever bold experimentation there had been now gave way to timidity. Discussion and debate within the church largely ceased, and any innovation tended to be viewed with suspicion. The papal condemnation of "Modernism"[37] in 1907 caused scarcely a ripple among American Catholics, although it did contribute further to the theological silence that was to characterize the Catholic Church in the United States for the next few decades.

---

[34] For Ireland's letter from Rome, dated February 24, 1899, see *ibid.*, 281.

[35] The term was coined by Felix Kelin, the leader of the Americanizing party in France. The fourth volume of his autobiography, *Americanism: A Phantom Heresy*, was published in an English translation in 1951.

[36] McAvoy, *The Great Crisis in American Catholic History*, 293, 296, 329.

[37] Reprinted in Smith, Handy, and Loetscher, II, 340–45.

Other Immigrant Faiths and Accessions

Although Roman Catholicism accounted for the largest number of the religiously affiliated among the new Americans, there were significant accessions to other churches, and several additional faiths were introduced for the first time. Buddhism, for example, made its appearance among Chinese and Japanese immigrants on the West Coast, and a Young Men's Buddhist Association was founded in 1898. The annexation of Hawaii, also in 1898, gave added strength to the Buddhist community.

Lutheran Accessions

Of the Protestant groups, the Lutherans benefited most from the growing immigrant tide. By 1910, the Lutherans had become the third largest Protestant denominational grouping, being exceeded in number only by the Methodists and the Baptists. From fewer than 500,000 confirmed members in 1870, they had increased to more than 2,225,000 communicants in 1910. During this period 3 million Germans had entered the country, with perhaps nearly two-thirds of them being of Protestant background; and during these same years 1.75 million Scandinavians had arrived, almost all of whom were Lutheran by heritage and tradition. Although many of these new Americans were intensely anticlerical and served to swell the ranks of the unchurched, others among them were deeply pious and zealously orthodox.

As far as influence in the general life of the nation was concerned, the Lutheran segment of American church life remained a sleeping giant until after World War I. There were several reasons for this situation. First, apart from some cities in the Midwest, the overwhelming proportion of Lutherans were located in largely self-contained and self-sufficient rural communities. Second, many of them were further isolated by language barriers. Third, their energies were absorbed by the taxing demands of the attempt to keep abreast of the multiplying population from their homelands. Fourth, they had no organizational unity, being badly divided by national origin, place and time of settlement, and doctrinal differences. Throughout the period prior to World War I, they kept splintering apart, regrouping, and then splintering again. Among German Lutherans, the major bodies were the General Synod, the General Council, the United Synod in the South, the Missouri Synod, and the Joint Synod of Ohio. Scandinavians were represented by the Swedish Augustana Synod, the United Norwegian Lutheran Church, the Norwegian and Hague synods, the Danish Lutheran Church, the United Danish Lutheran Church, and Finnish and Icelandic churches. By 1900, there were twenty-four different Lutheran groups, with the family tree so complicated by constant reshuffling that it was difficult to chart even their individual histories.

Other Protestant Accessions

Both the older German Reformed (Reformed Church in the United States) and Dutch Reformed (Reformed Church in America) churches profited by the arrival of recruits from abroad. The Christian Reformed Church, though small, gained strength from renewed Dutch immigration, and in 1904, Hungarian Reformed immigrants formed a church of their own. More significant statistically was the growth of the Evangelical Synod,[38] the American counterpart of the Prussian Union of 1817 (the Evangelical United Church of Prussia), which had brought both Lutherans and Reformed together in a single church. Although the Evangelical Synod had roots that antedated the Civil War, scattered groups of "unionizing" Germans, whose major centers of strength were in the Midwest, were not fully organized as a united body until 1877. Mennonites also multiplied as a result of successive infusions from Switzerland, Prussia, and Russia. But they remained small and divided, with a membership of 54,000 in 1910 distributed among eleven different Mennonite groups.

Judaism and Eastern Orthodox Christianity

Immigration from eastern Europe, which peaked during the two decades that bridged the turn of the century, introduced the ancient churches of the East to the American scene and brought to Judaism the large-scale accessions that made it a major religious community in the United States.

Between 1880 and 1900, more than a half-million Jews entered the country, fleeing the anti-Semitic pressures directed against them in Russia, Poland, Austria-Hungary, and Romania. During the next fourteen years, more than a million arrived. These were added to an estimated Jewish community of 250,000 in 1880. The figures, however, are somewhat deceptive, for only a small proportion became affiliated initially with a synagogue.

Eastern Orthodox Christians had a long history, antedating the gradual separation within the Roman Empire of the East from the West, the Greek from the Latin, the Byzantine from the Roman. The estrangement of eastern from western Christianity began in the sixth century, and the final breach occurred in 1054 when Rome and the ancient patriarchates of the East found it no longer possible to gloss over the divisive issue of Roman primacy. Of the eastern Christians, the Russian Orthodox have chronological priority in America by virtue of the purchase of Alaska in 1867. Apart

[38] The Evangelical Synod should not be confused with the Methodist-oriented Evangelical Association, which joined with the United Brethren in 1946 to become the Evangelical United Brethren Church and in 1968 became part of the United Methodist Church. The Evangelical Synod united with the Reformed Church in the United States in 1934 to form the Evangelical and Reformed Church, which united with the Congregational Christian Churches in 1957 to form the United Church of Christ.

from this former Russian territory, the Eastern Orthodox churches became statistically significant in America only in the twentieth century. By 1916, the Russian Orthodox and the Greek Orthodox churches each had a constituency of about 100,000 people. Although Bulgarian, Romanian, Serbian, Syrian, and Ukrainian Orthodox churches had their beginnings in the United States prior to World War I, they were subordinated initially to the jurisdiction of the Russian church.

Since Judaism and Eastern Orthodoxy both reached their full maturity in America after 1920 and since the course of their later development is intimately related to the problems raised and the issues faced in earlier years, a subsequent chapter provides a more meaningful context for a discussion of their initial growth (Chapter 13).

Difficult as were the growing pains experienced by the churches of the new Americans, the churches of the older Americans had problems of their own during these years. The homogeneity of an evangelical Protestantism that transcended and minimized traditional denominational affiliations had been weakened by newer ecclesiastical separations into northern and southern, black and white churches. Now, in the last quarter of the century, as Arthur M. Schlesigner, Sr., noted, these churches were to be beset with new "pitfalls and perils," being confronted simultaneously with "two great challenges"—the one to their "system of thought," the other to their "social program."[39] The first challenge focuses attention on the new intellectual climate of the post–Civil War period, and the second on the new urban and industrial environment. The response to this dual challenge is the concern of the next two chapters.

---

[39] Schlesinger's essay, "A Critical Period in American Protestantism, 1875–1900," in *Massachusetts Historical Society Proceedings*, 64 (1930–1932), 523–48, is reprinted in John M. Mulder and John F. Wilson, eds., *Religion in American History* (Englewood Cliffs, N.J., 1978), 302–17. For Protestantism's response to the twofold challenge, see Robert T. Handy, *A Christian America* (New York, 1984), 134–58.

CHAPTER ELEVEN

The New Intellectual Climate

During the post-Appomattox years when many of the Protestant churches were preoccupied with problems related to Reconstruction in the South and missionary expansion in the West and were devoting their energies to revival campaigns and Sunday-school work, crucial theological issues were being raised by radical changes in the intellectual climate—issues that could not long be ignored.

Within a decade after the Civil War, practically every important American scientist had been converted to Darwin's theory of biological evolution, and Herbert Spencer's "social Darwinism" was equally influential.[1] Indeed, as early as 1872, the *Atlantic Monthly* was able to report that within the scientific community "natural selection" had "quite won the day in Germany and England, and very nearly won it in America." This new intellectual current penetrated the public consciousness with astonishing rapidity. "Ten or fifteen years ago," Whitelaw Reid declared in an address at Dartmouth in 1873, "the staple subject here for reading and talk, outside study hours, was English poetry and fiction. Now it is English science. Herbert Spencer, John Stuart Mill, Huxley, Darwin, Tyndall, have usurped the places of Tennyson and Browning, and Matthew Arnold and Dickens." And the discussion was not limited to college students. Equally avid interest in the new scientific theories was displayed by the general public, if the amount of space devoted by the popular periodicals and newspapers to academic lectures and debates is an accurate index of what was being read and discussed.

---

[1] See Richard Hofstadter, *Social Darwinism in American Thought* (New York, 1959).

The new biblical studies were another feature of the postwar intellectual climate. These studies, stemming mainly from the German universities but partly the work of British textual critics, utilized the techniques of "scientific history" to exhibit the Bible as a varied compilation of poetry, prophecy, and folklore that had been assembled over a period of one thousand years. The extent of the popular interest awakened by these studies is indicated by the reception that was given in 1881 to the English Revised Version of the New Testament, which incorporated the results of scholarly analysis of the text. The *Chicago Times* and the *Chicago Tribune* both printed the entire text, and 200,000 copies of the revised New Testament were sold in New York within less than a week.

Furthermore, the study of comparative religion was coming to the fore as an academic discipline, and it soon became apparent that the non-Christian religions also were of fascinating interest to the reading public. James Freeman Clarke's sympathetic appraisal of *Ten Great Religions* went through twenty-one editions after it was published in 1871.[2] Toward the end of the century when a World's Parliament of Religions was held in connection with the Columbian Exposition of 1892–1893, more than 150,000 people attended its sessions.

Finally, before the century was out, the burgeoning "sciences" of psychology and sociology made their appearance as forces to be reckoned with in the intellectual life of the nation. Almost immediately religious phenomena were subjected to psychological and sociological analysis. E. D. Starbuck was one of the pioneers, and his *Psychology of Religion* (1899) was something of an overnight sensation. When William James published his Gifford Lectures, *The Varieties of Religious Experience* (1902), the interest was so great that within a dozen years it had been reprinted twenty-one times. Ten years later J. H. Leuba pointed up in provocative fashion the disturbing implications of the psychological approach in his *Psychological Study of Religion* (1912). In the meantime, William Graham Sumner had published *Folkways* (1906), a sociological study of human behavior that stressed the socially conditioned character of religion and rejected any notion of absolute or eternal truth.

Each of these several currents of thought constituted a threat to accepted understandings of the Christian faith. The psychological and sociological studies tended to reduce religion to a social phenomenon. The accounts of other religions raised questions with regard to the uniqueness of the Christian faith. Both Darwinian biology and the new biblical studies seemed to undermine the authority of the Bible. How could one reconcile Darwinism with the Genesis accounts of creation? How could one adjust the doctrine of biblical inspiration to take account of errors and

---

[2] Clarke's views initially were expressed in an article published in 1857, a portion of which is reprinted in H. Shelton Smith, Robert Handy, and Lefferts Loetscher, *American Christianity*, II, 160–64.

contradictions in the biblical text that were noted by the scholars? What was one to make of a composite authorship of the books of Moses, with fragments of the text being assigned to widely separated times? What happened to the prophetic character of the book of Isaiah if parts of it were written by a later, "second Isaiah" who was reporting events rather than predicting them? These were unsettling questions, and their disturbing implications were made plain to the thousands who listened to Robert G. Ingersoll—"the notorious infidel"—as he ranged back and forth across the land questioning basic tenets of Christian belief.[3] Other thousands read his lectures—*The Gods* (1872), *Some Mistakes of Moses* (1879), *Why I Am an Agnostic* (1896)—in printed form. On a less popular level, J. W. Draper sought to demonstrate the incompatibility of science and religion in his *History of the Conflict Between Religion and Science* (1874), a task also undertaken by Andrew D. White in his *History of the Warfare of Science with Theology* (1896).

The pattern of response among Protestants, Roman Catholics, and Jews to the challenge of scientific modes of thought was remarkably similar. There were some who resisted the new intellectual currents and rejected any modification of inherited theological formulations. There were others who came to believe that the traditional forms of faith were no longer relevant and must be discarded and replaced with idioms and practices that were forthright expressions of scientific worldview. A third group occupied an intermediate position between the two extremes, seeking to effect adjustments that would do justice both to the essential elements of the inherited faith and to the newer scientific patterns of thought. The radical tendency never loomed large on the American scene, and the moderate "liberal" tendencies in Roman Catholicism were arrested by papal intervention. But in both Reformed Judaism (see Chapter 13) and liberal Protestant evangelicalism were new modes of thought destined to flourish.

Protestant Liberalism

The challenges of the postwar era were enormous, and they provoked theological reform among Protestants. Henry Ward Beecher, pastor of Plymouth Congregational Church in Brooklyn from 1847 to 1887 and easily the most prominent preacher of his time, was one of the earliest to recognize that the mere repetition of ancient doctrines would no longer do. In 1872, as the first Lyman Beecher lecturer at Yale, he warned the students of the Divinity School of the danger they faced of being left behind by "the intelligent part of society."

---

[3] Ingersoll, the son of a Congregational minister, was a great orator who had electrified the Republican convention of 1876 with his famous "plumed knight" speech nominating James G. Blaine for the presidency.

There is being now applied among scientists a greater amount of real, searching discriminating thought . . . than ever has been expended . . . in the whole history of the world put together. . . .

If ministers do not make their theological systems conform to the facts as they are; if they do not recognize what men are studying, the time will not be far distant when the pulpit will be like a voice crying in the wilderness. And it will not be "Prepare the way of the Lord," either. . . . The providence of God is rolling forward in a spirit of investigation that Christian ministers must meet and join.

The one thing ministers cannot afford, insisted Beecher, is to become "apostles of the dead past" by letting "the development of truth run ahead of them." Consequently, many seminaries took steps to familiarize their students with the scientific worldview, a program that in the end produced mixed results for religion.[4]

The Fundamental Issue of Biblical Authority

The most heated initial debate centered on the notion of biological evolution, for it was a dramatic issue and, by its apparent contradiction of the Bible, Darwin's theory seemed to strike at the very root of a biblically grounded faith. Charles Hodge, the towering theological oracle of Princeton Theological Seminary, declared in 1874 that "a more absolutely incredible theory was never propounded for acceptance among men," and Mark Hopkins, the equally distinguished president of Williams College, denounced the whole concept as "essentially atheistic." A different verdict, however, had been pronounced three years earlier by Hodge's neighbor James McCosh, president of Princeton University. "I am inclined to think," he said, "that the theory contains a large body of important truths." If one distinguished the "major assumptions" of the biblical accounts of creation from their literary form, McCosh saw no reason why creation as described in Genesis should be regarded as inconsistent with developmental theories. Holding fast to the traditional doctrine of design in nature, he interpreted "natural selection" as the product of "supernatural design."[5]

A similar resolution of the problem was proposed by John Fiske. In his *Outline of Cosmic Philosophy* (1874) and subsequent volumes, he transmuted the struggle for survival into a struggle for the lives of others. Infusing the whole process with divine purpose, Fiske coined the sentence "Evolution is

[4] Lyman Beecher, *Yale Lectures on Preaching* (New York, 1872–1874), I, 87–89. See C. E. Clark, *Henry Ward Beecher: Spokesman for Middle Class America* (Champaign, Ill., 1978). A perceptive analysis of the forces behind Beecher's fears and the manner in which they influenced religion is James W. Turner, *Without God, Without Creed: The Origins of Unbelief in America* (Baltimore, 1985).

[5] See Charles Hodge, *What Is Darwinism?* (New York, 1874); and James McCosh, *Christian and Positivism* (New York, 1871).

God's way of doing things," which was later popularized as a slogan by Lyman Abbot. In the meantime, Henry Ward Beecher had given further impetus to this type of adjustment, announcing in the *Christian Union* (August 2, 1883) that he was "a cordial Christian evolutionist."[6] But perhaps the most reassuring evidence to many faithful Christians that evolutionary views could be assimilated without harm to the Christian faith was provided by Henry Drummond, the author of *Natural Law in the Spiritual World* (1883). This gifted young Scottish theologian was an intimate friend of Dwight L. Moody, and when Drummond visited the United States in 1887, Moody enlisted his aid both at Northfield and in his revival meetings.

The theory of biological evolution was actually the least serious of the intellectual problems that the churches were being compelled to face. Whereas the problem could be handled by construing the first chapter of Genesis allegorically or by contending that the Bible was never intended to be a scientific encyclopedia, other problems could not be sidestepped so easily. This problem was notably true of the issues that were being raised by the "scientific" study of the Bible, for the new biblical studies were making it increasingly evident that any attempt to justify even the "major assumptions" of the Christian faith by an appeal to the authority of Scripture was fraught with difficulty. Biblical scholars were demonstrating that at many points of Christian doctrine, conflicting evidence could be adduced from within the biblical text itself.

In 1867, these difficulties pointed out by Thomas F. Curtis of Bucknell University in *The Human Element in the Inspiration of the Sacred Scriptures* and the measure of the confusion he evoked are indicated by the reaction to his book of a fellow Baptist, Henry G. Weston, who was soon to become president of Grozer Theological Seminary. "I am all at sea," wrote Weston, "except so far as a dogged belief in inspiration goes, without being able to define what 'inspiration' is or what its metes and bounds are." Small wonder Weston was determined to hold fast to a belief in inspiration, for this had been the major line of defense of the whole dogmatic structure.[7]

The central issue was the authority of the Bible. Few great religions have been so dependent as Christianity upon a sacred book. Preaching elucidated its texts. Prayer claimed its promises. And theology and conduct alike were grounded on its teachings. Although both Protestants and Roman Catholics had long regarded the Bible as the inspired and inerrant Word of God, the Roman Catholic Church found it necessary at the Council of Trent (1545–1563) to supplement biblical teaching with that of

[6] For Henry Ward Beecher and Lyman Abbott, see Beecher's *Evolution and Religion* (New York, 1885), and Abbott's *The Theology of an Evolutionist* (New York, 1897).

[7] See J. W. Brown, *The Rise of Biblical Criticism in America, 1800–1870* (Middletown, Conn., 1969); and N. H. Maring, "Baptists and Changing Views of the Bible, 1865–1918," *Foundations* (July 1958), 52–78, (October 1958), 30–61.

"tradition," and at the first Vatican Council (1870) to affirm papal infallibility in the interpretation of Scripture and tradition. Protestants, on the other hand, had clung to the sole authority of Scripture, which in the first half of the nineteenth century was almost universally understood in terms of an inspired and infallible text. Since they had no recourse to any supplementary authority, the questioning of biblical inspiration was peculiarly threatening to Protestants. Once this point was surrendered, a thorough reconsideration of the basis of the Christian faith was required. Ultimately, Protestants worked out different ways of understanding biblical authority, but first many of them sought in "evangelical liberalism" and "scientific modernism" other sources of authority.

Evangelical Liberalism

The striking feature of the liberal movement in Protestantism that began to take shape during the 1870s was its conservative intent. Leaders of the movement were evangelicals, standing firmly within the church, cherishing their Christian experience, and uncompromising in their loyalty to Christ. They had little in common with the earlier rationalistic liberalism that became dominant in Unitarianism. The central concern was quite explicitly apologetic. They wished to preserve the truth of the gospel as it spoke to the hearts of men. In the face of what many feared might be fatal assaults on the Christian faith, they sought to restate the essential doctrines of evangelical Christianity in terms that would be both intelligible and convincing and thus establish them on a more secure foundation.

Although isolated individuals in various parts of the country helped fashion what came to be called the "New Theology" and "Progressive Orthodoxy," the most important contribution was made by a notable group of pastors in prominent New England pulpits, all of whom had been deeply influenced by Horace Bushnell. In neighboring churches on the New Haven green, Theodore T. Munger and Newman Smyth gave new luster to a tradition of distinguished theological preaching that had been exemplified in these same pulpits by Jonathan Edwards, Jr., and Nathaniel W. Taylor. Munger, at the United (Congregational) Church, was the author of *The Freedom of Faith* (1883), which the *New York Times* called the "most forcible and positive expression" of the new theology to appear in this country;[8] and Smyth, at the Center (Congregational) Church, had argued the same case in three pioneering volumes: *The Religious Feeling* (1877), *Old Faiths in New Light* (1878), and *The Orthodox Theology of Today* (1881). In Boston, Phillips Brooks at Trinity (Episcopal) Church and George A. Gordon at Old South (Congregational) Church were making Copley Square a center of the new theological outlook. Washington Gladden was

---

[8] C. H. Hopkins, *The Rise of the Social Gospel in American Protestantism* (New Haven, 1940), 61.

less philosophically inclined, but he was equally creative in his own way and was the most effective propagandist of the new point of view. As early as 1873, he had written for the *Independent* an editorial entitled "Immoral Theology," which exhibited the journalistic flair that won widespread circulation for his subsequent books dealing with current theological issues: *Burning Questions* (1886), *Who Wrote the Bible?* (1891), *Ruling Ideas of the Present Age* (1895), *Seven Puzzling Bible Books* (1897), and *How Much Is Left of the Old Doctrines?* (1899). By the time these books were published, Gladden had left New England in 1882 to accept a call to the First Congregational Church of Columbus, Ohio. All these young men were responding in the immediate post–Civil War years to the practical necessity of relating the Christian faith from week to week to questions that were uppermost in the minds of alert and inquiring congregations.

The mood was set by Horace Bushnell, who rejected a rationalistic response to the intellectual challenges to faith and proposed instead a response to the "heart," along the lines of Pascal's dictum that "the heart has its reasons, which reason does not know." Following Bushnell, theologians placed Christ at the center of the religious experience that they were seeking to defend. Egbert C. Smyth, writing in the journal of the recently liberalized Andover Theological Seminary, asserted that Christ alone "fulfills the aspirations and harmonizes the discords in man's religious history."

> The history of religion leads on and up to him, and he possesses all the resources requisite for its greatest possible future growth. He is the Alpha and Omega; the Absolute, revealed; the Infinite, personally disclosed; the eternal Power that makes for righteousness, realized in the Righteous One. . . . A theology which is not Christocentric is like a Ptolomaic astronomy; it is out of true relation to the earth and heavens, to God and the universe.[9]

Thus, although there was much that earlier generations had affirmed that could be surrendered as nonessential and much that had to be adjusted and accommodated to new knowledge, the person and work of Christ as the clue to the nature of God, the worth of human personality, and the meaning of life were indispensable. His life and teachings constituted "the final principle" of "interpretation," the standard by which all else must be judged. The goal of the New Theology, as William Adams Brown was to point out in 1898 in his inaugural address as professor of systematic theology in Union Theological Seminary, was no more than "the old cry, 'Back to Christ.' Let no theology call itself Christian which has not its center and source in him."

Although these evangelical liberals clung tenaciously to the Bible and repaired to it for consolation and inspiration, they viewed it as a document that recorded the historical experience out of which the Christian faith had emerged, a vivid personal record of suffering and travail that culmi-

---

[9] *Progressive Orthodoxy*, by the editors of *Andover Review* (Boston, 1886), 35–36.

nated in the disclosure in Christ of true and perfect communion with God. It was a record not of a theology but of an experience that was to be reproduced "in our own times and in our own souls." Although it told them what they knew of Christ, there was no need to seek "scientific arguments for Christian truth," for their own experience of Christ was self-authenticating. "The foundation of spiritual faith is neither in the church nor in the Bible, but in the spiritual consciousness of man."[10] The doctrines that "form the subject matter of theology," declared Brown in his inaugural address, are not "dogmas to be received on authority"; they are "living convictions, born of experience, and maintaining themselves in spite of all opposition because of the response which they wake in the hearts and consciences" of advocates of new ways of thinking.

The same impulse to reinvigorate the Christian witness by a less stultifying understanding of the Christian faith that stood at the heart of the New Theology found parallel expression in a related movement known by many names but most commonly called "the higher Christian life" theology.[11] Like the New Theology of evangelical liberalism, it stressed the centrality of religious experience and the work of the Holy Spirit, but was less interested in intellectual questions. Wesleyan holiness leaders had long been committed to the idea that conversion should be followed by a baptism of the Spirit, the primary effect of which was purity of life. The higher Christian life leaders, in contrast, thought of this second transforming religious experience as energizing and empowering believers to witness for Christ and thus to serve the church and society. So closely akin was the higher Christian life emphasis to some expressions of the New Theology that it is often difficult to tell within which camp different leaders should be classified. Both were rooted in churches of a Reformed rather than a Wesleyan background, both were similar in social and cultural status, and evangelical liberals were no less emphatic in appealing to the testimony of the heart and religious experience. Some of the latter did not hesitate to speak of a new apostolate of the Spirit.[12]

The great advantage of both forms of a revived evangelicalism was that proponents were enabled to maintain what to them was the heart of the inherited faith without coming into conflict with the intellectual climate of the modern world. The stress upon self-authenticating religious experience allowed the higher Christian life advocates to bypass for a time many potentially troublesome issues, whereas the same stress permitted evangelical liberals to bridge the gap between the natural and the supernatural and to give due recognition to the claims of science and the scientific

---

[10] See Lyman Abbott, *Reminiscences* (Boston, 1915), 451, 461–62.

[11] See Grant Wacker, "The Holy Spirit and the Spirit of the Age in American Protestantism, 1880–1910," *Journal of American History* (1985), 45–62.

[12] See *Walter Rauschenbusch: Selected Writings*, ed. W. S. Hudson (New York, 1984), 22, 25, 32–33.

method. The acceptance of the idea of development made it possible to view the Bible in a way that was congenial to both their religious and their cultural orientation, allowed them to share to varying degrees the growing confidence in man and his future, and fostered an open-minded attitude toward differing opinions and new modes of thought.

Scientific Modernism

Although evangelical liberalism continued to be the dominant liberal current in American Protestantism, a more radical approach to the issue of the relation of science to religion began to emerge in the first years of the twentieth century. Those who in retrospect have been called "scientific modernists"[13] stood in marked contrast to the conservative intent of evangelical liberals, for they viewed as a lost cause the endeavor of the evangelical liberals to maintain continuity with the inherited faith by abstracting religion from the realm of scientific verification. These men recognized that the sanctuary of the heart that the evangelical liberals sought to preserve inviolate had been invaded by the scientists. "Science," E. D. Starbuck had proclaimed in 1899, "has conquered one field after another, until now it is entering the most complex, the most inaccessible, and of all the most sacred domain—that of religion." The scientific modernists were impressed by the way in which psychological and sociological analysis was able to explain religious experience, doctrinal concepts, and ecclesiastical practice in terms of inner personal drives and conditioning social forces. Thus they were ready to grant "to the data of religious experience the same scientific status as the data of the physical sciences," and then to fashion a religious faith "out of the materials furnished by the several sciences."[14] They did not seek a complete break with the Christian past, as is made clear in Shailer Mathews's classic definition of modernism—"the use of the methods of modern science to find, state, and use the permanent and central values of inherited orthodoxy in meeting the needs of a modern world."[15] The values of orthodoxy were not to be ignored, but

---

[13] The term was coined by Sidney E. Mead. Although exact lines of demarcation between the evangelical liberals and the scientific modernists are difficult to draw, there was a clear difference of intention and emphasis. The liberals were committed first and foremost to the Christian tradition and from that vantage point attempted to effect any necessary adjustments. The scientific modernists took their stand with the presuppositions of science and then sought to reclaim what they could of the traditional faith. Complicating the picture is the fact that evangelical liberals frequently called themselves "modernists."

[14] E. E. Aubrey, "Religious Bearings of the Modern Scientific Movement," in *Environmental Factors in Christian History*, ed. J. T. McNeill, Shirley Jackson Case, Mathew Spinka, & Harold R. Willoughby (Chicago, 1939), 368.

[15] See the portion of Mathews's *The Faith of Modernism* that is reprinted in Smith, Handy, and Loetscher, II, 238–45.

"science" was the arbiter in determining what they were and how they were to be stated and used.[16] It is safe to assume, Mathews asserted, that "scientists know more about nature and man than did the theologians who drew up the Creeds and Confessions." The tendency was to become less concerned with a distinctively Christian witness and more interested in general religious affirmations based on a "scientific world view."

Unlike liberal evangelicalism, which initially was the product of the reflections of men who were pastors of churches, scientific modernism was indigenous to the theological seminaries. The great center was at Chicago, where William Rainey Harper and John D. Rockefeller had established their Baptist superuniversity in 1892, assembling for that purpose many of the most noted scholars in America. Many pastors found comfort and reassurance and themes for sermons in the reports that filtered down to them from the psychologists and sociologists that religious beliefs integrated personality, fostered mental health, and several socially useful ends; yet the theological professors at Chicago, with John Dewey, Albion W. Small, and George Herbert Mead numbered among their university colleagues, were compelled to face the fundamental theological issue that was raised by the empiricism upon which these new disciplines were based.

The Chicago approach to theology (they hesitated to call it more than a theological method) was not fully elaborated until after World War I, but its basic character was evident much earlier. The key figures of the Divinity School faculty, in addition to a distinguished corps of biblical scholars headed by Harper himself, were Shailer Mathews, George Burman Foster, Shirley Jackson Case, and Gerald Birney Smith; and Edward Scribner Ames—simultaneously professor of philosophy in the university, pastor of the University Church of the Disciples of Christ, and dean of the Disciples Divinity House—also provided strong leadership in the task of theological reconstruction. The dominant emphasis, exemplified preeminently by Mathews, was upon a sociohistorical approach to theology that viewed all doctrinal statements as reflections of historic cultural patterns, and consequently were functional and not normative, changeable and not permanent. They were to be tested and applied "in the same way that chemists and historians reach and apply their conclusions," and they must be stated in terms that would make sense to intelligent men and women within the contemporary cultural context. "The God of the scientifically minded will assume the patterns of science."[17]

In spite of the fact that some members of the Chicago group moved to a nontheist position and others found it difficult to find anything either unique or normative in the Christian faith, the influence they exerted in

[16] A typical monograph was that of George A. Coe, "What Does Modern Psychology Permit Us to Believe in Respect to Regeneration?" *American Journal of Theology,* 12 (1908), 353–68.

[17] Shailer Mathews, "The Faith of Modernism," in Smith, Handy, and Loetscher, II, 240–41; and Shailer Mathews, *The Growth of the Idea of God* (New York, 1931), 184.

the life of the churches was far from insignificant. This trend was partly due to the fact that for a period of thirty or forty years, a very large proportion of professors in other theological seminaries received their graduate training at Chicago. Scarcely less important was the fact that most of the key figures remained staunch churchmen and played a leading role in ecclesiastical affairs. Mathews, for example, was president of the Federal Council of Churches from 1912 to 1916 and of the American (Northern) Baptist Convention in 1915. Finally, the men at Chicago exhibited an intensely practical propagandist zeal. Harper set the pattern when he became superintendent of the Hyde Park Baptist Sunday School in order to put his theories into practice; and with the stimulus of Harper's interest, the University of Chicago pioneered in the new "scientific" approach to religious education. One of the most effective means of penetration was a scheme of adult education known as the American Institute of Sacred Literature, through which books, pamphlets, and study courses in a steady stream were made available and were widely used in Protestant churches throughout the Midwest.

Protestant Conservatism

Mounting accommodation within Protestantism to the new intellectual climate did not go unchallenged. From the beginning, resistance was both vocal and widespread, but the response was mainly limited to dogmatic denials grounded in a pietistic indifference to the new "scientific" studies. Charles Hodge, in an earlier debate, set the tone of the unyielding defensive posture of the conservative elements when he declared, "We can even afford to acknowledge our incompetence to meet them in argument, or to answer their objections; and yet our faith remains unshaken and rational."[18] The arguments broke out like wildfires at seminaries in the late nineteenth century. Heresy trials took place in virtually every Protestant denomination and resulted in dismissals of faculty from church seminaries as well as suspensions from the ministry. Such trials were widely reported in the public press and had the effect of both fomenting quarrels over points of doctrine and awakening sympathy for the "persecuted." When the trials tapered off early in the twentieth century, the centers of conservative strength were clear.

The theological climate of the country varied from section to section. By the time of World War I, New England had long been the great stronghold of Protestant liberalism. New York State, with its Yankee heritage and "New School" tradition, was scarcely less liberal in its dominant theological mood. The Midwest was generally moderate with leaders of both "right" and "left" exerting influence within the churches. This was the area in which the influence of the University of Chicago, through its "extension" activities, was widely felt. On the Pacific coast, the old-line denominations were not deeply

---

[18] *Princeton Review* (1857), 662.

rooted, but, with a few exceptions, their general tone was conservative. Perhaps more significant, especially in California, was a cultural rootlessness that was beginning to manifest itself in a number of new sects and cults. The South had witnessed a few attempts to break with orthodoxy. Alexander Winchell at Vanderbilt had contradicted the Genesis account of creation in 1878, thereby provoking a pointed censure by the General Conference of the southern Methodist church of those who bend "all the energies of their most exalted genius to the inculcation of theories which are calculated, if not designed, to destroy the credibility of the Holy Scriptures."[19] When Winchell refused to resign, the university abolished his position. The following year Crawford H. Toy was forced to resign from the faculty of the Southern Baptist Theological Seminary at Louisville, Kentucky, for teachings that allegedly undercut the absolute authority of Scripture. And in 1886, James Woodrow, uncle of Woodrow Wilson and professor at Columbia Theological Seminary, was condemned and dismissed from his post by the General Assembly of the southern Presbyterian church for suggesting that the theory of evolution could be reconciled with a "not unreasonable interpretation of the Bible."[20] Such incidents were significant only as an occasion for the closing of ranks by the southern churches against any departure from the inherited theological formulations. A placid and undisturbed orthodoxy continued to prevail throughout the South as a whole.

Pennsylvania and New Jersey stood in marked contrast to their neighboring states to the north, for they were dominated by a vigorous, articulate, and strongly entrenched conservatism. This was the Presbyterian citadel, and it was a Presbyterianism that was shaped by the unyielding orthodoxy of Princeton, Western, and Pittsburgh (United Presbyterian) theological seminaries. Also contributing to the conservative cast of the Middle Atlantic states was the strength of the denominations of German origin. The rallying center of the conservative forces was Princeton Theological Seminary, where the mantle of Charles Hodge had been bequeathed to his son Archibald Alexander Hodge and then to Benjamin Warfield, both of whom were as convinced as the elder Hodge that the truth of the gospel had been definitively set forth in the Westminster Confession of 1646. In response to the issues raised by biblical criticism, the younger Hodge and Warfield fashioned the "Princeton doctrine of Inspiration," which became a major defense of biblical inerrancy.

Meanwhile, throughout the northern half of the United States, a new movement was arising that was to give added strength to the conservative forces. This was a movement that found expression in "prophetic" Bible conferences held annually after 1875 at which premillennial views were discussed and advocated. Although differing interpretations of Scripture were represented, those adhering to the "dispensationalist" speculations of J. N.

---

[19] K. K. Bailey, *Southern White Protestantism in the Twentieth Century* (New York, 1964), 10.
[20] *Ibid.*

Darby (1800–1882) in England were ultimately to prevail and provide the standard by which all else was to be judged. Premillennialist sentiment in America was spearheaded by a few prominent pastors, a number of itinerant evangelists, and additional leadership supplied by newly established "Bible Schools." Displaying little concern for denominational peculiarities, proponents of the "prophetic" understanding of Scripture were making inroads by 1890 in most Protestant denominations. By 1900, varying views were being crowded out, and the victory of the Darbyites (the "any moment now" group) was sealed by the popularity of the *Scofield Reference Bible,* an annotated edition of the Bible prepared by C. I. Scofield and published in 1909. The Scofield Bible imposed a rigid schematization on the complex biblical materials by dividing Scripture into seven or eight distinct historical eras called "dispensations." According to this scheme, the present dispensation was to culminate "any moment now" in the return of Christ to reign in glory.[21]

Pushed by the rising tide of "dispensationalism," many advocates of "the higher Christian life" theology felt it necessary to choose between the harder-line premillennialism and the more benign evangelical liberalism. The result for those who adopted the premillennialist option was a curious blending of the "holiness" motif of the Keswick conferences in England[22] with the hardline dispensationalism of the Darbyite faction of the prophetic conferences.

Among the conspicuous leaders of the dispensationalist movement, after the publication of Scofield's Bible, were Reuben A. Torrey, J. W. Chapman, A. C. Dixon, and James M. Gray, all of whom were related in one way or another to the Moody Bible Institute in Chicago. These men tended to interpret every manifestation of theological liberalism as the work of Satan, and they constantly voiced their alarm. This preoccupation with heresy led them to identify specific items of Scripture—such as the verbal inerrancy of Scripture, the virgin birth of Christ, and his personal and imminent return—that could be utilized to spot a heretic by a few pointed questions.

New Departures

During these same years, much more radical attempts to come to terms with the new intellectual climate were taking place outside the established churches. Most of them were not numerically significant, but they are

---

[21] See C. N. Kraus, *Dispensationalism in America* (Richmond, 1958); C. B. Bass, *Backgrounds of Dispensationalism* (Grand Rapids, 1960); and F. E. Gaebelien, *The Story of the Scofield Bible* (New York, 1959). For the larger context of "dispensationalism," see E. R. Sandeen, *The Roots of Fundamentalism: British and American Millenarianism* (Chicago, 1970).

[22] The Keswick conferences were held each summer for the purpose of "promoting practical holiness" and had been initiated in 1875 by men who had been influenced by Dwight L. Moody during his British tour of 1873–1875.

important in illustrating the ferment that had been precipitated. Some were sober attempts at a thoroughgoing reconstruction of religion without a "supernatural" dimension, and others were impressed by "discoveries" in the field of comparative religion, but the most successful were those that constructed a new "science" out of evidence supplied by mesmerism and utilized it as the basic datum for a whole new system of religious belief. What bound these diverse groups together was a common revolt against any accepted understanding of the Christian faith.

The Religion of Humanity

In 1867, the Free Religious Association was formed by a militant group of young Unitarians who had become convinced that organized Christianity, even in its Unitarian form, had become the chief enemy of freedom and progress. They were devotees of science influenced by the positivist philosophy of Auguste Comte and were persuaded that with the tools of science, people could become masters of their own destiny.[23] But to release latent energies and to awaken the necessary idealism for the fashioning of a new society in which the peoples of the world would be united in universal brotherhood, they believed that the inspiration of religion was required. The religion they had in mind betrayed many overtones of the transcendentalism of Ralph Waldo Emerson and Theodore Parker, but its major thrust was toward an empirical and a scientific naturalism. Conventional theism was abandoned. This concept was made clear by Octavius Brooks Frothingham, president of the Association, when he declared the following in *The Religion of Humanity:*

> Whether there shall be peace or war, rule or misrule, purity or corruption, justice or injustice, . . . are questions which men must answer for themselves. There is no higher tribunal before which they can be carried; there is no super-human or extra-human will by which they can be dealt with. If things go well or ill rests with those who are commissioned to make them go.[24]

The fundamental convictions of the "religion of humanity"—as it was disseminated from the pulpit as well as the lyceum podium—were summarized in "Fifty Affirmations" which Francis Ellingwood Abbot published in each issue of the *Index,* the official organ of the Association. The Affirmations begin with the assertion that "religion is the effort of man to perfect himself." This is the oft-times hidden but universal element in all historical religions, and the objective of free religion is the perfecting of people by emancipating them from outward laws and winning them to a voluntary

---

[23] There were other, more explicitly Comtean societies, including the Positivist Society, which was formed in New York City in 1871, and two Societies of Humanity, one of which Leon Trotsky attended.

[24] Octavius Brooks Frothingham, *The Religion of Humanity*, 3rd ed. (New York, 1875), 171.

obedience to the inward fundamental law of true humanity. Perhaps the spirit of this free religion was best expressed in these lines of Walt Whitman:

> If I build God a church it shall be a church to men and women.
> If I write hymns they shall be all to men and women.
> If I become a devotee, it shall be to men and women.[25]

Although the Free Religious Association had its origin in Boston, it had representatives elsewhere. Abbot moved to Toledo in 1870, and the Association's most prominent pulpit was in New York City, where Frothingham preached each Sunday in the Lyric Hall to a congregation that included notable figures in the arts and letters. The watchwords of the movement were freedom and unity, and because its strong-minded members believed so wholeheartedly in freedom, there often was little unity and frequently considerable dissension.[26] By 1890, most of the Free Religionists had been reabsorbed into Unitarianism.

The "religion of humanity" found more permanent institutional expression in the Society for Ethical Culture, founded by Felix Adler in 1876. Adler had been trained for the rabbinate but had revolted against his religious heritage. For a time he was president of both his own society and the Free Religious Association. The Ethical Culture movement was never large. It enjoyed, however, a slow but steady growth as long as Adler lived. In 1926, there were six societies in the United States, with a membership of more than two thousand and perhaps an equal number of peripheral adherents.

Esoteric Wisdom from the East

Theosophy capitalized, on a more popular level, upon much the same interest that had led to the formation of the Free Religious Association. It also emphasized fundamental truths that lay behind all the great religions, assimilated in a curious way the discoveries of modern science, and stressed the godlike potentialities of men and the universal brotherhood of the human race. The founder of the movement was Madame Helena P. Blavatsky, who came to New York in 1872 and three years later established the Theosophical Society.[27] As the wife of a Russian general, she had led a peripatetic existence in the Orient where she had busied herself accumulating occult lore. She claimed that in Tibet she had been instructed in the esoteric wisdom of the ages by a group of "adepts" or "masters"—gifted

---

[25] C. J. Furness, ed., *Walt Whitman's Workshop* (Cambridge, Mass., 1928), 43.

[26] For the inability of the Free Religionists to act on the basis of complete freedom, see Stow Persons, *Free Religion: An American Faith* (New Haven, 1947), 93–94.

[27] See C. E. B. Roberts, *Mysterious Madame, Helena Blavatsky* (New York, 1931); and A. B. Kuhn, *Theosophy* (New York, 1930).

seers who stood in direct succession to Moses, Krishna, Lao-tze, Confucius, Buddha, Christ, and other great religious prophets. Her teaching combined many features of Spiritualism with a bowdlerized understanding of Buddhism, and interpreted reincarnation as an extension of the evolutionary process. Indicative of her central emphasis are titles of two of her many books: *Isis Unveiled: A Master Key to the Mysteries of Ancient and Modern Science and Theology* (1877) and *The Secret Doctrine: The Synthesis of Science, Religion, and Philosophy* (1893).

After Madame Blavatsky's death, the movement divided into two camps when Mrs. Annie Besant[28] began to replace some of the characteristic Buddhist doctrines with concepts derived from Hinduism. Mrs. Besant, with a suave and cultured Hindu brahmin sleeping outside her door to guard her against intrusion, was the leading sensation at the World's Parliament of Religions in 1893. But the conference with the words of Malachi as its motto—"Have we not all one Father? Hath not one God created us?"—provided an opportunity for other representatives of Eastern religions to gain a hearing. The Vedanta Society, a Hindu cult, had its American origin here in the teaching of Swami Vivekananda. A similar movement was the Yogoda Sat-Sanga, or Self-Realization Fellowship, which taught the Hindu practice of yoga. The Baha'i faith, of Muslim origin, received some notice in 1893 at Chicago, but its American adherents were more fully enlightened when Abdu'lu-Baha arrived in 1912. The new religion had been founded in Persia in 1853 when Mirza Husayn Ali announced that he was Baha'u'lláh—"the Glory of God." Operating from the premise that God is unknowable except through a "manifestation," he claimed to be the manifestation for this age commissioned by divine command to unify humanity within one faith and one order. When he died in 1892, he left a testament appointing his son Abdu'l-Baha—"the Servant of Glory"—as his authoritative interpreter. With its stress on human brotherhood and the unity of all religion, the Baha'i faith also insists on full and unquestioning acceptance of Baha'u'lláh as the authoritative manifestation of God.[29]

Science, Religion, Health

Interest in "mental healing" had been developing in America prior to the Civil War. It was based on experiments with hypnosis by a German physician, Franz Anton Mesmer (1733?–1815), who concluded that a mysterious magnetic fluid was the explanation for the mental power that one person could exercise over another. Phineas Parkhurst Quimby of Portland, Maine, was one of many who became intrigued by the therapeutic power of mesmerism. Ultimately he became convinced that disease could

---

[28] See the two-volume biography by A. H. Nethercot, *The First Five Lives of Annie Besant* (Chicago, 1960), and *The Last Four Lives of Annie Besant* (Chicago, 1963).

[29] R. H. Stockman, *The Baha'i Faith in America* (Wilmette, Ill., 1985).

be cured by cultivating healthy attitudes—positive thoughts instead of negative ones—through suggestion and without the use of hypnotism. Sickness, he insisted, was the consequence of wrong beliefs. The remedy, therefore, was to displace the erroneous ideas of the ill with healing truth.

One of Quimby's patients was Mary Baker Eddy, the founder of Christian Science.[30] As a child she suffered from nervous disorders. Her ill health continued to plague her through three marriages. Although she was helped by Quimby in 1862 and 1864, she and her followers have insisted that she was guided through her own experience to an original discovery of the divine law of life that surpassed in importance Newton's discovery of the law of gravitation when he saw the apple fall. Whether she built upon the foundation provided by Quimby or gained her insight from a unique revelation, Mrs. Eddy was soon embarked upon an independent healing career based upon the conviction that the Eternal Mind is the source of all being, that matter is nonexistent, that disease is caused by erroneous thought (compounded, to be sure, by the Malicious Animal Magnetism projected by one's enemies), and that power is released through Christian Science to overcome all the illusions that have troubled humanity. "The control mind holds over matter," she declared, "becomes no longer a question when with mathematical certainty we gain its proof and can demonstrate the facts assumed." In Christian Science this proof has been reduced to a scientific statement that "furnishes a key to the harmony of man and reveals what destroys sickness, sin, and death."[31]

In 1875, Mrs. Eddy formed a small group of adherents into a society at Lynn, Massachusetts, and published the first edition of the authoritative textbook of her doctrine, *Science and Health with Key to the Scriptures*. The movement did not prosper, however, until she moved to Boston and established the Massachusetts Metaphysical College to train "practitioners." In 1892, control of the movement was vested in the self-perpetuating board of trustees of "the Mother Church" in Boston. Membership multiplied rapidly thereafter, and the Church, especially through its official organ, the *Christian Science Journal* (later the *Monitor*), addressed a host of practical matters of social reform and family life. By the time of Mrs. Eddy's death in 1910, the Church of Christ, Scientist, with its various local units, had grown to almost 100,000 members.

There were other heirs of Quimby. The most important were his former patients Julius A. Dresser and Warren Felt Evans.[32] The latter was a former Methodist minister who had become a Swedenborgian. Evans began to

---

[30] Robert Peel, *Mary Baker Eddy: The Years of Discovery* (New York, 1966). See also E. F. Dakin, *Mrs. Eddy: The Biography of a Virginal Mind* (New York, 1929).

[31] Mary Baker Eddy, *Science and Health* (Boston, 1875), 9.

[32] See J. A. Dresser, *The True History of Mental Science* (New York, 1899); H. W. Dresser, *A History of the New Thought Movement* (New York, 1919); and C. S. Barden, *Spirits in Rebellion: The Rise and Development of New Thought* (Dallas, 1963).

practice "mental medicine" at Claremont, New Hampshire, and set forth the principles of the new science in a series of books: *The Mental Cure* (1869), *Mental Medicine* (1872), *Soul and Body* (1876), and *The Divine Law* (1881). In Boston other disciples of Quimby who had formed the Church of the Divine Unity were joined by Dresser in 1882. The movement spread rapidly under many names—Mental Science, Higher Thought, Higher Life, and Divine Science. The term "New Thought" was coined in 1889 by William Henry Holcombe, a homeopathic physician; and in 1894, this was chosen as the title of a little magazine published in Melrose, Massachusetts. The first national convention was held in San Francisco in 1894 under the auspices of the Divine Science Association, and five years later the name of the sponsoring body was changed to the New Thought Alliance. The annual conventions failed to develop any centralized organization, and the movement continued to be highly individualistic, with considerable variation in doctrine and with personal preference dictating the choice of name by local groups. One current, represented by M. J. Barnett's *Practical Metaphysics* (1889), interpreted New Thought doctrine within a theosophical context; another current was strongly influenced by Spiritualism. The most prolific of the New Thought writers were Ralph Waldo Trine (1866–1958) and Emmet Fox (1886–1951), whose books were widely read by people who had no connection at all with the movement. All these currents lived on in various forms of popular religious belief and acquired renewed importance in the late twentieth century.[33]

A less amorphous expression of the "mind cure" idea was the Unity School of Practical Christianity founded at Kansas City, Missouri, by Charles and Myrtle Fillmore.[34] They were attending New Though lectures in 1886 when "Truth" came to Myrtle Fillmore, as expressed in the affirmation "I am a child of God, and therefore I do not inherit sickness." As Myrtle's tuberculosis improved, people were attracted to the Fillmores and to Myrtle's notion that "spiritual truth is that you are God's own beloved child and that God is ever giving you his wisdom, love, power, life and substance."[35] The Fillmores began to advertise themselves as "Healers and Teachers" and gradually gathered a small group into the Society of Silent Help, a prayer ministry. In 1889, a periodical, *Modern Thought,* was launched to publicize their views, and two years later the name "Unity" was seized upon as more adequately expressing their basic principle.

> Unity! . . . Unity! . . . That's the name for our work! The name I've been looking for! . . . It embodies the central principle of what we believe: unity of

[33] See Robert Fuller, *Mesmerism and the American Cure of Souls* (Philadelphia, 1982), and *Alternative Medicine and American Religious Life* (New York, 1989).

[34] See J. D. Freeman, *The Household of Faith: The Story of Unity* (Lee Summit, Mo., 1951); and C. S. Braden, *These Also Believe* (New York, 1949).

[35] Myrtle Fillmore, *How to Let God Help You* (Unity Village, Mo., 1956), 13.

the soul with God, unity of all life, unity of all religions, unity of the spirit, soul, and body; unity of all men in the heart of truth.[36]

The name of the group subsequently was changed to the Society of Silent Unity, which later became simply Silent Unity, a "department of dedicated prayer" within the Unity School. In 1891, another periodical, *Unity,* was launched as the official organ of Silent Unity. The Fillmores denied that they were starting a new sect; they were only teaching a practical philosophy to supplement the teachings of the existing churches. Accordingly, the term "school" was chosen over "church" in 1914, when the Fillmores combined the various programs (e.g., Silent Unity, the publishing company, and a correspondence school) into the single corporation known as "The Unity School of Practical Christianity."[37]

Unity, for all its practical, down-to-earth emphasis, was far from simple. It developed a highly complex metaphysical system (including belief in reincarnation) that incorporated ideas from New Thought, Christian Science, Theosophy, the Christian Bible, Spiritualism, and Hinduism. The Fillmores advocated the repeated use of statements of denial and affirmation to assist in opening the mind to the "true self" and binding God's "wisdom, strength and holiness" to one's consciousness. For the Fillmores, only "those who have *meditated seriously* upon the source of existence and stirred up the inner substance and life make very substantial pictures in the universal ether or kingdom of the heavens." Serious meditation thus was not simply "the thought images of an intellectual thinker," but rather the activity "of one who has got access to the spiritual substance and life within."[38] Like other new faiths of the time, Unity promised not only physical health but also economic prosperity. "God will pay your debts," declared Charles Fillmore.

> Do not say money is scarce; the very statement will drive money away from you. Do not say that times are hard with you; the very words will tighten your purse strings until Omnipotence itself cannot slip a dime into it. Begin now to talk plenty, think plenty, and give thanks for plenty. . . . It actually works.
>
> Every home can be prosperous, and there should be no poverty-stricken homes, for they are caused only by in-harmony, fear, negative thinking and speaking.[39]

Unity grew into a vast publishing enterprise and a prayer ministry (Silent Unity). Both services claimed a large following beyond the official

[36] Freeman, 44, 61–62. Cf. Marcus Bach, *They Have Found a Faith* (Indianapolis, 1946), 223.

[37] Hugh D'Andrade, *Charles Fillmore: Herald of the New Age* (New York, 1974), 35–36, 67; Freeman, 56–57, 89, 105.

[38] Fillmore, *How to Let God Help You,* 44; Charles and Cora Fillmore, *Teach Us to Pray* (Unity Village, Mo., 1941), 70–71.

[39] Charles Fillmore, *Prosperity* (Kansas City, Mo., 1938), 103–4, 117.

Unity membership, including an astonishingly large number of persons from the conventional churches. During the movement's early growth, it was not uncommon for followers to meet in public places such as hotels to hear Unity teachers and to engage in study and prayer sessions. By 1925, however, Unity leaders had grown wary of non-Unity practices (e.g., occult seances, palm reading) creeping into the fringes of the movement. Though opposed to formal creeds and dogma, the church subsequently adopted a set of rules governing the teaching of Unity classes and the activities at Unity centers. As the activities at Unity centers acquired more definition and structure by the mid–twentieth century, they were referred to as churches.

Such were the disparate religious responses to the new intellectual climate. It was a difficult time for the churches, for their whole system of thought had been challenged at many points. But this was not the only problem with which the churches had to grapple. They had to come to terms at the same time with revolutionary changes in the economic and social order that were created by the rapid pace at which the country was becoming urbanized and industrialized. This challenge demanded changes in practice as well as in thought.

CHAPTER TWELVE

New Frontiers for the Churches

While the mind of America was being reshaped by the intellectual revolution of the years of midpassage from 1865 to 1918, the outward aspects of American life were undergoing swift and bewildering change as a result of rapid technological advance. "Steam and electricity have tremendously increased the pace of life," reported an observer in 1896.

> Everybody is in a hurry. . . . St. Martha is the patron saint of the women, and St. Vitus of the men. Nervous prostration is our characteristic disease. Leisure is a word for whose meaning we consult the dictionary. In the clatter of the train, in the click of the keys at the telegraph office, the spirit of the age finds speech.[1]

The click and the clatter were symbols of a surging industrial advance sped by a flood of inventions. In contrast to the fewer than 62,000 patents that had been issued prior to 1865, the number granted by the Patent Office in the following thirty-five years was in excess of 637,000. Large-scale steel production was made possible by the introduction of the Bessemer converter. The efficiency of the railroads was multiplied by automatic couplings and Westinghouse air brakes. Refrigerator cars made feasible the centralized slaughterhouses of the meatpackers. The discovery of oil, coupled with the use of tank cars and pipelines, gave further impetus to industrial development. The McCormick binder, the typewriter, the transatlantic cable, the telephone, the incandescent lamp, the electric motor, and the

---

[1] George Hodges, *Faith and Social Service* (New York, 1896), 6.

gasoline engine each fostered growing commercial enterprises. Before the end of the century, the linotype, the automobile, and the motion picture had made their appearance. Meanwhile, through an increasing utilization of machinery and the adoption of interchangeable parts, the factory system had been established in almost all areas of production. By 1894, the United States had become the leading manufacturing nation of the world, with its production of manufactured goods surpassing the combined output of its two closest rivals, Great Britain and Germany.

Many rubrics have been used to characterize the impact upon society of this massive industrial development. Some have viewed these years as "the gilded age"; others have called it "the tragic era." To some these were "50 years of progress"; to others they were "years of unrest and corruption." The most obvious label has been "the age of big business," for this was the era of the empire builders—the steel kings, the coal barons, the railroad magnates, the merchant princes, the Napoleons of finance, and the potentates of the stockyards, the oil wells, and the street railways. Another rubric has been "the rise of the city," for these were the years when cities were "springing up and growing great and splendid as it were in a night." A further facet of this adolescent period in the emergence of modern America has been suggested by Harold U. Faulkner's phrase "the quest for social justice." A key part of that social justice involved issues of gender, as women sought to undertake religious work in areas previously closed to them. And those who placed the period against a larger canvas have used the term "imperial America" to convey the expansionist spirit of an awakening industrial giant. All these aspects of this new industrial society—the problems and opportunities posed by the city, the economic order, and the outward thrust of imperialism—were to replace the West as urgent new frontiers for the churches.

The Roles of Women and Men

Churchgoing Women

In institutional life, and especially in daily and weekly worship and devotional activities, women participated to a greater degree than men. Early in the history of New England, Boston pastor Cotton Mather observed that "there are far more Godly Women in the World, then there are Godly Men; and our Church Communions give us a Little Demonstration of it." A seemingly endless string of eyewitness accounts reinforces the perception that women were more active in churches than men, and church records frequently confirm it.[2] In New England, the number of men who

---

[2] Cotton Mather, *Ornaments for the Daughters of Zion* (Cambridge, Mass., 1692), 44.

belonged to churches already had dipped below 50 percent by 1650. And by 1720, women thoroughly dominated—in terms of their numbers—those New England congregations.[3] The Protestant revivals of the eighteenth and nineteenth centuries (with the exception of the 1858 "Businessmen's Revival") also attracted many more women than men. By the end of the eighteenth century, nearly 80 percent of black converts to Methodism were women.[4] During the Second Great Awakening (1790–1835), women accounted for about two-thirds of persons joining the involved churches, and this figure by the end of the nineteenth century represented the membership in most large denominations. In some congregations the ratio was even more severe, whether it be in modest frontier revival churches or among the Episcopal elite of North Carolina, where some antebellum congregations recorded three or four times as many women as men.[5] By the early twentieth century, the Methodist Episcopal church as a whole counted 100 female members for every 67 males.[6] Immigrant Catholic churches—German, Irish, Italian, and Hispanic—frequently exhibited similar ratios, especially when it came to participation in devotional activities and everyday parish life.[7] And Jewish women—beginning with the Reform movement in the mid–nineteenth century—frequently outnumbered males in certain areas of institutional life.[8]

Is it true, as Philadelphia doctor and Revolutionary patriot Benjamin Rush proposed, that "the female breast is the natural soil of Christianity"? Is it as Ray Frank Litman, a Jewish woman who served as temporary rabbi for Jewish communities on the western frontier, wrote of women: "The weaker sex physically, it is the stronger spiritually, it having been said that

[3] Jon Butler, *Awash in a Sea of Faith: Christianizing the American People* (Cambridge, Mass., 1990), 170.

[4] Graham Russel Hodges, ed., *Black Itinerants of the Gospel: The Narratives of John Jea and George White* (Madison, Wisc., 1993), 4.

[5] Richard Rankin, *Ambivalent Churchmen and Evangelical Churchwomen: The Religion of the Episcopal Elite in North Carolina, 1800–1860* (Columbia, S.C., 1993), 53, 168, 169.

[6] Roger Finke and Rodney Stark, *The Churching of America, 1776–1990: Winners and Losers in Our Religious Economy* (New Brunswick, N.J., 1992), 11. See also the tables in Harry S. Stout and Catherine A. Brekus, "Declension, Gender, and the 'New Religious History,'" in *Belief and Behavior: Essays in the New Religious History*, eds. Philip R. Vandermeer and Robert P. Swierenga (New Brunswick, N.J., 1991), 27, 28, 30.

[7] Jay P. Dolan and Gilberto M. Hinojosa, eds., *Mexican Americans and the Catholic Church, 1900–1965* (Notre Dame, Ind., 1994), 62, 101, 124; Ann Taves, *The Household of Faith: Roman Catholic Devotions in the Mid–Nineteenth-Century* (Notre Dame, Ind., 1986), 17–19; Robert Anthony Orsi, *The Madonna of 115th Street: Faith and Community in Italian Harlem, 1880–1950* (New Haven, 1985).

[8] Ann Braude, "The Jewish Woman's Encounter with American Culture," in Rosemary Radford Reuther and Rosemary Skinner Keller, eds., *Women and Religion in America: Volume 1: The Nineteenth Century* (San Francisco, 1981), 155.

religion were impossible without woman"?[9] From the beginnings of the European settlement of North America, a chorus of observers down through the twentieth century have echoed this belief and have offered elaborations of it rich with symbolism and moral argument. One important part of the discussion of women's high visibility has focused on the manner in which women were identified as guardians of religion within the domestic sphere. The Protestant notion of women as pious, nurturing, moral exemplars, as defenders of the faith within the home, is rooted in Puritan thinking about the family. The idea is present in Catholicism with distinctive emphases. And even though Jewish men played a central role in domestic piety, the nineteenth-century Jewish periodical *Occident* declared, "It is ever so with women, and particularly so with the daughters of Israel, who are more deeply imbued with the true spirit of our religion than the 'sterner sex' and are . . . the *Guardians of the Faith*. . . ."

Historians' observation of the relationship between active piety in the Christian home and frequent church attendance was acknowledged by many Americans, including the author of a Methodist poem published in 1830:

> Women, excused from public care
> Designed for nobler service seem;
> God gives them time, in frequent prayer
> His handmaids to attend on Him:
> And more to piety inclined
> We always see the gentler kind.
>
> Women we own the foremost still,
> Where stated prayer is made to appear;
> They first the place of worship fill,
> They first the joyful tidings hear, . . .[10]

According to the poem, the essential link between women's spirituality and their domestic role is the fact of their dissociation from public life—or at least from the world of commerce and politics in which men operated. Untarnished by the worldly activities of business and government, women fashioned domestic life according to principles of love and care, sacrifice and devotion, and moral uprightness. In their wisdom and holiness, women guided their children in the cultivation of Judaeo-Christian virtue and the love of God, and in more than a few cases a woman succeeded in

---

[9] Quoted in Martha Tomhave Blauvelt, "Women and Revivalism," 3, and in Ann Braude, "The Jewish Woman's Encounter with American Culture," in Reuther and Keller, eds., *Women and Religion in America*, 184.

[10] Quoted in A. Gregory Schneider, *The Way of the Cross Leads Home: The Domestication of American Methodism* (Bloomington, Ind., 1993), 171–72.

reforming a wayward husband. Their piety bloomed in this hothouse of devotion and moral endeavor, and eventually overflowed into the churches, which, like extended families, provided a context for even more ambitious promotion of godly behavior and prayerful reliance upon the divine will. Typical is the opinion published in a Congregational journal just after the Civil War: "Men are engaged for the livelong day in the distractions and toils and worldliness of business. It is hard for them to leave these for the atmosphere of the prayer meeting. Woman is shielded from many of these withering and chilling influences," and, accordingly, more capable of engaging profitably in prayer meetings.[11]

This manner of framing women's religious life, which characterized the Protestant denominations and influenced Catholics and Jews, was adaptable to various settings. For some congregations, depending on class, race, and the particular denomination, a woman who was sheltered from the public world may indeed have developed religiously because her everyday life in the home amounted to a continuous immersion in culturally prescribed religious themes. For some women, in other contexts, different dynamics were involved, and additional theological ideas played determinative roles in their religious lives. Among some women, for example, the ideal of self-sacrifice was preeminent. The reason for this tendency is that the terms of the cultural myth of domesticity identified men as rulers over the household, and women, for all of their supposed spiritual superiority and insight, as submissive. Focusing on the image of Christ as servant, women sought to imitate that role in relation to their husbands and, to a certain extent, with their children. This cultural expectation for women to serve permeated Protestantism and was well represented in nineteenth-century Catholicism. The Catholic writer Bernard O'Reilly summarized it in *True Womanhood:* "Woman's entire existence, in order to be a source of happiness to others as well as to herself, must be one of self-sacrifice."[12]

Single women without children were expected to display the virtue and piety associated with married women, but without a brood at home to train in the discipline of Christian responsibility, they were not positioned for maximum participation in the domestic cult. On the other hand, in the cases of adolescent girls or very young women, Christian society sometimes exacted a display of moral purity and devotion exceeding that even of older women.[13] Among Catholics, women who remained single and then became nuns typically ran local parish schools. The "mother superior" and the other sisters stood before the schoolchildren as examples of piety and as teachers of virtue in a manner not unlike mothers in their households. The rapid growth of religious orders for women—between 1850 and 1900,

---

[11] Quoted in Barbara Brown Zikmund, "The Struggle for the Right to Preach," in Reuther and Keller, eds., vol. 2, 202.

[12] Karen Kennelly, ed., *American Catholic Women: A Historical Exploration* (New York, 1989), 4.

[13] Schneider, 174.

women in religious orders grew from 12.1 to 41.2 per 10,000 Catholics—is directly related to the ideal of "true womanhood" articulated by nineteenth-century Catholic writers, who pictured nuns as teachers of the women who would eventually marry and assume their own roles as teachers within the home.[14]

For other women—women who were comfortable with some aspects of domesticity but who actively resisted a submissive role—there was the option of Christianity as a religion of justice and equality. For such women, the church was a place to explore the meanings of the Pauline affirmation that in Jesus there was "neither Jew nor Gentile, male nor female, slave nor free." Over time, this message became the foundation for a more ambitious agenda among women, namely, the movement of women into the ranks of preachers and eventually into the clergy. "True womanhood" for some women accordingly came to mean a woman's calling to involve herself in teaching and leading within the formal framework of a denomination.

The Segregated Clergy

In the nineteenth century, women sought more active roles as preachers and ordained clergy. Women's efforts to enter into these ranks were resisted by churches, and the male leadership of the denominations generated a variety of arguments against female preaching and ordination. In some cases, church officials, in resisting widening women's roles in institutional life, drew upon the same set of ideas that had sustained the belief in the elevated spirituality of women. Church leaders argued that women flourished spiritually because they were protected from the troubles and temptations of the public world, that they were safe from worldly distractions while inside the refuge of the home. To give them broader responsibilities in the public world—as licensed preachers or ordained clergy— would draw them out of their domestic sanctuary and endanger their religious sensibilities.

Prior to the nineteenth century, there was little modification in the public roles of women. Among Protestants in the English colonies, women began challenging the religious order shortly after the migration to America, and they continued challenging it in uneven fashion through the eighteenth century. Churches met those challenges by demonstrating that women's opportunities for public ministry of any sort were slim or none. Frequently that demonstration was forceful. Anne Hutchinson, who in 1635 made public her theological differences with the ecclesiastical order in Massachusetts Bay, was banished from the colony. Other women were expelled from the community of the holy for various offenses, and in some cases were, like Hutchinson, suspected of witchcraft.

---

[14] Finke and Stark, 135; Kennelly, 17–18.

Among Catholics in New France and New Spain, opportunities for women were broader. Orders of nuns early on took active roles in the colonial drama. In Mexico, nuns (as well as women who joined the lay branches of the orders) organized and administrated the education of European and Indian girls on a large scale. In New France, nuns and lay women took on a more expansive role, serving not only as educators but also as missionaries, and as notable participants in the construction of civil and religious institutions. Such was the case of the Ursuline nun Marie of the Incarnation, who came to Quebec in 1639, founded a convent there, involved herself extensively in missionary work, and eventually wrote dictionaries in the Iroquois, Huron, and Algonquin languages. Most nuns resided in convents, undertook some measure of public activity, and answered to their female superiors. Outside of the accusations of Protestant nativists, few persons disputed the nuns' usefulness as either project organizers or as examples of religious devotion.[15]

The institutional role of Protestant women began to change about the time of the American Revolution. Sarah Osborn, a Newport widow, who led a local revival in 1766–1767, preferred the word "school" to "meeting" when describing the gathering of men and women who listened to her read, talk, and sing Psalms. Her role, nevertheless, was unmistakably public and authoritative.[16] Osborn broke new ground, but change came slowly, and decades would pass before women became vocal, even as participants in general revivals. By the end of the Second Great Awakening, signs of change were stronger, as manifestations of the religious authority of women increased noticeably. An important landmark was the testimony of women during the revivals preached by Charles Finney in the 1820s. Revivals frequently relied upon women's prayer groups as a base for involvement of the larger community. Departing from standard procedure, Finney incorporated the custom of women's speaking out loud at their own prayer meetings into gatherings at which both sexes were present. Such a practice was condemned by other ministers, such as the Presbyterian Ashbel Green, who, appealing to the authority of St. Paul, warned in 1825 that "women, are in no case, to be publick preachers and teachers, in assemblies promiscuously composed of the two sexes."[17] The practice nevertheless became accepted in many denominations by the end of the century and was important groundwork for the licensing and ordination of women in Protestant denominations.

---

[15] Asunción Lavrin, "Women and religion in Spanish America" and Christine Allen, "Women in colonial French America" in Rosemary Radford Ruether and Rosemary Skinner Keller, eds., *Women and religion in America: Volume 2: The colonial and revolutionary period* (San Francisco: 1983).

[16] Quoted in Rosemary Skinner Keller, "Protestant Laywomen in Institutional Churches," in *ibid.*, 86.

[17] Ashbel Green, quoted in "Women and Revivalism," in Ruether and Keller, eds., vol. 2, 35.

Women who sought official denominational credentials for preaching were driven by their certainty that they had been called by God to preach. Few were able to obtain the support of their churches, and those who were not licensed faced difficulties. A Maryland woman, who was the subject of a biography entitled *Elizabeth, A Colored Minister of the Gospel Born in Slavery,* was threatened with arrest when she began to preach in Virginia in the 1790s. Authorities declined to prosecute Elizabeth (b.1766) when she responded to their inquiries about the time and place of her ordination by asserting, "Not by the commission of men's hands; if the Lord has ordained me, I need nothing better."[18] The first female preacher of the Bethel African Methodist Episcopal Church in Philadelphia, Jarena Lee (b.1783), was, like Elizabeth, never ordained. But like Elizabeth, she was certain of her calling, and related it in no uncertain terms:

> Between four and five years after my sanctification, on a certain time, an impressive silence fell upon me, and I stood as if someone was about to speak to me, yet I had no such thought in my heart. But to my utter surprise there seemed to sound a voice which I thought I distinctly heard, and most certainly understand, which said to me, "Go preach the Gospel!" I immediately replied aloud, "No one will believe me." Again I listened and again the same voice seemed to say "Preach the Gospel; I will put words in your mouth, and will turn your enemies to become your friends."[19]

The best-known unlicensed female preacher in the nineteenth century was Phoebe Palmer (b.1807), who participated in over three hundred revival meetings and campaigns in the United States, Canada, and Britain. Author of ten books, including the popular *The Way of Holiness* (1845), Palmer preached a holiness theology that stressed Pentecostal spirit baptism. Her preaching, like that of the Baptist itinerant Nancy Towle and circuit preachers Harriet Livermore and Clarissa Richmond, was fundamental to the reemergence of lay ministries in the nineteenth century and paved the way for the activities of later-nineteenth-century preachers such as Dwight L. Moody.

The first fully ordained woman in a major American denomination was Antoinette Brown, who became a minister in the Congregational church in 1853. In the Methodist Episcopal Church, Margaret Newton Van Cott was licensed to preach in 1869. Anna Howard Shaw was ordained in the United Methodist church in 1880 but later encountered resistance to her work from the denomination. Few other women were given credentials by their denominations, however, and outspoken opposition to female ordination was common throughout the nineteenth century. The striking exception to the pattern was within the Society of Friends, which did not

---

[18] Quoted in C. Eric Lincoln and Lawrence M. Mamiya, *The Black Church in the African American Experience* (Durham, N.C., 1990), 279.

[19] Jarena Lee, *Religious Experience and Journal of Mrs. Jarena Lee* (Philadelphia, 1849), 14.

have an ordained ministry but promoted female leadership and preaching. Many of the nineteenth century's most effective women's rights leaders, including Susan B. Anthony, Abby Kelly, Lucretia Mott, Alice Paul, and the Grimké sisters, were Quakers.

Social Reform

Some women—such as Anna Shaw and Phoebe Palmer—became active social reformers in addition to answering their calls to preach. Social reform and religion have been closely linked throughout American history, and were especially so in the nineteenth and early twentieth centuries. Shaw eventually translated her Methodist ministry into full-time service as president of the National American Women's Suffrage Association. Palmer, through her influence in the Ladies Home Missionary Society of the Methodist Episcopal Church, pioneered Protestant social reform in New York slums and was acknowledged by Catherine Booth of the Salvation Army and Frances Willard of the Woman's Christian Temperance Union as the inspiration for their own ambitious agendas of reform.

The conceptual basis for women's involvement in social reform developed its characteristic features in the early nineteenth century. Charles Finney, who as we have seen supported an enlarged role for women in religious gatherings, was outspoken in his characterization of reform as a moral duty. Moreover, he rejected the gradualist approach of antislavery protest in favor of immediate political action. These ideas of Finney, together with an assortment of arguments and theories generated by women writers and reformers, encouraged a reconceiving of the nature of both men's and women's involvement in social causes. Reform increasingly came to be understood in terms of an urgent call to activism grounded in moral obligation. Women forcefully articulated that understanding with regard to their own participation, as in the case of Sarah Grimké, who stated, "Whatsoever it is morally right for a man to do, it is morally right for a woman to do; . . . confusion must exist in the moral world until woman takes her stand on the same platform with men, and feels that she is clothed by her Maker with the *same rights,* and, of course, that upon her devolve the *same duties.*"[20] Lucretia Mott asked an audience in Philadelphia in 1849, "Why should not woman seek to be a reformer?" Responding to criticism of the women's rights campaign and women's "exclusion from the pulpit or minstry," she inverted nineteenth-century rhetoric about "woman's sphere" to argue that the "true woman" was she who was involved in "the active business of life."[21]

---

[20] Nancy A. Hardesty, *Your Daughters Shall Prophesy: Revivalism and Feminism in the Age of Finney* (Brooklyn, 1991), 114–15.

[21] Quoted in Keller and Reuther, eds., 262–63.

Prior to 1840, almost all women's associations were church-related. Gradually, in urban settings,[22] those associations developed from their churchly base of operations into national organizations focused upon education, abolition, temperance, and other issues. By the 1870s, individual Protestant denominations supported reform societies of women, and by the end of the century, over 140 deaconess homes were training women for missionary activities abroad and among immigrants at home. Among Catholics, nuns carried forward almost all social causes—education, nursing, orphanages, "houses of protection" for women recently arrived in cities, and other such work—during the nineteenth century. In the last quarter of the century, Catholic laywomen became active in numerous organizations and causes. Mary Harris "Mother" Jones (d.1930) and Leonora Barry (d.1930) helped to organize the 2 million women in factories and domestic service in the late nineteenth century. Kate Kennedy (d.1890) and Margaret Haley (d.1939) worked to reform education and the teaching profession. Ellen Boyle Sherman (wife of Union General William T. Sherman) and Mary Haughery, the "Bread Woman of New Orleans," organized care of the indigent urban poor. Jewish women became the religious equals of male laity in the Reform movement of Judaism, and although this trend did not immediately lead to the development of Jewish women's reform societies, it provided groundwork for Jewish women's involvement in labor activism, educational reform, and Zionism by the end of the nineteenth century.

Three areas in which women were most effective as reformers were education, the antislavery movement, and the temperance movement. Catholic nuns were increasingly joined by laywomen of various religious backgrounds in establishing educational institutions for women in the nineteenth century. When a group of Jewish women started a coeducational Reform school in Charleston in the 1840s and when Mary Lyon founded Mount Holyoke Female Seminary in 1837, these undertakings were, in the words of Lyon, still an "experiment."[23] By the end of the century, institutions such as these formed a well-established part of the religious landscape.

The antislavery movement developed more rapidly, as it moved out of the churches and into a broad arena of public discourse in the early nineteenth century. At the forefront of this transition were Sarah and Angelina Grimké, who left the Episcopal Church in South Carolina to become Quakers and members of the abolitionist community in Philadelphia in

---

[22] Women in rural environments had little time for reform or social welfare societies. See, for example, Carol K. Coburn, _Life at Four Corners: Religion, Gender, and Education in a German-Lutheran Community, 1868–1945_ (Lawrence, Kans., 1992), 31–59, 158.

[23] Mary Lyon, _The Power of Christian Benevolence Illustrated in the Life and Letters of Mary Lyon_ (New York, 1858), in Keller and Reuther, eds., 268.

the 1820s. They actively campaigned from lecterns throughout New England during the 1830s and exercised a broad influence over the movement for decades afterwards through their writings. One of these writings, Angelina Grimké's *An Appeal to the Women of the Nominally Free States* (1838), marked the direction of a large part of women's reform activity by blending an appeal to religious duty with support for women's rights and a hatred of slavery: "The denial of our duty to act is a bold denial of our right to act; and if we have no right to act, then may we well be termed 'the white slaves of the North.' "[24]

Temperance, which began as an assortment of crusades to battle the "rum curse," eventually, like abolitionism, became centralized in a few large organizations. Chief among these was the Woman's Christian Temperance Union (WCTU) which, during the tenure of the Methodist reformer Frances Willard (d.1898), exercised great influence over national discussion of this issue. Willard, who wished to be ordained but was refused by her denomination, took leave of her work with the WCTU in order to lead revival meetings for women under Dwight L. Moody in Boston in 1877. Two years later she was made corresponding secretary of the WCTU, a post that she held for almost twenty years. Initially concerned with the damaging effects of alcohol on home life, she developed a view of temperance in relation to labor and women's suffrage and redirected a familiar metaphor in expressing her mission to reform the social order: "IT IS TO MAKE THE WHOLE WORLD HOMELIKE. . . . But 'home's not merely four square walls.' "[25]

Women's reform activities eventually also came to include the criticism of religious institutions themselves. In some cases, such criticism took shape as a defense of women's rights to engage in public life. Sarah Grimké, who was condemned by the Massachusetts Congregational ministry for her public speaking, accordingly responded, "I shall depend solely on the Bible to designate the sphere of woman. . . ." and in so doing avoid "the false translation of many passages of Holy Writ."[26] Other women tackled the matter of the historical religious impediments to equal rights in a more ambitious manner and with direct reference to the ways in which the Bible had been used to support their subjection. Elizabeth Cady Stanton (d.1902), who had been converted during one of Finney's revivals, eventually became a Unitarian and, finally, a skeptic. But before she disavowed Christianity, she guided the production of *The Woman's Bible* (1895, 1898), an attempt to purge the Christian Scriptures of antifemale interpretations. An immediate best-seller, *The Woman's Bible* threatened some of the tradi-

---

[24] Angelina Grimké, *An Appeal to the Women of the Nominally Free States* (Boston, 1838), 13.

[25] Frances E. Willard, *How to Win: A Book for Girls* (New York, 1886), 56. See also Barbara Leslie Epstein, *The Politics of Domesticity: Women, Evangelism, and Temperance in Nineteenth-Century America* (Middletown, Conn., 1981), 115–46.

[26] Quoted in Keller and Reuther, eds., 224.

tional bases for women's social work, and important women's organizations repudiated it, fearing that association with it would undermine their efforts to establish women's rights.

Religious Innovation

Women became more visible and more influential as religious innovators in the nineteenth century. Several instances stand out as examples of the manner in which women shaped religious sensibilities and built associations of like-minded persons into formalized religious groups. Shakerism, which acquired its distinctive shape at the end of the eighteenth century, broke important ground for later utopian and revivalistic movements, as well as for revision of gender roles within denominations. Under Mother Anne Lee and during the tenures of Joseph Meacham (1787–1796) and Lucy Wright (1796–1821), Shakers developed a notion of deity that stressed duality of gender. God as Father-Mother was eventually conceived as a pair identified as Holy Mother Wisdom and the Eternal Father. The leading attribute of the former was loving tenderness, and the latter was cast as a stern, potentially wrathful personality. Both figures were capable of love, justice, and power, however.[27] Authority within the organization was structured along parallel gender lines, with female leaders participating equally with male leaders in the government of the Shakers. The movement reached its apex in membership in the decades before the Civil War and diminished steadily afterwards. However, it remained important as an influence upon the religions of spiritualism and upon Christian Science, which emerged in the latter part of the nineteenth century.

Spiritualism, which excited broad religious interest after the Civil War, was especially attractive to women, and it allowed them comparatively large opportunity for participation and religious leadership. Spiritualism was not, however, organized in such a way as to situate it as a competitor to established denominations. Christian Science, on the other hand, was such a religion. The Church of Christ, Scientist, founded by Mary Baker Eddy in 1879, was grounded in Eddy's belief that human life in "Spirit" was "the sole reality of existence." To this she juxtaposed life in the "flesh" and belief in matter. For Eddy, God was not distinguished by any attributes associated with the flesh, including gender. God was, rather, unitary. Accordingly, Eddy spoke of God as both male and female, and she rewrote the Lord's Prayer as "Our Father-Mother God." Within the church, women served in the key role as "practitioners," who prayed with the sick and practiced healing by "demonstrating" the truth of spiritual life and the error of belief in matter, sometimes by reading from Eddy's *Science and Health*. This religion of "mind-cure" was but one of numerous endeavors emphasizing

---

[27] Stephen J. Stein, *The Shaker Experience in America: A History of the United Society of Believers* (New Haven, 1992), 195.

the spiritual nature of reality that emerged in the nineteenth century. Some were led by women, and a few—such as Katherine Tingley's Theosophical experiment at Point Loma, California—flourished for a time as alternative societies.

Women and men continued to generate language identifying God as androgynous or as female. Such theological fashioning led in the late nineteenth and early twentieth centuries to more ambitious projects. Women such as Matilda Joslyn Gage (who worked with Stanton on *The Woman's Bible*), Catherine Hartley, and Charlotte Perkins Gilman began constructing explicit critiques of Christian patriarchy and offering in its place a new religious vision informed by the experiences of women. Gage's *Woman, Church, and State* (1893), as one bookend on a century of dramatic change for women, marked an important step away from American thinking at the beginning of the nineteenth century, when ideals of female domesticity and self-sacrifice had held sway:

> The whole theory regarding woman, under Christianity, has been based upon the conception that she had no right to live for herself alone. Her duty to others has continuously been placed before her and her training has ever been that of self-sacrifice. Taught from the pulpit and legislative halls that she was created for another, that her position must always be secondary to her children, her right to life, has been admitted only in so far as its reacting effect upon another could be predicated. That she was first created for herself, as an independent being to whom all the opportunities of the world should be open because of herself, has not entered the thought of the church; . . .[28]

Masculinizing Religion

Women's numerical dominance in the churches did not mean that men did not meet to share a ritual life or moral vision. The nineteenth century incubated a host of religious and parareligious organizations for men. Men attended church services, served as church officials, were active in missionary societies, denominational social-reform organizations, broad-based labor activism, and similar enterprises carried out under the umbrellas of the Protestant, Catholic, and Jewish faiths. Men also figured prominently in the many urban religious movements that were geared to improving the everyday lives of poor, immigrant, and minority Americans. Overflowing into the twentieth century, this enterprise sometimes included organizations of several million members. Such was the case of the Peace Mission, led by the African American Father Divine, who preached morality, racial equality, and service to the needy in the decades after World War I.

---

[28] Reuther and Keller, eds., vol. 3, 15.

The extent of men's involvement in explicitly religious organizations was superseded by their membership in parareligious and fraternal organizations in the latter part of the nineteenth century. The rolls of such organizations swelled to 5.5 million adult men by the end of the century, so that one of every four adult males belonged to societies such as the Odd Fellows (810,000), the Freemasons (750,000), the Knights of Pythias (475,000), the Red Men (165,000), and other lodges.[29] Such figures disclose that among the white, urban, middle-class population, "the women were in the churches and the men were in the lodges."[30] Individual fraternal organizations often targeted specific social problems for remedy and worked alone or in concert with each other and church organizations to foster middle-class ideals of patriotism, morality, and benevolence. Organizations with an affluent membership were less active in reform but no less ambitious in their social involvements. Equally important, fraternal organizations provided a rich world of ideas about the cosmic order, as well as complex ritual environments for men. One organization, Freemasonry, with its pageantry, mystical symbols, and support for emotional bonding between men, functioned in general as an alternative religion for the 88 percent of its members who did not claim membership in a Protestant church.[31]

Some organizations, such as the Young Men's Christian Association, which was transplanted from London to Boston in 1851, enrolled those not yet ready for participation in lodge life. The Y.M.C.A. was especially successful in attracting young men who had left rural homes to pursue careers in the expanding cities. These clerks, delivery boys, dockworkers, apprentice craftsmen, and office trainees took their meals, read and conversed, and sometimes slept at the local Y.M.C.A. They were also indoctrinated with a view of sports that correlated moral vigor with athletic prowess. This understanding of Christian manliness eventually blended with the churches' calls for moral reform, the ideals of the emergent business culture, and Anglo-Saxon racism to yield "muscular Christianity." Promoted by nationally prominent religious leaders, such as the revivalist Billy Sunday, and reinforced by a literary outpouring that featured the writings of New Englanders Oliver Wendell Holmes and Thomas Wentworth Higginson, muscular Christianity became influential across the broad front of middle-class religiosity. It breathed new life into earlier notions of female domesticity and emotionality, while advancing an interpretation of Christianity as essentially a moral warfare for which masculine qualities of competitiveness, hardened realism, heroic action, and unrelenting purpose were required. It flourished well into the twentieth century in league with

---

[29] See Mark C. Carnes, *Secret Ritual and Manhood in Victorian America* (New Haven, 1989).

[30] David G. Hackett, "Gender and Religion in American Culture, 1870–1930," *Religion and American Culture,* 5 (Indianapolis 1995), 132.

[31] *Ibid.,* 132.

fraternal organizations that professed ideals of leadership, public involvement, loyalty, and moral strength. World War I provided a severe cultural shock to Americans, who came to view the war not only as a tragic loss of soldiers' lives but also as an exposé of American naiveté about instituting homegrown Christian morality worldwide. Muscular Christianity as a popular movement suffered as a result, but the ideals upon which it was based survived in sufficient strength to bolster various movements throughout the twentieth century.

The Challenge of the Cities

Urbanization spawned a wide variety of human needs, for in its wake came slums, poverty, vice, and political corruption. Each of these needs was to claim the attention of the churches, but the most pressing problem was the basic task of evangelism. Even before the Civil War, extensive sections of rural America had begun to experience a steady and persistent decline in population as people moved from farms and back-country villages to growing commercial centers and newly established mill towns. After the war the process was vastly accelerated. Previously tilled acres reverted to woodland, and whole villages disappeared, leaving only a few foundation stones as monuments to the past. The cities, in contrast, were lusty infants. During the three decades from 1860 to 1890, the population of Detroit and Kansas City grew fourfold, Memphis and San Francisco fivefold, Cleveland sixfold, Chicago tenfold, Los Angeles twentyfold, and Minneapolis and Omaha fiftyfold and more. Even such previously major centers as New York, Philadelphia, and Baltimore more than doubled in population. "There is a city of thirty-five thousand added to Chicago, and one of fifty thousand added to New York, every year," reported Josiah Strong in 1887. With the overwhelming proportion of the churches located in rural areas and with many of them left stranded to dwindle and die as people departed, it became more obvious than ever that the future influence of the churches in the life of the nation was to be conditioned decisively by their success or lack of success in evangelizing the cities.

At the outset, most of the urban inhabitants came from the farms and villages of the hinterland where many of them had been regular in church attendance. They may not have been conspicuous for piety, and they may not even have been church members, but they had been accustomed to going to church. When they pulled up their roots and moved to the city, this pattern of habit and custom was broken, the emotional ties to a particular church were severed, and the pressure exerted by the expectation of friends and neighbors was removed. In their new environment, the tendency was for these former churchgoers to drift into "indifference." Later the problem of reevangelization was complicated by the sweeping tide of population arriving from abroad.

In larger industrial communities, whether in America, Britain, or France (and presumably in the developing urban concentrations of Belgium, Germany, and nothern Italy), the working classes tended to be impervious to the message and ministry of the churches.[32] It was not that the churches had "lost" these people; they never had most of them. If people generally attended church from habit, most of the laboring group who were born in the city never had the habit. It was to this habit of nonattendance that newer additions to the urban labor force conformed.

Among other portions of the urban population, churchgoing was a normal, mannerly, and even a fashionable activity. Signs of the popularity of the churches abounded. The churches were well attended. Costly and imposing edifices were being built to match the increasing prosperity of their clientele, and congregations vied with one another to possess the tallest steeple as a symbol of wealth and prestige. Pipe organs were installed, paid soloists were employed, and the preachers were polished orators who ranked in status with the most substantial citizens. It was a time during which ministers enjoyed a status matched only by New England's earliest pastors, and it was a "golden age of preaching." The princes of the pulpit—men such as Henry Ward Beecher and T. DeWitt Talmage in Brooklyn, Phillips Brooks and George A. Gordon in Boston, David M. Swing and Frank W. Gunsaulus in Chicago, Russell Conwell in Philadelphia, and Washington Gladden in Columbus—were figures of national prominence, but every city boasted eloquent preachers who could hold their congregations spellbound and who were regarded with deference and respect. Their sermons often were published and were circulated widely among Protestants comfortable in their urban existence. Furthermore, the most influential leaders of business and society—Jay Gould, J. Pierpont Morgan, John D. Rockefeller, Samuel Colgate, Jay Cooke, Cyrus McCormick, Marshall Field, James J. Hill, William H. Vanderbilt, P. D. Armour, G. A. Sift, A. J. Drexel, John Wanamaker, and many others—were prominent churchmen, active in religious enterprises, and frequently Sunday-school teachers.

To many of the immigrants from abroad, the Roman Catholic Church was the one familiar landmark in a strange and alien land, and its role in easing the transition to a new life in America helped it to retain the loyalty of many of the urban workers. With this single major exception, the great evangelistic successes of the city churches were won among the white-collar workers who had come from the rural areas—not to work in a mill, but to "clerk" in a store or an office—and who aspired to win, if not a fortune, at least a comfortable competence in the city. These young men, with their

---

[32] K. S. Inglis, *Churches and the Working Classes in Victorian England* (Toronto, 1963), 10–13, 327. For France, see H. Desroche, *Archives de Sociologie des Religions,* VI (Paris, 1958), 197–98; cited by Inglis, *Churches and the Working Classes,* 327. The Roman Catholic Church in America provided the major exception, but the strength it developed among working people was closely related to the insecurities of their immigrant status.

wives and their children, constituted the greater portion of those who were recruited for the churches by the revival campaigns, the Sunday school, and the Y.M.C.A. Beyond this potentially middle-class group was the hard core of nonchurchgoers—the urban masses, they were sometimes called, the poor, the destitute, the day laborers—who were to constitute a continuing challenge to the churches.

New Techniques for City Churches

The United States Christian Commission (an agency that ministered to soldiers during the Civil War) discovered after the war that American churches did little in any systematic fashion for those "who neglect the house of God." The city mission societies and the Y.M.C.A., to be sure, sponsored street preaching and tract distribution, and occasionally there were citywide revival campaigns. Although these activities were to be encouraged, the Commission believed that the great need was to recover "the simplicity and entire consecration of the early Christians," when "every disciple was a missionary and every church a missionary society," so that the church itself would reach out to people where they live. The obvious means of doing this undertaking was by regular house-to-house visitation of working-class neighborhoods. Many of the poverty-stricken, it was contended, had been alienated "because in their affliction they were not visited," and the only remedy was "personal, living, love-convincing" contact between the churchgoer and the nonchurchgoer. This, of course, demanded lay effort. Pastors of churches in densely populated communities were urged to "seek out and employ all such talent in their congregations as they shall believe to possess qualifications for this important and pressing work."[33] The increased designation of women as deaconesses in Protestant churches for a time also became a part of this enterprise.

A second problem highlighted by the Commission and underscored in the actual process of house-to-house visitation was the fact that often no churches were located in the neediest neighborhoods. The city mission societies were encouraged to established mission chapels in these areas. Most of these were conventional in character. Much more dramatic were the "rescue missions" designed to reach and reclaim the dregs of society—vagrants, alcoholics, former convicts, jobless men, and prostitutes. The Water Street Mission in New York was the most famous and the Pacific Garden Mission in Chicago the most successful of these rescue operations, but by the 1880s, every city boasted one or more missions of this type. The real pioneer of the movement was Jerry MacAuley, who founded the Water Street Mission in 1872, and his own early career was typical of those to

[33] *Ibid.,* 12–13, 15, 33.

whom he sought to minister. He arrived in New York from Ireland at the age of thirteen. Living in the streets, he became a petty thief and then graduated to gambling, organized burglary, and drunkenness. At the age of nineteen, he was sentenced to a fifteen-year term in prison, and while confined he was converted by an ex-prizefighter. Back on the streets after being pardoned in 1864, he resumed his criminal career until he was finally redeemed by agents of the Howard Mission. He then established his own mission in his former neighborhood, ministering primarily to the men who congregated there.

Among both conventional and rescue missions, there was a growing conviction that attention must be given to immediate material necessities before spiritual needs could be met. The managers of the North End Mission in Boston put it bluntly: "Till the cravings of hunger are satisfied, we cannot develop the moral nature," adding that they believed this to be "the biblical way of reaching the heart."[34] As a result of this conviction, rescue missions of all types launched a wide variety of enterprises, which included model tenements for the poor, homes for working mothers, and hospitals for the care of sick children.

James Yeatman's *Circular of Inquiry* (1865), an analysis of urban religious needs, had emphasized the importance of "trained" leadership for the specialized tasks of city work, and a number of institutions were established to meet this need.[35] A further step in this direction was taken when followers of MacAuley organized the Convention of Christian Workers in 1886. John C. Collins, a Yale graduate and manager of the Union Gospel Mission in New Haven, was the guiding spirit. By means of annual gatherings, a type of "in-service" training was provided through the sharing of experience with new methods and techniques. Within little more than a decade, it had gained more than 2,500 members; and Graham Taylor, professor of Christian sociology at Chicago Theological Seminary, declared that the annual Convention of Christian Workers was "a great exhibit of the work and working forces of modern Christianity" and "as nearly ecumenical a gathering of the church in America as is held on this continent." The *Christian Union,* Henry Ward Beecher's personal journal, was equally enthusiastic, asserting that the stenographic reports of the conventions furnished "the best literature on practical Christian work that can be secured."[36]

---

[34] *Ibid.,* 36.

[35] Among these schools were Stephen H. Tyng's Home of the Evangelists (1870) in New York, T. DeWitt Talmage's Tabernacle Lay College (1872) in Brooklyn, and Dwight L. Moody's Moody Bible Institute (1886) in Chicago. The latter institution was designed "to raise up men and women who will be willing to lay their lives alongside the laboring class and the poor and bring the gospel to bear on their lives." They were to do work that ministers could not do—"get in among the people and identify themselves with the people." W. G. McLoughlin, *Modern Revivalism,* (New York, 1959), 272–73.

[36] Aaron I. Abell, *Urban Impact on American Protestantism,* (Cambridge, Mass., 1943), 97–98.

Mullen Alley. Typical of the tenement crisis, Mullen Alley was described
by the New York *Morning Journal* (February 12, 1888) as "seven feet
wide at the entrance, but narrows as you proceed, until at the other
end there is less than two feet of a space between the walls . . . twenty-
five or thirty families most of them having many children, live in each
of the two houses between which it lies." *(Mullen's Alley, circa 1898. Mu-
seum of the City of New York/The Jacob A. Riis Collection.)*

Meanwhile, a new instrument of urban evangelization made its appearance. This was the Salvation Army.[37] It had been founded in London in 1878 by William Booth, an ex-Methodist preacher. Booth had come to the conclusion that "we can't get at the masses in the chapels," and consequently he was determined to move out into the streets. Organized on the basis of strict military discipline, the Army was geared for a many-sided attack on the problems of the city. The program was spelled out in Booth's famous volume, *Darkest England and the Way Out* (1890). The familiar brass band and tambourines that were used to gather a crowd for street preaching was only an incidental feature of a broad range of activities. Booth aimed to supply the poverty-stricken people of England with at least the three things any dray horse enjoyed—"shelter for the night, food for its stomach, work allotted to it by which it can earn its own corn." In addition to the usual provision made by rescue missions for meals, lodging, and an employment service, the Army moved out into the community with its Slum Brigades, Sewing Battalions, and visiting nurses. Legal aid bureaus were opened, day nurseries for children set up, and rescue homes for prostitutes established. And to give men and women the benefit of a new and wholesome environment, farm colonies were founded. Although the Salvation Army was ultimately to take on the characteristics of a church, its initial intention was to serve only as a recruiting agent of the churches among the most neglected elements of the population.

The Salvation Army was introduced into America in 1880, but its major expansion took place after 1886 when Booth's son, Ballington Booth, was sent over to take charge. A schism occurred in 1896 when Ballington Booth refused to obey his father's order that he return to England. Instead he and his wife founded the Volunteers of America, which patterned its activities after the parent organization but was organized on a more democratic basis.

The Institutional Church

The "institutional church," a strange name, was proposed as a means of enabling churches to survive in central-city areas instead of moving. The problem was to entice new arrivals in changing neighborhoods into existing churches. The solution put forward was for churches to provide the newcomers with a variety of "services" or "added attractions." Edward Judson was the preeminent theoretician of an institutional ministry. He defined an institutional church as "an organized body of Christian believers, who, finding themselves in a hard and uncongenial social environment, supplement the ordinary methods of the gospel—such as preaching, prayer meetings, Sunday school, and pastoral visitation—by a *system of organized kindness,* a

---

[37] The English background is summarized by Inglis, 175–214. For its American career, see H. A. Wisbey, *Soldiers Without Swords: A History of the Salvation Army in the United States* (New York, 1955).

congeries of institutions, which, by touching people on physical, social, and intellectual sides, will conciliate them and draw them within reach of the gospel."[38] With the slogan "open church doors every day and all the day," institutional churches became hives of activity with gymnasiums, athletic programs, reading rooms, day nurseries, sewing classes, lecture series, choral societies, drama clubs, concerts, and entertainments.

The honor of establishing the first institutional church probably belongs to Thomas K. Beecher, one of the numerous Beecher progeny, who was pastor of the Park Congregational Church in Elmira, New York, from 1854 to 1900. In 1872, he induced his congregation to build a block-long structure equipped for a full range of services. Mark Twain, a summer resident, described the building with its gymnasium, lecture rooms, library, and free public baths in his *Curious Dreams and Other Sketches* (1872) and commented that "we have at least one sensible but very curious church in America." Within two decades there were many of these "sensible" churches, including Reuben A. Torrey's Open Door Congregational Church in Minneapolis. By 1900, one observer listed 173 churches with a full-blown institutional program and acknowledged that there were probably others that had escaped his attention. In addition, scores of churches were appropriating parts of the institutional program, including Roman Catholic programs such as the St. Louis Verein.[39]

When the Open and Institutional Church League was formed in 1894 to promote "educational, reformatory, and philanthropic" activities by the churches as an evangelistic device, its leaders self-confidently proclaimed that the question "how to reach the masses" had been "practically solved." It was true that institutional churches were experiencing phenomenal growth. By 1900, the Baptist Temple in Philadelphia, in process of fathering what was to become Temple University, had become the largest congregation in America. St. George's Episcopal Church in New York, which had been ready to close its doors when it had only six families left, now numbered 5,000 members. Congregationalists reported that their institutional churches had six times as many additions as the average church. But there were problems. For one thing, an institutional church was an incredibly costly enterprise. Not many churches could command the necessary financial support. St. George's was fortunate in having J. Pierpont Morgan as a member of its initial remnant. St. Bartholomew's, whose parish house was erected by Cornelius Vanderbilt and his mother, had an annual budget of over $1 million.[40]

---

[38] "The Church in Its Social Aspect," *Annals of the American Academy of Political and Social Science*, 30 (November 1908), 436. For an impressionistic appraisal of the institutional church, see G. G. Atkins, *Religion in Our Times* (New York, 1932), 69–85.

[39] Many new "suburban" churches also felt they should have a gymnasium with a stage so that they too could adopt the tactic of the "added attractions" by having made adequate provision for athletics and theatricals.

[40] Abell, 150–51.

Edward Judson's begging expeditions were successful in tapping the resources of John D. Rockefeller. Furthermore, as Judson noted, the involvements of an institutional program "are so difficult and fascinating that they easily absorb all a minister's time and energy." The tendency is for him to neglect "his study and the care of his flock," to lose "his priestly character," and to become "a mere social functionary."[41] Becoming absorbed in manifold activities that initially were intended to serve as a bridge into church membership, the ideal of mere humanitarian service tended to replace the earlier evangelistic concern. As a result, the congregations of institutional churches, as their novelty disappeared, dwindled almost as rapidly as they had increased. In the end, far from being a means of building up a congregation to support a ministry in areas of deterioration, many institutional churches became social agencies that other churches had to find money and leadership to support. Meanwhile, storefront churches began to make an appearance in the surrounding neighborhoods to demonstrate that "added attractions" were not needed to "draw" people "within reach of the gospel." Few noted the irony of this development.

The Churches and the Economic Order

The decade preceding the great railroad strike of 1877 has been described as the "summit" of American economic complacency. This complacency was as evident among churchmen as it was among other Americans. Leaders of the churches may have disagreed about many things, but they displayed remarkable unanimity in their approbation of the existing economic order and the "principles" or "laws" of political economy that provided its theoretical foundation. Gone was the radical criticism and ferment of the 1830s and 1840s. Henry F. May observed that "in 1876 Protestantism presented a massive, almost unbroken front in its defense of the social status quo."[42] This state of affairs was equally true of Roman Catholicism. Within a dozen years, however, this situation began to change when people were shocked from their complacency by outbreaks of violent social conflict. Roman Catholics remained cautious,[43] but by the 1890s,

---

[41] "The Church in Its Social Aspect," 437.

[42] H. F. May, *Protestant Churches and Industrial America* (New York, 1963), 91.

[43] Francis J. Lally has pointed out that Roman Catholics gave little evidence of being "socially progressive" prior to the New Deal years. The papal encyclical *Rerum Novarum* (1891) had little immediate impact in America, and the few occasions when Roman Catholics displayed an interest in social reform were "sporadic and mostly short-lived." This was true of the 1919 "Bishops' Program of Social Reconstruction," which did not receive strong support until the 1930s. Participation in the labor movement was the single notable exception to the generally conservative outlook. *The Catholic Church in a Changing America*, (Boston, 1962), 47–48. For an account of developing social consciousness among Roman Catholics, see A. I. Abell, *American Catholicism and Social Action* (New York, 1960).

vigorous demands for social reform were being voiced in every major Protestant denomination. A few leaders were calling for the complete reorganization of society. By the turn of the century, the adherents of two antithetical gospels—"the gospel of wealth" and "the social gospel"—were locked in combat and struggling for predominance.

The Gospel of Wealth

For many Americans the years following the Civil War marked the beginning of a period of unrivaled prosperity. Rapidly as the population increased, the nation's wealth multiplied three times as fast. Those who benefited by this tremendous economic expansion were confident that they were living in the best of all possible worlds. The American economy had been tested and had not been found wanting. This smug self-satisfaction lent an aura of eminent reasonableness and even sanctity to the laissez-faire economic doctrines that had been fathered by Adam Smith, popularized in America by Francis Wayland,[44] and given strong reinforcement by the teachings of Herbert Spencer. The most persuasive argument for allowing economic self-interest free play was the seemingly obvious fact that it worked for general economic betterment. Perhaps it worked, as the *Congregationalist* put it, because there were "thousands upon thousands of acres of magnificent soil" beyond the Mississippi that could be secured "at a merely nominal price" so that "no man who is blessed with health and willingness to work, be his family large or small, need come to the poorhouse."[45] But it worked nonetheless, at least for a time.

The classic statement of "the true gospel concerning wealth," obedience to which will "solve the problem of the rich and the poor," was written by Andrew Carnegie, the steelmaster of Pittsburgh, and was published in the June 1889 issue of the *North American Review*.[46] Carnegie insisted that "civilization depends" upon the triple law of the "sacredness" of private property, free competition, and free accumulation of wealth. This triple law, which allows free play to economic forces, is indispensable to all progress, and nothing should be permitted to interfere with its operation. Its indispensability is a fact of life that cannot be changed. One can only make the "best of it." It is true that a price is exacted, since the law of competition forces the employer "into the strictest economies, among which the rates to be paid to labor figure prominently," and this process creates fiction.

---

[44] Wayland was president of Brown University and the author of *The Elements of Political Economy* (1837), the most popular textbook on the subject.

[45] March 17, 1870; quoted by May, 55.

[46] Carnegie's brief dissertation on "Wealth" is reprinted, with other essays, in *Democracy and the Gospel of Wealth*, ed. Gail Kennedy, *Problems in American Civilization: Readings Selected by the Department of American Studies, Amherst College* (Boston, 1949).

But even if the operation of the law "may sometimes be hard for individuals," it is "best for the race, because it insures the survival of the fittest in every department" and produces "a wonderful material development" that benefits all. "The laborer has now more comforts than the farmer had a few generations ago," "the farmer has more luxuries than the landlord had," and the landlord has more than "a king could then obtain." This inequality is better than the "universal squalor" that would otherwise prevail.

Carnegie's harsh views were somewhat tempered by his view of the proper use of wealth. In words reminiscent of Wesley's slogan "Gain all you can, save all you can, give all you can," he declared that "the man who dies . . . rich, dies disgraced."[47] Instead of leaving vast sums to one's children or even making humanitarian bequests, Carnegie insisted that one's wealth should be distributed in ways that served the common good during one's own lifetime. Indiscriminate charity, of course, could only serve "to encourage the slothful, the drunken, the unworthy." The race has never been improved by almsgiving, for it rewards vice rather than aids virtue. "Those worthy of assistance, except in rare cases, seldom require assistance." The objective should be to help those who will help themselves. "The best means of benefitting the community is to place within its reach the ladders upon which the aspiring can rise." Parks, museums, libraries, schools are ways of returning surplus wealth to the masses in a form "best calculated to do them lasting good."

Carnegie's gospel of wealth was closely intertwined with the doctrine of stewardship of time, money, and talent that had been staple fare in Protestant moral teaching. It was but a small step for current principles of economics to be translated into laws of God's providential ordering of society. Phillips Brooks, Henry Ward Beecher, and lesser luminaries of the Protestant pulpit embraced the gospel of wealth with fervent devotion; but Russell Conwell—with his lecture on *Acres of Diamonds* (they are in one's own backyard) and his exhortation that everyone has a "duty to get rich"—was its most eloquent clerical spokesman.[48]

Roman Catholics, for the most part, represented an older conservatism that enjoined passivity and acceptance of one's lot in society; God permits poverty as "the most efficient means" of fostering "some of the most neces-

---

[47] Wesley's concern, of course, was different. "Religion," he said, "must necessarily produce both industry and frugality, and these cannot but produce riches." And "whenever riches have increased," religion "has decreased in the same proportion." "Is there no way to prevent this—this continual declension of pure religion?" What way "can we take that our money may not sink us to the nethermost hell? There is but one way, and . . . no other. . . . If those who 'gain all they can,' and 'save all they can,' will likewise 'give all they can'; then the more they gain, the more they will grow in grace." *The Works of John Wesley*, 4th ed. (London, 1840–1842), XIII, 246–47.

[48] For Brooks and Beecher, see May, 64–72. For Conwell, see W. S. Hudson, *The Great Tradition of the American Churches*, rev. ed. (New York, 1963), 180–86. There is no standard text of Conwell's *Acres of Diamonds*, for it underwent constant revision.

sary Christian virtues." Charity should be directed to the relief of suffering and not to its elimination, for "a country where there are no beggars" would be "a veritable branch of hell." It was suggested that "to let well enough alone is a very wise old saw." Liberal Catholics, on the other hand, took a more positive view of the benefits derived from the free play of economic forces. Bishop Spalding assured a graduating class at Notre Dame that "the organs of the social body" had never been so healthy, and Cardinal Gibbons applauded Carnegie's essay on "Wealth." Archbishop Ireland insisted that "respect" for capital "must be supreme," and he admonished Roman Catholics to stop considering money as evil and—with "will," "energy," "pluck," "push," and "ambition"—to set about acquiring some. "It is energy and enterprise that wins everywhere," he declared with the briskness of an entrepreneur; "they win in the Church, they win in the state, they win in business." In 1890, the *Catholic World* published a minor classic of the gospel-of-wealth literature that pointed out that the three men Christ restored to life were all men of wealth and recommended that, after praying for faith, hope, and charity, Catholics should add the petition: "O Lord! give me good sense. Give me hard, practical, everyday gumption. If I had a little of that, I shouldn't act as foolishly as I generally do; I shouldn't waste my time nor money." The ability to make "frequent and handsome donations" to the church is a "pretty" sure indication "that a man has the right sort of zeal."[49]

Many wealthy men had this "right sort of zeal," for this was a great age of philanthropy. Even without the incentive of benefit to be derived from income-tax exemption, benefactions were large and numerous. George Peabody, with gifts amounting to $8.5 million, was only one of many who, in the words of William Gladstone, demonstrated "how a man may be master of his fortune, not its slave." There were, of course, incongruities symbolized by the image of Daniel Drew as both "master fleecer of the lambs" and "founder of a theological seminary." Jay Cooke presented a curious picture as a skilled corrupter of legislatures and president of the Education Society of the Protestant Episcopal Church. Considerations of self-interest may have spurred the Armour brothers to lavish more than $1 million on a mission in Chicago. But many took their stewardship seriously. John P. Crozer, whose many benefactions included a theological seminary, was not exceptional when he confessed his perplexity "how I shall use, as I ought, the great and increasing stores of wealth which God has bestowed upon me."

> Excuses are so easily framed, and the heart of man so deceitful, that one can easily reason himself into the belief that, all things considered, he has done

---

[49] R. D. Cross, *Emergence of Liberal Catholicism in America,* (Cambridge, MA, 1958), 107–9, 111–12, 163–64.

pretty well. I find such a process of reasoning in my own mind, but calm reflection tells me that I have not done well. I am a very unprofitable servant to so good a Master.

Troubled lest the good he designed be lost in the mere satisfaction of giving, he asked the Lord to direct him "clearly and decisively" to the "path of duty and usefulness." Commenting on Crozer's careful assessment of his responsibility, Sidney E. Mead observed that "only the sneering souls of the mean in mind" could belittle such transparently "honest and consecrated devotion" to sacred duty.[50]

The Rise of Social Discontent

The prosperity of a booming economy was not equally shared by all sections of the population, and the result was smoldering discontent among both farmers and workingmen. The woes of the farmers, apart from the natural hazards of the weather and periodic insect infestations, were due to their growing dependence upon the railroads and a system of mass marketing, both of which were susceptible to manipulation by the "moneyed interests."[51] The earlier subsistence farming had been replaced by the production of money crops—bought, shipped, and processed by others. Selling in a distant market in open world competition, the farmer purchased his machinery, supplies, and personal necessities in a market subsidized by protective tariffs. And his shifting fortunes from year to year frequently made him dependent upon credit to finance his next crop. The great enemy was the triple alliance of railroads, banks, and tariff-protected industry.

Caught in a web woven by railroad monopolists, buccaneering market speculators, tight-fisted money lenders, and hardheaded industrialists, the farmers rose in sporadic movements of protest and revolt. The Grangers of 1867, the Greenbackers of the 1870s, the Farmers' Alliance of the 1880s, the Populists of 1891, and Bryan's "free silver" campaign of 1896 all were expressions of this agrarian discontent that sought to impose systematic government control over the economic life of the nation to mitigate the plight of the farmers. The *Congregationalist Record* of Boston represented the attitude of most eastern churchmen when it described the leaders of the agrarian protest as "dangerous characters of the inflammable and covetous West." Lyman Abbot of Plymouth Congregational Church in Brooklyn was probably equally representative when he spoke disparagingly of William Jennings Bryan as a western "medicine man" who set up his tent to

[50] Sidney E. Mead, *The Lively Experiment*, (New York, 1963), 149.

[51] See R. B. Nye, *Midwestern Progressive Politics: A Historical Study of Its Origins and Development, 1870–1950* (East Lansing, Mich., 1951).

hawk "one medicine which will cure all the ills to which humanity is subject."[52]

The plight of the workers was even more serious than that of the farmers. Wages were low, hours were long, and working conditions were almost uniformly bad. Where women and children were employed, they labored from dawn to dusk for a pittance. And the situation steadily worsened, for the mounting national wealth was being concentrated in fewer and fewer hands. As early as 1867, a magazine reported that ten men owned one-tenth of the taxable property in New York City, and it listed their holdings. By 1890, it was estimated that 1 percent of the families of the country received one-quarter of the national income, and seven years later one-tenth of the American people were said to own nine-tenths of the national wealth. Wages, to be sure, were rising. From 1860 to 1881, they increased 31 percent, but prices rose 41 percent and more than offset the gain.[53] The crises came, however, when workers were laid off in large numbers or had their pay cut as the result of recurring financial crashes. The crash of 1873 set off the first crisis. This was followed by the panic of 1884 and then by the disastrous depression of 1893, when Coxey's "army" marched on Washington.

Numerous workingmen's associations were being formed throughout these years, and their efforts to improve the lot of the workers led to large-scale labor warfare. Strikes were frequent and bloody. Four were particularly frightening to the nation as a whole. The first was the railroad strike of 1877 in which pitched battles were fought in many cities, arousing widespread fear of imminent revolution and anarchy. The second was the McCormick Harvester strike of 1886. On May 3, six pickets were killed in a clash with the police. The following day at a protest meeting of the workers in Haymarket Square, a bomb was exploded that killed a policeman and injured many others. In the subsequent riot, ten more persons died. The third was the Homestead strike of 1892 at the Carnegie Steel Plant in Pennsylvania where 10 were killed and 60 wounded in a battle between the workers and 300 "Pinkerton" men. The fourth, the Pullman strike of 1894, which affected rail transportation in 27 states, was accompanied by widespread burning, looting, and killing, and was finally brought to an end by President Cleveland's use of federal troops.

The reaction of the churches to the revolt of the workingmen was one first of shock and then of panic. Orthodox economic theory had taught them that labor was a "commodity," subject "like all other commodities" to "the imperishable laws of demand and supply," and that in a free country the sole responsibility of government to both capital and labor was "the

[52] *Ibid.*, 5.

[53] See Charles B. Spahr, *An Essay on the Present Distribution of Wealth in the United States* (New York, 1896), 128 ff.; Robert Hunter, *Poverty* (New York, 1912), 61 ff.; Washington Gladden, *Applied Christianity* (Boston, 1894), 120; W. E. Garrison, *March of Faith*, (New York, 1933), 62, 120.

simple duty of enforcing contracts" and preserving peace.[54] Thus they were more shocked by the riots of the strikers than by the conditions that caused the strikers to riot. The whole fabric of society seemed in danger of being torn apart, and many of the Protestant periodicals responded with almost incredibly brutal denunciations of the workers. The issue is between "law and anarchy," declared the *Independent* on July 26, 1877. The safety of society demands that no concessions be made to rioters. A week later its mood was near hysteria. "If the club of the policeman, knocking out the brains of the rioter, will answer, then well and good; but if it does not promptly meet the exigency, then bullets and bayonets, canister and grape . . . constitute the one remedy and the one duty of the hour." The *Christian Union* agreed. "There are times when mercy is a mistake," it asserted.[55] But there were others who were deeply troubled. Washington Gladden, for example, in the late 1860s had defended the cause of the strikers in North Adams, Massachusetts; and in 1876, he published his first book on social questions, *Workingmen and Their Employers.* By the 1880s, many were to share his concern.

Roman Catholics were often equally intemperate in their denunciation of strikes. James R. Bayley, archbishop of Baltimore, took a dim view of labor unions, insisting that "no Catholic with any idea of the spirit of his religion will encourage them," and a Catholic periodical asserted that the proper solution for economic troubles was for the workers to "Pray, Pray, Pray."[56] The Knights of Labor, the first mass labor union, was condemned in Quebec by papal decree in 1884, and Archbishop Corrigan of New York insisted that membership in the Knights was forbidden in the United States as well. Cardinal Gibbons, on the other hand, believed that many of the workers' grievances were just, and he was alarmed by the prospect of major defections from the church if the censure was maintained. In 1888, with the help of Ireland and Keane, Gibbons obtained a ruling from Rome that stated that the Knights could be "tolerated."

The Social Gospel[57]

Developing social concern among American Protestants was stimulated in part by influences from abroad. The writings of Thomas Chalmers, the Scottish theologian and philanthropist, exerted the earliest influence in

---

[54] *Watchman and Reflector,* June 4, 1874, quoted by May, 55; and the *Independent,* July 26, 1877, quoted by Garrison, 64.

[55] May, 92–93.

[56] L. R. Ward, ed., *The American Apostolate,* (Westminster, Md., 1952); Cross, 118.

[57] The term "social gospel" did not come into common use until after 1900. Prior to this the term most widely used was "social Christianity." See R. C. White and C. H. Hopkins, *The Social Gospel: Religion and Reform in Changing America* (Philadelphia, 1976); R. T. Handy, ed., *The Social Gospel* (New York, 1966).

this direction,[58] and immediately after the Civil War, interest in the distinctively English "Christian socialism" of Frederick Denison Maurice and Charles Kingsley was aroused by their books and novels.[59] Later the "Christian socialists of Germany and Switzerland contributed a strong theological emphasis upon the centrality of the doctrine of "the kingdom of God." The chief American precursors were Henry M. Dexter, a New England clergyman who published *The Moral Influence of Manufacturing Towns* in 1848, and Stephen Colwell, a Philadelphia iron merchant who became preoccupied with social problems in the 1850s.[60]

The social gospel leaders represented no unified point of view. They shared a common concern, and they were agreed that the people in the churches needed to be exposed to the "facts." Most Protestants were isolated from the scenes of industrial conflict and had no personal acquaintance with the lot of the worker. To remedy this situation, socially minded clergymen organized forums and study groups to discuss industrial problems, and they invited representatives of labor to speak before men's brotherhoods in the churches. In addition, they busied themselves with producing a voluminous literature dealing with social issues from a Christian point of view.[61] But beyond this common pattern of activity, there were deep divergences.

Gladden represented a mild "progressivism" that recognized the rights of labor, advocated municipal ownership of public utilities, and placed strong emphasis upon the Golden Rule as the royal law of brotherhood. The latter theme was picked up and romanticized by Charles M. Sheldon, minister of the Central Congregational Church of Topeka, Kansas, in a parable-novel that was destined to win a place beside *Uncle Tom's Cabin* and *Ten Nights in a Bar Room* as one of the great American tracts. *In His Steps, or What Would Jesus Do?* (1897)[62] was the story of the revolution that occurred

---

[58] Chalmers' *The Application of Christianity to the Commercial and Ordinary Affairs of Life* was reprinted at Hartford and at Boston in 1821, at Lexington, Kentucky, in 1822, and at New York in 1855. His *Christian and Civic Economy of Large Towns* was considered to be of such value that an abridgment was published in 1900 by Charles R. Henderson, professor of Christian sociology at the University of Chicago.

[59] English nonconformists, such as Andrew Mearson, A. M. Fairbairn, C. Silvester Horne, John Clifford, and Hugh Price Hughes, may have exerted even greater influence in America because they were not "handicapped by ties with an aristocratic and partly feudal establishment." May, 149, 150.

[60] Colwell's books were *New Themes for the Protestant Clergy* (1851), *Politics for American Christians* (1852), and *The Position of Christianity in the United States* (1854). He also wrote the Preface to William Arnot's *The Race for Riches* (1853).

[61] Typical in this respect was Gladden's own literary output, which included *Working People and Their Employers* (1876), *The Christian League of Connecticut* (1883), *Applied Christianity* (1886), *Tools and the Man* (1893), *Social Facts and Forces* (1899), *Social Salvation* (1902), *Christianity and Socialism* (1905), *The Church and Modern Life* (1908), and *The Labor Question* (1911).

[62] Its circulation has been estimated to have exceeded 20 million copies. Conwell's *Acres of Diamonds* occupied much the same place in the gospel-of-wealth literature.

in a small city when members of a single congregation resolved to live for a year in accordance with the teachings of Jesus. At the opposite pole from Sheldon's nonprogrammatic sentimentalism was the demand for a radical reconstruction of society voiced by such men as George D. Herron, professor of applied Christianity at Grinnell College, and W. D. P. Bliss, an Episcopal clergyman in Boston and guiding spirit of the Society of Christian Socialists. A "scientific" approach to social problems was represented by a Chicago coterie whose chief luminaries were Shailer Mathews, Graham Taylor, and Charles R. Henderson. Social melioration based upon careful sociological analysis was their forte, and they were strong advocates of the utility of "social settlements" in forwarding the necessary process of social adjustment.

The social settlements were patterned after Toynbee Hall, a pioneer settlement house established in London in 1884. Their purpose was to bring together a company of university-trained social workers who would live together in the slums where they could study conditions at first hand and initiate projects of social betterment. Two of the best-known American "settlements" were in Chicago—Hull House, founded by Jane Addams, and Chicago Commons, with Graham Taylor as its guiding light. Others were to be found in most of the major cities, usually being established in connection with either a university or a seminary.

In terms of continuing influence, Walter Rauschenbusch was the outstanding prophet of the social gospel. His social awakening occurred during ten years spent as pastor of a small Baptist church of German immigrants in New York City. Participation in Henry George's campaign for mayor helped shape his views, as did his experience among the tenements and his association with two other young pastors, Nathaniel Schmidt and Leighton Williams.[63] In 1897, Rauschenbusch was appointed to the faculty of the Rochester Theological Seminary, and in 1907, when *Christianity and the Social Crisis* was published, he was thrust into national prominence. Of equal note was his *Prayers of the Social Awakening* (1910), one of the few devotional classics that America has produced.

Rauschenbusch is difficult to classify in relation to other social gospel leaders. His fellow Baptists at the University of Chicago dismissed him as "rhetorical" rather than "scientific." He called himself on occasion a "Christian socialist," but he was careful to distinguish his reformist position from any doctrinaire socialism. Although he did not wholly escape the sanguine temper of his time, he showed few traces of the sentimental optimism that characterized so much of the social gospel literature. As early as 1892, he had rejected the "comforting" doctrine of "the inherent upward forces of nature," and in 1907, he spoke strong words of caution

---

[63] Henry George had an astonishing influence in awakening Christian social concern in England. Schmidt, Williams, and Rauschenbusch linked themselves in a Society of Jesus, which was later expanded to become the Brotherhood of the Kingdom.

to those who had imbibed the heady wine of inevitable progress. As the title of his last volume, *A Theology for the Social Gospel,* indicates, his interest was much more theological than most of the others, and his great contribution was to clothe the social gospel with passion and a sense of destiny. He did this by relating the social gospel in dynamic fashion to the concept of the kingdom of God, placing it in juxtaposition to the inherited, massive, and stubbornly resistant structures of the kingdom of evil.[64]

Apart from sincere concern to combat injustice, this official "social Christianity" was motivated by a desire to overcome an assumed alienation of the workingman from the churches. Gladden had noted that only one-tenth of his congregation were wage earners, whereas the census reported that almost one-fourth of the population were of the laboring class. It is "all too evident," he declared, "that the proportion of working people who attend church is much smaller than the proportion of churchgoers to the entire population."[65] The assumption was that the gap between the churches and the workingmen would be closed if the churches would only exhibit an interest in their plight and support them in their struggle for justice.

Middle-class Protestantism, however, was mistaken in assuming that there was such an alienation of workingmen. They simply did not belong to middle-class churches. Overlooked had been the existence of "a working-class social Christianity" running parallel to "the more widely known and well-studied social gospel" of middle-class critics of society. A study of labor periodicals has made it clear that Christian rhetoric, imagery, and motivation were characteristic of labor leadership and that the workingmen found religious sanction for their discontent and union activities in the evangelicalism of traditional American Protestantism.[66] The tactic of wooing workers into middle-class churches by a show of concern for their plight, however, met with little success. Immediate gains rather than expressions of sympathy interested them. Indeed, the 1896 election witnessed a massive shift in the labor vote from its traditional democratic affiliation to the Republican party of Mark Hanna and William McKinley.[67] Practical issues were decisive, for neither party in its urban strongholds (Republicans in Philadelphia and Chicago, Democrats in Boston and New York) offered programs of thoroughgoing social and economic reform.

---

[64] See the Introduction to W. S. Hudson, ed., *Walter Rauschenbusch: Selected Writings.*

[65] From "The Working People and the Churches," *The Independent,* July 23, 1885.

[66] Herbert Gutman, "Protestantism and the American Labor Movement: The Christian Spirit in the Gilded Age," *American Historical Review,* 72 (1966), 74–101.

[67] S. P. Hays, *The Response to Industrialism, 1885–1914* (Chicago, 1957), 46–47. Democrats did not recover their urban strength until the elections of 1928 and 1932.

The "Progressive" Movement

Middle-class support of "social Christianity" was related to Theodore Roosevelt's "Square Deal" and "Bull Moose" platforms. Most social gospel leaders were involved in "progressive" politics, and the 1912 Progressive party campaign had a strong religious flavor. The party convention had as its theme song "Onward, Christian Soldiers," a response to his ringing challenge to them before the convention met—"We stand at Armageddon and we battle for the Lord." Ministers campaigned openly from the pulpit for the party, and one justified himself by maintaining that, although "it is not the province of the pulpit to say that any man ought to be elected president," it is "the province of every pulpit to say that the principles of the Progressive party should guide the nation for the next four years."[68]

Progressivism, like the social gospel, was almost exclusively a manifestation of middle-class idealism. Middle-class opinion had been deeply shocked by the muckrakers' exposure of widespread vice and corruption, of the ruthless tactics employed by the trusts, and of the special privileges accorded "vested interests" by city governments, state legislatures, and the national Congress. The progressives had no consistent philosophy, and their program was a miscellaneous collection of reforms that included direct primaries, women's suffrage, the initiative, referendum, recall, regulation of interstate commerce, revision of banking and currency laws, effective antitrust legislation, municipal ownership of public utilities, the income tax, the eight-hour day, prohibition of child labor, safeguards against industrial accidents and occupational diseases, and either strict regulation of the liquor traffic or its outright prohibition.

The related issues of conspiracies in restraint of trade and the corrupting of government officials were the great objects of concern. When most of the reforms designed to curb the "vested interests," restore power to the people, and eliminate other abuses had been adopted, attention was concentrated upon women's suffrage and the abolition of the liquor traffic as the final goals to be achieved. Each was regarded as something of a universal panacea for the ills of society. The women's vote, it was believed, would strengthen at every point the cause of virtue, morality, altruism, and humanitarian endeavor. The crusade for prohibition, also integral to the progressive program, was viewed as a general panacea.

The liquor industry with its increasing monopolistic tendencies was regarded by the progressives as the most dangerous and predatory of all big business. It was lavish in its expenditures both to gain desired legislation and to thwart the enforcement of bothersome regulations adopted as concessions to public opinion. Often arrogant in its control of government, the liquor industry had been exposed again and again by the muckrakers

---

[68] *Ibid.*, 93.

as a principal source of political corruption and a strong ally of political re-action. Its links with vice and crime were more indirect but nonetheless real. As a progressive reform, prohibition drew upon the same moral idealism as the rest of the progressive program. It was popularly believed that the abolition of the liquor traffic would eliminate at a single stroke a primary cause not only of political reaction, corruption, vice, and crime, but also of poverty, disease, economic inefficiency, marital discord, and broken homes. Although some of the progressives disliked the reform, believing it to be too extreme, their withdrawal of support was more than compensated by that received from conservative Protestants. But the leadership that pushed the adoption of the Eighteenth Amendment remained with the socially liberal progressives.[69]

The temperance cause had long been gaining ground in the United States, and it had become much more vigorous with the organization of the Women's Christian Temperance Union in 1874. Through the efforts of Frances Willard, rhetoric about the physical and social consequences of alcohol consumption were framed within the view of temperance as a moral cause.[70] The emphasis shifted from temperance to total abstinence to a full-scale attack upon the saloon. By 1900, five of the forty-five states had adopted statewide prohibition laws that banned the manufacture and sale of intoxicating beverages, and others had made provision for local option. The big thrust, however, was launched with the formation of the Anti-Saloon League in 1895, an agency that was to become an instrument of sophisticated political action. It was amended by socially progressive Protestant churchmen and also enlisted the support of liberal Catholics.[71] As was true of the progressive movement as a whole, the drive for prohibition found its greatest strength in an alliance between the old-stock middle-class element in the cities and the rural and small-town population, both groups being staunchly Protestant and united in their determination to rid the cities of vice, crime, poverty, and corruption. Unless this goal was accomplished, it was feared that the growing influence of the cities would subvert the character of American society and thwart all further attempts at progress and reform. Men and women who favored the movement pledged their support in writing, sometimes signing a capital "T" alongside their name to indicate that they were opposed to consumption of any kind of alcohol, including beer and wine. Consequently, those entirely opposed to alcohol became known as "T-totalers."

---

[69] See J. H. Timberlake, *Prohibition and the Progressive Movement, 1900–1920* (Cambridge, Mass., 1963).

[70] The influence of the WCTU was great. For Frances Willard, the key figure in the organization, see Ruth Bordin, *Women and Temperance* (Philadelphia, 1981).

[71] Bishop John J. Keane attended the Anti-Saloon League's founding convention, Archbishop Ireland served as one of the vice-presidents, and Catholic clergymen regularly addressed subsequent conventions.

The drive to suppress the liquor traffic had the great advantage of enlisting the support of both liberal and conservative Protestants, and in the end it became a great Protestant crusade. By April 1917, twenty-six states had gone "dry," and before the end of the year, a constitutional amendment to ban the liquor traffic had been passed by Congress and was submitted to the states for ratification. With the approval of forty-five of the forty-eight states, the Eighteenth Amendment came into effect on January 16, 1920. Later in the same year, the Nineteenth Amendment, which established the right of women to vote, came into operation. Of the major reforms sought by the progressives, the only unfinished business was a federal ban on child labor. The national child labor statute was declared unconstitutional by the Supreme Court in 1918, and subsequent attempts to secure a child labor amendment were to be unsuccessful.

Imperialism and World Missions

A third frontier of the new industrial society of urgent concern to the churches lay beyond the seas. Conscious of its growing industrial power, the United States began to assume a more positive and vigorous role in international affairs. Foreign trade mounted rapidly, and American entrepreneurs were eager to exploit the untapped markets of Latin America and eastern Asia. James G. Blaine, as secretary of state under Presidents Garfield and Benjamin Harrison, championed vigorous action to expand American economic and political influence abroad, and negotiated reciprocal trade agreements and arbitration treaties to further American interests. As early as 1878, a U.S. naval base was established on the Samoan Islands, and the process of reducing the Hawaiian Islands to an American possession had begun. President Cleveland's bold defiance of Great Britain in the Venezuelan crisis of 1895 was symptomatic of the new temper that led to the Spanish-American War of 1898 and to the prompt support of Panama's revolt against Colombia in 1903. As an aftermath of the war with Spain, Puerto Rico, Guam, and the Philippines were claimed as U.S. possessions, and "protectorates" were established in several Caribbean countries. Meanwhile the United States was intervening in China to preserve an "open door" for American commerce.

Dollar Diplomacy and Religion

American imperial expansion was accompanied by a mounting enthusiasm among the churches for overseas missions. In its more bellicose form, this enthusiasm was utilized as an excuse for territorial aggrandizement and what came to be called "dollar diplomacy." This was the note struck by President McKinley when he sought to explain to some Methodist friends how he had come to change his mind with regard to the acquisition of the Philippine Islands.

> I am not ashamed to tell you, gentlemen, that I went down on my knees and prayed Almighty God for light and guidance more than one night. And one night late it came to me this way. . . . There was nothing left for us to do but to take them all and to educate the Filipinos and uplift and civilize and Christianize them, and by God's grace do the very best we could by them, as our fellow men for whom Christ also died.

Senator Albert J. Beveridge was not troubled by such hesitation and uncertainty, and his defense of annexation was positive and to the point.

> We will not renounce our part in the mission of the race, trustee under God of the civilization of the world. . . . He has marked the American people as his chosen nation to finally lead in the regeneration of the world. This is the divine mission of America. . . . The judgment of the Master is upon us: "Ye have been faithful over a few things; I will make you ruler over many things."

The possibility of a different interpretation of scripture was made clear when Senator George F. Hoar rose to his feet in response to Beveridge and quoted another biblical text: "The Devil taketh him up into an extremely high mountain and showeth him all the kingdoms of the world and the glory of them and saith unto him, 'All these things will be thine if thou wilt fall down and worship me.' "[72]

Without the results of public opinion polls, there is no way to determine which senator represented majority opinion in the churches. Many shared the militant spirit of Senator Beveridge, but influential churchmen who had supported the conflict with Spain as a war of liberation in keeping with America's anticolonialist tradition were appalled when it became an occasion for launching the United States on an imperial career of overseas expansion.[73] When their efforts to exclude provisions for annexation from the peace treaty were defeated, they mounted a continuing campaign to promote the cause of peace and international justice. Peace societies multiplied. Dollar diplomacy and the "big stick" (the naval construction program) were attacked. The newly organized Federal Council of Churches trained young people for foreign mission work, inspiring them with the ideal of human brotherhood and a warless world. On February 10, 1914, twenty-nine of America's most distinguished religious leaders—Protestant, Roman Catholic, and Jewish—formed the Church Peace Union to coordinate their separate activities into a single thrust for a peaceful settlement

---

[72] Charles S. Olcott, *The Life of William McKinley* (Boston, 1916), II, 110–11; Mark Sullivan, *Our Times, the United States, 1900–1925* (New York, 1926–1935), I, 47–48; Garrison, 174.

[73] W. S. Hudson, "Protestant Clergy Debate the Nation's Vocation, 1898–99," *Church History*, 42 (1973).

of international disputes. Andrew Carnegie provided an endowment to underwrite the program. So great was his optimism that he included as a proviso of his gift that "after war is abolished" the income may be used "to relieve the deserving poor . . . , especially those who have struggled long and earnestly against misfortune and have not themselves to blame for their misfortune."[74] The first project of the new organization was to aid in the establishment of the World Alliance for International Friendship through the churches. This was accomplished in August 1914, the month that marked the beginning of World War I.

The Evangelization of the World

When William R. Williams, a scholarly Baptist preacher, wrote in 1846 that "our heavenly Father has made us a national epistle to other lands,"[75] he was reiterating a conviction that had long been held by most American Christians. In the nineteenth century, however, Great Britain had taken the lead in the foreign-mission enterprise, and the United States was the junior partner. At the close of the century, this role was reversed.

The expansion of American commercial and political interests abroad riveted the attention of the churches upon the needy people beyond the seas. In 1885, Josiah Strong, in a little book entitled *Our Country*, summoned the churches of America to assume their full responsibility for the Christianization of the world.[76] American ideals, he insisted, rather than its national power should be the focal point of concern in America's relationship to other lands. The Anglo-Saxon race in general and the American people in particular, he contended, were the bearers of two great interrelated ideas—"civil liberty" and "spiritual Christianity." And but for the "salt" provided by the second, the first would "speedily decay." These in turn are the "two great needs" of all mankind.

> Without controversy, these are the forces which, in the past, have contributed most of the elevation of the human race, and they must continue to be, in the future, the most efficient ministers to its progress.

The obvious corollary of this fact was that "the Anglo-Saxon, as the great representative of these two ideas, the depository of these two great blessings, sustains peculiar relations to the world's future" and "is divinely commissioned to be, in a peculiar sense, his brother's keeper."[77]

---

[74] Charles S. MacFarland, *Pioneers for Peace Through Religion: Based on the Records of the Church Peace Union* (New York, 1946), 22.

[75] John R. Bodo, *The Protestant Clergy and Public Issues, 1812–1848* (Princeton, N.J., 1954), 241.

[76] Jurgen Herbst, ed., *Our Country: Its Possible Future and Its Present Crisis*, (Cambridge, Mass., 1963). The quotations that follow are taken from Chapters XIV and XV, 201–3, 205, 210, 212, 215–18, 252, 256.

[77] *Ibid.*, 203.

Strong's racism and anti-Semitism were complex, particularly in view of his thinking about the nature of Anglo-Saxon superiority. He believed that superiority was "due in large measure to its highly mixed origin," it being "almost universally admitted by ethnologists that the mixed races of mankind are superior to the pure ones." Thus the Anglo-Saxon is not to be defined in terms of a racial strain but as the heir of a dual tradition—"civil liberty" and "spiritual Christianity"—of which the Anglo-Saxon is the custodian. And the influence of these twin concepts served as a corrective to the inevitable temptation to exercise tyrannical domination over other peoples. In the United States, as a result of this cultural tradition, all immigrants by the alchemy of the "melting pot" were considered Anglo-Saxons. This transformation occurred as soon as they learned to speak English. Nor did Strong explain the energy and vigor of the Anglo-Saxon in terms of "blood" or "genes." It was largely the product of climate and diet.

As Strong reviewed past history, it was evident to him that, with "two hands," God had been "preparing in our Anglo-Saxon civilization the die with which to stamp the people of the earth" and at the same time, through the revolutionary ferment that contact of Christian with heathen was creating, had been "preparing mankind to receive our impress."

> The door of opportunity is open in all the earth; organizations have been completed, languages learned, the Scriptures translated, and now the triumph of the Kingdom awaits only the exercise of the power committed to the church.

Whether the perils that threaten to delay "the coming of the kingdom wherein dwelleth righteousness" will be permitted to retard its advance "is now being swiftly determined" by the men and women of this generation. Living as they do in one of the plastic moments of history, Strong declared, "it is fully in the hands of the Christians of the United States, during the next ten or fifteen years, to hasten or retard the coming of Christ's kingdom in the world by hundreds, and perhaps thousands, of years."

Spurred by the rhetoric of Strong and others, the missionary enterprise advanced. It was marked by widespread interdenominational cooperation. Not only did the mission boards recruit their personnel through the joint endeavors of the Student Volunteer Movement, but also they allocated territory on a comity basis in the mission fields and formed interdenominational councils in mission lands for purposes of consultation and sharing of experience. At home the work of the denominational boards was coordinated through the formation of the Foreign Missions Conference of North America in 1893, and later it was also coordinated through the International Missionary Council, which grew out of the Edinburgh conference of 1910. In 1902, the Missionary Education Movement was launched to quicken missionary interest in all the major denominations. A continuing problem, of course, was to provide sufficient financial support for the youth who were offering themselves in increasing numbers for missionary service. A Presbyterian layman, John B. Sleman, Jr., sought to meet this need. He had been deeply moved when thousands of college students had gathered in Nashville in 1906 for a Student Volunteer convention. As a result of his prodding, the Laymen's Missionary Movement was organized in the autumn of that year to challenge laymen throughout the nation to match the devotion of youth with the dedication of their dollars. Until the outbreak of World War I, the Laymen's Missionary Movement was carried forward with the same surge of enthusiasm that characterized the Student Volunteer Movement.

The years of midpassage following the Civil War had introduced many changes into American life and had presented the churches with multiple problems of adjustment. These problems had been met with varying degrees of success, but never were they tackled with more exuberance than during the first decade and a half of the new century, which Gaius Glenn Atkins described as "the age of crusades." The unusual moral idealism and superabundance of zeal that found expression in the allied enterprises of the missionary movement were channeled into a whole galaxy of causes, only a few of which have been noted in this chapter. World War I brought to an end all these peaceful crusades by diverting the idealism and zeal of the American people into the one great crusade to end war and make the world safe for democracy through military power.

World War I also marked the end of the years of transition. The great tide of immigration from Europe was cut off in 1914 when the German armies smashed through Belgium and into France. The economic effect of the war was to hasten the process of industrial development and to bring to maturity the urban world of modern America. In most parts of the country, the agrarian democracy of earlier years was to be little more than a memory as backcountry villages and smaller cities were brought within the orbit of great metropolitan centers.

The changes introduced by World War I were not immediately apparent. By the time the United States entered the war in 1917, the attention of the American people had long been absorbed by the dramatic news of the conflict in Europe. When the United States joined the struggle, President Wilson's "Fourteen Points" made the issues at stake seem clear-cut, and the churches responded to the national summons with zeal and unanimity. Few voices of dissent were heard as "preachers presented arms," utilizing their sermons to depict the iniquity of the Central Powers and the righteousness of the Allied cause. Prominent clergymen exhibited their enthusiasm for the president's crusade by volunteering to go abroad with the troops as Y.M.C.A. workers. Others served at home as "Minute Men," promoting the sale of Liberty Bonds. Then, with American troops having scarcely arrived on the field, the war ended. So quickly had it rushed to its conclusion that only the most perceptive had had time to contemplate the possibility that the old days were gone and that the world would never be the same again.

PART FOUR

Modern America
1918–

CHAPTER THIRTEEN

The Shifting Religious Configuration

By 1914, when the onset of World War I brought to an end the massive influx of new Americans, the religious configuration of the nation had been sharply modified. Mounting Roman Catholic immigration had continued to reduce the numerical predominance of Protestantism, and in the two decades preceding the outbreak of war, both Judaism and Eastern Orthodox Christianity made the striking gains that transformed them into numerically significant communities. At the same time, marked Lutheran growth, the emergence of new "disaffected" Protestant groups, and the growing strength of black churches had altered the Protestant spectrum.

Judaism

Of all the religious traditions and groups that emerged into relative numerical prominence for the first time at the turn of the century, Judaism had the longest history. As children of Abraham, the ancient Hebrews had known troubled times and prosperous times, times of strife and times of peace. Their epic included escape from bondage in Egypt, only to spend forty years in the wilderness before reaching the Promised Land. Recurring wars ended with exile in Babylon, from where many returned to rebuild the temple in Jerusalem. Greeks and Romans came as conquerors, followed by a heroic insurrection. Again the temple was destroyed, and the Jewish people were further dispersed into almost all parts of the known world. Here and there, scattered in small communities from Spain to India and from northern Africa to the Danube and the rivers of Gaul, the Jews survived. Sometimes they prospered, but frequently they were harried; and always the dispersion continued.

Jewish life found its focus in the giving of the Law to Moses some 3,000 years ago and in the consciousness of being a people chosen of God to exhibit both his righteousness and his mercy.[1] The Temple in Jerusalem was the center of Jewish worship. The synagogue appeared for the first time during the Babylonian exile and was given definite shape by Ezra after the return to Jerusalem, where it occupied a subordinate position to the renewed Temple worship. Among Jews of the Diaspora (those living outside Palestine), except for a rare pilgrimage to Jerusalem, the synagogue provided the sole opportunity for communal worship. Although its prayer services were modeled after the Temple service, the central emphasis was upon the instruction of the people rather than upon priestly acts performed in a sacred place. The Torah (the Law contained in the Pentateuch, the five books of Moses) was read and explained and then applied to the needs of daily life. When the Temple was again destroyed in A.D. 70, synagogue worship took on heightened significance as a corporate reminder of the ancient bond symbolized by the Temple and its Ark of the Covenant.

Closely related to the developing life of the synagogue were the rabbis. The rabbis, or teachers, were businessmen or workers who had devoted their leisure to studying the heritage of Israel and, as learned scholars, had been recognized as competent authorities of Jewish law. Although they had no official relationship to the synagogue, the rabbis had always played a prominent role in synagogue life as spokesmen and interpreters of God's claim upon his people. After the shattering events of A.D. 70, the rabbis gained a more central position. Broken and forlorn, the members of the scattered Jewish communities were groping for guidance and comfort. The rabbis gave them both. In their teaching they reinterpreted the Law to make it applicable to the new situation and combined this instruction with glowing words of encouragement and hope. Official leadership, to be sure, did not belong to the rabbis. Others conducted the services of worship, reciting the prayers and reading from the Torah. But it was the rabbis who won the full respect and esteem of the community. More than a millennium was to pass, however, before it became customary to provide the rabbis with a salary. Even as late as the fifteenth century, this was far from a universal practice.

Life in America introduced a significant change in Jewish life. In medieval Europe a pattern of Jewish life developed that was perpetuated in

---

[1] For Jewish faith and practice, see Milton Steinberg, *Basic Judaism* (New York, 1947), and Arthur Hertzberg, *Judaism* (New York, 1961). Jacob Neusner, *American Judaism: Adventure in Modernity* (Englewood Cliffs, N.J., 1972) and Joseph Blau, *Judaism in America* (Chicago, 1976) are compact accounts of the American Jewish experience.

some areas until the twentieth century. These European Jewish communities were tightly knit enclaves set apart from the larger community. An individual Jew had no independent civic status. But within the ghetto there was considerable self-government, with the Jewish leadership being responsible for maintaining order, levying taxes to satisfy the demands of the civil government, and imposing additional assessments to meet their own communal needs. The synagogue was but one of several communal institutions, and it both embraced and was controlled by the total Jewish community.[2] In America these self-contained Jewish enclaves disappeared. The synagogue became the primary institution of Jewish life, with membership a matter of individual choice. Instead of one synagogue, there could be several within a given area. And the synagogue was controlled by its own congregation rather than by the whole Jewish community. In some respects, this arrangement made adaptation easier.

Reform Judaism

Almost everywhere throughout the world, Jews had been forced to regard themselves as a separate entity, living apart from the general community and governing themselves, to the extent that they were permitted to do so, by Talmudic law.[3] In the United States the legal restrictions that fostered this isolated life were absent. Jews could become full citizens. They could be Americans of Jewish faith rather than an alien people. True, the United States was not a perfect society. Numerous ills needed to be remedied. But with political rights having been followed by economic advance and growing acceptance, Jews felt more completely at home than they had in the lands from which they came. They accommodated themselves to American society.

In this situation a growing number of Jews came to regard many of their ancient laws as anachronistic. Specific sources of embarrassment were some of the ancient folk customs associated with synagogue worship, and a perceived lack of decorum and dignity in the religious services. An initial attempt to simplify synagogue worship and to make it more comprehensible and appealing was made at Charleston in 1824. Although this attempt was abortive, a similar effort in 1836 was more successful. The first congregations that were founded to foster Reform were Har Sinai of Baltimore in 1842 and Emanu-El of New York in 1845.

American Jews, of course, were few in number. The great impetus for Reform came from Germany, where the Jews had been emancipated by constitutional changes. At Frankfort-on-the-Main in 1843, the Frankfort

---

[2] See Nathan Glazer, *American Judaism* (Chicago, 1972), 18–19.

[3] The Talmud is a distillation of the biblical interpretation and wise counsel of the ancient rabbis.

Society of the Friends of Reform was organized and issued the following declaration:

> First, we recognize the possibility of unlimited development in the Mosaic religion. Second, the collection of controversies, dissertations, and prescriptions commonly designated by the name Talmud possesses for us no authority from either the doctrinal or practical standpoint. Third, a Messiah who is to lead back the Israelites to the land of Palestine is neither expected nor desired by us; we know no fatherland except that to which we belong by birth or citizenship.[4]

These were to be the classic guiding principles of Reform Judaism. As a result of the storm of protest that the declaration aroused among the more conservatively inclined, many German Jews sympathetic to Reform emigrated to the United States, where they greatly strengthened the Reform cause.

The great leader of Reform Judaism in America was Isaac M. Wise, who arrived in the United States in 1846. He served as rabbi of a small congregation in Albany until 1854 and then spent the rest of his career in Cincinnati. His great concerns were to effect a national organization to give some unity to the independent Jewish congregations and to establish a college to train rabbis. Primarily through his efforts, the Union of American Hebrew Congregations was formed in 1873, and the Hebrew Union College was founded in 1875. His Reform views were promoted through the *American Israelite,* a paper that he founded and edited. In the area of doctrine, he discarded belief in a personal Messiah and in the resurrection of the dead. He also made a distinction between the Torah of God (the Ten Commandments) and the Torah of Moses (the rest of the Pentateuch), the latter being an application of divine truth to specific circumstances and becoming outdated as conditions changed. In terms of practice, he insisted upon equal rights for women (family pews, for example, instead of segregation by sex) and introduced into the service the use of both the English language and instrumental music. The prayer book he compiled was a simplification of the traditional liturgy modified to conform to his views. Other reformers were much more radical than Wise, making a sharper break with the past, introducing original prayers into the service, and substituting Sunday for Sabbath worship. Wise's adjustment to the problem posed by a Saturday morning service was to shift it to Friday evening, an innovation that had little support during the nineteenth century but that became the general practice by the middle of the twentieth century.

By 1880, Reform had become the dominant version of American Judaism, although a placid orthodoxy continued to find expression in scattered synagogues. The extent to which Reform leaders were willing to effect accommodation to American life, however, was soon to create a

---

[4] David Philipson, *The Reform Movement in Judaism* (New York, 1931), 122.

further division. The growing restiveness of a minority who were nominally within the Reform camp was brought to a head in 1883 by the serving of shrimp (a violation of the dietary laws) at a banquet honoring the first graduates of Hebrew Union College. This conduct produced a deep emotional shock among some of the more conservatively inclined. Rallied by Sabato Morais, the disaffected groups in 1886 founded the Jewish Theological Seminary in New York City, an institution that was to become the chief center of Conservative Judaism. Occupying a middle position between Reform and Orthodox Judaism, the Conservative synagogues did not prosper greatly until the atrocities of the Nazi era in Germany heightened the sense of Jewish identity and created a desire among Jews to reemphasize the historic continuities of Judaism.

The Great Immigration

The wave of Jewish immigrants who poured into the United States for three-and-one-half decades after 1880 introduced a new strain into American Judaism and changed the character of the whole community. In 1880, there were 250,000 Jews in the United States,[5] mostly German in background, and widely dispersed throughout the country. Most of them were related to the synagogue, that is, to a Reform Temple. By 1914, the Jewish segment of the population numbered 3 million. This new Jewish population was markedly different in cultural background and represented a quite different type of Judaism. The recent arrivals were refugees from eastern Europe. They were poverty-stricken and heterogeneous. Because they came from different lands, their common Yiddish tongue was spoken in varied dialects. Although a few were distinguished scholars, some were illiterate, and most were without skills. Unlike the older Jewish inhabitants, they crowded into the eastern cities.

The Jewish flight from eastern Europe was a response to harsh anti-Semitic pressures and pogroms. In 1882, the Russian government issued a series of decrees designed to make Jewish life impossible. The objective was stated with cynical frankness by the Czar's most trusted advisor: "One-third of the Jews will emigrate, one-third will be baptized, and one-third will starve."[6] A similar policy was pursued elsewhere in eastern Europe, most notably in Romania and Galicia (Austrian Poland). The pressure continued with varying intensity until the outbreak of World War I.

Among Jews of eastern Europe, there were three responses to the tragic condition in which they found themselves. The majority, without hope of

---

[5] Interpretation of Jewish statistics is complicated by the fact that until well into the twentieth century, numbers were computed in terms of "heads of families." Nor are Jewish statistics comparable to those of most other religious bodies, for they usually refer to total Jewish population rather than to synagogue membership.

[6] Bernard Jacob Bamberger, *The Story of Judaism* (New York, 1957), 324.

securing full status as citizens through the political and social assimilation in the lands of their birth, retreated into rigid orthodoxy, finding inner security in unquestioning piety and strict observance of the Torah. Their cultural outlook was little affected by cultural movements among the peoples about them. A second group, those who had some contact with contemporary thought, reacted in a fashion quite different from that of the Jews of Germany and America. Instead of seeking to create a Reform Judaism that would be consonant with modern culture, they tended to renounce Judaism and identify themselves with radical antireligious movements of social reform. The passion and intensity with which the religious Jews of eastern Europe clung to traditional forms of thought and practice made the prospect of altering these forms seem hopeless, whereas the political structures were so repressive and class-oriented that only a thoroughgoing social revolution seemed to offer the possibility of emancipation. Emerging from this second group was a third faction, rather insignificant at the outset, which cast its revolutionary fervor into a nationalistic mold. Taking their cue from the liberation movements of Poles, Czechs, Ukrainians, and other oppressed peoples of eastern Europe, these "Lovers of Zion" emphasized the national rather than the religious character of Judaism and began to think in terms of securing emancipation through the establishment of the Jewish state. Each group was represented in the east European immigration.

Nathan Glazer has reported that the Jewish immigrants who came from eastern Europe were "a frightening apparition" to "the established, middle-class, Americanized German Jews of the 1880s."

> Their poverty was more desperate than German Jewish poverty, their piety more intense than German Jewish piety, their irreligion more violent than German Jewish irreligion, their radicalism more extreme than German Jewish radicalism. It is not surprising that the American Jews viewed this immigration with mixed feelings, and some even suggested the possibility of deflecting or preventing it.

The American Jews did not know which was the most objectionable: the strident orthodoxy of the immigrants (as distasteful to the dignified Orthodox who opposed Reform as it was to the adherents of Reform synagogues), the antireligious views of the social radicals, or the political separatism of the Jewish nationalists. By the end of the century, however, the antipathy had been pushed sufficiently to one side for the leaders of the other Jewish communities to engage in strenuous efforts to "uplift" the immigrants and ease their adjustment to American life. One specific project of considerable future significance was the injection of new life into the Jewish Theological Seminary, which had slowly been dying as its original base of tradition-oriented synagogues had dwindled. Under the leadership of Cyrus Adler, the financial support of Reform Jews was enlisted to transform the seminary into an agency for "civilizing" the east Europeans by providing them with modern, English-speaking rabbis. A fund of more than $500,000 was collected for this purpose. Solomon Schechter was brought from England to be the new president, and a distinguished faculty was assembled.

Reconstructionism and Zionism

By 1920, 80 percent or more of the Jewish population in the United States was of east European descent, and adherents of Reform Judaism were far outnumbered by members of Orthodox synagogues. Those unaffiliated with any synagogue, however, exceeded the combined totals of all religious Jews, and the proportion of the unaffiliated was growing. The flight from Judaism, which had begun in the old country, was accelerated as a con-comitant of the process of Americanization. Repelled by the "foreignness" of the religious observances of their parents, children of Orthodox immigrants drifted into an indifference to religion. Few exhibited any inclination to transfer their loyalties to more modern synagogues. The results of a 1935 survey in New York City, which revealed that approximately 75 percent of Jewish young people between the ages of 15 and 25 had attended no religious service during the preceding year, were not regarded as atypical.[7] Social centers, growing out of such social agencies as the settlement houses and the Young Men's and Young Women's Hebrew Associations, were more often the focal points of Jewish life than the synagogues.

A creative response to this situation was the Reconstructionist movement led by Mordecai M. Kaplan of Jewish Theological Seminary. Kaplan's views evolved out of the synagogue center movement, which he had initiated in 1918. Others had experimented with making the synagogue more attractive by developing "institutional" temples patterned after the institutional churches of the Protestants, but Kaplan's aim was a new type of Jewish community, with its focus not religion but "Jewishness." His approach to religion was sociological. He sought to strengthen Judaism by relating it closely to all aspects of Jewish life—political, cultural, intellectual, and philanthropic. His central contention, fully elaborated in *Judaism as a Civilization* (1934), was that Judaism was not a religion but a religious civilization in which nonreligious as well as religious Jews shared. The synagogue should be the rallying center of Jewish people and Jewish culture, even for those who did not feel strongly about Jewish religion. Traditional rituals and ceremonies were viewed as important for their instrumental value as cement that helped bind the Jewish people together. In Kaplan's thinking, there was little place for the supernatural: "To modern man, religion can no longer be a matter of entering into a relationship with the supernatural. The only kind of religion that can help him live and get the most out

---

[7] Glazer, 85.

Jewish celebration of Sukkoth, a seven-day festival in the fall, is shown in this photograph from 1908. The occasion, which remembers the Israelite trek in the wilderness of Sinai, "living on the move," was especially meaningful for Jews who had moved to America. *(Corbis.)*

of life will be the one which will teach him to identify as divine or holy whatever in human nature or in the world about him enhances life."[8]

Conservative Judaism, with its ambivalent stance between Reform and Orthodox Judaism, was best equipped to assimilate Kaplan's Reconstructionist emphasis upon both traditionalism and modernity. In general, the Conservative synagogues adopted Kaplan's policy of fostering a broad, inclusive Jewishness while rejecting the more radical features of his philosophy.

Closely allied to Kaplan's view of Judaism as a civilization was the older Zionist view of Judaism as a nation. Zionism had east European roots among the nineteenth-century "Lovers of Zion" but was given its more definitive

[8] Mordecai Kaplan, *The Meaning of God in Modern Jewish Religion* (New York, 1985).

shape by Theodor Herzl, a Viennese reporter who was present in Paris at the trial of Captain Alfred Dreyfus. In 1894, Dreyfus had been falsely charged with treason and was subsequently convicted, a victim of virulent anti-Semitic feeling in the French army. In a state of high emotional excitement, Herzl wrote a pamphlet entitled *The Jewish State* (1896). The only salvation for Jews, he insisted, was national rebirth. This undertaking necessitated a homeland, preferably in Palestine. Herzl was hailed by many as a prophet, and in 1897, the first World Zionist Congress was held in Basel, Switzerland.

The Zionist issue became the subject of prolonged debate. Although Zionist leaders tended to be nonreligious, many Orthodox Jews embraced Zionism, since it could be reconciled with the ancient expectation of the restoration of Israel. Conservative Jews had even fewer reservations and tended to become ardent Zionists. Reform Jews, on the other hand, were generally hostile, viewing Judaism as a religion and advocating a policy of assimilation at other points. After Hitler's persecution of the Jews began in 1933 and thousands of German Jews emigrated to Palestine, the Zionist question became much less theoretical. By 1935, a majority of the Reform rabbis had moved into the Zionist camp, and in that year the Central Conference of American Rabbis abandoned its official policy of opposition to Zionism and adopted in its stead a position of neutrality. The subsequent Holocaust, in which 6 million Jews were murdered by the Nazi state, further strengthened both the Zionist cause and the sense of Jewish solidarity. When the State of Israel was established in 1948, American Jews rallied to ensure its survival by raising astonishingly large sums through the United Jewish Appeal to aid the resettlement of refugees who were streaming into Israel from many parts of the world.[9]

Jewish Religious Revivals at Midcentury

Although the Hitler years heightened Jewish self-consciousness and drew many into participation in Jewish activities, there was no great return to the synagogue. The surge of growth in synagogue membership was to be a phenomenon of the post–World War II period. In 1937, the American Jewish Year Book estimated that the Reform congregations had 50,000 member families. The Conservative congregations, having gained recruits from the children and grandchildren of Orthodox immigrants, numbered some 75,000 member families. The Orthodox congregations had the largest constituency, with about 200,000 families. Thus the combined synagogue membership represented between 1 and 1.5 million Jews, not much more than one-fourth of all the Jews in the country. By 1956, there was a marked change. Synagogue life was flourishing, with most of the gains having been made in the last decade. Member families of Reform temples numbered

---

[9] The total amount raised in 1948 was $201 million. In subsequent years the amount declined, but in 1955, it still exceeded $100 million.

255,000, a fivefold increase over 1937. The growth rate of Conservative synagogues was smaller, but their member families had almost tripled in number and stood at 200,000. Although Orthodox Judaism was a declining portion of the Jewish religious community, it too was exhibiting signs of vigorous life, and its intellectual center, Yeshiva College, had become a flourishing university.

Apart from numbers, there was a marked increase in the practice of piety. The proportion of Jewish population attending religious services at least once a month increased from 18 percent in 1947 to 31 percent in 1955. Even among Reform Jews there was a strong tendency to reemphasize traditional values, customs, and ceremonies. The Friday evening family Kiddush with its candle lighting became more common, and holidays were more widely observed. In the mid-1950s, it was said somewhat skeptically that the modern Jew "does more" but "knows less." This verdict was scarcely supported by available evidence. Not only had there been a vast increase in the number of children receiving a Jewish education through weekday classes, the Sunday school, and Jewish day schools, but also publishers had discovered that there was a growing market among adults for books dealing with Jewish theology and religious life.

The revival of synagogue life may have been related to a change in the Jewish community. In the 1930s, Jews had been predominantly working class in status, but by the 1950s, only a small segment could be classified as blue-collar workers. As a result of a zeal for education, second- and third-generation east European Jews were successful in imitating earlier Jewish immigrants by moving into business and the professions. Their children and grandchildren also shifted their place of residence from the inner city to better neighborhoods and then to the suburbs. Having become a more homogeneous and prosperous community, mid-twentieth-century Jews tended to conform to the churchgoing pattern of other middle-class Americans. They conformed in other ways as well: in their denominationalism, in the lay control and autonomy of congregational life (there was no "chief rabbi" as in Europe), and in their activism and emphasis on Judaism as a "way of life," not as doctrine.

By 1960, there were stirrings of a deeper religious concern. On university campuses some Jewish students, reacting against the affluent lifestyle and the seeming spiritual void represented by suburban temples, began to exhibit interest in discussing Jewish mysticism, spiritual discipline, and personal faith. A few sought to develop a renewed or parallel Judaism of their own in communes or "covenanted" communities. Although older members of the Jewish community did not resort to such drastic solutions, many shared the same longing for meaning that transcended their daily routine.

The establishment of the State of Israel also posed a problem for thoughtful Jews. It pushed to the fore the issue of defining Judaism in more specifically religious terms. Attachment to the land of Israel and hope for eventual return, whether Judaism was religiously or culturally defined, had been one of the bonds of Jews of the Diaspora (dispersion).

When it became clear that millions of Jews chose to remain where they were when the way to return was open, the need for a rationale for a continuing Diaspora became urgent. If a cultural Judaism was unable to satisfy the spiritual hunger of individuals, it was equally unrealistic to expect Jews in America to find a meaningful existence merely by living vicariously in another land. They had to live where they were, and no emotional tie to Israel, however strong, could provide the meaning derived from a common religious vocation to which Jews everywhere had a contribution to make.

With astonishing rapidity, Jewish scholars began to mine the rich resources of Jewish mystical piety. Some younger Jews were especially drawn to the Hasidic mystical enthusiasm that had its beginnings in eighteenth-century eastern Europe, attracted partly by the countercultural aspects of Hasidic communal life, but more interested in the Hasidic experience of encounter with God than in rituals and customs. Martin Buber had explicated the teachings of the Hasidic masters,[10] but youthful Jews set about exploring the riches of Hasidic texts for themselves. The mystical piety of Abraham Heschel, who had insisted that Jews by attuning their "yearning to the lonely holiness of this world" will "aid humanity more than by any particular service," became more influential than hitherto.[11] The issue of vocation, so important to Jews of the Diaspora, was a central concern for a group of distinguished scholars, including Eugene Borowitz, Norman Lamm, and Seymour Siegel. Known as "Covenant theologians," they defined the Jewish people in terms of a relationship with God, insisting that God established a special covenant with the Jews that imposes on them a special vocation that has relevance and meaning for all humanity. If Vatican II was to open windows and allow fresh air to penetrate the closed confines of Roman Catholicism, it is clear that a freshness of thought and a deepening of spirituality was also penetrating a Judaism that was in danger of ceasing to be a living religion.

Eastern Orthodox Christianity

The Eastern Orthodox churches also have a long history.[12] They look back to the early Christian Fathers, and to Athanasius, the Cappadocians, Pseudo-Dionysius, and "the seven ecumenical councils" as the source of their tradition. Perhaps Orthodox Christianity can best be identified in

---

[10] Martin Buber, *Hasidism and Modern Man* (New York, 1958).

[11] For a moving account of his views and lively faith, see Abraham Heschel, *The Earth Is the Lord's* (New York, 1950), and also *Man Is Not Alone* (New York, 1951).

[12] See Nicolas Zernov, *Eastern Christendom* (London, 1961); Ernst Benz, *The Eastern Orthodox Church: Its Thought and Life* (Chicago, 1963); and Timothy Ware, *The Orthodox Church* (Baltimore, 1963).

terms of the two separations that gave the Orthodox churches their geographical locus. The first separation, which took place in the fifth and
sixth centuries, was that of the smaller eastern churches—the Nestorians
of Syria, Persia, and ultimately China, and the Monophysites (the Jacobite
and Coptic churches) of Armenia, Syria, Egypt, and Ethiopia. The second
separation was the product of a growing cleavage between the Greek-
speaking and the Latin-speaking areas of the old Roman Empire. Although the ecclesiastical division was beginning to be apparent as early as
the sixth century, the final separation is commonly dated from 1054. As a
result of these two separations, Eastern Orthodoxy was bounded on the
east and the west, but it was able to expand to the north among the Slavic
peoples. As the Greek power of Byzantium dwindled, the newer Orthodox
churches of the north increased in importance. After the fall of Constantinople in 1453, Moscow—"the third Rome"—tended to assume Byzantium's role as protector of the Orthodox world.

The Orthodox Churches

Distributed throughout eastern Europe, in Russia, and along the eastern
coast of the Mediterranean, Orthodox Christianity is a family of self-
governing churches, united by a common faith and order. Apart from
areas of more recent expansion, these churches are the ancient Patriarchates of Constantinople, Alexandria, Antioch, and Jerusalem; the national churches of Russia, Romania, Serbia, Greece, Bulgaria, Georgia,
Cyprus, the Czech Republic, Slovakia, Poland, and Albania; and the Holy
Monastery of Sinai. Although the Patriarch of Constantinople is known as
the Ecumenical or Universal Patriarch and enjoys a position of special
honor, he has no power to intervene in the affairs of any church other
than his own. His position is much like that of the Archbishop of Canterbury in the Anglican communion, which is also composed of self-governing
churches spread throughout the world. Because the overwhelming proportion of Orthodox Christians (perhaps as many as 55 million) were for
many years behind the "iron curtain," it is difficult to estimate their total
number. The four ancient Patriarchates have more than 2.5 million adherents, and the churches of Greece and Cyprus have a combined total of almost 8 million adherents.

Although the Orthodox have much in common with Roman Catholics,
there are significant differences in emphasis, practice, and even doctrine.
The whole mood is much more mystical and much less legalistic. The
mode of baptism is triple immersion. Communion is in both kinds, the
communicant receiving both the bread and the wine. Infants are confirmed and receive communion immediately after being baptized. Because
statues (rounded images) are not permitted, in their stead, icons (paint-
ings and mosaics) are used. Priests may marry prior to ordination, but

bishops must be unmarried. The date of Easter is different (being reckoned by the Julian rather than the Gregorian calendar), and church architecture is distinctive. The doctrines of purgatory and the immaculate conception of Mary are not generally accepted; and instead of extreme unction for the dying, the sick are anointed for the recovery of health. The most crucial difference is the authority that Roman Catholicism confers upon the Roman Pontiff as the vicar of Christ and the infallible teacher and ruler of the faithful. Where Roman Catholics insist upon obedience to the Bishop of Rome, Orthodox Christians stress the role of the bishops in the government of the church and the authority of General Councils in the determination of matters of faith.

Orthodoxy in America

Eastern Orthodoxy had it beginnings in North America when missionary monks came to Alaska in the 1790s and succeeded in converting many of the natives. A seminary was established at Sitka in 1848, and a diocese was formed in 1867 when Alaska became a territory of the United States. In 1872, the seat of the diocese was transferred to San Francisco, and in 1905, to New York. In addition to the Russians, a few Greek communities had churches prior to 1900, but the major Orthodox influx came after the turn of the century. During the latter years of the great Jewish immigration, Slavic peoples (and Romanians) were also arriving from eastern Europe. Many of the non-Jewish east Europeans were Roman Catholic, but a large portion were Orthodox. Unlike the Jews, these other east Europeans did not crowd into the coastal cities. They had been recruited to labor in the mines and steel mills, and hence they were dispersed throughout Pennsylvania and along the periphery of the Great Lakes. The significant exception to this pattern of Orthodox settlement was represented by non-Slavic immigrants, principally Greeks and Syrians (including Armenians), who, as independent entrepreneurs, were widely scattered throughout the country.

From a total membership of not more than 100,000 in 1900, the number of Orthodox in the United States had risen to more than 2 million in 1960,[13] subdivided into at least fifteen national or jurisdictional groups. Before World War I, all Orthodox Christians in America were under the jurisdiction of the Russian church, since it was the Russians who first brought Orthodox Christianity to the United States. The subsequent multiplicity of jurisdictions was a consequence of the Russian Revolution of

---

[13] According to the *Year Book of the American Churches*, the total in 1960 was 2,680,633. This figure is no more than an approximation, for Orthodoxy, like Judaism, has tended to estimate its adherents in terms of total ethnic or national groups. Membership is generally reported in round numbers.

1917. With the Russian church becoming involved in a difficult and controversial relationship to the new Soviet regime, each of the Orthodox nationality groups formed separate organizations.

The Orthodox churches in America had a confused history in the post–World War I years as a result of the readjustments that then took place. The Greek church has been the largest (1.5 million members in 1962) and most stable, but it was troubled by such disorders and frictions that it was not until 1930 that its life was fully regularized as the Greek Archdiocese of North and South America. The Russians experienced a fourfold split based mostly on varying interpretations of their relationship to the Patriarch of Moscow. The Ukrainians in America not only separated from the Russians, but they also suffered a threefold division among themselves. The Albanian, Bulgarian, Romanian, Serbian, and Syrian Orthodox were not fragmented, but their churches did not become fully stabilized in organization until around 1930.

Troubled by cultural and administrative divisions, the Orthodox churches in America gained stability only after World War II. Several theological seminaries were established, and those in New York and Boston became distinguished centers of theological scholarship. There also was evidence of growing sentiment for unity. In 1954, the Council of Eastern Orthodox Youth Leaders of America was formed and drew together most of the Orthodox youth organizations; and in 1960, a committee of Orthodox bishops began periodic meetings under the presidency of the Greek archbishop. The Orthodox churches also exhibited vitality in adjusting to the American environment. The use of English in worship, the introduction of mixed choirs and instrumental music, the installation of pews, the development of parish organizations, and the adoption of church dinners as an important aspect of church life were the kind of adaptation that other immigrant bodies had made prior to becoming integrated into American life. There were several attempts, mostly by former Episcopalians, to form an indigenous Orthodox church that would be at the same time both more American and more "catholic," and thus would attract converts from other traditions. These attempts met with little success, received little encouragement from Orthodox leaders, and enlisted only a handful of adherents.

"Disaffected" Protestants

One consequence of religious liberty is the opportunity for disaffection to find free and open expression. Many groups born of disaffection in the nineteenth century lived on into the twentieth century, some growing in strength, others declining. Among those that have been discussed in preceding chapters are Mormonism, Millerism, and Spiritualism;

New Thought, Christian Science, and Unity; Theosophy, Baha'i, and the Vedanta Society. But other groups were to have a surge of growth in the post–World War I years. Of these, with the exception of the Fundamentalist movement, the Holiness and Pentecostal churches and Jehovah's Witnesses were perhaps the most conspicuous. These latter groups were more traditional in orientation than those previously considered. One might refer to them as "sects" rather than "cults."[14] They are best described as disaffected Protestants, for they claimed no new revelation and their intention was to recover past tradition.

The Holiness Movement

The quest for perfect sanctification or holiness is as old as Christianity. In nineteenth-century America it had received powerful reinforcement from the generally optimistic temper of the time ("Jacksonian perfectionism"), from the hunger for holiness generated by the revivals, and from the pervasive influence of the strong Wesleyan emphasis upon the doctrine of Christian perfection.[15] Among the non-Methodists who responded to this "perfectionist" climate of opinion, Charles G. Finney and his colleagues at Oberlin were the most prominent. Beginning in 1839, the Oberlin group exhibited a growing interest in "the higher Christian life," and through their influence the concern for sanctification penetrated most Protestant denominations during the decades immediately preceding and following the Civil War.[16] The holiness revival, however, found its preeminent expression among Methodists, where it was sparked in the North by the enthusiasm of a remarkable woman, Phoebe Palmer, and where it gained

[14] As is true of many words, "cult" and "sect" have a variety of meanings. In this context, "cult" is used to denote those groups that are based on a claim to new revelation and/or the authoritative teaching of a new prophet. A cult tends to be forward-looking and frequently is eager to come to terms with what is considered to be "modern" thought. On the other hand, "sect" (from the Latin *secta*, which means "school of thought") is used to denote groups that make no claim to new revelation but instead seek to recover what they regard as an important but neglected aspect of past tradition. In the process, they emerge as new and separate incarnations of tradition.

[15] Wesleyan perfectionism was defined by nineteenth-century Methodists in terms of a "second blessing"—a work of grace (sanctification) subsequent to conversion (justification) that imparted perfect love of God and liberation from sin. Wesley never claimed sanctification for himself, and sometimes he seemed to imply that it was the culmination of a growth in grace rather than an instantaneous experience. For Wesley's views, see Harold Lindström, *Wesley and Sanctification*, trans. H. S. Harvey (London, 1946).

[16] For Asa Mahan's statement of the Oberlin views, see selection in H. Shelton Smith, Robert Handy, and Lefferts Loetscher, *American Christianity*, II, 42–48. Wesleyan and Oberlin perfectionism had much in common, but the former tended to stress the instantaneous change wrought by the "second blessing," whereas the latter emphasized the more gradual change resulting from growth in grace. See Timothy L. Smith, *Revivalism and Social Reform* (New York, 1957), 108–12, and J. L. Peters, *Christian Perfectionism and American Methodism* (New York, 1956).

momentum through her evangelistic tours and through the organizational efforts of the National Association for the Promotion of Holiness. In the South, Mary Cagle contributed similar energy to the movement.

Methodism as a whole continued to be concerned with the quest for holiness in the latter half of the nineteenth century.[17] In spite of this unanimity, it was nonetheless a potentially disruptive emphasis, for it tended to cultivate an absolutist state of mind that brooked no compromise. This tendency was illustrated by the Wesleyan Methodist defection of 1843, which demanded moral perfection on the slavery issue. After the Civil War, the disruptive issue was the growing "worldliness" of Methodists.

Methodists had been a plain people—plain in dress, behavior, and worship. But as Methodism gained in numbers, wealth, social status, and signs of laxity began to appear. As early as 1856, the stringent rules prohibiting the use of specific items of dress were reduced in the *Discipline* to a general admonition—an admonition that was not sufficiently rigorous to deter Bishop Matthew Simpson's wife from appearing in ruffled silk, expensive lace, and fine jewelry. A similar loss of simplicity in worship occurred as costly edifices were built and as choirs, organs, and instrumental music were introduced. A correspondent of the *Christian Advocate* reported in 1868 that in the cities of the western states—in Ohio, Indiana, Michigan, Wisconsin, Illinois, and Iowa—the tendency was to erect "one hundred thousand dollar churches" where "wealth and style and fashion gather, and the poor have not the gospel preached to them." Two years earlier a writer in the same journal had noted with satisfaction that "by virtue of the habits which religion inculcates and cherishes, our church members have as a body risen in the social scale, and thus become socially removed from the great body out of which most of them were originally gathered." Although he regarded this development as "natural" and "not undesirable," there were some who regarded it as a betrayal of the summons to holiness.[18] By the end of the century, grievances were multiplying, with notice being taken of the "church theatricals" and "fairs" that were being held and of the increasing number of church members who "dance, play cards, attend theaters, [and] absent themselves from revivals."[19]

A foretaste of what was to be a continuing disaffection was supplied in 1860 with the formation of the Free Methodist Church at Pekin, New York. Taking its stance on the declaration that "those who are sanctified wholly are saved from all inward sin" and "all their thoughts, words, and actions are governed by pure love," the new church proceeded to denounce the

[17] Southern bishops constantly emphasized this theme, and northern bishops were equally firm, declaring in 1884 that "the mission of Methodism is to promote holiness." E. S. Bucke, ed., *The History of American Methodism* (New York, 1964), II, 614–18.

[18] W. C. Barclay, *History of Methodist Missions*, Vol. III (New York, 1957), 49; Henry F. May, *Protestant Churches and Industrial America* (New York, 1949), 62.

[19] Barclay, II, 624.

proud and aspiring, to voice opposition to all "superficial, false, and fashionable" Christians, and to demand of church members an affirmative response to the question "Will you forever lay aside all superfluous ornaments and adorn yourself in modest apparel . . . , not with broidered hair or gold or pearls or costly array?" Organs, instrumental music, and pew rentals were also condemned.[20]

The Free Methodist revolt was restricted to three relatively small areas in western New York, Michigan, and Illinois; but in the 1880s, evidence of more widespread disaffection found expression in the formation of numerous independent Holiness groups throughout much of rural America, and in some urban contexts as well. Although some of these "come-outer" groups were composed of people from various denominations, the larger portion were formed by dissident Methodists. By the 1890s, local fellowships had begun to coalesce into larger groupings. Most were to remain numerically unimportant, but a few were to exhibit a capacity for sustained growth during the first half of the twentieth century. One of these was the Church of God (Anderson, Indiana), founded in 1881 with a dual stress of holiness and Christian unity. From its initial base in the rural Midwest, it spread gradually into the South and to the Pacific coast. Another group, the Christian and Missionary Alliance, was founded by a Presbyterian minister, A. B. Simpson, in New York City in 1887. But the most successful was the Church of the Nazarene, established by a Methodist district superintendent at Los Angeles in 1895, which numbered 874,000 members by 1988. By this date the Holiness groups, including the Salvation Army, had a total membership of more than 2.5 million.[21]

Pentecostalism

Pentecostalism emerged out of various healing and holiness movements of the late nineteenth century. Although there are some accounts of scattered incidences of the signature pentecostalist "spirit baptism" within those movements (especially among students of C. F. Parham's Topeka Bible College in 1901), the genesis of the pentecostal movement is associated with worship at the Azusa Street Church in Los Angeles in the spring of 1906. The "speaking in tongues," or glossolalia, that was practiced by the worshipers there was taken as a sign of the presence of the Holy Spirit in that community, and specifically as an indication of individuals being "baptized" or "filled" with the Holy Spirit.

Pentecostalism embraced a restorationist view of history. That is, pentecostals sought to restore the practice of the primitive Christian religion, so as to form a religious community uncomplicated by church history and

---

[20] Ibid., 346, 352, 356, 357n., 359.

[21] See Timothy L. Smith, *Called unto Holiness: The Story of the Nazarenes* (Kansas City, Mo., 1962).

the various sediments of sacramental, clerical, and doctrinal tradition that had accumulated over the centuries. Pentecostals wanted a church free of the distracting and corrupting baggage of church history, and they derived from scripture an outline of what that church was in the first century of Christianity. As described by a sympathetic observer, Bennett F. Lawrence, in 1916, "This movement has no history. It leaps the intervening years, crying 'back to Pentecost.'" For Pentecostals, the vitality and authority of the primitive church rested above all in the events of Pentecost, when followers of Jesus who gathered for prayer shortly after his death experienced the "gifts" of the Holy Spirit. Those gifts, sometimes called the "latter rain," included healing, prophecy, miracles, and various other capabilities in addition to speaking in tongues. For many Pentecostals, the yearning for the experience of regeneration was intensified by their belief that the end of the world and the coming of Christ were imminent. Those who were not baptized in the Holy Spirit would suffer the terrible tribulations of the end times while the saved escaped them through the miracle of the "rapture."[22]

Several of the leaders of the Azusa Street revival in 1906 were students of Parham. William J. Seymour, an African American who received a minister's license from Parham earlier that year, was at the center of the revival as it built slowly over several months before finally attracting the attention of the press and the criticism of observers, including Parham, who denounced it in racist terms. The revival continued to grow, however, at Azusa Street and other missions in the neighborhood, claiming thousands of persons in its first few years. The meetings were, moreover, diverse in terms of the backgrounds of the participants. Whites and blacks, Native Americans, and persons of Mexican, Asian and Eastern European backgrounds joined the revival. Those who participated in the revival were less diverse in terms of their social status, however. Most came from farm families, had experienced economic misfortune, and had experienced social disapproval of their habitation of the periphery of the culture. Their embrace of the "apostolic faith" of Pentecostalism moved them even further to the periphery. Some of those who joined the revival, however, were of middle-class background. Their involvement in the first decade of the Pentecostal movement forecasted the shape of the movement at the end of the century, when Pentecostalism's embrace of popular culture represented its movement off the margins and towards the center of American life.[23]

The transformation of Pentecostalism in America over the course of the twentieth century has much to do with the fact that it "has always been an

---

[22] Edith Blumhofer, *Restoring the Faith: The Assemblies of God, Pentecostalism, and American Culture* (Urbana, Ill., 1993), 12–16, and Lawrence quoted, 13.

[23] Robert Mapes Anderson, *Vision of the Disinherited: The Making of American Pentecostalism* (New York, 1979); Grant Wacker, *Heaven Below: Early Pentecostals and American Culture* (Cambridge, Mass., 2001), 199–216.

audience-conscious popular expression of Christianity."[24] Its inclination toward the mainstream of American popular culture, characterized above all by its determination to present religion as a matter of mass appeal, has profoundly shaped its short history. Although in its early years it was often linked with a dim premillennial view of the future, it soon manifested a more positive and upbeat expression of religious faith, one that represented Pentecostals' sense of personal regeneration (complete sanctification), collective righteousness, and the spiritual legitimacy of life in the world. Pentecostals came to believe that God, through the Holy Spirit, had regenerated them and wanted them to prosper in the world into which He had placed them. Pentecostals who once saw the truth of their religion in terms of its modest numbers and its propagation of small, close-knit communities gradually came to believe that its genuineness and promise were to be evaluated precisely on the basis of its mass appeal, its dissemination throughout the population, urban and rural, rich and poor, black and white, North and South. Pentecostalism accordingly has vigorously appropriated the genres, themes, and technologies of popular culture in attempting to communicate its message to a wide audience. The "parallel" popular culture that they began to create in the second half of the twentieth century includes counterparts of the television programs, concerts, musical recordings, business manuals and self-help books, diet programs, sporting events, fashion, and other aspects of the secular culture, all massaged in such a way as to reflect a Christian viewpoint. Pentecostalism by the late twentieth century firmly embraced the culture of the Protestant middle class. One observer noted the following in analyzing the development of American Pentecostalism: "Since God's Holy Spirit did everything, Holy Spirit–filled Christians did nothing. But since Holy Spirit–filled Christians did nothing, they were free to do everything. That conviction, as inspiring as it was ironic, gave saints the two greatest goods that mortal existence had to offer: the life beyond in all its fullness, and the life at hand in all its richness. It was heaven below."[25]

The rapid growth of Pentecostalism and the consistent emphases on feeling and the display of emotion, alongside the overall adaptability and even malleability of the movement, have contributed towards its loose approach to doctrine. The essential features of the movement—salvation through Jesus Christ, entire sanctification, baptism in the Holy Spirit, and the evidence of tongues—historically have been sufficient for belief. Theological aspects of belief beyond those features might be the subject of discussion among individuals or occasionally might inspire ministerial quarrels, but for the most part, the history of the movement has not been marked by attempts to enforce acceptance of a detailed theological code.

---

[24] Blumhofer, 7.

[25] Wacker, 268–9; and "Pentecostalism" in *Encyclopedia of the American Religious Experience*, ed. Charles H. Lippy and Peter W. Williams (New York, 1988), 937–941. Blumhofer, 7–8.

For most of its life, Pentecostalism has remained flexible and adaptable, and at times it has even appeared to drift in the various currents of Protestant culture.

The institutional development of Pentecostalism is characterized both by the proliferation of independent congregations and the emergence of large denominations. The Azusa Street mission became a nursery of Pentecostal leadership, with Florence Crawford establishing headquarters in Portland, Oregon, and C. H. Mason and C. B Cashwell planting the seed in what proved to be the highly receptive soil of Appalachia. Located in Memphis, the mostly African American Church of God in Christ, the oldest Pentecostal denomination, was shaped and nurtured by Mason. The Church of God, the second oldest Pentecostal denomination, probably began in 1902 on the heels of the Camp Creek, North Carolina, Holiness revival. Moved by A. J. Tomlinson to Cleveland, Tennessee, in 1907, the church shares its name with several other Pentecostal groups located elsewhere. The Pentecostal Holiness Church took shape in 1911 as the merger of several Holiness churches in the Carolinas. It was headquartered in Georgia before relocating to Oklahoma City in 1973.[26]

A different sort of process led to the organizing of the Assemblies of God (AG), the nation's largest Pentecostal denomination.[27] As the blending of groups from several states, the denomination began as a conference of over one hundred delegates from Pentecostal congregations in Hot Springs, Arkansas, in 1914. The conference did not frame a statement of faith and put off a formal constitution until 1927. But the Assemblies of God flourished as an umbrella organization over ministries, which were scattered throughout the nation, that looked to the imminent Second Coming, embraced healing and evangelism, sought the evidence of tongues, and took a restorationist approach to religious life.[28] After several false starts, the group settled its headquarters in Springfield, Missouri, in 1918, and eventually developed ambitious missions, educational, and publications programs. It also experienced setbacks, especially in the form of scandals involving its leadership. In the 1980s, as the denomination was embracing the celebrity of its ministers and its reputation as a church for those who were successful in "this world," it was rocked by revelations of financial and sexual improprieties involving two of its most important leaders, Jim Bakker of North Carolina and Jimmy Swaggart of Louisiana. The Assemblies of God, however, has demonstrated its adaptability over the

---

[26] Wacker, "Pentecostalism," 938–942.

[27] The adult membership was calculated as 1.1 million in 2001 (Barry A. Kosmin, Egon Mayer, and Ariela Keysar, *American Religious Identification Survey* [2001]). The church itself claims over 2.5 million members nationally (of all ages). A note on the problems in counting pentecostals is in Wacker, *Heaven Below*, 271–2. Blumhofer reports that the worldwide membership of the Assemblies of God is 23 million (*Restoring the Faith*, 260).

[28] Blumhofer details the founding of the denomination in connection with its interest in restoring primitive Christianity (*Restoring the Faith*, 112–141).

course of many years and in numerous crises. The number of those who identify themselves as AG members rose over 50 percent during the decade of the 1990s. The ability of the denomination to attract Hispanics, African Americans, and non-Anglo immigrants—as well as a white middle class—has been important to that growth and an indication of the continued success of the denomination in casting its message in a popular genre that has appeal across cultural lines.

Healing has been of central importance to the Pentecostal movement since it began. This focus is not surprising, given that the movement emerged at a time in American life when healing was of interest to Americans generally. By the late nineteenth century, a number of religious groups have established themselves as in various ways invested in health. Mary Baker Eddy's Christian Scientists looked to "demonstrations" of right knowledge in healing. Mormonism, strongly influenced by Thomsonian ideas about diet and health, established a dietary code for its membership alongside a program of healing through prayer and the laying on of hands. Ellen G. White, the energetic prophetess of Seventh-Day Adventism, linked diet, prayer, and health as part of a program for preparing for the Second Coming of Christ. Pentecostal healing, which was grounded in faith in the gifts of the Holy Spirit, is one aspect of the orientation to healing in various parts of the nation's religious culture. Its role in Pentecostalism has waxed and waned over the last century in much the same way as interest in healing in other religious groups has varied over the course of the last century.

One of the best-known Pentecostalist healers was Aimee Semple McPherson, founder of the Church of the Foursquare Gospel. An itinerant faith healer before and after World War I, she eventually settled in Los Angeles, where she founded the 5,000-seat Angelus Temple in 1923. Credentialed at various times by the Assemblies of God, Methodists, and Baptists, she preached a streamlined Pentecostal message of tongues and healing. With a magnetic personality, striking beauty, a flair for the dramatic, and an ability to turn the unfavorable publicity generated by her sensational adventures to her advantage, McPherson attracted a large following. Emphasizing Christ as Savior, Healer, Baptizer, and Soon-Coming King, Sister Aimee became the most visible Pentecostal leader of the 1920s, a star in a city known for its stars. Her tumultuous revivals set the terms for the performance of faith healing in Pentecostal communities throughout the twentieth century.

Millennialism

Although premillennial views were held by some Holiness and Pentecostal groups, other disaffected Protestants seized upon the expectation of Christ's return to judge the quick and the dead as their major theme. This emphasis offered both present and future consolation to those who felt alienated by the "fashionable" churches of the privileged classes. Part of the comfort was the assurance that the established denominations were clearly apostate, and further consolation was gained from the belief that the tables would soon be turned, with the mighty being put down and the humble exalted, the hunger being filled with good things and the rich sent away empty.

The "dispensationalism" of the Darbyites and the Scofield Bible (see Chapter 11) had made significant inroads among members of many of the older churches during the latter years of the nineteenth century, and after 1920, it produced a growing number of independent Bible churches and gospel tabernacles. It also contributed to Fundamentalist defections. An older premillennial tradition in America, stemming from the Millerite excitement of the 1840s, was represented by the Seventh-day Adventists and the smaller Advent Christian group. After maintaining a modest witness for more than half a century, the Seventh-day Adventists, who had been known chiefly for their sanitariums and for fathering the breakfast-food empires of the Kelloggs and the Posts, experienced a surge of new life in the twentieth century. From 62,211 members in 1906, they grew to 110,998 in 1926, to 237,168 in 1950, and to 317,852 in 1960. But these statistics tell less than half the story, for twice this number of Seventh-day Adventists were to be found outside the United States as a result of far-flung missionary endeavor. Quite surprising in view of their firm belief in the imminent end of the world was their heavy investment in publishing houses, hospitals, homes for the aged, and especially educational institutions. Not only did they maintain numerous academies, colleges, graduate schools, and both a theological seminary and a medical and dental school, they also established a widespread network of elementary schools. Noting their many good works, one observer has commented that seldom, while expecting a kingdom of God from heaven, has a group worked so diligently for one on earth.[29]

Of all the Adventist or millennial groups, Jehovah's Witnesses have been the most conspicuous and vigorous.[30] After the onset of the depression in 1929, the Witnesses often seemed omnipresent, selling the *Watchtower* on busy street corners and ringing doorbells endlessly in an effort to gain an opportunity to present their message of salvation. Then with the end of World War II, Kingdom Halls began to multiply. But it was their encounters with the law that gained the Witnesses most notoriety. Much of their trouble stemmed from their refusal to salute the flag, register for the draft, and permit their children to receive blood transfusions. Not only did these several refusals bring them before the courts, but they also served to engender a popular hostility that found expression in attempts to harry the Witnesses by charging them with minor infractions of municipal codes—

[29] Edwin S. Gaustad, *Historical Atlas of Religion in America* (New York, 1962), 115.

[30] H. H. Stroup, *The Jehovah's Witnesses* (New York, 1945); Marley Cole, *Jehovah's Witnesses* (New York, 1955); and J. A. Beckford, *The Trumpet of Prophecy* (New York, 1975).

disturbing the peace, trespassing, violating Sunday "blue laws," and peddling without a permit.

The Witnesses have been known under a variety of names—Millennial Dawnists, International Bible Students, the Watchtower Bible and Tract Society, Russellites, and Rutherfordites. The founder was Charles Taze ("Pastor") Russell, a haberdasher and member of a Congregational church in Allegheny, Pennsylvania, who had been troubled by the notion of eternal damnation and by doubts as to the reliability of the Bible. "Stumbling," as he put it, upon an adventist preacher, he found help that was sufficient to reestablish his "wavering faith." By 1872, Russell was meeting with a group of earnest Christians to examine the teaching of Scripture "relative to the coming of Christ and his kingdom."[31] Soon he had elaborated a millennial scheme of his own. In 1879, he began the publication of a magazine. The following year he published his first book, *Food for Thinking Christians.* In 1884, he formed his adherents into the Zion's Watch Tower Society. To disseminate his message, Russell trained "preachers" and issued a constant stream of publications, including a multivolumed *Studies in the Scriptures.* Attention was focused on 1914 as the year when "the kingdoms of this world" will be brought to an end and "the full establishment of the Kingdom of God will be accomplished."[32] When the year passed without the expected heavenly intervention, a reexamination of Scripture disclosed that it was Christ's return "in spirit" that had taken place in 1914, and that this event was a prelude to his visible return to lead the righteous into battle against the hosts of evil. This imminent Armageddon would mark the beginning of the millennium.

When Pastor Russell died in 1916, his following was not large, but positions of leadership in the Society were sufficiently coveted to occasion a severe struggle for power. The victor was Joseph Franklin ("Judge") Rutherford, legal counsel of the Society and Russell's attorney in his imbroglio over the sale of "miracle wheat." Judge Rutherford injected new life into the Society, substituted his writings for those of Pastor Russell, popularized the slogan "Millions now living will never die," introduced the name "Jehovah's Witnesses" (1931), and equipped the Witnesses with phonographs so that they could utilize transcriptions of his talks in their house-to-house calls. As before, it was a personality-centered operation, with Rutherford replacing Russell as the authoritative teacher and leader. All these features changed when Rutherford died in 1942. This time there was no "palace intrigue," no struggle for control, for a collective leadership took over and the "personality cult" was eliminated.[33] A board of directors assumed control with Nathan H. Knorr as president. Unsigned pronouncements replaced the writings of Rutherford, and the portable

---

[31] Stroup, 4, 6.

[32] Charles Taze Russell, *Jehovah's Witnesses in the Divine Purpose* (Brooklyn, 1959), 55.

[33] Cole, 107–8.

phonographs disappeared. Henceforth, the Witnesses were trained to do their own talking instead of relying on the transcribed voice of a leader.[34]

With Rutherford's death, Jehovah's Witnesses entered the period of their greatest growth. Activity was stepped up both at home and abroad. During World War II, the worldwide membership almost doubled, increasing from 115,240 to 207,552. The rate of growth was even greater during the next five years, with membership reaching 456,265 in 1952. By 1960, the number of Witnesses throughout the world was nearly 1 million, with the United States accounting for slightly more than one-quarter of the total.

The message, elaborated successively by Russell, Rutherford, and the directorate headed by Knorr, was calculated to appeal to the multiple resentments of those who were euphemistically described as the "culturally deprived." The central contention was that Satan's power is wielded through "the religious, commercial, and political combine" that is united in oppressing the righteous.[35] These three elements in society are so intimately linked that each does the bidding of the others. All these churches and religious organizations are "tools of Satan" and are utilized by the clergy as a means of securing cash income. The clergy both support and are supported by the proud and arrogant commercial class, which dominates, subjugates, and exploits the poor. The wealthy in turn are protected by the governments of the world, all of which are equally wicked, since they are ruled by Satan. The righteous, however, are not without hope, for the evils of the world are soon to be rectified at the battle of Armageddon when the forces of Jehovah led by Jesus will defeat the hosts of Satan.

Although few of the Holiness, Pentecostal, and millenarian groups were as direct or as comprehensive in their appeal to the frustrated and the resentful as were the Jehovah's Witnesses, they all tended to thrive among those who for one reason or another felt either alienated or disinherited. And since this was a common feeling among many upwardly mobile, lower-income Americans, these diverse expressions of disaffection—including the related Fundamentalist groups—represented a combined membership in 1960 of almost 8.5 million persons.

The Black Churches

In many ways, black religious life reflected the patterns and trends that prevailed in the general religious life of the nation. Most larger "white" denominations had black members. Some of these black members belonged

---

[34] Ibid., 211–12.
[35] See Stroup, 155–61.

to predominantly white congregations, but most were in separate black congregations. These "integrated" churches, however, accounted for only a small fraction of black church membership, for the overwhelming proportion of blacks belonged to black denominations. Outwardly these denominations closely resembled the churches of the white majority, but this outward resemblance was somewhat deceptive.

As a result of social forces to which blacks were subjected, a separate black world had been created. The black church was partly the product of this segregated society, with a distinctive life of its own.[36] The worship featured liturgical innovations designed to encourage group participation. The theology stressed both the consolations of heaven and the this-worldly promise of a near-approaching Day of Jubilee. Congregational singing was deeply moving. Both the emotional pitch of the services and their eschatological focus found expression in the "spirituals," which have been called the most original and enduring contribution of the black church.[37] With most avenues of social expression cut off and with the ministry one of the few professions open to blacks, the church assumed an importance that has seldom been duplicated among other groups.[38] Since there was little opportunity elsewhere for a black person to gain recognition and exercise authority, there often was a scramble for leadership. This highly competitive situation led to numerous schisms, withdrawals, and reorganizations. Black Methodists splintered into at least eight denominational bodies, the largest ones being the African Methodist Episcopal Church; the African Methodist Episcopal Church, Zion; and the Christian Methodist Episcopal Church. Perhaps as many as 70 percent of black church members were Baptists, and their strength is explained at least in part by the ease with which an individual pastor could pursue an independent course. But the Baptists suffered a major denominational schism in 1917 when the National Baptist Convention split into two rival organizations—the National Baptist Convention, Inc., and the National Baptist Convention of America. A later breach resulted in the Progressive National Baptist Convention.

The large-scale movement of black population into the major industrial centers of the nation, which began during World War I and continued

---

[36] See C. G. Woodson, *The History of the Negro Church* (Washington, D.C., 1945), and E. F. Frazier, *The Negro Church in America* (New York, 1974). For the ambivalent relationship to the larger American community, see G. S. Wilmore, *Black Religion and Black Radicalism* (New York, 1972); L. I. Sweet, *Black Images of America* (New York, 1976); and James M. Washington, *Frustrated Fellowship: The Black Baptist Quest for Social Power* (Macon, Ga. 1986).

[37] See Howard Thurman, *The Negro Spiritual Speaks of Life and Death* (New York, 1947), and D. J. Epstein, *Sinful Tunes and Spirituals: Black Folk Music to the Civil War* (Champaign, Ill., 1977).

[38] By the 1930s, a larger proportion of blacks were church members than was true of members of the white population.

thereafter at a steadily mounting tempo, introduced marked changes into black church life. Many urban churches became much more formal and restrained. The emotionalism of earlier days declined, "spirituals" were sung less frequently, and preaching, although still the foundation of church life, gave less emphasis to otherworldly aspects of the faith. Attention was increasingly devoted to advancing the interests of blacks through practical action. The Supreme Court decision of 1954, which put an end to the "separate but equal" doctrine in public education, triggered a massive civil rights movement in which the black churches played the predominant role. A spectacular illustration of this involvement was the bus boycott in Montgomery, Alabama, in 1955 to 1956, which was sparked by Rosa Parks's refusal to move to the back of the bus, was led by the local black clergy, and made Martin Luther King, Jr., a national figure. Subsequent "freedom rides" to eliminate discrimination in interstate travel, "sit-ins" and "demonstrations" to obtain equal access to public accommodations, and voter registration drives were usually planned and organized in the black churches, and often were led by their pastors.

The growing decorum and "worldliness" of many of the city churches produced much the same reaction among some of the new black urban dwellers as had occurred among segments of the white population. Tiny storefront churches, which had produced the intimacy and informality of the rural churches, multiplied, and the Holiness and Pentecostal movements found ready recruits among blacks who looked back with nostalgia to the uninhibited emotionalism of their childhood religious experience. A whole cluster of new black denominations emerged—the Church of God in Christ, Christ's Sanctified Holy Church, Church of the Living God, House of the Lord, Apostolic Over-coming Holy Church of God, Fire-Baptized Holiness Church of God, Triumph the Church and Kingdom of God, Church of Our Lord Jesus Christ of the Apostolic Faith, Bible Way Churches of Our Lord Jesus Christ, Kodesh Church of Immanuel, and Free Christian Zion Church of Christ. Most were small—some almost minuscule in membership—but taken together, they had almost 750,000 adherents in 1960. The Church of God in Christ accounted for half of this total. Founded in 1897 with a stress on sanctification and on the gift of tongues, the Church of God in Christ experienced rapid growth after 1936, numbering 392,635 members in 1960.

Like urban whites who experimented with the teachings of Psychiana, the Rosicrucians, the "Mighty I Am," and Zen Buddhism, blacks also developed cults in the urban environment.[39] The House of Prayer for All Nations of Bishop "Sweet Daddy" Grace was a product of the Depression years that gained added income from the sale of Daddy Grace coffee, Daddy Grace cold cream, and Daddy Grace toothpaste. Although Daddy

---

[39] See A. H. Fauset, *Black Gods of the Metropolis* (Philadelphia, 1971).

Where it all began. Rosa Parks being fingerprinted in Montgomery, Alabama, for refusing to move to the back of the bus on September 1, 1955. *(Photograph from AP/Wide World Photos.)*

had given God a vacation, the faithful were assured that they need not despair, for they could still be saved by grace—Daddy Grace. The Peace Mission of Father Divine was equally unusual, for he claimed to be God and his followers to be "angels." In 1932, he established "heavens" in Harlem, where he fed thousands. Later, Philadelphia became a major center. After World War II, the Peace Mission lost much of its momentum. Both Daddy Grace and Father Divine emphasized nonracial brotherhood, but other movements took an opposite tack. The "Black Jews" of W. S. Crowdy, F. S. Cherry, and W. A. Matthew, for example, stressed black separateness and superiority. A similar view was represented by Marcus Garvey's "Black Nationalists," who appealed to "the God of Africa," and by Drew Ali's "Moorish Americans," who rejected the white gods and turned for inspiration to the Qur'an. Important developments in the African American embrace of Islam occurred, as we shall see, at midcentury.

Mid-Twentieth-Century Religious Profile

An accurate assessment of the balance of religious forces in the United States is difficult to make. Several shifts took place during the first half of the twentieth century, but available statistics are not always comparable. As officially reported, Protestant church membership in 1960 was approximately 64 million, the Roman Catholic total was 42 million, the number of Jews was 5.5 million, and the Eastern Orthodox total was roughly 2.65 million.[40]

Within Protestantism, significant shifts in numerical strength took place during the post–World War I period. Methodists increased from 7.6 million to 13.15 million between 1916 and 1960, but they were displaced as the largest Protestant grouping by the Baptists, who had grown from 7 million to 21 million. Lutherans surged forward from 2.5 million to 8 million to become the third largest Protestant group. Presbyterians and Reformed slipped to fourth place with a gain from 2.8 million to 4.8 million. The growth of the Protestant Episcopal Church from 1.1 million to 3.3 million was somewhat deceptive, for the first figure was communicant membership and the second was the total number of baptized. The merger of the Congregational Christian Churches with the Evangelical and Reformed Church put the United Church of Christ in sixth place with 2.2 million members in 1960. A group that had only a tenuous relationship to Protestantism, the Latter-day Saints, or Mormons, had grown from 450,000 to 1.6 million between 1916 and 1960.[41]

Although interesting and illuminating in some respects, such a traditional classification of the relative strength of various Protestant groupings

[40] Information supplied by the U.S. Bureau of the Census and the American Institute of Public Opinion indicates that the Protestant–Roman Catholic membership figures give a rather accurate picture of proportionate strength. A census bureau study in 1958 reported that of 119,330,000 Americans fourteen years of age and older, 66.2 percent (78,952,000) regarded themselves as Protestant, 25.7 percent (30,669,000) regarded themselves as Roman Catholic, 3.2 percent (3,868,000) regarded themselves as Jewish, 1.3 percent (1,545,000) identified themselves with other faiths, and 3.6 percent (4,300,000) claimed no religious preference or were not reported. Protestant predominance is reduced to rough conformity with official membership figures when active identification, as reflected in church attendance, is taken into account. A survey by the America Institute of Public Opinion in 1958 reported that 44 percent (34,740,000) of those who considered themselves Protestant attended church the preceding Sunday, whereas 74 percent (22,700,000) of those who considered themselves Roman Catholic attended.

[41] The long-established smaller religious groups met with varying success in the twentieth century. The Mennonites doubled their membership in the 1916–1960 period (from 80,000 to 160,000), as did the Church of the Brethren (100,000 to 200,000). The rapid growth of Christian Science ended about 1940, after having tripled in number of churches during the preceding three decades. Quakers, Unitarians, and Universalists, on the other hand, had steadily declined during the first forty years of the century, but each of them made small but significant recoveries after World War II.

serves to obscure one of the most significant shifts that was taking place in twentieth-century Protestantism. The traditional classification was largely based upon differences in polity and church government, which had little relationship to the divisive issues of the twentieth century, for the latter were theologically and sociologically grounded in a way that bypassed the older distinctions. The traditional classification fails to give adequate weight, for example, to the 1.5 million members of Holiness churches, the 1.5 million members of Pentecostal bodies, and the 500,000 members of Adventist or premillennialist groups. Moreover, some of the smaller Baptist, Methodist, Presbyterian, and Reformed groups should more properly be classified as part of the 4.8 million members of Fundamentalist denominations. And the Fundamentalist total ought to be even larger to take into account many individual churches, such as the Park Street Congregational Church in Boston and the Tenth Presbyterian Church in Philadelphia, which held Fundamentalist views and actively supported Fundamentalist agencies.[42] What is needed in place of the traditional grouping of Protestants into denominational families is a classification that takes into account the actual realignment within American Protestantism.

The old-line Protestant group at midcentury was composed of those mildly "liberal" or "progressive" denominations affiliated with the National Council of Churches. Frequently referred to as "cooperative Protestantism," these bodies represented a constituency of some 37 million members. Approximately 24 million conservative Protestants were "noncooperative" in the sense that they were not affiliated with the National Council of Churches.[43] These included such major groups as the Southern Baptists with over 10 million members, and almost 5 million Lutherans belonging to the American Lutheran Church and the Lutheran Church–Missouri. In addition, there were 8.5 million "disaffected Protestants," members of Fundamentalist, Adventist, Holiness, and Pentecostal churches. This classification does not produce neat packages, for it does not take into account the fracturing of Protestantism along racial lines. Nor do the formal figures give any hint that "disaffected Protestantism," having given up hope of gaining control of the major denominations of "cooperative Protestantism," continued to exhibit astonishing vitality during the 1930s and 1940s and was succeeding in penetrating old-line denominations at the grassroots level.[44] Many individuals and congregations

---

[42] Their respective pastors, Harold J. Ockenga and Donald Grey Barnhouse, were prominent Fundamentalist leaders.

[43] Some did have their own cooperative organizations, such as the National Association of Evangelicals, the smaller American Council of Churches, and a variety of cooperative missionary, evangelistic, educational, and publishing agencies. See Joel A. Carpenter, "Fundamentalist Institutions and the Rise of Evangelical Protestantism, 1929–1942," *Church History*, 49 (1980), 62–75.

[44] Ibid., 65–68.

grouped with "cooperative Protestantism" actually were providing major support for the institutions of the "disaffected."

The emergence of Judaism and Eastern Orthodox Christianity as prominent components of an American religious scene that was becoming ever more multiform and diverse has been discussed in some detail. Major Protestant and Roman Catholic developments during the period that followed World War I, however, were more complicated and need further attention before the bubbling ferment affecting all religious groups in the 1960s, followed by a turn to conservatism, can be assessed.

CHAPTER FOURTEEN

Protestantism's Uneasy Journey to the Comfortable Fifties

For American Protestantism, World War I marked the end of an era. Kenneth Scott Latourette observed that "Protestant Christianity had entered the nineteenth century on a rising tide" and noted that it had come to the end of the century "on a rapidly ascending curve."[1] The momentum of almost two hundred years of vigorous advance had not yet been spent, and the new century found Protestantism at the peak of its apparent strength and influence. Churches were crowded, financial support was generous, programs were proliferating, and a host of good causes elicited eager and ardent devotion. It was a time of unusual moral idealism generated in part by a widespread determination among church members to "win the world for Christ in this generation." By the time Warren G. Harding was installed in the White House, however, much of the contagious enthusiasm exhibited by the churches had begun to be dissipated. By 1925, the usual indices of institutional health—church attendance, Sunday school enrollment, missionary giving—showed a downward trend that was to continue for at least a decade. Although not many at the time were aware that the forward thrust was seriously blunted, it is clear in retrospect that by the middle 1920s, an ebb tide had set in.[2]

---

[1] Kenneth Scott Latourette, *A History of the Expansion of Christianity* (New York, 1937–1945), IV, 458; VI, 5.

[2] See Robert Handy, "The American Religious Depression, 1925–35," *Church History*, 29 (1960), 2–16.

The Transitional Years

The blunting of the long Protestant advance was foreshadowed by the fate of the Interchurch World Movement of 1919 and 1920. This was an ambitious enterprise, launched with a flourish of trumpets, that was designed to push to rapid completion the task of Christianizing the world, a Christianizing that was defined in terms of "the complete evangelization of all of life." The major Protestant denominations cooperated to make a detailed survey of urgent needs both at home and abroad, to chart a common strategy for meeting them, to allocate specific responsibilities to the different mission boards, and then, through a concerted campaign patterned after the great wartime drives for funds, to secure the necessary financial resources to carry out the plans.[3] Each denomination had its own financial goal and its own "movement" or campaign for funds, and these coordinated drives were to be supplemented by a general campaign that would tap the supposedly vast potential support of public-spirited citizens who could not be reached through denominational channels. At first a goal of $300 million was suggested, then $500 million, and the final figure was $1 billion, with $335 million to be raised initially. Although large sums were raised by the participating denominations,[4] the joint campaign was a costly and dismal failure that left the denominational mission boards saddled with debts incurred in the cooperative phases of the endeavor.

The failure of the Interchurch World Movement can be attributed in part to the economic recession of 1920–1922. Prospects for success also were blighted by the report of the Movement's commission of inquiry, which surveyed the needs of the steelworkers and their families. The inquiry coincided with the 1919 strike of the steelworkers, which sought the elimination of the twelve-hour day and the seven-day week. The sympathetic tenor of the commission's report was not calculated to win the support of wealthy public-spirited citizens, which was one of the objectives of the campaign. But there were more deep-seated reasons for the failure. A marked shift in the mood of the American people was perhaps the most

---

[3] For objectives of the Movement, see H. W. Schneider, *Religion in the Twentieth Century*, (Cambridge, MA 1952), 95ff. The scope is indicated by a survey to ascertain "all the facts about the religious, social, moral, physical, and economic environments through the world." D. B. Meyer, *The Protestant Search for Political Realism*, (Berkeley, 1960), 9. The full story is told by Eldon Ernst, *Moment of Truth for Protestant America* (Missoula, Mont., 1974).

[4] The New World Movement of the Northern Baptists was the most successful on the basis of per capita giving, but only half of the $100 million goal was raised. Methodists, with five times as many members, raised the largest total amount. The much more modest $40 million goal of the Methodist Centenary Movement was far exceeded, with more than $100 million being subscribed. But in the end, the Methodists had many unpaid pledges and soured hopes.

important. Moreover, long-smoldering tensions within Protestantism broke out into open conflict at the close of the war, diverting to internecine strife the energies that might have been otherwise employed. And finally, Protestantism was beginning to reap the consequences of a long period of acculturation.

The Postwar Generation

For two decades, Protestants had been engaged in a series of crusades to refashion the face of America and to reshape the life of the world (see Chapter 12). World War I itself was but the greatest of these crusades, enlisting as it did the idealism generated by the churches in "a war to end war" and to "make the world safe for democracy." The United States had entered the conflict with banners flying, but it proved to be a dirty, unheroic war that few participants remembered with anything but distaste. The peace proved equally disappointing. Little idealism was apparent in the treaty negotiations at Versailles, and Woodrow Wilson was pilloried at home as a fool trapped by the wily diplomats of Europe. Harding's call for a "return to normalcy," a summons to put aside idealistic crusades and farflung responsibilities, mirrored the mood of a tired and disenchanted people. Small wonder, in this climate of opinion, that the new crusade envisioned in the Interchurch World Movement met with so disappointing a response.

The postwar generation, however, was suffering from a more severe malady than mere weariness with crusades. Nor was the disenchantment that stemmed from the machinations of the diplomats at Versailles sufficient to account for the waning of idealism. The latter was more largely the product of a profound revolution in morals. Wars tend to be followed by a breakdown in public and private morality, and World War I was no exception. For many people the war was a liberating experience. Young men were uprooted and introduced for the first time to the amoral standards of army life. Women were drawn from their homes to engage in war work. The movement of population into the cities was accelerated. Each of these factors represented a break with accustomed patterns of life. But the war also imposed its own restrictive discipline. Those at home were driven to strenuous exertion by the effort to win the war, and those in the army were subjected to the unpleasant regimentation of military life. From this perspective, it was the end of the war that brought a welcome release from the stern requirements of duty and evoked a heartfelt desire to relax and enjoy the satisfactions of a less-disciplined existence. This mood, quite apart from the brutalizing effect of war, was normal for a postwar period. Parallels in other postwar epochs can be found for the scandals of the Harding administration and the heedless preoccupation of the business community with making "a fast buck." But these were symptoms only of a widespread moral change that was mostly covert and did not represent an open flouting of accepted standards of morality. Somewhat more significant was a candid and undisguised revolt that bluntly attacked the whole system of traditional manners and morals.

The revolution in morals of the 1920s is most frequently depicted in terms of "flaming youth" and the "jazz age," of "speakeasies" and "gang wars." But it was more than this. It was a revolution that affected all classes of society and tore people loose from their old moorings. It can be seen in part as an aftermath of war, but its fundamental rootage was more remote. Technological advance had multiplied material satisfactions and weakened religious sanctions, and the booming prosperity of the 1920s was a heady experience. The "status revolution" that undercut the authority of those who traditionally set the moral standards—the "professional" classes (ministers, lawyers, teachers), the "rural gentry," and the "urban patricians"—was also involved. Not least important were changes in family life brought about by increasing urbanization. But it was the popular appropriation of insights derived from the teachings of such men as John Dewey and Sigmund Freud that contributed as much to the new culture as anything else. "Self-expression" and "self-fulfillment" became magic words, and anything that smacked of "repression" was regarded as a threat to the "psyche." These tags of popular understanding distorted carefully devised philosophies, but they had the effect of giving a supposedly scientific imprimatur to self-indulgence.

The prophets of the moral revolt were literary figures—Theodore Dreiser, Sinclair Lewis, H. L. Mencken, George Jean Nathan, F. Scott Fitzgerald, Ernest Hemingway, and other luminaries. Their rebellion took the form of a frontal attack on what they called America's "puritanism"—an epithet for anything that interfered with the new freedom. Religion was dismissed as antiquated, false, and absurd—a blend of prudery, cant, and sanctimoniousness from which individuals must emancipate themselves if their spirits were not to be suffocated. To Joseph Wood Krutch, "sin" and "love" were empty words, and he insisted that "all the capital letters in the composing-room cannot make the words more than that which they have become—shadows, as essentially unreal as some of the theological dogmas which have been completely forgotten."[5] Concerned with the individual rather than society, with private rather than public experience, these writers had no interest in social reform. "Doing good" was either a dull business or, as Mencken insisted, "in bad taste." "The great problems of the world—social, political, economic, and theological—do not concern me in the slightest," wrote Nathan.

[5] Joseph Wood Krutch, *The Modern Temper: A Study and a Confession* (New York, 1929), 191–92.

> If all the Armenians were to be killed tomorrow and if half of Russia were to starve to death the day after, it would not matter to me in the least. What concerns me alone is myself and the interests of a few close friends. For all I care the rest of the world may go to hell at today's sunset.[6]

Not all were as blunt and callous as Nathan, but social nihilism was a fundamental theme of the avant-garde novelists and poets. Even the care with which most of them avoided adjectives and sought to make do with unadorned nouns and verbs was part of a studied and self-conscious rejection of all idealistic sentiment.

Although the cynical hedonism of the novelists and poets and literary critics blazed the way for many, the revolution in morals found more temperate and prosaic expression in the population as a whole. Spurred on by handbooks of popular psychology and carried forward in home and classroom, the revolution produced a less sin-ridden and more self-indulgent people. But, unlike the despair of the "intellectuals," the popular mood of "the booming twenties" was optimistic, and the new freedom was geared to an undisciplined pursuit of more tangible forms of personal fulfillment. Whereas the intellectuals had lost faith in progress, the great mass of Americans were content to believe that the promises of the past had become the realities of the present. Here the waning of idealism had complacency, and even smugness, as its hallmark, and it manifested itself in the demise of the Progressive Movement. The only alarm was that directed against those who seemed to threaten the existing order.

In 1912, progressivism, with its zeal for reform, had been triumphant. In a three-cornered race, Taft had been far outdistanced by both his progressive rivals—Woodrow Wilson and Teddy Roosevelt. Moreover, Eugene Debs, the Socialist candidate, had amassed almost a million votes. Four years later Wilson and Hughes, who were almost equally progressive in outlook, had vied for the White House. But in 1920, progressivism was buried under the Harding landslide, and only a remnant could be resurrected by the LaFollette-Wheeler banner in the 1924 campaign.

The churches were not unaffected by this shift in mood of the American people. The demise of progressivism was accompanied by the decline of the social gospel that in prewar years had given American Protestantism much of its verve and contagious enthusiasm. As a typical social gospel project, the Interchurch World Movement was one of the first casualties of the fading idealism. It is true that interest in social Christianity survived in some circles, just as there were still progressives to be found, but it was mostly confined to clerical ranks and had ceased to be important as a powerful ferment in church life. Clergymen who continued to issue social pronouncements were generals with few troops. They were tolerated by their

---

[6] Quoted in William Edward Leuchtenburg, *The Perils of Prosperity* (Chicago, 1958), 150.

congregations, but their summons to action sparked little response.[7] Even among the clergy, much of the social concern was diverted into a pacifist crusade. Shamed and humiliated by the role of churchmen in propagating hatred during World War I[8] and revolted by the horrors of trench warfare, a large percentage of the clergy vowed that the church should not bless war again and that they would neither support nor participate in any future conflict.

The Fundamentalist Controversy

If the Protestant advance was blunted by the shifting mood of the American people, it also was impeded by an intramural conflict that broke out in 1920 within Protestantism. The protagonists were "Liberals" or "Modernists," who sought to adjust the inherited faith to the new intellectual climate, and "Fundamentalists," who insisted that the old ways of stating the faith must be preserved unimpaired.[9]

Theological tension had been developing for a long time, but it subsided after the heresy trials of the latter years of the nineteenth century. A common enthusiasm for reform made it possible to subordinate theological differences and to gloss over divergent theological positions with pious ambiguities.[10] Almost every prominent professional evangelist regarded himself as being engaged in a work of social reformation. A few, like B. Fay Mills, went all the way with the social gospel. Others, like Sam Jones, Milan B. Williams, Burke Culpepper, William E. Biederwolf, and Rodney "Gypsy" Smith, limited themselves to "civic reform" and stressed "social service." Some, like J. Wilbur Chapman, placed primary stress on personal morality. But whatever emphasis, they tended to be welcomed as allies in the progressive movement for human betterment and were drawn unwittingly into its orbit.[11] And they, in turn, tended to mute points of theological dis-

---

[7] A failure to make this distinction weakens Robert M. Miller's otherwise cogent demonstration of a continuing interest in social Christianity in his *American Protestantism and Social Issues, 1919–1939* (Chapel Hill, N.C., 1958).

[8] See R. H. Abrams, *Preachers Present Arms* (New York, 1933), as qualified by J. F. Piper, "The Social Policy of the Federal Council of the Churches of Christ," Duke University Ph.D. thesis (Durham, N.C., 1964).

[9] Stewart G. Cole, *The History of Fundamentalism* (New York, 1931), is an early account of the controversy. See also G. M. Marsden, *Fundamentalism and American Culture: The Shaping of Twentieth-Century Evangelicalism, 1870–1925* (New York, 1980); E. R. Sandeen, *The Roots of Fundamentalism* (Chicago, 1970); and T. P. Weber, *Living in the Shadow of the Second Coming: America Premillennialism, 1875–1925* (New York, 1979).

[10] See William G. McLoughlin, *Modern Revivalism* (New York, 1959), 305–54, 361–63, 386–87, 393, 397, 402, 411.

[11] Biederwolf and Gypsy Smith, for example, were active in the Men and Religion Forward Movement of 1911–1914, liberal in leadership with a strong social emphasis.

sent. Not everyone, to be sure, was bemused by this happy state of affairs. The more ardent "dispensationalists" within the revivalist camp were primarily responsible for introducing discord into the general harmony.

Unlike other professional evangelists, the "dispensationalists" had their own scheme of reform, which reflected the general expectancy and enthusiasm of the time, a scheme expressed in terms of their premillennial views. Furthermore, they were not of a mind to compromise their convictions by glossing over theological differences. In 1905, Amzi C. Dixon, shortly to become minister of the Moody Church in Chicago, published a book in which he announced that there could be no reconciliation between science and religion any more than socialism and free enterprise could be reconciled. The duty of the church was to convert individuals, to keep out of politics, and to remember that there could be no true revival that was not led by "believers in the inspiration and infallible authority of the Word of God."[12]

With the help of Reuben A. Torrey, superintendent of the Moody Bible Institute, Dixon prepared a counterattack that culminated in 1910–1915 with the publication of twelve small volumes entitled *The Fundamentals*, which sought to reduce the Christian faith to clear essentials. These brief treatises were written by various men but were edited by Dixon and Torrey, and their distribution was financed by two wealthy residents of Los Angeles, Milton and Lyman Stewart. They were sent free of charge "to every pastor, evangelist, missionary, theological student, Sunday school superintendent, Y.M.C.A. and Y.W.C.A. secretary" whose address could be obtained, and eventually 3 million copies were distributed.[13] It is likely that serious strife would have been provoked then had not the agitation been interrupted by the outbreak of World War I.

The career of Billy Sunday—the professional baseball player turned evangelist—bridged the prewar and postwar periods.[14] He was a transitional figure, whose early popularity was derived in part from the alacrity with which he jumped on the bandwagon of civic reform and moral uplift, and who then rode to fame on the crest of the wave of reaction against the social gospel. Even during the early phase, his denunciations of liberal theology were frequent and coarse. He had no use for the "bastard theory of evolution" or for the "deodorized and disinfected sermons" of "hireling ministers" who gave up the old faith to please their liberal parishioners. Furthermore, he complained of those who tried to "make religion out of social service with Jesus Christ left out." He exhibited nonetheless a marked

[12] McLoughlin, 348, 352–53.

[13] *Ibid.*, 352, 370; N. F. Furniss, *The Fundamentalist Controversy* (New Haven, 1954), 12. Charges that fright among wealthy laymen aroused by radical social views accounts for Fundamentalist financial support at this time are unfair.

[14] See W. G. McLoughlin, Jr., *Billy Sunday Was His Real Name* (Chicago, 1955), and *Modern Revivalism*, 400–54.

ability to blend his "old-time religion" with the progressive emphasis on reform. He advertised his revivals as "civic clean-ups" that would make any
town a better place in which to live. He appropriated many of the indict-
ments leveled by the "muckrakers," and this treatment led many progressive
and social gospelers to believe that he was buttressing their cause. Even his
vulgarity and "vaudeville stunts" were defended as a necessary means of
reaching the masses. One contemporary observer was confident that "it is as
a reformer that Mr. Sunday has warmed the hearts of all who desire better
things." His ideas of reform, however, turned out to be extremely limited,
not extending much beyond the suppression of the liquor traffic.[15]

Sunday was quick to respond to changing climates of opinion. From the
beginning he had preached a masculine "muscular" Christianity that
equated salvation with decency and manliness ("the man who has real,
rich, red blood in his veins instead of pink tea and ice water") but that
stressed as well a strongly emotional rather than a mechanical piety
("Some people pray like a jack-rabbit eating cabbage."). Under the excitement of war, this masculine Christianity was transformed into a barn-
storming, tub-thumping "100 percent Americanism" that insisted that
"Christianity and patriotism are synonymous terms" just as "hell and trai-
tors are synonymous." Soon he was attributing German atrocities to the
baneful influence of biblical criticism upon the German people. And
when labor unrest developed at the close of hostilities, he was in full cry
after all foreign-inspired, godless social radicalism.

In spite of Billy Sunday's diatribes, most prominent Protestant leaders at
the end of the war believed that the struggle to win acceptance for new
ways of understanding the Christian faith had been won, and they were
prepared to resume the humanitarian advance of the prewar years.[16] But
Sunday was demonstrating how hostile sentiment could be aroused in the
postwar climate. The American people were in no mood for any further
tampering with the social order, and it was easy to demonstrate to the satisfaction of many that "modernism" and "communism" were but reverse
sides of the same coin.

A decisive factor in thrusting the controversy into public attention was
the championship of the Fundamentalist cause by William Jennings Bryan,
the "peerless leader" of the old populist element in the Democratic party.
When Bryan entered the fray in 1920, he was able to claim a national audience and to use his magic voice and moving rhetoric to transform isolated
protests into a more-or-less unified crusade. Soon every denomination was
embroiled in conflict. Strenuous efforts were made to ferret out evidence
of heresy accompanied by demands that remedial action be taken to guarantee doctrinal orthodoxy. Harry Emerson Fosdick, a Baptist preacher fill-
ing the pulpit of the First Presbyterian Church of New York City, added

[15] McLoughlin, 399, 410–12, 429, 437.

[16] For the eager enthusiasm of church leaders, see Meyer, 12–13.

fuel to the flames in 1922 when, dismayed by the demoralizing effects of the Fundamentalist attacks that he had observed on a visit to the mission fields of Asia, he seemed to fling down the gauntlet in a sermon entitled "Shall the Fundamentalists Win?"

The qualifying phrase describing the Fundamentalist movement as "more or less" unified is important, for it did embrace diverse elements. The Bible School "dispensationalists" sought to detect heresy by a summary of key points of faith, including the verbal inerrancy of Scripture, the Genesis account of creation, and the premillennial return of Christ, as the standard of orthodoxy. But this was initially a fringe position. The movement derived much of its strength at the outset from men who stood more squarely within the traditional life of the churches.[17]

Curtis Lee Laws, Baptist editor of the *Watchman-Examiner* who coined the label "Fundamentalist" in 1920 to designate those who were prepared to battle for the "fundamentals" of the faith, was associated with a large body of genuine "conservatives," whose concern was to conserve and defend the integrity of the Christian faith. The key issue, as they saw it, was the authority of the Bible, for Protestantism historically claimed the authority of Scripture for the whole structure of its thought. While continuing to revere the Bible as a treasury of religious devotion, there had been a growing tendency in liberal circles to reject it as being normative. It was suitable for historical study and useful for devotional purposes, but the canons of truth were to be found in religious experience. It was this tendency to forget that the Christian faith had any objective standard of truth that alarmed the conservatives. These men were not obscurantist in their attitude toward modern knowledge. Although they centered attention on the question of biblical authority, few wished to make an issue of evolution, biblical inerrancy, or premillennialism. They represented the type of reaction to the more extreme modernist tendencies that had long been present in Protestant seminaries. The views expressed by John A. Faulkner at Drew Theological Seminary in *Modernism and the Christian Faith* (1921) and by Augustus Hopkins Strong, former president of Rochester Theological Seminary, whose *Outlines of Systematic Theology* was widely used as a textbook in the more conservative seminaries, were typical of this broad current of concern. Nevertheless, critics such as those at the University of Chicago warned that fundamentalist premillennialism essentially gave up on the world and consequently conveyed a message that threatened world security.

Strong frankly accepted the doctrine of evolution and the methods of biblical criticism. "Neither evolution nor the higher criticism has any terrors to one who regards them as parts of Christ's creating and educating process." The composite authorship of the Pentateuch and the existence of two Isaiahs did not disturb Strong. "Any honest Christian," he affirmed, ". . . has the

---

[17] For this distinction, see the chapter by Norman H. Maring, "Conservative But Progressive," in *What God Hath Wrought*, ed. G. L. Guffin (Philadelphia, 1960), 17–28.

right to interpret Jonah and Daniel as allegories rather than histories." The Bible, he insisted, is the record of a progressive revelation, "shaped in human molds and adapted to ordinary human intelligence." It is a "human composition," but it is also "God's Word," presenting "divine truth in human forms." The danger of historical criticism of the Bible, he declared, is not the method but the presuppositions of those who use it. "'The historical method' of Scripture interpretation, as it is often employed, ends without Christ because it begins without him." It makes the mistake of "treating Scripture as it would treat any unreligious or heathen literature" and ignores the fact that to interpret the Bible properly, one must adopt a confessional stance. The point is "not how man made the Scripture for himself, but how God made the Scripture through the imperfect agency of man." To abandon the Bible as the authoritative testimony of Christ and thus in a derivative sense the authoritative ground of faith, Strong contended, would cut the "taproot" and imperil the very existence of Protestantism.[18]

The moderate Fundamentalists, however, were quickly upstaged by more radical elements, whose quarrel seemed to be with almost every facet of modern life. Viewed from this perspective, Fundamentalism can best be understood as a phase of the rural-urban conflict, drawing its strength from the tendency of many who were swept into an urban environment to cling to the securities of their childhood. Although this characterization does less than justice to the moderate wing of the movement, it does point up the fact that in many ways, Fundamentalism was as much the product of a cultural as a religious concern. It is significant that it arose among rural-oriented people in the cities before it penetrated the small towns and villages of the countryside. Furthermore, the mores that were emphasized as dispensable to the Christian life had, in the words of H. Richard Niebuhr, "at least as little reaction to the New Testament and as much connection with social custom" as did those aspects of behavior that were condemned, and the cosmological and biological notions that were stressed as integral to the gospel were equally culturally conditioned.[19] Fundamentalist sentiment also was not unrelated to the sweeping tide of hyperpatriotism that was so conspicuous a feature of the early 1920s. "One hundred percent Americanism" was regarded as the normal corollary of "old-time religion," and "Back to Christ, the Bible, and the Constitution" was a typical slogan. Isolationism and renewed nativism were two features of the "siege mentality" that emerged in particularly vivid terms during the "Red Scare" of 1919–1920.[20]

---

[18] Augustus Hopkins Strong, *Outlines of Systematic Theology* (Philadelphia, 1903), ix, 55–62. See also Strong's *Tour of Missions* (Philadelphia, 1918), 177, 181, 186–87, 191, 203.

[19] H. Richard Niebuhr, *Christ and Culture* (New York, 1951), 102.

[20] Official Roman Catholic opposition to "modernism" and "Americanism," and advocacy of a return to tradition, likewise contributed to the formation of a siege mentality that mixed well with the conservatism of the period.

The great body of Protestants was never fully committed to either side of the controversy, but when the more belligerent Fundamentalists formed themselves into a power bloc intent on seizing control of various Protestant denominations by placing them in a rigid theological straitjacket, the effect was to push middle-of-the-roaders into a defensive alliance with the liberals. By 1925, when a national comedy was acted out in the "monkey trial" at Dayton, Tennessee, with William Jennings Bryan and Clarence Darrow in the starring roles, the violent language and "smear" tactics of the more vociferous Fundamentalists so alienated public opinion generally that there was little prospect that the Fundamentalists would gain control of any major Protestant denomination. Fundamentalism nevertheless maintained itself in many local congregations and expanded its influence through the formation of independent Bible churches and the capture of some smaller denominational bodies. A continuing source of strength was its ability to supply, through graduates of Bible schools, ministerial leadership to impoverished churches.

Merchandizing Religion

Theological tensions, large-scale social change, the economic roller coaster, and demographic trends placed the churches under considerable pressure in the decades after World War I. Uncertain as to their role, the churches struggled to rekindle the spirit of their congregations. Less and less reliance could be placed on habit and custom to maintain active participation in church life. In addition to the free and easy atmosphere generated by the revolution in morals that enabled many to ignore the Sabbath and neglect church attendance without compunction, there were other features of American life that made the task of the churches more difficult. The population was increasingly urban and mobile. Once within the urban orbit, there were many who did not stay put long enough to develop strong ties to a church. Nor could the churches count on the family as an ally to the same extent as formerly, as was made evident by the rising divorce rate and the sharp decline in the practice of family devotions. Automobile production soared at almost a geometric rate, vastly extending the range of an individual's freedom, providing easy access to multiplying golf courses and setting up the family weekend outing as a counterattraction to the church. Motion pictures and the radio joined the press as rivals of the churches in setting the tone of society.[21] Almost everything—the

---

[21] The press provided much less support for the churches than heretofore. The circulation of religious periodicals dwindled, and there was a marked change in the attitude of the nonreligious press. One study has indicated that, whereas about 78 percent of published views of religion in 1905 could be classified as favorable, by 1930 the situation was almost reversed with 67 percent unfavorable. Hornell Hart, "Changing Attitudes and Interests," *Recent Social Trends* (New York, 1933), I, 403.

popular mood, the churches' own sense of uncertainty, urbanization, mobility, competing attractions, the decay of family solidarity—militated against vigorous church life.

One response to this situation was a frenzied effort by some churches to "merchandise" religion with the huckstering methods of Madison Avenue.[22] "Early to bed and early to rise, preach the gospel and advertise," ministers were admonished. "Selling Religion—that is the only business of the Church," proclaimed Lewis S. Mudge, stated clerk of the Presbyterian General Assembly, in supplying the churches with five surefire tips on how they might best vend their goods. "The old idea that a minister is above stooping to commercial devices must disappear if the church is to grow," the Methodist *Zion's Herald* informed its readers, for "ministers are salesmen with a wonderfully fine 'line' to sell their congregations." The use of printer's ink and brightly illuminated signs to advertise their services, churches were told, could change the cry of "S.O.S." to "S.R.O."—standing room only. Bruce Barton, an advertising executive, made his contribution to the cause by writing a biography of Jesus, *The Man Nobody Knows* (1925), which for two years headed the nonfiction list of best-selling books. Jesus was pictured as a master salesman, psychologist, and forceful young executive, who forged twelve men from the lower ranks into the best management team of all time. As the merchandising of religion became more sophisticated, abuses occurred. Guy Ballard's "I AM" movement, which combined ideas from a wide range of religious traditions and popular religious belief, was put on trial in the 1930s in New York for hoodwinking the elderly with promises and taking their money.

Churches responded to the multiple exhortations with snappy slogans and promotional stunts. "A friendly church" became a familiar slogan that compared favorably with more flashy punchlines such as "Be a Sport—Come to Church" or the hard-sell "Worship Increases Your Efficiency" and "Business Success and Religion Go Together." Catchy sermon topics—"The Irishmen of the Old Testament," "Two in a Bed," "The Mae West of My Bible"—were used as teasers to draw a crowd.

Churches with a more sedate and prosperous clientele sought to maintain their prestige and popularity by the more dignified expedient of constructing impressive gothic cathedrals, and even the less prosperous invested heavily in modest gothic structures. In 1921, the total spent on new church buildings was $60 million. Five years later the total had risen to $284 million. John D. Rockefeller, Jr., explained his interest in spending large sums on the construction of a new home for the Park Avenue Baptist Church on Riverside Drive by saying that he did not want the business

---

[22] See R. Laurence Moore, *Selling God: American Religion in the Marketplace of Culture* (New York, 1994).

community to look down on the churches.[23] Some attempted to make Sunday morning worship more attractive by decorating it with liturgical innovations borrowed from other traditions. Unlike earlier forms of church architecture and liturgical practice that expressed the common faith of the congregation, the new eclecticism betrayed little discernible relationship to any fundamental theological convictions.

These same churches also adopted "progressive" programs of religious education, geared to the immediate interests and capacities of the child. According to George A. Coe's *Social Theory of Religious Education* (1917), the aim of the new educational program was "the growth of the young toward and into mature and efficient devotion to the democracy of God, and happy self-realization therein." The basic conviction was that religious consciousness is a natural and progressive experience that emerges out of "an experimental pupil-teacher quest for growing values."[24] With this emphasis upon "growth" and a "continuous becoming," there was little point to the old Sunday school "Decision Day." Far from involving any crisis of conversion, church membership was regarded as a routine stop in the normal unfolding of human life.

Much church life, of course, remained untouched by these newer expedients, for many congregations refused to adopt cheap appeals to attract a crowd and did not have the financial resources to embark upon a building program or to launch a full-blown program of "progressive" education. Moreover, many of them were still old-fashioned enough to believe that a "life-centered" Sunday school curriculum was no adequate substitute for specific instruction in the Bible. But whatever course individual churches pursued, nothing could obscure the fact that most Protestant churches were suffering a loss of prestige and authority. It was upon churches thus weakened that the blow of the economic depression of the 1930s fell, and the churches suffered from the crippling effect of the economic disaster along with the rest of the nation. Budgets were slashed, benevolent and missionary enterprises were curtailed, and some churches were forced to close their doors.

Protestant "Revivals"

Many people expected that the depression into which the nation was cascaded following the crash of the "great bull market" of 1929 would produce a return to religion. A people shorn of their material possessions, it

---

[23] *Ibid.*, 25.

[24] See H. Shelton Smith, "Christian Education," in *Protestant Thought in the Twentieth Century,* ed. A. S. Nash (New York, 1951), 241.

was believed, would turn to God in some spectacular way. By-and-large they did not. Samuel P. Kincheloe of the Chicago Theological Seminary explained that secularism had become so pervasive that a general revival was impossible.[25] Even churchgoing people looked to Washington instead of to God in their extremity. But there were exceptions. A somewhat sub-rosa revival did occur among less secularized portions of the population as indicated by the rapidly mounting membership of what Kincheloe dismissed as "minor fundamentalist groups," the most striking gains being made by Holiness and Pentecostal churches.

At the opposite end of the social spectrum, a quickening religious interest found expression in the "First Century Christian Fellowship" of Frank Buchman.[26] Since 1921, Buchman had been engaged in personal evangelism among students. Becoming convinced that Park Avenue needed conversion as much as the Bowery, a mission to America was launched in 1930 with headquarters in the Calvary Episcopal Church in New York City. The focus was upon "four absolutes" of perfect honesty, purity, unselfishness, and love, and upon "the five C's" of confidence, confession, conviction, conversion, and continuance, which were the five stages of a "changed" life. The basic "house party" technique was supplemented by a traveling team, and sophisticated use was made of news media and propagandist literature, with such titles as *For Sinners Only* (1932), *I Was a Pagan* (1934), *Life Began Yesterday* (1935), and *How Do I Begin?* (1937). In 1939, after the movement was renamed Moral Re-Armament, 30,000 people filled Hollywood Bowl for its second World Assembly. Buchman's emphasis was highly individualistic and no great renewal of church life was effected, but many prominent people confessed to have had their lives changed in the "quiet times" of the house parties.

Theological Reassessment

As early as 1928, Episcopal Bishop Charles Fiske was convinced that there was "evidence of a sad disintegration of American Protestantism," a view shared by Unitarian writer William L. Sullivan. In an article on "Our Spiritual Destitution," Sullivan noted that religion had become "timorous, unimaginative, quick with comment upon the contemporaneous, but unable in the authentic manner of its great tradition to judge the contemporaneous by categories that are eternal."[27] Further discontent with

[25] Samuel P. Kincheloe, *Research Memo on Religion in the Depression* (New York, 1937), 45 ff., 95.

[26] See A. W. Eister, *Drawing-Room Conversion* (Durham, N.C., 1950), and W. H. Clark, *The Oxford Group: Its History and Significance* (New York, 1951). For the later Moral Re-Armament phase see *Moral Re-Armament: A Study of the Movement Prepared by the Social and Industrial Council of the Church Assembly* (London: Church [of England] Information Board, 1955).

[27] William L. Sullivan, *Confessions of a Puzzled Parson* (New York, 1928), 191; *Atlantic Monthly*, 133 (1929), 378.

Protestantism's theological void and accompanying acculturation was voiced by Edwin Lewis, *Christian Manifesto* (1934), H. Richard Niebuhr, *The Kingdom of God in America* (1937), and Joseph Haroutunian, *Wisdom and Folly in Religion* (1940). Even more stirring was Reinhold Neibuhr's devastating polemics, *Moral Man and Immoral Society* (1932) and *Reflections on the End of an Era* (1934).[28] In spite of the prescience of such men, not more than a handful of ministers were ready to engage in a fundamental theological reconsideration. Harry Emerson Fosdick was a significant exception, having announced in a widely publicized sermon that "The Church Must Go Beyond Modernism."

There were several reasons for the lack of response. In the midst of a depression, the working clergy were overwhelmed with the mere task of seeing that bills were paid and church doors kept open. Whatever time was left for reflection tended to be absorbed by efforts to mitigate the plight of their parishioners. Additional energy was siphoned off in an effort to qualify themselves to deal more adequately with the personal problems of anxious and distraught people. More important was the lingering impact of the Fundamentalist controversy. Attention had been centered on peripheral issues, with both parties driven to more extreme positions than they otherwise would have adopted. Alarmed by the controversy's threat to institutional concerns, denominational officials took charge and, in the interest of harmony, were largely successful in ruling theological discussion out-of-bounds in church assemblies.

It was otherwise in the seminaries, where indications of a theological revival had begun to surface in the 1930s. This revival, however, is difficult to characterize, for it found expression in no single theological system or school of thought. Its most common feature was represented by Henry Nelson Wieman's announcement in 1932 of his intention henceforth "to promote a theocentric religion as over against the prevalent anthropocentric one." Influenced by Alfred North Whitehead's process philosophy, Wieman, Douglas C. Macintosh, and also Walter M. Horton moved in a new theological direction that rejected the philosophical idealism of the older liberalism. Destined to be much more influential, however, were views derived from Europe,[29] where the shattered optimism of the postwar years had produced an earlier theological reassessment. Although European-oriented theology in America was generally labeled "neo-orthodox," it was multiform and varied, borrowing insights from such diverse sources as the Jewish thinker Martin Buber, the Russian Orthodox theologian Nicholai Berdyaev, the Spanish existentialist Miguel Unamuno, the French neo-Thomist Jacques Maritain, and the Swedish Lutheran theologians

---

[28] Other important books were Walter Lowrie, *Our Concern with the Theology of Crisis* (Boston, 1932), and George Richards, *Beyond Fundamentalism and Modernism* (New York, 1934).

[29] See S. E. Ahlstrom, "Continental Influence on American Christian Thought Since World War I," *Church History*, 37 (1958), 256–73.

Anders Nygren and Gustaf Aulén. While recognizing the diversity, the European influence can best be summarized as an intermingling of neo-Reformation and existentialist emphases, with Karl Barth and Emil Brunner representing primary stress on the Reformation heritage and Paul Tillich, who came to America in 1933, drawing more heavily on the "existentialism" of Søren Kierkegaard.

Karl Barth was the towering figure of the theological revival. Although fully accepting the historical criticism of the liberal era, Barth took his stand firmly on the Scriptures as interpreted by the Protestant reformers and insisted that it is through Jesus Christ alone that God's Word addresses man. Emil Brunner was not quite so uncompromising in the rejection of natural theology and was at first more influential in the United States than his Swiss colleague. Americans found Brunner's strong emphasis on one's apprehension of God being derived from a deeply personal "I-thou" encounter less forbidding than Barth's seemingly more harsh statement of much the same position. Although both Barth and Brunner had been influenced by "the melancholy Dane," Americans were directly exposed to Kierkegaard's writings through translations provided by Walter Lowrie and David Swenson. In differing ways, a type of existentialism represented by Kierkegaard was mediated by the writings of Rudolf Bultmann and Dietrich Bonhoeffer, the German martyr. Preoccupied with the problem of the agonized conscience (the sense of guilt, estrangement, and frustration that once had been so prominently displayed in revival meetings), these men manifested much the same personal concern and introspective analysis that had become fashionable among the literati. The self-acceptance they stressed, however, was grounded in the biblical message of justification by faith alone.

Although the tendencies of the theological revival cannot be reduced to a single consistent point of view, major themes can be identified.[30] The first was a reassertion of the sovereignty of God. Even such a neonaturalist as Wieman thought in terms of a religion of "grace." Second, there were a much less optimistic evaluation of the human situation and a much more radical stress on the demonic power of sin. Third, there was a renewed appreciation of the centrality of biblical revelation. Fourth, there was a revival of interest in Christology. Fifth, there was a deepening concern to recover a sense of fullness and wholeness in the life of the church. Finally, there was a tendency among many, while moving to the "right" theologically, to move to the "left" politically. The tone was set by Reinhold Niebuhr's remark in *Reflections on the End of an Era:* "In my opinion, adequate spiritual guidance can come only through more radical political orientation and more conservative religious convictions than are comprehended [at present] in the culture of our era."

---

[30] Several of these themes are illustrated by selections reprinted in Smith, Handy, and Loetscher, *American Christianity*, II, 438–71.

For at least three reasons, the theological revival was abortive, having little impact beyond the seminaries. First, attention to theological issues was diverted by World War II. Second, attempts at theological reconstruction never got out of the classroom and into the pulpit, to say nothing of making the transition from pulpit to pew.[31] Most important of all, serious theological reflection was overwhelmed by the surging popular "religious revival" that peaked in 1957 when Billy Graham had his "finest hour" in New York City.

The Religious Revival of the Fifties

By the 1950s, it was evident that the United States was in the midst of a religious revival. Critical voices became muted, and religion was riding the crest of a wave of popularity. Church attendance soared, contributions mounted, and unprecedented sums were spent on new church buildings.[32] This trend was equally true of Protestants, Catholics, and Jews. Publishers discovered that religious books were profitable. The more popular volumes dominated the best-seller lists for extended periods of time. Seldom had religion been held in greater public esteem. The pledge of allegiance was amended to include the phrase "under God," prayer breakfasts were attended by the president and members of his cabinet, a prayer room was installed in the national Capitol, and both the American Legion and the National Advertising Council launched "Back to God" and "Go to Church" campaigns. In 1957, the U.S. Bureau of the Census indicated that more than 96 percent of the American people cited a specific religious affiliation in response to the question "What is your religion?" Many names among the 96 percent did not appear on any church membership roll, but the fact that they so identified themselves is significant.

The "return to religion" of the 1950s was formless and unstructured, manifesting itself in many different ways and reinforcing all religious faiths quite indiscriminately. It was a comfortable time for the churches, but it cannot be understood apart from the trauma of World War II and its aftermath. Unlike the brief involvement of the United States in World War I, four long years elapsed after Pearl Harbor before peace was restored. Husbands and wives were separated and marriages postponed for what seemed to be an unending period of time. Those left at home spent long hours in

---

[31] Presbyterians attempted to make the transition with their *Christian Faith and Life Series* of church school materials, but an ill-equipped laity found it difficult to teach, and it was gradually phased out. For the point of view of the series, see Maurice W. Armstrong, ed., *The Presbyterian Enterprise*, (Philadelphia, 1956) 301–3.

[32] From a base of $26 million in 1945, the amount spent on new churches rose steadily: 1946—$76 million; 1948—$251 million; 1950—$409 million; 1954—$593 million; 1956—$775 million; 1958—$863 million; 1959—$935 million; 1960—$1,016 million. After 1960 a decline set in.

the workforce on assembly lines and loading platforms, not for a few months as in World War I, but for two, three, or four years. The developing nostalgia was for the recovery of the quieter time and ties of family, home, and church. Back to normalcy meant the reunion of loved ones and the establishment of new family formations or the reestablishment of old ones. These were the years of the baby boom and of the housing explosion in the surburbs. Seldom had the joys of home and family been more cherished and celebrated. These joys were given added importance by an undercurrent of anxiety. The Depression of the 1930s had been a sobering experience, but among the more thoughtful, the "immense and indomitable optimism" of the American people was given a heavier blow when the bombing of Hiroshima and Nagasaki in 1945 demonstrated the potential destructiveness of the unleashed powers of the atom. The uneasy peace of the "Cold War" that followed, with its recurring cries and continuing conflicts, heightened the sense of anxiety and insecurity.

As a result of what Robert Maynard Hutchins, president of the University of Chicago, called "the good news of damnation," even the world of the secular intellectuals was prepared to listen to the theologians, most notably to Reinhold Niebuhr and Paul Tillich, in a way and to a degree that had not been true for almost half a century. The comment of *Time* magazine in 1956 that Tillich was an intellectual whom even the intellectuals regarded with awe may have been overly exuberant, but it nonetheless reflected the shift in attitude that had occurred. For the most part, however, the revival flowed through more popular channels.

Heirs of the Fundamentalists gave the revival its most vigorous leadership. The way for their new surge of activity had been prepared by the National Association of Evangelicals (N.A.E.), Youth for Christ, and a handful of scholars determined to develop an effective Fundamentalist apologetic. The N.A.E. was formed in 1942 to unite the forces of moderate Fundamentalism,[33] and under the leadership of Harold J. Ockenga, it adopted a conciliatory policy designed to capitalize upon the demoralization of the "modernists" and to penetrate the life of major denominations by persuasion from within rather than by leveling criticism from without. In pursuing this goal they successfully appropriated for themselves the name "evangelical" to avoid the Fundamentalist label. Youth for Christ, the second organization spearheading the Fundamentalist recovery, was founded in 1943 to sponsor Saturday night rallies for young people. It quickly became both a recruiting instrument and a training ground for the new "evangelical" leadership. The activity of these two agencies was strengthened by a coterie of young theologians who were willing to engage in the give-and-take of reasoned theological discussion.[34]

[33] See J. D. Murch, *Cooperation Without Compromise* (Grand Rapids, 1956).

[34] The most prominent were Carl Henry, Edward Carnell, and Cornelius Van Til. See A. W. Hearn, "Fundamentalist Renascence," *Christian Century*, 75 (1958), 528–30.

The thrust of the new "evangelicalism" was brought into focus by Billy Graham, who had been recruited by Youth for Christ in 1945 to serve as an itinerant evangelist at its rallies. Four years later at a tent meeting in Los Angeles, Graham gained widespread attention through the conversion of three minor celebrities—a local television star, a former Olympic athlete, and an alleged associate of the notorious racketeer Mickey Cohen. The Los Angeles success was followed by an eighteen-day campaign at the Park Street Church in Boston and in 1950 by a citywide revival in Portland, Oregon. Under the tutelage of Ockenga, Graham expressed a distaste for interdenominational feuds, deplored "fumbling Fundamentalists" who destroyed their effectiveness by intolerance and sectarianism, and announced a decision to refuse any invitation to conduct a revival that was not tendered by a majority of the Protestant clergy of the host city.[35]

Several factors, in addition to his dashing youthful appearance and generally irenic spirit, combined to further Graham's growing prominence and popularity, which culminated in his dramatic "invasion" of England in 1954. One factor was a skillful use of sophisticated organizational techniques and an adroit exploitation of publicity media, including his weekly "Hour of Decision" radio broadcast. The second was the care he took to marshal support among all denominations. But the real key to his success, perhaps, was the mounting public anxiety that reached a peak during the Korean conflict and the Red-hunt of the McCarthy era.

The political flavor of Graham's gospel had great appeal to ultraconservative segments of the population. Drawing a contrast to the Garden of Eden where there were "no union dues, no labor leaders, no snakes, no disease," Graham depicted the United States as "falling apart at the seams" as a result of deficit spending, "giveaway" foreign-aid programs, "immorality in high places," the influence of "big labor" and "pinks and lavenders" in Washington, and "the infiltration of the left wing" into schools and churches. The "betrayals" at Yalta and Potsdam, the war in Korea, the bungling United Nations ("they set the policies and we shed the blood and pay the bills") were cited as evidence of the "deadly work" of Communism boring from within and were used to demonstrate that "we are living in the latter days." Since Communism was "masterminded by Satan," it was a mistake to think that Satan can be defeated with "flesh and blood and guns and bullets." Only through a great revival, purging America of "the rats and termites" that are weakening "this nation from within," can the United States be saved and the battle won, for "the greatest and most effective weapon against Communism today is a born-again Christian." The altar call was simple and direct: "If you would be a true patriot, then become a

---

[35] See John Pollock, *Billy Graham: Evangelist to the World* (New York, 1979); Marshall Frady, *Billy Graham: A Biography of American Righteousness* (Boston, 1979); W. G. McLoughlin, *Billy Graham: Revivalist in a Secular Age* (New York, 1960); L. I. Sweet, "The Epic of Billy Graham," *Theology Today*, 37 (1980), 85–92.

Christian. If you would be a loyal American, then become a loyal Christian." In a political atmosphere charged with suspicion and fear—represented above all by the witch hunts of Senator Joseph McCarthy and the House Un-American Activities Committee—the combination of religious conservatism and anti-Communism proved to be appealing to many.[36]

The patriotic motif did not represent the full scope of Graham's message. There was much traditional doctrine, and he often spoke to the more personal needs of people. Here the stress was upon the role of religion as a consolation that brings "peace of mind, peace of soul, peace of conscience." This latter emphasis points to another prominent feature of the surge of piety of the 1950s—the "cult of reassurance" of which Norman Vincent Peale, minister of the Marble Collegiate Church in New York City, has been called the "high priest."

New Thought, Christian Science, and the Unity School of Christianity had long exploited the reassurance theme in religion, but the full-blown cult of reassurance dates from the publication of Joshua L. Liebman's *Peace of Mind* in 1946, which quickly achieved a phenomenal sale. Liebman was a Jewish rabbi, and preachers of all persuasions, including Monsignor Fulton J. Sheen with his *Peace of Soul* (1949), capitalized upon this newly awakened religious interest.

Of the "peace of mind" evangelists, Norman Vincent Peale most fully captured the public imagination. From his base in New York City, he issued a stream of books, including the fabulously successful *The Power of Positive Thinking* (1952). His was a simple "do-it-yourself" faith, calling for the replacement of "negative thought" with "positive thinking," that was strongly reminiscent of the teachings of Charles and Myrtle Fillmore. You can "make your life what you want it to be through belief in God and in yourself," he informed his readers. You must "think, believe, visualize success"—"think big," "believe big," "pray big," "act big." How does one "practice faith?" he asked. "First thing every morning before you arise say out loud, 'I believe,' three times."[37]

Peale was referred to by some as "the rich man's Billy Graham," and the two men did hold each other in high esteem. Although they differed theologically, they shared common political and economic views. Peale was a sponsor of Graham's New York Crusade, and if the number of decision cards received from the Graham organization was an accurate index, his church reaped the largest harvest. Graham in turn regarded Peale as "a born-again Christian" in spite of his obvious self-help Pelagianism.[38]

---

[36] McLoughlin, *Modern Revivalism*, 505–12.

[37] Norman Vincent Peale, *The Power of Positive Thinking* (New York, 1952), 154; *Stay Alive All Your Life* (Englewood Cliffs, N.J., 1957), 22, 104, 211, 263.

[38] Pelagius was a British monk of the fourth–fifth century who denied original sin and the need for divine grace for salvation.

Although the popular "religious revival" of the 1950s can most easily be depicted by vivid personalities, its substratum was much broader than that suggested by personality cults. Religion-in-general, any religion and all religion, was thoroughly popular, reflecting a simple belief that religion was a "good thing." President Dwight D. Eisenhower stressed the importance of having "faith in faith." Belonging to a church was widely regarded as a badge of respectability. This was the real revival of the 1950s, expressing itself in increased church attendance, increased church giving, increased church building, and increased public esteem.

Other Manifestations of Religious Vitality

In spite of the experimental mood of the time, many of the clergy and coteries of church members continued their attempts to deal realistically, from a more traditional Christian perspective, with some of the urgent problems of national life.

During World War II, the churches demonstrated that they had learned a lesson from the uninhibited exuberance with which they had blessed World War I. The new conflict was viewed much more soberly. The halting of totalitarian aggression was accepted as a necessity. It was recognized, however, that if the ensuing peace was to be secure, the requirements for the establishment of international order must be clearly defined before the victory was won. To this end a conference was summoned in 1942 to meet at Delaware, Ohio, to draft a report on the prerequisites for a "just and durable peace."[39] Seldom has a report received more serious consideration by the churches. Study guides were prepared, and few congregations failed to make use of them. Key political leaders declared that the report was of decisive importance in creating the favorable climate of American opinion that was indispensable to the establishment of the United Nations.

Later in the McCarthy era, the Protestant churches performed yeoman service in calling a halt to the witch hunt of those years. All major denominations repeatedly expressed alarm at the threat to freedom implicit in the practice of character assassination, imputation of guilt by association, use of loyalty oaths as a means of thought control, and curtailment of individual rights on the basis of credence given accusations by undisclosed informers. The boldest action was taken by the Presbyterian General Council in a statement of October 21, 1953, to be read to each congregation, which declared that "detestation of Communism" was becoming a "new form of idolatry" that could be as dangerous as Communism itself, that dissent and treason are not identical, and that true believers in God will not

---

[39] The "Statement of Guiding Principles" is reprinted in Smith, Handy, and Loetscher, II, 522–26.

play fast and loose with truth to preserve freedom.[40] The firm strictures of official church bodies played no small part in heartening the defenders of liberty in this difficult time and in encouraging the U.S. Senate to meet the issue without equivocation.

Still later the racial crisis elicited the strong leadership of many churchmen.[41] Two years prior to the 1954 Supreme Court decision outlawing segregation in the public schools, the National Council of Churches adopted an official statement, *The Churches and Segregation*, which declared racial segregation to be "diametrically opposed" to the Christian faith. When the decision of the Court was announced, the National Council quickly issued "Suggestions for Action" to guide the churches in helping speed compliance with the law. Unfortunately, instead of proceeding with "all deliberate speed" to carry out the directive, many southern states adopted a "massive resistance" policy that served to create smoldering discontent in black communities. A tragic aspect of the situation was the abdication of responsibility and leadership by southern white churches. After passing a mild resolution commending the Court's decision, the Southern Baptist Convention retreated into silence. The record of other denominations was not notably better, although some local congregations exhibited firm and courageous leadership.

A new phase of the struggle began in 1956 when blacks of Montgomery, Alabama, put an end to segregated seating in the city's public transportation by a mass bus boycott. The leader of the boycott was a young black Baptist minister, Martin Luther King, Jr., who became the principal architect of a drive to attack all forms of segregation through nonviolent action.[42] Other clergymen and particularly black college students rallied to his support, as did leaders of northern white churches. Several organizations, including the Southern Christian Leadership Conference of which King became president, were formed to push a program of nonviolent resistance. By 1962, the movement had spread to northern cities, where the local point of concern was discrimination in housing, employment, and de facto school segregation.

With a succession of "long hot summers" of increasing tension in prospect, the National Council of Churches created a committee on Religion and Race to coordinate the activities of member denominations. Action programs were set into motion. Special funds to aid victims of economic and legal harassment were established. Prominent churchmen joined picket lines, street demonstrations, and "sit-ins," and the top echelon of official leadership was conspicuously present in the massive "March on Washington" on August 28, 1963, when King stirred the conscience of

---

[40] The statement is reprinted in *ibid.*, 549–55.

[41] See Robert Root, *Progress Against Prejudice: The Church Confronts the Race Problem* (New York, 1957).

[42] See his *Stride Toward Freedom: The Montgomery Story* (New York, 1958).

the nation with his emotion-packed and unforgettable refrain, "I have a dream." In the autumn the nation was shocked by the tragic murder of four black Sunday school children in the wanton Sunday morning bombing of a Baptist church in Birmingham. The following spring, during the Senate debate on the Civil Rights Bill of 1964, a Daily Protestant Assembly was maintained at the Lutheran Church of the Reformation on Capitol Hill. The prayer services of the Assembly were followed by briefings for those who came to make their views known to their legislative representatives. But it was the marshaling of support in local congregations that was of decisive importance in bringing the debate to a successful conclusion.

A further feature of old-line Protestantism at midcentury was a growing trend toward unity. Throughout the nineteenth century, Protestants were accustomed to work together in voluntary societies of individuals. Most believed "there were sufficient targets to hit without firing at each other." In the twentieth century, these voluntary modes of cooperation were replaced by "official" interdenominational agencies to coordinate home-mission, foreign-mission, and Christian education activities. The final step in the consolidation of Protestant cooperation was taken in 1950 when these several agencies came together to form the National Council of Churches.[43] The national coordinating structure was paralleled by state and local councils of churches. In rural areas a "grass roots" unity movement developed with the formation of federated and community churches to solve the problem created by a declining rural population. Although there were dissident voices, H. Richard Niebuhr was probably correct when he observed that "the increasing unity of American Protestantism" was "more striking than its apparent diversity."[44]

The typical Protestant pattern in America had been to unite in service while preserving diversity in polity and worship, but the vision of organic unity has had recurrent spokespersons. Numerous proposals for broad-scale union were made, but the suggestion that won most serious consideration was made in 1960 by Eugene Carson Blake, stated clerk of the United Presbyterian Church, speaking in the San Francisco Episcopal cathedral at the invitation of Bishop James A. Pike. A Consultation on Church Unity (COCU) was convened in 1962 to forward a plan of union that would be "both catholic and reformed." High hopes were awakened, and nine denominations participated in the continuing consultations.

Denominational "reunions" had more success than more broadly based mergers. Three Methodist bodies came together in 1939 to form the Methodist Church, becoming the United Methodist Church in 1968 with the addition of the Evangelical United Brethren (German Methodist) Church. The twenty-four Lutheran groups of 1900 were gradually reduced

---

[43] *Christian Faith in Action: The Founding of the National Council of Churches* (New York, 1951). See also Samuel McCrae Cavert, *Church Cooperation and Unity in America* (New York, 1970).

[44] H. Richard Niebuhr, *The Purpose of the Church and Its Ministry* (New York, 1956), 16–17.

Martin Luther King, Jr. "I have a dream . . . black and white together." This was the theme at the peak of his career when he spoke to the multitude assembled at the Lincoln Memorial during the famed March on Washington in 1963. *(AP/Wide World Photos.)*

in number until by 1960, almost all Lutherans (96 percent) belonged to three major bodies—the Lutheran Church in America, the American Lutheran Church, and the Lutheran Church–Missouri Synod. Several mergers followed, so that by late 1988, the newly created Evangelical Lutheran Church in America included most Lutherans. Meanwhile in 1958, the United Presbyterians had merged with the northern Presbyterians, and in the 1970s, northern and southern Presbyterians were brought together to form one church. A merger that bridged traditional denominational lines of division was the formation of the United Church of Christ in 1957 by the Congregational Christian Churches and the Evangelical and Reformed Church.

Closely related to movements of Christian unity in America was a growing concern for ecumenical or worldwide unity, which found expression in the formation of the World Council of Churches in 1948. Several currents of interest combined to produce the World Council. The first stemmed directly from foreign-mission fields, where divisions imported from the West seriously impaired the task of evangelism and weakened the small Christian communities that were struggling to maintain themselves in non-Christian societies. Periodic missionary conferences to chart common strategies culminated in the formation of the International Missionary Council at the Edinburgh Conference of 1910. This conference inspired two Americans to pursue alternate paths to unity. Bishop Charles H. Brent, believing that churches should engage in theological discussion to learn from one another and to discover their common faith, was instrumental in organizing the Faith and Order Movement. Charles S. MacFarland took an alternate route. Believing that the way to bring churches together was to have them address themselves jointly to common social tasks, he took the lead in helping initiate the Life and Work Movement. Leaders in all three areas had become accustomed to working together in the World's Christian Student Federation, organized in 1905, and it was natural for them to envision the consolidation of their efforts in an inclusive ecumenical body. Though its formal organization was delayed by World War II until 1948, the World Council immediately achieved a status far exceeding the hopes of those who labored to bring it into being.

The Protestant phase of the "religious revival" has often been dismissed as an expression of mere religiosity—a booming, surging, culture religion, without depth and with little commitment, which was utilized to lend divine sanction to "the American way of life." Although there is evidence to support this indictment and although there was much that was superficial in Protestantism at midcentury, there were deeper currents that were never wholly submerged.

CHAPTER FIFTEEN

The Maturing
of Roman Catholicism

When Pius X issued the apostolic constitution *Sapienti Consilio* on June 29, 1908, he recognized that the Roman Catholic Church in the United States had come of age by bringing to an end its missionary status. Hitherto the church in the United States had been under the jurisdiction and control of the Congregatio de Propaganda Fide in Rome. Henceforth, it was to be administered on a basis of equality with the older branches of the church in Europe. But it was not until after World War I that the Roman Catholic Church in America began to exhibit the full marks of maturity as an indigenous expression of the Roman Catholic faith.

The External Marks of Maturity

Maturity is an ambiguous word, which may refer to external manifestations of adulthood or which may connote an inner temper of mind that is no longer plagued by the insecurities and anxieties of adolescence. Generally in the maturing process, outward evidence of maturity precedes the inward maturation. Here the initial concern is with the external aspects of a "full-grown" American Catholicism.

The Effect of World War I

The outbreak of war in 1914 cut off the massive influx of immigrants that had contributed so largely to the numerical growth of Roman Catholicism. After the war, restrictive legislation put an end to renewed large-scale immigration. Thus for the first time, the Roman Catholic Church had an opportunity to become stabilized in the American environment. Throughout the nineteenth century, it had been a church of immigrants—heir of many different national traditions. Parishes were identified by national constituencies—Irish, Polish, German, Portuguese, Italian, French, Slovak, Croatian, Hungarian, and Spanish. It often was difficult to think of them as constituting a single, indigenous church. With the curtailment of immigration, the nationality and language distinctions normally would have tended to disappear over a period of two or three generations, but the process was hastened by the strong Americanizing pressures that were so prominent a feature of World War I and its immediate aftermath. Immigrant languages were abandoned as quickly as possible, and there was a scramble by immigrants to demonstrate that they were 100 percent American. Almost within a single decade thereafter, Roman Catholicism ceased to be thought of as an immigrant's church, and by 1955, acculturation had to a great extent weakened the identification of religion with specific national origins.[1]

A second consequence of the war was a greatly increased organizational unity that was achieved through the formation of the National Catholic Welfare Conference. The last plenary council was held in 1884, when the triumvirate of Gibbons, Ireland, and Keane was intent on limiting diocesan autonomy in the interest of a unified national policy. Since that time, the papal delegate and an annual meeting of the archbishops were the only channels through which the activities of the church could be coordinated. In practice, this arrangement meant that each bishop set his own policy. Neither the delegate nor the archbishops had the necessary administrative staff for overall planning. Although the delegate could intervene in a diocese if an emergency situation developed, the authority of the archbishops was limited to the influence that they could exert by persuasion and example. The war, however, created a situation in which specific and detailed centralized action was necessary if wartime needs were to be met effectively. For this purpose the National Catholic War Council was formed in 1917. So "sensible, visible, practical, efficacious" was its work that many bishops became convinced that a peacetime coordinating agency should be continued. After some delay occasioned by a few bishops who feared that their independent powers would be jeopardized, the National Catholic Welfare Conference (N.C.W.C.) was established in 1921.

Initially the work of the N.C.W.C. was divided into five departments—Education, Lay Activities, Press, Social Action, and Missions. Later it was reorganized to embrace almost every area of Catholic interest and

---

[1] See Will Herberg, "The Triple Melting Pot," *Commentary* (1955), 101–8, 243. Later the massive influx of Spanish-speaking Catholics from Puerto Rico, Cuba, Mexico, and elsewhere posed the question of whether this surging tide could be assimilated in similar fashion within two or three generations.

concern. The Conference had no independent authority, existing solely to advise and assist the bishops. Nonetheless, it gained such prestige that it became an affective instrument for establishing national policy, for issuing pronouncements in the name of the entire hierarchy, and for fostering a sense of unity and solidarity among American Catholics.

Another mark of growing maturity was the changing role of American Roman Catholics in the field of foreign missions. For almost a century, they had been the recipients of assistance from abroad. The war shut off this source of help, and by bringing mass immigration to an end, the war also lessened the need for such aid. The Society for the Propagation of the Faith, with headquarters in Europe, had long been a chief channel through which mission funds had been sent to the United States, but after the war, Americans began to supply much of its income. By 1957, about 65 percent of its total budget was being met by gifts from the United States. In terms of foreign-mission personnel, the story was much the same. The Maryknoll Fathers had been funded in 1911, but it was not until 1918 that the first missionaries were sent out. By midcentury, however, Maryknoll Fathers were at work in Asia, Africa, Central and South America, and the islands of the Pacific. Meanwhile, other American orders joined the enterprise, and by 1960, Americans represented about one-ninth of the total Roman Catholic foreign-mission force.

Increase in Numbers and Wealth

Growing homogeneity, increasing unification, and vanishing dependence upon aid from abroad were not the only signs of maturity. In terms of numbers, the Roman Catholic Church was far more than a lusty infant. By 1920, the *Official Catholic Directory* reported a total of 17,885,000 baptized members.

With the flow of recruits through immigration reduced to a trickle, there was hope of strengthening the church through converts. The number of converts did increase, many the result of mixed marriages. This, of course, was a two-way street, with a Gallup Poll indicating that the movement in both directions was roughly in balance.[2]

Other defections stemmed from the natural tendency of many people to shirk religious obligations, but Roman Catholicism was remarkably successful in holding its own during these years. The officially reported membership was 20,203,702 in 1930; 21,284,455 in 1940; 28,634,878 in 1950; and 42,104,900 in 1960.[3] The last figure reflects the triple effect of a

---

[2] "Conversion Poll Ends in a Dead Heat," *Christian Century*, 72 (1955), 411.

[3] Inadequate collection of data resulted in an underreporting of membership at least through 1940. Statistical procedures were gradually improved thereafter. See G. A. Kelly and Thomas Coogan, "What Is Our Real Catholic Population?" *American Ecclesiastical Review*, 100 (1944), 377.

swelling birthrate, the influx of the refugees following World War II, and the "religious revival." In terms of any realistic standards of membership, the church in the United States had become the largest national grouping of Roman Catholics in the world.

In addition to numerical size, the Roman Catholic community in the United States was distinguished by its success in developing the largest private educational system in the world. By 1964, there were 10,902 Catholic elementary schools with more than 4.5 million pupils; 2,458 high schools with 1,068,424 students; 295 colleges and universities with more than 350,000 students; and 596 seminaries with 48,750 seminarians preparing for the priesthood. This success was accomplished with little or no direct aid from public taxation.

A third indication that American Roman Catholicism had moved far beyond its period of infancy was the fact that it had become the wealthiest national church in the Roman Catholic world. By 1920, it had achieved its financial independence and rapidly became a chief contributor to foreign-mission funds. Moreover, as early as 1937, it was estimated that half of Rome's current income was supplied by Americans.[4] A decade later, Communist takeovers in Poland, Czechoslovakia, Hungary, and Yugoslavia increased the reliance of the Vatican on American support.

Representation in the College of Cardinals is often an index of the importance that Rome attaches to a particular segment of the church. Until 1921, there was never more than one prince of the church in the United States, but thereafter the number gradually increased. By 1959, there were six American cardinals, a number approximating Spanish representation and exceeded only by that of France and, of course, Italy. The number of American priests appointed to offices in the Curia and in the Holy See's diplomatic service also reflected the enhanced importance of American Catholicism in the eyes of Rome.

Changing Status of Catholics in American Life

In the first half of the century, attention often was called to the contrast between the number of Catholics and their representation in national leadership positions. The failure to attain prominence in proportion to their numbers was commonly alleged to be the result of a conscious discrimination designed to keep Catholics out of posts of leadership. Few would contend that there were no instances of discrimination, but as an explanation of the lag in status of Catholics in American life, it requires elaboration.

First, such an explanation fails to take into account the source of a large portion of Roman Catholic strength. It was derived from recent immigrants who were drawn from the underprivileged classes of Europe and

[4] William Teeling, Pope Pius XI and World Affairs (New York, 1937), 133, 158f.

who arrived without financial resources. Many were illiterate; of those who were not, many were isolated from the general culture by language barriers. It normally takes at least a generation for children of immigrants to secure education necessary to qualify for professional positions. More often it is not until the third generation that this achievement occurs.

Second, much of the isolation of Roman Catholics was self-imposed. To hold immigrants true to the faith, tightly guarded enclaves were often created. Language barriers were perpetuated, and children were separated in parochial schools from other children in the community. The Knights of Columbus, the Catholic Youth Organization, the Newman Clubs, and Catholic War Veterans, and even Catholic "Junior Leagues" served to retard assimilation into the general community and thus made it more difficult for Catholics to gain positions of community leadership.

Third, the Catholic Church often projected a negative image. It was most successful in conveying an image of what it was against—birth control, divorce, euthanasia, and therapeutic abortion. The Legion of Decency, founded to encourage the production of better motion pictures, became much better known for the films it blacklisted than for those it approved. At several points, including issues relating to public education and American policy toward Franco Spain, Catholic opinion was at variance with that of other citizens. Quite apart from any religious prejudice, Catholic aspirants for public office were sometimes defeated simply because they did not represent majority opinion.

Studies based on information gathered in 1939 to 1940 and in 1948 indicated that Roman Catholics moved up the economic ladder much faster than generally had been assumed.[5] By the latter date, differences in class affiliation were rapidly disappearing. No appreciable distinctions in class, occupation, and education were found between Roman Catholics, Baptists, and Lutherans; and the disparity between Roman Catholics and Methodists was not great enough to be statistically significant.

Roman Catholics gained political prominence at an even earlier date. As was to be expected, urban centers where their strength was concentrated provided the arenas where Catholics first gained roles of political leadership. Later they moved in increasing numbers into positions of consequence in state capitals. If Roman Catholics were underrepresented in some state governments, it was presumably not because of their religion but because of the apportionment of state legislatures, which gave undue predominance to rural rather than urban interests.

The nomination of Alfred E. Smith in 1928 as the Democratic candidate for president signaled that Roman Catholics had come of age politically on the national scene. This success reversed his failure to gain the nomination in 1924. Even so, Smith faced a hopeless prospect. In 1928, Smith as

[5] See appendix to Herbert W. Schneider, *Religion in Twentieth Century America*, (Cambridge, MA, 1952), 255–38.

the Democratic candidate was seeking office in a time of booming prosperity, and he had as his opponent a man with a towering reputation as a great humanitarian. Also, Herbert Hoover, the opponent, as secretary of commerce had guided the nation into such affluence that the slogan "two chickens in every pot and two cars in every garage" did not seem unrealistic. Moreover, Hoover had the benefit of Republican alliances with big-city machines and organized labor. Later it was said that Smith's religion cost him votes.

Anti-Catholic votes were cast in the election. Methodist Bishop J. M. Cannon of Virginia urged Protestants to "vote as you pray," and in the South the traditional Democratic vote was reduced. But prohibition was as decisive as religion in this defection. Elsewhere "the noble experiment" was not yet a sufficiently emotional issue to cause very many to vote against their pocketbooks. Four years later, a vote for one's pocketbook coincided with a vote to end prohibition. Smith's Catholicism apparently gained him more votes than he lost. What else would account for his astonishing achievement in lifting the Democratic percentage of the total vote from 34 percent in 1920 and 28 percent in 1924 to 40 percent in 1982?[6] It is likely that a Protestant would have fared much worse. Not only did Smith lift the Democratic total from 8 to 15 million, but he also did better in proportion to the Democratic vote for congressmen than any other twentieth-century Democratic candidate prior to Franklin D. Roosevelt. After the election of 1932, Catholic political participation at the national level became commonplace, and John F. Kennedy's election in 1960 finally put to rest the myth that a Catholic could not be elected president of the United States.

Expressions of New Vitality

European Roman Catholics often referred to the "activism" of American Catholicism. With rapidly proliferating parishes to staff, churches to build, and schools to be established, money to be raised and ecclesiastical supervision to be maintained, there was ample cause for energetic busyness. The preoccupation with immediate tasks may explain the absence of any native-born citizen in the ranks of the saints. Mother Cabrini, of course, was elevated to sainthood in 1946, but she was of Italian birth. It is also true that Elizabeth Bayley Seton was canonized in 1970. But on the whole, American Catholics have been distinguished for virtues other than those calling for veneration by the faithful. It is appropriate, therefore, to begin

[6] R. C. Silva, *Rum, Religion, and Votes: 1928 Re-examined* (University Park, Pa., 1962), 4. Also E. A. Moore, *A Catholic Runs for President* (New York, 1956).

a consideration of currents of thought and concern that have characterized American Catholicism by centering attention on its "social program."

The Social Program of the Church

For two decades after its founding, the National Catholic Welfare Conference was regarded in public esteem as almost synonymous with its Social
Action Department, headed by John A. Ryan, professor of moral theology
at Catholic University.[7] In 1919, Ryan wrote a pamphlet, "Social Reconstruction: A General Review of the Problems and Survey of the Remedies,"
which became known as the "Bishops' Program of Social Reconstruction."[8]
The document pointed to the need for minimum-wage legislation, regulation of child labor, protection of the right of labor to organize, public
housing, a national employment service, and unemployment, industrial-
accident, and old-age insurance. With one or two exceptions, the recommendations of the Ryan document became part of the New Deal
legislation of the early Roosevelt years. In Ryan's writings, in Catholic
urban projects such as the St. Louis Verein and in Father Edward
McGlynn's programs of humanitarian reform, there existed a loosely organized Catholic initiative that was similar to the Protestant Social Gospel in
its religiously grounded call for social reform.

Meanwhile, other Catholics forwarded the cause of economic justice.
The Catholic League for Social Justice was established in 1932. A year
later, Dorothy Day helped found the Catholic Worker movement. In 1937,
the Association of Catholic Trade Unionists was formed. Numerous "labor
schools" were established to train union members and to help them combat both racketeering elements in the unions and Communist infiltration.
Moreover, Charles E. Coughlin, the radio priest of the Shrine of the Little
Flower in Royal Oak, Michigan, won a large following in the 1930s as a
spokesman for social justice. When his weekly broadcasts became tinged
with anti-Semitic sentiment, however, his ecclesiastical superiors gradually
inhibited him from political activity.

Although the "Bishops' Program of Social Reconstruction" was based on
the authoritative papal encyclical *Rerum Novarum* (1891), the stance of the
church was ambiguous. Some bishops were lukewarm in their support, and
many of the laity were recalcitrant. The cooling of social ardor was especially noticeable after World War II when much of the Catholic press became scornful of "do-gooders" and "bleeding hearts." The disposition to
give only nominal acceptance to the "social encyclicals," Bishop William

---

[7] See F. L. Broderick, *Right Reverend New Dealer: John A. Ryan* (New York, 1963).

[8] Reprinted in H. Shelton Smith, Robert Handy, and Lefferts Loetscher, *American Christianity*,
II, 407–14.

Mulloy declared in 1952, "tended to paralyze the force of the teaching Church in modern American society."[9]

Roman Catholic policy was more firm during the 1950s in the area of racial justice. Ever since the Civil War, work among blacks had followed a segregated pattern, but in the 1920s, a series of conferences focused attention on segregation in Catholic institutions. The movement began to bear fruit when the Archbishop of St. Louis in 1947 ended segregation in the schools of his diocese. The following year the Archbishop of Washington followed his example, and in 1953, the Bishop of Raleigh, North Carolina, defied the opposition of Catholics in his diocese and opened the churches, schools, and hospitals under his jurisdiction to people of every race. After the Supreme Court in 1954 declared public-school segregation unconstitutional, the unequivocal stands of Archbishops Robert E. Lucey of San Antonio and Joseph F. Rummel of New Orleans were a heartening feature of the situation in the South.

The tenor of Catholic political thought contrasted sharply with the progressive character of other aspects of the church's social program. Tendencies toward accommodation of Catholic tradition to basic assumptions of American democracy had been arrested by Leo XIII's condemnation of "Americanism" in 1899. The alternative, in terms of official teaching, was to look back to the Middle Ages for normative models, and this alternative was commanded by Leo XIII's encyclicals "The Christian Constitution of States" (1885) and "Christian Democracy" (1901), which rejected doctrines of popular sovereignty, government by consent of the governed, and pernicious notions of freedom of religion, freedom of speech, freedom of assembly, and freedom of the press.[10] The encyclicals conceded that, because of circumstances in any given nation, a full Christian political order may not always be possible or practical. Under certain conditions, therefore, the church will not judge it "blameworthy" for "the people to have a share, greater or less, in the government." Indeed, under certain conditions, "such participation . . . may even be of obligation." This concession was the "out" seized upon by American Catholics familiar with papal teaching to effect a practical adjustment to the necessities of American political life. The theory was explicated by John A. Ryan and Moorhouse F. X. Millar in the widely used textbook, *The State and the Church* (1922).[11] In the area of political thought, since he was forced to acknowledge that Catholic teaching involved "hard sayings" that smacked of intolerance, Ryan was cast into the role of a reactionary.

---

[9] Robert D. Cross, *Emergence of Liberal Catholicism*, (Cambridge, MA, 1958), 218–19.

[10] For the encyclicals, see W. S. Hudson, *Understanding Roman Catholicism*, (Philadelphia, 1959).

[11] Later revised and republished by John A. Ryan and Francis J. Boland under a new title, *Catholic Principles of Politics* (New York, 1940).

By the late 1940s, however, Catholic theologians began to challenge Ryan's conclusions. Jesuits John Courtney Murray and Gustave Weigel took the lead with a more dynamic view of Catholic political theory, placing it in historical context and demonstrating that political democracy could be firmly grounded on Catholic principles.[12] Their views were widely accepted. Whatever Ryan's intention may have been, the views expounded in his textbook made it possible for many Catholics in the 1950s to defend Senator Joseph McCarthy's activities on the assumption that they were based on "Catholic" teaching.

Intellectual Life

As early as 1928, in *The Catholic Spirit in America*, George N. Shuster voiced the complaint that American Catholicism was intellectually asleep and exhibited "a terrible contempt for thought." In 1940, he renewed the charge that the church had "virtually no use for intellectuals." The absence of a strong intellectual tradition may be attributed to several causes. For one thing, American Catholics had been too engrossed in "brick-and-mortar" enterprises—constructing churches, schools, and other institutions—to allow much energy and imagination to be devoted to intellectual pursuits. Moreover, the average immigrant family lacked both the educational background and the financial resources to foster intellectual interests. Symptomatic of this state of affairs was the fact that in the late 1940s, not a single member of the hierarchy was the son of college-educated parents. Furthermore, the Catholic educational system had emphasized "safeness" at the expense of "excellence" and creative inquiry. But the major reason was the inhibiting effect of the condemnation of "Americanism" and "Modernism." The authoritarian (as opposed to critical-intellectual) style of the Catholic Church, coupled with a sacramentalism that required for its efficacy the participation of church authorities (e.g., priests, bishops), intensified the problem, so that an outright anti-intellectualism developed among Catholics in America.

The retreat into "separatism" from American culture that followed Leo XIII's letter of 1899 to Cardinal Gibbons was strongly reinforced by Pius X's comprehensive attack in 1970 on the "modernist" heresies flowing from the historical researches of certain European Catholic scholars. Bishops were instructed to exercise minute supervision of both teachers and students. Three years later, a decree was issued requiring all Catholics in positions of responsibility to take a detailed antimodernist oath. Although few in America held the condemned opinions, the effect of the condemnation was to heighten timidity and give full reign to an unquestioning orthodoxy. The spirit inculcated was reflected in the counsel given a young

---

[12] See John Courtney Murray's essays, *We Hold These Truths* (New York, 1960), and Gustave Weigel, "The Church and the Democratic State," *Thought*, 27 (1952), 165–75.

Paulist who was perplexed by intellectual problems. He was advised to "preach the moral law and let dogmas alone."[13]

After World War II, the situation began to change. The mingling, especially of priests, with non-Catholics in the armed forces ended Catholic isolation. Also, the educational level of the Catholic population was rising, thrusting to the fore those questions that hitherto had been regarded as "too hot to handle." And an awareness of new theological trends in Europe began to seep into academic cloisters. But the decisive factor may have been such verdicts as that expressed by an English observer that "the Catholic church in America has counted for astonishingly little in the formation of the American intellectual climate." In 1955, John Tracy Ellis of Catholic University created a minor sensation with an indictment of American Catholics for their intellectual abdication, and three years later, Thomas F. O'Dea contributed an even more detailed analysis of the problem.[14]

In the meantime, a vigorous controversy developed between those who were convinced that the general culture was important to Catholics and necessitated their active involvement in it and those who insisted that a strongly guarded defensive posture was indispensable, since Catholicism and modern cultural tendencies were diametrically opposed. The first position commanded massive Jesuit support, with John Courtney Murray and Gustave Weigel the outstanding protagonists. Stressing the obligation of the church to the pursuit of truth and drawing heavily upon new biblical and theological studies in Europe, they believed that one who turned aside from apologetic opportunities involved in friendly contact with non-Catholic scholars was "only a half Catholic." The conservative citadel was the faculty of theology at Catholic University, where Joseph C. Fenton and Francis J. Connell took the lead in viewing the "openness" of the Jesuits as verging on indifferentism. "Polemics" rather than "irenics" was emphasized as the proper approach to error, because any minimizing of the hard sayings of dogma to avoid offense to outsiders was to trifle with the salvation of the faithful.[15] By 1960, the ranks of the "liberals" were swelled by recruits from non-Jesuit orders, new scholarly journals were being published, and a number of Catholic colleges and universities were beginning to be

---

[13] W. L. Sullivan, *Under Orders* (New York, 1944), 111. T. T. McAvoy spoke of the "theological silence" that descended on the church. See *The Great Crisis in American Catholic History*, (Chicago, 1957), 344.

[14] D. W. Brogan, *U.S.A.: An Outline of the Country, Its People and Institutions* (London, 1941), 65; John Tracy Ellis, *American Catholics and the Intellectual Life (Chicago*, 1956); and Thomas F. O'Dea, *American Catholic Dilemma; An Inquiry into the Intellectual Life* (New York, 1958).

[15] See Joseph C. Fenton, "The Direction of Catholic Polemic," *American Ecclesiastical Review*, 122 (1950), 48–55; "The Church and God's Promises," *ibid.*, 123 (1950), 295–308; "The Lesson of Humani Generis," *ibid.*, 359–78; and "Catholic Polemic and Doctrinal Accuracy," *ibid.*, 132 (1955), 107–17. See also Francis J. Connell, "If the Trumpet Give an Uncertain Sound," *American Ecclesiastical Review*, 188 (1948), 23–30; and "Theological Content of Humani Generis," *ibid.*, 123 (1950), 321–30.

distinguished by the quality of their scholarly contributions and the vigor of their intellectual life.

The Religious Revival

Fulton Sheen and Thomas Merton were two major symbols of the post–World War II religious revival among Roman Catholics. In public esteem, Sheen ranked with Billy Graham and Norman Vincent Peale as the preeminent spokesmen of religion during these years. A teacher of philosophy at Catholic University with a gift of speaking intelligibly and convincingly to a mass audience, Sheen gained fame as a radio and television preacher and then as the author of several widely read books. His role in a number of prominent conversions, both before and after being appointed auxiliary bishop of New York, also made him a focus of attention. These conversions, however, did not prevent him from gaining a wide hearing among Protestants as well as Catholics, since he seldom stressed distinctively Roman Catholic doctrine. Merton was a disillusioned sophisticate who had sought peace in many places, including Greenwich Village, and finally found it in the silence of a Trappist monastery in Kentucky. His autobiography, *The Seven Story Mountain* (1948), was on the list of best-sellers for months, and his subsequent writings also aroused widespread interest.

Merton's pilgrimage was part of a striking movement to which his autobiography gave added impetus. Although a Trappist monastery had been established in America early in the nineteenth century, contemplative monasticism, with its vows of perpetual silence and rigorous austerity, failed to prosper in the American environment. At the end of World War II, however, a startling change occurred when hundreds of young men began to forsake the world and give themselves fully to a life of prayer.

The surge of interest in a contemplative life, of course, was restricted to a spiritual elite. A more typical expression of the religious revival was the mounting lay participation in the life of the church, much of it associated with the burgeoning parishes of the suburbs. The lay movement was the product of the wedding of traditional American activism with postwar religious enthusiasm and the increased stress of Pius XII on the importance of the lay apostolate. So marked was the development that one clerical observer could speak with confidence of "The Coming Era of the Catholic Layman."[16]

Closely related to the lay movement was a developing liturgical interest that sought to revitalize corporate worship. The religious revival had expressed itself initially among Roman Catholics in the growing popularity of many special nonliturgical devotions—the Forty Hours Adoration of the

---

[16] This was the title of an article by W. R. Fleege in the *Homiletical and Pastoral Review*, 54 (1953), 134–39. For the lay movement, see Leo R. Ward, *The American Apostolate* (Westminster, Md., 1952), and *Catholic Life, U.S.A.* (New York, 1959).

Blessed Sacrament; novenas to Our Lady of Perpetual Help, Our Lady of Sorrows, Our Lady of Fatima, Our Lady of the Miraculous Medal; and devotions to favorite saints such as St. Ann, St. Jude, St. Anthony, and St. Rita. But attendance at Mass was often little more than fulfillment of solemn obligation. Worshipers sometimes had little understanding of the service and sat as mere spectators or performed private devotions by reciting the rosary. This was scarcely an adequate expression of their role as a Christian people or of their lay priesthood, nor did such routine attendance readily relate life to their apostolate in the world. It was out of concern to renew the life of the church through truly corporate worship that the liturgical movement was born.

The main center of the liturgical revival in America was the Benedictine Abbey at Collegeville, Minnesota, where Virgil Michel was the outstanding pioneer. Through his initiative, the periodical *Orate Fratres* (later known as *Worship*) was founded to promote liturgical renewal. In 1940, annual Liturgical Weeks, conferences for those interested in liturgical renewal, began to be held. In addition to seeking to instruct the faithful in the meaning of the liturgy, two chief goals of the movement were the use of the vernacular instead of Latin and adoption of the dialogue Mass in which the people recite the prayers with the priest. Other aims included restoration of the Holy Week Liturgy, encouragement of daily attendance at Mass, and the use of "people's altars" placed in the midst of the worshiping congregation.[17] By 1960, liturgical renewal was receiving widespread support, many innovations had been introduced, and the movement was influencing the architecture of new church buildings.

Hispanic Catholicism

Catholicism originally took root in the Americas through the efforts of Spanish Franciscan, Dominican, and Jesuit missionaries in Mexico and the Caribbean, and eventually in Central America, Peru, and the rest of South America. Financed by the gold-rich royal treasury, over 15,000 missionaries came from Spain to the Americas between 1493 and 1820. The missionary endeavor as a whole was greatly expedited by a proclamation of the crown that every exploration include two priests who were to undertake the conversion of the Indians encountered along the way. The Spanish missions that were thus founded were highly organized centers of learning, agriculture, the arts, and religion. Missionaries learned the native tongues, taught the Indians to read and write Spanish, catechized them, and introduced

[17] E. B. Koenker, *The Liturgical Renaissance in the Roman Catholic Church* (Chicago, 1954); P. B. Marx, *Virgil Michel and the Liturgical Movement* (Collegeville, Minn., 1957); and A. H. Reinhold, *The American Parish and the Roman Liturgy* (New York, 1958).

Spanish ways of farming and animal husbandry. Sometimes the missionaries were extraordinarily successful. At other times they failed to persuade
the Indians to convert, and not infrequently they were wiped out by
uprisings.

In the course of expanding the mission system, the Spanish developed a
tolerance for native religious beliefs and customs. Although they sought to
curb practices that they considered idolatrous or superstitious, they nevertheless accepted to some degree the Indians' desire to retain certain aspects of their religious traditions. Accordingly, the Catholicism that
developed in Mexico and the American Southwest was marked by the interweaving of local religious custom with Catholic devotions. In Mexico,
folk healing and a rich vein of animism survived alongside Catholic doctrine. The widespread display in Mexico of images of the Virgin of
Guadalupe, who reputedly appeared to the Indian Juan Diego in 1531,
represents something of the supernaturalistic tone and the distinctive emphases of Spanish Catholicism as it developed in the New World.

From Mexico, Spanish missionaries made their way northward to Southwest territories ranging from Texas to California. In these territories,
which came into the union following war with Mexico in 1848, and in
Florida, the labors of the missionaries bore fruit for a time. With the arrival of Anglos, however, the Protestant churches rapidly proliferated, so
that Catholicism remained dominant only in New Mexico.

In the mid–twentieth century, a series of waves of immigration from the
Caribbean, Mexico, and Central America took place. Following World War
II, Puerto Ricans settled in extreme poverty in New York City, where diocesan officials who did not speak Spanish were ill-equipped to incorporate
them into church life. Middle-class and professional Cubans who came to
south Florida after Fidel Castro's revolution in 1959 adapted more easily to
their new surroundings and became a strong Catholic presence. Most important were the many millions of Mexican Americans who flowed contin-
uously into the Southwest in search of economic opportunity. The
expanding Spanish-speaking American churches found themselves in a
difficult relationship with an Irish-American hierarchy that disapproved of
the folk religion aspects of Mexican American Catholicism. However, as
Mexican Americans became more visible, not only in the Southwest but
also in cities such as Chicago, Detroit, and Atlanta, they exercised a
stronger influence on church life, as in the appointment of Patrick Fer-
nandez Flores, a Mexican American, as bishop of El Paso in 1978.

The dramatic increase in the Hispanic population of the United States
in the latter part of the twentieth century significantly affected the religious landscape. The Hispanic population stood at 35 million, or 12.5 percent of the nation's 2000 census, with about 77 percent of Hispanics
associated with Catholicism. Seventy-one percent of the growth in Catholicism since 1960 was Hispanic, and at the end of the century, as much as

38 percent of all U.S. Catholics were Hispanic, making them the largest ethnic group in the Catholic church.

The continuing difficulties faced by Catholic leaders in addressing this large Hispanic constituency have been represented most visibly in the ratio of clergy to laity among Hispanics (1:9,925) in relation to clergy for U.S. Catholics as a whole (1:1,230). Part of the problem of the shortage of clergy in Hispanic communities stems from linguistic differences. Only 17.9 percent of parishes had a Hispanic ministry at the end of the twentieth century. Most non-Hispanic Catholic clergy are unequipped to function in religious environments where Spanish is the primary language, and they are often unfamiliar with the distinctive emphases of Hispanic religiosity. And in many parishes where English- and Spanish-speaking Catholics worship, Hispanics attend their own masses in Spanish, usually at off-peak times and not always in the main church sanctuary. The marking of difference between Hispanic and non-Hispanic Catholics through separate worship schedules and even worship places is often duplicated at other levels of parish life. The United States Conference of Catholic Bishops reported in 1999 that Hispanics "rarely have the same level of representation on the parish pastoral council as non Hispanics, and frequently rely on volunteers to manage their own parish programs."[18]

There is much diversity within Hispanic Catholicism. Cuban, Puerto Rican, Mexican, and Salvadoran groups, to name just a few, embrace Catholicism in their own ways. Nevertheless, a common feature of Hispanic religious life across these various groups is the blending of folk customs and traditional ethnic practices with Catholicism. This popular religion, which has been more easily accepted by church leadership since the Second Vatican Council in the 1960s, is a distinguishing mark of Hispanic worship and is visible in the ways that Hispanic groups integrate family, community, and church in their parishes. Popular religion is also present in Hispanic Protestantism, and as Protestantism continues to claim more American Hispanics, that style of religion will become increasingly prominent in some of the Protestant denominations.

The *religiosidad popular* of Hispanics arises, like all popular religion, through a complex interweaving of local traditions and experiences with institutional forms. Popular Catholicism arguably is everywhere apparent, in every place where there are Catholics. Its usefulness as a term lies largely in its capability to describe the process of blending that takes place in religious life, rather than in any distinctions it might suggest between "pure" religion and "syncretistic" religion. Popular religion is to a certain extent spontaneous, in that it is not imposed upon a group by religious

---

[18] Rev. Gerald R. Barnes, Chairman, "Hispanic Ministry at the Turn of the New Millennium: A Report of the Bishops' Committee on Hispanic Affairs" (National Conference of Catholic Bishops, 1999).

leaders who seek uniformity in ritual, symbol, and myth within a religion, but, rather, it arises out of the devotional themes imbedded in everyday life. Hispanic popular religion specifically is formed from Spanish Christian tradition, Native American religiosity, and African faiths. The Amerindian influence in Hispanic religion is especially revealed in Mexican American religious life. A worldview grounded in a trust in the wholeness of life, of the interrelatedness of all cosmic phenomena, is characteristic of that life, as is the valuing of community and belief in the transcendence, of the presence of the divine quality in nature. The African element in Hispanic religion, which emerged more visibly as the slave trade increased, includes dance and music, and a belief, as well, in a world populated by spirits of various sorts. Also important in shaping Hispanic popular religion is the Spanish Catholicism of the sixteenth through eighteenth centuries, which itself was characterized by its accommodation of religious ideas and practices from a variety of Mediterranean backgrounds and which brought a strong mystical strain to the conversionist enterprise in the Americas. In recent years, protestant Pentecostalism has made strong inroads into Hispanic populations in Latin America and the United States. Offering emotional satisfactions and being largely amenable to the interweaving of indigenous traditions with Christianity (e.g. healing and narrative, but with some exceptions, such as processions, which are discouraged), Pentecostalism has become dominant in some Hispanic communities, possibly, according to some observers, because Hispanic Catholics experience church authority as a threat to their social survival in the same way that they perceive the dominant non-Hispanic society to endanger their way of life.[19]

The religious calendar of Hispanic Catholics features an assortment of religious practices that are distinctive. The Mexican American *posada*, which is celebrated outdoors as part of a novena leading up to Christmas, is a reenactment of parts of the nativity narrative. The story of the search by Mary and Joseph for a place in which to stay is told in hymnody, one group singing the parts of Joseph and Mary, and the other group reenacting the role of the innkeepers. The *posada* culminates in prayer and feasting after Joseph and Mary are eventually welcomed into the home. In Puerto Rican communities, a similar religious exercise, the *parrandas*, which focuses on the visit of the Three Kings to Bethlehem, also takes place at Christmastime, and it likewise includes special hymns, foods, and prayers. The *quince años*, which is celebrated on a girl's fifteenth birthday,

---

[19] Kenneth Davis, "Brevia from the Hispanic Shift: Continuity Rather Than Conversion?" in *An Enduring Flame: Studies on Latino Popular Religiosity*, eds. Anthony M. Stevens-Arroyo and Ana Maria Diaz-Stevens (New York, 1994), 208; Pedrito U. Maynard-Reid, *Diverse Worship: African-American, Caribbean & Hispanic Perspectives* (Downers Grove, Ill., 2000), 167–180; William A. Christian, Jr., "Spain in Latino Religiosity," in *El Cuerpo de Cristo: The Hispanic Presence in the U.S. Catholic Church*, eds. Peter Casarella and Raul Gomez (New York, 1998), 325–330.

ritually marks the movement from childhood to adulthood. The *quinceañera* renews her baptismal vows, pledges to make contributions to her family and community, and accepts from the community symbols of her faith and commitment, such as a medal of the Virgin, a rosary, or a ring. Like much Hispanic popular religion, this event is overwhelmingly a family occasion. Although the teenage girl is the center of attention, the occasion is structured as a way for affirming family bonds. Parents, godparents, siblings, and friends all have roles to play in the *quince años*. The tone of the proceedings is serious—the mastery of a catechism is required—as much as it is celebratory, and the often substantial amount of money spent on the occasion by families of modest means indicates its central importance to the religious and social maturation of a Hispanic girl.

Distinctive rituals of mourning, and especially the observation of *Día de los Muertos*, are also present in the *religiosidad popular* of Hispanics. The festival dedicated to children and the dead that originally was celebrated by the Aztecs in late July (as long ago as the second millennium B.C.) was moved by Spanish Catholic missionaries in Mexico to All Hallows Day in the hopes that the coincidence would result in the gradual triumph of the Christian observance. Celebrated on November 2, the day of the dead instead has remained a vital part of the religious life of many Mexican Americans, and especially those in California. The centerpiece of the celebration is an altar erected in the home and decorated with the various items of the *oferenda*, or offering. Those items include photographs of the deceased, sugar skulls, toys, cigarettes, bread, corn and other harvest produce, candles, artwork of various sorts, flowers, incense, money and liquors. An effort is made to place upon the altar things that were valued by the deceased. This family event, usually but not always celebrated in the home, shares meaning with the *novenario*, a nine-day ritual of mourning when a family member dies, that includes the daily praying of the rosary as well as the erection of an altar.

In Hispanic religious life, women take responsibility for domestic religion. They pass on the traditions, organize the special occasions, and foster an awareness of the sacred within the home. And the figure of Mary is usually at the center of religious devotions both within the home and outside it. Hispanic Catholic churches frequently feature a statue of Mary over the main altar, with a crucifix above a sanctuary to the side if there is one. Persons with Mexican backgrounds make pilgrimages to sites associated with Mary: Our Lady of Guadalupe (Mexico City), Our Lady of Los Lagos (Guadalajara), and Our Lady of the Lake (on the Texas-Mexico border). In Hispanic Christianity brought to the United States from the Caribbean, women play the leading role in spiritual healing and discernment.

The quest for social justice is an essential part of Hispanic religion, both Protestant and Catholic, in the United States. Hispanics are disproportionately poor and lacking in education when compared with other Americans. The moral dimension of religious life includes for many Hispanics a commitment to reform of institutions that limit their ability to participate fully in American society. Though rarely an application of an explicitly "liberation theology," much Hispanic theological reflection, as well as the construction of agendas for social action, is oriented toward social justice. The figure of Jesus as a reformer, as an exemplar of struggle against oppression, looms large in Hispanic Christianity in America. Discourses stressing human rights are common in Hispanic religious communities, and base Christian communities (*communidades eclesiales de base*, or CEBs)—activist neighborhood groups grounded in theological legitimations of struggle—frequently form within parishes or congregations.

Interfaith Relationships

The middle decades of the twentieth century were marked by increasingly friendly interfaith relationships. The National Conference of Christians and Jews, founded in 1928, was one of the instruments for promoting understanding between adherents of different faiths, utilizing local committees to combat prejudice, ill feeling, and strained relationships. Broad Protestant and Jewish support was enlisted, but Catholic participation was extremely limited. Francis J. Connell voiced the prevailing sentiment when he declared that "the association of Catholics with non-Catholics in such organizations and meetings is a grave menace to the faith of our people."[20] This aloofness from interfaith relationships was in striking contrast to the generally warm, friendly, and even cordial attitudes of Protestants and Jews. Even the Eastern Orthodox churches, while maintaining their doctrinal integrity, felt sufficiently secure to accept membership in both the national and the world councils of churches. The Catholic problem was complicated by tension at several points of social policy and also by an unresolved difference of opinion as to the proper strategy to be pursued in a religiously pluralistic society.

Although uncomfortable feelings were exacerbated by Roman Catholic intransigence on issues of public policy, the greatest problem in reducing tension was the self-imposed Roman Catholic policy of isolation. As the ecumenical movement gained momentum in the 1920s and 1930s, it was hoped that Catholics would participate. This hope was dashed in 1928 when Pius XI issued an encyclical on "Fostering True Religious Unity" (*Mortalium Animos*) in which he declared that it was unlawful for Catholics to "take part in these assemblies" and that by giving "such enterprises their encouragement or support," they "would be giving countenance to a false Christianity quite alien to the one Church of Christ." Throughout the 1940s, however, there was growing restiveness at this blanket prohibition.

[20] Cross, 212.

In retrospect, it is clear that a basis for a new attitude was being pre-pared by a revival of biblical studies that made it possible to distinguish the spiritual from the physical body of Christ. This dual understanding of the church was susceptible of being interpreted to justify the regarding of Protestants as "separated brethren" and "brethren in Christ." Although European scholars initiated this new type of thinking, a number of Ameri-can Catholics recognized the necessity of breaching the wall of ignorance that separated Catholics and Protestants in the United States. In 1957, when John A. Hardon published *The Protestant Churches of the United States*, he noted that Catholics "often have only the vaguest notion of what Protes-tants believe, how they worship, and what their religion means to them."[21] Nor was Hardon alone in his concern. In 1955, George H. Tavard pub-lished *The Catholic Approach to Protestantism*, and in 1957, Gustave Weigel contributed *A Catholic Primer on the Ecumenical Movement.*

The elevation of Angelo Giuseppe Roncalli to the chair of Peter as John XXIII late in 1958 inaugurated a new era in the Catholic Church. On Jan-uary 25, 1959, he announced his intention to summon a General Council of the Roman Catholic Church to bring the church up-to-date (aggiorna-mento) through purification and renewal. By opening a few windows, he hoped to introduce "some fresh air" into the church and thus to make it more effective in dealing with the problems of the twentieth century and to provide a basis for furthering Christian unity. When the first session of the Second Vatican Council convened on October 11, 1962, seventeen non–Roman Catholic churches had responded to an invitation to send "of-ficial observers," and the impact of their presence was felt throughout the church.

In the United States, John XXIII's initiatives led to a dramatic shift in the atmosphere of interfaith relationships. Even in terms of pressing social problems, there had been little interfaith cooperation, but within a month of the close of the first session of the Second Vatican Council, Protestants, Roman Catholics, and Jews met in a national meeting to chart a common strategy for dealing with the racial crisis. "The bishops were holding back from these meetings out of fear—fear of Rome," one theologian ex-plained. "Now Pope John has given the Church a freedom from fear."[22] The most impressive consequence of the new spirit was the flowering of in-terfaith discussion in city after city throughout the nation. Reticence gave way to openness and friendliness, and for the first time in more than half a century, Catholic clergy with ease of mind could talk freely with represen-tatives of other faiths about points of difference. Equally impressive was

---

[21] Two years later, historian Jaroslav Pelikan, a Protestant, made a similar admission in the In-troduction to *The Riddle of Roman Catholicism*, stating that many Protestants "know more about the batting averages of the Yankees or the marriages and divorces of Hollywood than they do about the life and workings" of the Roman Catholic Church.

[22] R. B. Kaiser, *Pope, Council, and World* (New York, 1963), 254.

the warmth of the response by clergy of other faiths. No surrender of doctrinal positions was intended or expected, but sympathetic understanding
was no longer foreclosed by estrangement.

The several tendencies of growing maturity within American Roman
Catholicism—a deepened sense of responsibility to society, a heightened
emphasis upon intellectual pursuits, a greater stress on the role of the laity,
and an intensified concern for liturgical renewal—had been brought into
focus and reinforced by John XXIII and the Second Vatican Council. But
this remarkable pontiff, who had been expected to serve only a caretaker
role, made a further contribution. By the openness to the "world" that he
displayed, American Catholics were enabled to shed the last vestiges of an
immigrant mentality, and with Americans of other faiths they were learning, in the presence of diversity, to live together in a way that was mutually
enriching rather than impoverishing. Learning this latter lesson was to be
especially important for the years ahead, for both churches and nation
were about to enter a troubled time that would tax the wisdom, strength,
and resources of everyone.

CHAPTER SIXTEEN

"Old and New Centers"

Religious revivals sometimes succeed in bringing persons into the churches. The Great Awakening and the revivals of the early nineteenth century substantially increased the rolls of local congregations in certain parts of the country. And later revivals, such as those associated with Dwight L. Moody and Billy Sunday, left in their wake at least a temporary increase in the numbers of churchgoers in the host city.

Revivals can also represent cultural change. They frequently emerge in contexts fraught with conflict between old and new theological ideas, and with economic turbulence, dislocation of populations, and shifting patterns of authority. In cases in which change is very rapid and thoroughgoing, revivals are less significant as a means of religious renewal than as a signal of approaching religious disarray. The revivals and innovations of the 1950s for a short time functioned as a means of lending stability to Jewish, Protestant, and Catholic denominations. By the end of the 1960s, however, it was clear that the old religious order would not be revived. In its place emerged a host of new emphases and movements. These movements spun away from the old center—or, more appropriately, old centers—of religious gravity.

The Fracturing of Protestantism

Protestant Disarray

In 1957, according to a Gallup Poll, only 14 percent of Americans believed that religion was losing influence. A decade later, 57 percent held this opinion. In 1970, those who believed that religion was losing influence increased to 75 percent. After 1957, church attendance leveled off and then declined. In 1968, ten of the largest Protestant bodies had fewer members than in the preceding year. The United Methodist Church, a denomination that once outpaced all others, leaping forward like a brush fire, in 1972 reported a net loss of 518,000 members in the previous four years.

The old-line churches of cooperative Protestantism continued to post declines in membership throughout the 1970s and into the 1980s. Statistics drawn from the 1970 and 1985 *Year Book of American and Canadian Churches* show the losses sustained by the following typical old-line denominations:

Christian Churches (Disciples of Christ) declined 27.8 percent.

Episcopal Church declined 14 percent.

Presbyterian Church in the U.S.A. declined 15.4 percent.

United Church of Christ declined 16.3 percent.

United Methodist Church declined 14.5 percent.

When measured against growth in population, the actual declines were even greater. The American Lutheran Church and the Lutheran Church in America fared somewhat better with a combined loss of 10 percent during the same years, whereas the ultraconservative Lutheran Church–Missouri Synod, its rapid growth checked by controversy, had a 3.7 percent loss.

While the old-line churches were declining, other parts of Protestantism were growing. During the 1970s and 1980s, those parts, located outside the official structures of long-established denominations, had a distinctly conservative cast. Southern Baptists were one exception. With their own brand of regional and Baptist identification, Southern Baptists had surged forward after 1920 to become the largest Protestant body in the United States. After 1940, they became increasingly noncooperative with mainline Protestantism. Although many were unhappy with this trend, by the 1970s, Southern Baptists, who were victims of a power struggle, had begun to move steadily in an extreme fundamentalist direction that brooked no dissent. From the large base of over 11 million members reported in the 1970 *Year Book of American and Canadian Churches*, Southern Baptists posted a 25 percent gain in the next fifteen years. Apart from Southern Baptists, who kept to themselves, new Protestant vitality was represented by parallel and sometimes overlapping movements that had taken on new life after being on the scene since early in the century. These movements were what once would have been called the holiness-pentecostal-fundamentalist fringe of Protestantism. By the 1970s, they were commonly referred to as "the new evangelicalism" and "the new pentecostalism."[1]

If the religious landscape looked different at the end of the 1980s, it was partly the result of the new confidence and thrust of the evangelicals—what the press called "the born-again movement." To some, the new evangelicalism seemed little more than a renamed, and perhaps reborn, version of the old fundamentalism. There were continuities, including an insistence upon a conversion experience, a reliance upon the authority and inspiration of the Bible, and an acceptance of the birth, miracles, and resurrection of Christ as supernatural events. But there were also differences. The movement was less monolithic[2] and more broadly based and more socially respectable. The leadership was better educated and more prone to identify with middle-class America. And there was a strong tendency to identify with overtly right-wing politics.

A growing awareness of evangelical strength led *Newsweek* to label 1976 "the year of the evangelical." This choice was perhaps a salute to the election of Jimmy Carter as president. But the editors could have cited other evidence. Evangelical book publishers were flourishing, penetrating the commercial book market with titles that reached the top of the best-seller lists. Also, student organizations such as Intervarsity Christian Fellowship and Campus Crusade were eliciting strong student support at a time when conventional campus religious groups were dwindling. But the most telling evidence, to the public mind, was the fact that it was becoming almost fashionable to be "born again." The ranks of the reborn included rock stars (Bob Dylan), folk singers (Johnny Cash), and a long list of movie stars, professional athletes, and U.S. senators.

An equally striking manifestation of the turn to conservatism was the mushrooming of the "new pentecostalism" within conventional Protestant denominations and the Roman Catholic Church. For fifty years, charismatic gifts of healing, miracles, prophecy, tongues, and the interpretation of tongues (I Cor. 12:1–11) had been the domain of small Pentecostal denominations. But late in the 1950s, "the pentecostal experience" began to

---

[1] During the same fifteen-year period for which churches of cooperative Protestantism reported losses, the Christian and Missionary Alliance posted a gain of 80 percent; Church of God (Anderson, Ind.), 25 percent; Church of God (Cleveland, Tenn.), 103 percent; Church of the Nazarene, 40 percent. The Assemblies of God led the numbers parade, tripling their membership from 626,660 to 1,992,754.

[2] Many were moderate, irenic, and cooperative. But others were contentious and ready to fight along narrowly defined lines. Some were still proud to call themselves fundamentalists, and some of these believed in "biblical separation," not separation of church and state nor separation from the world, but separation of the races.

penetrate major Protestant churches without producing defections. It was primarily a lay movement, informal groups being drawn together by mutual unhappiness with a lackluster spiritual life and a common longing for an intimate experience of God's presence.[3]

In terms of national publicity, the charismatic movement, as it was now called, surfaced in 1960 when sensational treatment was accorded Dennis J. Bennett's announcement to his 2,000-member Van Nuys, California, Episcopal congregation of his "pentecostal experience." Within the decade, Presbyterians, Methodists, Lutherans, and Baptists also were involved.

The most important institutional bridge between the old and new pentecostalism was the Full Gospel Businessmen's Fellowship, founded by a wealthy California dairyman, Demos Shakerian. The intent was to provide an opportunity for laypersons in the older pentecostal denominations to promote pentecostal renewal without supervision of denominational officials. Meetings of the fellowship were often held in luxury hotels, and their nondenominational character was attractive to persons in conventional churches who did not wish to sever their old affiliations. Oral Roberts also played a key role in transmitting the old pentecostalism to the new charismatic movement. Ordained by the Pentecostal Holiness Church, Roberts began a full-time faith-healing ministry in 1948. By 1954, his healing services were being carried live on network television. Determined to spread the pentecostal message more effectively, Roberts became a United Methodist in 1968 and founded Oral Roberts University as the world's first charismatic university. He also erected a sixty-story hospital, "the City of Faith," next to the campus as testimony to his emphasis on the health of the "whole person"—spiritual, intellectual, physical, and even financial. In 1980, the *Christian Century* named Oral Roberts as one of the ten most influential religious leaders of the decade.

The eruption of pentecostalism within Roman Catholicism began in 1967 with a lay faculty prayer group at Duquesne University in Pittsburgh. An Episcopalian woman invited them to attend an informal pentecostal prayer group at the home of a Presbyterian woman. Shortly thereafter, early in 1967, four of them received a Spirit baptism. Later, at a "Duquesne weekend," about 30 students were touched by the Spirit. The excitement spread to Notre Dame, Michigan State, Michigan, and other university centers. In the late 1970s, 20,000 to 30,000 persons were attending an annual "National Conference on Charismatic Renewal in the Catholic Church" at Notre Dame. Although there was much going and coming between Protestant and Catholic pentecostals, Protestants tended to stress tongues as evidence of the initial baptism in the Holy Spirit, whereas

---

[3] See D. E. Harrell, Jr., *All Things Are Possible: The Healing and Charismatic Revival in Modern America* (Bloomington, Ind., 1975), and Richard Quebedeaux, *The New Charismatics* (Garden City, N.Y., 1976).

Catholics regarded tongues as one of many possible manifestations of the Spirit.

Evangelical and pentecostal influence was most evident in their successful use of radio and television to reach a mass audience. Seventy percent of religious radio programming and 90 percent of religious television programming were produced under their auspices. Estimates of the amount of revenue raised by the programs varied from $500 million to $1 billion annually. Whatever the sum, the lion's share was garnered by fewer than a dozen ministries.

The "big league" television programs were individually produced. They included "Pat" Robertson's "700 Club" from Virginia Beach, Virginia; Jerry Falwell's "Old Time Gospel Hour" from Lynchburg, Virginia; Rex Humbard's "Cathedral of Tomorrow" from Akron, Ohio; and Jim Bakker's "PTL Club" from Charlotte, North Carolina. Others with audiences and revenues in the millions were Jimmy Swaggart in New Orleans, James Robison in Fort Worth, and two stars in California—Gene Scott in Glendale and Robert Schuller in Garden Grove.[4] Schuller with his "possibility thinking," derived from his mentor Norman Vincent Peale, was sharply criticized by both liberals and conservatives. Still, it is clear that his nationally syndicated television program, "The Hour of Power," strongly appealed to theologically unsophisticated evangelicals.

There were differences among the leaders of the "Electronic Church." Some were pentecostals; others steered clear of charismatic gifts. A few were nonpolitical, but most did not hesitate to use their programs to promote right-wing causes that often had no visible connection with religion. The similarities, however, among these electronic superstars were much more striking. All directed their message to upwardly mobile people. All were intensely ambitious. All, except Schuller, perceived themselves as modern-day prophets, fervently ringing a tocsin to warn of a perilously close day of final judgment.

"Armchair religion" was the label some attached to the Electronic Church. Nothing much was demanded beyond mailing in a weekly or monthly check. Still, the influence in shaping the mind-set of the listener was tremendous. Although viewers of evangelical television programs could relax religiously in their armchairs, they were exhorted to be active politically. When Hodding Carter reviewed David Broder's *Changing of the Guard* (1980), which analyzed the shifts in political power in America, he noted one striking omission. Nowhere did Broder mention "the newly politicized religious fundamentalists" as a significant influence in "the coming years."[5] Traditionally, these doctrinally rigid people had been

---

[4] Billy Graham and Oral Roberts could be included, but their broadcasts began in the 1950s and were not the central focus of their ministries.

[5] *Washington Post Book World* (August 31, 1980), 2.

much less inclined to register and vote than the population as a whole. But by 1980, this trend was no longer true.

Since the 1950s, there had been vocal right-wing, fundamentalist, anti-Communist organizations such as Billy James Hargis's "Christian Anti-Communist Crusade" and Carl T. McIntire's American Council of Churches. But not many paid these organizations much attention. What was new in the last years of the 1970s was the development of heavily financed evangelical organizations designed to elect right-wing conservatives to national office.[6] On the West Coast, Richard Zone established Christian Voice, which boasted 200,000 active supporters, a mailing list of 5 million names, and a $3 million treasury. And in Texas, where television evangelist James Robison never hesitated to link the gospel to extremist politics, several thousand ministers were brought together from the mid-South in the summer of 1980 to listen to Ronald Reagan and to encourage voter-registration drives.

The largest of these organizations was the Moral Majority, founded in 1979 by Jerry Falwell. Falwell had organized the Thomas Road Baptist Church in 1956, meeting with a humble congregation of 35 faithful in the abandoned Donald Duck Bottling Company building in Lynchburg, Virginia. In television broadcasts of his "Old-Time Gospel Hour," Falwell addressed from a fundamentalist perspective the leading issues of the day, including abortion, the Equal Rights Amendment, prayer in public schools, and civil rights. A national audience responded to his preaching by joining the Moral Majority. By the fall of 1980, it reportedly had nearly a half-million members, claimed to have registered 3 million voters, and signed up 72,000 clergymen to serve as precinct workers, in addition to accumulating a million-dollar war chest. As religion mixed with politics in the activities of the Moral Majority and similar organizations, such goals as increasing defense spending, curtailing the powers of regulatory agencies, repealing the Panama Canal Treaty, and reinstating diplomatic recognition of Taiwan became major tests of religious orthodoxy.

Evangelical leaders were cultivating grassroots support in ways that the churches, with the exception of black churches, had not done since early in the century. And they were doing it more efficiently by means of computerized technology. Grassroots opinion had been neglected by the politically active leadership of the conventional churches, a neglect that limited their effectiveness as spokespersons in forwarding causes for which they had marshaled only partial support among people in the pews. It was not clear at the outset whether evangelicals would be more successful in turning their flocks into a solid voting bloc. In the end, in spite of running

[6] Not all evangelicals were wedded to right-wing politics. A number of young evangelicals sought to relate biblical faith to the problems of hunger, racism, and sexism through such magazines as *The Other Side, Sojourners,* and *Daughters of Sarah.* See also Robert Webber, *The Secular Saint* (Grand Rapids, Mich., 1979).

against a highly visible "born-again" Christian (Jimmy Carter), Ronald Reagan in 1980 gained great support in areas of evangelical strength. Evangelical support was even more evident in 1984. An indication of this support was the contrasting figures obtained in two surveys of 1,000 Southern Baptist ministers. A 1980 poll revealed that 29 percent of these ministers were registered Republicans. Four years later, 60 percent reported that they were registered Republicans.[7]

The politicizing of conservative Protestantism, however, should not be misconstrued as a process whereby fundamentalists were drawn away from their traditional theological orientation. For all of their investment in reforming society, fundamentalists continued to believe in the literal return of Christ in the Second Advent, and they were inclined to interpret geopolitical events according to a religiously grounded scheme that led them to expect the end of the world. Billy Graham had preached regularly about the end since the 1950s, and Hal Lindsey's vision of doom in *The Late Great Planet Earth* (1970) sold to millions throughout the 1970s and 1980s. And Jerry Falwell, in "Nuclear War and the Second Coming of Jesus Christ" (1980), predicted that the world would end in 1985, following a period of accelerated decay of traditional values. Millennialism and political action were not easily reconciled, but in the fracturing of Protestantism after the 1960s, they emerged nevertheless as leading features of the conservative worldview.

Conservative Protestants, in spite of some victories at the polling place, failed in their bid to transform American politics—a failure confirmed by the ill-fated 1988 presidential campaign of "Pat" Robertson. Some of the strident tone of evangelicalism was lost as Presbyterian, Baptist, and Methodist churches, and even to some extent the Roman Catholic Church, had made some room within their ranks for the "born-again" style of religion. Of more importance, the public face of evangelicalism suffered from scandals involving its most visible figures. Jim and Tammy Bakker left the "PTL Club" in disgrace amid charges of sexual improprieties and financial misdealings (the latter resulting in a fifty-year jail sentence for Jim Bakker, later reduced). Jimmy Swaggart, discovered in a sexual relationship with a prostitute, confessed to his audience, "I have sinned," and faded into a minor-league ministry. Oral Roberts, threatening that God would "call him home" if he did not raise a large sum of money by a certain date, lost credibility as well.

Conservative evangelicals remained politically engaged in spite of setbacks. The most important of the various right-wing political organizations that evangelicals embraced at the end of the twentieth century was the Christian Coalition, founded by Pat Robertson, which identified itself as "America's Leading Grassroots Organization Defending Our Godly

---

[7] *Christian Century* (August 14–21, 1985), 729.

Heritage." The movement, which distributes millions of voter's guides each election season, has made itself visible largely through its vigorous antiabortion, antipornography, and antitax stances. In 2002, it claimed two million members, as well as the responsibility for putting into office a number of Republican party governors, as well as United States senators and congresspersons. Its influence frequently has been debated, both by Republican party leaders who downplay its control over the party agenda, as well as by moderate and liberal groups who claim that it has had an inordinate amount of influence on state and national politics. The Christian Coalition eventually was stripped of its tax-exempt status for its blatant political action, and the organization has also been the object of legal action by persons claiming that it practices racial discrimination.

The enduring influence of conservative Protestantism at the institutional level was to be found in the Southern Baptist Convention, where evangelical conservatives embarked on a successful program of power politics within the denomination. Conservatives eventually gained nearly complete control of the national and state organizational apparatus, including a majority of the denomination's fifty one colleges and six seminaries. Striking institutional gains also were registered by the Assemblies of God under a variety of names for the local units, and the Church of God in Christ continued to exhibit remarkable numerical growth.

Roman Catholic Euphoria, Vacillation, Dissidence, and Retrenchment

The rate of Roman Catholic growth peaked in 1959. Thereafter, a slowly eroding plateau was maintained until 1965, when the erosion accelerated. The decline in accessions was partly obscured and partly arrested by the heady excitement following John XXIII's election to the papal office in 1958, by John F. Kennedy's election, and by the surprising events of Vatican II. Of the three, the Vatican Council (1962–1965) had the most important consequences. Not since the Council of Trent in the sixteenth century had the Church been subjected to such transformation. Few aspects of church life were left untouched—shape and language of worship, devotional practices, ecclesiastical administration, relationships to other Christians, attitudes of clergy and laity. Ripples set in motion by the Council ran far and wide.

Euphoria and Vacillation

If Vatican II initiated profound changes in the Church, expectation of change often outran the speed and extent of reform. The response of most American bishops was hesitant and cautious. They were slow to move, partly out of habit and partly because they had other pressing problems. The heady anticipation of reform made the problems seem less pressing to others, but bishops were not permitted the luxury of ignoring urgent day-to-day needs. The Church was in trouble.

A dramatic decline in conversions was paralleled by declines in accessions by birth and immigration. More serious were declines in the number of seminarians and of religious vocations among young women, accompanied by increases in the number of priests and members of teaching orders returning to lay life.[8] Parochial schools also demanded attention. Even with enrollment dropping and schools closing, the loss of low-paid personnel precipitated a crisis, for this meant greater dependence on more highly paid lay teachers. The problem was aggravated by a questioning of the value and quality of parochial education.[9] There also was the problem of parishes left stranded by the shift of Catholic families from slums to suburbs. New churches had to be built in the suburbs, and inner-city churches were left with half-empty houses of worship and inadequate means of support. Thus, bishops had to make agonizing reappraisals of priorities and allocation of resources.

The Roman Curia and the National Conference of Catholic Bishops were slow in issuing guidelines for reforms approved by the Council, and individual bishops were often tardy in instituting reforms once guidelines were provided. The "Constitution on the Sacred Liturgy," for example, was promulgated in 1963; but Cardinal Thomas McIntyre of Los Angeles, who believed that lay participation distracted attention from "contemplation of the mystery of the Eucharist," kept the liturgical life of Los Angeles unchanged throughout the decade. Most bishops were less laggard, but few kept pace with expectations. Eager young priests with enthusiastic support of youthful parishioners took things into their own hands, embarking on liturgical experiments that sometimes took the form of "underground" or "house" churches but more often were unauthorized innovations introduced into regular worship. Official changes were dramatic enough—use of English instead of Latin, freestanding "people's altars" with the priest facing the people, congregational responses, singing of (often Protestant) hymns.

Gradually other reforms were instituted. The laity were given more active roles. Advisory school boards and parish councils were established. Diocesan priests' councils were set up, and in 1968, these were linked in a National Federation of Priests' Councils. In 1966, bishops sought greater coordination among themselves by electing a president of the National Conference of Catholic Bishops.

---

[8] Seminarians dropped from 48,046 in 1966 to 22,963 in 1972; nuns from 181,421 to 146,914; lay brothers from 12,255 to 9,740.

[9] See Mary P. Ryan, *Are Parochial Schools the Answer?* (New York, 1964).

Dissidence

A curious result of Vatican II is that it created dissidence both right and left. Apprehension was aroused, as well as exhilaration and expectation. The "fish on Friday" syndrome is a convenient way to illustrate the disquiet that followed the ending of compulsory Friday abstinence. Of little consequence in itself, "Friday's fish" was of great symbolic importance in distinguishing Catholics from other Americans. When such a symbol is changed, much else is called into question. And alterations were introduced in other areas of symbolic importance. With the changes, gnawing identity anxieties were awakened.

The Latin Mass was symbolically the most important feature of traditional church life, and the introduction of a vernacular liturgy was a point at which conservative opposition first coalesced. The Catholic Traditionalist Movement issued its first manifesto in 1965. Other groups, such as Catholics United for the Faith, were organized. The National Federation of Laymen urged the withholding of funds from parishes that allowed their schools to teach "humanistic" and "Freudian" values. An anomaly of traditionalist dissidence was that it led to open disobedience of Church authority and to blunt criticism of the Pope. Of Paul VI, William Marra of Fordham grumbled, "He looks at all the heresy that is rampant in the chanceries, and all that he can do is weep."[10]

Among "progressives," the vacillation of the bishops also precipitated a crisis of authority. The Church's teaching began to be questioned on subjects as diverse as the Incarnation, birth control, celibacy of priests, and papal infallibility. The issue of obedience was publicly dramatized in 1967 at Catholic University when Charles S. Curran was denied a promotion recommended by the faculty. To the consternation of authorities, this action led to a boycott of classes by faculty and students, including large numbers of graduate student priests and nuns. The ecclesiastical authorities capitulated, and Curran was promoted.[11]

Caught up in a crisis of change, younger priests were unsure of who they were and what they were to do. Responding to this malaise, the bishops in 1967 sponsored sociological and psychological studies to ascertain the scope of the problem. The results were illuminating. Customary devotional practices were being abandoned. Of younger priests, 60 percent did not pray privately each day, 85 percent did not say the breviary each day, and 50 percent did not say it at all. Of those under age thirty five,

[10] "Catholic Right," *New York Times*, March 14, 1971.

[11] The capitulation was eased by J. E. Walsh's redefinition of a Catholic university's role being "the Church learning" instead of being part of the "teaching function of the Church." *Academic Freedom and the Catholic University*, ed. Edward Manier and J. S. Houck (Notre Dame, Ind., 1967), 109. Twenty years later Curran was again charged with deviation from Catholic doctrine in his ethics courses and was barred from teaching in that area at Catholic University. He subsequently left that school to teach elsewhere.

87 percent did not support the official teaching on birth control. Sixty percent of all priests did not think divorce was forbidden by divine law.[12]

The identity crisis of priests was accentuated by the relaxing of their psychological isolation. The 1964 decree on "Ecumenism" led to an extraordinary fraternizing with non-Catholics. Some priests used their new freedom to engage in dialogues and to experiment with "sensitivity" training. Others began to think of their rights, demanding the right to be heard and to elect their own bishops. Still others sought relevance by going into the streets. Participating in the civil-rights march on Selma, Alabama, was an exhilarating experience. Even more dramatic were open-housing marches in Milwaukee led by Father James Groppi and involving angry crowds, stern-faced police, and multiple arrests. Opposition to the Vietnam War enlisted articulate groups of priests and led to highly publicized acts of civil disobedience. The celebrated folk heroes of the movement were Fathers Daniel and Philip Berrigan.[13]

Members of women's religious orders also were in revolt. At the 1972 Berrigan conspiracy trial, Sister Elizabeth McAlister was a codefendant. On April 30, 1972, a dozen nuns disrupted a Mass conducted by Terence Cardinal Cooke at St. Patrick's Cathedral in New York City to protest Catholic apathy toward the Vietnam War. The nuns prostrated themselves in the center aisle before the Cardinal until police dragged them from the cathedral and arrested them for disorderly conduct.

Emancipation of nuns began in 1954 with the founding of the Sisters Formation Conference. Small progress was made until the number of sisters dropped alarmingly. Changes were then rapid and startling. There were changes in garb (street clothes were adopted by some orders) and experiments in living in small groups without a superior. Many wished to be treated as individuals, to be able to relate more freely with outsiders, and to be relevant to their own moment in time. On July 20, 1967, *The Saturday Evening Post* featured an article on "The New Nuns," and in December the cover story of *Newsweek* was "The Nun: Going Modern." In 1972, the National Coalition of American Nuns issued a "Declaration of Independence," demanding full equality in churches, including women priests.

Episcopal authority was in obvious disarray when priests no longer hesitated to criticize their bishops on issues of policy. The Association of Chicago Priests in 1971 publicly rebuked John Cardinal Cody for failing to represent their views at the National Conference of Catholic Bishops. The focus of their anger was his "silence" on the issue of celibacy when he knew from the survey commissioned by the hierarchy that the majority of priests favored optional celibacy.

---

[12] Andrew Greeley, *Priests in the United States* (Garden City, N.Y., 1972), 55–56, 65–66; D. P. O'Neill, *The Priest in Crisis* (Dayton, Ohio, 1968).

[13] See Daniel Berrigan, *No Bars to Manhood* (Garden City, N.Y., 1970), and Philip Berrigan, *Prison Journals of a Priest Revolutionary* (New York, 1970).

Most of the laity seemed unaffected by the stress and strain among the clergy. But the cork was out of the bottle, and the froth had begun to fizz. Unlike their grandparents, who docilely accepted the word of their bishops and priests, the laity were making up their own minds. A 1971 Gallup survey reported these findings: attendance at Mass was taken less seriously (only 52 percent attended regularly, and 42 percent did not regard absence as a sin); confession was neglected (63 percent had not made confession in eight weeks); 60 percent neither prayed together as a family nor said the rosary as a private devotion; 78 percent believed that their children could still be saved if they left the church. Oddly, when confused about what to believe, almost as many relied on Billy Graham as looked to the teachings of the Pope. There was no open revolt. The teachings of the church were simply quietly ignored by many. This trend was notably true in matters relating to sex. Seventy-five percent of those of childbearing age believed that good Catholics could use contraceptives. Nearly half favored liberalized abortion laws, and 60 percent did not believe that a remarried divorced Catholic was living in sin.

Retrenchment

The 1978 election of a Pole, Karol Wojtyla, as the first non-Italian bishop of Rome in more than four hundreds years inaugurated a dramatic reversal in the Roman Catholic Church. Unlike the grassroots turn to conservatism in Protestantism, the return to old ways in Roman Catholicism was imposed from above by the new pope.

John Paul II stood in marked contrast to the conventional image of occupants of the papal office. Much younger, he was bold, colorful, and charismatic in personality. With a quick wit and a keen sense of humor, laughter came readily. He related easily to ordinary people, did not hesitate to lead them in singing folk songs, and established instant rapport with great crowds as well as small groups. He was a poet, a sophisticated philosopher, and a skilled linguist. Above all, he had learned the techniques and discipline needed for the church to survive in the hostile environment of a land under Communist rule.

The new pontiff turned his attention immediately to the task of reinvigorating his worldwide flock. His technique was to make dramatic and triumphant visits to carefully targeted countries. In January 1979, he visited traditionally anticlerical Mexico and was followed by millions of people as he toured the nation. In June, he overwhelmed Poland, his native land, in an eight-day visit that astonished the world. It was as if he were implicitly challenging the government to interfere. At the end of September, he made a three-day visit to Ireland, where he was welcomed and heard by over half the population. This visit was followed by a seven-day, six-city conquest of popular sentiment in the United States. Six months later, in May

1980, he visited six new nations in central Africa. And two months later, he was in Brazil for a whirlwind tour of that vast and diverse country.

It was clear that John Paul II was not marching to any drum except his own. Wherever he went, he neither shortened his step nor lengthened his stride to accommodate local opinion, and he used every opportunity to spell out how he intended to restore order to the Church. A sympathetic observer commented that he was a man with an open heart but a closed mind. He faced issues without equivocation. He was sensitive to human need but unwavering on matters of doctrine and discipline. He was mild with the faithful but stern with the clergy.

During his visit to the United States, John Paul II spoke sharply against abandoning priestly celibacy and ordaining women. Priestly celibacy is a sign of total consecration to God and a reminder of the loyalty that priests owe their superiors in the hierarchy. Nor is the priesthood a proper calling for women, and John Paul urged nuns who had discarded their habits to resume their traditional garb.

Perhaps as compensation for the subordinate role assigned to women in the church,[14] the new pontiff made every effort in his travels to revive, restore, and exalt the cult of the Virgin—which had been the center of much popular piety but had been played down following Vatican II. To strengthen devotion to Mary, he made it a point to visit the most prominent shrines to the Virgin, as at Guadalupe in Mexico, at the shrine of the Black Madonna in Poland (where he led a half-million pilgrims in consecrating their country to Mary), and at Knock in Ireland. John Paul's concern to give renewed prominence to Mary was also related to her role as a model for women in their day-to-day life as mothers. Strengthening family life was strongly stressed, and the Pope made plain his unswerving opposition to birth control, abortion, divorce, extramarital sex, and homosexual relationships.

In Washington and in Brazil, John Paul met with leaders of other Christian churches. In Chicago, he spoke of his desire to pursue the ecumenical vision of Vatican II, but he insisted that Catholic doctrine must not be compromised. Meanwhile, steps were taken at the Vatican to bring theologians into line with teaching that received papal approval. By the end of 1979, members of theological faculties had been put on notice. Hans Küng, one of the most liberal and by far the best-known scholar, was notified that he was no longer recognized as an official theologian and was therefore no longer qualified to serve as a member of the Roman Catholic faculty at Tübingen, Germany. Elsewhere scholar-priests were reassigned to different duties. Then, during the next six years, other theologians were rebuked, censured, even silenced.

---

[14] In Philadelphia, in a special mass celebrated by the Pope for those with a religious vocation, the nuns were seated in the basement with closed-circuit television while the priests were ushered into the sanctuary above.

At the same time, John Paul was using his appointive powers to secure control of the Vatican bureaucracy and to consolidate his hold on the bishops. Those who shared his views were rewarded. John O'Connor of New York and Bernard Law of Boston, who were the two American archbishops to be made cardinals in 1985, were among the most vocal in stating that, because of her qualified stand on abortion, Roman Catholics could not in good conscience vote for Geraldine Ferraro, the Democratic candidate for vice-president. The same issue came into play in attempting to force a number of nuns publicly to retract their views under threat of being expelled from their orders.

For many Catholics in the United States, the Pope demanded radical readjustments. His stand on birth control and divorce ran counter to the practice or the opinion of most Roman Catholics. His stand on priestly celibacy was opposed by a majority of both priesthood and laity. His views on the role of women were out of step with the views of many. His lagging approach to ecumenism was foreign to the easy relationships that had developed in the United States. His theological traditionalism was not in tune with the thinking of many scholars in Catholic universities and seminaries. For those who had embraced the collegial and innovating spirit of Vatican II, as well as for those who already had one foot outside the church, the conservatism of the Pope was one more reason to move away from the old center of Roman Catholicism.

New Centers

For most of the nation's history, a conglomeration of various Protestant denominations—or centers of Protestant religious life—wielded a dominating influence. But America always has featured an assortment of religious centers, Protestant and non-Protestant. Different populations, identifiable by region, ethnicity, and other factors, have had their own religious centers, their own distinctive brands of religious life, even during the long period of Protestant dominance. These centers became increasingly visible in the aftermath of the 1960s. The rapid growth of religions once considered "marginal," the expanding American interest in world religions, the rise of new religions, and the wholesale reform of other religions, represent that trend.

The Jesus Cult

No one knows where or when it began, but by 1967, there were traces of reviving interest in Jesus among the "street people" of California. Perhaps it began with rock music. The turning of rock to protest themes led to secularized religious themes in order to express and convey messages of alienation. The rock musical *Hair* had religious overtones. These became explicitly Christian themes in *Jesus Christ Superstar* and *Godspell.* Then "Amazing Grace" and "O Happy Day" hit the top of the charts.

New Christians among hippies, flower children, and drug addicts quickly became known as Jesus Freaks or Jesus People. They were a variegated lot, having no common origin. Although there were spontaneous beginnings elsewhere, the Jesus cult first gained public attention in California. An early group in San Francisco was related to Ted Wise, a sail maker from Sausalito who had been deeply involved in drug use. Late in 1967, he established a coffeehouse known as The Living Room, forerunner of a commune called The House of Acts. Then Lonnie Frisbee founded a similar commune in southern California, The House of Miracles. Members of these groups dispersed to New Knoxville, Ohio, Rye, New York, and Eugene, Oregon, to extend the influence of the Jesus Way.[15]

By 1970, there were Jesus groups everywhere, representing a surprisingly wide range of ideology. The appeal of Jesus to youth who had become apathetic to organized religion was not unlike the appeal of Asian religions to some of their friends. With a pervading sense of emptiness and futility, they found in simple gospel texts a meaning and direction that released them from drug-oriented routes of escape. Their new commitment, although it did not change their counterculture lifestyle, did result in a shift to sober, disciplined living, coupled with new excitement and purpose. Although diverse, Jesus people shared some common emphases: a nonintellectual insistence on the simple gospel, a belief that they were living in the last times, an espousal by some of pentecostal gifts, a tendency toward communal living, a bias against organized Christianity, and a utilization of the music and vocabulary of the youth culture.

It is difficult to assess how many were involved with the Jesus people. There was much coming and going. For some it meant no more than the first step in going back to Kansas, back to a more conventional life. But numbers were not as important as influence. As a result of media attention, Jesus definitely was "in." He even became commercial, and thus organizations of conservative bent capitalized on the new interest.

The Authoritarian Strain

The Children of God, founded by "Moses" Berg, began as "Teens for Christ" in Huntington Beach, California, in 1968, and demonstrated the appeal of intensely rigid authoritarian discipline. When acutely distraught "flower children" discovered that the counterculture of the street provided little support, it is not surprising that some retreated to the security of a group gathered about a dictatorial father figure. Bluntly antiestablishment

---

[15] See R. M. Enroth, Edward E. Ericson, C. B. Peters, *The Jesus People* (Grand Rapids, Mich., 1972).

and legalistic, the Children of God demanded complete separation (including rejecting their parents) from the world that was soon to perish.[16]

In addition to the Children of God, there were two other rigidly authoritarian groups that gained notoriety in the 1970s. One such group gained worldwide attention in 1978 with a macabre murder-suicide ritual in Jonestown, Guyana. Jim Jones had gathered poor blacks and white social activists into his Indianapolis People's Temple, moving them in 1965 to rural Redwood Valley in California. A Stanford Law School graduate joined the Temple in 1969 and helped facilitate a move to San Francisco. The People's Temple had a different clientele from the Children of God, garnering its followers not from among the "flower children," but from among those who had been active in civil-rights marches, anti–Vietnam War demonstrations, and organizing farm workers. They turned to the charismatic leadership of Jones as a last hope for securing a more humane and just society. The discipline of the Temple was intense. Jones patterned his style of leadership after Father Divine, becoming the personification of God. This role may have helped cloak his growing paranoia. In 1973, an agricultural commune was established in Guyana as a refuge from a hostile world, a venture that ended on November 18, 1978, with mass suicide and slaughter.

A third and more stable authoritarian group was generally known as the "Moonies," members of the Reverend Sun Myung Moon's Unification Church. Moon, a Korean, founded his Holy Spirit Association for the Unification of World Christianity in 1954, mingling messianism with anti-Communism while amassing a private fortune. In 1973, he shifted his primary base to the United States, being preceded by emissaries who sought converts by warning of the approaching doom of America because of crime, alcoholism, drug abuse, college radicals, and Communists. Later at a "God Bless America" rally in Yankee Stadium, Moon said that his purpose was to restore confidence in the American dream.

There was more involved than the American dream. As the self-proclaimed Messiah commissioned by Jesus on a Korean mountainside to finish his task, Moon's teachings were to be accepted unquestioningly as divinely revealed. Aided by a Stanford graduate as director of training, Moon won recruits not from the "street" but from psychologically troubled middle-class youth who had yet to make a break with home and family. Enticed by fellow students to conferences where they were surrounded by loving concern, potential recruits were persuaded to attend marathon training sessions that left them exhausted and scarcely able to think for themselves. God's plan for salvation was spelled out, and they were offered one last chance for salvation. Moon was called "father," and his command was "What I wish must be your wish." When parents objected, recruits were taught to regard them as agents of Satan. Ever smiling and neatly dressed,

---

[16] The date for the end most recently predicted by them is 1993.

Moonies were conspicuous as they solicited money for vague humanitarian causes.

Beyond the fringe of conventional religion in the United States, there always have been groups based on fresh revelations and authoritarian leadership. Some of them—most notably the Mormons, the Seventh-day Adventists, and Jehovah's Witnesses—survived and prospered in the years following World War II, even winning adherents worldwide; and their momentum increased in the 1970s and 1980s. None of these three, of course, would be happy to be placed in a classification with the others, for they have little in common beyond illustrating the appeal of self-enclosed groups in an uncertain world.

For Jehovah's Witnesses, the 1970 and 1985 issues of the *Year Book of the American and Canadian Churches* indicate a dramatic increase of 91 percent for a total of 428,046 adherents in the United States, but some say that this figure does not take into account recent losses. The Church of Jesus Christ of Latter-day Saints (Mormons) with 3,602,000 members maintained its remarkably rapid growth, posting a gain of 65 percent for the same comparable period. Seventh-day Adventists had a 56 percent gain and a membership of 623,563.

Intramural strife was present within both the latter groups. The issue for Seventh-day Adventists was, What happened in 1844? Did Christ enter the heavenly sanctuary at that time to begin judging people in preparation for his return? Or did he begin raising up a people as a prerequisite to his return? The issue was raised in 1979 by an Australian scholar, Desmond Ford, at the Adventists' Pacific Union College in California. He insisted that the latter doctrine was necessary to sustain the worldwide outreach of the church. The hidden agenda was the exact authority of Ellen Gould White. One scholar phrased the question, "Are we prepared to test Mrs. White by the Scriptures?" A year later the official answer was given when Ford's ministerial credentials were withdrawn.

Mormons achieved the height of respectability following World War II as a thoroughly American church with a claimed rootage far in the American past. Although its growth was worldwide, it projected an image of all-American young men and women—clean-shaven, well-dressed, and devoted to the virtues of honesty, diligence, thrift, sobriety, and obedience—as they spread out across the nation from their Utah heartland. Both the church and its members prospered, the latter achieving high posts in business, industry, and government. Still, Mormons were troubled by gnawing problems. The disturbing issue of the place of blacks in the scheme of salvation was partially solved in the 1970s. But the ejection from the church in 1982 of some housewives and mothers who spoke out against the church's organized opposition to the Equal Rights Amendment indicated that the church was not ready to yield to public opinion on every issue. A more serious problem was posed in 1985 by some bombings that were related to the surfacing of letters (later proved to be fraudulent) that raised questions about Joseph Smith's early life and his later account of the finding of the golden plates.

Religion and Identity

The rituals, myths, and symbols of religion are some of the most effective means for the preservation and transmission of cultural meanings, as well as for protest against cultural systems that are experienced as confining or unjust. Religion, accordingly, often encodes a sense of identity for a specific population. It reveals what has been important about the past, about the words and deeds of a people over many generations. It offers direction for the future in the form of expectations, and, sometimes, promises. And by offering guidelines for everyday life—moral codes, patterns of worship, models of authority, and so forth—it enables people to construct an everyday world that will point them to that future.

For African Americans, Hispanics, Jews, Native Americans, and other minorities in America, identity often is closely intertwined with religion. That is, religion has served as an especially effective means of articulating a sense of identity, of marking the distinctiveness of a people's experience as a racial or an ethnic minority in America. It does so by publicly representing the core beliefs and values of a group, as well as by making explicit the differences between that group and others. Minority groups continue to participate in the broad cultural life of the nation, to embrace American ideals of democratic government, justice, equality, and so forth. But Americans are a nation made up of persons from many backgrounds, and religion both expresses those differences and enables people to preserve them.

The 1960s witnessed religious innovation on a large scale, and some of the most striking of the changes occurred within the African American community. Martin Luther King had marshaled a mass following under the banner of a theology of reconciliation. But in the years after 1966 when Stokeley Carmichael raised the cry of "Black Power" during James Meredith's march to Jackson, Mississippi, an independent course began to be pursued that, unlike the emphases of King, had few affinities with traditional theology. Labels were changed. Negro theologians became black theologians. The stress was on black pride, black church, black religion, black theology, black liberation. The look was back to Africa for "roots," and Afro-American studies became a respected academic discipline.

Two major spokesmen for the theology of black liberation were Albert B. Cleage, Jr., and James H. Cone.[17] Cleage, with a black Christology brought into focus in his Church of the Black Madonna in Detroit, sought to bring black religion into the service of political action, economic pres-

---

[17] See Albert B. Cleage, Jr., *The Black Messiah* (New York, 1968), and James H. Cone, *Black Theology and Black Power* (New York, 1969).

sure, and black separation. Cone related a theology derived from black experience to biblical themes—the bondage of the Israelites in Egypt, the oppression of Christians under Roman rule, the manifestation of Jesus as the Black Christ. Black theology was a strategy for freeing the black mind from beliefs and attitudes that frustrated the thrust for liberation. The cause of liberation took priority over any suffering servant claim of the gospel. "Black theology must say: 'If the doctrine is compatible with or enhances the drive for black freedom, then it is the gospel of Jesus Christ. If the doctrine is against or indifferent to the essence of blackness as expressed in Black Power, then it is the work of the Antichrist.'"[18] Black liberation theology had great influence, especially in theological schools, but it did not go unchallenged. Others, no less concerned with black awareness, self-esteem, and liberation, held fast to Martin Luther King's vision of a redeemed society of mutual reconciliation. Still, even this perception involved a degree of separation as a prerequisite to full mutuality. Some African Americans, as we shall see, found meaning alternatively in Islam.

Few people were more wedded to the American tradition of liberty, both civil and religious, than the Jews; and few exhibited more idealism and compassion for the rights of the underprivileged. They constituted an important component of what once was referred to as the cultural consensus. Although widespread euphoria was generated among Jews by Israel's speedy triumph in the Six-Day War of 1967, a few, most conspicuously in Brooklyn, were less than euphoric. They were more concerned with their immediate situation. Crime in the streets had become common in America, and the push for integration precipitated many forms of backlash. Both elements were present in Brooklyn, where Jewish neighborhoods were in transition and hazardous places to live, while "affirmative action" policies threatened the security and advancement of Jews long entrenched in the school system. What made Brooklyn distinctive was not that the backlash was more intense than elsewhere. Rather, it was the historical dimension given the plight of the Jews by Rabbi Meir Kahane, who, not willing to be intimidated, organized the Jewish Defense League in 1968 with the slogan "Never Again." Too long, he insisted, Jews had responded passively to threats to their existence.

Kahane's language and tactics embarrassed leaders of the Jewish community and found scant support among the rank and file. But there was a growing feeling of the precariousness of life, a feeling that was reinforced by Israel's near defeat in the Yom Kippur War of 1973. The consequence among some Jews was a shift to conservative politics, in both domestic and foreign policy. And among other Jews, there was a stronger emphasis upon Jewishness and Jewish roots.

An important instance of the emphasis upon Jewish tradition has been the resurgence of the Lubavitcher Hasidic community in the Williamsburg

---

[18] Cone, 121.

neighborhood of New York. By the early 1960s, this community, which included many Holocaust survivors, was all but written off by Jewish and non-Jewish observers alike. Made up of a mostly lower-class population, it appeared to be disintegrating as younger members, as well as financially secure older ones, abandoned it for other neighborhoods. Lubavitchers strictly observed Jewish dietary rules, wore distinctive dress and hair styles, embraced a rich and varied worship, and kept an ambitious calendar of holy days. The men often wore tefillin, the leather strap-and-box devices attached to the head and left arm for weekday morning prayers, and men and women alike scrupulously observed the Laws of Family Purity, which govern sexual relations. The members of the community are fiercely loyal to their rabbis.

Led by rabbis Yoel Teitelbaum and Menachem Schneerson (who was thought by some of his followers to be the Messiah), the Lubavitcher community underwent a remarkable turnaround beginning in the 1960s. Unwilling to abandon their orthodox lifestyle in the Williamsburg neighborhood, Lubavitchers—over 50 percent of whom lived below the poverty line—undertook a campaign to shore up defections from the community and reestablish it as a viable social and economic entity. The success of that venture has been described as a victory of "valuational over ecological and economic factors in the dynamics and structure of a community."[19] Williamsburg in the 1990s was a larger, more active, more economically viable community than at any point in its history. It had become even more important a center of orthodox Judaism than it had been before 1960.

Hispanic movements to define identity and to claim social justice have been closely intertwined with religion since the 1960s. Some of the background for this relationship lies in the Liberation Theology that emerged in force in Latin America in the 1960s as a protest to injustice there. Liberation Theology, as it took shape within Roman Catholicism following a bishops' conference in Colombia in 1968, voiced the interests of the poor, articulated their rights, and criticized the exploitation of the Third World by the developed nations. As formulated by Gustavo Gutiérrez (*A Theology of Liberation,* 1971) and other Catholic thinkers, the theology served as a point of departure for political organizing and popular resistance to Latin American governments. Although Liberation Theology per se did not translate directly to America—the Vatican actively discouraged it and most American bishops did not recognize its relevance to the American scene— it helped to set the tone for religious and social activism in Hispanic immigrant communities. Those communities, inspired by the spirit of reli-

---

[19] George Kranzler, "The Economic Revitalization of the Hasidic Community of Williamsburg," in Janet S. Belcove-Shalin, ed., *New World Hasidism: Ethnographic Studies of Hasidic Jews in America* (Albany, N.Y., 1995), 182; See also, by the same author, *Hasidic Williamsburg: A Contemporary American Community* (Northvale, N.J., 1995).

giously inspired political activism in the southern hemisphere and informed by their own Catholic traditions closer to home that had long
blended social causes with religious visions, utilized the church as a focal
point for the organization of reform efforts. From the United Farmwork-
ers Movement led by Cesar Chavez to the broadly defined mission of the
National Council of La Raza to reduce poverty and discrimination in the
Hispanic community, reformers have built bases of power in Catholic congregations (and in a few cases, in Protestant congregations). Their efforts
have resulted in practical improvements in the lives of American Hispanics, and their successes have reinforced the linkage between religion and
reform in ethnic self-understanding among Hispanics.

As we have seen, religion is of essential importance to Native American
life. In the twentieth century, this relationship has been tested in several
instances, because Native Americans have resisted on religious grounds an
assortment of governmental challenges to their way of life. They have organized for social justice and in protest against discrimination in much the
same way as African Americans, Jews, and Hispanics, by claiming a religious standpoint for their actions. In such cases, the articulation and defense of Native American identity frequently becomes a matter of
expressing religious beliefs and expecting those beliefs to be respected.
Identity as a Native American and as a person of specific religious orientation thus almost always go hand in hand in the process of self-definition.
Two instances in the latter part of the twentieth century made clear the
role of religion in the affirmation of identity. In the first case, Native Americans challenged the excavation of pre-Columbian archaeological sites that
resulted in the disinterment of Indian remains. Protesting the disruption
of their ancestral grave sites and casting those protests in religious language, Indian groups were able to persuade Congress to pass legislation
that protected grave sites from further tampering and also that required
the repatriation of Indian remains to sacred ground. The National Mu-
seum of the American Indian Act (1989) required the Smithsonian (which
held upwards of 16,000 sets of remains) to inventory, document, and, if re-
quested, repatriate culturally affiliated human remains—as well as ritual
artifacts taken from graves—to Native groups. The following year, the Native American Graves Protection and Repatriation Act (NAGPRA) was applied nationally to museums, federal agencies, and academic institutions.
Likewise significant in terms of its assertion of the centrality of religion to
ethnic identity was the legal battle over the use of peyote in Native
American religious ritual. In the case of *Oregon v. Smith* (1990), the U.S.
Supreme Court ruled against Klamath Indian Alfred Smith, and Galen
Black, his coworker at a drug rehabilitation center, for their sacramental
use of peyote (a controlled substance) in ceremonies of the Native
American Church. The subsequent outcry from a diverse array of religious
groups eventually led to the passage in Congress of the American Indian Religious Freedom Act Amendments (1994), which specifically

guaranteed the right to use peyote. During the years when the case was debated, the religious aspect of Native American identity was profoundly visible as various parties testified before lawmakers and as both Native American tribal spokespersons and non-Native religious groups issued statements supporting religious freedom.

World Religions in America

The arrival of Europeans on these shores in the late fifteenth century began a long period of Christianization of the North American continent. Christianity, however, was not the first religion of Americans—Native American religions existed here long before the creation of Christianity. And it is clear that Christianity will not be the only world religion for Americans in the twenty-first century.[20] With the liberalization of immigration laws in the 1960s, religious leaders and missionaries from all of the major religions of the world came to the United States. These leaders have served growing bodies of immigrants, especially from Asia and the Middle East, as well as native-born Americans who have converted to Buddhism and Islam and other non-Christian religions.

Islam

A world religion of 1.2 billion that numbered approximately 6 million North American adherents in 1996, Islam, which means "submission," coalesced in the seventh century around the teachings and example of Mohammed, the Prophet of Allah. From Arabia, it spread quickly throughout Africa, across Asia to Mongolia and Indonesia, and into southern and central Europe. Early in the Spanish exploration of the New World, "Isfan the Arab" accompanied Franciscans to Arizona. Some of the slaves who had been brought to southern plantations from the east coast of Africa were Muslim, and individual Muslims had settled here and there in North America from the sixteenth century. Outside of slaves, the first wave of Muslims who came to North America immigrated in the 1880s. Among these were the Druze, who began arriving from the area around Damascus in 1881. Others, primarily from the Middle East, followed, in spite of anti-Muslim sentiment stirred up by Americans such as John A. Dowie, a Catholic priest in Illinois, who hoped to put an end to Islam through prayer: "I pray to God that the day of destruction of Islam draw nearer.

---

[20] See Diana L. Eck, *On Common Ground: World Religions in America* (New York, 1997). (Also on CD-ROM.)

O God! Do like that, O God, bring destruction to Islam."[21] Thriving Muslim communities gradually grew up in places such as Dearborn, Michigan, adjacent to the automobile manufacturing plants, and Quincy, Massachusetts, around the shipbuilding works. Canadian cities such as Toronto also became centers for immigrant Muslims.

If the moment of critical mass for Islam in the United States is determined by the beginnings of mosque construction, then we should recognize the period of the 1920s and 1930s as key. The first mosque was built in 1919, in Highland Park, Michigan. Construction of mosques and Islamic centers proceeded slowly, however, and it was not until 1952 that the Federation of Islamic Associations of America was established as an umbrella organization of approximately two dozen mosques. The next important step was the completion of the Islamic center in Washington, D.C., in 1957, which came into being as a joint project involving American Muslims and the governments of a number of Islamic nations. A model of Islamic architecture, it inspired the subsequent construction of over a hundred mosques in America. In the 1970s, as funds from Arab states became available to North American Muslim communities, another round of mosque building commenced. These places of worship, together with other buildings converted to mosques, numbered over 1300 at the end of the twentieth century. Most of them were built after the mid-1970s, especially in New York and California, and in metropolitan areas such as Washington, D.C., where there are over thirty mosques. As many as a thousand Muslim community centers, in several hundred cities, supplemented these mosques.[22]

The mosque, from the Arabic *masjid* meaning "a place of prostration" to God, is a holy place for prayer. It is a courtyard-like open space (usually with a roof) that includes several characteristic design features. The *mihrab*, a semicircular niche that is located in such a way as to point to Mecca, is where the imam leads prayer. To the right is the *minbar*, or the pulpit. The *khatib*, who delivers the Friday sermon, climbs its steps just short of the top, out of respect for the higher authority of the prophet Mohammed. The *minbar* represents as well something of the relationship between religion and the state in Islam, as it early on served as well as a place for the broadcasting of proclamations by the civil authority, in the form of the Caliph or other government leaders. Schools are often attached to mosques, and in many places the mosque has served as the court of justice.

Because Islam prohibits the making or display of images of Muhammad or other holy personages, the walls inside the mosque have no pictures or statues, nor are ritual objects displayed. Verses from the Qur'an may decorate the walls, however. There are no ordained clergy in Islam, but besides

---

[21] Quoted in Yvonne Yazbeck Haddad and Jane Idleman Smith, *Mission to America: Five Islamic Sectarian Communities in North America* (Gainesville, Fla., 1993), 60.

[22] Jane Smith, *Islam in America* (New York, 1999), 152–3.

the leader of prayer (*imam*),[23] other persons may be visible because of their special roles. Chanters (qurra') may chant the Qur'an within the parameters of a highly defined system of vocalizations (but there is no singing or musical performance in mosques). The floor of the mosque, where worshippers kneel and bow as they perform the ritual cycle of prayer (*salat*), is covered in carpets or mats. A mosque is identifiable from the outside by its *minaret*, or tower, from which the *muezzin* calls the faithful to prayer five times a day: in early morning, at noon, in midafternoon, at sunset and at evening. People enter the mosque only after taking off their shoes, moving the right foot first across the threshold while blessing Mohammed. Mosques often have been closed to women, who pray at home instead (as do many male Muslims as well, although prayer in the mosque is understood to be more meritorious). However, as American Muslims increasingly affirm the mosque as a place for family worship, women are more likely to enter the mosque (though usually by a separate door) for public worship. Women sit apart from men in the mosque, usually behind a partition, in a balcony with their children, or, in more conservative communities, in a room equipped with audiovisual apparatus that displays the worship service taking place in another part of the building. Those who attend the Friday *salat* (at noon) prepare themselves by bathing, dressing for the occasion, and perfuming themselves.

Worship is one of the essential features of Islam, one of the Five Pillars, which include, first of all, testifying to Islamic faith, that is, a statement of orthodoxy ("doctrinal correctness"). The following four pillars—almsgiving, pilgrimage to Mecca, worship, and seasonal fasting—have to do with orthopraxy, or "correct practice." Whereas the mosque and the Islamic community centers represent institutional Islam in communities, a primary context for the practice of Islam is the home and family. Marriage between Muslims and non-Muslims is permitted under Islamic law, but Muslim men and women are strongly encouraged to marry other Muslims. The common understanding among Muslims is that men and women complete and fulfill each other in marriage, and Muslims expect to have children early and often. A childless marriage, or even one with a single child, can be distressing to Muslim couples. The business of raising children is framed with reference to the extended family. Relationships with aunts and uncles, cousins, nieces and nephews, and grandparents form a rich matrix for family identity, which carries over in many ways into social life in general. In some cases, family activities provide almost the entire range of recreational activities for Muslims: meals, visits, discussions, and

---

[23] For Sunni Muslims, the *imam* is the leader of prayer. Shi'ite Muslims understand the *imam* to be a holy person leader raised up by God to lead the community, and a direct descendant of the Prophet.

play are conducted largely within the context of the extended family. Parents, however, accept the necessity, and even the desirability, of contact with non-Muslims; and in America, they increasingly have adopted a broader view of the nature of social life for their children. In such cases, there are still limits that remain on the ways in which children may conduct themselves outside the family circle. Although attendance at public schools might be permitted, dating or attendance at school dances is unacceptable. Young people do have broader options for social life as they grow older and can participate in conferences and activities organized by Muslim organizations such as the MYNA (Muslim Youth of North America), can join Muslim Boy and Girl Scout troops, and can take part in locally based initiatives. Such initiatives are directed especially toward teenagers who are seeking to come to grips with their distinctiveness and their visible difference from other American teenagers—differences that are represented in everyday life by the *hijab* (a veil worn by Muslim females) and by dietary practices.

If family life is a center of gravity for Muslims, then meals are the focal point of much family interaction and consequently a key aspect of religious practice. The discussion and debate, the expressions of concern and support, and the playfulness of table talk are of course a large part of the cultivation and maintenance of an Islamic ethic within the family. But mealtimes are also times to praise and thank God, and so in some Muslim communities in America—and in many in other parts of the world—eating takes precedence over conversation, and a quiet, worshipful attitude toward God takes precedence over recreational banter. Muslims, like Jews, are also careful about what they eat, certain foods (those that are *halal*) being permitted them and others forbidden. Beef must be slaughtered in a religiously prescribed fashion in order for it to be edible. Pork cannot be eaten. Shellfish (unlike the case in Jewish law) may be consumed, but predators (both mammalian and avian) are *tayyib*, or impure. The drinking of wine and other alcoholic beverages is not permitted. In America, where much food is processed, observance of dietary restrictions can make the creation of a menu complicated, because of the fact that forbidden items might be present in small amounts in prepared foods. A growing number of companies specialize in the production of foods that meet *halal* standards, so that observant Muslims can eat everything from marshmallows to Vienna sausages and still be confident that the food has been prepared in keeping with dietary requirements.[24] Having spread the table with dishes that are *halal*, Muslims sit down to eat, always using the right hand, as the left hand is for unclean duties having to do with the toilet. In some parts of the Muslim world, the men eat first, followed by the women and children, but in America this is not a widespread practice.

[24] Frederick M. Denny, *An Introduction to Islam*, 2nd ed. (New York, 1994), 283–4; Smith, 144.

As we have noted, there is significant debate among Muslims in America about appropriate dress, and especially for women. Although clothing is not regulated in great detail, there are certain aspects of dress for which guidelines exist. The wearing of silk and gold, because they are luxuries, is discouraged for men, who are expected to provide for charity rather than display their status in dress. Clothing that presents the body in a sexually alluring way is not allowed, and neither sex may wear clothes associated with the other. As a general rule, dress must be modest. Some women who present themselves in public in the conservative fashion—long sleeves, a scarf or other head covering, the legs, ankles, and feet unexposed—have encountered difficulties in their careers and accordingly have challenged dress traditions. Others, and especially African American and Anglo converts to Islam, continue to embrace the conservative style of dress (which actually began to appear after the Arab defeat in the 1967 war with Israel) as requisite for Islamic life in the United States.[25]

African American interest in Islam in the twentieth century has developed under the umbrellas of several different groups. Though estimates vary, it is likely that thousands of blacks brought as slaves to North America were Muslim. However, their practice of Islam was for the most part prohibited on the plantations where they lived, with Christianity being pushed upon them instead. It therefore was only with the emergence of leaders in the black community who called for a return to the religion of their African past that Islam became a visible and eventually a vibrant religion among African Americans. Those leaders linked the embrace of Islam to the struggle against white racism and framed it as a critical step in recovering the African identity that white slave-owners had taken from them.

One of the most important early voices for the African American rethinking of religion and identity was Marcus Garvey, whose Universal Negro Improvement Association (UNIA), which he founded in Jamaica in 1914, took root in Harlem in 1917. Garvey preached racial purity (and ironically, the UNIA was acceptable to the Ku Klux Klan for that reason), and he proposed a return to Africa, where the practice of Christianity would be purified of the racist overtones of its American incarnation. Garvey was influenced by Noble Drew Ali (born Timothy Drew in North Carolina in 1886), whose Moorish Science Temple was likewise both religious and political in its view of the African American predicament. In his oral teachings and in *The Holy Koran of the Moorish Holy Temple of Science*, a sixty-four page document that had nothing in common with the Qur'an of orthodox Muslims, Ali taught economic independence for blacks, argued for their Asiatic origins, and urged them to reject the roles assigned to them by whites. He established the first temple in Newark in 1913, and others

---

[25] Smith, 108.

followed until Ali's death in 1929, when the movement experienced schism, one stream eventually taking shape as the Nation of Islam.[26]

Founded by Wallace Fard Mohammed in Detroit in 1930, the Nation of Islam built upon the messages of Garvey and Drew in attracting an African American following in a number of urban settings. Declaring that he had recently arrived in Detroit from Mecca, he preached that blacks were part of the ancient lost tribe of Shabazz, that they had been taken from Mecca in the mid–sixteenth century, and that he would lead them back to their origins. Asserting that blacks were the "original people," he proclaimed that "the original people must regain their religion, which is Islam, their language, which is Arabic, and their culture, which is astronomy and higher mathematics, especially calculus." As a peddler, Fard sold silks and other items door-to-door, an activity that gave him access to people's homes, where he presented to them his interpretation of Islam. Although that interpretation coincided in some ways with ideas and practices characteristic of orthodox Islam (submission to Allah, no consumption of alcohol or pork, etc.), it departed from, or outrightly contradicted, Islam in other ways. By 1934, Fard had attracted about 8,000 followers. They began meeting in a rented hall and undertook an assortment of initiatives that included a University of Islam, a training program for women called the Muslim Girls Training and General Civilization Classes, and the organization of a group of bodyguards and security persons known as the Fruit of Islam. Fard experienced legal troubles in Detroit. He located to Chicago in the spring of 1933, was soon arrested there, and then disappeared in 1934.

One of Fard's followers, Elijah Muhammed (born Elijah Poole in Georgia in 1897), who was the son of a Baptist minister, rose quickly in the ranks of Fard's ministerial staff. He founded Temple Number Two in Chicago in 1932, and after Fard's disappearance, he became the leader of the Nation of Islam (whose members are known as "Black Muslims," which is not to be confused with references to orthodox Muslims who are black). Prior to his disappearance, Fard had come to be known as the Great Mahdi, or Messiah; and Elijah Muhammed, who had accepted that identity for Fard, eventually presented himself as a "messenger" of Islam. Though such claims are heresy to orthodox Islam, they proved persuasive to urban blacks who continued to hold the Bible, alongside the Qur'an, as the revealed word of God. Elijah Muhammed stressed the necessity for a black nation apart from racist America, and he urged the worship of Allah. He taught that blacks were the "chosen people" and that whites were

---

[26] E. David Cronon, *Black Moses: The Story of Marcus Garvey and the United Negro Improvement Association*, Foreword by John Hope Franklin (Madison, 1969), 190. Kambiz GhaneaBassiri, *Competing Visions of Islam in the United States: A Study of Los Angeles* (Westport, Conn., 1997), 140.

"blue-eyed devils" (a rhetoric that he softened in his later years). Jews were singled out as especially evil. He foresaw the demise of white America and urged his followers to envision themselves as a black Nation apart from it. He was jailed in 1942 to 1946 for advising his followers to avoid military service in a war that was not being fought for their Nation. As the leader of the Nation of Islam (NOI), he was successful in reaching poor and unedu-cated African Americans, especially males, drawing them under the um-brella of the strict code of conduct for members of the religion and inculcating them with belief in black economic self-determination. The high turnover rate in membership nevertheless indicated that living as a member of the Nation of Islam required a lifestyle that many ultimately could not embrace. Members prayed five times a day, observed dietary re-strictions, and gave alms (as in orthodox Islam).[27]

Malcolm Little converted to the Nation of Islam in a Massachusetts prison in 1947. Elijah Muhammed gave him the name "Malcolm X" until such time as he demonstrated his commitment to his new life, at which time he would be given a Muslim name. Malcolm wore his "X" like a badge, a protest against the institution of slavery that had stolen his African identity. Charismatic and articulate, he became the best-known ad-vocate of the NOI during the 1950s and early 1960s, when politics within the organization, together with his own growing doubts about the legiti-macy of some of the movement's doctrines, brought him to the periphery of the movement. In 1964, he made the journey to Mecca, where he was impressed by the cooperation of persons of all races and backgrounds in the *hajj*, or pilgrimage. His experiences there led him to several important conclusions about his religion and his life as a black man in America, which he described in his *Autobiography*. Malcolm X observed of the African American that "the religion of Christianity had failed him." He ex-pressed a profound sense of belonging to the Islamic community: "In the Holy World, away from America's race problem, was the first time I ever had been able to think clearly about the basic divisions of white people in America. . . . In my thirty-nine years on this earth, the Holy City of Mecca had been the first time I had ever stood before the Creator of All and felt like a complete human being." He consequently declared: "I have learned that not all white people are racists. I am speaking against and my fight is against the white *racists.*" And he came to question the authority of Elijah Muhammad: "I believed in him not only as a leader in the ordinary *human* sense, but I also believed in him as a *divine* leader. There on a Holy World hilltop, I realized how very dangerous it is for people to hold any human being in such esteem. . . ." After returning to the United States, Malcolm X, now an orthodox Muslim, changed his name to El Hajj Malik el Shabazz, broke with the Nation of Islam, and founded a new group, the

---

[27] Asma Gull Hasan, *American Muslims: The New Generation* (New York, 2000), 63–4.

Muslim Mosque, Inc. He was severely criticized by the NOI, and he became the subject of close surveillance by law enforcement agencies. Within a year he was dead, murdered by gunmen while speaking in New York. Three men, including two Black Muslims, were sentenced in his death.[28]

The growth of orthodox Islam in the African American community was facilitated by the emergence of Wallace Muhammed (Warith Deen Mohammed after 1980) as the leader of the Nation of Islam upon the death of his father Elijah Muhammed in 1975. Having made a pilgrimage to Mecca some years earlier, Wallace Muhammad, like Malcolm X, had begun to question some of the doctrines of Elijah Muhammed. Stressing Islam as a religion rather than a political posture, he taught that whites were not devils and that blacks should not pursue separate nationhood. He abolished the Fruit of Islam and divested the organization of the businesses that his father had built, in the interest of focusing on religion. He promoted the study of Arabic and the Qur'an, and the practice of orthodox Islam. Under his leadership, the group changed its name several times, until, in 1985, he proposed that an organizational name suggesting a distinct kind of Islam was no longer necessary, since the members were all part of the larger global community of Sunni Islam. As Imam of the Muslim American Society, he was the first Muslim to deliver an invocation at the U.S. Senate (in 1992), and his place as the leader of the Muslim community in the United States has been recognized by the World Mission of Imam Administrators.

The Nation of Islam did not die out, however. In 1978, Louis Farrakahn, who opposed Wallace Mohammed's initiatives to change the direction of the organization, reorganized the NOI along the lines of a black supremacist and separtist movement. Because most of the earlier members had followed Wallace Mohammed into orthodox Islam, the reorganized Nation of Islam built its membership through conversions in the African American community. A former minister of the New York Temple of the NOI and a close associate of Elijah Muhammed, Farrakahn provided a highly visible profile to the media, often through an extreme rhetoric that he reportedly deployed on one occasion in 1984 to picture Judaism as a "gutter religion" and Hitler as a "great man"—a pronouncement doubly controversial because of presidential candidate Jesse Jackson's anti-Semitic reference at the same time to New York as "Hymietown." During the 1980s, however, Farrakhan began inching the NOI closer to orthodox Islam by encouraging prayer and fasting along with the observance of dietary laws preached by Elijah Muhammed. The movement became more actively involved in politics in the 1980s and 1990s as well, and it received significant attention for Farrakahn's leadership of the Million Man March in Washington in 1995. Although recognized for its social programs—largely

---

[28] *The Autobiography of Malcolm X as told to Alex Haley* (New York, 1965), 372, 374.

in Chicago, its headquarters—its ongoing embrace of key doctrines and practices begun by Elijah Muhammed have kept it, for the most part, outside the body of the Islamic community in America.[29]

Orthodox Islam saw steady growth in the late twentieth century, and part of that growth took place through conversions in prison. The majority of those who convert to Islam in prison are African Americans, most of whom are converted by Sunni Islamic groups. Approximately 30,000 persons convert to Islam in prison each year. In New York state, forty full-time Muslim chaplains are employed to minister to prisoners. In New York City, approximately 30 percent of those in jail are Muslim. Nationally, there are as many as 300,000 Muslims in prisons, of whom most converted to Islam while in prison.[30]

The emergence of African American Islam in recent decades has enlarged the scope of an already diverse religion in America. From early in the twentieth century, there has been significant ongoing discussion in the Muslim community about the nature of Islam in America. In places where the community formed in the late nineteenth and very early twentieth centuries, there has been some Americanization of Islam, such as in the rescheduling of services from Friday to Sunday, the creation of Sunday schools for religious education, and an increased focus on the mosque as a representation of religious life. Newer immigrants, especially those who began immigrating in the late 1960s, have brought with them more traditional religious views, including Islamicist ideologies that have been forged in reaction to the process of Westernization in nations such as Egypt and Pakistan. This change has resulted in tensions in American Muslim communities, because Muslim students, especially, have sought the reconstitution of American Muslims as part of the revivalist understanding of *'umma*, a worldwide Muslim community that transcends language, geography, and ethnicity.[31]

One unexpected consequence of the rise of Islamic nationalism and its transmission to American Muslims in the form of ideas about community has been the reinforcement of ethnic differences among Muslims. The making of Muslim identities in America accordingly has been linked to political discourse and activity. And to some extent, this connection in turn has hastened the process of defection from the practice of Islam by the children and grandchildren of the immigrants. Some Muslims today participate in religious observances only during festivals once or twice a year.

---

[29] Hasan, 81; Smith, 94, 95; GhaneaBassiri, 157.

[30] Sonsyrea Tate, *Little X: Growing up in the Nation of Islam* (New York, 1997), 77; Aminah Beverly McCloud, *African American Islam* (New York, 1995).

[31] Yvonne Yazbeck Haddad and Jane Idleman Smith, eds., *Muslim Communities in North America* (Albany, N.Y., 1994), xxi; and Laurel D. Wigle, "An Arab Muslim Community in Michigan," and Barbara C. Aswad, "The Southeast Dearborn Arab Community Struggles for Survival Against Urban 'Renewal,' " in Barbara C. Aswad, ed., *Arabic Speaking Communities in American Cities* (Staten Island, N.Y., 1974), 53–83, 155–67.

Immigrants who arrived before the relaxation of immigration laws in 1965 have to a large extent intermarried with non-Muslims and assimilated. But even among these "unmosqued" Muslims, certain aspects of Muslim religious culture remain intact. The everyday Muslim culture of family, diet, the organization of social life, manners, and gender roles continues to shape Muslim life in various way, for those in the process of assimilating as well as among the traditionalists.[32]

Islam in America Post-9/11

The consequences of the terrorist attacks of September 11, 2001, have been unprecedented for both Muslims and non-Muslims in America. In the weeks after the attack, there were many incidences of anti-Muslim violence, including the vandalizing of mosques, Muslim community centers, and businesses, as well as attacks on persons who, because of their appearance, were thought to be Muslim (especially including Sikhs, who dress in a manner similar to that of terrorist Osama bin-Laden, but who are not Muslims). In Washington, D.C., politicians condemned such crimes and repeatedly declared that the nation was not at war with Islam, but with terrorists. Non-Muslim legislators spoke of Islam as a religion of peace, and many governmental leaders urged their constituents to recognize that American Muslims were moral, upright, and patriotic Americans, not subversives. American Muslim and Arab American groups vigorously condemned the Al-Qaeda attacks on New York and Washington, pledged their support to Washington's campaign against terrorism, and stressed the incompatibility of terrorism with Islam. At the same time, they made efforts to educate the American public about Islam and especially, to demonstrate that it shared a moral and spiritual view of life with other American religions.

Although there were attacks on American Muslims in the period just following the September 11 attacks, national polls revealed that in the wake of the attacks, many Americans in fact formed a more positive view of Islam. One widely cited survey indicated that in May 2001, 45 percent of Americans had a favorable view of Islam. Two months after 9/11, that figure had risen to 59 percent, and among conservative Republicans, the change was even more dramatic, from 35 percent to 64 percent.[33] Data gathered by other polls eventually indicated that many Americans had known little or nothing about Islam until 9/11 and that once they began

---

[32] Denny, 356–58; Haddad and Smith, *Mission to America*, 23–48; Catherine L. Albanese, *America: Religions and Religion*, 2nd ed. (Belmont, Calif., 1992), 298.

[33] "Post September 11 Attitudes: Religion more prominent; Muslim-Americans more accepted," a survey conducted by The Pew Research Center for the People and the Press, December 6, 2001, available at: http://people-press.org/reports/display.php3?ReportID=144. The survey of 1,500 adults was based upon data gathered in mid-November 2001.

to learn about it, they found little to object to in terms of its moral vision or its general compatibility alongside other religious viewpoints in America. There were some exceptions. Some conservative Christian religious leaders complained that Islam was incompatible with what they believed to be a Christian America, preacher Franklin Graham calling it a "wicked, violent" religion. Such rhetoric was in keeping with a 1995 poll indicating that seven out of ten born-again Christians believed that the impact of Islam on American life was negative. But in general, non-Muslim Americans separated the agenda of the Al-Qaeda terrorists from the practice of Islam.[34]

In terms of the religious views of Americans, one of the most important consequences arising out of national reflection on 9/11 was the realization that America was linked to other parts of the world through the religion of its citizens, and more broadly than had previously been thought. During the nineteenth and twentieth centuries, and especially during times when large numbers of persons were immigrating to the United States, Americans had by degrees come to terms with the fact of their complex religious connections to Europe. American awareness of links between Jewish communities in America and Jewish populations overseas, and awareness of Roman Catholic and Orthodox connections to foreign communities developed gradually as immigrants found places within American society. The case of Islam, as well as the case of Asian religions, has been somewhat different. Viewing Islam (incorrectly) as a religion unrelated to the Jewish/Christian background of the vast majority of American religions, Americans historically have had difficulty placing it in relation both to American life and to the cultures of those places where it has flourished—the Arab countries, Indonesia, Africa, and so forth. The intense discussions about Islam and about American Muslims since 9/11 have raised American awareness not only about the size and diversity of Islam in America but also of the ways in which it connects the nation, through its citizens, to other cultures previously considered far-off and exotic.

Buddhism

The founder of Buddhism, Siddhārtha Gautama (563?–483? B.C.) reached spiritual enlightenment after rejecting his aristocratic life at the age of twenty-nine and then setting out upon a course of asceticism and medita-

---

[34] Conservative Protestant reaction to the attacks are Jerry Falwell at http://www.falwell. com/, dated 2001-SEP-14; Pat Robertson, "Pat Robertson's statement regarding terrorist attack," Christian Broadcasting Network, 2001-SEP-14, at http://www.cbn.com/partner/ Article_Display_Page/; Franklin Graham, "Christian leader condemns Islam: Preacher Franklin Graham calls Islam 'wicked, violent,' " MSNBC Nightly News, at http://www. msnbc.com/news/659057.asp. See also the 1995 poll results of: "Prejudice of Americans Towards Those of Other Faiths" at http://www.religioustolerance.org/amer_ intol.htm.

tion. As a teacher, he outlined a method by which others could likewise attain the spiritual goal of nirvana, or, liberation from desire. Fundamental to his teaching are the Four Noble Truths: suffering, the cause of suffering (desire), the end of suffering, and the path to that end. According to Gautama, the Buddha, it was possible to end desire by living in the world without becoming attached to it. Laypersons as well as communities of monks and nuns consequently set out upon the Noble Eightfold Path articulated by the Buddha as the religion spread from India throughout Asia. In time, Buddhism split into different schools, some of which are represented in America. The most significant overall division is between Mahayana Buddhism, which has been popular in China and Japan and which encourages the development of religious sensibilities in community, and Theravada Buddhism, which is centered in Southeast Asia and places more emphasis on religious exercises performed by the individual that lead to enlightenment.

Buddhism came to America initially through the Chinese who began immigrating into California, first in small numbers in the 1840s and then in large numbers after the discovery of gold in 1849. The first Chinese temple was built by the Sze Yap Company—one of the Six Companies who sponsored Chinese immigrants and served as their liaison to China—in San Francisco in 1853. By the time of the Civil War, approximately 10 percent of the population of California was Chinese, and during the decades following the war, Chinese Americans built hundreds of temples along the Pacific coast. Those temples represented a mixture of Taoism, Confucianism, and Buddhism wrapped together under the umbrella of Chinese popular religion. Early Chinese immigrants were sometimes met by nativist violence, such as arson and lynching, or by mass expulsion, as in the case of Tacoma, Washington, in 1884, where the entire Chinese population was rounded up and expelled from the town in railroad boxcars. Chinese Buddhists nevertheless found occasional legal support for the practice of their religion, notably in a California Supreme Court decision in 1859, which found no reason to limit the public performance of Buddhism.[35]

A different style of Buddhism—Pure Land Buddhism—arrived in North America with Japanese farm laborers who came to work in the Hawaiian Islands' cane plantations in the late 1880s. By 1897, the islands employed 23,000 Japanese, 96 percent of whom were officially listed in the census as "non-Christian." In that year, the Buddhists in Honolulu wrote to church authorities in Japan complaining of the "fraud and trickery" of impostor priests and asked for help: "We request that a suitable attention be given to the matter and that a suitable priest be sent to reside in the Teaching Hall

[35] Rick Fields, *How the Swans Came to the Lake: A Narrative History of Buddhism in America* (Boston & London, 1992), 70–76; Charles Prebish, "Buddhism" in *Encyclopedia of the American Religious Experience*, eds. Charles H. Lippy and Peter W. Williams (New York, 1988), 670, 671–82.

so that we can be healed from this thirst for the Buddha's teaching." Buddhists in Kyoto responded, and in 1900, Jodo Shinshu services were held for the first time in the Temple of the Original Vow in Hawaii. Bishop Yemyo Immamura and the four priests from the outside islands officiated.[36] Jodo Shinshu, a branch of Pure Land Buddhism, was grounded in devotion to Buddha Amida, whose love was so great that all persons who faithfully prayed the invocation "Hail to the Buddha of Infinite Life and Love" would attain Enlightenment. Jodo Shinshu, which stressed faith in a benevolent deity over a program of self-help meditation as the key to spiritual advancement, thus was structurally similar to Christianity. This similarity hastened the process of acculturation of Japanese Buddhists to an American culture dominated by Christian ideas that included belief in a loving and saving deity. As Japanese Buddhists settled on the mainland, they adjusted rapidly to the new cultural environment, and the various congregations of Pure Land Buddhism coalesced as the Buddhist Churches of America, which numbered over 100,000 members by the late twentieth century.

The determinative event for the growth of Buddhism in North America was the World's Parliament of Religions, a gathering of representatives of many religions from around the world, held in Chicago in 1893. The Rinzai Zen master Soyen Shaku presented a paper entitled "The Law of Cause and Effect as Taught by Buddha," in which he urged calm reflection and overcoming the distractions of feelings of pleasure and pain, love and hate. Rinzai Zen stressed sudden enlightenment, such as might come from insight derived through meditation on a koan, an alogical riddle, such as "Where was your face before you washed it this morning?" The paper attracted the attention of Paul Carus, an Illinois editor, who asked Soyen to assist him in translating Asian religious writings for publication in America. Soyen refused but suggested Daisetz Teitaro Suzuki in his stead. Consequently, in a series of visits to the United States over the course of about twenty-five years, Suzuki translated, lectured, and wrote about Rinzai Zen, and he became its most effective popularizer. A cluster of "beat generation" poets and writers advanced the visibility of Zen in the 1950s and 1960s, and significant numbers of white, middle-class Americans experimented with it during that time and afterwards.

During this period of rising American interest in Buddhism, several additional forms took root in America. Soto Zen deemphasized the role of the roshi, or master, in attaining Enlightenment, and encouraged "just sitting," or meditation on breathing. The Chicago Buddhist Temple and the San Francisco Zen Center, which were founded in the 1950s, served as springboards for the growth of Soto Zen elsewhere in America. During the 1960s, Nichiren Shoshu, which stressed encounter with a particular book

---

[36] Louise H. Hunter, *Buddhism in Hawaii: Its Impact on a Yankee Community* (Honolulu, 1971), 61.

of Buddhist scriptures, *The Lotus Sutra of the Mystical Law,* also gained in popularity. Yoshigirai Kawai, the Japanese representative of the sect at the 1893 Chicago World's Parliament of Religions, had explained that Buddhahood was attainable by any person willing to repeat the invocation "Namu-myo-ho ren-ge-kyo," or, "Hail to the Lotus Sutra." That message was driven home to a receptive audience through aggressive missionizing on the part of the sect in America in the 1960s and 1970s. By the early 1980s, as many as 200,000 non-Asian Americans had joined the "church" of Nichiren Shoshu.

With the advent of large-scale immigration from Asia beginning in the late 1960s, Buddhism in America grew both broader and deeper. Chinese Buddhism, through the efforts of the newly organized Sino-American Buddhist Association, was revitalized and enlarged. The first native-born American was ordained in a 108-day-long ordination ceremony in 1972, and the organization established a monastery and university. Southeast Asian Buddhist immigrants of the Theravadin orientation, who numbered about 750,000 in 1995, transplanted numerous organizations and teachers to North America after the fall of Saigon, Vietnam, in 1975 and in the years of tumultuous political instability in the neighboring countries of Southeast Asia following that event. Some of the 142 centers of Theravada Buddhism in America, such as Wat Dhammaram in Chicago and Dharma Vijaya Buddhist Vihara in Los Angeles, have become Americanized in recent years—especially in terms of increasing emphasis on the laity—as non-Asian Buddhists and immigrants alike adapt Buddhism to the local environment.[37] Tibetan Buddhism, aided by the popularizing work of American scholars and visits from the Dalai Lama and other Tibetan teachers, likewise has increased in membership in North America in the last twenty-five years.

Non-Asian Americans have long been curious about Asian religions. Such curiosity is present in the literary musings of nineteenth-century New Englanders Ralph Waldo Emerson and Henry David Thoreau, and in the poetry of Walt Whitman, as well as in the poetry of Gary Snyder and Allen Ginsberg in the 1950s. We find it in the development of the academic study of Asian religions in American universities in recent decades. And it is manifest above all when Americans embrace Buddhism as a sacred path. To some extent, all of this interest is shaped by the American tendency to exoticize Asia and things Asian, to see the "Orient" as a land of mystery, transcendence, ancient wisdom, difference. The white American encounter with Buddhism—more so than the encounter with Islam and Hinduism—has produced specific emphases of interpretation that may or may not eventually square with styles practiced by Asian immigrants and their descendants. Accordingly, Buddhism in America is still a largely

---

[37] Paul David Numrich, *Old Wisdom in the New World: Americanization in Two Immigrant Theravada Buddhist Temples* (Knoxville, Tenn., 1995), xxi, 140–47.

ambiguous phenomenon, in certain contexts displaying a dedication to conserving tradition, and in other contexts embodying a willingness to innovate and adapt.

Hinduism

Hinduism is a multifaceted religion that took shape in India over the course of thousands of years. It is grounded in complex philosophical ideas, elaborated in rich traditions of ritual and the worship of gods large and small, and guided by the theological doctrines embedded in the Vedas, which date from about 1000 B.C., and in the Upanishads, holy writings that took shape during the period 700–400 B.C. The goal set by Hinduism is spiritual perfection through escape from karma, the cosmic law requiring consequences for one's actions, good or bad. Until one is able to achieve release from the bondage of karma, one is reincarnated in a series of lives that populate the spectrum from plants and animals on the one hand to the privileged status of a Brahmin on the other. Brahmins are the priestly caste and the highest level of the caste system in India. The methods by which a person can escape reincarnation and merge with Brahma, the Universal Soul, vary but can be generally comprehended under three categories. The path of action offers deliverance through the faithful performance of one's role in the cosmic order of things, specifically, the duties of one's stations in life. By living in accord with the expectations and responsibilities of one's caste, age, and sex—in short, by acting in agreement with one's dharma—spiritual advancement is made possible. The path of knowledge stresses the acquisition of wisdom through reflection on the meaning of the eternal order and the nature of Brahma. Hindus who are embarked on this path commonly employ meditative techniques (as do most other Hindus) and specific physical disciplines (e.g., breath control and the mastery of ritual postures, as in some forms of yoga) in their pursuit of elevated consciousness and spiritual insight. The third path is the way of devotion, or bhakti, the cultivation of love for a god or goddess. By losing oneself in delight for the deity (such as Shiva or Vishnu), one is transformed.

Hinduism came to America through a combination of vectors. Initial interest was triggered by the nineteenth-century publication of books about Asian religions and later by translations of Hindu sacred writings. After the mid–nineteenth century, the firsthand accounts of missionaries and world travelers were fundamental to the American discovery of Indian religious life. And beginning in the 1880s, Americans hosted Indian religious leaders, who lectured and organized Hindu religious societies. Certain persons and organizations in America encouraged study of Hinduism, especially its philosophies. Ralph Waldo Emerson and Henry David Thoreau, *The North American Review*, Theosophy, and the American Oriental Society founded by Boston clergy and missionaries in 1842 laid the groundwork for the manner in which Americans engaged Hinduism. The sense of intellectual kinship between East and West represented in the undertakings of these people and organizations was well articulated by Thoreau's comparison of the spiritual glories of life at pristine Walden Pond with the ancient traditions flowing in the most holy of Indian rivers: "The pure Walden water is mingled with the sacred water of the Ganges."[38]

The first Hindu guru to visit the United States was Protap Chunder Mazoomdar, who spoke in 1883 to a group gathered at the house in Massachusetts where Ralph Waldo Emerson had died the previous year. Mazoomdar returned ten years later to the World's Parliament of Religions in Chicago, together with Swami Vivekananda, founder of the Ramakrishna Mission, a Hindu monastic order. Vivekananda proved to be the more charismatic figure, and by the following year, he had established a Vedanta Society in New York, the first of a dozen in American cities. The Hinduism of the Vedanta Society stressed a way of knowledge that dovetailed with certain aspects of Christianity and consequently was accessible to a largely Christian audience in the United States. Vedanta was a nondualistic, intellectual form of Hinduism that promoted a religious life characterized not only by the pursuit of insight into cosmic order but also by a structured religious life through church services. Moreover, as Vivekananda explained in his "Address to the Parliament," Hinduism was the embrace of timeless truths and therefore was no impediment to persons because of potential conflicts with Christian doctrines: "The Hindu religion does not consist in struggles and attempts to believe a certain doctrine or dogma, but in realizing; not in believing, but in being and becoming."[39]

The intellectual, monastic emphasis of Vedanta was the first but not the only style of Hinduism that took root in the United States. Swami Yogananda, who arrived in Boston just after World War I, remained for thirty years, founding the Self-Realization Fellowship in 1925. He taught the yogic discipline of meditation, as well as kriya yoga, which utilized various physical and mental techniques for organizing the seven energy centers of the body, which lay along a line from the base of the spinal column to the top of the head. Yogananda was successful in reaching a wide audience, and the organization that he founded numbered forty-four centers and had spawned an assortment of similar groups (led by other swamis) across the country by the mid-1980s. Few immigrant Indians belonged to the Self-Realization Fellowship or to Vedanta societies. Located almost entirely in California, small groups of Indians built temples in San Francisco and Los Angeles, and as an ethnic community, they had little influence upon the process by which Americans engaged Hinduism.

[38] Henry David Thoreau, *Walden* (New York, 1942), 198–99; William Bysshe Stein, ed., *Two Brahman Sources of Emerson and Thoreau* (Gainesville, Fla., 1967).

[39] Swami Vivekananda, "Address at the World's Parliament of Religions," in *Eastern Spirituality in America: Selected Writings*, ed. Robert S. Ellwood (New York, 1987), 56. See also 45–47.

With the repeal in 1965 of the 1917 Asian Exclusion Act, the immigrant Indian community expanded. Highly educated and cosmopolitan, the majority of Indian immigrants acculturated rapidly. But drawn from a broad background of geography and language, these immigrants frequently differ both in terms of the content of their religious practice as well as in the extent to which they are involved in that practice. It therefore is misleading to describe a common denominator of immigrant Hinduism. But, in general, those who have retained Indian traditions embrace a religion that involves communal worship in temples, the ritual structuring of important life-cycle occasions such as marriage, observance of a religious calendar, attention to diet, and devotion to gods and goddesses.

Religious leaders who were willing to translate Hinduism into terms understandable by Western audiences also came to the United States in larger numbers after 1965. Within a very short period of time after arriving in the United States, most of these leaders attracted impressive followings. Their success was due in part to the fact that Americans had not had access to Indian spiritual mentors during the time of restricted immigration, and with the opening of the borders, the new supply of gurus, or religious teachers, met a need that had gone unaddressed for two generations. In the words of one American scholar, "It was not so much that Eastern faiths suddenly struck a responsive chord in the American counterculture as their growth had been artificially thwarted until then. With the barrier removed, normalization occurred."[40]

One example of a fast-growing American movement grounded in Hindu devotion is the International Society for Krishna Consciousness (ISKCON). Its devotees are sometimes referred to as "Hare Krishnas" because of the repetitive chant they make to Krishna, who is considered the Supreme Personality of the Godhead: "Hare Krishna Hare Krishna Krishna Krishna Hare Hare Hare Rama Hare Rama Rama Rama Hare Hare." Founded by A. C. Bhaktivedanta Swami Prabhupada in New York in 1965, the movement stresses a strict personal discipline that includes celibacy (or limitation of sexual intercourse exclusively to procreation), vegetarianism, and a monastic lifestyle centered on the temple and on care for the images of Krishna and the founding figures of the movement enshrined there. The ecstatic dancing and chanting of devotees is understood as part of a process of overcoming false consciousness. This concept was explained by Bhaktivedanta in a lecture on the "transcendental vibration" of chanting, at the San Francisco temple in 1968. The "Hare Krishna" chant "is the sublime method for reviving our transcendental consciousness. . . . By chanting this transcendental vibration, we can cleanse away all misgivings within our hearts. . . . Krishna consciousness is not an artificial imposition on the mind. This consciousness is the original

---

[40] Roger Finke and Rodney Stark, *The Churching of America* (New Brunswick, NJ, 1992), 244.

natural energy of the living entity."[41] The movement peaked in the 1970s and then became progressively less visible as the counterculture of the 1960s to 1970s faded. Nevertheless, in the late 1980s, about 2,500 persons still lived in approximately sixty temples in the United States. Several thousand others visited those temples more or less regularly for worship services.[42]

Other religious movements grounded in Hinduism have attracted the interest of Americans. Some of those movements, such as the Divine Light Mission, which stressed devotion to the young guru Maharaj Ji, attracted tens of thousands of "blissed out" followers before losing its momentum in the cultural changes of the 1970s.[43] Transcendental Meditation, or TM, on the other hand, took shape initially in North America in 1959 as japa, a meditative practice involving the repetition of the names of Hindu deities, and has attracted hundreds of thousands of persons to its training sessions. The success of TM hinges partly on the claim of the movement's leaders that meditation brings desirable physical consequences, such as the reduction of stress and improved powers of concentration. TM centers point to laboratory experiments conducted with biofeedback machines to underscore the effectiveness of the technique in producing healthful states of mind and body.

At the end of the twentieth century, a wide variety of religious movements and organizations derived from Hinduism were alive and well in America. In some instances—as in the case of ISKCON—Asian immigrants have joined the ranks of non-Asian Americans who originally supported those movements. This enlarged membership has provided a certain amount of ballast to these movements, reinjecting Indian cultural traditions into them and in the process giving them more recognizably ethnic contours.

The Marketplace of Religion and the American Mission

The American traditions of religious freedom and the separation of church and state have furnished Americans with the opportunity to choose their religions. Lacking the guaranteed support of public funds— there is no state church in America, as there is in many other nations— churches in America have had to compete for members. To some extent, they have had to learn to market religion. Some churches have become

---

[41] Robert S. Ellwood, *Alternative Altars: Unconventional and Eastern Spirituality in America* (Chicago, 1979), 104–5.

[42] John Y. Fenton, "Hinduism," in Lippy and Williams, eds., vol. 2, 693.

[43] James V. Downton, Jr., *Sacred Journeys: The Conversion of Young Americans to the Divine Light Mission* (New York, 1979), 148, 221–25.

proficient in this enterprise, making use of the printing press, public spectacle, word-of-mouth campaigns, electronic communications, and so forth. For without members, that is, consumers, a church, just like a business, cannot survive. The varied and imaginative marketing strategies[44] employed by the churches are rooted in the conception of religion as a product. And, like businesspeople anywhere, religious leaders sometimes have altered or fine-tuned that product in such a way as to command more market share. The marketplace of religion in the late twentieth century was dynamic and complex, and Americans who have the opportunity to choose from this vast religious smorgasbord have become increasingly savvy buyers, looking for the best match between their needs and desires and the religious product.

These characteristics do not mean that religion in America is less "religious" than in other places, nor do they stamp American religions as artificial or corrupt. They do, however, affect the way in which Americans view the relation between religion and the future, or destiny, of the nation. As we have seen, Americans in the past frequently have connected religious faith with trust that God would bless the American "City on the hill." Blending religious ideas with devotion to democratic government, linking the rhetoric of salvation to rhetoric about equality and liberty, Americans envisioned a process of missionizing that would bring all the nations of the world under the umbrella of the American way. For many Americans, this was the national mission, a program of global proportions, blessed and sustained by God.

The late twentieth century ushered in an era in which global concerns challenged local concerns, and national priorities were weighed more carefully against the mass of world politics, economics, ecology, and cultures. And as the marketplace for all things has become increasingly global, Americans can choose from a broader assortment of religious options. The American embrace of Asian religions, the growth of Islam in America—especially among African Americans—the emergence in America of a host of religious options that were not present a century ago, all suggest that the mission of America as conceived in the eighteenth and nineteenth centuries is no longer viable.

Whether Americans will retain a notion of national mission in a reconceived form remains to be seen. Internal as well as external factors complicate such a project. Religion may play an important role in such a reconceived mission, or religion may be progressively unlinked to a national sense of purpose. The lively growth of religious and political fundamentalisms around the world that occurred in the late twentieth century

---

[44] These have been cataloged and analyzed by R. Laurence Moore in *Selling God: American Religion in the Marketplace of Culture* (New York, 1994).

may affect the course that Americans take, provoking either wholesale embrace of fundamentalism or reaction to it.[45] The ongoing opening of the global marketplace—in every area of human life—certainly will shape American thinking about the relation between religion and nation. It is, after all, the populus, the American people, who, by choosing to join or not to join, by choosing this religion over that, by choosing one church over another, will, one by one in numbers adding up across the national front, determine the course of change.

Religion, Nature, and Health

Nature Religion and Holistic Living

In the nineteenth century, Americans had shown considerable interest in religions that were focused on health, especially those that featured "mental healing." In the 1960s, that interest reemerged as a manifestation of "nature religion."[46] Nature religion in America was neither an institutional religion nor an organized denomination; nature religion was not characterized by a set system of rituals or by systematic theology or by the presence of seminary-trained leaders. It was essentially a perspective on nature, a recognition of a religious dimension to nature, that generated a wide range of behaviors and practices.

Nature religion has deep roots in the nation's past and has appeared in many forms, ranging from Puritan awe at the wilderness of the New World to twentieth-century revivals of pagan religions (from the Latin word *paganus*, which refers to a person from the countryside).[47] We might speak of Henry David Thoreau's experiment at Walden Pond as a form of nature religion. The same could be said of the lifelong mission of the naturalist John Muir. The numerous nineteenth-century attempts to articulate a sense of cosmic order based on theories about magnetism, electricity, and mesmerism likewise were species of nature religion. And the health-reform

---

[45] See three collections edited by Marty E. Marty and R. Scott Appleby: *Fundamentalisms Observed* (Chicago, 1991); *Fundamentalisms and the State* (Chicago, 1993); and *Fundamentalisms Comprehended* (Chicago, 1995).

[46] Catherine Albanese, *Nature Religion in America: From the Algonkian Indians to the New Age* (Chicago, 1990), proposes the term, and I have adopted it here. She writes that "the term nature religion is my own name for a symbolic center, and a cluster of beliefs, behaviors and values that encircle it" (p. 7). She identifies numerous and varied manifestations of nature religion, ranging from early American attitudes toward the wilderness to twentieth-century holistic health movements.

[47] See Margot Adler, *Drawing Down the Moon: Witches, Druids, Goddess-Worshippers, and Other Pagans in America Today* (Boston, 1986).

movements of the nineteenth and twentieth centuries—with their emphasis on diet, on clean living, on balance and harmony in everyday life—embodied a strongly religious perspective on nature. Sometimes, as in the
case of nineteenth-century reformer Sylvester Graham (who invented a
cracker that still bears his name), a religious perspective on nature was expressed against a background of Christian ideas.[48] In other cases, non-
Western, folk, or Native American traditions served as vehicles to express
that sensibility.

"Holistic health" emerged in the 1960s as one form of nature religion,
particularly in its incarnation as the "health-food movement." As Americans became increasingly conscious of ecological issues and as "country living" acquired symbolic power over urban life, so did "natural foods." If the
slogan of the nineteenth-century migration from rural America to the city
was "The country for health, the city for wealth," so too was it an accurate
expression of the attitudes of health-food advocates in the 1970s, but with
the emphasis reversed to reflect the desirability of communing with nature
and the physical, and rejecting the moral corruption of urban life. The religious dimension to the movement was apparent in the fact that many natural foods stores were operated by religious groups, and particularly by
those that favored the wisdom of the East. But the movement had a distinctly moral tone to it as well, as shown by the best-selling natural foods
cookbook *Diet for a Small Planet*, wherein a moral argument about the most
efficient use of grain to feed the world's hungry was coupled with meatless
recipes. Organically grown fruits and vegetables became, in this atmosphere, more than pesticide-free nutrition. They symbolized American re-
discovery of a harmonious relationship with nature.[49]

The health-food movement was an example of the "wellness" approach
that often was associated with holistic health. That is, it was predicated on
the belief that a proper diet and style of living would prevent illness, improve the quality of life, and promote moral behavior. Other movements
associated with nature religion were focused not as much on wellness as on
the healing of disease. One such movement, Reiki, which began in Japan
and became popular in America in the 1970s, was founded on the belief
that a properly trained healer could serve as a conduit for a life force energy to flow into a diseased person. The cure of a person's illness in this
way, through the mediation of a Reiki master, was understood to be the
consequence of a process of bringing harmony and balance into the body
and the mind. Healing was understood essentially as a process of "attune-
ment" to natural energy.

[48] See Stephen Nissenbaum, *Sex, Diet and Debility in Jacksonian America: Sylvester Graham and
Health Reform* (Westport, Conn., 1980).

[49] David J. Hofford, "Contemporary Folk Medicine," in *Other Healers: Unorthodox Healing in
America*, ed. Norman Gevitz (Baltimore, 1988), 222.

Other forms of spiritual healing besides Reiki—such as gemstone (crystal) healing, shamanism, Swedenborgian movements, and so forth—were a part of the religion of the "New Age," which began to take shape in the pages of the *Boston East-West Journal* in the early 1970s and which from there took root among the middle class and especially among upwardly mobile adults. New Age discourse, which featured an emphasis on cosmic harmony, quantum physics, and personal openness to spiritual energy, provided a twentieth-century framework for the reconstitution of nineteenth-century spiritualist impulses.[50]

Development of a Health Ministry

The involvement of the mainline denominations in health concerns had been well established since the mid–nineteenth century, when immigrant Irish Catholics and German Lutherans began constructing their own hospitals. Presbyterians, Baptists, Disciples, Methodists, and Seventh-day Adventists likewise founded a wide-ranging network of sanitariums and health-care institutions shortly thereafter. These denominations viewed their roles first of all as providers of medical care, but they conceived that enterprise as one wing of their overall ministry, so that the hospital served as a setting for the exercise of pastoral care of a specifically religious sort as well. With the rise of the hospital as a market institution in the twentieth century, however, the denominations gradually surrendered control to business administrators. Consequently, there was a deterioration of the formal connection between religion and the hospital that marked late nineteenth-century health care.[51]

The denominations by no means lost interest in religion and health, however. Because they continued to view the hospital as an inviting ground for pastoral work, they set about developing pastoral clinical education programs that trained counselors to appreciate the therapeutic aspect of ministry. Drawing on theoretical works about religion, psychology, and healing—such as Rollo May's *Art of Counseling* (1939), Carl Rogers's *Counseling and Psychotherapy* (1942), and Erich Fromm's *Psychoanalysis and Religion* (1950)—some Protestant theologians advocated the exploration of religion itself as therapy.

---

[50] Gordon Melton, *Encyclopedic Handbook of Cults in America* (New York, 1986), 108, 116; Meredith G. McGuire with Debra Kantor, *Ritual Healing in Suburban America* (Brunswick, N.J., 1988); Robert C. Fuller, *Alternative Medicine and American Religious Life* (New York, 1989).

[51] E. Brooks Holifield, *Health and Medicine in the Methodist Tradition* (New York, 1986); Paul Starr, *The Social Transformation of American Medicine: The Rise of a Sovereign Profession and the Making of a Vast Industry* (New York, 1982). See also the essays in *Caring and Curing: Health and Medicine in the Western Religious Traditions*, ed. Ronald L. Numbers and Darrell W. Amundsen (New York, 1986).

By the 1960s, the pastoral counselor who blended psychological and sometimes medical training with a religious perspective on health had become a fixture in the health-care (and especially the mental-health) field. In the 1950s, the National Institute of Mental Health reported that among persons who pursued counseling for their emotional disturbances, 42 percent first turned to their ministers for help. This impulse rapidly was translated into a process of institutionalizing the minister's role in such cases, with 149 pastoral counseling centers established by 1963.[52] The 1970s and 1980s witnessed further enlargement of an educational infrastructure for the training of pastoral counselors. Although such training revealed some sympathy with the mentality of New Age religion, in most cases it nevertheless remained rooted in theological orthodoxy. This trend was partly a consequence of warnings by theologians that the goal of therapy was compatible with, but not identical to, traditionally religious concerns about faith and morality.[53]

As religion and health increasingly were linked in both theory and practice, Americans also spoke more of death. The popularity of works such as Elisabeth Kübler-Ross's *On Death and Dying* (1969) and the wide circulation of accounts of "near-death experiences" in the popular press signaled a departure from previous habits of "evasion and concealment"[54] that characterized the American approach to death. Although evasion continued, perhaps most visibly in the rise in popularity of cryonic suspension of the body, there were signs that a new perspective was emerging. Not the least of these signs was the widespread initiation of programs for clergy and laity aimed at developing means to help the dying and the bereaved come to terms with death.

American concern about both health and death intensified during a time in which there was little sense of how all of the various strands of religion in America might join together in such a way as to suggest a new religiously grounded consensus. Lacking the kind of cultural guidance that was available to an earlier generation, frustrated Americans circumscribed their lives a bit more narrowly. Intensely personal matters such as health and death acquired a new prominence, and reflection upon such things formed a large part of the framework for new or resurrected understandings of cosmic harmony and balance.

---

[52] E. Brooks Holifield, *A History of Pastoral Care in America: From Salvation to Self-Realization* (Nashville, 1983).

[53] Don Browning, *Religious Ethics and Pastoral Care* (Philadelphia, 1983), and Charles Gerkin, *The Living Human Document* (Nashville, 1983).

[54] William F. May, "The Sacral Power of Death in Contemporary Experience," *Social Research*, 39 (1972), 469.

Epilogue

In 2001, the Graduate Center of the City University of New York conducted a massive survey of religion among American adults. The *American Religion Identification Survey* (ARIS) results indicated that 81 percent of American adults identified with a religious group. That figure, a sharp drop from the 90 percent identification demonstrated in a similar survey in 1990, was further detailed in numbers regarding adherence to specific religions and denominations. That part of the population that identified as Christian fell from 86 percent to 70 percent during the decade of the 1990s. In terms of sheer numbers, the population of Americans who indicated no adherence to any religion more than doubled, from 14.3 million to 29.4 million, or in terms of the overall adult population, from 8 percent to 14 percent. Those who claimed actual membership in a religious group decreased from 61 percent to 54 percent. Non-Christian identification increased slightly, from 3.3 percent to 3.7 percent. The numbers of Sikhs more than quadrupled, Hindus and Baha'is tripled, Muslims doubled, and Buddhists increased by 160 percent. Those identifying themselves as Wiccans increased sixteenfold. More women than men, and more older persons than younger, identified themselves as religious.[1]

In the midst of significant downward trends in the numbers of persons identifying themselves as religious, several aspects of religion in America—diversity, adaptation, and experimentation—have become much

[1] Egon Mayer, Barry A. Kosmin, and Ariela Keysar, *American Religious Identification Survey* (2001), http://www.gc.cuny.edu/studies/aris_index.htm.

more visible. Americans at the beginning of the twenty-first century are vigorously exploring new theological ideas and perspectives. The growth of religions such as Buddhism, Hinduism, and Islam in America has been dramatic. Christian Pentecostalism has developed rapidly in terms of its overall numbers since 1990 at the same time that it has found expression in the ongoing emergence of new denominations and congregations, each with different emphases. Americans likewise continue to refashion their religious lives by creatively combining elements drawn from an assortment of traditions, a process typically American in its experimentalism, pragmatism, and boldness.

Sometimes religious groups that recently have emerged in the process of American refashionings of traditions have been grouped under the misnomer "New Age Religions." But many of the ideas embraced by these groups are not "new"; nor, in themselves, do these ideas constitute "religions." Some ideas, such as reincarnation, astrology, healing arts, and goddess-worship, predate Judaism and Christianity. Other ideas, such as the belief that "all spiritual truth and wisdom is within me," are largely the products of the Renaissance and the Enlightenment humanism of the fifteenth through the eighteenth centuries. Some of this religious thinking overlaps with so-called secular humanism in its approach to social justice, democracy, separation of church and state, morality, and ultimacy. And ethnic religious emphases—practices and beliefs often found attached to the standardized religious life of mainstream or "elite" religions—are part of the mix as well.

We can reasonably expect Hindus in America to believe in reincarnation, because that idea is a part of the Hindu system of beliefs. Likewise, we find among American Indians a complex set of religious beliefs and rituals regarding healing of the body. And within Reconstruction Judaism and Unitarian Universalism, certain aspects of humanist thought are pronounced. There are, however, many examples of persons who are satisfied with their membership in well-established congregations, in traditional denominations, who nevertheless embrace popular beliefs that are not sanctioned by their churches, such as "the law of karma," communication with the dead, and panentheism (or, the belief that "the world is a part of God"). A recent study concluded that in six Protestant denominations, belief in New Age ideas among "satisfied" adherents has grown up alongside traditional beliefs, even when there are seeming contradictions between the two. So, for example, a sample of Lutherans, Methodists, Presbyterians, Baptists, Christians (Disciples of Christ), and members of the United Church of Christ hold that the truths of Christianity have been revealed in the Bible and through the direct involvement of God in the world. Nevertheless, a third of those surveyed believed at the same time that "all spiritual truth and wisdom is within me" and that "an individual should arrive at his or her own beliefs independent of any church." Some also believe in reincarnation, astrology, and communication with the dead.[2]

To speak of New Age beliefs and rituals—among Protestants, Jews, Catholics, or any other religious groups in America—is to speak of popular religion, of religion that grows up alongside denominational religious life, alongside religion as shaped by mature institutions. During some periods of history, officials of established churches vigorously attacked popular religion whenever it arose. Popular religion and "elite" religion accordingly have sometimes engaged each other as adversaries, and nowhere more dramatically than in medieval and early modern Europe. On occasion, elite authorities have prevailed, wiping out or limiting popular religion. But in some cases, popular religions have proven so attractive to people and have grown so quickly, that they have overwhelmed the institutional bases of their competitors and established themselves alongside dominant religions. In American religious history, Mormonism, Jehovah's Witnesses, and Christian Science are just a few religions that began in such fashion.

It has often been the case that popular religious beliefs and/or rituals have served primarily as a supplement to elite religion. In certain cases, and most visibly in instances involving ultimacy and death, Americans have looked beyond their denominational affiliations to ideas and symbols of a popular sort. Popular religious ideas are always somewhat ambiguous. They are a topic of conversation, passed from person to person by word of mouth, and they are sometimes sketched in novels or in general nonfiction writing, or now in cyberspace through the Internet. They only rarely manifest the precise definition, careful ordering, and complex expression that characterize elite religions. They flourish in the interstices, in the cracks, between formal institutional structures. People adopt them as they need them and discard them if and when they no longer need them. The appeal of popular religious ideas to individuals is stronger at some times than at others, as when a loved one dies or when there is a personal crisis. But none of these characteristics makes popular religion any less meaningful for individuals who are attracted to them or any less significant within the religious landscape of late-twentieth-century America. Popular religion has always played a role in shaping American religious life, alongside denominational religion. In the late twentieth century, it is an important component of the religious life of the nation.

Religious diversity in America has created an environment hospitable to popular religion. Christianity, Judaism, Islam, Buddhism, Hinduism,

---

[2] Michael J. Donahue, "Prevalence and Correlates of New Age Beliefs in Six Protestant Denominations," *Journal for the Scientific Study of Religion*, 32 (1993), 182. See also Table 1, p. 179. The six denominations are the Evangelical Lutheran Church in America, the Presbyterian Church (U.S.A.), the Southern Baptist Convention, the Christian Church (Disciples of Christ), the United Methodist Church, and the United Church of Christ.

Native American religions, and other ancient traditions are visible in an assortment of American contexts and locales. Alongside them are the many younger religions that either were born on American soil or were brought here by immigrants. The spectacle of religious diversity, which is unmistakable in America, and especially in urban settings, contributes to shaping the American mood of receptivity toward new religious perspectives. The vitality of popular religion, in short, is directly related to the fact of religious diversity in the late twentieth century. Popular religion, which is as much about the borrowing and blending of ideas and traditions as it is about the articulation of novel visions, flourished in the rich, complex, multifarious denominational environment of the late twentieth century.

The facts of diversity and fluidity of religion in America at the end of the millennium have not led to significant changes in relations between religions and the state. As has been the case for most of the nation's history, civil authorities scrutinize religions that depart from the familiar Judaeo-Christian emphases of the dominant culture. The state, claiming authority to intervene where the safety of the citizenry is in question, continues to monitor ideas and rituals that emerge in connection with popular religion. In some instances, courts have sought to limit religious practice, as in the case of Native American ingestion of peyote, a powerful drug, in religious rituals. On other occasions, governments have supported the interests of the state above the claims of religious groups, as in state insistence upon autopsies of Hmong people, who believe that such exercises negatively affect the spiritual future of the deceased. The ambiguous and sometimes difficult relations between government agencies and emergent religious groups have been most visibly represented in the disaster at Waco, Texas, where dozens of men, women, and children lost their lives in a conflagration that took place in the course of a federal investigation of the Branch Davidian community there.

Religion at the same time remains closely involved with the political life of the nation. In recent decades, this relationship has been particularly true of conservative Christian denominations, which have systematically cultivated relations with politicians and have exercised influence over public policy. Among such groups, The Christian Coalition, which organized support for a conservative political agenda in the 1990s, has been the most visible. Individual congregations, representing the spectrum of political opinion, also remain actively involved in reform at the local level.

Religious change has been accelerated by the rapid development of communications technology and by the initiative that religious groups have shown in exploiting it. Religious-oriented television and radio programming airs around the clock. Computer networks disseminate a huge volume of information, opinion, first-person accounts of religious experiences, and religious art, and provide easy means for association with like-minded persons. The marketing of religion is increasingly efficient, and the recruitment of persons to religious groups is more sophisticated. The role of electronic communications in fostering the spread of religious ideas was well represented in the case of the Heaven's Gate group, whose members committed mass suicide in 1997. Prior to their demise, members of the group operated a computer Internet business, advertising their views and attracting members through a sophisticated homepage website.

But not everyone is seeking converts to their religion on the Internet. For many persons, cyberspace is simply a means for the expression of their own religiosity. People tell their religious stories, periodically updating the account of their spiritual development and revising and refining their spiritual insights. These people who tell stories, profess spiritual insights, and articulate new visions have been a standard feature of religion in America throughout its history. Only a very few attract disciples. Most, instead, represent the American inclination publicly to disclose personal spiritual life. This project of bridging private experience and public life represents the American trust that religion—even in cases where it is a customized, select blending of denominational rituals, popular religious ideas, and personal reflection—is about collective life. Religion in America is about the experiences of individuals as much as it is about the development of religious institutions. Above all, it is about the dynamic relationship between people and the institutions that they create, destroy, alter, and envision.

Suggestions for Further Reading

The development of electronic databases and the refinement of access to documents through the Internet has transformed the nature of research and learning. Primary and secondary sources bearing on American religious history are widely available to persons interested in exploring the religious lives of Americans and historical interpretations of those lives. Some useful sites are the searchable *Project Muse* (http://muse.jhu.edu/) and the *JSTOR* (http://www.jstor.org/) collections of academic journals and the *Making of America* electronic library of books and periodical literature (http://cdl.library.cornell.edu/moa/ and http://moa.umdl.umich.edu/). Some journals not available through those sites are accessible through their own sites. Some, such as *Religion and American Culture* (http://www.ucpress.edu/journals/rac/) are available through subscription, whereas others, such as the *Journal of Southern Religion* (http://jsr.as.wvu.edu/index.html) are freely available to all persons.

For those wishing to sample some recent scholarship on various topics in American religious history, there are several useful volumes, including Thomas Tweed, ed., *Retelling U.S. Religious History* (Berkeley, 1997); David G. Hackett, ed., *Religion and American Culture: A Reader* (New York, 1995); and Jon Butler and Harry S. Stout, eds., *Religion in American History: A Reader* (New York, 1998). A number of dictionaries and encyclopedias likewise are available. The most comprehensive of these is the excellent three-volume *Encyclopedia of the American Religious Experience*, ed., Charles H. Lippy and Peter W. Williams (New York, 1988). Also helpful are two works edited by J. Gordon Melton, *The Encyclopedia of American Religions* (Detroit, Mich., 1989), and *Religious Leaders of America: A Biographical Guide to Founders and*

Leaders of Religious Bodies, Churches, and Spiritual Groups in North America (Detroit, Mich., 1991). Other reference works, some with a topical or regional focus are the following: Samuel S. Hill, ed., *Encyclopedia of Religion in the South*, reprint edition (Macon, Ga., 1998); Sam D. Gill, ed., *Dictionary of Native American Mythology* (Santa Barbara, Calif., 1992); Daniel G. Reid, Bruce L. Shelley, Robert D. Linder, and Harry S. Stout, eds., *Dictionary of Christianity in America* (Downers Grove, Ill., 1990); Michael Glazier and Thomas J. Shelley, eds., *The Encyclopedia of American Catholic History* (Collegeville, Minn., 1997); Bill J. Leonard, ed., *Dictionary of Baptists in America* (Downers Grove, Ill., 1994); D. G. Hart and Mark A. Noll, eds., *Dictionary of the Presbyterian & Reformed Tradition in America* (Downers Grove, Ill., 1999); H. W. Bowden, *Dictionary of American Religious Biography* (Westport, Conn., 1977); John J. Delaney, *Dictionary of American Catholic Biography* (New York, 1984); and Kerry M. Olitzky, ed., *An Encyclopedia of American Synagogue Ritual* (Westport, Conn., 2000).

Although many bibliographies are available online (see, for example, Charles Cohen's "Readings in American Religious History to 1860" at http://history.wisc.edu/cohen/963syl.pdf), some of the print bibliographies that remain helpful are Arthur P. Young and E. Jens Holley, *Religion and the American Experience, 1620–1900: A Bibliography of Doctoral Dissertations* (Westport, Conn., 1992); Robert Singerman, *Judaica Americana: A Bibliography of Publications to 1900* (New York, 1990); Kerry M. Olitzky, Lance J. Sussman, and Malcolm H. Stern, eds., *Reform Judaism in America: A Biographical Dictionary and Sourcebook* (Westport, Conn., 1993); Dorothy C. Bass, *Women in American Religious History: An Annotated Bibliography and Guide to Sources* (Boston, 1986); and Diane Choquette, *New Religious Movements in the United States and Canada: A Critical Assessment and Annotated Bibliography* (Westport, Conn., 1985). On religion in the South, see Charles H. Lippy, *Bibliography of Religion in the South* (Macon, Ga., 1985), and especially the valuable essays introducing each chapter. Also valuable is the two-volume collection of essays edited by John F. Wilson, *Church and State in America: A Bibliographical Guide* (Greenwood, Conn., 1986, 1987). Other older but still reliable sources are Ernest R. Sandeen, *American Religion and Philosophy: Guide to Information and Sources* (Detroit., Mich., 1978), and Nelson R. Burr, *Religion in American Life: Goldentree Bibliography* (New York, 1971). The latter is a condensation and supplement to Burr's two-volume *A Critical Bibliography of Religion in America*, published as part of *Religion in American Life* (Princeton, 1961).

Recent atlases of religion in America include Bret E. Carroll's streamlined *The Routledge Historical Atlas of Religion in America* (New York, 2001); William M. Newman, *Atlas of American Religion: The Denominational Era, 1776–1990* (Lanham, Md., 1999); and S. Kent Brown, Donald Q. Cannon, and Richard H. Jackson, *Historical Atlas of Mormonism* (New York, 1994). A mid-twentieth-century picture of religion in America is Edwin S. Gaustad, *Historical Atlas of Religion in America* (New York, 1962), which has also been updated and presented for a young adult readership as Edwin S. Gaustad, Philip L. Barlow, and Richard W. Dishno, *New Historical Atlas of Religion in America* (New York, 2000). The vast possibilities for the presentation of religious data as maps in searchable electronic form is exemplified in John Corrigan and Tracy Leavelle, *Spanish and French Missions in Colonial America* (Berkeley, Calif.: Electronic Cultural Atlas Initiative and California Digital Library, http://www.ecai.org/). Although not an atlas, the data made available by Roger Finke and Rodney Stark in *The Churching of America, 1776–1990: Winners and Losers in Our Religious Economy* (New Brunswick, N.J., 1992) can be used to supplement the reading of the religion atlases.

Ann T. Fraker has detailed a wide range of resources for classroom use in *Religion in American Life* (Urbana, Ill., 1989). Primary sources useful as supplementary reading in the classroom are collected in E. S. Gaustad's two-volume *A Documentary History of Religion in America* (Grand Rapids, Mich., 1982–1983).

Other surveys that approach religion as part of the whole of American life are Peter W. Williams, *America's Religions: Traditions and Cultures* (New York, 1990); Martin Marty, *Pilgrims in Their Own Land: 500 Years of Religion in America* (Boston, 1984); Catherine L. Albanese, *America, Religions and Religion* (Belmont, Calif., 1981); Richard E. Wentz, *Religion in the New World: The Shaping of Religious Traditions in the United States* (Minneapolis, 1990); Edwin S. Gaustad, *A Religious History of America* (San Francisco, 1990); Jon Butler, *Awash in a Sea of Faith: Christianizing the American People* (Cambridge, Mass., 1990); and Robert T. Handy, *A History of the Churches in the United States and Canada* (New York, 1976). Also useful is George M. Marsden, *Religion and American Culture* (San Diego and New York, 1990). R. Laurence Moore describes the historical roles and cultural contributions of religious groups not associated with the Protestant mainstreams in *Religious Outsiders and the Making of Americans* (New York, 1986).

Index